LIBRARY AUTOMATION
Issues and Applications

Dennis Reynolds

R. R. BOWKER COMPANY
New York and London, 1985

Published by R. R. Bowker Company
205 East Forty-Second Street, New York, NY 10017

Copyright © 1985 by Xerox Corporation

Printed and bound in the United States of America

Library of Congress Cataloging in Publication Data

Reynolds, Dennis.
   Library automation.

   Includes index.
   1. Libraries—Automation.   2. Library science—Data
processing.   I. Title.
Z678.9.R38   1985   025.3′028′54   84-6272
ISBN 0-8352-1489-3

Contents

Preface

Library automation is a process that has brought and will continue to bring profound changes to the library world, in terms of both technology and the involvement of people. Its scope can be defined quite narrowly or quite broadly. This book surveys the wide spectrum of applications for which automation in libraries is appropriate and has been attempted. The treatment and level of detail are such that it is useful to a variety of audiences, ranging from those whose exposure to library automation is relatively new, to those who could benefit from a review of selected aspects of automation, to those whose involvement is substantial.

Library Automation: Issues and Applications is divided into three parts and sixteen chapters (chapter content is discussed in detail in the Introduction). Chapters 1–6 in Part I, History and Background, provide a historical perspective—from early technical support systems to online technical support systems, the public catalog, information retrieval services, and interlibrary lending. Part II, Planning and Preparation, contains four chapters that deal chiefly with the two most important aspects of automation in the library. They cover recurring themes and present trends, and the options and resources basic to planning, preparation, selecting, procuring, and introducing automated systems. Converting bibliographic records to machine-readable form also is considered. Part III, Applications, Chapters 11–16, deals with applying the principles of automation to the workings of the library today, and covers the role of bibliographic utilities, characteristics of technical support systems, the user interface (dialogue languages, search logistics, and bibliographic displays) of the online catalog, online search services, and the organization and administration of the search service. Chapters 13 and 14 contain numerous illustrations from online catalogs that indicate how various library systems in operation handle different aspects of the search process.

In a market as rapidly changing as the one that surrounds library automation, there is a certain amount of risk in referring to and using examples from various vendors and systems in use at the time of manuscript preparation. The reader should be aware that changes may have occurred to the systems and examples used throughout this book. It is recommended that readers with specific needs for accurate and up-to-the-minute information use this book as a starting point for their own data gathering.

For readers of every level of involvement, *Library Automation: Issues and Applications* is a comprehensive treatment of expanding technology and human intervention. As automation is a process that will touch every library facility to one degree or another, so this book can aid every librarian and administrator in coming to terms with the issues that must be faced and decisions that must be made concerning automation in the library.

I

History and Background

1

Introduction:
A Perspective

Libraries have long sought technological aids to facilitate and enhance their services. The introduction of the typewriter into libraries was a revolutionary concept in the late 1800s. Innovations ranging from printing presses to microcomputers have effected a wide spectrum of library operations, extending from how an item is described, to how it is circulated to the reader, and even to the format in which it is read.

The impact of automation on librarianship has long been an inviting subject for discourse at library conferences and in the professional literature. Some enthusiasts have projected an electronic future void of paper, with libraries only slightly if at all resembling their traditional form. Other observers have been equally extreme in the opposite direction, foreseeing only a minor impact of automation on the overall role and form of libraries. Some have welcomed the challenge of new technology, others have left the profession because of it, and more than a few, including the nineteenth-century librarian J. Y. W. MacAlister (1897), have greeted it with skepticism:[1]

> My critics will tell you that the more time-saving apparatus is used the more time the librarian will have to cultivate his intellect and discourse with his readers on the beauties of Browning or of Byron. But is the time saved by mechanism used in this excellent way? I am afraid not. The taste for such things grows on what it feeds, and the librarian who has invented an appliance for supplying his readers with books ... by means of an automatic ticket-in-the-slot machine will not be happy, or spend any time in reading Browning, until he has invented one which will, by the touching of a button, shoot the book into the reader's home.

3

Close to 90 years after those words were spoken before the Second International Library Conference in London, libraries still do not exactly "shoot books" into readers' homes. Yet we have been moving increasingly toward what MacAlister envisioned as the ultimate technological boundary. It is possible in Colorado Springs, Colorado, to stand in a grocery store and examine the contents of the catalog of the local public library, or to dial into it from a home microcomputer. Some readers in various cities in North America have been able, at least on a trial basis, to charge out library materials simply by punching a button on a device connected to their television set.

Although perhaps approaching MacAlister's most extreme prophecy, the preceding examples are not inventiveness for its own sake as MacAlister warned against. Rather, they are attempts to address some very traditional library concerns: the description of, provision of, and access to recorded knowledge. Automation has been paramount in enabling libraries to provide broader and more convenient access to some very traditional forms, and some less traditional forms, of information. Improving access to recorded information, with all the logistical details it involves, has been a primary concern of libraries for a long time. This pursuit has never been the library's exclusive province, but libraries have carved out a deserved role for themselves. This role may at some time in the future be relegated to obsolescence for the library as we know it, or it may be changed dramatically. But to the library of the 1980s, the provision of access to automation is central, and the use of automation in facilitating this role is the subject of this book.

The scope of library automation can be defined quite broadly or quite narrowly. The phrase "library automation" has been used on occasion almost synonymously with "library mechanization." This is not quite accurate. At the other end of the spectrum, it would be convenient to equate library automation with "computerization." While it is reasonable to regard computerization as an operational requirement in most aspects of library automation given the context of the 1980s, it is not entirely justified in a historical context.

Before the advent of computers, International Business Machines (IBM) and Remington Rand led the way in business technology through the introduction of such equipment as keypunch machines and electromechanical card sorters and collators. Although these devices were not computers, they had certain similar qualities. Namely, they could read, compute, and manipulate data recorded in reusable form. A photocopy machine can read and reproduce data, but it cannot compute or manipulate data to appear in a form or sequence different from the document being copied. A basic mechanical adding machine can be used to compute data, but that data must be entered manually each time an operation is required.

The precomputer IBM and Remington Rand machines, on the other hand, could perform all these functions. A punched card had to be typed, but once a set of cards was prepared, the manufacturer's machines could assist in sorting and rearranging the cards while simultaneously computing data appearing on different cards within the set. These machines could "read" what had been typed onto a card, compare it to data appearing on another card, and perform an action based on the results of that comparison. In turn, the cards used for one operation could be saved and used again for similar or quite different manipulations at a later date, such as merging new cards into the file in proper sequence or rearranging the cards into an entirely different sequence. The revolutionary concept here was that information could be "stored" on cards and reused and that the machines could take these cards and, "programmed" to do so, examine them and perform a predetermined operation according to the result of that examination.

Reusability of data and flexibility in manipulating it are what the earlier IBM and Remington Rand machines had in common with their successor, the computer. These same characteristics constitute the technological foundation for what is examined in this book under the title of "library automation." Thus, photocopy machines, electronic security systems, time stamps, and many other such aids do not fall under this definition. Computers and information stored in and manipulated by that equipment do fall squarely into the context of this book, as do a few other devices not commonly thought of as "computers," but sharing the characteristics of reusable data and machine manipulation.

The perspective from which this book is written, however, views library automation as a process far broader than simply the technology it employs. In the context of computerization, machines with appropriate capabilities and software that has been properly written are prerequisites to any successful venture into library automation. But beyond these prerequisites, library automation is as much a human process as a technological one. Even the most sophisticated automated systems only provide a solid base from which to work. Equally important as ingredients for successful automation are very human elements having to do with how skillfully the technology is selected, introduced into a setting, and used.

Given this perspective, there are several themes central to the approach employed in this book. First, there are certain aspects of planning and implementing automated systems that demonstrate far greater stability than the technology itself. The technology of library automation changes rapidly, but there are analytical and managerial considerations related to evaluation, selection, purchase, implementation, and ongoing use of systems that cut across the boundaries of what is the state of the technological art in library automation at a particular time.

A second theme is that many of these same analytical and managerial considerations can also cut across a number of different applications for which automation in the library is appropriate. Obviously, the specifics of an approach to automation and the points of emphasis will vary according to application, but whether a library is automating a cataloging operation, introducing microcomputers for use by the library public, acquiring telefacsimile equipment, or is involved in some other automation project, an emphasis on analysis of options, careful planning, and attention to human consequences is essential.

A third underlying theme in this book is that applications of library automation must be viewed within the context of the broader issues surrounding them in the external environment. One can examine an aspect of library automation, like the bibliographic utilities, for example, strictly from a point of view of technical and functional operation. But the evolution of these networks, and the role they play in American librarianship, are best understood only against the background and within the current context of the conditions that have contributed to their growth.

With the overall perspective and these themes in mind, then, the book is divided into three major parts. The first is an overview of trends and landmark development in the evolution of library automation through the 1970s and into the turn of the decade. This background is purposeful not just from a point of view of academic appreciation, but also in terms of examining the practical principles that have emerged in library automation as a broader process involving more than simply the state of the technology on which it is based at any given time. The turn of the decade represents a convenient point of demarcation between the historical context and the more current context of library automation, but its selection is more than simply a matter of convenience. While the 1960s witnessed the emergence of computer applications in libraries and the 1970s ushered in the online era, it has only been in the 1980s that automation has become a feasibility, rather than a goal for the future, for large numbers of libraries. This simple fact is extremely important. It makes the first half of the 1980s quite different from the previous decades; at the same time, the successes and failures of the past did establish the pattern that has led to the present, and those important lessons are as applicable now as they have ever been.

The second part of the book focuses on general considerations in library automation as a planning process. Chapter 7 examines the current environment of library automation as a context for planning, including recurring themes, present trends, and three particular technologies—microcomputers, optical digital disks, and telecommunications—which are central to current and emerging developments in library automation. Chapter 8 presents a brief overview of the broad technological approaches available for automation, and the human resources that are likely—out of choice or necessity—to play a role in the overall process. Chapter 9 focuses on several more specific stages of planning for automation, particularly in an environment in which many libraries can be expected to purchase systems rather than design their own. Chapter 10 deals with a topic that cuts across several applications of automation: the conversion of manual bibliographic records to machine-readable form.

The third section of the book deals with applications of automation to what can generally be considered as rather traditional library operations and services. The specific focus, however, differs from one application to another, depending on what is felt to be the most crucial aspects given the current environment of automation in that area. Because of the importance of the role they play in American libraries, the bibliographic utilities are included in this section. In Chapter 11, the major utilities are examined not only in terms of their functional capabilities, but also in terms of the relationship between these networks and the issues surrounding their recent and future roles in American librarianship. Chapter 12 examines the automation of technical processing operations. The specific focus is on evaluating functional characteristics of systems, or modules, within integrated systems, designed to handle cataloging, acquisitions, serials control, and circulation operations. Chapters 13 and 14 discuss online public access catalogs. A treatment of online catalogs could be approached in a variety of ways, and there are a number of equally valid issues that could be addressed. But one of the foremost stems from the characteristic that most differentiates the use of online catalogs from the use of online technical processing systems: the fact that the systems are used primarily by the library public rather than by the library staff. As such, the mode of dialog that occurs between a system and a user of a system takes on an added dimension with online catalogs, and it is the "user interface" that constitutes the focus in the chapters on online catalogs. Chapters 15 and 16 examine a particular service in libraries that has come to be commonly referred to as "online searching." Although identified by generic terminology, this usually refers to those library operations through which users may submit requests to conduct searches on remotely stored databases. Unlike the focus in the chapters on other applications, neither

Chapter 15 nor Chapter 16 review these systems in terms of their technical or functional characteristics. Some of the present trends and issues pertaining to online searching are particularly dynamic and interesting, and several of the foremost of these are examined in Chapter 15. Chapter 16 then focuses on a variety of concerns relating to the organization and administration of an online search service in a library.

The contents in this book are arranged in such a way as to present a comprehensive overview, but at the same time allowing for convenience of use by those with a more specifically defined need concerning a particular application or a part of the overall process. Most of all, the book is intended to stress the importance, to all readers, of the human elements that go into planning, implementing, and using automation in the library; these are the key ingredients for successfully applying technology.

Notes

1. Quoted in Melvin J. Voight, "The Trend Toward Mechanization in Libraries," *Library Trends* 5 (October 1956): 195.

2

Early Technical Support Systems

To discuss library automation as a process and to place it in the context of the mid-1980s, it is necessary first to understand the general directions of the past. Perhaps the primary lessons that the history of library automation teaches are that it has been evolutionary yet abrupt at times and consistently overlapping in levels of sophistication, and that it has been a sometimes rewarding, sometimes painful, learning experience. In Chapter 1, machine readability and manipulation were established as primary criteria for library automation. Examining these criteria in historical perspective, we find three major developments over the years: (1) the introduction of unit-record equipment; (2) the move to offline computerization; and (3) the evolution to computerization in an online interactive mode. These developments have evolved in time from one to another, but in the general sense. Some libraries were just beginning to implement a system based on unit-record equipment when others had already moved on to offline computerization, and even a few to online systems. So long as we keep in mind these overlapping qualities, we can still trace some significant patterns in the evolution of library automation.

This chapter and Chapters 3–6 examine the general evolution of library automation. This chapter looks specifically at pre-online automation of technical support systems before online in libraries, including cataloging, acquisitions, serials control, and circulation. Chapter 3 examines the transition to online technical support systems, and Chapters 4, 5, and 6 deal more with systems related to public service. Although technical and public services support systems are separated here for purposes of description, there can be a very narrow line between the two. The application of automation to cataloging can have considerable impact on the nature and even the form of the public catalog. The automation of acquisitions, serials control, and circulation also affects the reference function. The clearest example is perhaps drawn from circulation systems. Circulation is a technical function of the library, but it is also clearly a public service function and more narrowly a reference support system. Even apart from automated systems, libraries that keep the circulation file or one component of it in call number order are in fact performing a reference function by being able to assist library users in locating items owned by the library but not on the shelf at a particular time. The existence of automated systems that serve the dual purpose of circulation system and public catalog further obscures the distinction between technical and reference support systems. This more obvious merging of technical and reference functions and the tools they draw upon is encouraging, but it too has been an evolutionary process and one in which distinctions still exist.

Even in the case of the automated circulation control system/public catalog, two quite different functions are involved: (1) a technical operation by the library in entering and maintaining the bibliographic, holdings, and circulation data; and (2) a reference operation by the patron in retrieving and examining that data for his or her own purposes. Because such distinctions still do exist and were even clearer in the past, they are retained here for purposes of discussion. Automation of technical operations in libraries has historically preceded efforts to introduce automation into public service functions; therefore, technical support operations are dealt with first.

Unit-Record Systems

Circulation Control

Perhaps nowhere else in the library has there been a greater need for automation in some form than in circulation control. While other technical operations have often been stowed away in back rooms out of view of the public, circulation has been exposed to the clear view of all. Bottlenecks, inefficiencies, and inability to keep pace with the work involved in circulation are played out on the central stage of the library, often with a long line of patrons watching. In addition to dealing with queuing problems, circulation control historically has been plagued by the enormous amount of staff time required to maintain files, as well as by problems seemingly inherent to the nature of the files themselves.

Ideally, a library circulation file should have several access points, including files of charges by due date to expedite issuance of overdue notices; files by call number or bibliographic access points to serve a reference function; and files by patron name to provide a public service function as well as a control operation if the number of charges per patron is restricted. In actual fact, very few manual systems maintained all three types of files. It was not simply a technological problem, since carbon forms could supply the required quantity of records to maintain multiple files. But the staff work involved in filing three charge slips for each item in separate files was more than most libraries were willing to take on. Upon return of an item, the charge slips would have to be removed from each of three files, thus adding to the already time-consuming task of maintaining multiple files.

Background

Different techniques were introduced into libraries in the first half of the twentieth century with the express purpose of streamlining circulation. These procedures were aimed at achieving one or more specific goals:

to reduce the amount of work required of the patron in charging out materials

to reduce the time and amount of paperwork required at the circulation counter in charging out an item

to maintain more versatile circulation files

to place an item back on the shelf more quickly after it had been returned

to make the overdue process less cumbersome

and, as a corollary to all these improvements, to reduce the amount of staff time required and the cost of the overall operation.

By and large, any efforts earlier in this century to improve circulation methods revolved around finding better ways to maintain manual systems. There were some attempts to introduce mechanization to expedite certain tasks, usually to reduce the work required by the patron to charge an item and the time required at the circulation desk to perform the operation. The Dickman book charger, introduced in 1927, automatically stamped an impression of a borrower's embossed metal registration card, along with a preset due date, on the book card for an item being charged. This basic machine considerably reduced borrower effort and streamlined the overall charging process. Five years later, Gaylord introduced the first electrical charging machine, almost identical in function to the Dickman machine.

In the 1940s, two innovative methods of circulation control—photo-charging and audiocharging—were introduced. Photocharging is credited to Ralph R. Shaw at the Gary, Indiana, Public Library. When a book was presented for charging, the desk attendant placed under a special camera the borrower's registration card, the book card, and a stamped date due card, which also included a sequential transaction number. Each transaction required an amount of film ranging from 1/32 to 1/8 of an inch, and since the camera could hold rolls of film ten feet long, a significant number of transactions could be recorded before having to change film. An important strength of photocharging was that it reduced patron effort to presenting a registration card and the items to be charged. This was also an advantage of audiocharging, first introduced at the St. Louis, Missouri, County Public Library by Stewart W. Smith. Instead of photographing the essential information, the desk attendant read it into a tape recorder.

Although both these systems required less work of the patron, each had its own special problems. For example, the Tulsa, Oklahoma, Public Library, using photocharging, had to send the required special film to Dallas, Texas, for developing; a roll was sent only about once every ten days.[1] This essentially meant that the "circulation file" on film was inaccessible until many of the items for which charges were recorded had already been returned. This certainly saved the amount of paperwork and staff time required, but it did not supply a very flexible file!

One of the greatest choruses of complaints about photocharging came from clerks responsible for issuing overdue notices. The transaction numbers of overdue items could be identified without consulting the film, but the borrower's name and the bibliographic identification of the item noted by the transaction number could be determined only by examining the developed film. The fact that the images were so small and difficult to read was greatly unappreciated by overdues clerks and led to experiences similiar to that of the Charlotte, North Carolina, Public Library in which, the librarian reported, "The eyestrain led to glasses for one clerk and later to the loss of another employee."[2]

The Charlotte library subsequently abandoned photocharging in favor of audiocharging. That technique, as applied in libraries, had its own problems. It soon became apparent that some patrons were not particularly fond of having an attendant read aloud their name and the list of materials they were checking out for everyone to hear. One library found a simple, and faster, solution by reading aloud an accession number rather than the author and title of an item.[3] Another library solved the problem by installing the microphone in "a sound absorbent half-size telephone booth by which the assistant's voice is muffled."[4] On occasion, a lack of audio clarity caused by an attendant's hurried dictation led to subsequent misinterpretation by an overdues clerk transcribing the author and title. Such was the case when a patron of the St. Louis County Public Library, who had charged out *Augustus Caesar's World,* received an overdue notice for *Augustus Feeds the Squirrels.*[5] Of more serious concern, however, were the difficulties of locating overdues on the tapes and handling holds placed on charged items.

Although the electrical devices did help alleviate some of the congestion problems at the circulation desk and did reduce the effort required of patrons, they did little to enhance the circulation file as a usable tool. It is true that both photocharging and audiocharging greatly reduced the amount of staff time needed in circulation file maintenance, but this was realized only at the expense of rendering the film or tape file practically worthless as a tool to assist in determining whether a specific item was in circulation. Their use in compiling circulation statistics for administrative purposes was limited to counting the total number of charges over a given period of time, but even this capability was related to the use of sequential transaction numbers rather than to the mechanical nature of the equipment.

Early Unit-Record Systems

Several years before the advent of photocharging, a quite different system was being introduced into the main library on the University of Texas campus. This system made use of Hollerith punched cards and equipment manufactured by IBM, and in contrast to the systems already described, it focused at least in part on machine-readable data. (Although the terms "Hollerith cards" and "IBM cards" are not strictly interchangeable, they became practically so in common usage.) The procedure for charging books, as described by Ralph Parker, then circulation librarian at the university, was similar in many respects to manual methods used in many other academic libraries at the time. The borrower filled out his or her name, address, and student number on a call slip, along with the author, title, and call number of the item to be charged. The borrower presented the slip at the circulation desk. The slip was then sent to a library assistant in the closed stacks who retrieved the item and returned it and the call slip to the circulation desk. The desk attendant stamped the due date in the book and on the call slip. The book was issued to the patron and the call slip dropped into a box for later filing into the main circulation file.

The only feature of the Texas system that distinguished it at this point from many others was the nature of the call slip. It was an

80-column IBM card. At the end of each day, the IBM cards for all materials checked out that day were collected and, rather than being filed immediately, were inserted into an IBM machine; a due date was punched into each through a "gang-punch" function on the machine. The IBM cards were then filed, in call number order, into the general circulation file.

By the one simple step of keypunching the due date into the cards, the University of Texas had in effect merged two traditional circulation files into one. The single circulation file, arranged by call number, was removed daily and placed in an IBM machine called a sorter. A control was set on the machine; as each card in the circulation file passed through the sorter, those on which the punched due date had expired were mechanically separated out of the file. This process eliminated any need to maintain a separate date due file in addition to the call number file. As Parker enthusiastically projected, "Every auxiliary file that has grown up to meet the needs of large libraries can be safely cast aside. . . . "[6] With one file it would indeed require a run of the entire file through the sorter to separate cards based on criteria other than the principal arrangement of the file, but this posed little problem since one could "select any group of cards from the general file with lightning speed,"[7] which at the time was 400 cards per minute. Compared with today's technology, that IBM sorter operated at a snail's pace, but in 1936 it was indeed "lightning speed."

During the subsequent quarter-century, a number of other libraries incorporated IBM equipment into their circulation procedures. Most, however, did not take full advantage of its capabilities. Even at the University of Texas in 1936, for example, the daily charge cards were integrated into the general file manually rather than by machine, as Parker had calculated that, given the comparatively small number of new charges and the much larger size of the existing file, the merging could be done more quickly by hand than on the IBM equipment. Most academic libraries that adopted IBM machines for use in circulation followed the University of Texas pattern fairly closely, although with occasional modification. These libraries tended to favor using the IBM card itself as a call slip on which the patron would fill out borrower and bibliographic information, and, upon charging, the IBM cards were retained and formed the basis of the circulation file.

In contrast, public libraries frequently used the IBM card as a transaction card; the patron filled out borrower and bibliographic information on a traditional paper, nonmachine-readable call slip and presented it at the circulation desk. The attendant took an IBM card from a stack of prepunched, sequentially numbered cards retained at the circulation desk. The number on the IBM card was the "transaction number," and the card was referred to as the transaction card. The transaction number, along with the due date, was stamped or written on the call slip. The IBM card with only the transaction number was inserted into the book pocket and the due date stamped in the book. The call slip was retained and filed in the circulation file, arranged by transaction number. When an item was returned, the IBM transaction card was pulled from the book pocket, and the item was immediately reshelved. At periodic intervals, groups of these pulled cards representing returned books were arranged in transaction number sequence with the help of IBM equipment. Missing numbers in the sequence logically represented charged items not yet returned. This process was generally coordinated with due dates, and thus the missing transaction cards represented overdue charges. The corresponding paper call slip, containing borrower and title information, was pulled from the circulation file and an overdue notice prepared. Call slips corresponding to returned IBM cards were discarded.

In contrast to photocharging and audiocharging, the use of IBM equipment in libraries focused on the problems of file maintenance rather than patron convenience. In each of the procedures using IBM cards, the patron was required, for each item, to write the author, title, and call number along with certain borrower registration information, either on the IBM card itself or on a paper call slip. Even in the early 1960s, in a procedure adopted at the University of California, Los Angeles, which merged the call card and transaction card concepts by using a two-part perforated IBM card, the borrower was still required to fill out the record in considerable detail.[8] By and large, then, the use of IBM unit-record equipment and machine-readable data in library circulation departments was limited to identifying overdues and reducing the time and effort expended in file maintenance. It certainly did not represent radical departures from established routines, nor did it introduce a sophisticated level of automation into those routines.

The Montclair System

Against this background of a very slow and functionally limited evolution of unit-record automation in circulation departments, there was one rather outstanding exception. In the early 1940s, IBM was searching for a library to automate with state-of-the-art techniques. The president of IBM was acquainted with the president of the board and with another trustee of the Montclair, New Jersey, Public Library. After a series of consultations, IBM selected Montclair as the setting for an experiment, which resulted in the most sophisticated automated circulation system in the precomputer era.

The essentials of the Montclair charging system consisted of IBM punched book cards and borrower cards, and a device called a record control unit, which contained two slots for card insertion and a keyboard wired to a keypunch machine. Implementing the system required the large-scale effort of converting bibliographic records to machine-readable form on IBM cards. Very abbreviated bibliographic data were keypunched into a two-part perforated IBM card for each item in the library—the left-hand portion became an inventory card; the right-hand portion, into which similar bibliographic identification had been punched, became the book card and was placed in the book pocket of the described item. The borrower registration files were also converted to machine-readable form on two-part perforated IBM cards—the left-hand part was retained by the library; the right-hand part was removed and became the borrower's library card.

Once the system was implemented, the borrower merely presented the punched library card and the items to be charged out. The desk attendant inserted the patron's card into one slot on the record control unit, removed the book card from an item to be charged, and inserted it into the other slot on the unit. The attendant then depressed one key on the keyboard attached to the unit. This command triggered the punching machine, the final piece of equipment in the charging operation, to punch a new IBM card on which item and borrower information was merged from the two cards in the record control unit. This third card became the transaction card. Then the book card was inserted back into the book pocket and the borrower's library card was returned. The transaction card was retained by the library, and all such cards generated on a given day were mechanically merged into the general circulation file.

The Montclair system "modernized" the circulation process in a variety of ways. Far less work was required of the patron than in many conventional systems, less staff time was needed in maintaining the files since much of the filing could be performed mechanically, and the resulting file was more flexible and could be manipulated quite easily for statistical or other purposes. Automated procedures centering on the punched-card IBM equipment were devised by Montclair to more easily handle holds, overdues, and the recording of fines.[9]

Despite the proven success of the Montclair system and more limited successes in other libraries employing less sophisticated configurations, the use of automated unit-record equipment in circulation never reached great proportions in libraries. The most common complaint, despite vociferous reports to the contrary by libraries using the unit-record system, was that it was simply not cost-effective.

Acquisitions

Machine-readable records in the form of IBM punched cards were in limited use in circulation departments of American libraries in the mid-twentieth century, but they were even less extensive in acquisitions, serials control, and cataloging operations, and usually took only partial advantage of the capabilities of available equipment on the market. In acquisitions, for example, the punched cards were sometimes used only as an aid in financial administration, leaving intact the manual procedures for preparing multipart order forms and for file maintenance.

There were a few cases, however, where the use of machine-readable punched cards made a much greater impact on procedure in the acquisitions department. One was the Decatur, Illinois, Public Library, which adopted unit-card IBM equipment at the comparatively recent date of 1960. Under the newly implemented system, when a decision had been made to order an item, the appropriate selection documents such as reviews or advertisements were sent to a keypunch operator. The operator made three punched cards for each copy of each title being ordered. The information on each card included author, title, copyright date, volume number, edition, department, item order number, source, list price, and encumbered price. An IBM machine was used to print the list of orders to Decatur's book jobber. When an item was received by the library, one of the IBM cards was pulled and the actual cost keypunched into it. In addition to reducing paperwork, one of the main advantages cited by the library was the improvement made on traditional financial administration. Not only was the system used for purchasing materials for the collection, but it was also used in the acquisition of supplies and in payroll.

The Decatur system, although admittedly introduced later than a number of others using similar equipment, was nevertheless significant in that it represented one of the more comprehensive operations based on use of unit-record equipment. After an item was received and a punched card updated with the actual cost, both the item and the card were sent to the cataloger. After determining the appropriate call number and subject headings, the cataloger returned the card to the keypunch operator, who entered the call number and abbreviated numerical codes for the subject headings assigned. Duplicate cards were mechanically reproduced and served as shelflist cards in cataloging and as book cards for use in the library's circulation system. Although a number of other activities, such as serials control and the production of catalog cards, remained manual, Decatur had surpassed many of its predecessors in approaching an integrated system based on unit-record equipment.[10]

Serials Control

Punched cards and unit-record equipment in serials control work basically involved three forms. One was tied to the acquisitions process. Even by 1946, the University of Texas had converted certain aspects of serials acquisition to punched cards and IBM equipment. For each current subscription, an IBM punched card was made showing title, country of publication, subscription expiration date, department benefited, account charged, location within the library system, and source from which it was ordered. As invoices were paid, the subscription price and binding costs were written on the cards; the actual keypunching of these pieces of information was deferred until the end of the fiscal year. Once the subscription price and binding costs were keypunched for all subscriptions, the punched cards could be manipulated for a variety of purposes. IBM equipment was used to mechanically sort the cards by department and calculate and print financial data. At the beginning of a fiscal year and before renewals were placed, a list of titles benefiting each academic department was printed and submitted to the department for review and suggestion of possible cancellations or additions.

One of the greatest benefits cited by those using a machine-readable process in serials was the ease of preparing bidding lists. Alexander Moffit, discussing the procedures used at the University of Texas, pointed out the propensity of many libraries to renew subscriptions with the same agent year after year simply "because of the assumption that any increased discount received [by switching to a less expensive agent] would not compensate for the labor cost and inconvenience involved."[11] With the pertinent data on machine-readable cards, the IBM equipment made preparation of bidding lists comparatively easy.

The printing of bidding lists, department review lists, and financial records suggested a second use for punched cards in serials control— the printing of serials lists for public use. The Massachusetts Institute of Technology, for example, carried out a conversion of 3,200 titles to machine-readable punched cards in the late 1950s exclusively for this purpose. No ordering information was detailed on the cards, just essential bibliographic, locational, and holdings data for each title. The total cost of the project was estimated at $3,500 for converting the titles and producing 24 copies of the serials list.[12]

A significant lesson from this and other projects using the IBM punched-card method was that the bulk of the cost was in the initial conversion. The result of the conversion, however, was a reusable file. There were labor costs in updating holdings, adding titles of new subscriptions, and so on, but the changes could be incorporated into the deck of existing cards. Subsequent editions of the list did not require retyping information for all titles to be included.

The third automated punched-card application for serials control involved check-in. Of all technical library procedures, serials check-in has been one of the most difficult to automate. The unpredictability with which even scheduled issues arrive, the diabolically ingenious frequency patterns of many journals issued on a "regular" basis, the annoying proportion of titles that do not even claim to be issued on a regular basis, and misnumberings and other discrepancies all conspire to make automation of serials check-in difficult, to say the least. Automation operates on a principle of controlled, or at least defined, options, and the issuance of serials has always had little respect for such requirements.

Although computers were used after 1960 to handle serials check-in more efficiently, the earlier IBM unit-record equipment was seldom used to support that operation. In those few instances where it was used, the procedure was to punch "arrival cards" for each subscription that included an expected date of receipt for each issue. All arrival cards with expected receipt dates during a particular interval, such as during a given month or quarter, were filed together alphabetically by title. When an issue arrived, the corresponding punched card was manually removed from the file. The cards remaining at the end of the period represented issues on which a claim decision had to be made. Although such a system could assist in the serials check-in procedure, it was essentially a manual operation and did not generally offer much of an improvement over other manual systems designed to serve the same purpose.

Cataloging

One of the traditionally most time-consuming technical operations in libraries is cataloging. The cataloging process describes the content of each item in a collection, organizes those descriptions into a coherent structure of relationships, and provides a tool in the form of a catalog as an avenue of access to the library's holdings. A host of specific tasks must be performed to achieve these ends. An item must be described in summary, a process referred to rather generically as cataloging and classification. Most libraries attempt to limit this procedure to a defined and systematic structure of description involving the application of cataloging codes and rules and various levels of authority work. There must be a method for representing the resulting description in a public catalog, centering on the essential decision concerning the basic form of the catalog itself. There are also many other tasks, such as preparing spine labels and book pockets.

In terms of tasks performed, some characteristics of the cataloging procedure are significantly different than other library operations. In circulation, acquisitions, and serials control, there is a level at which each item may be treated as any other, or at least at which limited numbers of categories of items can be defined. In circulation, for example, such categories may include young adult books with two-week loan periods, 24-hour circulating reference works, and so on; in serials control, categories may be defined according to frequency, renewal date, and other parameters. The ability to categorize items to be treated identically is a condition that is most conducive to automation, and the absence of this condition impedes the automation of the first and most important function in the cataloging operation—the description of an item. At this level, cataloging is a purely intellectual process; although a standard set of requirements may dictate what types of information are to be included in the description, the actual selection of information is discrete to each item. There have been successful attempts to automate the part of the process that summarizes subject content, but for the most part, descriptive and subject cataloging have remained in the realm of human intellectual endeavor.

Although the intellectual work involved in cataloging is very time-consuming and not easily automated, libraries have long tried to reduce the amount of time and effort involved. Since there is a certain amount of overlap between library collections, there are obvious advantages in cooperation so that the burden of intellectual work does not have to be repeated in each institution. Until the 1970s, the primary method for reducing duplicate effort in cataloging was through the Library of Congress (LC) Card Distribution Service, begun in 1901. By ordering cards from LC, a library could significantly reduce the time and effort spent in deriving cataloging information. And there was another potential time-saving element for a library that had such a service; it could adopt, in toto, a built-in authority structure for names and subject headings. Most libraries that ordered cards, however, only partially incorporated this structure, maintaining their own authority file based primarily on the Library of Congress structure but with notable and sometimes numerous local variations.

Some libraries, for a variety of reasons, chose not to use the LC Card Distribution Service or any of several similar services offered by commercial vendors. Beginning in the 1940s, these libraries could still take advantage of LC's intellectual work (although with considerable delay) by basing their own cataloging on data supplied in the printed LC author catalogs and later the *National Union Catalog;* they did, however, have to prepare their own catalog cards.

A basic problem with card reproduction methods used in libraries was that the reproductions were just that—exact copies of the original—and this did not entirely eliminate the need for typing, since an appropriate heading still had to be added on each card. An exception, by the late 1950s, was the tape-producing automatic typewriter, the Frieden Flexowriter being the most commonly used in libraries. With this equipment, information could be typed so that basic cataloging data for an item appeared on one tape and a list of headings on another. The unit-card tape containing basic cataloging data for an item was then placed on one reader as a continuous loop, and the headings tape for that item was placed on a second reader. Activating the two readers resulted in a set of catalog cards complete with an appropriate heading on each card. Unlike systems that were strictly reproducing machines, this made use of machine-readable data and could alleviate entirely the need for manually typing headings onto each card in a set. Manually changing the single-item tapes on the reader did, however, require a great deal of time. An American Library Association publication in 1965 even concluded that the time required ". . . is so great that using these machines cannot be considered an acceptable process for card reproduction."[13]

In the whole process of catalog card production, unit-record equipment had little to offer unless a library was willing to drastically change the form of cards in its public catalog. IBM did bring out a document-writing machine that could be adapted to prepare standard 3×5-inch cards, but that did not really have an impact on the form of the catalog in some libraries that replaced the card catalog with a book catalog. (This development is discussed in greater detail in Chapter 4.)

Unit-record equipment did offer promise in solving certain types of problems in libraries, but it was not adopted widely and in some cases was greeted with skepticism or resistance. Many felt that purchase or rental of the needed equipment was simply too expensive for the advantages gained. Some advantages in the use of unit-record equipment, such as in preparing statistical reports or sorting on a variety of access points, were not seen as high enough priorities to justify capital expenditures on equipment. Furthermore, although unit-record equipment did provide these types of additional capabilities, staff still had to operate the equipment, reload card decks, and so on, which could be quite time-consuming. In addition to these drawbacks, unit-record equipment was designed for handling numerical information. For alphabetical data, the sorting process was quite cumbersome. For all of these reasons, by the late 1950s, the practice of automation in terms of the machine-readable record had not become very widely established in American libraries.

Offline Computer Applications in the 1960s

The interest in computer applications that surfaced during the 1950s reached a broader level in the 1960s and began to culminate in the actual implementation of systems in libraries. During that one decade there was much more widespread adoption of computer systems than there had been of unit-record equipment during the entire quarter-century before 1960, a fact that is understandable from a viewpoint of technological capabilities. Some important influences other than just the technology itself, acted as additional incentives for computerization of library operations. Burgeoning student enrollments combined with relative prosperity in education and social services during the 1960s resulted in more library users and more acquisitions funds than had been available before.

Over and over in the library literature of the 1960s, reports appear from academic libraries to the effect that time-tested manual systems were simply falling apart under the pressure of increased circulation and acquisitions activity. At the same time, the use of computers was growing in all segments of society, including local governments and academic institutions. In many cases, the city, university, or corporate computer system became available to a library. Significant in this regard was the fact that local governments, university administrations, and corporations often perceived computer services as a centralized activity and a separate budget line item. These services were often made available to departments at a rate significantly below the actual operating costs of the computer center. In some cases, the services were offered at virtually no direct charge at all to the department. This milieu of overburdened manual library systems and the availability of more sophisticated technology that could improve the level of service, often at the same or even less cost to the library itself, presented an extremely favorable environment for librarians to realize applications for their growing interest in computers.

With a few exceptions later in the decade, computer applications in libraries during the 1960s involved offline batch processing. Computers were used to enhance operations in circulation, acquisitions, serials control, and cataloging. As compared with unit-record equipment, computers changed some essential features of these operations, but in many instances the main impact was to enable the same operations to be carried out faster and with less human effort. Printing circulation lists, for example, was an activity performed in several libraries before 1960 using unit-record equipment at a rate of 100 lines per minute. In contrast, the IBM 1403 printer used in many of the computerized systems during the 1960s did this same work at a rate of 1,100 lines per minute. For printing its serial lists, the library of the University of California Lawrence Radiation Laboratory used a high-speed printer that reportedly operated at the rate of 30,000 lines per minute.[14] The library daily produced its entire 160,000-line list of serials in slightly more than five minutes; older models of IBM unit-record equipment would have taken nearly 27 hours of machine time to complete the same job. For libraries with large circulation, serials, or order files, printing on unit-record equipment had simply been too slow to make frequent lists a feasible option. In computer systems, the data could be both processed and printed at such a faster rate that frequently updated lists became a possibility.

In addition to the importance of speed in processing and printing data, computers had other advantages over unit-record equipment. One of these was input and storage of data on medium other than 80-column cards, such as paper tape and magnetic tape. Many libraries continued to provide input on cards, but others began to record data on tape. Even if the input remained in the form of cards, tape storage eliminated the need to maintain the cards throughout the life cycle of a transaction, thus considerably reducing the size of card files that had to be maintained. This, combined with speed, resulted in a significant feature of computerized systems: removal or at least reduction of both the file and file maintenance operations around the library work station. And this was particularly true for computerized circulation systems, where the file could be reduced to a computer printout, which, because of the computer's speed, could be updated and printed out in multiple copies, if desired, on a daily basis. Most of the tasks involved in maintaining the file could be removed from the circulation station itself, which meant far less congestion and fewer people attempting to perform several different tasks on the same file at the same time.

Circulation Control

As with unit-record equipment, much of the focus in computerizing library operations centered on circulation. A survey conducted by Creative Research Services for the American Library Association (ALA) and the Special Libraries Association showed that by the mid-1960s, more than 80 libraries in the United States were using computerized circulation systems.[15] The LARC (Library Automation Research and Consulting) Association's survey a few years later identified more than 150 libraries using computers for circulation control.[16] Although neither survey was thoroughly comprehensive, both did include most of the libraries large enough to have computerized systems.

Among the 80 libraries in 1966 with computerized circulation control systems and another 40 with computer-based "classified document control" loan systems, the Creative Research Services survey identified 64 different computer models manufactured by ten different companies. Almost invariably, the computer equipment was housed in a centralized data processing facility outside the library. Although there may have been considerable diversity in the computer models available, the most predominant in the early 1960s belonged to IBM—the 1401 and the 1620. These later gave way to various models in the 360 and 370 series, along with a growing number of computers manufactured by other companies.

Techniques

More common than the model of mainframe during the 1960s was the equipment used to gather circulation information to serve as input into the computer. This consisted of the IBM 357 Data Collection System. The 357 operated in principle very much like the Montclair Public Library circulation system in use since the 1940s. The 357 machine had two slots. A punched borrower ID card was inserted into one slot. An IBM book card with the previously recorded call number, accession number, or other item identifier was inserted into the other slot. A borrower merely presented his or her ID along with the items to be charged. The desk attendant removed the punched card from the book and inserted it into the appropriate slot on the 357, inserted the borrower ID into the other slot, and either typed the date due on an attached keyboard or inserted a date due cartridge into the unit. This activated a keypunch machine, which combined borrower ID number, item identifier, and date due from the three separate pieces of information into a single punched "transaction card." The borrower's ID was returned, the book card was replaced in the book pocket, and the transaction card was retained by the library for later computer processing.

Some variations of this system connected two keypunch machines to the 357 unit; thus two identical transaction cards were keypunched for each charge. One card was retained by the library for processing, and the other was placed in the book pocket along with the book card. When the item was returned, the second transaction card was removed and served essentially as a discharge card for computer processing. Under the one-card system, it was necessary to generate a discharge card at the point of return. The book card was removed from the item and put into one slot on the 357; a special "return" badge, similar to a borrower ID card, was inserted into the other slot. This activated the keypunch machine to generate a discharge transaction card. In addition to patron badges and return badges, most libraries that had the 357 unit used special badges for fines payments and for charging items to the reserve book collection, interlibrary loan, the bindery, or any other location off the shelf.

In typical situations involving the 357 in the library and a computer in a remote facility, all charge, discharge, and other situational transaction cards for a given day were taken late that same evening to the data processing center that housed the computer and where the main circulation file was stored on magnetic tape. Before the opening of the library the next morning, the new transaction cards were run against the main file on the computer. New charges were added to the file, charges for returned items were deleted, overdues were identified, and fines calculated. The computer invariably had a peripheral printer attachment for generating output, and in the case of library circulation systems, this output took the form of lists of items currently in circulation, overdue and fines notices, and a variety of other lists and statistical tabulations. By the time the library opened, it had a completely updated circulation printout plus various other printed products.

Of course, there were variations on the above. Some libraries, for example, did not have overdue and fines notices printed at data processing, but they continued to be typed in the library. In contrast, other libraries not only had such notices printed, but developed programs incorporating borrower files, which would actually address the notice to the delinquent borrowers.

The 357 data collection system was predominant, but some libraries had other methods of generating input. The Johns Hopkins University Library, Baltimore, Maryland, for example, used a computer in its circulation procedure, but added an intervening step. Items were charged with the use of photography; the borrower's ID was photographed, along with the books to be charged, photographed in such a way that call numbers on spines could be read on the developed film. A date due sticker was pressed onto the back of each item being charged, before filming, thereby eliminating the need to open the book at all during the charging process. Using the developed film, a keypunch operator prepared a punched transaction card with call numbers, due date, and borrower ID. The same photographic and keypunching sequence was used for discharge. All transaction cards that resulted from these procedures were processed on an IBM 1401 housed in the library, and appropriate lists were printed.[17] In retrospect, this procedure appears much more cumbersome than those based on the 357, but it did circumvent the need to prepare and insert book cards as well as the need to handle any cards at the point of charging.

Despite the variety in the systems and in the specific applications, most realized a common set of advantages. Minimal effort was required both of patrons and of library staff in charging and discharging materials. The speed of computer processing and printing meant that a library's entire circulation file could be updated daily, at the same time eliminating bulky card files and maintenance congestion in the circulation department. The computer greatly reduced the traditionally considerable amount of library staff time spent on identifying overdues, calculating fines, and printing notices.

Conversion of Records to Machine-Readable Form

Although computerized circulation systems did have all the previously noted advantages, their effectiveness revolved around the availability of machine-readable information; specifically two types of machine-readable information, one identifying the borrower and the other identifying the items to be charged. Especially in academic libraries, machine-readable borrower identification proved little if any problem, since machine-readable numbers often had already been punched into student identification cards for purposes of registration and records. In some cases, these cards required minor modifications and in some cases were not at all compatible. But in many instances with the library's equipment, the identification cards could be used in charging units such as the 357 with no change at all.

Converting item records to machine-readable form was another matter. Except for those with systems that did not use machine-readable book cards, such as at Johns Hopkins, libraries were typically confronted with a massive task in preparing a machine-readable record for each item in the collection. In many cases the conversion effort was total: a book card was keypunched for virtually every item in the circulating collection before implementing the computer-based system. There were exceptions, such as the University of British Columbia Library, which did not prepare a machine-readable book card for an item until it actually circulated under the new system. This evened out the conversion process over time and considerably reduced the portion of the collection for which book cards had to be prepared. In this manner, an easily identifiable "collection within a collection" was also created of items that had not circulated since implementing the automated system and that, therefore, at some time in the future might be prime candidates for storage or removal.

In total conversion efforts, the shelflist usually provided the basis for conversion, with keypunch operators going through the shelflist one card at a time and preparing a machine-readable IBM book card for each item in the collection. Because of the magnitude of the project, often involving the preparation of book cards for several hundred thousand items, it was common to limit the information keypunched for each item to the least amount that would still provide sufficiently unique identification, perhaps just the call number or accession number. Some of these massive conversion projects used optical character recognition techniques instead of manual keypunching. The Southern Illinois University Library at Edwardsville, for example, used special mark-sensing pencils to code call numbers onto worksheets, eight items to a page. The coded sheets were then read by a computer and the call numbers converted to magnetic tape. The tape, in turn, was run to generate the IBM punched book card for each item.[18]

Total conversion, by whatever method, was time-consuming and costly. It is a commentary on the 1960s that many, although certainly not all, conversions were carried out at a time when data processing centers and their services, even keypunching, were heavily subsidized by the host institutions.

Shortcomings

The introduction of computers to library circulation in the 1960s was successful and greatly improved many aspects of the procedure. It did not, however, solve all problems. Although manual systems in some libraries had reached such a level of disarray that the circulation file was anything but an up-to-the-minute record, the batch processing character of the offline computerized circulation system inherently also had a temporal blind spot. The circulation printout prepared the previous night at the data processing center was current when the library opened the following morning, but would not be so again until the next update, usually after one full day's activity. The absence of easily determined records for the current day, however, was not a great price to pay given the advantages of a computerized system, especially since many manual systems also used batch filing procedures and thus had an updating delay of similar duration.

Another bottleneck that offline computerization could not entirely ease was the problem of identifying "holds." The 357 Data Collection System had no way automatically to determine if a hold had been placed on an item being discharged, and the procedure for dealing with holds largely remained manual. Some libraries maintained a file of holds in nonmachine-readable form, which was simply checked manually against returns before allowing reshelving. At the Texas A&M University Library, unit-record equipment was incorporated into the holds procedure. The accession number of an item placed on hold was punched onto an IBM card, and the file of these cards was matched on a collator against accession numbers on return transaction cards for recently returned items before reshelving.[19]

The American University Library, Washington, D.C., was one of the few to attempt to computerize the holds procedure. When a hold was placed, the library notified the data processing center, and a special value was indicated on the outstanding charge record stored on magnetic tape. When the item was returned and its return transaction card processed, the special value on the charge record caused the return card to be separated from the others. The only problem with this procedure was that all returned items had to await the next processing run before being reshelved. Since transaction cards were processed once daily after the library closed, this invariably meant that all returned items had to be held overnight before being reshelved.[20]

Acquisitions

The evolution from unit-record equipment to computers had profound implications for circulation work, as it significantly changed the amount of work and procedures required of both patrons and library staff. This transition in technology had a similar, although perhaps less dramatic, impact in acquisitions and serials control. In acquisitions, the changes introduced by the computer over a manual system were in essence the same as those achieved in some of the more sophisticated systems based on unit-record equipment. There was, however, an enormous difference between unit-record and computer equipment in the amount of time required to process and print acquisitions data.

In discussing the acquisitions system at the University of Illinois, Chicago campus, during the 1960s, Louis Schultheiss revealed that speed of printing was the decisive factor in opting for a computer-based system over unit-record equipment.[21] The importance of this can be demonstrated by the example of the University of Michigan Library, whose cumulative orders outstanding list, printed monthly, required about 2,800 pages.[22] The speed with which data was processed and printed by the earlier unit-record equipment, although faster than any alternative before the computer, was still too slow to make its use practical in the acquisitions departments of many larger libraries. The computer made it possible for such libraries to automate part of their acquisitions process and thereby gain greater control over their operations with more up-to-date information than was possible under manual or unit-record systems. The computer was used to generate orders, authorize payments, update and print orders outstanding lists, provide acceptably current fund reports, identify potential claims, and print notices if desired.

As in circulation, the computer in acquisitions allowed the transfer of at least some part of the relevant files in the library to the more compact medium of magnetic tape stored at the data processing center. The main orders outstanding file in systems based on unit-record equipment required storing at least one punched IBM card for each item on order from the moment it was ordered until the time it was received, paid for, and often cataloged. This could, and did, result in a very bulky central file. In a computer-based system, this same master file could be stored on magnetic tape. The computer did not totally eliminate the use of punched cards, since they generally served as the input medium for adding new orders, reporting changes in the status of outstanding orders, and deleting completed orders from the main file. Nevertheless, the master file itself could be stored much more compactly, and once any change could be incorporated into it, the punched card that was used to make the change could be thrown away.

Serials Control

In serials control the primary application of the computer was in the updating and printing of serials lists, the same emphasis as in the earlier use of unit-record equipment. During the early 1960s, several libraries attempted to go beyond this listing capability by implementing procedures for check-in and claiming. One of the first to do so was the University of California, San Diego (UCSD). Check-in revolved around the "arrival card" concept, and it was basically a computerized version of the unit-record systems already in use in a limited number of libraries. The San Diego project was started in 1961 with a conversion of records for 100 serials titles to machine-readable form and, after an initial test, was expanded over two years to include the remainder of UCSD's subscriptions. For each title, necessary information was keyed into machine-readable code, including title, call number, location, fund, source, subscription expiration date, number of issues per year and per volume, and so on. These data were stored on magnetic tape to serve as the master serials file, which could be updated and printed according to a prescribed schedule. The check-in and updating processes were based on generation of an IBM punched card containing issue-specific information for each issue of any title expected to be received during a month. All cards for the month were kept on file in the library; when a periodical arrived, its punched card was manually removed from the file. At the end of the month, the cards that remained in the file represented potential claims. Cards for issues that had arrived—and that had therefore been removed from the arrival card file—were run on the computer to update holdings on the master serials tape, and a new listing was printed. At that time, the next month's arrival cards were automatically generated.[23]

In due course, the arrival card method revealed four weaknesses with automating the check-in procedure: the myriad frequencies even for regularly issued periodicals; the unpredictability of the date of receipt even of titles with stated frequencies; the complexity and length of serials titles; and the amount of time required for checking in an issue. During the 1960s, several modifications were introduced to alleviate these problems. The library at the University of Washington School of Medicine developed a frequency coding scheme designed to make the generation of arrival cards follow a more discriminant pattern and to make identification of potential claims more efficient.[24] However, even the most accurate system for coding the dates on which issues of a title were supposed to be published in no way ensured that such issues actually would be published, or received by the library, anywhere near those or any other predictable dates. The frequent and seemingly unpredictable discrepancies between cover date and actual date of publication or receipt by the library became such a problem that some libraries ceased viewing the arrival card as a "prediction" card in any sense. The emphasis shifted to regarding the card as simply a convenient mechanism for keeping track of receipts and updating the master file.

Perhaps the most sophisticated effort to deal with the question of predictability and frequency was introduced in the late 1960s at UCSD. A "double calendar" was established for each title published monthly or less frequently. Each calendar had 12 positions. On the first calendar, each month was coded in which an issue was supposed to be published. The number of the calendar month in which the issue actually arrived was recorded on the second calendar. Thus, data were recorded for both cover date and actual date of receipt. In addition to allowing greater flexibility in coding frequency patterns for serial publications, this plan helped to predict more accurately long-range title-specific and even issue-number-specific arrival patterns, which in turn could improve the efficiency of the claiming procedure.[25]

The complexity and length of serials titles were another problem in the arrival card method. Only one punched card was generally used for each expected issue, but it had to include a considerable amount of detail. As a result, the amount of space for listing the title on an 80-column card was severely restricted; in many cases the title had to be greatly abbreviated. This often produced indistinguishable or very similar shortened titles, a critical problem since arrival cards were filed alphabetically. One solution was to use arrival lists in place of or as a supplement to the punched arrival cards, a strategy used by the University of Minnesota Biomedical Library. Rather than the computer punching all pertinent information on an 80-column card for each title, only a coded numerical title identifier was punched on the card. These arrival cards were then placed in a file arranged in numerical identifier order. The computer printed the title and all other pertinent information, including the numerical title identifier, on a paper list using as many lines for each title as necessary to provide clear and convenient identification. When an issue was received, it was checked in on the printed list by marking a designated column. The corresponding arrival cards, still necessary for updating the master serials file by computer, were manually removed from the arrival card file by matching the numerical title identifier on the printed list with those on the cards.

Perhaps most inhibiting of all, computer-assisted check-in systems did not seem to reduce the amount of staff time required as compared with even a strictly manual Kardex system. The computer assisted in generating arrival cards and filing them in a prescribed sequence, but the cards had to be manually removed when an issue arrived, and this required as much or even more time than checking in an issue on a Kardex file. This comparison, however, is not one of exactly equal function, for the arrival card also served as input for updating a machine-readable file of holdings from which serials lists could easily and frequently be printed, and it could also be helpful in quickly identifying potential claims.

The advantages of a computer-assisted procedure for check-in did not rest strictly in the check-in function itself, but rather in its relation to a broader concept of serials control. This was convincing enough reason for some libraries during the 1960s to tolerate, and even try to alleviate through design, some of the more obvious shortcomings of automated serials check-in.

Cataloging

The primary impact of unit-record equipment as it concerned cataloging in the library had been in facilitating the printing of book catalogs. For those libraries not wishing to abandon the card catalog, unit-record equipment did not readily lend itself to the task most in need of streamlining, namely, reproducing catalog card sets from a single unit entry. The most promising developments in this area had been automatic typewriters capable of producing machine-readable paper tapes, but even these were slow and required a great deal of staff work throughout the process.

In the early 1960s there were indications of improvements in the automatic typewriter method. Perhaps the foremost was a machine from Itek Corporation, which could automatically "expand" a unit entry on a punched paper tape into a full set of entries, complete with headings, onto a second tape. The second tape was run through an automatic typewriter to produce catalog cards. Some libraries already had automatic typewriters to perform essentially this task, but there was an important distinction between the capability of such a typewriter and the added value gained by using the Itek Crossfiler. With the automatic typewriter setup, a set of catalog cards could be produced for only one title at a time. It was necessary to manually change the unit entry and add entry tapes for each title. The Crossfiler allowed the library to eliminate this continuous handling by preparing a single input tape containing a number of unit entries and expanding it onto a continuous tape containing full sets of entries with appropriate headings for all titles included on the original tape. This continuous tape, when run through an automatic typewriter, produced catalog cards for all entries without further manual intervention. In the original application of the Crossfiler, a computer was used in place of an automatic typewriter for the printing of the catalog cards. Although cards could be printed faster on a computer, the Crossfiler was designed to be used in libraries that might have an automatic papertape typewriter but no access to a computer, and its main function of "expanding" unit entries into full sets of entries did not depend on a computer.[26]

The Itek machine was a promising innovation, but it was introduced at a time when some libraries were beginning to experiment with computers to perform essentially the same operation. Machine-assisted expansion of a unit entry into a full set of entries was achieved almost effortlessly by a computer, evidenced by the joint venture of the medical libraries at Harvard, Yale, and Columbia universities during the early 1960s. The procedure began with a cataloger preparing a worksheet for each item cataloged, with information written in catalog card format. A keypunch operator punched an IBM card for each line on the cataloging worksheet, thus requiring a sequence of several punched cards to form a unit entry for an item. Information on the unit entry was coded to identify headings, and the computer was programmed to make as many separate machine-readable records for an item as necessary based on the number of headings indicated. This expanded set of full records was then stored on magnetic tape.

The function of the Harvard-Yale-Columbia procedure served the same purpose up to that point as the Itek Crossfiler: automatic reproduction of machine-readable entries with appropriate headings. The next step in the computerized project, however, underscored a fundamental difference in capabilities between the computer and the Itek machine. The entries were sorted by the computer into filing order, so that when the final catalog cards were produced, they were alphabet-ized by heading, which was not possible with the Crossfiler. Initially, the computer output in the Harvard-Yale-Columbia project consisted of punched IBM cards produced from the alphabetically sorted machine records. These cards were then run through an automatic typewriter to transfer the data onto catalog card stock.[27]

Experimenting with the Machine-Readable Record

Other experiments during the early 1960s differed in many respects, but they all had the common purpose of producing, from a single unit entry, complete sets of catalog cards with appropriate headings automatically typed. They were also intended to break the constraints of the "80-column" syndrome. With unit-record equipment, it had been desirable to restrict information describing an item to one 80-column card, not only because this was more convenient for machine manipulation, but also because the punched cards had to be retained as a master file for further processing, and so there was emphasis on conserving storage space and reducing processing time. With the introduction of computers and tape storage, the convenience of 80-character description was less significant. For circulation book cards and arrival cards in serials check-in systems, it was still desirable to describe pertinent information as briefly as possible on a single IBM card. In acquisitions work, however, the 80-character limit presented extreme difficulties, and in cataloging it was even more problematic if an adequate amount of information was to be represented for each record.

An added difficulty in library work, and particularly in bibliographic description, was that the number of characters needed to describe an item could vary considerably. The traditional way of identifying input data for manipulation by unit-record equipment was to define a certain fixed range of positions on a punched card or cards for each distinct category of information: Positions 7 through 10 would be defined for one type of information, positions 11 through 20 for another type, and so on. These same positions were reserved on cards for the same element, such as call number, author, title, and so on, for each item cataloged.

For bibliographic information and the wide variety of possible types of data that might appear on cataloging records, a prescribed fixed length became a problem. There was no problem in providing data consisting of fewer characters than the maximum number of positions reserved for a particular category of information; the unused positions merely remained blank. The difficulty, however, was in defining the optimum number of positions to set aside for each category of bibliographic information. For example, to make sure that there would be room on a card or cards for the title of any item being cataloged, it was necessary to set aside a large number of positions to accommodate long titles even though most titles would take up far fewer positions than the number available. As a result, a long string of blank positions would usually appear before the start of the position range for the next information category, such as place of publication. Fixed length, when applied to cataloging data, had to result either in a far greater number of positions than were needed to describe most items or in a lesser number, sufficient to accommodate many items, but insufficient for others.

Solutions to these limitations imposed by fixed-length "fields" rested in the capability of computers to recognize coding structures. Schemes were devised and programmed into the computer that established a structure allowing variable-length input. The number of positions or the sequence reserved for the title could vary from one item to another, so long as the computer had some means for distinguishing where the title began and ended.

One of the most interesting proposals emerging during the early 1960s for allowing variable-length input was drawn up by the Florida Atlantic University Library in Boca Raton. Citing research conducted at the University of Illinois, Chicago campus, the Florida Atlantic design was based on applying a numerical coding scheme to bibliographic information. For example, the numerical value 10 on the computer input medium would always be followed by a main entry, the numerical value 23 by a title and edition statement, and so on. The numbering scheme remained consistent from one bibliographic item to the next. The computer could always identify the main entry of any work by the appearance of a numerical code 10 directly preceding a string of characters; a title and edition statement was identified by a numerical code 23 before a string of characters, and so on. Thus, the identification of and distinction between different types of bibliographic data were made on the basis of this coding scheme, regardless of the number of positions occupied by the text following a numerical value. Data were therefore not tied to rigid, fixed-length positioning on the input medium. Such numerical identifiers, referred to in early Florida Atlantic system descriptions as "knots," are generally known today as "tags."[28]

The Florida Atlantic tagging scheme was only one aspect of the automation activities charted by that library during the early 1960s. The university was a new campus in the state system, and plans for the new library, under the direction of Edward Heiliger, symbolized the visions of the most enthusiastic proponents of computer applications in libraries during that period. Acquisitions, cataloging, serials control, and circulation were all to be automated into one integrated, total library system, extending also into the public and reference services. The focus of professional librarians interested in automation, enthusiasts and skeptics alike, was squarely on Florida Atlantic.

As described by William Axford in the *Encyclopedia of Library and Information Science*, the application of Florida Atlantic's projects fell far short of their anticipated goals, and by 1967 "it became apparent that the experiment which had been launched with such confidence and such fanfare had failed."[29] The automated serials system was abandoned in 1966, followed the next year by the end of the automated acquisitions program and computer-generated book catalogs. Only the circulation system survived relatively intact.

The Florida Atlantic experience was a disappointment, but, in retrospect, its significance cannot be understated. Perhaps as much as any other automated activity in libraries during the early 1960s, it was Florida Atlantic's well-publicized development plans that fostered interest, debate, and self-assessment in the library profession with regard to the role of computer applications. The concept of a comprehensive system integrating traditionally separate functions through automation was an appealing idea. In the mid-1960s, some libraries, such as at Washington University School of Medicine, came closer to attaining this goal than Florida Atlantic ever did, but it was Florida Atlantic that had made the most far-reaching pronouncements and had leaped from a design stage headlong into an attempted total implementation.

Parts of the technical design at Florida Atlantic showed admirable foresight and ingenuity, most notably the coded knots, or field tags, to identify discrete types of variable-length information on a machine-readable record. Even this was abandoned early in the actual implementation of automated activities, but at least on a design basis it foreshadowed one of the most important developments in library automation during the decade of the 1960s, the evolution of the Library of Congress MARC format.

Library of Congress and MARC Format

In descriptions of unit-record applications in libraries, an advantage often cited was that a machine-readable unit record created once for an item could be built upon and used repeatedly for a variety of purposes, including acquisitions, cataloging, circulation, and serials inventory, if appropriate. However, a companion emphasis in any application was on brevity of description, due in large part to the 80-column card and the time required to manipulate large amounts of data, particularly in alphabetical arrangement. Even in the production of book catalogs, the general trend had been toward abbreviated entries limited to an 80-character length. The 80-column limitation stymied the versatility of the record. Furthermore, there had been little attempt by libraries to use any standard positioning or coding structures that could have facilitated the transference of records between libraries.

With their faster processing speeds, compact storage, and use of input and storage media extending beyond the punched card, computers more closely accommodated the concept of the full-entry, machine-readable bibliographic unit record. Since the early 1900s, in one form or another, the Library of Congress had been a major source of full-entry cataloging data for use by libraries in the United States, and in the 1960s this role took on an added dimension in the supply of bibliographic data in machine-readable form. Beginning in 1964 and culminating with the start of a distribution service in 1968, the evolution of the LC MARC (Machine Readable Cataloging) format through a design stage, trial application, and revised version represents an achievement of truly important magnitude in American librarianship.

The development of the MARC II format, which became available to libraries in 1968 and is still in use, was the result of a series of studies, proposals, and evaluations over the several previous years. An important step was taken in 1964 when the Council on Library Resources awarded Inforonics, Inc., a grant to study the feasibility and possible methods of converting information on Library of Congress catalog cards to machine-readable form. Inforonics submitted its report in November,[30] and the following January a Conference on Machine-Readable Catalog Copy was held at the Library of Congress. Several important conclusions were reached, and the Library of Congress was urged to proceed with the design of a standard machine-readable format for the transfer of bibliographic data. In June 1965, LC issued *A Proposed Format for a Standardized Machine-Readable Catalog Record.*[31] This report and supplementary comments were the focus of the Second Congress on Machine-Readable Catalog Copy held at LC in November. The following month, the Council on Library Resources awarded LC a grant for design and programming to represent LC cataloging data in machine-readable form and to initiate a pilot project involving use of that data by 16 libraries (expanded to 20 during the course of the project).

The format devised by LC included a series of both fixed-length and variable-length fields on the machine-readable record. The first 108 positions on the record consisted of 25 fields of fixed length for which bibliographic or control data could be specified or coded. The remainder of the record was a structure of numerically coded field tags identifying the types of variable-length data that were to follow. The distribution of cataloging data on magnetic tapes on a weekly basis to participants in the MARC pilot project was to begin in September 1966 and continue through June 1967, with each tape cumulating all machine-readable records created since the beginning of the project. Programs were written by a contracting firm to facilitate use of the tapes by participants. Each participant was to experiment with the tapes and evaluate the format, method of distribution, and general value of distributing LC cataloging copy in machine-readable form.

Regular distribution of the tapes was postponed until November 1966. The tape programs written by the contracting firm were problematic at best. The difficulty in modifying these programs or in writing completely new ones at each institution initially dampened several of the participants' enthusiasm. At least two of them felt that debugging programs or writing new ones to manipulate the MARC tapes was not economically feasible given the nature and duration of the project, and most of the remaining libraries that did rectify the problem spent considerable time and expense in doing so. Although some participants reported that the data processing centers of their institutions were extremely helpful, others noted less than friendly service, and one library was unable to participate in the project primarily because of some confusion over city government administration of the data processing department.[32]

In spite of these setbacks, there was generally strong support for the idea of distributing machine-readable LC cataloging copy. The participants that did manage to successfully manipulate the tapes found them helpful in the printing of preorder bibliographic listings, catalog cards, and sample book catalogs. Rice University, Houston, Texas, for example, reported that "Our best estimate is that three years and considerable sums of money have been saved by our participation in the MARC project."[33]

Apart from problems with supplied programs, participants noted several areas in which the distribution service could be made more effective. One was in the coverage of information. In the pilot project, only titles for English-language monographs were included on the tapes; expansion of this coverage to other formats and languages was recommended to enhance the value of the service. Participants felt that cumulating coverage on each new tape was unnecessary and that it would actually be easier if each weekly tape included only new information generated since the previous week. Several participants were critical but understanding of the unacceptably high incidence of typographical and tagging errors on records. Timeliness of records was another area of concern. Most participants kept comparisons of the appearance of cataloging copy on the MARC tapes with the arrival of LC proofslips and found the latter generally to be available a week or two before the tapes. Finally, most of the participants offered concrete suggestions concerning the system of tagging used in the MARC format to identify elements of bibliographic description.

Identifying these shortcomings was an integral part of the purpose of the MARC pilot project. In order to evaluate the worthiness of the service and make it an effective program, it was necessary to test it, pinpoint needed improvements, and incorporate these into the final product. Despite some blatant shortcomings, participants felt that the project represented a potentially valuable service. As for the MARC format itself, revision was underway almost as soon as the pilot project was begun and continued throughout the duration. The result was the MARC II format in 1968. Although subject to continual revision, MARC II has remained an important standard in American libraries to this day.

When the MARC Distribution Service was made generally available on a subscription basis, the Argonne National Laboratory temporarily assumed the role of copying and distributing the LC tapes to subscribers. By the end of the first year, there were nearly 80 subscribers. It was apparent, however, that not all were actually integrating the tapes into their library operations. Hillis Griffin of the Argonne National Laboratory reported that of 74 subscribers contacted in late 1969, he could identify only 13 that were actually using the tapes.[34] It would only be a matter of time, however, before the MARC Subscription Service, and even more so the MARC II format, would have a strong impact on librarianship in the United States.

Although there were important achievements during the 1960s in the application of offline batch processing computerization to library procedures, its existence as state-of-the-art technology was short-lived. Even by the middle of the decade, it was apparent that online, interactive systems would be within the grasp of libraries before too long. Lessons had been learned with both the unit-record and offline computer applications. The experience sometimes might have been painful, but inevitably automation clearly showed great promise in traditional technical library operations.

Notes

1. Allie Beth Martin, "Tulsa Finds New Aid in Photographic Charging," *Library Journal* 74 (October 1, 1949): 1476.
2. Tera Bailey, "Charlotte Experiments with Audio Charging," *Library Journal* 75 (June 15, 1950): 1066.
3. *Ibid.*, p. 1067.
4. Lillian M. Speer, "Charging Books the Audio Way," *Wilson Library Bulletin* 25 (September 1950): 58–59.

5. "Audio-charging: A Misunderstood Orphan?" *Library Journal* 87 (May 15, 1962): 1845.
6. Ralph H. Parker, "The Punched Card Method in Circulation Work," *Library Journal* 61 (December 1, 1936): 904.
7. *Ibid.*
8. James R. Cox, "Circulation Control with IBM Unit Record Equipment at UCLA," in *IBM Library Mechanization Symposium, Endicott, New York, May 25, 1964* (White Plains, N.Y.: IBM Data Processing Division, 1965), pp. 95–131.
9. For a description of the Montclair system, see Ralph H. Parker, *Library Applications of Punched Cards* (Chicago: American Library Association, 1952), pp. 31–37.
10. For a description of the Decatur system, see Mary T. Howe and Mary K. Weidner, "Data Processing in the Decatur Public Library," *Illinois Libraries* 44 (November 1962): 593–597.
11. Alexander Moffit, "Punched Card Records in Serials Acquisitions," *College & Research Libraries* 7 (January 1946): 12.
12. Natalie N. Nicholson, and William Thurston, "Serials and Journals in the M.I.T. Library," *American Documentation* 9 (October 1958): 307.
13. *Catalog Card Reproduction* (Chicago: American Library Association, 1965), p. 39.
14. John B. Verity, and Elizabeth L. Crocker, "A Computer-Based System for Serials Records at Lawrence Radiation Laboratory," *Journal of the American Society for Information Science* 21 (July/August 1970): 248.
15. Cited in C. D. Gull, "Automated Circulation Systems," in *Library Automation: A State of the Art Review*, Stephen R. Salmon, ed. (Chicago: American Library Association, 1969), p. 139.
16. Barbara Evans Markuson, "Application of Automation in American Libraries; An Analysis of the LARC Survey Returns," in *Survey of Automated Activities in the Libraries of the U.S. and Canada*, 2nd ed. (Tempe, Ariz.: LARC Publications Office, 1971), p. 2.
17. Benjamin Courtright, "The Johns Hopkins University Library," in *Proceedings of the 1966 Clinic on Library Applications of Data Processing* (Urbana, Ill.: University of Illinois Graduate School of Library Science, 1966), pp. 18–33.
18. L. R. DeJarnett, "Library Circulation Control Using IBM 357s at Southern Illinois University," in *IBM Library Mechanization Symposium, Endicott, New York, May 25, 1964* (White Plains, N.Y.: IBM Data Processing Division, 1965), p. 87.
19. Bruce W. Stewart, "Data Processing in an Academic Library," *Wilson Library Bulletin* 41 (December 1966): 390.
20. Patricia Ann Stockton, "An IBM Circulation Procedure," *College and Research Libraries* 28 (January 1967): 39.
21. Louis A. Schultheiss, "Data Processing Aids in Acquisitions Work," *Library Resources and Technical Services* 9 (Winter 1965): 66–67.
22. James M. Thomson, and Robert H. Muller, "The Computer-Based Book

Order System at the University of Michigan Library," in *Proceedings of the 1968 Clinic on Library Applications of Data Processing* (Urbana, Ill.: University of Illinois Graduate School of Library Science, 1969), p. 59.

23. George Udovin, Melvin J. Voight, David Newman, and Clay Perry, "Computer Processing of Serials Records," *Library Resources and Technical Services* 7 (Winter 1963): 71–80.

24. See Irwin H. Pizer, Donald R. Franz, and Estelle Broadman, "Mechanization of Library Procedures in a Medium-sized Medical Library: I. The Serial Record," *Bulletin of the Medical Library Association* 51 (July 1963): 328–329.

25. Don L. Bosseau, "The Computer in Serials Processing and Control," in *Advances in Librarianship,* vol. 2 (New York: Seminal Press, 1971).

26. For a description of the Itek Crossfiler, see Paul J. Fasana, "Automating Cataloging Functions in Conventional Libraries," *Library Resources and Technical Services* 7 (Fall 1963): 350–365.

27. For a description of this project, see Frederick G. Kilgour, "Development of Computerization of Card Catalogs in Medical and Scientific Libraries," in *Proceedings of the 1964 Clinic on Library Applications of Data Processing* (Urbana, Ill.: University of Illinois Graduate School of Library Science, 1965), pp. 25–35.

28. For a description of the Florida Atlantic coding scheme, see Edward M. Heiliger, "Use of a Computer at Florida Atlantic University for Mechanized Catalog Production," in *IBM Library Mechanization Symposium, Endicott, New York, May 25, 1964* (White Plains, N.Y.: IBM Data Processing Division), pp. 165–186.

29. Axford H. William, "Florida Atlantic University Library," in *Encyclopedia of Library and Information Science,* vol. 8 (New York: Marcel Dekker, 1972), p. 547.

30. Lawrence F. Buckland, *The Recording of Library of Congress Bibliographical Data in Machine Form* (Washington, D.C.: Council on Library Resources, 1965).

31. Henriette D. Avram, Ruth S. Freitag, and Kay G. Guiles, *A Proposed Format for a Standardized Machine-Readable Catalog Record* (Washington, D.C.: Library of Congress, 1965).

32. Henriette D. Avram, *The MARC PILOT Project* (Washington, D.C.: Library of Congress, 1968), p. 119.

33. *Ibid.,* p. 119.

34. Hillis Griffin, "MARC Users: A Study of the Distribution of MARC Tapes and the Subscribers to MARC," in *Proceedings of the 1970 Clinic on Library Applications of Data Processing* (Urbana, Ill.: University of Illinois Graduate School of Library Science, 1971), p. 31.

3

Online Technical Support Systems

The use of computers and the creation of a standardized MARC format were significant achievements in the evolution of library automation, but their full impact was best realized within the context of other important developments occurring between the mid-1960s and the mid-1970s. The cornerstone of these developments was a radical change in mass market computer technology, characterized by faster processing, increased storage capability, and decreasing hardware prices. Systems such as the IBM 1401, popular in library use during the early and mid-1960s, comprised what came to be known as second-generation computers. Faster and incorporating far greater memory in less physical space than the vacuum tube based computers of the 1950s, the second-generation machines were based on solid state circuitry. Such rapid and quantum advances were made in solid state computer technology that, even by the mid-1960s, newer models of computers were so much more powerful than the IBM 1401 that a third generation was hailed. The magnitude of technological advancement even within the third generation can be shown by comparing two disk transport systems, the IBM 2314 and the IBM 3330, from the late 1960s and early 1970s. The 2314 utilized removable pack, rotating disk memories of about 29,000,000 characters per pack; a piece of information could be assessed in an average of 75 milliseconds (75/1000 of a second) and read into core memory at 300,000 characters per second. The capacity of each pack in the 3330 system was 100,000,000 characters; the time of access was reduced to 30 milliseconds, and information could be read into memory at a rate in excess of 800,000 characters per second.[1]

As processing speeds and storage capabilities were increasing, the size and price of the machinery were decreasing. By the early 1970s, computers appeared on the market that were comparatively so small and inexpensive that they warranted the label of "minicomputer." Slower and less powerful than their contemporary larger counterparts, minicomputers possessed capabilities that matched and exceeded the most sophisticated second-generation computers of barely a decade before, and at a mere fraction of the price. In a 1977 issue of *Library Technology Reports,* William Scholtz put the comparison in perspective:

> In 1960, the IBM 1620 computer needed a room that was approximately 20 by 30 feet. . . . In 1974, a similar machine in terms of capability took up a space that was approximately 3 feet by 3 feet . . . [and] could perform identical tasks to those performed by the IBM 1620 in about one quarter the time. And finally, the cost to *buy* the 1974 machine was about what it cost to *rent* the IBM 1620 for one month.[2]

The chief implication of these technological advancements in terms of library application was to usher in the era of online automation. Although the minicomputer would play its own role in this development, earlier online library systems in the late 1960s were based on use of the larger third-generation computers. The computers for these systems were shared among a number of users and invariably were located outside the library in a centralized data processing facility.

Another difference between second- and third-generation facilities was the extent of the latter's timesharing capacity. Second-generation systems were generally not capable of timesharing; the computer processed one job before moving to the next job in the queue. The remarkable advancements in speed, all tasks associated with design, and storage capacity in third-generation systems allowed them to process a number of jobs simultaneously—or so it seemed. In actual fact, the computer still performed one task at a time, but could handle several jobs coincidentally and execute tasks so quickly that it appeared to each user that the computer was interacting exclusively with their programs, files, and commands.

Although the technological environment for online library systems has been in place since the late 1960s, their realization by the late 1970s was still in a stage of infancy if viewed within the context of the totality of libraries in the United States. Despite the decrease in computer hardware prices that characterized the late 1960s, the design, implementation, and maintenance of an online system were still prohibitively expensive for all but a few libraries during the late 1970s, and even most of these required special grant funding.

Between the late 1960s and late 1970s, three trends evolved in the development of online library systems. The first consisted of pioneering in-house projects in single institutions. The second centered around the evolution of what came to be known as "bibliographic utilities." The third trend was the emergence of private enterprises developing prepackaged "turnkey" (plug it in and turn it on) automated library systems. These three trends are discussed in the remainder of this chapter.

In-house Circulation Developments

Much as with unit-record equipment and computerized offline batch processing, the earliest online library systems focused on circulation.

Illinois State Library System

One of the first online systems was at the Illinois State Library in Springfield, in late 1966, at a time when many other libraries were designing fully offline systems. The backbone of the system was an IBM 1620 computer located in the state processing facility. The equipment in the library consisted of IBM 1033 printers and 1031 card readers, which were similar in operation to the 357 Data Collection System, requiring insertion of machine-readable book cards and borrower identification badges. Rather than producing transaction cards or recording transaction data on tape, however, the 1031s at the Illinois State Library transmitted data directly to the computer.

By later standards, the online system at the library was primitive. Although transaction information was conveyed directly to the computer as it occurred, it was stored on a separate daily transaction pack and was merged with the main circulation file only on a once-a-day batch processing basis. The system did not include item-specific online query, so that it was still necessary to use offline batch-produced circulation lists to trace circulation information pertaining to a given item. For these purposes, the system was much like wholly offline batch processing systems. What set it apart from those, however, was its ability to perform two important functions online: checking borrower registration numbers for validity and checking each returned item against an online holds file. Each time a borrower identification card was inserted into the designated slot of the 1031, the borrower number was automatically checked against a computer-stored file of valid borrower numbers. If the borrower's number did not have a counterpart in the file, that fact was generated immediately on the 1033 printer. This was a major improvement over completely offline operations, where such validation, if done at all, could be performed only by manual lookup in a printed directory of borrower numbers.

The other important online function of the Illinois State Library system was checking holds, and that had equally important implications. When the book card of a returned item was placed in the 1031 for discharge, the call number was checked against an online list of call numbers of items placed on hold. If the call number of the returned item matched a call number in the holds file, a message was automatically generated on the 1033 printer showing call number, identification number of the patron who had placed the item on hold, and the date when the hold had been placed. In this manner, greater control over holds was realized than was possible in offline batch processing computerized circulation systems.[3]

Midwestern University System

Another early online circulation system was implemented in late 1967 at Midwestern University in Wichita Falls, Texas. The Midwestern system was unique in that it was, at least insofar as its designers knew, the first and perhaps only online circulation system to operate on an IBM 1401 computer, a decidedly second-generation machine.[4]

Like the Illinois State Library system, Midwestern used IBM 1031 input stations and 1033 printers, validated borrower identification numbers, and checked items against an online holds file. But it went further than the Illinois system in several important respects. Not only did the Midwestern system check borrower numbers during a charging operation for general validation, but it also determined if a borrower had any outstanding overdue items or unpaid fines. If so, the computer generated an immediate list of the charges on the 1033 printer. The Midwestern system had an online query capability, albeit restricted to searching on a borrower number. The keying in of a number prompted the computer to respond by printing a list on the 1033 containing all items charged to that borrower. But perhaps the fundamental difference in the Midwestern system was that the main circulation file was online in the strict sense of the term, with the file being updated immediately upon completion of each transaction, rather than in a batch mode.

Eastern Illinois University System

In September 1968, the Booth Library at Eastern Illinois University in Charleston began to operate its own version of an online circulation system using a third-generation IBM 360/Model 50 computer and the IBM 1031 input stations and 1033 printers. The Booth system had the basic functional characteristics of the Midwestern system, but with an important additional query feature. The Midwestern system had query capability by patron number; the Booth system supplemented this with item query by call number. By entering a particular two-digit code followed by a call number, a terminal operator could retrieve bibliographic information and current circulation data about a specific item. Queries of this nature were made using an IBM Cathode Ray Tube (CRT) terminal located at the circulation desk.

A further extension of this search capability was a scanning command that displayed bibliographic entries in call number sequence. Since the Booth Library online file was an inventory file containing an abbreviated bibliographic record for nearly every item in the library— not just items currently charged out—the scanning capability allowed shelflist searching of the entire library collection. The structure and search capabilities of this system suggested possible extension as a public-access tool, and in fact plans were announced to locate a public-access CRT terminal near the card catalog in fall 1971.[5] By 1973, however, these plans had not been realized.[6] Still, the known item query capability of the Eastern Illinois system allowed more immediate information about the circulation status of an item—even if the query had to be generated by a circulation attendant—than was possible in an offline system.

Minicomputer-based Hybrids

In the early 1970s, a number of academic libraries began to incorporate minicomputers in their circulation operations. A significant feature of these systems was that at least part of the processing hardware was located in the library itself, although a larger computer, outside the library, still played an integral role. Typically, the minicomputer in the library contained certain files for immediate online access and captured transaction data for later batch transmission to a larger computer located outside the library on which the main circulation file was stored. While some of the operations remained offline, this setup realized the benefits of online processing for certain critical purposes.

One of the more common minicomputers in this type of configuration was the IBM System/7, in use in circulation control in at least six libraries by early 1974.[7] In the system operational at the University of Pennsylvania in Philadelphia, five online files were stored in the minicomputer. Each of these contained critical information against which various types of transactions were checked. There were three item files against which renewal attempts and discharges were checked. A call number file contained the call number of all items placed on hold, the access number file contained a list of all items recalled, and a reserve book file contained all items for which a request had been placed to transfer the item to a reserve book collection upon its return. Another file, against which all patron identification numbers were checked, was the restricted patron file, containing a list of borrower identification numbers of all users whose further attempts to charge materials were to be blocked for some reason. The fifth online file was the daily transaction file, which recorded the day's activity. Once a day, this file was transmitted to the main computer, an IBM 370/Model 168, located at the university data processing center, for batch updating of the main circulation file. This transmission, usually involving information for about 3,000 transactions, required about 30 minutes.[8]

For the most part, improvements gained in the online circulation systems of the late 1960s and early 1970s over what was possible in an offline system were focused on immediate access to information about restricted items, such as holds, and better control of patron privileges. Although improvements regarding access to information about restricted items enhanced public service by allowing more rapid reshelving of returned items and a better system for regulating holds and ensuring identification upon return, these benefits were not always immediately evident to the average library user. The second common capability, immediate access to online delinquent patron files, could as likely cause ill feelings as goodwill between the library and its users. The lack of reliable backup measures, inexperience in dealing with online systems, and continued reliance on batch-produced circulation lists combined to make early online circulation systems less than revolutionary in terms of public service. At least one facility, the Simon Fraser University Library, had so many problems and so much user discontent with its online system that it abandoned online and reverted to its earlier offline system.[9]

Ohio State University System

Perhaps the outstanding example during the early 1970s of an online circulation system that could, in fact, facilitate user services to a degree not possible in an offline system was demonstrated by Ohio State University's Library Control System. The entire philosophy behind the design and application of the system for the Ohio State University libraries was, as described by Hugh Atkinson, "that the system should be one which would speak to the problems of its users rather than simply the problems of the library."[10] These problems included, among others, a decentralized library structure consisting of a main library and more than 20 branches. Only one catalog—the main library's—contained complete information for all items in all 21 libraries.

Similar to several earlier online circulation systems, Ohio State opted for an "inventory" file approach in which the main machine-readable database contained records for all items in the libraries rather than an "absence" file, which would have contained records only for those items in circulation. This principle was fundamental at Ohio State since the system was to be used as a locator file as well as for circulation operations. A massive conversion effort—perhaps the largest of its kind carried out by any library to that date—was contracted to a vendor, which put into machine-readable form records containing call number, unique item number, author, title, date of publication, Library of Congress card number, language code, form of publication code, and holdings for each of 1 million distinct titles and 2.5 million items.

The key to the Ohio State system was its item query capability. Searching was possible by call number, title key, and a combination author/title key. When the desired item was retrieved, it was possible to see which library or libraries on campus owned a copy of the item, and whether each copy was charged out. Search terminals were available in the main library and in most of the branches. Thus, the entire union catalog of the libraries' holdings could be assessed from any library in the system. Although this in itself was a monumental improvement over the single union catalog in the main library, the online system went even further with a remote charging capability. An item not already checked out in one library could be charged on terminals located in any other library. Thus, if a patron in a branch library requested an item and a copy was found to be available in a different branch library, the circulation attendant could issue a command that would generate a charge slip in the branch library that had the copy. The item would be retrieved in that library and placed on a shelf to await later pickup by the patron. The online union catalog, showing location and circulation status of each item throughout the system, combined with the capability of remote charging to remove much of the patron uncertainty that was inherent under prior circumstances.

The Ohio State University library system, like all other online systems, was not entirely free of problems,[11] but many of them could eventually be alleviated by design changes, and the system was such an improvement over earlier conditions that the problems were of comparatively minor consequence. The impact of this system on library service was probably best exemplified by the fact that, during the first 18 months it was in operation, circulation at the Ohio State University libraries increased by more than 40 percent.[12] The system was an important achievement owing to its scale of implementation, its query capabilities, and its emphasis on public service problem solving. The same system was later taken by Atkinson to the University of Illinois and implemented; today it is the basis of an important networking system in libraries throughout Illinois.

Acquisitions, Cataloging, and Serials Control Development

Apart from circulation, the late 1960s and early 1970s saw the development of a number of online technical processing systems. One of the earliest acquisitions systems was designed at the Washington State University Library in Pullman and was implemented in 1968; an online serials control system was up and running at Université Laval in Quebec the same year. Predating both of these was the beginning of a comprehensive online library system at the Redstone Scientific Information Center in Alabama. Some parts of the system were operational as early as 1966, and by the early 1970s, acquisitions, cataloging, authority control, serials check-in, and circulation were online.[13]

Offline computerization had been an important development in acquisitions, providing for machine-assisted production of purchase orders, improved methods of fiscal control, and more timely updating and generation of status lists. Still, a significant amount of form handling and paper file maintenance remained in many of these systems. The online acquisitions systems developed in the late 1960s and early 1970s represented major improvements by reducing the amount of manual handling and maintenance of paper products, as well as further enhanced those functions that had been performed well in offline computerized systems.

Acquisitions

One of the more ambitious projects in the late 1960s was carried out at the Oregon State University Library at Corvallis. Christened LOLITA, this online acquisitions system required nearly seven "staff years" in programming, systems, and clerical labor to develop. It contained three online files: order/in-process, vendor, and fund accounting. Each online record in the order/in-process file contained three display screens of information input when an order was placed, and updated as an item passed through the acquisitions and cataloging procedures. The first screen included basic bibliographic data, the second screen contained accounting data, and the third screen allowed for local cataloging information such as call number and location. The amount of time and file maintenance that this system saved the staff, particularly when compared with a manual system, was considerable.[14]

LOLITA generated four paper copies of each order, two going to the vendor, one later used as a cataloging workslip, and one retained as a general hard copy record for the library. The two copies for library use were a reduction over most offline systems, and some libraries went even further. With the online acquisitions systems in use at the University of Massachusetts Library and the Dartmouth College Library, neither library retained any paper copies of the order form in technical processing at all.[15]

One of the greatest contributions made by online systems in general was the expansion of access points, and these early acquisitions systems were no exception. It was possible with an offline system to produce lists or maintain paper copies of order forms by more than one point of access, such as by order number, author, and title if desired, but that merely increased the number of lists to be consulted or files to be maintained. As a result, the number of listing parameters was usually minimized in offline systems. In online systems, all files and their indexes could be maintained in the computer, and multiple access points to a single record would not mean an increase in hard copy materials to be consulted or maintained. LOLITA, however, only provided two access points, order number and author, to each record in the system.

The early online acquisitions systems retained some of the capabilities that had been included in their offline predecessors, but the newer systems were much improved in quality, speed, and ease of handling. LOLITA, along with several other early systems, provided for handling of partial shipments and authorization of partial invoice payments, capabilities that were handled, if at all, only with some difficulty by offline systems. The fund accounting component of LOLITA was also successful. A year-end encumbrance report could be generated in 20 minutes, and LOLITA was not only much faster, but also judged more accurate and detailed in a controlled comparison with manual ledgers.[16]

Perhaps the most important characteristic of online acquisitions systems was that, in most cases, it was only one part of a broader integrated technical processing system that brought the acquisitions and cataloging functions closer together. The online order record, upon receipt of an item, became an online cataloging record. This greatly reduced duplication between acquisitions and cataloging and also provided an end product consisting of a machine-readable bibliographic record for each item entering the collection. In LOLITA, the final steps in the online processing after an item had been received were for a cataloger to verify the bibliographic information originally entered by the acquisitions department and then complete the record by adding local cataloging data. The completed record was removed from the online file, but not before it had been copied onto magnetic tape as a permanent machine-readable record.[17]

An important feature in the development of online technical processing systems was the incorporation of Library of Congress MARC records. Records on MARC tapes were transferred into the local online systems in various ways. A common feature across systems was that each new order was searched against a locally maintained MARC file, and when a match occurred, the appropriate MARC record entered the local system as the source for bibliographic information for ordering and eventual cataloging.

One of the most comprehensive uses of MARC records evolved in the University of Chicago Library Data Management System. Orders could be searched against the MARC files, and there was a retrospective searching capability whereby incoming MARC records were searched against the local bibliographic file to identify previously created local records as potential candidates for bibliographic upgrading by the new matching MARC record. These features in one form or another could be found in other systems, but an interesting feature of the Chicago system was its use of MARC tapes as a collection development tool. Subject profiles, defined by Library of Congress classification numbers and ranges of numbers, could be maintained online, and each incoming MARC tape was matched against them. The result was an offline list of items falling into each subject profile for use in identifying potential orders for the library. The system also allowed access to these lists online if a bibliographer wished. Supplementing the LC class number profiles were certain national bibliography online profiles used to identify potential orders from an area studies perspective. In addition to profiles designed to identify items of potential interest for the library, the University of Chicago system also included a capability designed to assist in better control over blanket orders from publishers. The first four digits of an International Standard Book Number (ISBN), MARC field 020, are unique to each publisher. Each record on the MARC tapes was automatically searched on these first four digits at Chicago. The system could then generate lists of items published by each publisher with whom Chicago had a blanket order arrangement, and these lists could be used to assist in monitoring receipt of blanket order items.[18]

BALLOTS

Several of the largest research libraries in the United States were interested in the concept of an online integrated technical processing system as early as the mid-1960s, although actual systems could be implemented at these institutions only after several years of planning, design, and experimentation. Three of the more well publicized of these large-scale efforts included the Northwestern Online Total Integrated System (NOTIS), the University of Chicago Library Data Management System mentioned earlier, and Stanford University's Bibliographic Automation of Large Library Operations using a Time-sharing System (BALLOTS). Without minimizing the importance of achievements elsewhere, BALLOTS was perhaps the most sophisticated online technical processing system developed in the early 1970s. Because of its later adoption as the online bibliographic component of the Research Libraries Group (RLG), its impact on American librarianship during the 1970s and early 1980s has been greater than any other system originally designed for use by a single institution.

An experimental version of BALLOTS was brought online as early as 1969, but it was not until 1972, after further design and modification, that the system was fully implemented. It ran on the Stanford University campus computer, an IBM 360/Model 67, with a Digital Equipment Corporation PDP 11 minicomputer in the library as a front-end communications processor. The terminals initially selected for accessing the system were programmable Sanders PDS 804s.

The hardware for BALLOTS was in itself an important achievement. The selection of terminals with a programmable capability was based on the design requirements for the terminal display features desired. Two important functional considerations were to allow for protected fields in an online record that could not be modified by a terminal operator, and at the same time to permit line insertion to allow expansion in length of certain nonprotected fields. At the time BALLOTS was being designed, either one of these features could be incorporated by using a nonprogrammable terminal, but not a combination of the two. Only a programmable terminal, such as the Sanders model, could allow both protected and expandable fields. In addition, it was possible for several programmable terminals to share a single communications line rather than each requiring its own dedicated line.[19]

BALLOTS was designed around several modules and contained four online files critical to technical processing. One was a MARC file, which held the most recent 6 to 12 months of MARC records from the Library of Congress. A second was an In-Process File (IPF), which contained a record for each item anywhere in the processing stage from initiation of an order to final cataloging. Once received and cataloged, the record was transferred into a third file, the Catalog Data File (CDF), which contained an online record for each item fully processed on BALLOTS. Fourth was a Reference File (REF), which included see references, see also references, and explanatory and history references.

When a request for an order was submitted, a terminal operator first searched the MARC file to see if a corresponding MARC record was available. If a match was found, the operator requested an online ordering work form, which contained mnemonic fields into which information could be entered. Appropriate bibliographic data were automatically transferred from the MARC record to the work form, requiring the terminal operator to input only the additional information pertaining to the order, such as vendor code and accounting data. An online order record could easily be created for an item where there was no available MARC record, but this naturally required more time since bibliographic information had to be supplied from other sources and typed onto the online work form. Offline products, such as purchase orders, a cataloging workslip, and a temporary order slip, were printed each evening for all items entered into the In-Process File during the day. Stanford found the traditional 3″ × 5″ slip too small for its purposes and, as described by Veaner, "because copies of certain forms no longer had to be filed, the forms themselves could be designed around their data requirements rather than a filing cabinet size."[20]

The online order form was updated as its status changed, such as when an item was received. After receipt was indicated, the item was given to the cataloging department for final processing. One of the helpful features of BALLOTS was its tracing procedure; the location of an item within the processing unit was kept up-to-date online even to the name of the specific cataloger handling the final processing. It was the responsibility of the cataloging department, with item in hand, to verify and, if necessary, modify the information on the online record created in acquisitions and to add any additional pertinent data. Catalog cards and spine labels were then printed offline, with the day's production of all cataloging cards sorted into filing order sequence. The online record was transferred into the Catalog Data File as the permanent bibliographic and holdings inventory record.

BALLOTS had a number of built-in features that made input and modification of records easy for a terminal operator and at the same time reduced the likelihood of operator error. Fields that were inappropriate for operator input or modification were automatically protected so the operator could not even place the cursor in those positions on the screen display. After entering information into a nonprotected field, the operator could move the cursor to the next nonprotected field simply by depressing the shift and tab keys. Throughout the procedure were default protocols that assumed the operator's next most logical step but these could be overriden by the operator if an item required atypical treatment.

The system also had validation capabilities for certain types of information such as account codes. When an account code was entered by an operator onto the online order work form, the system checked the code validity. This check did not prevent a valid inaccurate code from being assigned to an item, but it did insure that nonexistent accounts could not be charged.

Ordering selected volumes of a multipart set had always been a problem in acquisitions systems, but BALLOTS handled this in a way that minimized the work of the terminal operator and still allowed flexibility in subsequent processing. If, for example, volumes 1, 2, 3, 8, and 9 were being ordered, the operator merely typed 1–3 and 8–9 in an appropriate field on the order work form, and the system automatically "exploded" the record into five distinct records, one for each volume ordered. These separate records for each volume allowed receipt of partial shipments and individualized processing.

One of the strongest features of the BALLOTS system was its search retrieval capabilities. Unlike most other technical processing systems, BALLOTS offered a wide complement of searchable fields and allowed searching on truncated words, variant forms of entry, and keywords. A terminal operator could search the MARC file by Library of Congress card number, personal name, corporate or conference name, and title. The Catalog Data File allowed for searching by all these elements, but also by Library of Congress subject headings, call number, and BALLOTS ID number. Searching of the In-Process and Reference files was more restricted than searching of the Catalog Data File, but less restrictive than searching the MARC file.

As an automated technical processing system, BALLOTS was a landmark project far more sophisticated than earlier offline systems and more successful than its online contemporaries of the early 1970s. As might be expected, it had a tremendous impact on Stanford's operation, such as integrating technical processing functions more closely than before. The Acquisitions and Cataloging departments, although remaining under separate supervision, were physically consolidated. They had previously been located on different floors of the library. In addition, the number of staff was reduced. One-third of the staff positions in the Order Division were eliminated, as were several positions that previously had been responsible solely for typing unit entry cards, duplicating and typing headings on them, and sorting them into filing order: all functions that were computerized under BALLOTS.[21]

By the mid-1970s, automated efforts in technical processing were turning to shared systems. BALLOTS remained an exemplary illustration of an in-house system, and itself became the basis of a networking system, first among several libraries in California, then in a wider geographic area in the western United States, and still later among a number of major research libraries across the country.

Serials Control

Although serials control is an integral part of technical processing, development of automated systems for serials handling has usually been carried out somewhat independently of acquisitions and cataloging. This had been the case with unit-record and offline batch processing systems and was equally typical of online development. The offline batch processing serials systems had generally revolved around the "arrival card" concept described in Chapter 2. Offline systems allowed libraries greater control in some aspects of the serials operation, particularly in claiming, and enabled holdings lists to be updated and printed much more frequently and with far less staff effort than in unit-record systems. A considerable amount of manual card and paper handling still was required, however, and the offline lists were a problem in that they tended to be generational, with periodic supplements to other periodic supplements to less frequent master cumulations. Online capabilities offered the potential of reducing the amount of handling and making available up-to-date records of holdings in one place.

In the early 1970s, and on perhaps a somewhat less dramatic scale, the system developed at the UCLA Biomedical Library was to serials what BALLOTS was to acquisitions and cataloging and what the Ohio State University system was to circulation. Although not the first online serials control project to be implemented, the UCLA system was generally considered more sophisticated and flexible than its contemporaries. Design objectives included, among others, the elimination of all card handling and the generation of fewer hard copy lists. By 1972, there were records in the serials control database for about 12,000 titles, slightly more than half the library's current subscriptions. The format of the online records was similar to MARC, but with fewer fields. When an issue of a title was received, the operator retrieved the online record and updated it by keying a simple code. Other codes were defined for updating holdings when back or skipped issues were received.

In addition to the check-in operation, the system had automatic overdue detection and binding status monitoring. Keyword searching of the database could be performed, an especially crucial capability given the complexity and similarity of serials titles. The search component also allowed retrieval of titles by fixed field values, such as language, with resulting online display or offline listing of all titles in the database that had an identical value in a given fixed field.[22]

Online systems had many advantages over those based entirely on batch processing. The volume of paperwork and hard copy files was reduced, as well as the amount of staff time required for their maintenance. Although the "up-to-the-second information" characteristic of online was highly touted, many of the earlier systems only partially had this capability, as evidenced by some circulation functions that used minicomputers as front-end communications systems. Nevertheless, even those systems were able to store some of their more critical files in virtually current status.

One of the most important characteristics of online systems was search retrieval capability. Again, some of the early ones were very restricted in inquiry capability, but others were considerably sophisticated, such as at Ohio State University, Stanford, and the UCLA Biomedical Library described earlier. The design, implementation, and continuing operation of the more sophisticated online systems were landmark achievements, but their costs were correspondingly high. In many instances, funding was aided through grants or heavily subsidized by the host institution's general operating budget; the costs were far out of reach of the vast majority of libraries. It was estimated, for example, that the continuing production and development costs in operating BALLOTS for a single month in 1974 were $34,225,[23] and this figure pales in comparison to the design and development costs incurred before the system's implementation.

Bibliographic Utilities

Left with an alternative of in-house, single-library development projects, only the largest and most well endowed libraries could have used an online system for any technical support systems during the 1970s. As early as 1967, however, a second alternative was being formulated, and the outgrowth of this and similar efforts was the evolution of four systems—OCLC, RLG, WLN, and UTLAS—whose use by the early 1980s, extended into several thousand libraries on the North American continent.

OCLC

Although some libraries continued to develop their own in-house systems for certain library functions, it was apparent by the mid-1970s that automated cataloging in particular was evolving in a different direction. The basis of this transformation was the Ohio College Library Center (OCLC), a system based on the simple premise that, recognizing minor local variations, cataloging data for a given item were essentially similar from library to library. The Library of Congress MARC project had been a major breakthrough in the concept of shared cataloging information in an automated environment, but the general pattern of sharing had been unidirectional and on an institution-by-institution basis. MARC tapes were sent from the Library of Congress to subscribing institutions, each of which then loaded the tapes and manipulated the data on its own computer. The idea that evolved for OCLC was a central file of cataloging records that could be maintained on a single computer system and accessed through terminals sharing dedicated communications lines connected to that computer. Not only would this enable libraries to share a MARC file, but it would centralize development costs of the system and virtually eliminate the need for each participating library to use the host institution's computer system.

Because the Library of Congress cataloged only a portion of the universe of materials received by libraries, and since the MARC tapes included only prospective and not retrospective cataloging, an important feature of the OCLC online system was the capability for allowing original input of records, using the MARC format, by the participating libraries themselves. The impact of this is seen by the fact that even by the end of the decade, less than one-fourth of the master bibliographic records in the OCLC database had been supplied by the Library of Congress.[24]

OCLC was chartered in 1967 and Frederick G. Kilgour named as its executive director. System production first began with offline batch processing in 1970; 54 member academic libraries in Ohio submitted punched IBM cards with Library of Congress card numbers of items for which they wanted catalog cards produced. The punched cards were searched against a file consisting of the Library of Congress MARC records, and when a match occurred, catalog cards were generated and sent back to the requesting library within two weeks. In 1971, OCLC went online, installing terminals that allowed each library to search the growing OCLC On-Line Union Catalog (OLUC), the bibliographic database of the system. The library could order catalog cards merely by depressing a couple of command keys on the keyboard attached to the CRT display terminal.

During the first several years of OCLC online operation, a number of far-reaching decisions were made that would enhance—and sometimes plague—the cooperative effort. The display format revolved around the concept of a bibliographic "master record"; in theory there was to be only one record in the database for any given bibliographic entity. When this master record for an item was retrieved by a library, any of the MARC fields could be modified to reflect local practices with respect to subject headings, forms of name entry, local call number, and so on; virtually any element in the record could be modified.

All local changes were reflected on the catalog cards printed offline at OCLC and mailed to the library (and eventually on the library's magnetic tapes of its cataloging activity when this service became available). These modifications, however, were not stored permanently online for the library. Therefore, when a library retrieved a record it had previously used for cataloging, the bibliographic master record was displayed online, without the local modifications that the library had previously made.

The lack of capability to permanently store local information was probably justifiable in OCLC's initial stages. The amount of storage required to maintain this data for each cataloging use of each record by each library would have been enormous, especially since most members of OCLC at that time had a low incidence of adding copies for titles they had already cataloged once. Nevertheless, it was not long after the system went online that some members began to express concern over the lack of a permanent online record containing local modifications for previously cataloged materials.

A characteristic of OCLC during the 1970s was a perpetual gap between announced plans and actual implementation, and the permanent storage and display of local cataloging data—or at least of a scaled-down version of local holdings from selected fields—perhaps provides the most exemplary illustration. In early 1974, "Definition and Use of the 049 Holding Field,"[25] detailing a critical field used to record local data for card production and tape purposes, was published by OCLC partially in anticipation of an impending change, which would allow storage and display of modifications to master records. The actual change proved far less than imminent. Five years later, in 1979, OCLC's development schedule projected the capability of local holdings display for current cataloging records to be available to members in January 1980, with access to local information for previously cataloged materials available sometime later. But less and less discussion of this capability emanated from corporate headquarters and the capability eventually disappeared from all development schedules.

The strategy initially used in creating the online file of bibliographic master records in OCLC revolved around the creation of as large a database as possible in as little time as possible. This may be overgeneralization, but there is little doubt that it was prevalent enough so that a great many of the permanent master records entered into the database by member libraries in the early years suffered in quality and completeness of information. Master records, particularly for retrospective cataloging entered into the database, were frequently created from a description taken solely from the shelflist card of the first member library to convert the title. Thus quality and completeness depended in great part on any given library's past shelflisting practices, on the library's policy for input of new records into the database, and, beyond that, on the accuracy of the terminal operator.

The philosophy of rapid creation of a database at the expense of detail and completeness of record could be seen in OCLC's approach in 1975 to providing records for serials titles, for which a specifically designed MARC format had only recently become available. To greatly increase the number of serials records in a short time, tapes of the Minnesota Union List of Serials (MULS) were loaded into the OCLC database. Although MULS contained accurate information as far as it went, it was primarily a locational tool and provided very abbreviated bibliographic data for cataloging purposes.

Perhaps the greatest quality control complication in the long run was the extreme difficulty of upgrading master records when a mistake was detected or information found to be incomplete. Written forms had to be completed by a member library and mailed to OCLC; when received, the master record was examined by OCLC staff and modified according to the reported additions or changes. This process was time-consuming and cumbersome for member libraries, and not exactly a foremost staffing priority at OCLC. The result was that a library could easily retrieve a master record containing an obvious typographical error that presumably had been modified locally by any number of other libraries for their own card production, but that remained in the master record due to backlogs at OCLC in record upgrading. Owing to the prominent role of the OCLC database in the Conversion of Serials (CONSER) project, a limited number of libraries were given the capability of making permanent online modifications to OCLC serials master records from their own terminals, thus bypassing the manual error reporting procedure. This proved a tremendous success. The possibility of enabling a small number of libraries a similar online capability for records in other formats was a topic of discussion for several years, and was finally initiated in mid-1984.

The approach used in creating its database and the difficulty in correcting errors in master records earned OCLC a reputation in some quarters as a "dirty database." To be certain, many early records in the database did suffer from lack of quality control. An often overlooked factor by critics, however, was that OCLC was an experiment without direct precedent and included among its membership a segment of the library community that had virtually no previous experience with any type of library automation. OCLC was not the first online system used for collective representation of cataloging data for a number of independent libraries, but immediate predecessors were based on centralized input and thus centralized control.[26] This was quite different from the structure of OCLC, in which any member library could input an original bibliographic master record for an item. Given this degree of autonomy and decentralization, combined with the lack of previous experience with library automation on the part of most of its members, and a lack of precedence to gauge the implications of shared databases, the early 1970s were an individual and cooperative learning experience for OCLC members, which served to demonstrate both the strong points and the problem areas of cooperative ventures in library automation.

During its first year of online operation, OCLC remained a cooperative venture of Ohio academic libraries. During 1972, membership was extended to Ohio nonacademic libraries, and in 1973 to libraries outside the state. Although the major computer facilities were to remain centralized at OCLC headquarters, a decentralized approach to the provision of general support services emerged by the mid-1970s. OCLC and various independent state and regional agencies entered into contracts for the brokering of OCLC services and for provision of training and ongoing assistance. Some of these networks had predated OCLC; others were formed in direct response to the need for an agency to provide OCLC services in a particular area. Two exceptions to the general pattern of independent brokering were the formation of OCLC Western (referred to as PACNET—the OCLC Pacific Network), consisting of several branch offices on the Pacific Coast, and OCLC Europe, both being service agencies under the direct administration of OCLC. The independent affiliate networks, which have usually numbered about 20, have remained administratively separate from OCLC, a relationship that has at times worked to the benefit of OCLC and at other times served as a source of conflict. (The relationship between OCLC and these affiliate networks is discussed in greater detail in Chapter 11.)

Within four years after OCLC's decision in 1973 to expand its base of participation beyond Ohio, the number of libraries using the system had increased to more than 800. Increasing numbers of public and special libraries were joining, but the majority of new members continued to be academic libraries. These included many members of the Association of Research Libraries as well as medium-sized university libraries, but an influx of new participants continued from among the ranks of four-year colleges, a pattern that underscored OCLC's role in introducing automation into smaller institutions. A major factor in the opportunity for these smaller academic libraries to join OCLC during these years was the availability of implementation grants from the Kellogg Foundation.

By 1977, it had become apparent that OCLC's governing structure had not kept pace with the growth of the system. General "membership" and positions on the board of trustees were still restricted to libraries in the state of Ohio, with libraries in other states defined as "participants" and having no elective say in the governing body. The Arthur D. Little firm in Cambridge, Massachusetts, was commissioned to study OCLC's governing structure and to suggest alternatives. With recommendations based on a report submitted in June 1977, the Ohio OCLC membership later that year voted to adopt a new governing structure to reflect its national character. During the same year, OCLC changed its official name to the acronym by which it had become known, and in 1981 it adopted the name of OCLC Online Computer Library Center.

RLIN

The concept of resource sharing was the basis for the formation of a number of formal cooperative ventures during the 1970s. One such, begun in 1974, was the Research Libraries Group (RLG), comprised of Harvard, Yale, Columbia, and the New York Public Library. Its broad goals focused on the sharing of resources, collection development, and preservation and conservation of library materials. RLG felt that a common automated bibliographic system would enhance cooperative efforts among member libraries. By early 1978, the four systems under final consideration for adoption included OCLC, Stanford's BALLOTS, the University of Chicago Library Data Management System, and the New York Public Library bibliographic control system.[27]

In spring 1978, RLG announced agreement with Stanford for the use of BALLOTS as the group's automated bibliographic component. Although RLG may merely have chosen what it considered to be the best available system, the choice drew strong reactions from within and outside the group. In June of that year, Harvard announced withdrawal from RLG, although Director of Libraries Douglas Bryant indicated that the choice of BALLOTS was not the motivating factor.[28] A wide spectrum of emotions was expressed throughout the library community concerning RLG's decision not to go with OCLC, which many saw as the emerging national bibliographic network.

In comparing the online features of BALLOTS and OCLC, there is no question that BALLOTS was the far more sophisticated and flexible technical processing system. Unlike OCLC, it also provided for online storage and display of an individual library's cataloging data in a network environment, as well as other features such as searching by title keyword and subject, not available on OCLC. Although on a smaller scale than OCLC, BALLOTS had also proved capable of serving as a shared system as early as 1975 when seven public libraries in California entered into a networking arrangement with Stanford, and the number of libraries using it has increased since then.

The greatest source of resentment among OCLC libraries about RLG's selection of BALLOTS was probably not so much the choice itself as it was the accompanying implicit, and sometimes explicit, attitude that OCLC and its "dirty database" were unacceptable, and that the needs of RLG members were somehow quite apart from those of the rest of the library community—including those of many prestigious research libraries that remained ardent supporters of OCLC. Equally crucial in the reaction, OCLC had come to be recognized by then as much more than a shared cataloging database. Because of library identifier symbols attached to each bibliographic record, OCLC had grown into a tremendous tool for facilitating interlibrary lending and, to many, was the most current and reliable source of locational information available in the United States. The selection of another system by RLG virtually cut off those libraries and their collections from this source of information and erected a major obstacle to their participation in resource sharing on a broader scale. To many OCLC libraries and even to those using neither system, this detachment seemed a conscious and motivated effort to minimize the role of RLG members in the broader context of American library cooperation.

The reaction to RLG's choice of BALLOTS may have been emotional and exaggerated, but RLG did little at that time or later to discourage the image of elitism. Full membership in RLG, in essence, required a library to be a member of the Association of Research Libraries (ARL), and this restricted potential membership in RLG to a pool of barely 100 libraries. RLG permitted other libraries to apply for participant status, meaning a library could use and contribute cataloging data, but the feeling was that this did little to soften the image of elitism.

BALLOTS, which in the RLG environment became the Research Libraries Information Network (RLIN), may have been functionally superior to OCLC as a technical processing system, but not all of its distinctions were carried over into the new network. At Stanford, the system had been, and remained, a full technical processing system, which traced an item and built on its online record from the initial point of ordering to its final point of cataloging. Crucial in this progression was the In-Process File (IPF), described earlier in this chapter. Although any RLIN member library had searching access to Stanford's IPF, there was no capability for other members to build a similar file for their own institutions. Thus, one of the strongest features of the original BALLOTS, which provided the continuity for its realization as a more complete technical processing system, did not exist under RLIN in its earliest manifestation for any library other than Stanford.

WLN

During the 1970s, work was also being conducted at the Washington State Library on the design of an online bibliographic system. Supported by a $1.2 million start-up grant from the state legislature, the system went online in 1977. By 1978, the Washington Library Network (WLN) was being used in 12 public and 9 academic libraries in the state, along with 2 libraries in Alaska. Later that year, 3 libraries in Idaho and 1 in Oregon joined WLN.

From the start, it was apparent that WLN was a well-designed and highly sophisticated system. It included retrieval of local information, subject access, and, not long thereafter, authority control. WLN took a cautious approach to building its bibliographic database. As in RLIN and OCLC, Library of Congress MARC tapes were loaded, but unlike the other two utilities, WLN established a standing policy to centrally review all records input by member libraries.

In January 1979, the library press reported that the National Library of Australia had signed for membership in WLN.[29] This turned out to be a slight misinterpretation. Instead, WLN had sold its system software to the National Library. The distinction was significant. All three of the major utilities—OCLC, RLIN, and WLN—were based on a centralized computer system linked through telecommunications lines to terminals in member libraries; none of the utilities up until that time had attempted to transfer any part of its system for use in another computer.

In 1978, it was not entirely clear to the American library community what role WLN would assume in national bibliographic networking. Although WLN was focusing on regional cooperation in the Pacific Northwest, OCLC had also been a geographically limited system at one time, and BALLOTS had been implemented in a single library. It seemed possible that a third nationally competing system may have been emerging in the form of WLN. In 1979, however, the network reaffirmed its regional emphasis, adopting a policy that expansion outside the Pacific Northwest would be restricted to sale of the WLN software in a manner similar to what had taken place with the National Library of Australia. In the years immediately following, a number of such transactions occurred, including sales to the Southeastern Library Network (SOLINET), the University of Illinois, and the University of Missouri. Membership in the WLN network in the Pacific Northwest had increased to 60 members by 1980 and, as OCLC had done slightly more than two years before, WLN modified its governing structure to reflect the expansion of its membership base beyond a single state.

UTLAS

Although its impact in the United States has been limited, the University of Toronto Library Automated System (UTLAS) was a fourth major online bibliographic networking system to have emerged on the North American continent during the 1970s. Implemented in an online networking mode during the mid-1970s, UTLAS had increased its membership to more than 200 libraries by the end of the decade.

UTLAS membership was limited primarily to Canadian libraries, with some important exceptions. In 1980, the network signed its first member in the United States, the Rochester, New York, Institute of Technology. The following year, UTLAS signed a million-dollar agreement with a Japanese firm to broker UTLAS in Japan. The system did not make concerted efforts to expand into the United States, but it is noteworthy that in 1981, in a comprehensive comparison of the four major utilities, the University of California at Berkeley ranked UTLAS first in overall technical capability. The University did not, however, opt for UTLAS. In 1984, UTLAS opened a U.S. branch office in New York, and it will be interesting to see what impact this will have on its position in the nation.[30]

Over the years, each of the four bibliographic utilities has strived to become more than simply a shared cataloging database. Development efforts by one or more have gone into acquisitions subsystems, serials check-in capabilities, circulation systems, interlibrary loan communications, online union lists, provision of Computer Output Microform (COM) catalogs, and terminal compatibility for searching other databases. (Some of these activities are described in greater detail in Chapter 11.)

WLN, OCLC, and RLIN made a tremendous impact on librarianship in the United States during the 1970s in terms of providing online cataloging capabilities, but their impact in circulation control, acquisitions, and serials check-in was negligible. Some libraries continued to develop their own in-house systems to handle these functions. However, another alternative emerged, particularly in the area of online circulation, in the form of commercial vendors of automated library systems.

Commercial Online Systems

Commercial enterprise played a pivotal role in library automation long before the advent of online systems. Automation via unit-record equipment had been almost the exclusive domain of IBM. Remington Rand offered unit-record equipment comparable to IBM's, but its impact on the library market was negligible. IBM continued its domination into the early 1960s when offline computer processing came into use in some libraries. As the decade progressed, however, computers manufactured by other firms began to appear in universities, corporations, and municipal facilities. By the end of the decade, IBM was still the predominant name in computers for library applications, but it no longer maintained the exclusivity it had once enjoyed.

During its years of dominance, IBM had been responsive in devoting time and effort to assist in applying its equipment to the library environment. Libraries certainly did not receive an undue share of attention, but IBM representatives were often assigned to help libraries with implementing applications, and the corporation published descriptions of and guides for use of its equipment in library applications. The company also sponsored seminars, the most notable being a symposium held in Endicott, New York, in 1964.[31]

Although IBM and its new competitors expressed at least nominal interest in library applications during the 1960s, it was evident that this was an infinitesimal share of the total computer market. According to estimates in the early 1970s, less than one-tenth of one percent of the computers in the United States were being used by libraries in any way.[32] To make these facilities still less conducive as a market, even those with computers were inevitably using equipment purchased by host institutions for a variety of applications, the foremost usually not being those of the library. Libraries had little control in either the selection of equipment or in the decision to replace one manufacturer or model with another. As long as large-scale, multipurpose mainframes were the only available computers, libraries were essentially at the mercy of their host institutions. Although some libraries established excellent relations with their computer centers and did play a role in automation decisions, procurement was an unpredictable and uncontrollable environment for many.

The advent of minicomputers radically altered the computer field for libraries, enabling at least the larger ones to perhaps purchase their own equipment and create a more predictable environment. A number of libraries did purchase their own equipment and designed applications software in-house in the 1970s, but another alternative began to emerge in that decade—the library-specific commercial vendor of automated library systems. In terms of the total computer market as viewed by larger corporations, libraries were too few to attract a great deal of attention, but the potential volume demonstrated a suitable market for smaller and specifically library-oriented commercial ventures.

CLSI and Circulation

One early commercial venture came from Computer Library Systems, Inc., later shortened to CL Systems, Inc., and later again simply to CLSI. The company's first automation efforts involved acquisitions systems, and one of its first installations, in 1972, was at the Cleveland Public Library, which had been using a batch processing system on IBM equipment for eight years. In a description of the CLSI system at Cleveland Public, Richard Palmer observed that, over a five-year period, the cost of the new online system was expected to be less than one-half the cost of the IBM batch processing system, had it been continued.[33] In addition, the new system offered broader and more library-specific features.

CLSI soon turned its attention toward circulation control. Its LIBS 100 system and other vendor-supplied systems introduced subsequently came to be known as "turnkey," a reference to the premise that, upon delivery and installation, virtually all that was required to make the system work was to plug it in and turn it on. Although in practice this has not always exactly proved to be the case, the idea was essentially sound and formed the basis on which these systems would become cost-effective alternatives to in-house development. As so many libraries had learned in implementing their own online or even batch processing systems, the costs of design and development were considerable. With a mass-marketed system, such up-front development costs could be distributed among many customers and hence would be far less for each library than independent design and development. With a turnkey system, programming expertise was not required of the library staff or even at the host institution. Perhaps most importantly, the library's minicomputer could be operated and maintained within the library itself, and the software was marketed by vendors whose entire business was specifically library applications.

Other vendors joined CLSI in the online circulation control market during the early and mid-1970s, but for several years the field was fairly unstable. Various companies entered and left the market, were purchased by other companies, and radically redesigned their systems. By 1975, five commercial vendors were offering turnkey automated circulation systems with varying degrees of online and offline capacity. Two years later, three of them had ceased marketing efforts in the United States and another had been sold and its system totally redesigned. CLSI provided the only continuity in this short span of time.[34]

The year 1977 was pivotal, however, in that several new vendors of circulation control systems entered the market and would prove more stable than most of their predecessors. Among these were Data Phase,

Geac, and Universal Library Systems. Entering the 1980s, CLSI was still the leading force in the commercial market, with 177 installations and more than 300 other libraries remotely accessing computers located at one of the installation sites. The fastest growing competitor was Data Phase with 50 installations, followed by Geac with 22. Gaylord, active since 1978, had 11 installations by 1981. Although not actively marketing in the United States since about 1977, the Plessey online circulation system popular in Great Britain had 9 users in the United States and Canada.[35]

Acquisitions, Serials Control, and Cataloging

With the exception of early CLSI efforts, commercial activity in online acquisitions and serials control has lagged behind circulation control and did not really begin to make an impact until the late 1970s and early 1980s. The primary source of commercial developments also differed between the two areas. For the most part, vendor-supplied online circulation control systems have resulted from new commercial ventures into the library marketplace. In acquisitions and serials control, in contrast, many of the earliest efforts came from long-established library vendors; book jobbers for acquisitions and subscription agents in serials control.

Baker and Taylor's offline BATAB system was available to libraries since the 1960s, and by the late 1970s the system had been redesigned, enhanced, and offered online as LIBRIS. Around the same time, Brodart also announced availability of an online acquisitions system. By the early 1980s, book jobbers had been joined by other vendors, such as Ringgold and Innovative Interfaces, in offering online acquisitions, as well as by each of the four bibliographic utilities. In addition, several vendors of circulation systems were in the process of testing acquisitions modules, promising even more competition.

Commercially available online serials control systems have appeared comparatively recently. Two major subscription agencies, Ebsco and Faxon, each announced plans for an online system in 1981, capable not simply of ordering, but encompassing functions such as check-in and claiming, and not limited to titles ordered through the respective agency. Ebsco eventually abandoned development of its own online check-in component, while Faxon did incorporate one into its online system. Also in 1981, the MetaMicro Corporation of San Antonio, Texas, announced a serials control software package for minicomputer application, although active marketing of this system eventually ceased. Activity in the not-for-profit sector also showed signs of life in the early 1980s, exemplified by marketing of the CHECKMATE serials control system by the California Library Authority for Systems and Services (CLASS) and by OCLC planning efforts to make its rather dormant serials check-in subsystem more attractive. Changes in the OCLC subsystem were made in 1983, but had a negligible impact in attracting new users. An interesting activity occurred with CHECKMATE, as Ebsco began to market that system when it abandoned development of its own online check-in module.

Although the bibliographic utilities emerged during the 1970s as the clearly predominant supplier of automated cataloging systems, there were a few commercial attempts to penetrate the cataloging market. One of these was the BIBNET system, announced by Information Dynamics Corporation in 1974. BIBNET was to operate similarly to OCLC in a number of ways: it was principally intended to be a shared cataloging database; it was to contain member input master records as well as LC MARC records; the master database was to be stored on centralized computers; and library identifier symbols were to be affixed to each bibliographic record as an aid to interlibrary loan.

Several features of BIBNET were planned conspicuously different from OCLC and attempted to answer some of OCLC's more pressing problem areas. Keyword-in-title search capability was to be available, along with plans for the eventual introduction of subject searching of the database. BIBNET users would be encouraged to access the system through a minicomputer housed in the library to facilitate local production of offline products and to reduce telecommunications costs. By using a minicomputer, libraries could retrieve records from the master database, copy them onto a cassette tape, and then break the telecommunications link. Master records copied onto the cassette would then be displayed on a CRT terminal connected to the minicomputer, modifications made to the records, and the revised records copied onto a second cassette. Catalog cards and other offline products could be printed locally, based on the modified records on the second cassette. Although access to BIBNET could be gained through means other than a minicomputer, the front-end interface was strongly promoted as the most useful for allowing flexibility.

Information Dynamics had ambitious intentions for BIBNET. Not only was it to contain post-1968 LC MARC records, but there was a plan to centrally input access points into the online system for more than 3.5 million Library of Congress manual cataloging records created between 1953 and 1968. When a library retrieved such an index entry, it could notify Information Dynamics through the system that it would like a full record in the database for that title. Information Dynamics would then create a record in MARC format for the title requested and load it into BIBNET within four days.[36]

BIBNET'S entry into the marketplace coincided with the rapid and successful expansion of OCLC. The system simply never established a firm position. A more successful venture was launched several years later by Informatics, Inc., with the introduction of MINIMARC. It was minicomputer-based, but with no pretense as a networking system. The entire LC MARC database was supplied on floppy diskettes. The library retrieved these records locally on its minicomputer and modified them according to need. For titles not found on the LC MARC database, the library could create and input records into its own working file. Catalog cards and other offline products could be locally produced.

Since a premise of MINIMARC was local processing, the system did not incur the telecommunications charges as did use of a bibliographic utility, and the overall costs were not as per-unit-dependent. On the other hand, the initial investment could be as much as tenfold that of joining a bibliographic utility, and monthly maintenance and other costs were substantial enough to make participation in a utility more economical for smaller libraries. A limiting feature of MINIMARC was that, as a nonnetworking system, its core database was restricted to LC MARC records and was therefore smaller than those of the bibliographic utilities. Since its emphasis was so much on being a local system, it did not serve in any capacity as an interlibrary loan locational tool. In 1981, however, Informatics, RLG, and the California Library Authority for Systems and Services (CLASS) announced availability of an interface whereby MINIMARC users would be able to search the RLIN database through their MINIMARC system equipment, an arrangement that would enhance MINIMARC as a local system with access to a broader utility. By 1981, more than 30 libraries had installed MINIMARC, and the number has increased steadily since then.[37]

Another successful commercial venture into automated cataloging was the Carrollton Press REMARC project. In 1980, Carrollton announced a five-year project in which it would convert more than 5 million Library of Congress cataloging records, not included on MARC, to machine-readable form. Libraries could submit brief data to Carrollton, such as Library of Congress card numbers or bibliographic search keys, in either machine-readable or nonmachine-readable form, to match against both the LC MARC database and the REMARC database being created by Carrollton. For items for which a record could be found, Carrollton would supply machine-readable bibliographic records containing relatively complete LC cataloging data.

In addition to MINIMARC and REMARC as alternatives to the bibliographic utilities, a number of commercial book jobbers and COM vendors were maintaining machine-readable cataloging databases for their customers. These were really a quite different matter, since initially with these stored databases, a customer did not have direct online access to its own database. This circumstance has been changing, as some of these vendors now provide online access.

In the late 1960s, the only choice for libraries implementing an online system was to design and develop it in-house and use a large mainframe computer housed in central facilities at the host institution. During the 1970s, additional alternatives emerged: systems designed and developed by bibliographic utilities and commercial vendors; systems that could be operated on library-owned minicomputers and, more recently, on microcomputers. What was once a very restricted environment has broadened into an increasing range of options. As with unit-record equipment and batch processing computerized systems, the use of online has been a learning experience for those libraries implementing their own systems, for the bibliographic utilities, and for the commercial vendors. Libraries implementing online systems in the late 1960s and throughout the 1970s provided a valuable basis of experience upon which other institutions could draw. This building on experience has helped to create a more solid foundation of general principles and specific tenets for automation of technical processing operations, but changes in technology and increasing competition in the marketplace certainly give assurances that the options available to a library are not likely to become stagnant or mundane. (Some of these options and their comparative advantages and disadvantages are examined in greater detail in Chapter 12.)

Notes

1. Philip L. Long, "Computer Technology—An Update," in *Annual Review of Information Science and Technology*, vol. 11 (Washington, D.C.: American Society for Information Science, 1976), pp. 218–219.
2. William H. Scholz, "Computer-Based Circulation Systems—A Current Review and Evaluation," *Library Technology Reports* 13 (May 1977): 243.
3. For a description of the Illinois State Library System, see Robert E. Hamilton, "The Illinois State Library 'Online' Circulation System," in *Proceedings of the 1968 Clinic on Library Applications of Data Processing* (Urbana, Ill.: University of Illinois Graduate School of Library Science, 1969), pp. 11–28.
4. Calvin J. Boyer, and Jack Frost, "On-Line Circulation Control—Midwestern University Library's System Using an IBM 1401 Computer in a 'Time-Sharing' Mode," in *Proceedings of the 1969 Clinic on Library Applications of Data Processing* (Urbana, Ill.: University of Illinois Graduate School of Library Science, 1970), p. 135.
5. Paladugu V. Rao, and B. Joseph Szerenyi, "Booth Library On-Line Circulation Systems (BLOC)," *Journal of Library Automation* 4 (June 1971): 101.

6. Richard Phillips Palmer, *Case Studies in Library Computer Systems* (New York: R. R. Bowker, 1973), p. 44.
7. Lois M. Kershner, "Management Aspects of the Use of IBM System/7 in Circulation Control," in *Proceedings of the 1974 Clinic on Library Applications of Data Processing* (Urbana, Ill.: University of Illinois Graduate School of Library Science, 1974), p. 52.
8. For a description of the University of Pennsylvania system, see Kershner, "Management Aspects of the Use of IBM System/7," pp. 43–53.
9. M. Sanderson, "On-Line and Back at S.F.U.," *Journal of Library Automation* 6 (June 1973): 87–102.
10. Hugh C. Atkinson, "The Ohio State On-line Circulation System," in *Proceedings of the 1972 Clinic on Library Applications of Data Processing* (Urbana, Ill.: University of Illinois Graduate School of Library Science, 1972), p. 23.
11. For a description of some of the problems encountered, see A. Robert Thorson, "Operation of an Automated Circulation System," in *An Automated On-Line Circulation System: Evaluation, Development, and Use,* Irene Braden Hoadley and A. Robert Thorson, eds. (Columbus, Ohio: Ohio State University, Office of Educational Services, 1973), pp. 25–46.
12. Atkinson, "The Ohio State On-line Circulation System," p. 26.
13. For a description of the Redstone system, see Jane F. Bentley and Leo J. Cooney, "Automation at the Redstone Scientific Information Center—An Integrated System," *Library Resources and Technical Services* 18 (Summer 1974): 259–267.
14. For a description of LOLITA, see Larry Auld and Robert Baker, "LOLITA: An On-line Book Order and Fund Accounting System," in *Proceedings of the 1972 Clinic on Library Applications of Data Processing* (Urbana, Ill.: University of Illinois Graduate School of Library Science, 1972), pp. 29–53; and Frances G. Spigai and Thomas Mahan, "On-line Acquisitions by LOLITA," *Journal of Library Automation* 3 (December 1970): 276–294.
15. Palmer, *Case Studies,* pp. 143, 194.
16. Auld and Baker, "LOLITA," p. 35.
17. *Ibid.,* p. 44.
18. Charles Payne, Rob McGee, Helen F. Schmierer, and Howard S. Harris, "The University of Chicago Library Data Management System," *Library Quarterly* 47 (January 1977): 9.
19. Wayne Davison, "Minicomputers and Library Automation: The Stanford Experience," in *Proceedings of the 1974 Clinic on Library Applications of Data Processing* (Urbana, Ill.: University of Illinois Graduate School of Library Science, 1974), pp. 87–89.
20. Allen B. Veaner, "BALLOTS—The View from Technical Services," *Library Resources and Technical Services* 21 (Spring 1977): 140.
21. Project BALLOTS and the Stanford University Libraries, "Stanford University's BALLOTS System," *Journal of Library Automation* 8 (March 1975): 41–43.
22. For a description of the UCLA Biomedical Library serials system, see the following articles by James Fayollat in the *Journal of the American Society for*

Information Science: "On-line Serials Control System in a Large Biomedical Library, Part I: Description of the System," 23 (September/October 1972): 318–322; "Part II: Evaluation of Retrieval Features," 23 (November/December 1972): 353–358; and "Part III: Comparison of On-line and Batch Operations and Cost Analysis," 24 (March/April 1973): 80–86.

23. Project BALLOTS, "Stanford University's BALLOTS System," p. 47.

24. Based on statistics provided in *Cataloging File Statistics* (Columbus, Ohio: OCLC, Inc., 1982).

25. "Definition and Use of the 049 Holding Field" (Columbus, Ohio: OCLC, Inc., 1974).

26. One of these earlier systems was the cataloging system brought online by the Shawnee Mission, Kansas, Public Schools. For a description, see Ellen Wasby Miller and B. J. Hodges, "Shawnee Mission's On-line Cataloging System, *Journal of Library Automation* 4 (March 1971): 13–26. The same authors presented an update the following year: "Shawnee Mission's On-line Cataloging System: The First Two Years," in the *Proceedings of the 1972 Clinic on Library Applications of Data Processing* (Urbana, Ill.: University of Illinois Graduate School of Library and Information Science, 1972), pp. 94–108.

27. "Research Libraries Group Goes for BALLOTS," *Library Journal* 103 (April 1, 1978): 916.

28. "Major Consortium Votes for BALLOTS; Harvard Quits Group," *American Libraries* 9 (June 1978): 309.

29. "WLN Reports Beachhead Down Under," *LJ/SLJ Hotline* 8, no. 4 (January 29, 1979): 2.

30. Socio-Economic Systems, Inc., "Computer-Assisted Evaluation for Four Technical Processing System Bids," sensitivity analysis, p. 2.

31. *IBM Library Mechanization Symposium, Endicott, New York, May 25, 1964* (White, Plains, N.Y.: IBM Data Processing Division, 1965).

32. Diana Delaney, "Technology: Present Status and Trends in Computers," in *Library Automation: The State of the Art II*, Susan K. Martin and Brett Butler, eds. (Chicago: American Library Association, 1975), p. 19.

33. Palmer, *Case Studies*, pp. 184–185.

34. William H. Scholz, "Computer-Based Circulation Systems—A Current Review and Evaluation," *Library Technology Reports* 13 (May 1977): 249–250.

35. "C. L. Systems Holds Commanding Lead among Circulation Systems Marketers," *Advanced Technology Libraries* 10 (August 1981): 1, 5, 7.

36. For a description of BIBNET, see David P. Waite, "The Minicomputer: Its Role in a Nationwide Bibliographic and Information Network," in *Proceedings of the 1974 Clinic on Library Applications of Data Processing* (Urbana, Ill.: University of Illinois Graduate School of Library Science, 1974), pp. 136–157.

37. "MINIMARC Systems Installed, RLIN Link to Home," *Advanced Technology Libraries* 10 (June 1981): 2.

4

The Public Catalog

In terms of historical development, the primary focus of library automation has been on internal operations not immediately visible to the user. The ultimate goal of such efforts, however, has been to improve the quality of service that is available to the user. Automating the cataloging, acquisitions, serials check-in, and circulation operations has made materials available to the library public more rapidly and more reliably. Yet, with the exception of automated circulation systems, the user had very little exposure to automation in the library, and even in the case of circulation systems, involvement has been as an observer rather than as a participant.

Since the early 1950s, libraries in increasing numbers have sought to automate one element of their operations that was visible to the library user—the public catalog. In certain forms, use of automated catalog has required about the same effort by patrons as the card catalog. In more sophisticated forms, the automated catalog has required the user to become an interactive partner. Despite differences in degree of effort required by the user, three forms of the automated catalog—book, microform, and online—have shared the common goal of trying to alleviate the shortcomings of manually maintained card catalogs.

The Card Catalog Crisis

Until the latter part of the nineteenth-century, the prevalent form of catalog in American libraries was the book catalog. Increasingly, however, the book catalog came to be seen as somewhat of a dinosaur, ill-suited to the changing environment in which it existed. Library collections were growing in number and size and were changing more rapidly and on a broader scale than ever before. It became obvious that a more flexible tool was needed for coping with those conditions. Book catalogs were costly, impossible or at least extremely difficult to modify on a timely basis, and out-of-date almost as soon as they were printed. A less expensive yet more dynamic form of catalog was needed, and it was to be found in the card catalog. A catalog of individual cards was conducive to change and currency. Bibliographic descriptions of additions to the collection and changes to existing descriptions could be made simply by inserting new cards or by modifying existing ones. The entire catalog did not have to be reprinted to reflect those changes.

By the last quarter of the nineteenth century, it was apparent that the card catalog would usurp the book catalog as the predominant form in American libraries. And once so established, it remained virtually unchallenged throughout most of the first half of the twentieth century.[1]

Despite the advantages of the card catalog, it was not perfect, and inadequacies were recognized early on. But until the 1950s, there did not seem to be any feasible alternative. During the third quarter of the twentieth century, the environment of American libraries was beginning to change in a direction that made the inadequacies of the card catalog even more pronounced, and at the same time gave evidence that new technology might offer suitable alternatives.

Although in theory the card catalog could be an up-to-the-minute reflection of what was held in a library collection, in practice this did not always prove to be the case. Particularly during a period of growth in acquisitions budgets, such as during the 1960s, the maintenance of card catalogs frequently lagged behind. Increases in personnel budgets often did not keep pace with increases in acquisitions budgets, one result being a substantially greater number of catalog cards to be filed without the personnel to do so. The growing complexity of cataloging rules and more widespread adherence to standards merely made the task of maintaining a card catalog even more formidable.

Since the structure of the catalog revolved around the concept of several discrete entries for a single item, the task of modifying any piece of information about an item required considerable duplication of effort. When such changes were required for a whole category of items, the implications were even more profound. Making a change in terminology for a frequently assigned name or subject heading was a task of prohibitive dimension, requiring changes to large numbers of author, title, and subject entries. An alternative to massive amounts of modifications and refiling was to rely on a complex web of cross-references in the form of "see" and "see also" cards, usually posted in the catalog in such a way that only the best-informed or luckiest catalog user could find them. The most convenient solution for the library was simply not to change terminology. Librarians were conscious, however, that this often-adopted answer to the problem was a disservice to library users who had never used a "water closet" or read about an "aeroplane."

As the maintenance of the card catalog was becoming an increasingly complex and expensive task, some libraries that had been using such a catalog for several decades were also discovering another problem—the catalog, or parts of it, was simply wearing out. The older card stock was deteriorating and writing or typeface on the cards was fading. Especially in large or rapidly growing libraries, the amount of physical space occupied by the card catalog was another concern. If the total amount of available library space remained stable and had to accommodate a growing collection, the prospect of a card catalog that needed an ever increasing amount of space was not a pleasant one. Libraries that could ease their general space pressures by establishing branch or departmental facilities were faced with a different, but equally uninviting, dilemma: it was necessary to create and maintain new card catalogs for all branches, which sooner or later would be subject to all the problems described above.

Book Catalogs

In the 1940s, an alternative form of catalog began to appear in the United States. Actually it was not a new form, but the reappearance of an old one—the printed book catalog. The dozen or so major book catalogs published during the 1940s were not issued with the intention of replacing a card catalog, but were tools for librarians and researchers working in very specialized areas. The most ambitious project of the decade was the publication of the 167-volume *Catalog of Books Represented by Library of Congress Printed Cards.*[2] As its title implied, the *Catalog of Books* was not an alternative to a card catalog, but rather a printed book version of it. Other printed book catalogs of the 1940s were, like the *Catalog of Books,* photographic reproductions, not replacements, of card catalogs.

Unit-Record Equipment

The photographic reproduction of catalog cards in book form may have made legitimate once again the concept of the book catalog in the United States, but it was not until the 1950s that a few libraries began to introduce book catalogs as an alternative to the card catalog. Production of book catalogs in the 1950s was sometimes based on the use of machine-readable data and IBM unit-record equipment. One of the first libraries to engage in this was the King County, Washington, Public Library, which produced catalogs for its branch libraries.[3] Between the early 1950s and early 1960s, a handful of other libraries adopted methods similar to those used by King County for the production of book catalogs. In most cases, these libraries were public, usually county, systems encompassing a number of branch or independent libraries. It was this collective character of the projects that, more than anything, was responsible for bringing into focus the advantages of book catalogs produced on unit-record equipment as a viable alternative to the card catalog.

In most public or county systems producing a book catalog with unit-record equipment, each branch had previously maintained a card catalog of its own holdings. The replacement of these separate catalogs with centrally maintained and produced systemwide book catalogs provided not only a cost-effective alternative to maintaining separate catalogs in each library, but also provided a more service-effective tool by including in one catalog all titles held throughout the system.

Despite the advantages for some, the actual number of libraries and library systems that produced a printed book catalog on unit-record equipment during the 1950s and early 1960s was very small. Although the book catalog did have some benefits over the card catalog, its cost-effectiveness in general was restricted to situations such as those in county or branch systems, where it could serve as a substitute for not one but several card catalogs. There were the advantages of incorporating a broader range of locations into a single catalog, and of distributing copies to multiple locations. But the speed at which the equipment operated did warrant some service tradeoffs. Printing the master copy of the catalog was a slow and cumbersome process on unit-record equipment. As a result, a high priority was placed on abbreviations and the inclusion of minimal data, usually restricted to one 80-column IBM card for each bibliographic entry. The King County catalog, for example, included all pertinent information on a single card, which meant a maximum of 27 characters for the title of any item.[4]

Computer-Produced Book Catalogs

The advent of the computer alleviated some of the problems with the use of unit-record equipment for producing printed book catalogs. The manipulation and printing capabilities of the computer were much faster than unit-record equipment. This made the production of book catalogs for larger collections more feasible than it had been with unit-record equipment and allowed more frequent publication of updated catalogs. By the mid-1960s, libraries had become much more sophisticated in their ability to input variable-length data into computers, so that more information could be represented for catalog entries than was generally possible in the title-a-line book catalogs produced with unit-record equipment. Furthermore, despite the terminology used to identify unit-record equipment, in actual practice libraries using such equipment to produce book catalogs had invariably prepared, or at least reproduced, separate cards for each entry point in the catalog, such as for author, title, and each appropriate subject heading. With the computer, a single card or deck of cards could be entered for each title and expanded by machine to produce multiple entries, which reduced the amount of staff effort required in keying catalog data.

Many of the computer-generated catalogs used in public and academic libraries during the 1960s evolved from circumstances much like those of their predecessors, namely, in relation to multilibrary situations or with the opening of a new library or libraries. Although county library systems continued to figure prominently in the expanding use of book catalogs during the decade, some academic libraries also began to produce book catalogs by computer. One of the earliest examples was in conjunction with the Ontario New Universities Library Project. The Ontario government in Canada announced the creation of five universities in the province and sought assistance from the University of Toronto Library in setting up libraries in each one. Part of the task involved creating a catalog for each facility.

Confronted with the creation of five separate card catalogs, the University of Toronto began to explore, and then decided in favor of, the production of a union catalog for the five libraries using a computer and machine-readable data stored on punched cards. As with the county system catalogs, cost savings were possible only because the production of one multilibrary union catalog was an alternative to several card catalogs. Had a catalog been required for only one library, it would have been less costly to create and maintain a card catalog.[5]

In the United States, two early computer-generated book catalogs appeared at Florida Atlantic University Library in Boca Raton and the Stanford University undergraduate library. In each instance, the catalog was created in conjunction with the opening of a new library. These catalogs represented departures from the general trend in public and academic libraries at the time, for although they were created under conditions where no previous card catalog existed, each was to describe the contents of a single library rather than several.

The relative ease of duplicating and distributing multiple copies of computer-generated book catalogs was a crucial argument in their favor during the 1960s, and the libraries that adopted them generally took full advantage of this feature. The Montgomery County, Maryland, Public Library, for example, distributed copies of its union book catalog not only to each library in the public system, but also to each public secondary school library, plus a copy of the children's portion of the catalog to each of the 115 public elementary schools in the county.[6] And a most ambitious plan was suggested in the initial planning of the book catalog for the Stanford undergraduate library—to distribute a copy of the catalog containing titles in the core collection to each freshman enrolling at the university.[7]

Advantages and Disadvantages

One advantage in a machine-readable database as the basis for production of a book catalog, whether on computer or unit-record equipment, was the ability to distribute copies of the catalog to multiple locations. Another benefit was the ease with which specialized catalogs could be produced using the same data. The Baltimore County Public Library produced a separate index of plays and another of phonograph records included in its catalog,[8] and both the Los Angeles County Public Library and the Montgomery County Public Library generated separate catalogs of their foreign-language holdings.[9]

In addition to the advantages of multiple copies and flexibility in producing specialized catalogs, computer-generated book catalogs alleviated some of the problems created by the increasingly large and complex card catalogs. They clearly required less physical space for storing and consulting. Filing new entries became an automated procedure, and making a change in terminology was tremendously simplified. To change a name or subject heading in some systems, for example, the new terminology merely had to be keyed once, along with instructions concerning which old term the new one replaced, and the change would be reflected throughout the catalog in its next edition. And although machine-readable cards or tapes might deteriorate over time, "refreshing" the medium by copying onto new cards or tapes could be handled by machine with relatively minimal demands on staff time.

Although there were numerous benefits with automated book catalogs, there were drawbacks, too. Some were more the result of lack of experience with automation and book catalogs than with anything inherent in the technology itself. Libraries had to rely on outside agencies for the actual programming and production work, and more than a few surprises cropped up in finished products.

One of the most frequent complaints by libraries was the failure of outside agencies, such as a city or university data processing center, to meet promised delivery schedules. The Montgomery County Public Library originally planned to begin production for its book catalog in early 1962, but the project had to be deferred for an entire year because of "various local governmental problems outside the control of the department."[10] Delivery of the first edition of the computer-generated book catalog for the library of the University of California, Santa Cruz, was by one account delayed 20 months,[11] and by another account the photocopying and final distribution of copies of subsequent cumulations of the catalog were taking six months and longer to complete.[12]

Computer generation of book catalogs, like the automation of technical processing operations, also fell prey to a lack of understanding between librarians and data processing personnel, resulting sometimes in minor problems and sometimes in major ones. Preparing the book catalog of the Stanford undergraduate library involved a novel printing technology, capable of printing lowercase as well as uppercase alphabetical characters, and also capable of printing special diacritical marks. Although the programming allowed for variable-length input, there was an upper limit to the number of characters for any given field as well as for the total record. The library worked within the constraints of these upper limits, but at first without knowing that any uppercase character required two computer storage positions rather than one. Fortunately, this turned out to be a very minor problem since few fields or records approached their upper limits of allowable characters.[13] But a somewhat larger problem was discovered by the Baltimore County Public Library staff examining the first run of its printed book catalog. Whenever an added author entry was included in the catalog, the entry under the primary author of the work was entirely omitted from the catalog![14]

Two characteristics of computers of the 1960s—their standard filing capabilities and their rigorous literal interpretation of input data—led to two other types of problems in the production of library catalogs. First, the computers' filing sequence was very simplistic compared with the complex filing rules to which libraries had become accustomed with card catalogs. During the programming for its undergraduate library book catalog, the University of Illinois at Chicago investigated the possibility of programming the ALA Filing Rules. It found that such an effort would require not only extremely complex programming, but would also necessitate extensive manual coding of input.[15] Most libraries came to accept that the rules by which the computer filed entries would not cause trouble for catalog users, and in fact might even make the catalog easier to use.

The second type of filing problem was more serious. Because computers interpret data so literally, any input inconsistencies in spacing or spelling, as well as even minor transcription errors, could result in serious separation or improper sequencing of entries. With a card catalog, library staff have a tendency to overlook or miss certain types of mistakes, and so become a correcting influence where minor typographical errors are concerned. For example, a card with a subject heading *U.S.—Foreign Relations—Algerie* would quite possibly find its way into a card in proper sequence under the heading *U.S.—Foreign Relations—Algeria*. In a computerized system, however, that would never be the case; the subheading "Algerie" would always be filed after all the entries under the subheading "Algeria."

One example of the potential cumulative effect of input errors was described by Malinconico in the mid-1970s.[16] A Library of Congress MARC record at that time contained an average of 116 characters in all access points in the record: name, title, and subject headings. Even if a typist made only one error per 1,000 characters, approximately one of every nine records would have a typographical error in one of its access points in the catalog, and thus would probably be filed out of sequence. The more staunch defenders of computer-generated catalogs argued that, in fact, the incidence of errors was probably no greater than in typical card catalogs. Whether that was the case, it was true that errors in computerized catalogs tended to "jump out" at the reader. Since users of a card catalog examine entries on a one-by-one basis, serious misfilings are likely to be discovered only by accident. The page layout of a book catalog with multiple entries per page, on the other hand, exposes errors and misfilings more openly. Of course, this fact could actually be a long-term benefit for the book catalog, since errors could more easily be detected and noted for correction in the next edition.

Multiple copies of many of the book catalogs of the 1960s were produced through photographic methods. Since the number of pages in a catalog had a direct bearing on the catalog's overall expense, concerted efforts were made to minimize the number of pages. This was achieved to some extent by careful selection, albeit judgmental, on the librarian's part concerning how much bibliographic description to allow in each entry. But another common method for controlling catalog size was by reduction in the photographic process. In 1965, Irwin Pizer echoed a concern expressed by a number of librarians throughout the decade: "In today's catalogs produced by photographic methods, an optimal size type for ease of reading and mental well-being is repeatedly ignored."[17] The type in the catalogs produced by the Ontario New Universities Library Project was, for example, photographically reduced to 60 percent of its original size,[18] and in a number of other book catalogs the print was reduced by similar proportions.

Type size was not the only area in which user convenience was sacrificed for the sake of economy and convenience of production. Volumes of book catalogs were often several hundred pages or more in length, and their sheer weight affected their portability and ease of handling. Invariably, certain assumptions were made about what the user wanted and needed in a catalog. Although the systemwide county library book catalogs had the positive feature of containing all titles held throughout the system, in many cases specific holdings libraries for any given item were not listed. That data could be determined only by consulting a librarian, who would then call the central library which maintained a detailed holdings record. The decision of one library to exclude specific systemwide holdings information in its book catalog was based on the assumption that: "Experience so far has tended to prove that the public seldom pays any attention to the holdings indication, especially when they learn that they can obtain any title listed either by reserve or by interbranch loan."[19]

Placement of data elements within entries could also be a potential source of confusion for the catalog user. When the Baltimore County Public Library contracted with a commercial vendor for the production of its book catalog, each record in the machine-stored database was assigned a unique identification number by the vendor. Rather than placing the call number to the left of each entry in the printed catalog, a practice most library users are familiar with, the vendor placed the call number to the right of the entry and placed its own identification number to the left. As might be expected, this led to confusion for a number of catalog users, who interpreted the vendor's number as a call number.[20]

One of the most persistent and disquieting problems with computerized book catalogs of the 1960s remained the same as it had been a century before with noncomputerized book catalogs—currency and cumulation. Although filing into the card catalog may have been backlogged in many libraries, adopting a new catalog form that by its very nature was out-of-date upon publication was a concession not all libraries were comfortable with. Computer-generated book catalogs were cost-effective only under certain conditions, one of which was that updated full editions would be published relatively infrequently. Despite the speed of the computer, frequent publication of an entire catalog was simply too time-consuming and expensive.

Although standard computer printer devices, such as the IBM 1403, printed at a rate of 1,100 lines per minute, this was still prohibitively slow considering that some book catalogs of the 1960s contained several thousand pages. Further complicating the printing speed problem was the fact that the actual rate of speed was often far less than even the standard 1,100 lines if the library wished to include diacritical marks or both uppercase and lowercase alphabetical characters. The joint development of an expanded print train in the early 1960s by the University of Toronto Library, the Florida Atlantic University Library, and the Yale Medical Library was an important achievement that allowed libraries greater flexibility in computer-generated products, but it also reduced the effective printing speed to a rate as low as 200 to 400 lines per minute.[21]

In an effort to lower printing costs, most libraries issued a full catalog only about once a year, with interim supplements to show what had been added to its collection since the last full edition. The chief drawback of the supplement strategy was that it required the library user in some instances to consult more than one catalog to determine whether a library owned a particular item. In most catalogs, the supplements were cumulative; that is, each new supplement included the contents of all earlier supplements issued since the most recent full edition. In that case, library users had to consult a maximum of two catalogs. Other libraries, however, issued noncumulative or only partially cumulative supplements.

An example was the catalog of the Ontario New Universities Library Project. After a full annual edition had been published, two noncumulative monthly supplements were published and then cumulated in a quarterly supplement, which was followed by two more noncumulative monthly supplements, with all of the preceding then cumulated in a semiannual supplement. This cycle repeated through the second half of the year before publication of the next annual full edition of the catalog.[22] At the extreme, this schedule meant that a library user consulting the catalog during the month directly preceding the new annual edition may have had to look at as many as five separate catalogs—the most recent annual edition, the semiannual cumulative supplement, the third-quarter supplement, and two monthly noncumulative supplements! Such publication patterns were often a financial necessity, but they obviously imposed their own brand of hardship on the user.

The book catalog was a snapshot of what the library owned at a given time, or in the case of supplements, of what the library had added since its most recent full edition. As such, not even the supplements could be entirely up-to-date; there was always at least a brief period when the newest additions were not listed in any part of the catalog.

Items withdrawn or lost from the collection posed a further problem. Once a title was listed in an edition or supplement, the entry could not be deleted from the catalog until the next edition or cumulative supplement was published. As a temporary measure in the current catalog, the entries could be marked out or annotated, but this was extremely difficult to coordinate and nearly impossible if copies of the catalog had been distributed to a variety of locations outside the library.

The relative merits and shortcomings of computer-generated book catalogs weighed quite differently according to the situation. To replace a number of separately maintained catalogs, or when large quantities of distribution copies were essential, the computer-generated product was usually a cost-effective and service-effective solution. Under other circumstances, however, its contribution to service-effectiveness was negligible and its cost-effectiveness marginal at best. Particularly for large collections, computer-generated book catalogs were simply too expensive. Yet, at the same time that some libraries were implementing book catalogs, a few others were beginning to experiment with a newer alternative to card catalogs—computer output microform.

Computer Output Microform (COM) Catalogs

In the late 1950s and early 1960s, techniques were developed that merged a new technology, the computer, with a more established one, microphotography. The library community was already familiar in some degree with microfilm, but its use had largely been relegated to such tasks as providing backup copies of paper documents, and for distributing copies of specialized materials, and so on. As Malinconico observed, a pervasive attitude among many was that microforms were "something which one hopes he does *not* have to use."[23]

By the mid-1960s, a few libraries in the United States and Great Britain were beginning to experiment with this technique as a means of producing library catalogs. At the Lockheed Technical Information Center, staff keypunched data about each item in the collection onto 80-column IBM cards and forwarded them to the data processing center, where the information was transferred onto magnetic tape. Up to this point, the procedure was similar to that used by many libraries in generating computer-produced book catalogs. The output process, however, was radically different. Rather than using a line printer as the output attachment to the computer, a computer output microfilm (COM) recorder was attached. This device recorded the information onto miniature film. As with any microform, the finished product had to be mounted on special viewing equipment that magnified the filmed images to eye-readable size.[24]

The outstanding advantage of COM over printed book catalogs was in production and distribution costs. Some savings occurred at the stage of producing the first copy of the catalog. COM recorders generally operated at speeds at least ten times greater than line printers, thereby requiring only a fraction of computer time to produce the master copy. The significant reduction in computer time translated into a direct and substantial savings in cost. The processes involved in reproducing additional copies of a COM catalog were quite different from those used for a book catalog and represented further savings. Since COM catalogs were invariably lighter in weight than book catalogs, there was even a savings in distribution costs when copies had to be mailed to various locations.

Some of the savings realized in producing COM catalogs were offset by the need to buy special viewing equipment. However, the total investment for COM readers usually paled in comparison with the savings realized in production.

Not all libraries implementing COM took full advantage of the potential annual savings over the amount that would have been required for production of a book catalog. Instead, at least part of the savings were applied to improving service to library users through more frequent publication of full editions and supplements of the catalog.

Even after investing in equipment and publishing more frequent editions, libraries with COM catalogs often realized substantial cost savings. Yet, despite COM's financial attractiveness, most libraries producing computer-generated book catalogs in the late 1960s were not convinced of its suitability as a replacement. Libraries using card catalogs had equally serious reservations when considering COM during its earlier years on the market. Part of the reluctance may have had to do with a general distrust of an unfamiliar medium, but, in truth, the state-of-the-art technology of both the production process and viewing equipment left much to be desired.

There evolved two broad categories of microform available to libraries for the production of COM catalogs—microfilm and microfiche. Within each one, however, production standards were ill-defined. As a result, critical differences in format existed from one COM manufacturer or bureau to the next, with little regard for compatibility or standardization.

The two common containers for microfilm were cartridges and cassettes. The microfilm cartridge was a single-core device; the cassette was a double-core container. Cassettes were preferable because the film itself was encased; it could be removed from a reader without having to be rewound. A cartridge, on the other hand, had to be rewound before removal, requiring more time and effort on the part of the catalog user. Because film was not encased, a cartridge also required more frequent and open handling, which meant greater likelihood of abrasion and other wear and damage to the film.

During the late 1960s and early 1970s, the limits of technology meant that microfilm cassettes or cartridges repeatedly had to be mounted and removed when consulting a library catalog. The maximum length of film on a cartridge or in a cassette was 100 feet, capable of holding the equivalent of 2,000–4,000 hard copy pages. This was not long enough to contain all catalog entries of most libraries using COM. The catalog of the Lockheed Technical Information Center, containing slightly more than 1 million name, title, and subject entries, required 40 cartridges of film to comprise a single set of the catalog,[25] and this collection was not outstandingly large. By the early 1970s, reels of 215 feet were in common use, but this was still not enough to eliminate the need for multiple reels of film to contain the entire catalog of most libraries.

Once a film cartridge or cassette was mounted on a COM reader, it could take considerable time to find the desired entry. If the entry was located near the end of a cartridge, the user had to wind through nearly 100 (or later 215) feet of film before locating the right frame. Eventually, the film, if on a cartridge, would have to be rewound and the cartridge removed before other parts of the catalog could be mounted. The film cassette did eliminate some of this bother since it did not have to be rewound before removal, but the amount of time and effort required to locate a specific entry once the cassette had been mounted was still unacceptable to some.

Fiche vs. Film

As an alternative to film, microfiche offered certain advantages for the COM catalog. Microfiche readers were less expensive than film readers. A single unit of fiche was generally easier, or at least no more difficult, to mount on the viewing equipment than a cartridge or cassette. Once fiche was mounted, a specific entry could, on average, be located much more rapidly than on film. When mounted on viewing equipment, the fiche could be moved vertically or laterally. Locating any given entry on a unit of fiche required essentially the same amount of time as locating any other entry, quite unlike the strictly sequential access required with roll film.

Along with the relative merits of fiche over film, however, there were some liabilities. Perhaps the greatest concerned the amount of information that could be held on a single unit. A 100-foot roll of microfilm generally contained the equivalent of 2,000–4,000 hard copy pages of data; a single fiche usually contained only about 208 page-equivalents at 24:1 reduction or 270 pages at 48:1 reduction. A library catalog was likely to require multiple units of either film or fiche, and a catalog on microfiche was bound to require several times as many individual units as the same catalog on microfilm. The greater the number of units, the greater the likelihood of problems in keeping the units properly filed. In reports by libraries opting for film over fiche, another frequently cited concern was that, although with cassettes the film was encased in a container and therefore not handled directly by a catalog user, fiche required direct handling and thus was open to greater likelihood of abrasion, wear, and other damage.

Growth in the 1970s

The quality and reliability of COM readers, particularly film readers, were often less than acceptable. One of the most concise and incisive reports of the types of problems encountered with viewing equipment came from Great Britain as late as 1977.[26] Advances had been made by that time, particularly in North America with the introduction of the Information Design ROM 3 microfilm reader and similar models. But the complaints registered in Great Britain in 1977 during a meeting between librarians and COM bureau and manufacturer representatives were indicative of the frustration traditionally expressed with equipment design. Attendees complained, for example, about poorly designed placement of winding handles, lack of signs over switches, and type of finish on the equipment, which seemed to have the sole function of repelling instructional signs and notices. The equipment manufacturers replied that they had not received complaints about these features from other users—mainly, machines used by the business sector, which did not require use by the general public. The representative of one compay related that 95 percent of the company's business was for fiche, and there was little likelihood that it would bother to modify its film equipment.

Another suggestion by those who attended the meeting was that film reader manufacturers might consider making attachments for the readers in which cassettes could be conveniently stored. One manufacturer did supply such a device, but it was a side-mounted rack and, as the author of the report observed, "Unfortunately, the racks are horizontal, with the result that a user sitting in front cannot see the end of the cassettes,"[27] which contained contents labels. Complaints were heard also about the short life span of the light bulbs supplied with the readers, as well as about film products, such as slippage of film on cassettes and the poor quality of images. Further problems, not mentioned in the report but often voiced elsewhere, included poor and uneven illumination of screens and noise levels of readers.

Beginning in the early 1970s, the situation improved; strides were made in standardization and improvements in the quality and capability of equipment. One of the most important achievements was the introduction in the United States, in the mid-1970s, of more sophisticated microfilm readers, such as Information Design's ROM 3. This model and others could handle a roll of film up to 1,200 feet in length, a twelvefold increase in capacity over cartridges of less than a decade before. Although in some instances this capacity was still not sufficient to enable entire catalogs to be placed on a single roll of film, it was close enough to allow permanent mounting of different portions of the catalog in different readers, which eliminated the need for patrons to handle the cassettes themselves. The readers were motorized and had eye-readable odometers posted on the front of the machine to guide the user to the section of film on which a desired entry could be found. With these innovations, microfilm catalogs became far more convenient for both users and library staff than had been the case only a few years before.

As circumstances surrounding the production and display of COM catalogs improved, their use in libraries increased. Although prone to some of the same shortcomings characteristic of computer-generated book catalogs, COM catalogs also shared one of the most attractive features of book catalogs (and at a lower cost), which was the relative ease of duplication and distribution. Many libraries in the United States adopting COM had previously relied on computer-generated book catalogs. The Los Angeles County Public Library, the Enoch Pratt Free Library in Baltimore, the Baltimore County Public Library, the Fairfax (Virginia) Public Library, the Salt Lake County (Utah) Library System, the Clark County (Nevada) Public Library, and the Austin (Texas) Public Library were just a few of those that had made a transition from book to COM catalogs by 1978.

Although many of the libraries using COM were from the same group of city, county, and branch library systems previously using book catalogs, it was significant that other types of libraries were also adopting COM, and not necessarily small or medium-sized ones. Perhaps the clearest example of the increased demand for and decreased costs of COM over book catalogs was the announcement in 1976 by the University of Toronto to adopt COM. Eleven years before, Ritvars Bregzis had concluded that, based on his work at the University of Toronto with book catalogs for the five new Ontario University libraries, the cost-effectiveness of computer-generated catalogs for large research collections was yet to be realized.[28] By 1976, COM technology, combined with other changes in the environment, was apparently bringing about that realization.

User Acceptance

A constant question about COM catalogs was the level of library user acceptance. As important as that question was, there were few reports of studies of user reactions. Of the studies that were carried out, a number were poorly conducted or based on responses from a very small number of users. Even the better studies were inconclusive, and results were often positive or negative depending on interpretation. In a study conducted at the University of Oregon, for example, James Dwyer reported that responses to a question comparing ease of use of a card versus microfiche catalog showed that:

> The largest group, 43 percent of the sample, reported that the fiche was slower, 23 percent thought both took the same amount of time, and 31 percent considered the microfiche faster. The optimistic interpretation is that more than half of the people discovered that the microfiche is as fast or faster to use than cards. The pessimistic view is that nearly two-thirds think it is the same or even worse than an already ungainly access tool.[29]

The results of the University of Oregon study raised a number of questions about user acceptance of microform catalogs, but a study conducted at the Los Angeles County Public Library showed more favorable responses. Still, comparisons with other forms of catalogs were, as in the Oregon study, favorable to the degree one wished to interpret them. Although 66 percent of the users felt that the film catalog was easier to use than a card catalog, the results were less conclusive for the comparison between film and book catalogs. Forty-five percent felt that the COM catalog was easier to use; 37 percent felt that the two were about the same; and 17 percent felt that the book catalog was easier.[30] Optimistically, therefore, 82 percent felt that the COM catalog was at least as easy or easier to use than the book catalog; pessimistically, 54 percent felt that it was as difficult or more difficult to use.

The overall evidence concerning user attitudes toward COM catalogs was not entirely conclusive one way or another. Most librarians in institutions employing book or COM catalogs were of the opinion—admittedly subjective but based on everyday experiences with library users—that COM was relatively well accepted. From the patron's point of view, the catalogs were sometimes easier to use and less cumbersome than card catalogs. The ability to distribute multiple copies allowed far broader access to a library's catalog, and where multilibrary systems adopted a union approach to their COM catalogs, users were given access to a considerably expanded collection. With such benefits, annoyances such as equipment failure or the need to consult supplements were perhaps tolerable.

Parallels with Card Catalogs

In terms of a library's internal operations, computer-generated catalogs had the potential to alleviate some of the increasingly complex
problems of card catalogs. Once created, a machine-readable database
provided a more manageable source of information than catalog cards,
and one to which additions and modifications were easier and less
demanding of valuable staff time. In addition to enhancing the level of
library service through their greater adaptability to change and the
ease of distribution to multiple locations, computer-generated catalogs
proved to be, under certain circumstances, a more cost-effective form
of catalog.

Although the computer-generated catalog differed from and improved upon the card catalog in many respects, it closely mirrored
traditional card catalogs in certain important respects. The level of
bibliographic description provided and the depth of access to materials
in computer-generated book and microform catalogs seldom departed
from the established practices of card catalogs.

Concerning the bibliographic description for individual entries in the
catalog, any departure from traditional card catalog practices often
resulted in less information rather than more. This was particularly
true in many of the earlier book catalogs where, for economy and ease
in processing, a premium was placed on limiting input to a single
80-column IBM card for each entry. This restriction frequently meant
the shortening of long titles and names of authors, omission of certain
elements of description, and virtual elimination of any summary or
contents notes or other lengthy annotation.

As for access points to items contained in the catalog, depth of indexing generally remained unchanged. In the case of subject headings in
particular, the practice of assigning a minimal number of headings
defined at the broadest possible levels usually remained constant in
making the transition from manually maintained card catalogs to computer-generated book and microform catalogs.

Special Libraries

Many public and academic librarians have long argued for more
detailed descriptions of, and broader access to, materials in their collections through the medium of the public catalog. With offline computerization, however, these were realized to any extent only in a few
special libraries. Because of the nature of their parent organization,
and the role that they played in the organization, some special libraries
were in a particularly strong position to incorporate the use of a computer into their operations to the fullest extent possible.

The category of "special libraries" is enormously broad and generally defined more by exclusion of other categories—public, academic, school—than by any well-conceived notion of responsibilities or organizational roles. At one extreme, some loosely defined special libraries have been barely more than a collection of stockpiled materials that no one at the parent institutions knew what else to do with; at the opposite end, some special libraries have played an integral role with far-reaching responsibilities in the information sources critical to the everyday and long-range operations of their institutions.

For the special library, catalogs have served the same essential function as in public and academic libraries. In terms of materials described, however, there have traditionally been important differences. Even when considering only written documents and not graphics, special libraries playing a crucial role in the parent agency's operations have often been responsible for handling different, and sometimes quite diverse, categories of materials, which include a broader range of documents than those that make up the core of public and academic library collections. Internally and externally generated technical reports often comprise an important part, and sometimes the major scope, of the special library's collection. Many of these reports are outside public distribution channels and the mainstream of bibliographic control. Added to the responsibilities of handling such material, many special libraries have been asked to organize and maintain a wide variety of internal records, ranging from correspondence to contract documentation to any other documentation that concerns the agency's business. To exercise control over such a broad range of materials traditionally outside the scope of the main collections of public and academic libraries, a more detailed approach was often taken to describe the contents of the material. Not only did these specialized collections demand their own vocabularies and classifications, but in practice they often required indexing procedures far more thorough and detailed than was in general practice in academic and public libraries.

Uses and Services

In the early and mid-1960s, special libraries and information centers in high technology corporations and agencies were in an excellent position, by virtue of the tools of the trade employed by their parent institutions, to experiment with computer applications. In many cases, this led to the design and implementation of a processing system that included production of computer-generated book catalogs. These catalogs had many of the positive attributes of those used in public and academic libraries, such as relative ease of reproduction and distribution in quantity, elimination of manual filing into a catalog, and reduction of the amount of work required to add a new record to the database or modify an existing one.

In addition to such benefits, special libraries using computer-generated catalogs generally took fuller advantage of machine capabilities than did public and academic libraries in providing a broader range of subject access points to materials in the collection. This was partly the result of a traditional tendency on the part of special libraries to assign a far greater number of subject descriptors to documents than public and academic libraries commonly did. The procedure was still manual insofar as determining, coding, and actually keypunching descriptors for input into the system. However, by taking advantage of processing capabilities, special libraries did not have to repeat the entire bibliographic entry for each descriptor or code assigned in order for the full entry to be listed in the catalog under each. A fast and effective method to establish at least a partial list of the appropriate subject descriptors for a document was to select terminology from the title, abstract, or other selected parts of the document itself.

Several special libraries and technical information centers that maintained machine-readable databases of catalog information offered an automated current awareness service offline. Machine-readable patron profiles indicating subject interests were periodically loaded into a computer and matched against new records entered into the database. A listing of all recently acquired documents relevant to each profile was compiled, printed, and delivered to the particular patron for whom a standing profile had been written. This listing service was an application that went beyond the general use of machine-readable catalog databases in academic and public libraries during the 1960s. Rather than simply processing and printing a general listing, computerized current awareness services focused on the needs of the individual information user and exploited the computer's tremendous speed and capacity for manipulation to best serve these interests.

The use of computers for generating custom-tailored searches for the individual patron was not restricted only to periodically matching user interests against new acquisitions. Some libraries offered a retrospective search service; a user could submit a request to have the entire database automatically searched for all previously cataloged documents pertaining to a term or a combination of terms. Most systems used for searching were programmed to handle Boolean logic, in which multiterm searches could be specified in a manner that broadened or narrowed the parameters of the subject of interest. The use of "OR" as a logical operator connecting search terms would retrieve any records in the database indexed with any of the terms so connected; the use of "AND" would retrieve a record only if it was indexed under all terms thus connected; and the logical operator "NOT" would retrieve a record only if it was indexed under the first search term but not under the second. In the 1960s, these special service search applications were generally carried out by keying the search strategy and entering it into a computer via batch mode for comparison with the database.

The use of computers to maintain bibliographic and other records in special libraries during the 1960s was, as in public and academic libraries, limited in terms of the total number of libraries. Computerization was still beyond the financial reach of most libraries, and the special libraries in the technological forefront were able to computerize not usually because of an independent endowment or their own financial resources, but because of the nature of their parent corporation's or agency's business. Special libraries and information centers that did use computers, however, were generally a step ahead of their public and academic counterparts in terms of the level of service-oriented offline applications.

Online Public-Access Catalogs

During the late 1960s and much of the 1970s, most efforts to create online bibliographic databases did not focus on providing access to the holdings of a particular library, but rather on recording and providing distributed access to all or at least a major portion of all available published literature in a targeted field of specialization. In some cases, the difference between the two approaches was minor in degree; a subject-oriented database might in fact be largely based on the holdings of a single library or other information center collecting as comprehensively as possible in that area. The evolution of the use of these subject-oriented databases in libraries is discussed in the next chapter. The focus of the remainder of this chapter is on the evolution of what have come to be known as online public access catalogs (OPACs), which detail the holdings of a particular library or group of libraries and to which users have direct access.

Changes

A few libraries were experimenting with online access to their catalog databases as early as the mid-1960s, when computer-generated book and COM catalogs were coming into greater use. Most of these early online catalogs were, by later standards, fairly limited in capabilities, but their existence at least confirmed the great potential of the computer for public service library uses. The most immediately visible differences between these and computer-generated book and microform catalogs were currency of available information, interaction between user and catalog, and flexibility of access to records in the catalog.

With book and COM catalogs, the machine-readable catalog database was distinct from the final product available to the user; in an online catalog, the database and its associated index files *were* the catalog. Its currency was restricted only by the timeliness with which libraries entered new records and made changes to existing ones. These new records and changes did not have to wait, as with catalogs generated offline, until the next printed edition or supplement. As with online technical processing systems, this currency and instant supplementation were one of the major advantages of online over offline catalogs.

Online catalogs required a fundamental change in the manner in which the patron interacted with the library catalog. With card, book, or microform catalogs, the user may form a search strategy in his or her mind and then proceed directly to examine the specific section of the catalog appropriate to that strategy. The user is not required anywhere in the process to translate mental strategy into verbal or written form to gain access to the catalog. In using an online catalog, however, the user must not only form a mental search strategy, but must also be able to articulate it simply to gain access to the contents of the catalog. And in many online catalogs, the user must make still another transition. Although users of a card, book, or microform catalog may not fully understand the cataloging and filing principles that were used to arrive at and arrange access terms, those terms are generally expressed in a basic vocabulary form similar to the one used in the patron's mental research strategy. For access to some online catalogs, the user must translate the search strategy into certain codes or truncated terms prescribed by the system: the user must learn the system's mode of dialog simply to gain entry into the catalog.

Although it may require a greater amount, and certainly a different type, of effort on the part of the user, there were clearly attractive benefits to be gained by accessing a library catalog online. An important feature of a number of online systems implemented since the mid-1960s is the increased flexibility of access to individual records in the database, even to the point where theoretically a catalog entry may be retrieved on almost any term appearing anywhere in the machine-stored record for that entry. This degree of flexibility presents its own set of problems, and in practice few online systems have tried to carry their retrieval capability quite that far. On a less exhaustive scale, however, the expansion of access points to entries in an online catalog has introduced a level of search and retrieval flexibility not found in card, book, or COM catalogs. Efforts toward this end have included such capabilities as enabling retrieval of a catalog record for an item by entering any significant word in its title or any term in an assigned subject heading phrase regardless of the position of the terms within the complete title or heading. Added to the increased number of access points are capabilities for refining or expanding searches through such means as Boolean logic and user-designated qualification of term searches by additional parameters like date of publication, language, and so on.

Even by the late 1970s, online public-access library catalogs with this level of search and retrieval capability were something of a rarity. The initial efforts in online catalogs in the mid- and late 1960s were even more limited. In some cases, online catalogs were not really public access, in that although a user could request a query of the system, the search was actually performed by library or information center staff. Such was the case, for example, in the early stages of the online library catalog at the Missile and Space Division of General Electric. As of 1966, at least, the library staff conducted the queries for patrons. The contents of the system comprised only a partial catalog in that a search of subject terms retrieved and displayed only a list of accession numbers of documents in the library indexed under those terms. Bibliographic information was not displayed online.[31]

INTREX Project

One of the most ambitious explorations of the potential applications of computer technology to library service was Project INTREX (INformation TRansfer EXperiments), conducted at the Massachusetts Institute of Technology (MIT) between 1965 and 1973. The project involved the creation and maintenance of a bibliographic database for a narrowly defined category of library materials, the storage of the full text of each item represented in the database, online access to the bibliographic database both in a controlled and an open library environment, and automatic retrieval and display of the full text of indexed documents upon request.

The materials selected for coverage by the INTREX database included journal articles appearing in periodicals received by the libraries at MIT in the areas of microwave spectroscopy, quantum electronics, high-temperature metallurgy, solidification and casting, and structural strength of materials. The bibliographic record created for each article included a broad range of descriptive elements. Some of these elements, such as author's name, title of article, and bibliographic citation, were straightforward and similar to those appearing in manual library catalogs or printed bibliographies and indexes. But a variety of other information was also entered into a record, including an abstract of the article. Since retrieval by subject was to be the core of the online system, a great deal of emphasis was placed on the in-depth assignment of subject terms to documents represented in the database. These terms were extracted from titles, abstracts, and other portions of the article, but descriptors not appearing anywhere in the article could also be assigned. The vocabularly used for subject descriptors was uncontrolled; that is, there was no predetermined set of acceptable terms from which the descriptors had to be drawn.

The INTREX bibliographic database was stored on the computer, but computer storage of the full text of all documents represented by the database would simply have been too expensive. Therefore, the full text of each article was stored on microfiche. The microform storage and retrieval units were designed in such a way, however, that the full text of articles could be immediately retrieved and displayed on viewing devices adjacent to the terminal used to access the online bibliographic database. In 1970, a terminal model was installed allowing display of both bibliographic records and the full text of articles on the same piece of equipment. Access terminals were located in the MIT Electronic Systems Laboratory, where controlled studies were carried out on use of the system; in MIT's Barker Engineering at MIT; and eventually in the Division of Engineering and Applied Physics at Harvard.

Users could search the INTREX database by keying in an author or a subject term. When an online search of the bibliographic database was keyed in at one of the access terminals, the system responded by informing the user of the number of records in the database matching the search strategy entered. In the INTREX experiments, an average number of about 400 references matched the search strategy initially entered by the user. Inevitably, the user would refine the strategy in an attempt to narrow the number of references. The user could examine the full bibliographic record for any reference, and could also have the abstract of any of the articles displayed by keying an additional command. The user could then request a display of the full text of any of the documents represented by the bibliographic display. As already noted, the full text of articles was stored on microform, but their automatic retrieval and display was rapid and effective. If the user decided an article was relevant, a hard copy could be requested and printed out immediately at the access station.

The INTREX system was designed for direct access by the library user, albeit a fairly limited audience of specialists working in certain areas of scientific and technical research. The INTREX staff devised a number of aids to assist the user in operating the system. Some of these were instruction manuals, providing detailed descriptions of about 30 pages; others were abbreviated guides. Neither proved to be terribly effective. A large instructional wall chart did not fare too successfully either, nor did an instructional slide-tape kit. The most effective aid proved to be online assistance in the form of prompts. At any given stage during a search, these prompts instructed the user as to options and commands that were available at that point in the dialog. Although this lengthened a search, the system also incorporated a short mode, whereby users familiar with the system could omit the detailed instructions and be afforded other time-saving procedures. In the Barker Engineering Library, reference staff were trained to assist users upon request.

Between 1967 and 1971, bibliographic records for about 20,000 articles were entered into the INTREX database. The storage of the full text of these articles required about 1,500 microfiche cards. Although the INTREX "augmented catalog" encountered its share of difficulties during its operation, it was far ahead of its time in demonstrating the potential of computer applications to library service. It demonstrated, too, that the application of such comprehensive systems on a wide scale was not yet financially feasible. The project was supported largely through grant funding, which by mid-1971 totaled nearly $2.5 million and had come from such diverse sources as the Carnegie Corporation, the Council on Library Resources, the U.S. Department of Defense, the Independence Foundation, the National Science Foundation, and the Sloan Foundation.[32]

With the exception of INTREX, the few online public-access catalogs implemented in libraries between the mid-1960s and mid-1970s continued to remain largely outside the public and academic sectors. In the early 1970s, the library at the IBM Los Gatos Laboratory brought up its Experimental Library Management System, which offered online retrieval of catalog records for books and technical reports in the library.[33] In Great Britain, an online catalog was developed for the Technical Information Systems Department of Strip Mills Division of the British Steel Corporation. The bibliographic database could be searched directly by users, and access could be gained not only at the library, but also remotely through terminals located elsewhere.[34]

By the mid-1970s, there was increasing recognition among public and academic librarians that online public-access catalogs would be feasible, if not immediately, at least within the next decade. For some libraries, the path to this eventuality was seen to be through OCLC, an expectation expressed by several of the respondents to Kenneth Bierman's survey in 1975.[35] OCLC had proved an undeniable success in leading hundreds of libraries into automation for the first time, and the system seemingly lacked only a few features that would allow it to become an effective public-access tool. These essential features seemed fairly easily identifiable—subject access, the display of local modifications of master records, and redesigned display formats being among the most obvious. Even without these, several libraries were already experimenting with public access to OCLC and were finding library users receptive.[36]

OCLC did not develop the critical capabilities that would have made the system even minimally acceptable to most libraries as a local public-access catalog. Online display of local holdings information was kept on OCLC's development schedule but was never realized. A similar fate befell subject-access capability. Display formats were never redesigned in a way that would be conducive to public access. System performance—downtime and response time—proved to be further limitations on the feasibility of the centralized OCLC system ever having become a viable alternative as a public access catalog.

Ohio State University

During the mid- and late 1970s, a few academic and public libraries introduced online public access catalogs. One of the first to do so was the Ohio State University (OSU) Libraries. As described in the preceding chapter, Ohio State had introduced a comparatively sophisticated online circulation system in the early 1970s and its equally noteworthy role in introducing an online public catalog was related to that earlier development. The OSU online catalog, like most others implemented before 1980, was an outgrowth of its circulation system.

Because of the nature of its system, OSU was more easily able to broaden it into a versatile public-access tool than were other libraries with the circulation systems they had developed. Many online circulation systems implemented during the early 1970s had been designed around an "absence" system: the database, at any given time, contained records only for items in circulation at that moment. Generally, access was provided only by call number or other local system control number and by patron ID number. Although public use of a system with these features would have been feasible, it would obviously have been limited in scope. In contrast, OSU's circulation system had been designed with a broader range of access points and contained permanently stored records for nearly every item in the libraries.

Limited public access to OSU's system was introduced in 1975 with the placement of a few terminals in public use areas of the main library. It was an integral part of the plan that the online system was *not* to be an immediate replacement of the card catalog, and the two would coexist until the electronic version encompassed all varieties of access available in the card catalog. Through 1977, the online system allowed access by author, title, a combination of author and title, and call number. Records retrieved contained only brief bibliographic information, such as author, title, and date of publication, along with local information including call number, location, and circulation status. During 1978, subject access was introduced, along with capability for viewing more complete bibliographic information for titles cataloged since 1977. The provision of online cross-references was still in the planning stage.

As the OSU system evolved, author access was possible through two approaches: by entering the full name of the author or by entering an abbreviated search key using the first six letters of an author's surname (or the first word of a corporate name) and up to the first three letters of the first name (or of the second word of a corporate name). Either strategy might retrieve multiple records, in which case the system could display up to 30 very abbreviated bibliographic entries on three stored sequential screens. The user could see more complete bibliographic or local information about the desired item by keying in the line number corresponding to the brief entry. A search by title required the user to type the initial four characters of the first word of the title followed by the first five characters of the second. A combined author/title key required the user to enter the first four letters of the author's surname (or the first word of a corporate name) followed by the first five characters of the first word of the title. The technique for displaying more complete bibliographic or local information when multiple entries were retrieved followed the same procedure used in refining author searches.

An exact call number search was available, as was a shelflist position search, a form of subject browsing. When a user entered a call number, the system responded by displaying that number and brief bibliographic records for the 11 shelflist entries preceding it and the 18 following it. Subject term searching was introduced in 1978 and was also designed to facilitate browsing. Although the subject system was based on Library of Congress headings, the user could enter a term or phrase in any form, and the system would respond by displaying the 11 LC subject heading terms alphabetically preceding the search term or phrase and the 18 alphabetically following it. Beside each term was shown the number of entries in the online system that had been assigned that heading. By selecting the desired heading, the user received a display of brief bibliographic records of titles indexed under the heading. The major problem with this form of subject access was the same as with a card catalog; the user could key in a term alphabetically quite unlike the appropriate Library of Congress subject heading. Although it would not solve the problem entirely, the development of an online authority structure and cross-reference display was an important step in at least partially alleviating it. Only after this capability was added to the OSU system in 1982 did the library feel that the online catalog fully met the range of access available in the card catalog.[37]

An important public service feature of online catalogs based on circulation systems was that they provided the user not only bibliographic and holdings information, but also data on whether an item was presently available for circulation. This was a critical feature, setting these catalogs apart from other forms such as card, book, and COM. The user could have a fairly accurate idea of the status of an item *before* going to the stacks. Whether because this capability required an additional user command to call up a circulation status screen or because of habit, librarians at OSU found that users often did not take advantage of it; and after finding the call number for an item, many users went directly to the stacks rather than checking the circulation status online. On the other hand, other users consulted the online system almost exclusively for this purpose, having first obtained the call number of an item from a search in the card catalog.

Even with the advantage of containing circulation status information, online catalogs evolving from circulation systems sometimes suffered from the features that were designed to carry out the original intention of the system. This was recognized at OSU, for example, where the design of the circulation system in the early 1970s was based on an assumption that users would be library staff with training in use of the system. As a result of this assumption, online prompting of commands and online instruction were minimal. The display format of records and identification of bibliographic elements on a record also assumed training. When public access was made available, design limitations represented potential sources of confusion or difficulty for the library user. The evolution of a circulation system into a viable public-access catalog was thus an evolving process for libraries that have taken this approach to developing an online catalog. Ongoing revisions to the system were necessary to make it more easily understandable and usable for the general public.

While online systems like OSU's usually did not initially take full advantage of the sophisticated retrieval capabilities possible with computers, they served a vital role in demonstrating that online, interactive catalogs could be successfully used by the general library public. Their development during the 1970s foreshadowed the intense activity that would begin to occur in the 1980s.

Into the 1980s

The early 1980s represented an intense period in the development of online public-access catalogs, enough so that several apparent trends began to emerge. In contrast to earlier catalogs based on circulation systems, some of the online catalogs developed during the early 1980s were designed in and of themselves as public access catalogs, not as an extension of an up and running system formerly reserved for other purposes. One such catalog was developed by the Minnesota State University System Project for Automated Library Systems (MSUS/PALS), frequently referred to as the Mankato State System for the Minnesota State University campus where it was first implemented. From the beginning of its design, MSUS/PALS was developed for public access, which allowed the creators to grapple from the outset with the question of accommodating users in terms of access, display, and system guidance and assistance. Like MSUS/PALS, the MELVYL prototype online catalog developed by the University of California Systemwide Division of Library Automation was first implemented as a public-access catalog; both systems intended to incorporate a circulation function at a later date.

Another trend was the development of integrated systems in which the public-access catalog was just one component of a broader online system. The most long standing examples are systems such as those described above, that both control a library's circulation function and provide patrons access to at least a portion of the library's catalog through the same system. Many of the systems developed during the 1980s have strived to encompass other functions as well. The Total Library System (TLS) developed by the Claremont Colleges brought together acquisitions processing, circulation, and an online catalog in a single integrated system by early in the decade. Both the Integrated Library System (ILS) originally implemented at the National Library of Medicine's Lister Hill National Center for Biomedical Communications and the Bibliographic Access and Control System (BACS) developed at the Washington University School of Medicine Library in St. Louis incorporated serials control as well as circulation into their public-access systems. Integrated online systems have long been expounded and were to some extent realized in some of the landmark technical processing systems during the 1970s, but the expansion of functions to include public access has been an important achievement, largely of the 1980s.

Another trend in the development of online library catalogs during the early 1980s was their design to accommodate multi-institutional arrangements. Both MSUS/PALS and MELVYL were designed as multi-institutional systems. In both cases, users in a specific library could search the catalog of their own library, the catalog of another library sharing the system, or a systemwide union catalog. The online catalog marketed by Carlyle Systems, Inc., was designed on a similar basis.

As with online technical processing systems, the options available to a library in the implementation of an online catalog expanded rapidly in the early 1980s. Many of the online catalogs developed in-house by libraries during the late 1970s and early 1980s were being offered for sale, sometimes through commercial handlers, sometimes by the library itself, and sometimes through arrangements whose complexity defies either of these categories. The MSUS/PALS system, Northwestern University's system, the Virginia Tech Library System (VTLS), and several more recently designed systems have been actively marketed by one means or another. OCLC planned to market Claremont's TLS with modifications, but these efforts were later abandoned. The University of California chose not to actively market MELVYL, but the chief officers of the university's Systemwide Division of Library Automation established Carlyle Systems, Inc., and used their expertise to develop TOMUS, which they began to market commercially. The software for Lister Hill's ILS has been available very inexpensively from the National Technical Information Service (NTIS), but it is supplied through that agency virtually without such important support services such as installation, training, modification, or ongoing assistance. At least two commercial firms—Online, Inc., and Avatar—began to offer modified versions of ILS, the latter company being formed by some of the original creators of ILS at NLM. In 1983, OCLC concluded agreements with both companies to assume marketing rights for the modified ILS versions. In addition to the marketing of online catalogs developed by libraries, most vendors of large-scale automated circulation systems have introduced online catalog modules.

Although sharing the common purpose of trying to provide the library user a more flexible tool than had been offered through the medium of card, book, or microform catalogs, the online catalogs that emerged during the 1970s and early 1980s have differed greatly in approach. Some represent, in essence, a continuous supplement to the card catalog, with the former containing records for items brought into the collection after a certain date and the latter containing records for materials in the collection before that date. In some libraries, the two forms of catalog coexist concurrently, even for new materials coming into the collection. In yet other libraries, the card catalog has been discarded and completely superseded by the online catalog. Just as noticeable are the differences in the command languages used, the range of access points available, and the format and content of records as they are displayed. These important variables in the design of online catalogs—the command structures governing dialog, the access points, and display format and content—are examined in detail in Chapters 13 and 14.

Notes

1. For a history of pre-twentieth-century book catalogs, see James Ranz, *Printed Book Catalogs in American Libraries: 1723–1900* (Chicago: American Library Association, 1964).
2. U.S. Library of Congress, *A Catalog of Books Represented by Library of Congress Printed Cards* (Ann Arbor, Mich.: Edwards, 1942–1946).
3. For a description of the King County catalog, see Dorothy Alvard, "King County Public Library Does It with IBM," *PNLA Quarterly* 16 (April 1952): 123–132.
4. *Ibid.*, p. 124.
5. For a description of the University of Toronto project, see Ritvars Bregzis, "The Ontario New Universities Library Project—An Automated Bibliographic Data Control System," *College and Research Libraries* 26 (November 1965): 495–508; see also the report by the same author "The ONULP Bibliographic Control System: An Evaluation," in *Proceedings of the 1965 Clinic on Library Applications of Data Processing* (Urbana, Ill.: University of Illinois Graduate School of Library Science, 1966), pp. 112–140.
6. George B. Moreland, "An Unsophisticated Approach to Book Catalog and Circulation Control," in *Data Processing in Public and University Libraries* (Washington, D.C.: Spartan Books, 1966), p. 58.
7. Robert M. Hayes, Ralph M. Shaffner, and David C. Weber, "The Economics of Book Catalog Production," *Library Resources and Technical Services* 10 (Winter 1966): 62–63.
8. Paula Kieffer, "Book Catalogs—To Have or Not to Have," *Library Resources and Technical Services* 15 (Summer 1971): 292.
9. Stephen R. Salmon, *Library Automation Systems* (New York: Marcel Dekker, 1975), p. 44; and Moreland, "Unsophisticated Approach," p. 61.
10. Moreland, "Unsophisticated Approach," p. 59.
11. David C. Weber, "Book Catalog Trends in 1966," *Library Trends* 16 (July 1967): 159.
12. Kenneth John Biermann, "Automated Alternatives to Card Catalogs: The Current State of Planning and Implementation," *Journal of Library Automation* 8 (December 1975): 285.
13. Richard D. Johnson, "A Book Catalog at Stanford," *Journal of Library Automation* 1 (March 1968): 18.
14. Kieffer, "Book Catalogs," p. 293.
15. Wesley Simonton, "The Computerized Catalog: Possible, Feasible, Desirable?" *Library Resources and Technical Services* 8 (Fall 1964): 405.
16. S. Michael Malinconico, "The Library Catalog in a Computerized Environment," *Wilson Library Bulletin* 51 (September 1976): 57.
17. Irwin H. Pizer, "Book Catalogs Versus Card Catalogs," in *Book Catalogs*, Maurice F. Tauber and Hilda Feinberg, eds. (Metuchen, N.J.: Scarecrow, 1971), p. 43.

18. Bregzis, "The ONULP Bibliographic Control System," pp. 116–117.
19. Charles W. Robinson, "The Book Catalog: Diving In," *Wilson Library Bulletin* 40 (November 1965): 264.
20. Kieffer, "Book Catalogs," pp. 294–295.
21. Bregzis, "The ONULP Bibliographic Control System," pp. 116–117.
22. Bregzis, "The Ontario New Universities Library Project," p. 503.
23. S. Michael Malinconico, "The Display Medium and the Piece of the Message," *Library Journal* 101 (October 15, 1976): 2145.
24. For a description of the procedure used at the Lockheed Technical Information Center, see W. A. Kozumplik and R. T. Lange, "Computer-produced Microfilm Library Catalog," *American Documentation* 18 (April 1967): 67–80.
25. *Ibid.*, p. 68.
26. James F. Hadlow, "Some Problems with COM Catalogues," *MICRODOC* 16 (1977): 75–82.
27. *Ibid.*, p. 79.
28. Bregzis, "The ONULP Bibliographic Control System," p. 125.
29. James R. Dwyer, "Public Response to an Academic Library Microcatalog," *Journal of Academic Librarianship* 5 (July 1979), p. 139.
30. Brian Aveney and Mary Fischer Ghikas, "600 Users Meet the COM Catalog," *American Libraries* 10 (February 1979): 83.
31. For a description of the General Electric Missle and Space Division library catalog, see Lawrence I. Chasen, "Information Retrieval Systems and Technology in an Aerospace Library," *Special Libraries* 57 (December 1966): 687–691.
32. For brief overviews of the INTREX project, see Carl F. J. Overhage, *Project INTREX: A Brief Description* (Cambridge, Mass.: Massachusetts Institute of Technology, 1971); and Carl F. J. Overhage and J. Frances Reintjes, "Project INTREX: A General Review," *Information Storage and Retrieval* 10 (1974): 157–188.
33. For a description of ELMS, see Ruth Winik, "Reference Function with an Online Catalog," *Special Libraries* 63 (May/June 1972): 217–221.
34. For a description, see M. N. Patten, "Experience with an In-house Mechanized Information System," *ASLIB Proceedings* 26 (May 1974): 189–209.
35. Biermann, "Automated Alternatives," pp. 283–284.
36. W. Stuart Debenham, Jr., Kunj Rastogi, and Philip Schieber, *OCLC Public Use Terminals: Report of a Survey of Users of OCLC Public Use Terminals, 1974–1975* (Columbus, Ohio: Online College Library Center, 1976).
37. A number of articles about LCS appeared in the professional literature during the late 1970s and early 1980s. A couple of the more general descriptions include Susan L. Miller, "The Ohio State University Libraries Online Catalog," in *Closing the Catalog,* D. Kaye Gapen and Bonnie Juergens, eds. (Phoenix, Ariz.: Oryx Press, 1980), pp. 79–84; and Susan L. Miller, "The Evolution of an On-line Catalog," in *New Horizons for Academic Libraries* (New York: K. G. Saur, 1979), pp. 193–204.

5

Information Retrieval Services

As described in the previous chapter, the public catalog is one of the public services functions in libraries that has been affected by automation. Since the 1960s, and particularly since the mid-1970s, two other public services functions have become increasingly automated. One is in the provision of access to subject-oriented indexes, abstracts, and similar reference sources. Through use of such services as DIALOG Information Services, System Development Corporation (SDC), and Bibliographic Retrieval Services (BRS), many libraries have incorporated online database searching into the routine complement of services available to users. As a reference function in libraries, searching and retrieval from machine-readable databases offered through these services is only about a ten-year-old phenomenon. The other public services function to be increasingly automated has been interlibrary lending.

Both database searching and interlibrary lending are library services that predate computers. Automated database searching has a direct precedent in subscription to printed indexes and abstracts covering general or specialized bodies of literature. As for interlibrary lending, libraries relied on printed catalogs, telephones, mail, and assorted other means of document delivery long before the advent of the computer.

There is a logical continuum between these two services, both in their noncomputerized and their computer-assisted forms. Indexes and abstracts are likely to provide the library user with references to materials that are not available on the immediate premises, and it is at this point where an interlibrary loan service takes over. For purposes of discussion, however, these two services are examined separately here: the evolution of online databases in this chapter and the use of automation in interlibrary lending in the next chapter.

Background

In a constantly increasing number of libraries, subject-oriented printed indexes and abstracts, such as *Chemical Abstracts, Sociological Abstracts,* and *Modern Language Association Bibliography,* are being replaced or supplemented by online access to machine-readable versions of the same publication. Use of these databases is through a service agency that provides access to many such databases. Simply by dialing a telephone number, a terminal in a library is connected via one of several telecommunications networks to the service agency's computer. Through a simple identification, the searcher specifies which database on the computer is to be searched and then proceeds through interactive dialog to retrieve citations that are pertinent to a user's search request.

Machine-readable databases that are accessible in the manner described above and the computers on which they are stored are so numerous, so constantly changing, and so undocumented that they defy estimation. Therefore, discussion is limited here to services that have targeted libraries as a primary commercial concern. Even so, it is possible to arrive at meaningful estimates only by setting up fairly strict criteria for inclusion. Martha Williams, for example, estimated that by the end of the 1970s there were 650 "bibliographic-textual-natural language" databases searchable either online or in batch mode and "publicly available" on "major U.S. and Canadian bibliographic retrieval systems."[1]

These parameters make it somewhat easier to identify the major bibliographic retrieval systems and services within a library context. In the past, very few actual *producers* of these databases—primarily the indexing and abstracting services—have felt it economically viable to offer online access themselves. Instead, these producers have generally concentrated efforts on just creating machine-readable files of bibliographic information, the "raw material" for a retrieval system. The producer then licenses the machine-readable database to a database vendor (or "information retrieval service"), which has developed a retrieval system and has mounted many such databases on its computers. It is the vendor, then, that provides libraries and other institutions online access to the content of the databases. Since most of the major vendors have this type of arrangement with a number of database producers, there are far fewer database vendors than producers.

In some cases, the relationship between the information retrieval service, the retrieval system it uses, and the databases to which it offers access is fairly straightforward. For example, System Development Corporation (SDC) offers a service through its internally developed ORBIT retrieval system, with access to more than 70 distinct databases. In other cases, the relationship is less direct. For example, Bibliographic Retrieval Services (BRS), another major online service, uses a version of the STAIRS system developed by IBM. Perhaps the most complex relationship, especially in a historical sense, concerns the National Library of Medicine (NLM), which acts both as a database producer and as a vendor of its own databases. The retrieval system used in NLM's own service is ELHILL-2; the earliest version was developed by SDC, based in large part on ORBIT.

Adding to all this complexity is the fact that a number of the databases available from major vendors are not offered by only one service, but rather by two or three or more. For example, access to portions of NLM's most comprehensive database, MEDLARS, is offered not only by NLM directly, but also through BRS and DIALOG. The ERIC database compiled by the National Institute of Education is offered through BRS, DIALOG, and SDC. As one might expect in such cases of parallel service, there is a significant amount of professional literature that compares the retrieval effectiveness of different services for databases offered through more than one service.

Origins and Emergence

Two of the practical advantages that online indexing and abstracting databases have over their printed counterparts are the same as in online technical processing systems and public-access catalogs: currency of information and flexibility in searching. In terms of implementation, the earliest of the online technical processing systems, and even online public-access catalogs, predated use of formally established information retrieval services by libraries. This is not to say, however, that the design of the latter was in any way based on the former. The fact that the information retrieval services did not really emerge until the early 1970s in a publicly available forum (with the exception of the SUNY Biomedical Communications Network) was not due to a lack of developed systems, but rather to other factors. The early online systems described in Chapters 3 and 4, for cataloging, acquisitions, serials control, circulation, and public catalogs, actually owed a great deal to the lessons learned from experimental and operational online systems developed by some of the retrieval services as far back as the early 1960s.

The various information retrieval services had several features in common that distinguished them from online library catalogs and systems for technical processing applications. Some of these distinguishing features included:

1. Subject orientation, covering material pertinent to a particular discipline, in some cases narrowly defined and in others quite broadly defined, rather than the holdings of a particular library.
2. An emphasis on indexing and abstracting of the periodical literature rather than books.
3. An emphasis on remote access to centrally stored databases by a number of different users.
4. Use limited to searching and retrieval of information; data in the master file could not be permanently added to or purged from the database by remote access users.

In addition, the vendor-based information retrieval systems of the 1970s and their predecessors in the 1960s shared a distinguishing emphasis in the direction of system capabilities. Almost without exception, the earliest online library operations systems of the 1960s were very rudimentary in certain features, such as depth of indexing of machine-stored records and breadth of retrieval capabilities for accessing those records. In contrast, bibliographic storage and retrieval systems developed by the information retrieval services had placed their most concentrated focus on precisely those features so lacking in sophistication in the early online library systems. They were designed with primary emphasis on in-depth indexing of records and exploited the tremendous power of computers in order to provide more sophisticated avenues of retrieval.

TIP System

One of the more successful initial efforts in the design of an online bibliographic retrieval system was in conjunction with the Technical Information Project (TIP) at the Massachusetts Institute of Technology in the early 1960s. The database created for the project included citations to articles in more than 20 journals in the field of physics; by 1966, the database included about 35,000 citations. The input for each source article consisted of a citation that included the name of the journal, the issue and pagination on which it appeared, the author and title, the institutional affiliation of the author, and a list of all references cited in the article.

The procedure for retrieving citations from the TIP database required the searcher first to specify the parameters of the search, such as which issues of which journal were to be searched. Next, the user entered a search strategy, instructing the system to retrieve all citations of articles, for example, by a given author or with a certain term in the title. Boolean searching could be performed and the system also allowed for retrieval on truncated search terms. In entering more than one term in a title search, a user had the flexibility of specifying whether these terms had to appear anywhere within a title or whether they had to appear exactly in the same order as specified in the search statement.

The decision not to assign additional subject descriptors for each article was based in part on the premise that if very sophisticated search and retrieval capabilities were designed into the system, subject-access avenues might be available that would not depend on manual selection and assignment of subject terms. Such an experiment had profound implications for creating information retrieval databases, for it reduced the input procedure to a clerical task not requiring the additional, purely intellectual, time and effort involved in selecting and assigning subject terms.

The nontraditional form of subject access in the TIP system was based on manipulation of citations listed as references in source documents. A searcher could enter an author's name or a title of a work and retrieve records for all source documents that had cited that author or title as a reference. One extension of this capability was bibliographic coupling. A searcher could enter two authors' names or two titles, for example, and would retrieve records for all source documents that had cited both authors or both titles.

The premise for citation retrieval and bibliographic coupling as a form of subject access was that there exists a strong correlation between the subject of an article and the subject of works cited therein. Further, the more references any two articles have in common, the more closely related the subjects of those two articles are likely to be.

For a searcher who was aware of important works in a particular field that were likely to be cited, these retrieval capabilities represented a viable form of subject access. Recognizing that this was only a partial approach and would have assumed that the user was already aware of articles likely to be cited, the TIP retrieval system design incorporated features that automatically assisted the search process. A most interesting strategy was a set of procedures referred to in TIP as Strategy A. The user did not have to execute all of the steps involved, but merely had to initiate the strategy by entering a search term that was likely to appear in titles of source documents on a subject in which he or she was interested. After retrieving records for all source documents with this term in the title, the system automatically examined all references cited in those documents and ranked the references according to the number of documents citing them. Given a cut-off point, the system then took the most commonly cited references and searched for other source documents in the database, which, even though lacking the original search term in their title, cited these same references. Once this second file of source documents was compiled and added to the first, the system then examined all titles to identify the most frequently appearing terms apart from the original search term. It then went back through the entire database to retrieve still other source documents with these secondary terms in their titles. This interplay continued until no new records were retrieved.[2]

In addition to citation-retrieval and bibliographic-coupling techniques such as those designed into the TIP system, other retrieval techniques developed during the 1960s explored the computer's potential for eliminating the need for human indexing and at the same time for assisting in making judgments about the relevance of records in the database to any given search query. In contrast, a number of other experimental systems were designed in which human indexing of source documents played an integral role. The retrieval effectiveness of these systems was evaluated with regard to such variables as depth of indexing, selection of index terms from various portions of the source documents, use of controlled versus uncontrolled indexing vocabulary, and construction of thesauri.

The 1960s were indeed an exciting period for exploring a broad range of issues related to bibliographic storage and retrieval on computers. A more detailed discussion of these issues and the specific retrieval techniques and systems developed to study them during the 1960s is beyond the scope of this book, but a source that may be of interest, and particularly appropriate for developments during that decade, is Lancaster's and Fayen's *Information Retrieval On-Line*.[3]

DIALOG and ORBIT

The sophisticated techniques devised for the TIP project and for other systems during the 1960s provided the theoretical basis that would be used in the early 1970s. Some of the vendors of that time had, in fact, been in the forefront of information retrieval systems design during the 1960s. Of the systems developed in those years, the two that have had the most long-standing impact on libraries are the DIALOG system, developed by the Lockheed Corporation, and the ORBIT system, by System Development Corporation (SDC).

By 1964, the Information Sciences Group at Lockheed's Palo Alto, California, Research Laboratory was experimenting with an online information retrieval system called CONVERSE. In its initial version, CONVERSE was a primitive effort compared with what it would soon lead to. Searching a database of 100 document citations, experimenters selected prepunched cards on which possible search terms had been recorded, and read these "search cards" into the system through a one-card reader. The system searched the database to find records for source documents containing the search terms, and responded on a teletype machine, showing either full bibliographic information for each citation retrieved or only the document citation reference number, depending on the number of citations retrieved. If the search retrieved more than 15 citations, the system sent a message to this effect and the searcher had to refine the search strategy.[4]

By 1967, through constant refinement and introduction of more sophisticated capabilities, CONVERSE was transformed into DIALOG. The impetus for the initial application of DIALOG was Lockheed's contract with the National Aeronautics and Space Administration (NASA) to develop a remote retrieval capability for the NASA database, to be used by the NASA Ames Research Center in California. A year earlier, NASA had awarded a contract to the Bunker-Ramo Corporation for development of a prototype system to allow three other NASA centers remote access to a NASA database stored on Bunker-Ramo's computer in New York City.

The 300,000-citation NASA database was mounted on a computer at Lockheed's Palo Alto facility. A remote-access terminal was placed at the Ames Research Center, from which engineers and scientists accessed the database through the DIALOG retrieval language.

A subsequent contract was awarded to Lockheed to provide a similar retrieval system that could be mounted at NASA's own facilities. The resulting system, called RECON (REmote CONsole), was based largely on DIALOG. The rights for future development of RECON were retained by NASA, and in the early 1970s, NASA in fact removed its database storage from Lockheed to mount on its own computer. About the same time, NASA awarded the contract for maintenance and further development of the RECON system to Informatics, Inc., a Lockheed competitor during the early 1970s in the emerging information retrieval services industry.[5]

The System Development Corporation had participated in the design of interactive retrieval systems as early as 1960. This experimental retrieval system, called PROTOSYNTHEX, incorporated a full-text searching capability with the text of the *Golden Book Encyclopedia* serving as its database. During the mid-1960s, SDC continued to work on the design of online information retrieval systems. One result was BOLD (Bibliographic On-Line Display), which was tested on a database of several thousand bibliographic records and abstracts for technical reports issued by the United States Documentation Center. Another SDC system during that period was COLEX (Central Information Reference and Control On-Line EXperimentation), used by the Foreign Technology Division of the U.S. Air Force Systems Command at Wright-Patterson Air Force Base in Ohio.

ORBIT (On-Line Retrieval of Bibliographic Information Time-shared) emerged at SDC from experiences gained through the design of such systems as BOLD and COLEX. An important development in SDC's information retrieval systems history occurred in 1970 when it was awarded a contract by the National Library of Medicine (NLM). The contract called for a portion of NLM's MEDLARS machine-readable database to be loaded on a computer at SDC's facilities in Santa Monica, California, and for SDC to develop a retrieval system and to provide remote access to approximately 30 libraries and hospitals throughout the United States. The project came to be known as AIM-TWX (Abridged Index Medicus TeletypeWriter EXchange Network). Much as Lockheed had done for NASA, SDC developed a retrieval system specifically for use with the MEDLARS database. Given the name ELHILL, the system was very similar to SDC's own ORBIT. Beginning in June 1970, the AIM-TWX service enabled any of the participating institutions to dial into SDC's computer over the TWX or standard telephone network and conduct online searches of the NLM database using the ELHILL retrieval language.[6]

In 1971, after several months of experience with the AIM-TWX project, NLM mounted a portion of the MEDLARS database on its own computer and, using the ELHILL system, established its own online search service called MEDLINE. For a while, SDC ran a parallel service, with a portion of the MEDLARS file mounted on its computers and accessible through ORBIT. In the mid-1970s, however, NLM terminated that arrangement and withdrew its database from SDC.

Among information retrieval systems developed during the 1960s, ORBIT and DIALOG eventually had the greatest impact on the broadest range of libraries. But another important system appeared late in the decade that would also gain library use—the Mead Data Central system developed by Mead Corporation. Its first applications were in providing online access to the Ohio Bar Automated Research (OBAR) legal database of the Ohio State Bar Association, the Epilepsy Abstracts Retrieval System (EARS) database provided by the National Institute of Neurological Diseases and Stroke, and the machine-readable bibliographic files of the National Technical Information Service. Mead narrowed its scope during the 1970s, concentrating largely on providing access to LEXIS, an outgrowth of OBAR, and to NEXIS, a news-oriented database.

SUNY BCN

Applications of online retrieval systems during the 1960s were generally limited to use in government agencies and by corporations. Probably the first information retrieval "service" used by libraries other than in those agencies or corporations was not provided by Lockheed or SDC, but by the State University of New York Biomedical Communications Network (SUNY BCN). Under the direction of Irwin Pizer, SUNY BCN became operational during fall 1968. It provided nine medical libraries access via direct telephone lines to a database stored on a computer at the SUNY Upstate Medical Center in New York. The libraries included seven in New York State, the Countway Library of Medicine at Harvard, and the National Library of Medicine.

As information retrieval services emerged in the early 1970s, SUNY BCN was somewhat distinctive in that it was neither the major producer of the database used nor the developer of the information retrieval system used to access it. The original retrieval system used was the Document Processing System (DPS) developed by IBM, replaced in 1973 by IBM's STAIRS (STorage And Information Retrieval System). Although it is true that the database was in part created by direct input from member libraries, much of it consisted of MEDLARS records provided by the National Library of Medicine.

The SUNY BCN database was broader in purpose than those eventually accessible through other information retrieval services. By 1969, it included MEDLARS files dating back to 1964, bibliographic records for monographs and serials titles cataloged by NLM since 1967, for all monographs cataloged in three of the participating libraries since 1962, for a portion of monographs cataloged by the Countway Library since 1968, and records for a 25,000-title union list of serials held by libraries on campuses of State University of New York and in several others.[7] Not all of this data was permanently available online, but requests for searching the files stored offline could be submitted over the same terminal used for online searching. These requests were then batch searched and the results mailed.

In terms of retrieval capabilities, the early version of the IBM Documented Processing System was not as sophisticated as some of the systems being developed elsewhere. Once entered, a search could not be interrupted by the user until it was completely processed. Even more restrictive, the system could return only ten citations in response to any search query. If the search retrieved more than ten citations, the system printed out only the ten most recently published. If the user wished to see more than ten, the search strategy could be reentered and processed again to retrieve ten more citations.[8] This was an awkward and time-consuming procedure, particularly since the terminals communicated at comparatively slow speeds.

Many of the design limitations imposed by the IBM Document Processing System were alleviated when SUNY BCN converted to the STAIRS system. SUNY BCN grew from its original 9 participants in 1968 to 32 by 1973 and continued in operation until 1977.

Early Databases Online

As is evident from the description of the early information retrieval systems and services that were to have the strongest impact on libraries, the machine-readable MEDLARS database played a key role in their development. By late 1971, the MEDLARS database or portions of it were available through at least three different services: SDC, SUNY BCN, and the National Library of Medicine itself. NLM may have had one of the largest bibliographic machine-readable databases, but other government agencies were also creating such files and mounting them for information retrieval purposes. Lockheed, based on its proven success with the NASA project, was in the forefront of providing government agencies with retrieval services through the DIALOG system. In 1969, it mounted the *Nuclear Science Abstracts* database for use by the Atomic Energy Commission, and the ERIC database containing machine-readable records for citations in *Research in Education* and *Current Index to Journals in Education* for use by the U.S. Department of Education. Between 1970 and 1972, other information retrieval services began providing access to databases created by government agencies: SDC made the ERIC database available through ORBIT; Mead briefly provided access to the NTIS database; and Informatics, Inc., maintained the TOXICON (later TOXLINE) retrieval system for the National Library of Medicine.

Of equal importance to the increase in the number of databases produced by government agencies was the mounting of nongovernment databases by the information retrieval services. By 1972, SDC was offering online access through ORBIT to the *Chemical Abstracts Condensates* database; Mead was offering access to the *Psychological Abstracts* database; and Lockheed was providing access to PANDEX, created by the McMillan Company and covering scientific and technical literature.

Packet-Switching Networks

During the early 1970s, online access to at least some of these databases was becoming publicly available. In essence, any institution could gain access if it was willing to pay the fees charged by the service on whose computers the databases were stored. But there were a couple of problems that stood in the way of an immediate outburst of enthusiasm on the part of librarians. One was a basic unfamiliarity with such services, their technology, and the procedures involved. Beyond this, however, was the question of costs, and most particularly of communications costs. In accessing a database through one of these services, it was necessary to dial the computer via standard telephone lines or, in some cases, through a TWX network. Since the service's central computer might be located at some distance, this was not an inexpensive venture, and communications costs could comprise a substantial portion of the total cost of the search.

This obstacle was partially overcome during the early 1970s with the introduction of publicly accessible packet-switching networks, such as TYMNET and TELENET. Circuit-switched networks, such as used for telephone and TWX communication, reserved a fixed bandwidth over which communication occurs for the entire duration of a connection. Packet switching, on the other hand, sends messages over communications networks in smaller blocks of information. It is ideally suited for communications in a computer network, since the network is activated for any particular user only when a message is ready to be sent. It does not maintain a permanent connection between points over a field bandwidth during the entire course of a communication, which would include time spent in formulating search strategy, keying the strategy, computer processing of a request, and so on.

Extensive research on the cost-effectiveness of packet-switching communications networks had been conducted by Rand as early as 1964. Commissioned by the U.S. Air Force to conduct a feasibility study, the Rand Corporation in fact recommended that the Air Force adopt such a network, which would not only be less expensive but would also provide a defensively more secure communications network than was available through existing systems. The Air Force did not act on the recommendation. In the late 1960s, however, the Advanced Research Projects Agency (ARPA) of the U.S. Department of Defense funded development of a packet-switching network. By December 1969, ARPANET was declared operational, linking four computers located at different sites. By 1971, the network had grown to include 20 computers.[9]

In the late 1960s and early 1970s, work proceeded on establishing similar networks for a broader audience of users. These efforts culminated in the formation of the TYMNET and TELENET networks, the latter created by some of the people who had worked on ARPANET. Each of these "value added" networks established nodes in a number of major U.S. cities. Each node consisted of a minicomputer, which acted as a communications link and as an interface device between remote terminals and host computers, such as those on which databases were being stored at Lockheed and SDC.

In order to establish a connection between a terminal and a host computer, the user still had to dial into the computer, but in using TYMNET and TELENET, the standard telephone link occurred only between the terminal and the minicomputer at the nearest network node. Messages received by the minicomputer were then sent over telephone lines leased by the networks to another node, and so on through the network until the message reached the host computer. Messages returned from a host computer to a remote terminal followed the same procedure. The exact route any message might take through the networks was determined dynamically by the network itself and depended on the flow of traffic at the precise moment of communication.

The bottom line of the packet-switching networks was that they dramatically reduced telecommunications costs. As a measure of the magnitude by which these costs were reduced, Davis McCarn at the National Library of Medicine estimated in 1974 that with the introduction of packet-switching networks, the average cost of communications for MEDLINE searching immediately dropped from $24 per hour to $5 per hour—a decrease of about 80 percent.[10] A further innovation was the pricing structure. Unlike the telephone system, the packet-switching networks charged a flat hourly rate for communications, regardless of which node a message emanated from and regardless of where it was sent.

During the same period that the packet-switching networks were being introduced commercially, computer hardware costs were declining sharply. This was no small consideration for the information retrieval services as they added new databases to their collections. By mid-1974, for example, SDC was offering service on about 11 databases with a collective 3.5 million bibliographic records. These required in the vicinity of 3.3 billion bytes of storage on disks that had a capacity of 200 million bytes each.[11] These dual-density disks were in fact a relatively recent breakthrough on the market, improving upon disks that had a storage capacity in the range of only half that amount. The decrease in costs for telecommunications and per-unit computer storage brought the price of these services into a more acceptable range for libraries and other institutions. As the number of users began to grow and maintenance and development costs could be distributed across a larger number of users, prices decreased still further. The increased revenues, in turn, could be used to license new databases and make additional enhancements in order to attract still more users. As an indication of the total impact of these and other factors on pricing during the early 1970s, the cost of searching through Lockheed's service in 1973 was less than half of what it had been in 1970, and between 1973 and 1975 the cost was again reduced by about half.[12]

Growth and Use

Although it is difficult to trace the magnitude by which the use of information retrieval services grew during the 1970s, one way is to examine the growth of the services themselves. In 1971, there were less than half a dozen services that offered access to bibliographic databases, and each of those had only between one and three databases available. The considerable changes introduced even by 1974 are illustrated in Table 5-1. Lockheed and SDC each offered service to more than ten databases, and NLM had broadened the number as well, although some were essentially spin-offs from the main MEDLARS file. SUNY BCN continued its service and in fact entered an arrangement with NLM for its computer to act as a backup for searching MEDLARS. As Table 5-1 indicates, there was substantial overlap among the services in database coverage, particularly for some of the larger and more widely used databases such as *CA (Chemical Abstracts) Condensates,* ERIC, MEDLARS, *Psychological Abstracts,* and *Science Citation Index.*

New Services

One of the new services to appear in the early 1970s was the New York Times Information Bank (NYTIB). Its database had been available for in-house use at the *New York Times* office since 1971. In 1973, access became publicly available exclusively through the *Times'* own new commercial information retrieval service, using a retrieval language designed by IBM. Coverage included not only articles from the *New York Times* dating back to the late 1960s, but also selected items from more than 60 other newspapers and periodicals indexed back to 1971.

The depth of the NYTIB indexing was extremely thorough, based on the use of a controlled vocabulary. This was at times cause for annoyance, especially given the fact that this database was a source for material on current events. One user, for example, wrote of the frustration in attempting to retrieve articles about migration to the "sunbelt states" at a time of extensive news coverage of that phenomenon. The controlled vocabulary used by the NYTIB did not include such a term, nor did it have any term that corresponded to the geographic area being described. Although the descriptor "Southern Rim States (U.S.)" was eventually added to the list of acceptable index terms and an at-

TABLE 5-1   BIBLIOGRAPHIC DATABASES OFFERED BY MAJOR
INFORMATION RETRIEVAL SERVICES, 1974

Database	Subject	Service Offered By	Approx. No. of Records Online
Databases offered by 3 or more services			
CA CONDENSATES	Chemistry	Lockheed, SDC, SIA	1,200,000
ERIC	Education	Lockheed, SDC, SUNY BCN	157,000
MEDLARS	Biomedicine	NLM, SDC, SUNY BCN	530,000
NTIS	U.S. Government Technical Reports	Lockheed, SDC, SIA	400,000
Psychological Abstracts	Psychology	Lockheed, MEAD, SUNY BCN	125,000
Databases offered by 2 services			
ABI/INFORM	Business	Lockheed, SDC	14,000
COMPENDEX	Engineering	Lockheed, SDC	300,000
NAL/CAIN	Agriculture	Lockheed, SDC	450,000
SCISEARCH	Life sciences	Lockheed, SDC	400,000
TOXLINE	Toxicology	Informatics, NLM	340,000
Databases offered by 1 service			
API/LIT	Petroleum	SDC	154,000
API/PAT	Petroleum patents	SDC	80,000
BIOSIS	Life sciences	SUNY BCN	unavailable
CATLINE	Biomedicine	NLM	140,000
Chemical & Electronic Market Abstracts	Business	Lockheed	60,000
CHEMLINE	Chemistry	NLM	60,000
COMPFILE	Biomedicine	NLM	352,000
Engineering Index	Engineering	Lockheed	300,000
Excerpta Medicine	Biomedicine	Informatics	1,200,000
GEOREF	Geosciences	SDC	200,000
INSPEC	Physics, computers, electronics, mechanics	Lockheed	700,000
MEDFILE	Biomedicine	NLM	533,000
NASA/RECON	Aerospace	NASA	1,000,000
New York Times	News	NYTIB	500,000
Nuclear Science Abstracts	Nuclear science	AEC	unavailable
PANDEX	Science, technology	Lockheed	530,000
Predicasts	Business	Lockheed	300,000
SDILINE	Biomedicine	NLM	20,000
SERLINE	Biomedicine	NLM	5,000

tempt made to reindex some of the material in the database retrospectively with this term, such efforts required time.[13] This aspect of a controlled vocabulary was certainly not unique to the NYTIB; it is one faced by any database using a controlled vocabulary for searching. In 1980, the *New York Times* introduced a coexisting version of the primary database, Information Bank II, on which free-text searching could be performed.

Martha Williams estimated that in 1974 approximately 700,000 on-line searches were conducted in the United States on remote-access bibliographic retrieval systems other than OCLC.[14] To illustrate how pivotal a period this was for the commercial information retrieval services, in December 1972, SDC could claim less than one-half dozen organizations using its search service. Within six months, this number had grown to more than 40, and by early 1974 the number of sub-scribers approached 150.[15] Another author stated that the number of searches on Lockheed's DIALOG in 1975 was more than seven times the number conducted in 1973.[16] Already by 1974, there were more than 500 organizations searching MEDLARS through either NLM or SUNY BCN services,[17] and Cuadra estimates that in 1975, "well over 2,000" organizations were conducting searches through the various on-line information retrieval services.[18]

With such a rapid growth rate, there were constant changes and new problems. One very basic problem for the services themselves was how, despite advances in technology, to keep their computer configurations of sufficient size to handle the enormous number of machine-readable records included in the databases to which they offered access. One solution was to maintain records online only for the most recently published materials, often a two- to five-year span. SDC used an ap-proach whereby databases were rotated during the course of each day, making some available for the entire day but others for only a few hours, a decision that resulted in a one-half to two-thirds savings in storage costs over what would have been necessary had all databases been mounted all the time the system was available.[19]

Continued Growth

Between the mid- and late 1970s, the information retrieval services continued to grow. The years 1975 through 1977 saw some fundamen-tal changes and controversies in the information retrieval service indus-try. By 1975, the National Library of Medicine, although continuing to provide SUNY BCN with its MEDLARS file, had withdrawn MED-LARS from SDC and TOXLINE from Informatics, Inc. SDC, of course, already had a broad range of other databases. Informatics, meanwhile, attempted to expand its services by offering online access to the Excerpta Medica database compiled by the Excerpta Medica Foundation in Amsterdam. There was significant overlap between this and MEDLARS, and although Informatics continued to offer Excerpta Medica for several years, it was an uphill battle all the way. NLM and its MEDLARS database were subsidized operations, and Roger Summit of Lockheed tersely observed the resulting impact on competition in 1975: "NLM with MEDLARS and Informatics with Excerpta Medica are in competition at prices of $15 ($8 off shift) and $120 per hour respectively. Competition?"[20]

NLM was not the only government agency whose direction was of concern to the commercial services during the mid-1970s. In 1975, for example, the U.S. Energy and Research Development Association (ERDA) began offering a restricted group of government agencies several databases that were also being offered through commercial services, but ERDA's charges were far lower. The commercial services saw government subsidization as the reason for the wide discrepancies in pricing between their services and those offered through the public agencies for searching the same databases.

In 1976, a significant new commercial enterprise announced plans to enter the informational retrieval business. In its *Final Prospectus*, the Bibliographic Retrieval Service (BRS) explained its rationale as follows:

> At the end of 1975, a survey of the available online database search services disclosed that the existence of a wide gap between the cost of those services available from the public sector (government and university services) and those for sale by private information companies. . . . Access to the public services was generally at cost-recovery levels, averaging between $10 and $15 per connect hour, including communications costs, while the cost of accessing commercial services ranged from $25 to $150 per connect hour, *excluding* communication costs. . . . Unfortunately, the online services provided by the public sector were limited either by their narrow subject scope or regional communication networking, and yet the comparatively high cost of commercial services precluded many interested libraries from using them as an alternative supplier. . . . Thus the information needs of a major segment of the potential user base for these new services were simply not being met. . . . The BRS was established to fill this gap by making it possible for the national community of libraries and information centers to search a variety of major bibliographic databases online at connect hour costs ranging from as low as $10 per hour to a maximum of $30 per hour.[21]

The idea behind the formation of BRS, and indeed even some of its staffing, stemmed from SUNY BCN, which phased out its services a few months after BRS began operations in early 1977. Using the IBM STAIRS retrieval system, BRS provided an initial offering of ten databases. Two were MEDLARS and TOXLINE from NLM; the remaining eight covered a rather broad range of topics, and each was also available through either DIALOG, SDC, or both.

Another new service on the market in 1977 was Dow Jones News/Retrieval (DJNR). Its database consisted of items appearing on the Dow

Jones News Wire, in the *Wall Street Journal,* and in *Barron's* magazine. The appearance of DJNR was part of a significant trend beginning in the 1970s and continuing into the 1980s, which saw a number of news, financial, and popular literature databases enter the market. With few notable exceptions, databases of this type had been conspicuously absent up to this time.

Most of these newly emerging producers chose not to go the route of DJNR in setting up their own services, but rather vended their databases to one of the existing major services. One of the most successful new producers to emerge in the late 1970s was Information Access Corporation (IAC), first with its Magazine Index (MI) database, and soon after with its National Newspaper Index (NNI). Both became available on DIALOG. The MI indexed nearly 400 popular periodicals, including not coincidentally, all those covered in the *Reader's Guide to Periodical Literature,* published by the H. W. Wilson Company. NNI coverage included the *Wall Street Journal,* the *Christian Science Monitor,* and, quite interestingly, the *New York Times.*

Beginning in the mid-1970s, Martha Williams monitored the growth of library-related information retrieval services and databases through the maintenance of a Database of Databases. The growth of the Database of Databases during the second half of the 1970s lends some insight into the magnitude of growth in the industry. Whereas 177 U.S. databases were recorded in the Database of Databases in 1975, the number had grown to 208 by 1977 and to 259 by 1979. An even greater rate of growth occurred in the number of non-U.S. databases, from 124 in 1975, to 154 in 1977, and to 269 by 1979. The number of records available on these databases also showed impressive growth, from about 46 million in 1975 to 93.5 million by 1979 on U.S. databases, and from 6 million in 1975 to 54.5 million by 1979 on non-U.S. databases. One must remember, too, that these figures were only for bibliographic databases available through major online retrieval services and subject to other criteria for inclusion as well. Not all the databases or records included in Williams's statistics were available for online searching; some were accessible only offline. It is indicative of the intensity of activity during that period that while in 1977 only about 47 percent of the records on both U.S. and non-U.S. databases were available online, this proportion had increased to 83 percent by 1979.

The number of online searches of databases through major U.S. and Canadian systems, according to Williams, just about doubled every two years during the last half of the 1970s. In 1975, about 1 million online searches were conducted through these services; in 1977, there were approximately 2 million, and in 1979, about 4 million.[22]

Into the 1980s

During the 1980s, the information retrieval service industry has continued to grow. Several new services have emerged, and scores of new databases have appeared that are of central interest to libraries. Their use of these services and databases has also continued to increase.

But the changes in the information retrieval service industry have not simply been a matter of expansion in numbers. There has been innovation in form and content as well as increased competition, and recent and merging technologies have presented a host of new challenges and opportunities. The first half of the 1980s has seen the microcomputer become almost commonplace in libraries, and these machines are being used in new and interesting ways in connection with online searching. By 1984, the ability to store enormous amounts of text on compact devices—optical disks, in particular—is no longer a vision of the future but a reality of the present. Online full-text databases—containing not just citations to documents, but the entire text of the documents themselves—number more than just a few, and the quantity is increasing. While the prices for accessing online databases through the major services fluctuated during the 1970s, the basic pricing *structure* remained relatively fixed. In the 1980s, technology and other factors have forced database vendors and producers to review the basic way they charge for service. Online searching of remotely stored databases is now common in libraries large and small, but the above factors provide assurance that the environment will be a dynamic one for information retrieval services, database producers, and libraries. Some of these forces of change, as they impact on online searching in libraries, are examined in greater detail in Chapter 15.

Notes

1. Martha E. Williams, "Highlights of the Online Data Base Field," in *National Online Meeting Proceedings—1981, New York, March 24–26, 1981* (Medford, N.J.: Learned Information), pp. 1–5.
2. For a description of the TIP, see M. M. Kessler, "The Technical Information Project of the Massachusetts Institute of Technology," in *Proceedings of the 1966 Clinic on Library Applications of Data Processing* (Urbana, Ill.: University of Illinois Graduate School of Library Science, 1966), pp. 7–17.
3. F. W. Lancaster and E. G. Fayen, *Information Retrieval On-Line* (Los Angeles, Calif.: Melville Publishing Company, 1973).
4. See D. L. Drew, R. K. Summit, R. I. Tanaka, and R. B. Whitely, "An On-line Technical Library Reference Retrieval System," *American Documentation* 17 (January 1966): 3–7.
5. For the development of NASA's RECON system, see especially Roger K. Summit, "DIALOG Interactive Retrieval System," in *Encyclopedia of Library*

and Information Science 7 (New York: Marcel Dekker, 1972), pp. 161–169; and Van A. Wente, "NASA/RECON and the User Interface Considerations," in *Interactive Bibliographic Search: The User/Computer Interface,* Donald E. Walker, ed. (Montvale, N.J.: AFIPS Press, 1971), pp. 95–104.

6. For a description of the AIM-TWX project, see Robert V. Katter and Davis B. McCarn, "AIM-TWX: An Experimental On-line Bibliographic Retrieval System," in *Interactive Bibliographic Search: The User/Computer Interface* (see note 5 above), pp. 121–141.

7. Irwin H. Pizer, "A Regional Medical Library Network," *Bulletin of the Medical Library Association* 57 (April 1969): 103.

8. Janet Egeland, "User-interaction in the State University of New York (SUNY) Biomedical Communication Network," in *Interactive Bibliographic Search,* pp. 109–110.

9. See Lawrence G. Roberts, "The Evolution of Packet Switching," *Proceedings of the IEEE* 66 (November 1978): 1307–1313.

10. Davis B. McCarn, "Trends in Information," in *Proceedings of the ASSS Annual Meeting, v. 11, 1974* (Washington, D.C.: American Society for Information Science, 1974), p. 149.

11. Carlos A. Cuadra, "SDC Experiences with Large Data Bases," *Journal of Chemical Information and Computer Sciences* 15, no. 1 (1975): 48–50.

12. Lee G. Burchinal, "Bringing the American Revolution On-line—Information Science and National R&D," *Bulletin of the American Society for Information Science* 2 (March 1976): 27.

13. Lois Seulowitz, "All the News That's Fit to Printout," *Online* 1 (January 1977): 58.

14. Martha E. Williams, "Progress and Problems of the Data Base Community," *Journal of the American Society for Information Science* 26 (September/October 1975): 305.

15. Cuadra, "SDC Experiences," p. 49.

16. Burchinal, "Bringing the American Revolution On-line," p. 27.

17. McCarn, "Trends in Information," p. 147.

18. C. A. Cuadra, "Problems of Growth in On-line Information Services," in *The On-Line Age: Plans and Needs for On-Line Information Retrieval: Proceedings of the EUSIDIC Conference, Oslo, 4th–5th December 1975,* Gordon Pratt and Susan Harvey, eds. (London: ASLIB, 1976), p. 54.

19. Cuadra, "SDC Experiences," p. 50.

20. R. K. Summit, "Problems and Outlook for the Information Services Industry," in *The On-Line Age,* p. 113.

21. *BRS Final Prospectus* (Latham, N.Y.: Bibliographic Retrieval Services, Inc., 1976), p. 1.

22. Martha E. Williams, "Database and Online Statistics for 1979," *Bulletin of the American Society for Information Science* 7 (December 1980): 29.

6

Automation
and Interlibrary Lending

Although technology and other factors since the 1950s have helped to bring about dramatic changes in interlibrary lending and the way it is conducted, such innovation was introduced into a context of long-standing tradition. The first issue of *Library Journal* in 1876 contained a letter by Samuel S. Green captioned "The Lending of Books to One Library by Another,"[1] and addressed a topic concerning already established precedents in American library practice. Statistics on the level of interlibrary lending have always been sparse, but by 1917 there was enough activity for a committee of the American Library Association to issue the first Code for Interlibrary Loans, revised in 1940, 1952, 1968, and 1979, and renamed along the way.

Beyond the initial, most basic step of identifying what is to be borrowed—which libraries assist by providing bibliographies, printed abstracting and indexing journals, and more recently online information retrieval services—interlibrary lending is a process involving several steps. This chapter focuses on the steps that involve the greatest degree of coparticipation by libraries and groups of libraries: distribution of locational information; communication of interlibrary loan requests and related correspondence; and physical delivery of materials from one library to another. It excludes, for the most part, steps that are important in the overall process but are primarily internal to each of the participants: retrieval of materials from bookstacks at the lending library, wrapping and preparing materials for shipment, bookkeeping functions, and so on.

Background: Locational Aids

Before the 1950s, the tools used in communicating interlibrary loan requests and delivering materials changed very little. Communication was by mail or telephone, and delivery was generally by mail, with bus or automobile courier services sometimes playing a role. The area of greatest progress during the first half of the twentieth century involved refining the ways to determine the location of an item to be borrowed. The most pertinent developments included union lists, surveys of resources, union catalogs, and bibliographic centers. Although these developments were not a result of automation, they are a necessary background to the events that were to follow after 1950.

The most specific aids for locating materials were union lists and union catalogs. A popular form during the first half of the twentieth century consisted of compilations of periodicals or serials holdings. Many of these compilations were published and distributed, although a significant number were maintained only in card form and stored at one of the participating institutions.

Union Lists of Serials

Possibly the first printed union list of serials was the *List of Serials in Chicago*, published in 1901.[2] If that was indeed the first, it was followed not long after by several others, and in subsequent decades union lists of periodicals and serials were compiled in a great many locations. The late 1930s was a period of intense activity for union lists of serials and periodicals, as well as for union catalogs of broader scope. Ralph Esterquest noted that in examining the cumulation of *Library Literature* for 1936 through 1942, one could find references to union listing projects in Atlanta, Boston, Denver, Maine, New York, Ohio, Philadelphia, San Francisco, southern California, Tennessee, and the southern United States in general, and these represented only projects being reported in the professional literature.[3] Although there was considerable activity in compiling union lists at the local level, there were also significant projects conducted on a broader regional and even national scale. Prominent was the publication by the Library of Congress in 1926 of the *Union List of Serials*, containing 75,000 titles and representing the holdings of 225 libraries. A second edition was published in 1943, containing 115,000 titles and representing the holdings of 650 libraries.

National Union Catalog

At the local level, the most elementary form of a union catalog containing more than periodicals or serials holdings consisted of the exchange of catalog cards between two or more libraries. This also occurred beyond local projects, exemplified at the most comprehensive level by the National Union Catalog (NUC), assembled by and housed at the Library of Congress. It was started in 1901 as a main entry union card catalog, and its contributors included government libraries in the Washington, D.C., area, the Library of Congress itself, and several prominent libraries throughout the United States, including the New York and Boston public libraries, Harvard, the University of Illinois, and the John Crerar Library in Chicago. Additional libraries joined the effort, and by 1927 the catalog contained nearly 2 million holdings. By 1954, it contained cards for nearly 7 million titles and 13 million holdings contributed by more than 500 libraries.[4]

In the mid-1950s, the first monthly, quarterly, annual, and five-year cumulative printed editions of the *National Union Catalog* were published in book form. This still left the question of what to do with the contributions of the previous 50 years, which remained available only in card form at the Library of Congress and various NUC card depository libraries around the United States, where duplicate catalogs were maintained. A contract for publishing the earlier holdings was eventually awarded to Mansell, Ltd., and in 1968 the first volumes of the *Nation Union Catalog, Pre-1956 Imprints* appeared. More than a decade later, the last volume of the more than 700-volume set was printed and distributed. Carried out largely during a time of increasing reliance on computers for bibliographic and locational information, the publication of the *Pre-1956 Imprints* remains a landmark in library cooperation.

Bibliographic Centers

The National Union Catalog represented the most ambitious union catalog compilation, but it was complemented by a host of others. The mid- and late 1930s saw particularly intensive activity in the initiation of union card catalogs. Most of these were carried out with funding from the Works Progress Administration (WPA), and as Ralph Esterquest later observed, were "brought to birth" by WPA funding and then "left to languish—often to die—when no one could be found to pay the high cost of perpetual maintenance."[5] Some did survive, however, at least for several decades. Three of the largest were the *Philadelphia Union Catalog,* the *Regional Union Catalog* maintained by the Bibliographical Center for Research (BCR) in Denver, and the union catalog maintained by the Pacific Northwest Bibliographic Center (PNBC) in Seattle. All three provided a crucial link for interlibrary lending among libraries in their respective regions. Many libraries contributing titles and holdings to these catalogs did not contribute directly to the National Union Catalog maintained at the Library of Congress; among the three centers, only Philadelphia contributed duplicates of all cards in its catalog to the NUC.

Although these bibliographic centers sometimes provided additional services pertaining to cooperation among libraries, their most significant role was in maintaining a union catalog in order to inform libraries of locations of materials for purposes of interlibrary lending. In 1950, the bibliographic centers in Philadelphia, Denver, and Seattle, with a total salaried staff of seven professional librarians and ten non-professional assistants, searched nearly 72,000 requests for locations.[6]

The functions that these centers served were probably enough to keep them operating, but their financial state was perpetually a matter of concern. The cost of maintaining the catalogs and providing location services was high. By the 1970s, these costs, along with an increasingly prominent role played by the bibliographic utilities as locational tools, were responsible for reducing the role union card catalogs played in interlibrary lending. PNBC was dissolved in June 1981, with location services from the union catalog being assumed by the University of Washington. By the mid-1970s, BCR had made a transition to library-related technology as its service base in brokering OCLC and other information retrieval services. Filing into the catalog ceased in 1977. In a 1979–1980 study, Segal and Reynolds demonstrated that the catalog was still a more viable tool for determining regional locations for pre-1976 publications than either OCLC or the *National Union Catalog*.[7] But the cost of the location service and of rent for housing the catalog, combined with a declining level of usage, all pointed toward an end to the service. In June 1982, the service did cease and the catalog was removed from the BCR offices to the Colorado State Library in Denver. The *Philadelphia Union Catalog*, into which filing also ceased, is housed at the University of Pennsylvania. PALINET, an OCLC affiliate network based in Philadelphia, is still providing a location referral service from a microfilm copy of the catalog.

Resource Directories

Of the major tools maintained or published during the first half of the twentieth century to assist libraries in locating materials for borrowing through interlibrary loan, a less item-specific type than either the union list or union catalog was the directory of resources. Such directories seldom attempted to identify specific titles held by libraries, but rather described the general nature of various library collections, particularly noting areas of emphasis and strength. One early work was

William C. Lane's and Charles K. Bolton's *Notes on Special Collections in American Libraries,* published in 1892.

Descriptive guides to resources published during the first several decades of the twentieth century, like union catalogs and union lists, varied a great deal in scope and content. Some focused on resources in a particular type of library: either within a limited geographic locale, such as resources in special libraries in an urban area; on a broader region, such as academic libraries within a particular state; or even on a national scale, such as the Special Libraries Association's four-volume *Special Library Resources,* published between 1941 and 1947. Other directories of resources placed their primary focus on geographic parameters and encompassed all or most types of libraries within those bounds, ranging from a city, such as Robert Downs's *Resources of New York City Libraries* published in 1942, to a broad region, such as the *Resources of Southern Libraries,* 1938, also prepared by Downs. The purpose of these directories extended beyond their application in interlibrary loan, but given the state of title-specific bibliographic control at the time, they often provided general clues as to where materials might most likely be found if specific locations could not be determined from other sources.

Other Developments

The lending of books between libraries is only one part of a broader concept of library cooperation. The tools and institutions described above—union lists, union catalogs, bibliographic centers, and surveys of resources—were the most important aids in determining locations during the first half of the twentieth century. But there were other aspects of library cooperation that also had an impact on the way interlibrary loan was conducted or on the level to which it was used. Such developments included cooperative acquisitions projects and cooperative collection development programs. Some of the larger-scale activities led to the founding of special interlibrary collection centers during the 1940s and early 1950s. Some of these centers, such as the New England Deposit Library, were primarily cooperative storage areas, with little attempt by participating libraries to organize the materials into an integrated collection. Others, such as the Hampshire Inter-Library Center (HILC) and the Midwest Inter-Library Center (MILC), started off mainly as storage centers but developed into something more. The materials stored by members were merged into a collection and duplicates were often purged. Important materials that members did not wish to acquire independently were published collectively, stored at the center, and borrowed from there through interlibrary loan.

Of all the centers established in the 1940s and early 1950s, the most successful has been the Midwest Center. Established in Chicago in 1951 by ten midwestern research libraries, the center changed its name in 1965 to the Center for Research Libraries (CRL), reflecting its broadened geographic basis beyond the midwest, and has continued to operate and expand its scope of activities.

Two important technological innovations introduced into libraries before the 1950s, which had implications for interlibrary lending, were microfilm and photocopying. Microfilming and photocopying could potentially ease a lending library's conflict between the desire to cooperate with other libraries and its primary allegiance to its own clientele. By sending a microfilm or photocopy of a document rather than the document itself, the lending library could fill an interlibrary loan request without having to remove the original document from the immediate premises for an extended period. Photocopying emerged as the preferred and more frequently used technique and eventually became the primary method for providing journal articles and briefer documents requested through interlibrary lending.

Alternative Communications Technologies, 1950–1967

With the exception of microfilming and photocopying, the tools to facilitate interlibrary lending before 1950 were aimed almost exclusively at one aspect of the process—determining the physical location of materials. Until the 1960s, and actually until the early to mid-1970s, there was little change in the technology even in these tools. Libraries continued to rely on printed sources—surveys of resources, union lists, and cards in union catalogs—as their primary sources for locating items. Although such sources may have grown in number and scope through the 1950s and early 1960s, the methods of producing them did not.

Teletype

Using tools created in the first half-century, libraries in the 1950s began to look at another aspect of the interlibrary loan process—communications technology. For the next decade and a half, this attention would focus primarily on the adoption of teletype machines as a way of transmitting interlibrary loan requests and associated administrative correspondence.

The use of teletype, or TWX (TeletypeWriter EXchange), significantly reduced the time required for communication when compared with mail services. Although the telephone was as speedy as TWX, it required another person's immediate attention at the receiving end; TWX did not. Furthermore, a TWX transmission resulted in a printed request at the receiving end, while a verbal request required the receptor to jot down details. Using TWX, communications time, and therefore cost, could be minimized by taking advantage of automatic features on the machine. TWX machines equipped with a paper-tape device allowed an operator to type a message onto a machine-readable paper tape in the local, noncommunicating mode. After recording the full message on paper tape, the TWX number of the receiving library was dialed. Once a connection was established, the paper tape was fed through automatically and its message transmitted at 60 to 100 words per minute.

Teletype technology had been available long before its more widespread adoption in libraries. As early as 1927, the Free Library of Philadelphia installed teletype machines for internal communication between the circulation desk and the bookstacks, but it was not really until the early 1950s that libraries began to adopt the technology for communicating with each other. As with any alternative communications technology, there was some reluctance to adopt TWX since its usefulness to libraries would be realized only when there was an ample number using the same technology. As a result, many of the instances in which TWX was adopted during the 1950s involved groups of libraries that had already developed, or were developing, an established and predictably high level of communication with each other.

One of the earliest examples of TWX use for interlibrary communication was between the Milwaukee and Racine public libraries in Wisconsin, dating back to 1949. With a high volume of interlibrary lending, the two libraries felt TWX to be an economical alternative to the telephone. On a broader scale, the Midwest Inter-Library Center installed TWX in 1951 as an alternative means of communication with its members, and by 1954, 14 of the then 16 members of the center had installed TWX in their libraries. Also in the early 1950s, TWX machines were installed in the Michigan State Library, the Detroit and Grand Rapids public libraries, and the University of Michigan for rapid transmission of interlibrary loan requests and other messages among the four. About the same time, libraries on the eight campuses of the University of California installed TWX for interlibrary communication.

By the mid-1950s, the costs associated with TWX equipment had escalated considerably over what they had been just a few years before. Several libraries that had installed TWX during the early 1950s decided that the level of use did not justify the continued rental of the machines, and had them removed. Michigan did so, as did some members of the Midwest Inter-Library Center, at least on a temporary basis.

In fact, in a 1958 survey, James Mack could account for only 24 libraries with TWX installations,[8] probably an underestimation of the total number of libraries in the United States using TWX for communications, but nonetheless indicative that TWX was hardly a common means of interlibrary communication at that time.

The use of TWX in libraries increased during the early 1960s. In 1964, a directory of TWX subscribers listed 64 libraries as having their own equipment. By the following year, the same publication listed 130 libraries. This dramatic increase can be accounted for by the emergence of several networking situations that adopted TWX in 1965 as their primary means of communications. Included among these were the National Library of Medicine and several medical libraries along the Atlantic coast and in the Southeast, and a few state networks such as in Indiana, where 25 libraries installed TWX in 1965. The state networks and their almost universal adoption of TWX as the primary means of communication between major network nodes were an important development in interlibrary lending during the mid- and late 1960s and are discussed in greater depth later in this chapter.[9]

Facsimile Transmission

Although teletype equipment was being installed in a gradually increasing number of libraries between the early 1950s and the mid-1960s, its use in interlibrary lending was necessarily restricted to the transmission of requests and associated brief correspondence rather than of the materials themselves. Both at the beginning and end of this period, some libraries experimented with electronically transmitting the actual text of the materials requested. These efforts, which focused on the use of telefacsimile equipment, were few in number, generally experimental, and in most cases short-lived.

The first major experiment with facsimile transmission of documents from one library to another was carried out by the Oak Ridge National Laboratory in Tennessee in 1951. The system, developed by RCA, consisted of two primary pieces of equipment. In the parlance of the day, one was a "reader-transmitter" located at the central library, and the other a "recorder" located at a test site eight miles away. When activated, the reader-transmitter photographically scanned a page of printed matter and converted the impulses of reflected light into electrical signals. These signals were then transmitted over a normal telephone line to the recorder equipment at the receiving site. When received, the signals were converted through an electrolytic process back into appropriate images on a sheet of paper, forming a facsimile of the original document. From the time of placing a page of a document on the reader-transmitter, it took 4.5 minutes for the facsimile copy to be completed at the receiving end.[10] In retrospect, one of the most interesting aspects of the Oak Ridge experiment was that the reader-transmitter was capable of copying from a bound volume, a capability that is still not available on any telefacsimile equipment commercially produced in the United States today.

It was not until the mid-1960s that libraries began to re-examine the implications of telefacsimile technology for interlibrary lending. The telefacsimile technology of the mid-1960s operated on the same basic principle described earlier, but was greatly improved over what it had been in the early 1950s. In 1966 and 1967, three important experiments and programs were initiated by libraries. Two were funded by the Council on Library Resources (CLR) and involved academic libraries in the western United States, and the other was carried out in connection with state networking activities in New York.

The first of the CLR-funded experiments, in 1966, was based at the University of Nevada at Reno (UNR) and involved facsimile transmission of documents from the UNR library to the campuses of the University of Nevada at Las Vegas and the University of California, Davis.[11] The second CLR-funded study, in 1967, involved facsimile transmission of documents from the University of California, Berkeley, to the University of California, Davis.[12] The equipment used in these studies consisted of different models of devices manufactured by Xerox, and the type of communications channel was also different: the earlier experiment transmitted over normal telephone lines, and the latter over a dedicated telephone line.

Although the results of these two experiments differed in detail, some similar general conclusions were reached. In the 1967 study, Shieber estimated that if personnel activities were better organized, the cost of document delivery via telefacsimile would be about $1 per page inclusive of equipment, staff, and communications charges. In the 1966 UNR study, Morehouse estimated a cost of about $0.685 excluding communications, which could range from hardly anything to as high as $3 per page depending on distance and whether communications were via normal telephone line service, WATS service, or leased line. Both reports stressed the circumstantial nature of costs given the short duration of the experiments, and pointed out that in long-term practice, costs would depend a great deal on factors such as volume of activity and type of communications link. There were incidences of equipment failures in both experiments, and the quality of reproduction at the receiving end of the transmission was not always satisfactory, particularly for smaller-point type, such as that used in footnotes, charts, and tables. Schieber reported that in the 1967 study, 14 of 65 respondents to user questionnaires expressed dissatisfaction with the quality of reproduction.

An interesting focus of one part of the 1967 study was on the distribution of time for various tasks during an interlibrary loan transaction. Although a copy of most article-length documents could be transmitted within an hour, delays in processing meant that the average time between receipt of a request at Berkeley and receipt of a copy of the item at Davis was more than 6 hours. The average time between receipt of a copy at Davis and the sending of a notification to the borrower was 3 hours. These figures were based on a 9-hour workday and 5-day week; on a stricter scale, taking account of a 24-hour day and weekends, the time required for completion of each of these tasks averaged about 21 hours and 9 hours, respectively. The clear implication is that, even with rapid transmission, the other tasks related to the handling of an interlibrary loan request interjected substantial delay in overall delivery performance. It is also interesting to note that for these same requests, the average time between a patron's notification of receipt of material at the library and actual pickup was 8 hours. This was on a 9-hour, 5-day-per-week schedule; in actual time calculated on a 24-hour, 7-day-per-week basis, the average pickup time was nearly 62 hours after notification.

Between January 1967 and March 1968, the New York State Library incorporated a facsimile transmission program, FACTS, as part of its statewide interlibrary loan network. It was broader in scope than the CLR studies, not only in duration and magnitude, but also by the fact that a request for a facsimile document could be submitted from virtually any library in the entire state. The request was channeled through the state TWX communications network to the state library or eventually to one of several referral sites having telefacsimile equipment. Not all libraries in the state, of course, had such equipment, and thus the geographic distribution of FACTS receiving sites relative to libraries where requests originated imposed some limitations on the system. Nevertheless, the FACTS program operated for 14 months and transmitted facsimile copies of nearly 4,000 documents requested through interlibrary loan. The program ended in 1968 for several reasons, some of which echoed the conclusion of the CLR studies. One of the two equipment models was mechanically unreliable and the other was prone to faulty transmission. Of the patrons responding to postcard questionnaires, 22 percent suggested that the quality of copy be improved, almost the same proportion that complained about copy quality in the 1967 CLR experiment.

The complex operation of the statewide system through which requests had to be channeled, combined with routine processing time and processing backlogs, resulted in an average time lapse of several working days between the time a patron submitted a request and the time that material was available for pickup. An interesting aspect of this time lag was that 70 percent of the users responding to a question on the postcard survey indicated that the FACTS program would be useful even if it took two or three days longer to receive the requested material.[13]

Although the two CLR-funded studies and the FACTS program were the most important, other programs based on facsimile transmission among libraries was occurring around the same time. By 1966, the State Library of Hawaii was transmitting copies of documents via facsimile to each of three regional libraries located on the outer islands. Unfortunately, a detailed evaluation of that program was apparently never carried out, and the only description of the system was an enthusiastic account in 1966 very soon after it had been implemented.[14] In the same year, several university libraries in Pennsylvania installed telefacsimile equipment. Its use was continued until 1975, but essentially it served for most of that time as an alternative means for communicating interlibrary loan requests and other brief correspondence rather than as a system for transmitting the full text of requested materials.

State-Based Interlibrary Networks

Since the early 1950s, many of the libraries installing TWX equipment for interlibrary communications had done so in a relatively informal way, enhancing an already existing pattern of relationships with neighboring libraries or with libraries connected by some other common bond, such as membership in an interlibrary center. In the mid-1960s, this same technology began to be adopted by large numbers of libraries in a quite different context, one of considerable structure and formality. This context was the state-based library network. Within most states, informal ties had developed between groups of libraries over the years, but these patterns were seldom organized into a coherent whole.

In 1956, the United States Congress passed the Library Services Act, providing federal funds to assist development of public library services in rural areas. The money was allocated on a state-by-state basis to be administered through a central agency in each state, usually the state library. Although the Library Services Act did not directly establish the basis for networking that emerged a decade later, it laid a crucial foundation by establishing the need for statewide organization to plan and administer federal funds, and by recognizing state libraries as the agencies to serve in this capacity.

During the next several years, the Library Services Act underwent a variety of changes broadening its scope, and in 1964 its name was changed to the Library Services and Construction Act (LSCA). Although the act had provisions to support interlibrary cooperation as a legitimate end for assignment of funds, Congress added more specific legislation in 1966 as Title III, providing for funding for "the establishment and operation of systems or networks of libraries, including state, school, college and university, public, and special libraries, and special information centers. . . ."[15]

During the late 1960s, a number of states created TWX-based networks, whose major function was the routing of interlibrary loan requests. It would be a mistake to attribute these communications networks solely to federal funding under LSCA Title III. In the first place, until 1970, the federal LSCA monies required a matching amount from the states. Second, some states had already laid the organizational groundwork for state networking, although only public libraries were usually involved. What the Title III funding and its matching state allocations provided in most instances was the financial force to accelerate these plans and to broaden their scope.

The state-based interlibrary loan networks were established in response to the ever-increasing demand for interlibrary loan services and were structured in such a way as to address some of the more pressing problems characteristic of interlibrary lending patterns during the preceding years. Apart from scattered local union lists and catalogs, there were only a few major sources, such as the *National Union Catalog*, the *Union List of Serials*, and major state or regional union catalogs, on which libraries had been able to rely for title-specific holdings information. The libraries contributing their holdings to these major sources were relatively few in number when viewed in a larger context, and they were generally the largest libraries in the country or a region. There was a resulting imbalance in the flow of interlibrary loan requests to the larger libraries, which had, indeed, made their holdings known through these sources. This imbalance was compounded by the fact that many librarians, who did not have access to any of the major locational sources, sent their requests to libraries they thought most likely to own an item, which usually meant the same large libraries that were also being inundated with known-location requests.

The most direct measure for alleviating these imbalances would have been the compilation, publication, and widespread distribution of more broadly based statewide union catalogs, but in the mid- and late 1960s such a solution was not yet practical. In lieu of this, interlibrary loan communications networks were established and designed to alleviate at least some portion of the imbalances by providing a structure to redirect the pattern of interlibrary loan traffic among libraries in the state. The structures usually entailed a three- or four-tier hierarchy through which interlibrary loan requests were channeled, with libraries at upper levels usually using TWX equipment to communicate with one another. A local library either telephoned or mailed an interlibrary loan request to a regional system headquarters, often housed at the largest public library in that area. If the request could not be filled by that library, it was sent via TWX to a library in the next level of the hierarchy, usually one of several designated major resource libraries participating in the network. In some states, there were one or two intervening levels in addition. The impact of such structures on the largest libraries was to remove them one or two steps from the flow of traffic, thereby filtering out a portion of the requests that would have otherwise been sent directly to them. Although this was the case in terms of proportions, its impact was often countered by significant growth in the overall volume of activity that was fostered by a formal network and by changing attitudes toward interlibrary loan. Thus, the large libraries were still receiving as many requests as they had previously. Many states used Title III and other federal and state funding to establish a reimbursement schedule for lending, thereby alleviating at least part of the financial burden of interlibrary lending operations at the large libraries.

NYSILL

One of the earlier state-based networks was the New York State Interlibrary Loan Network (NYSILL). Legislative groundwork for networking in New York State began as early as 1950, and in 1958 a library systems law was passed, backed by a stronger program of state aid. In 1966, NYSILL was formally established as an interlibrary loan communications network funded with part of a $700,000 appropriation by the state legislature. The network included 22 regional systems, 3 geographic referral libraries, and 9 subject referral libraries, with the state library acting as both a resource center and as a switching center between regional systems and referral centers.

When a library in the state other than one of the above wished to borrow something, it telephoned or mailed the request to the facility that served as its regional system library. The system library tried to fill the request from its own collection, but if unable to do so, it transmitted the request via TWX to the New York State Library. If the state library was unable to fill the request from its collection, it transmitted the request via TWX to one of the three geographic referral libraries, determined on the basis of the region in which the library originating the request was located. If the request could not be filled by the geographic referral library, it was transmitted back to the state library, and from there to one of the nine subject referral libraries, determined on the basis of the subject content of the item requested. If the request could not be filled at the most likely subject referral library, it was transmitted back to the state library. Some requests that went through this cycle without being filled were then transmitted to yet another of the subject referral libraries, but in most cases they were sent back down the hierarchy as unfilled. When any library along the hierarchy could fill a request, the material was mailed directly to the originating library.[16] As described earlier in this chapter, copies of documents for some requests filled through NYSILL in 1967 and early 1968 were delivered via facsimile transmission through the FACTS program.

The interlibrary loan TWX networks established in other states followed patterns similar to NYSILL, with local variations. In Illinois, for example, the state library was not a separate level of the hierarchy as in New York, but rather served as one of the four research and reference centers, with requests transmitted from any of the 18 regional systems in the state to any of the four research and reference centers. In states where the state library did not have a strong collection of its own, the largest public library in the state frequently assumed the role of switching center. In states where there were large union catalogs, such as in Pennsylvania, Colorado, and Washington, the bibliographic centers housing these catalogs often played a role in the networking systems, either as a switching center or as a bibliographic resource center for requests that had not been filled by the time they reached a specified level within the state hierarchy.

MINITEX

One of the least-tiered networks established during the late 1960s and early 1970s was the Minnesota Interlibrary Teletype Exchange (MINITEX). Instead of several levels of communications hierarchy and a multiplicity of referral centers at the highest level, libraries with TWX machines in Minnesota communicated directly with a single center, the MINITEX offices headquartered at the University of Minnesota. MINITEX drew upon the collections of the university and surrounding libraries in the Minneapolis-St. Paul vicinity to fill requests. Delivery to eight locations in the state was made via MINITEX-funded couriers, and delivery to other locations was through United Parcel Service. By 1974, 74 libraries in the state, including 18 regional public libraries, had installed TWX equipment. The MINITEX fill rate in 1973 was around 85 percent, and in three-fourths of these cases, the materials lent or copied had been delivered to the requesting library and were awaiting patron pickup within three working days after the request had been received at MINITEX.[17]

Other Networks

There were a few other state interlibrary loan communications networks that conformed neither to the hierarchical type as exemplified by NYSILL nor to the more centralized structure such as MINITEX. The Iowa Interlibrary Teletype Exchange (I-LITE), for example, consisted of three separate round robin teletype wheels, one for eight public libraries and systems centers, another for ten smaller academic libraries, and another for four major university libraries. A request was entered on the appropriate type-of-library wheel and circulated with other requests from one library to the next on a daily round robin until it had been filled or had circulated to all libraries without being filled by any. A request unfilled on its own type-of-library wheel could be placed on one of the other wheels the following day. The state library acted as a switching center among the three wheels.

Beginning in the mid-1960s, the number of states implementing interlibrary lending communications networks steadily increased. By 1970, there were 17 states with formal TWX communications networks. By 1980, there were about 40 states with interlibrary loan communications networks. Some had replaced, or were about to replace, their TWX machines with other types of equipment, teleprinters being among the most common. In 1982, Montana adopted microcomputers as communications devices for its state network, using a round robin setup similar to Iowa's I-LITE, but simplifying matters by having only one wheel rather than three. During the 1970s, at least a dozen state libraries experimented with facsimile transmission as a possible means for communicating interlibrary loan requests and other brief correspondence to libraries in the state network, but these tests proved unsuccessful in all but about three states.

Structure and Policy

In nearly every instance where a formal interlibrary loan communications structure was established, there were significant changes in interlibrary lending in the state with respect to volume of activity, pattern of traffic, and extent of participation. Although they made an enormous impact, these networks by no means ever embraced all interlibrary loan activity among libraries in their respective states. The volume of traffic outside the formal state structures remained high and continued to grow as the general level of interlibrary lending activity increased on the broader scale.

Some libraries viewed the network structure in their state as designed to actually discourage participation. Even in multitype state networks, there was a common tendency among academic and special libraries to see the networks as emphasizing primarily public and school libraries. Historically, the role of most state libraries had been in public library development. Combined with this precedent was a cooperative tradition in American librarianship that tended to focus on single-type library cooperation. In many cases, the reluctance of academic and special libraries to participate enthusiastically in state networks may have been based more on the psychology of these factors than on any direct evidence of discriminating practices or policies. In other cases, this psychology was reinforced by statutory policies that actually prevented some types of libraries from participating and allowed participation for others only on a restricted or specially designated basis. In Illinois, for example, certain categories of academic libraries could participate only as associate members of systems for many years, and some libraries felt that in practice this translated into lower priority handling of their interlibrary loan requests at the system level. The type of library most commonly prevented statutorily (or interpretively) from any type of participation in state networks was the corporate library.

A more common constraining policy in many state networks, particularly during the late 1960s, was the definition of what types of material could or could not be requested. For example, materials for which requests could not be sent through NYSILL at that time included multivolume sets, in-print paperbacks, and current publications in general. Requests for fiction, textbooks, children's books, and a broad category of nonresearch materials including self-help books, cookbooks, and books on sports, recreation, and hobbies could be sent up the hierarchy to the state library, but would not be sent beyond there to any geographic or subject referral libraries unless accompanied by a statement that the materials were to be used for serious research.[18] Such restrictions conformed to stringent interlibrary loan codes, but they did not necessarily conform to user demands nor to the desires of local libraries to satisfy those demands. A study by Nelson Associates of the early operation of NYSILL showed how great this problem could be. Of 46,000 requests received by the New York State Library during a six-month period in 1967, nearly 15,000 could neither be filled by the state library nor were eligible for referral to a geographic or subject resource center.[19] This meant that each month an average of nearly 2,500 unfilled requests for materials that fell into the nonreferral categories described earlier were sent back down the hierarchy from the state library as unfilled requests. Having exhausted the formal network channels, further attempts by the local or system library to fill these requests required going outside the channels.

Perhaps the main reason that some libraries conducted all or part of their interlibrary borrowing outside established state networking channels was their perception of network performance. And for libraries that had been actively involved in interlibrary lending for a long time and had established good working relationships with other libraries, this perception unfortunately proved all too often to be accurate. The multitier structure of most state networks could not help but result in processing delays for requests not filled at a lower level of the hierarchy. This could be particularly frustrating when a library was requesting an item known to be at one of the upper-level referral sites and extremely unlikely to be found at any of the intervening levels. In such a case the originating library might reasonably feel that the request should be sent directly to the referral library that was known to own the item, but mechanisms were set up in many state networks to discourage this practice. Compensation for in-state lending was sometimes paid to referral libraries only for loans processed through normal state network channels, and in many cases referral libraries had a policy of not accepting direct requests from in-state libraries, at least of less than a certain size.

These state networks created during the mid- and late 1960s had little on which to draw in the way of precedent. The environment in which they were established was characterized by an increasing level of interlibrary loan activity and an inadequate level of title-specific locational information in distributable form. These two conditions worked toward opposite ends, and a highly structured communications network was seen as the most appropriate available mechanism for coping with the circumstances.

Despite their sometimes cumbersome operation, state networks were not unresponsive to change, and the agencies responsible for their administration tried in many cases to streamline operations, broaden the scope of materials that could be borrowed, and incorporate new procedures or policies as need arose. Perhaps most importantly, the networks provided a place to which many local libraries with little or no previous experience in interlibrary loan services could turn for assistance, and a formal mechanism for those libraries to gain access to a far broader base of resources. Two years after the creation of NYSILL, S. Gilbert Prentiss, former New York assistant commissioner for libraries, said of the performance of NYSILL and similar networks: "The mere establishment of a system almost inevitably builds in a degree of inflexibility and cumbersomeness which in certain situations will be comparatively slow and costly, even though it expedites service to most users most of the time."[20]

Automation and Locational Tools—1970s

Against a background of increasing levels of interlibrary lending, state interlibrary loan communications networks carried out important functions as agents for regulating the flow of requests within a state and for providing a structure for locating requested items. These functions were needed in part because of the lack of comprehensive tools providing known locations of books, serials, and other items that might be requested through interlibrary loan. The hierarchical structure of most networks provided a mechanism for locating items in at least some libraries whose holdings were not likely to be reported in such tools as the *National Union Catalog*, thereby diverting some requests from those libraries at the top of the hierarchy whose holdings were available on a wider basis. It is uncertain whether greater knowledge of title-specific holdings information encompassing more libraries would have entirely obviated the need for the formal networks established in many states. It is certain, however, that the lack of such knowledge was a major obstacle in the interlibrary loan process.

Although more prolific in number, locational tools available even by the late 1960s had changed little in form or nature of compilation from precedents established during the first half of the twentieth century. Although more and more libraries had been gaining experience in the automation of internal operations through the use of computers, and unit-record equipment before that, there had as yet been little application of these tools in coordinated projects involving several different libraries. Union catalogs of a sort had been produced on unit-record equipment as early as the 1950s, but these were invariably intrasystem projects encompassing libraries under one administration, such as a public library or regional system and its branches. In several instances, even through the 1960s, these catalogs contained only bibliographic information about items held within the system, and information on specific locations for each item remained available only on a central union card catalog shelflist.

The major difficulty in automating interlibrary union projects was that few libraries had bibliographic records in machine-readable form, and even those that did were almost certain to have recorded them in a format different from that used by any other library. As a result, machine-readable records created by a library for its own internal operations could not easily be combined with those of another library to establish a common database for generating a union list or catalog. The automation of a union project, therefore, had to be well thought out and coordinated in advance to ensure the greatest possible compatibility and consistency in format; it could not be carried out as an afterthought.

Early Projects

A few interlibrary union projects were initiated during the early 1960s using unit-record equipment. One, focusing on monograph holdings, was a joint project involving the Niagra Falls and Lockport public libraries in New York in 1964. The scope of the catalog was fairly limited and did not entail conversion of records for items existing in the collections before the start of the project. Also in the mid-1960s, the Rio Grande chapter of the Special Libraries Association (SLA) issued a union list of serials, printed on unit-record equipment, to which about 30 special libraries contributed. In a similar venture, the Minnesota chapter of the SLA generated a 130-page union list of serials in 1963, containing about 3,500 entries.

Union Lists and Catalogs

As with other library applications, unit-record equipment had limited applicability for the preparation of union lists and catalogs because of the speed at which it operated. Already by the mid-1960s, a few groups of libraries were beginning to engage computers for union listing projects. One of the earliest was realized in the 1964 publication of the 13,000-entry *North Carolina Union Checklist of Scientific Serials*, containing titles and holdings information for scientific serials in five university libraries in the North Carolina Research Triangle. The *Kansas Union List of Serials*, 1965, contained more than 17,000 titles and reported holdings in six of the largest academic libraries in the state. The Medical Library Center in New York City began in 1964 to create a machine-readable database of holdings information for serials titles in a number of medical libraries in the city. In 1967, the first edition of a printed list, the *Union Catalog of Medical Periodicals* (*UCMP*), was issued, containing the more recent and active titles with holdings information for more than 50 medical libraries in the metropolitan area. Three years later, a copy of the *UCMP* machine-readable file was sent to the regional headquarters of the TALON Regional Medical Library Program, where it served as the starting point for creation of a regional union list of serials holdings in major medical libraries in Arkansas, Louisiana, New Mexico, Oklahoma, and Texas.

These examples were representative of computer-based union projects during the 1960s. Most were targeted exclusively toward periodicals, or serials, and encompassed libraries limited either by type or geography. During the 1970s, and often backed by LSCA Title III funding, a number of states initiated computer-assisted union listing projects. In some cases, these statewide efforts were based on previous or existing projects of lesser scope. In Kentucky, for example, a title checklist for collecting holdings information from a large number of libraries in the state was generated from the machine-readable database being created by the Kentuckiana Metroversity consortium of academic libraries in the Louisville area and in southern Indiana. Data from the returned checklists were converted to machine-readable form and stored on a computer at the University of Louisville. The original intention was to send checklists and forms for adding titles not yet on the lists to about 100 of the nearly 300 libraries in Kentucky. This number was eventually pared to 51, but it represented a range of academic, public, and special libraries. In 1972, the first edition of the computer-generated, 16,000-title *Kentucky Union List of Serials*, with about 37,000 holdings, was printed and distributed.

As early as 1968, funding had been appropriated in Indiana for preparing a broadly based *Indiana Union List of Serials* using computer facilities at Purdue University in West Lafayette. Considerable difficulty was encountered along the way, but in January 1970, a preliminary computer-printout listing was issued, containing about 46,000 entries with nearly 50 libraries in the state contributing. The reception was not overwhelmingly enthusiastic; criticism was aimed primarily at the format and filing order in which entries were listed. A second preliminary catalog issued in early 1971 was not much more favorably received.[21] After a great deal of reworking of data and software programs, the *Indiana Union List of Serials First Cumulative Edition* was issued in late 1973, containing more than 90,000 entries with more than 150,000 holdings.[22]

Minnesota also mounted a concerted effort to compile a broadly based union list of serials. With responsibility for coordination awarded to MINITEX, the Minnesota Union List of Serials (MULS) project was formally initiated in 1971. A preliminary two-volume edition, containing about 37,000 entries and 20,000 cross-references and added entries, was issued a year later. The first official edition was published in late 1974 in five volumes with more than 70,000 titles and contained holdings for 122 libraries. The machine-readable MULS database served as one of the three serials files, along with those of the Library of Congress and the National Library of Canada, used to create the initial CONSER (CONservation of SERials) file loaded into OCLC.[23]

The generation of a broadly based union list of serials from machine-readable data represented a substantial undertaking in the early 1970s, but it still paled in comparison with the effort and expense required to generate a union catalog that would have included bibliographic and holdings information for monographs and other materials for the same number of libraries. In 1968, the Connecticut State Library announced its intention to coordinate such an effort, to be backed by an infusion of $500,000 of LSCA funding over a five-year period. By 1971, however, the project had been abandoned and was replaced by a plan to microfilm various card catalogs and store copies at the state library as tools for assisting libraries in finding interlibrary loan locations.[24]

Compiling a machine-readable database representing monograph holdings of a number of libraries posed some serious problems that would have had to be solved pertaining to uniformity in bibliographic format, magnitude of converting manual records to machine-readable form, and the enormous amount of computer space required to store the records. A few states, however, invested in a less ambitious form of union locational tool known as the numerical register. Rather than indicating full bibliographic information for each item held by reporting libraries, the entire "catalog" consisted of Library of Congress Card Numbers (LCCNs) and location symbols showing which libraries owned an item represented by an LCCN. The idea was that when a known-item interlibrary loan request was submitted by a library user, its LCCN could be determined through a number of sources, such as the *National Union Catalog*, in which LCCNs were provided as part of the bibliographic entry. These numerical union registers, such as the one published in Louisiana in 1971, did circumvent the problems of bibliographic uniformity and did reduce conversion effort and the amount of computer storage space required, but they had obvious limitations. The scope of coverage was restricted to items cataloged by the Library of Congress, and a mechanism was required to assist smaller libraries that might not have adequate tools for determining the LCCN of an item requested by a patron.

Of all the efforts during the late 1960s and early 1970s to produce monographic union catalogs with the assistance of a computer and a machine-readable database, the most ambitious was the University of California's *Union Catalog Supplement*. Published in 1972, it was a 48-volume, 42,000-page book catalog of all monographs cataloged by libraries on all nine university campuses between 1963 and 1967. The time, effort, and expense involved in such a project were out of the question for most states and university systems to even think of attempting a similar feat. It was perhaps a fitting monument to the end of an era that the *Supplement* was one of the largest—and one of the last—computer-produced monographic union catalogs to be published in book form. Large union catalogs of monographic holdings would be published in the future, but their medium would be computer output microform rather than paper. They would also invariably be based in large part on the offline products of a type of union catalog emerging in the early 1970s, the online union catalog.

OCLC

One of the earliest online union catalogs in the United States, and the one that established itself by the mid-1970s as the most broadly based in American libraries, was OCLC. Its emergence in an online mode in 1971 as a shared cataloging system soon had important implications for interlibrary loan. Each time any member library cataloged an item using an OCLC bibliographic record, its location symbol was affixed to that record. Although many libraries joining OCLC had been reporting holdings to the *National Union Catalog*, the vast majority had not. For most, OCLC was the first opportunity to have their monographic holdings known to other libraries. A large number of libraries chose not simply to catalog their current acquisitions on the system, but also entered holdings for materials already in their collections before joining OCLC. As the shared database grew through the 1970s and as more libraries joined the system, OCLC evolved into one of the most powerful interlibrary loan locational tools available.

In some ways, the locational aspect of the OCLC system competed or conflicted with the role that had been carved out for state interlibrary loan communications networks. It represented an alternative for finding interlibrary loan locations. Point-to-point communication between libraries relying on OCLC for holdings information, even if located in different states, often meant that requests were handled more promptly than through state networking channels. In the most extreme cases, OCLC was seen by certain agencies as an intruder impinging on an already established area of responsibility and as an alternative threatening to reintroduce the unchanneled, free flow of requests that had typified interlibrary loan before the creation of the state networks. In many other cases, however, state networks were more open to OCLC and incorporated it into the network structure as an additional tool for locating items both within and outside the state.

COM Catalogs and Other Tools—Late 1970s

OCLC and the other bibliographic utilities that emerged later not only provided online union catalogs of locations, but they also enabled participating libraries to build their own machine-readable databases supplied on magnetic tapes. The difference between these institution-specific, machine-readable databases and those created by libraries during the mid- and late 1960s was in the degree of format compatibility from one library to the next. The credit for this compatibility rested in the widespread adoption of the MARC II format by libraries and bibliographic utilities as a standard for machine-readable representation of bibliographic data. This standardization allowed the information on one OCLC library's magnetic tape to be merged with another's with a minimum of effort, or even the records of an OCLC library with the records of an RLIN or WLN library, and so forth. There were minor problems in merging due to slightly differing interpretations of the MARC format by utilities and even individual libraries, but in essence the records were compatible.

During the mid- and late 1970s, a number of states took advantage of this compatibility by merging records of libraries with MARC-based machine-readable files into a single statewide database to be used in a union Computer Output Microform (COM) catalog. The statewide union catalog served as an indispensable tool for smaller libraries unable to afford membership in a bibliographic utility, and in some states it bridged the gap between libraries using different utilities or other systems that could not be cross-examined in an online mode. Alabama, Colorado, Florida, Kansas, Maryland, Mississippi, and Nebraska were among the states that developed statewide COM catalogs by the early 1980s, and many are still in existence and are updated periodically.

The 1970s was the most active decade in the history of American libraries in the distribution of holdings information on a nationwide scale, and this activity continued into the 1980s. By mid-1984, the OCLC system alone contained more than 150 million holdings for its nearly 11 million bibliographic records, and there were millions of other holdings in the RLIN and WLN databases. In addition to the birth and growth of the online bibliographic utilities during the 1970s, the 700-plus volume *National Union Catalog: Pre-1956 Imprints* was completed. In the early 1980s, several union lists and union listing capabilities were brought online. The California *Union List of Periodicals* became available through BRS; the OCTANET combined serials check-in, union listing, and interlibrary loan system was activated; and the OCLC union listing capability was implemented and by mid-1984 contained more than 50 local, state, and regional online union lists.

Activities on regional and nationwide systems were supplemented by efforts at the state and local levels. With the assistance of computers, a multiplicity of localized union lists and catalogs was being generated. Another important development was the evolution of clustering arrangements in automated circulation systems and online catalogs, whereby libraries share a central computer and are also able to search each other's online file.

Interlibrary Loan Requests

During the 1970s, when the distribution of holdings information was progressing at a rapid pace, there was little change in the techniques used to communicate interlibrary loan requests and associated correspondence between libraries. More libraries installed TWX machines or similar equipment, but the changes were of magnitude rather than kind. During the latter half of the 1970s, this began to change as some existing online systems introduced enhancements to link two previously distinct parts of the interlibrary loan process: identifying locations and communicating requests. The earliest precedents were found in remote-access circulation systems, such as the system developed for use by the 21 libraries on the campus of the Ohio State University.

In 1979, two existing systems were expanded to provide a link between location identification and transmission of requests in networking environments. One system, OCLC, had existed in a networking environment for several years, but had not had an interlibrary loan communications capability. The other system, the Library Computer System (LCS) in Illinois, had not previously existed in a networking environment beyond a single campus, but had already incorporated a link between identification of locations and transmission of requests to borrow.

OCLC's Interlibrary Loan Subsystem

Before 1979, the OCLC online union catalog was an important finding tool for interlibrary loan locations, but once locations were identified, the request itself had to be transmitted via other means, such as mail, telephone, or TWX. After a three-month test among 20 libraries in early 1979, OCLC introduced an interlibrary loan communications capability that provided an alternative to mail, telephone, and TWX. With this new capability, once a library retrieved an OCLC bibliographic record for an item it wished to borrow, it could select up to five potential lenders from among the OCLC membership. By keying in a simple command, it could then request an online interlibrary loan work form for the item. Bibliographic information from the OCLC record was automatically transferred onto the work form along with the identifier symbols of the libraries designated as potential lenders. The borrowing library then merely had to complete the work form by keying in its address and, if it wished, other information such as a patron's name.

When the online work form was completed, a simple command sent it to the central computers in Ohio and immediately into an online message file of the first potential lending library specified by the borrower. The potential lender retrieved the online request and replied that it either could or could not supply the item. If the lender responded that it could not, the online request went into the message file of the second potential lender, and so on. When a lender responded that it could supply the item, the request was subsequently updated online by the borrower and lender at various points of the transaction to indicate its precise status at any given time: shipped, received, renewal requested, returned, and so on.

Immediately upon its introduction, the subsystem was well received by the OCLC membership. In most instances, it enabled the library to combine bibliographic verification, identification of holdings, and transmission of a request into a single continuous step requiring only one session at the same terminal. These features, combined with instantaneous transmission, the ability to designate a routing chain of up to five libraries, and the automatic referral from one potential lender to the next after a negative response, reduced the elapsed time between request initiation and document receipt for most libraries, and resulted in a higher overall fill rate than had previously been the case in most libraries.

The results of five studies on the performance of the OCLC interlibrary loan subsystem are shown in Table 6-1. In all but the Florida Library Information Network (FLIN) study, the fill rate consistently exceeded 90 percent. Another consistency in these studies concerned the distribution of filled requests by position of potential lenders in the lender chain. Except in the first New York study, the first lender to which requests were sent filled between 52 and 57 percent of all requests that were eventually filled, and the second lender accounted for between 21 and 29 percent. Although not reported in Table 6-1, three of the studies compared average elapsed time between initiation of a request and receipt of the document for requests sent via the OCLC subsystem and those sent through the mail. In Illinois, Reynolds reported an average elapsed time of 10.8 days for requests sent via the OCLC subsystem during its first two months of availability. This compared with an average of 15.9 days for requests sent through the mail during the preceding two years when OCLC was used only to identify locations.[25] In the first New York study, comparative averages were 17.0 days for requests sent via OCLC and 27.4 days for those sent through the mail during the same period. Comparative averages for the second New York study were 16.3 days and 22.1 days, respectively.[26]

Use of the OCLC communications capability remained largely out-

TABLE 6-1   PERFORMANCE OF THE OCLC INTERLIBRARY LOAN
SUBSYSTEM

	WILC Reynolds* 1979	CUNY Taler[†] 1979	CUNY Taler[†] 1981	OCLC Dodson et al.[‡] 1981	FLIN Gorin[§] 1981
No. of requests sent via OCLC interlibrary loan subsystem	70	79	130	509	1,660
No. of requests filled	65	79	123	471	1,256
% fill rate	92.9	100.0	94.6	92.4	75.6
Distribution of filled requests by position in lender chain					
% filled by 1st position	52.3	63.3	56.9	57.1	52.6
% filled by 2nd position	29.2	31.6	23.6	25.1	21.4
% filled by 3rd position	10.8	2.5	9.8	10.5	16.4
% filled by 4th position	4.6	2.5	7.3	5.3	6.9
% filled by 5th position	3.1	—	2.4	2.0	2.7

*Reynolds, Dennis J. "Regional Alternatives for Interlibrary Loan: Access to Unreported Holdings." *College & Research Libraries* 41 (January 1980): 33–42.

[†]Taler, Izabella. "Automated and Manual ILL: Time Effectiveness and Success Rate." *Information Technology and Libraries* 1 (September 1982): 277–280.

[‡]Dodson, Ann T., Paul P. Philbin, and Kunj B. Rastogi. "Electronic Interlibrary Loan in the OCLC Library." *Special Libraries* 73 (January 1982): 12–20.

[§]Gorin, Robert S. *Florida Library Information Network: A Comparative Study of OCLC, TWX, U.S. Mail and Closed-Circuit Teletype, February 2, 1981–March 31, 1981, with Recommendations.* Tallahassee: State Library of Florida, 1981.

side formal state networking channels. Just as there had been earlier reservations about how OCLC as a locational device would affect the established channels of communications within a state network, so was there a reluctance after 1979 by many state systems to test the communications capability of OCLC. By the late 1970s, many state networks had finally incorporated OCLC as a locational tool, placing terminals in some or all of their systems and resources modes. But when the communications capability became available, there was a tendency in many state networks to continue to use OCLC only as a locational tool, relying on previously established modes of communication such as TWX for actual transmission of requests. There were some early exceptions to this general tendency, such as in Texas, where the state networking system adopted OCLC as its primary interlibrary loan communications system.

LCS

A second major online system to combine holdings information with transmission of requests in 1979 was the Library Computer System

(LCS) of the University of Illinois. LCS was not an interlibrary union catalog like OCLC, but rather a circulation system on which initially the files of one library, and later others, were available for remote searching and charging. The initial database on the system was comprised of records for most of the holdings of the University of Illinois Urbana-Champaign libraries. In December 1979, hard-wired LCS terminals were placed in each of the 18 ILLINET regional systems headquarters. Terminals were later placed in a number of other locations in Illinois, and several libraries in the state loaded their own machine-readable databases onto LCS and were using the system for circulation control.

The databases of the various libraries were maintained separately on LCS. Each library, however, was able to search the holdings of the other libraries and could directly charge out items online from them. When a charge command was entered, a page slip was printed at the lending library and the material was retrieved and sent to the borrowing library. A real advantage of LCS was that each online bibliographic record displayed the circulation status of the item. With this information, the borrowing library had a fairly good idea as to whether the item was indeed available for immediate loan by the library whose file it was searching.

Other systems had integrated functions of location identification, communication, and circulation charging before this time, but they were largely in libraries under a single administration or within a single jurisdiction. A unique aspect of the Illinois experience was that the LCS participants were administratively independent libraries located thoughout the state.

Other Developments

Systems providing a communications as well as a locational capability helped to streamline interlibrary loans. In 1981, enhancement to the RLIN system enabled its members to more quickly and easily identify all recorded locations among RLIN libraries for any title in the database. In 1982, a sophisticated online interlibrary loan communications capability was introduced.

Another development along different lines but also receiving considerable attention was the emergence of electronic mail services (EMS), such as TYMNET's On-Tyme II system. These systems have a wide spectrum of potential applications for libraries. In terms of communication for interlibrary lending, they are less expensive under some circumstances, but their capabilities are also less sophisticated than the interlibrary loan subsystems of utilities such as OCLC and RLIN. Messages can be sent to one location at a time or to several simultaneously, but stepwise referral from one lender to another is semiautomatic at best, and bibliographic information has to be keyed in its entirety into a request rather than any portion being automatically transferred from an outside source bibliographic record.

Document Delivery Revisited

Electronic mail services, shared circulation systems, and the interlibrary loan subsystems of some of the utilities were all playing an important role in interlibrary loan by the early 1980s. But even with the improvements in locating materials and transmitting interlibrary loan requests, a persistent problem remained the matter of actually delivering the documents themselves. Improvements on the time factor in document delivery during the 1970s were the result of better organization and exploitation of traditional means of delivery rather than the result of technological innovation. Both on an informal and formal basis, increasing numbers of libraries in local cooperatives and state networks began to exchange materials via courier delivery. Some of the information retrieval services and database vendors also began to offer document delivery services. Although copies of documents were still sent through the mail by these services, a high priority was placed on rapid handling of orders and mailing via the fastest postal class available.

Although there had been some experimentation with telefacsimile transmission throughout the 1970s, it was isolated and fairly narrow in scope. In 1979, however, two important experimental projects were funded. Eventually merged under one administration, one project was the Federal Library Network Prototype Project (FLNPP), in which 12 federal and 3 nonfederal libraries in various parts of the United States participated. The other was the Telefax Library Information Network (TALINET), with five sites in the Midwest and Rocky Mountain regions, which were experiencing rapid population and economic growth, a result of an influx of energy-related industries. Several different types of equipment and capabilities were tested during these experiments. Some transactions involved interlibrary loan requests for copies of articles; others were requests for answers to reference questions; still others were requests for online literature searches. In general, the TALINET and FLNPP project team felt the results were favorable. One of the principal participants whose library served as a central processing location for the experiment summarized:

> Facsimile is close to being the *least* costly delivery methodology. Any breakthrough in: facsimile equipment, such as a two-minute facsimile over the four-minute facsimile; reduction in telephone charges; utilization of satellites; or development of an entirely new delivery system such as a National

Periodicals Center, could tip the scales in favor of telefacsimile as a cost-effective methodology to deliver all or a large part of the information flow to and from libraries.[27]

Since the FLNPP and TALINET projects in 1979, there have indeed been important developments in telefacsimile technology. Machines are now widely available that transmit at a rate of one minute per page or faster, and the cost of equipment has decreased considerably. There has been a great deal of library experimentation with these machines during the first half of the 1980s. Some of these activities, and the equipment they have been using, are described in Chapter 15.

Although telefacsimile technology appears to be rendering more favorably for libraries and the service is becoming more cost-effective, there have been, and remain, some very fundamental questions about the suitability of telefacsimile for the transmission of documents in interlibrary lending. One question concerns the level of need. It seems an almost irreproachable tenet in the library profession that it is desirable to deliver information to the library user by the fastest means possible. Yet in the 1967 CLR-funded telefacsimile experiment, library users frequently did not pick up materials for two or more days after they had arrived. In the New York FACTS project, more than 70 percent of the respondents to a questionnaire indicated that the material would have been just as useful to them had it arrived two or three days later. In the TALINET project, only about 28 percent of the requests were "time critical"; answers to the majority of requests "could have been handled by conventional means (mail) and still have been useful."[28]

A significant factor in these user responses, of course, may have had to do with learned levels of expectation. It has always been true that interlibrary loan does not provide same-day delivery, or sometimes even same-week or same-month delivery, and library users have grown to accept or work around this fact. If this is indeed a significant factor, then one cannot discount the importance of or need for more rapid delivery of documents for at least some types of requests.

Beyond the question of user expectations, however, is an equally important consideration: the processing priorities assigned by the libraries involved. The actual time spent in transmitting a copy of a document can be greatly reduced through the use of telefacsimile equipment, but the mere substitution of one mode of delivery technology for another will not in itself insure what some individuals would perceive as rapid document delivery. In several major experiments with facsimile transmission, there were significant time delays in delivery owing to processing backlogs at any of several stages in the interlibrary loan process. There were delays before the transmission of requests, upon receipt of transmitted requests, in retrieving and preparing documents for facsimile transmission, and in notifying end users that requested materials had been received. The relationship of facsimile transmission to the overall interlibrary lending process was put into rather blunt perspective by S. Gilbert Prentiss in a discussion of the New York FACTS program and the decision to discontinue it in 1968:

> What may be the greatest difficulty stems from the whole interlibrary loan procedure, which moves so deliberately and majestically that the introduction of a single, highly sophisticated speedup factor has about the same effect as the installation of racing tires would have on the overall speed of a dump truck.[29]

Fortunately, considerable strides have been made in nearly every part of the "whole interlibrary loan procedure" since that assessment in the late 1960s. But Prentiss's remarks are still valid in underscoring the complexity of interlibrary loan as a multifaceted procedure, a breakdown in any part of which will negate some degree of advancement made in the others.

Although these questions are still important in regard to the use of telefacsimile transmission among libraries, what may turn out to be of even greater significance during the 1980s is the emergence of other, more sophisticated forms of document delivery. Telefacsimile transmission, although practical regarding copies of retrospective documents and even many current ones, may be on its way to becoming something of a technological dinosaur with respect to transmissions of other documents. Two developments in the 1980s eventually promise to have considerable impact on interlibrary loan. One is the emergence of on-line access to full texts of documents through commercial services. The second is the appearance of optical digital disks for storage of bibliographic information and the full text of documents. Although still in their infancy, these developments are no longer topics for speculation in the mid-1980s; they are realities. The scope and implications of both are examined in greater detail in subsequent chapters. Suffice it to say here that they do promise to have important implications for libraries, and not only for what is traditionally thought of as interlibrary lending, but in a far more pervasive sense for the activities and role of the library as a whole.

Notes

1. Samuel Green, "The Lending of Books to One Library by Another," *Library Journal* 1 (September 30, 1876): 15–16.
2. Mary Margaret Fischer, "Library Cooperation," *Catholic Library World* 39 (January 1983): 336.

3. Ralph T. Esterquest, "Co-operation in Library Services," *Library Quarterly* 31 (January 1961): 78.
4. Louis Round Wilson and Maurice F. Tauber, *The University Library: The Organization, Administration, and Functions of Academic Libraries*, 2nd ed. (New York: Columbia University Press, 1956), p. 462.
5. Esterquest, "Co-operation," p. 74.
6. Janice W. Sherwood and Eleanor E. Campion, "Union Library Catalogue: Services, 1950. Quo Vadis?" *College and Research Libraries* 13 (April 1952): 106.
7. JoAn S. Segal and Dennis Reynolds, "The Regional Union Catalog and BCR's Interloan Service," *Colorado Libraries* 7 (March 1981): 28–33.
8. Cited in Brigette L. Kenney, *Survey of Interlibrary Communication Systems* (Boston: EDUCOM, 1967), p. 15.
9. A summary of some of the early installations of TWX is provided by Kenney, *Survey of Interlibrary Communication Systems*.
10. Cedric Larson, "A Facsimile System for Reference Service," *Wilson Library Bulletin* 26 (January 1952): 394–395.
11. For a report, see Harold G. Morehouse, *Equipment for Facsimile Transmission Between Libraries: A Description and Comparative Evaluation of Three Systems* (Reno: University of Nevada Library, 1967).
12. For a report, see William D. Schieber and Ralph M. Shaffner, *Telefacsimile in Libraries: A Report of an Experiment in Facsimile Transmission and an Analysis of Implications for Interlibrary Loan Systems* (Berkeley, Calif.: Institute of Library Research, University of California, 1968).
13. For a report on the FACTS program, see Nelson Associates, Inc., *The New York State Library's Pilot Program in Facsimile Transmission of Library Materials* (New York: Nelson Associates, 1968).
14. James R. Hunt, "The System in Hawaii," *ALA Bulletin* 60 (December 1966): 1142–1146.
15. Quoted in Russell Shank, "Networks," in *Bowker Annual of Library and Book Trade Information, 1970* (New York: R. R. Bowker, 1970), p. 291.
16. For an overview of the early history of NYSILL, see S. Gilbert Prentiss, "The Evolution of the Library System (New York)," in *Library Networks—Promise and Performance*, Leon Carnovsky, ed. (Chicago: University of Chicago Press, 1969), pp. 78–89.
17. A description of the early workings of MINITEX is provided by Alice E. Wilcox, "Networks Descriptions of Operational Systems—MINITEX," in *Networks and the University Library*, LeMoyne W. Anderson, ed. (Chicago, Ill.: Association of College and Research Libraries, 1974), pp. 23–29.
18. New York State Interlibrary Loan Network, *NYSILL Manual*, rev. ed. (Albany, N.Y.: State University of New York, 1970), p. 7.
19. "Summary of Nelson Associates' Study of the New York State Library's NYSILL Pilot Project and a Report of Decisions Relating to Continuation of the NYSILL Program," *Bookmark* 27 (July 1968): 365.
20. Prentiss, "The Evolution of the Library System," p. 85.
21. William L. Corya, Gary L. Lelvis, and Bonnie A. Siiss, "Indiana Union List of Serials Project," *Library Occurrent* 24 (August 1974): 458.

22. *Ibid.,* p. 456.
23. Lois N. Upham, "Minnesota Union List of Serials," *Serials Librarian* 3 (Summer 1979): 289–297.
24. "$500,000 Union Catalog Planned for Connecticut," *Library Journal* 93 (April 1, 1968): 1405; "Computerized Union Catalog Abandoned in Connecticut," *Library Journal* 96 (May 15, 1971): 1662.
25. Dennis J. Reynolds, "Regional Alternatives for Interlibrary Loan: Access to Unreported Holdings," *College and Research Libraries* 41 (January 1980): 39.
26. Izabella Taler, "Automated and Manual ILL: Time Effectiveness and Success Rate," *Information Technology and Libraries* 1 (September 1982): 279.
27. Telecommunications and Libraries (White Plains, N.Y.: Knowledge Industry Publications, 1979), p. 118.
28. *Ibid.,* p. 105.
29. Prentiss, "The Evolution of the Library System," p. 86.

II

Planning and Preparation

7

Foundations: Recurring Themes and Present Trends

Library automation has come a long way, over an often uncertain and unpredictable path, since the 1930s when a few libraries began to incorporate IBM unit-record equipment into their circulation procedures. The evolution of automation in libraries has often been rather abrupt, characterized by landmark developments that usher in a new phase of activity or mode of application. In the broad sense, the emergence of unit-record equipment, batch processing on computers, and online computerization represent a few of the more pronounced technological benchmarks that have influenced the course of library automation. In the narrow sense, certain isolated projects or systems can be cited as pioneer efforts that brought each of these and other technologies into the realm of library application.

Although major "first" projects have a special role in the evolution of library automation, the ultimate test is the extent to which any such project is successful for setting the stage for adoption in other and greater numbers of libraries. In viewing library automation in the broad sense, the special mark of the 1980s is likely to be the magnitude of this transition from experimentation and limited use to commonplace occurrence. Because of advances in technology, lowering of costs, and changes in attitude among librarians, sophisticated means of automation are no longer an option for just the largest or most well-endowed libraries. After nearly a quarter-century of computer applications in libraries, circumstances in the mid-1980s, more than ever before, favor automation as a normal part of the routine operations in a large number of facilities. This is an exciting prospect for libraries, especially since it is occurring within a context of what has come to be known as the information age. It is a time of new challenges in the way that libraries conduct—and even define—their basic business.

Along with increased feasibility for automation has come a broadening of the possible approaches and an increase in the number of products and services available in this now intensely active library automation marketplace. In planning for automation in such an environment, a library must be aware of the major influences that shape how decisions must be made and activities carried out. After a look at the relationship between libraries and technological development in general, this chapter focuses on three particularly important influences during the mid-1980s. The first constitutes a "background for planning," the several recurring themes in library automation that should always be taken into account during the planning process. These considerations *have been* part of the library automation scene for a long time, but they are generally as relevant today as ever. Yet, such hard-learned lessons are still, far too often, overlooked in planning for automation; the net result can be disappointment or failure in a project. The second influence consists of present trends, which, unlike the recurring themes, are quite sensitive to changes over time. Since so many libraries are turning to the commercial market for automated products and services, the emphasis is on trends within or pertaining to that environment. The third influence examined here focuses on three particular techniques: microcomputers and their applications in libraries, optical digital disk and its implications, and telecommunications technology. While certainly not the only technologies playing an important role during the mid-1980s, these three have been assuming an increasing role in recent years and are likely to take on even greater significance in shaping the options for library automation during the remainder of the decade.

Libraries and Technological Development

Mainframe computers, minicomputers, and microcomputers have all found their way into service in libraries, and instruments ranging from satellites to optical disk recorders are becoming part of the library environment, rather than being strange technologies used in mysterious ways by governments and giant corporations. Just as libraries now may embrace and certainly are affected by many of the technical advances that have evolved in recent decades, they will feel the impact of others just now beyond the experimental stage, and still others either unforeseen or in only a speculative stage of development. The relationship of libraries to some of these technologies will be passive, to others only minimally participatory, and to still others quite active. Whether any particular technology will be adopted in libraries—and if so, when, to what extent, and for what purposes—will not depend on one single factor or steadfast set of rules, but rather will be the result of many and ever-changing influences acting on one another in ways that are sometimes not at all predictable.

As changes appear, and in order to examine the present environment in a broader context, it is important that developments—past, present, and future—be viewed against a larger backdrop of the relationship between libraries and technological development. Libraries are generally adaptors rather than innovators of technology. Of course, libraries do sometimes make major modifications in existing technology to adapt it for their own purposes, but the basic technologies were likely first developed and used by and for organizations mainly in the private sector or government. In an age when development of information-handling technology is advancing rapidly, it is easy to become carried away about possible repercussions of any particular item for libraries. Such enthusiasm is one of the most positive and creative forces responsible for the refinement and application of information technology in libraries, but it can be a double-edged sword if not tempered by a realistic notion about what is involved in the development, implementation, and capability of the technology on a broader scale.

Pace of Technological Development

Remarkably rapid advances have been made in information-handling technology since the 1950s, and the pace of development is greater now than at any time in the past. Hardly a day passes without the announcement of some new device or improvement that promises to carry information handling a full step further. Major advances seem to pop up almost overnight. While the rate of technological change is indeed staggering in an overall sense, it can also be deceptive if one attempts to apply the general pace to individual happenings. When someone involved in telecommunications technology announces a quantum leap in product capability, it is usually not the result of days or weeks or even months of development, but often years. This applies to applications of existing technologies as well. An example in the library world was the implementation in 1982 of the Library of Congress DEMAND system for storing catalog card images on optical disks. This represented an important achievement in the 1980s, but the planning and design for the project began as early as 1978.

Just as an announcement of a new product or application may signify the end result of a substantial period of research and development, glittering announcements of a research and development phase or a trial project usually mean that some time will pass before a finished product will be ready for the open market. And once the first model appears for commercial consumption, there is likely to be a further period of refinement, improvement, and the appearance of competing models suited to a broader range of applications before the technology becomes appropriate or affordable to markets such as libraries.

But even exercising restraint, it is impossible not to become excited about the implications for libraries of advances in technology. And for many of these, it is not really a matter of "if" they will be applied in libraries, but "when." In the case of optical disk, for example, at least four commercial vendors by mid-1984 were demonstrating its use for storage of bibliographic files in automated library systems. After investments in development technologies such as optical disk have been made and applications have started to reach beyond experimental and trial stages, they do not simply go away. They are refined and improved until superceded by some even newer technology or advance. But, in general, it is important to recognize that with an emerging technology, there is bound to be a time lag between research and development stages and emergence in experimental forms, another lag between experimental and marketable forms, another between early products and more refined ones, and often still another between the early competitive market and more widespread appropriateness or affordability for adaptive markets.

An equally important but sometimes overlooked consideration is that the ultimate success of a technology and the pace at which it is accepted are not determined solely by its own merits. There is a broader technological complex involved, and a host of social, economic, and political considerations will have bearing on the acceptance of any new technology, product, or service.

An example of the importance of the role of the broader technological complex can be found in Carlton Rochell's discussion of the development of steam power. The ancient Greeks had invented a steam engine of sorts, but its most advanced use was as a child's toy. Upon rediscovery of its principles two millenia later, the steam engine became an integral technology because there were by that time other technologies to which, and with which, it could be applied.[1] Although this is a rather dramatic example, some information technologies today are simply too recent to know precisely how, and even if, their respective roles will be affected by the existence of each other. For example, in the area of information technology, an interaction that will be extremely interesting to watch is between online systems that emphasize remote access to centrally stored files and optical digital disk technology, which promises to enable huge files of information to be rather inexpensively mass-produced and distributed for local storage and retrieval. It is not yet apparent to what degree or for what purposes these technologies will co-exist and even be complementary, and to what degree they will be competitive as alternative means for the delivery of the same types of information.

Not only will the fate of different information-handling technologies be influenced by how they relate to each other and the broader technological environment, but also by how they interact with economic, social, and political factors in the environment into which they are introduced. In some cases, these factors can inhibit adoption of a form of the technology in libraries or elsewhere. In a broad sense, what is technologically feasible is not necessarily what a potential audience is prepared to accept. An interesting example is videotex as a mass market technology. There are still some fundamental human barriers to its acceptance. One is the very speculative issue about whether people want to access textual information through their television sets. Until this question is answered, potential investors are likely to proceed with at least some degree of caution. And even if investors do take the risk, there remains a legalistic quagmire surrounding the delivery of electronic text, especially over such a medium as television. There are also questions about standards—or the lack—that need to be resolved before potential videotex entrepreneurs will be willing to invest even larger sums of money to develop, test, and refine systems according to specifications that might later be incompatible with a new or revised standard. These types of factors interject uncertainty into the development and broader implementation of new technologies.

Even if all of these specific concerns are answered, there remains another, broader factor governing the acceptance of a new technology or major advance, namely, the economic climate into which it must be introduced. For example, it is technically possible to store the full text of hundreds or even thousands of monographs on a single optical digital disk. And once a master copy of such a disk is produced, subsequent copies may be made at a cost of between $10 and $20 per copy. With this kind of know-how and such a mass-marketable product, it would seem that soon the full text of hundreds or even thousands of titles will be available for about the cost of a single hard-bound book. Yet such a projection is based on considering only the technological possibilities and the cost of materials, not on the realities of the economic and commercial markets. These markets being as complex as they are, it is just not going to be possible in the immediate future—legally, at least—to purchase a disk containing hundreds of mass-market, book-length current publications for a few dollars. Economic infrastructures and laws and social attitudes do change and the rate is often rapid, but it is seldom overnight.

Library Adaptation

In the midst of an information age, libraries can justifiably take pride in the fact that they have been in the information business longer than just about any other modern institution. And because of their involvement in gathering, storing, and organizing information, it seems quite logical that libraries should be among the earliest beneficiaries of new information technologies. With a few notable exceptions, however, this has generally not been the case. Libraries exist in a society that revolves around commercial activities and government priorities. The for-profit sector and the government make the investments in technology, information-related or not, and they are generally the first to benefit.

The challenge of applying a new technology to an adaptive environment like libraries is paramount, and the costs are high. Early innovators in computerizing library operations used technology that was already available, but the library's unique requirements meant that enormous sums of money had to be expended to develop software tailored to library-specific needs. However, there indeed did come a point at which computerization made the transition from simply being "potentially relevant to libraries" to being tested and used in the daily operations and services of at least some libraries. These major steps from anticipation to implementation were realized when a certain balance was achieved among technological considerations, costs, and perceived usefulness in the library environment. And as that balance has continued to shift more favorably through the years, the use of computerized systems and services has passed into still another phase, characterized by the feasibility of automation in far greater numbers of libraries than ever before. But it is important to note that it has taken more than 20 years to arrive at this point. Perhaps basic computerization in a wider scale in libraries has been such a crucial hurdle that other technologies or major advances will be adapted in libraries far more rapidly, but that remains to be seen. Whatever the longer-range future may hold, the mid-1980s are an intensively active period in library automation, and the next few years are likely to be even more so.

Background for Planning

The adage that "the more things change, the more they stay the same" is hardly an accurate description of information technology and library automation. But in spite of the enormous changes witnessed during the past quarter-century, a number of themes have remained fairly stable amid the technological changes and are still appropriate during the mid-1980s. Although the strength of some of them is eroding, these recurring themes still do surface in automation projects and can lead to problems and disappointments in the planning, implementation, and use of automated systems and services if not anticipated.

The following explains some of the most important lessons learned and relearned by librarians in their experiences with automation. An awareness of them will not be a guarantee against all problems that may arise, but acknowledging their existence will enable a library staff to be on guard and to try to prepare for them.

1. *Automation is almost always more expensive than initially anticipated.* The costs of library automation have decreased fairly consistently over the past two decades. However, it seems that expectations concerning costs have increased at about an inversely proportional rate. As a result, there is still often a discrepancy between the anticipated and the actual costs of implementing a system. In this age of microcomputers, there are still a few librarians who begin to investigate systems with a firm belief that a sophisticated microcomputer-based integrated library system capable of handling a fairly large collection and a high level of circulation can be purchased for a few thousand dollars. Maybe this will be true someday, but that day has not yet arrived. In cases with such a wide discrepancy between expectation and reality, little harm is usually done since the investigation will not advance very far before discovering that costs were seriously underestimated. The incident can be chalked up to a learning experience, and the whole matter of automation can then be examined from a more realistic perspective.

More prevalent are cases where basic system costs are clearly understood, but less obtrusive costs are not. When purchasing an automated system, libraries tend to focus on the costs of the hardware, software, and maintenance spelled out in the contract or on the purchase order. The importance of other costs associated with the system or service is often overlooked or underestimated. These may include site preparation expenses, the cost of converting manual records to machine-readable form, unrealistic expectations about post-implementation staff levels, failure to anticipate the need to expand the system in the not-too-distant future, and so on. If something will cost "more or less," experience in library automation has shown that it is likely to cost more. This is not some kind of mystical imperative, but is almost always the result of failing to take into account all auxiliary cost factors. The best protection against underestimating is careful and realistic assessment of all known factors in a project that are likely to have expenses associated with them. Careful planning and budgeting do not provide full insurance against the possibility of cost overruns, but they will help to reduce the gap between anticipated and actual final costs, and may even allow projects to be carried out within the estimated budget.

2. *Librarians and computer personnel still have problems in communicating with one another.* When the only option for libraries to automate was to use the computer of the parent institution and to have software written by local computer center personnel, effective communication between the library and the computer center was a persistent difficulty. Computer personnel generally were used to dealing with numbers and fixed length data, quite different from library requirements, and librarians did not know very much about computers. The two sides did not use the same terminology, and even when they did, the same words often had radically different meanings in library jargon and computer-ese. Over the years, this problem has declined somewhat, as many libraries have turned to turnkey automated systems that do not require involving local computer personnel. But even in the libraries that do opt for designing and operating a system through a local computer center, the situation has improved as librarians have learned more about computers and as computer center personnel have become more used to alphabetical and variable length data and more sophisticated retrieval requirements.

These more accommodating environments are often found where libraries and local computer centers have developed a working relationship on other projects in the past. But for libraries that are investigating their first venture, especially requiring use of a university, municipal, or corporate computer, the lessons of the past are still appropriate. Despite the prominence of the turnkey market, some libraries will continue to rely, either by choice or circumstance, on a local computer center to assist with some portion of their work. Even if the assistance does not include the design and operation of a full-scale system, there are sometimes special projects or peripheral services that may involve the center. And when this is the case, even in the mid-1980s problems in communication can arise. A new OCLC library in the Rocky Mountain region recently discovered this, much to the detriment of its budget. Upon receiving its first subscription tape from OCLC, the library wanted to be certain that the tape was not defective. A number of library vendors and networks offered such a service, the annual cost in the vicinity of $100 to $200. The computer center of the library's parent agency also said that it could perform this same work plus some elementary additional manipulation far less expensively on its own IBM computer. The computer center did eventually do the work—and then sent the library an interdepartmental bill for several thousand dollars to cover the cost of programmer time in figuring out exactly how to handle the tape!

At the risk of overgeneralization, and recognizing that sterling examples to the contrary do exist, many computer centers that have not worked with libraries before still seem to view bibliographic data and library system requirements in a way that librarians feel does not ensure a flexible and maximally useful system. Lest the potential problems be presented as too one-sided, it should also be noted that librarians who are unfamiliar with programming and the finer points of computers often have a tendency to underestimate what is involved, especially in major software design and in running a system. If a library and its local computer center work together on an automated project, it is not always an easy venture, especially the first time around. Both parties must be willing to explain, listen, and expend the effort to achieve effective communication and understanding of each other's requirements.

3. *Librarians and vendors have misunderstandings.* Many libraries, it is true, have avoided the tribulations associated with local system development by purchasing a turnkey system. But this solution is not without its own problems in communications. The relationship between librarians and vendors of automated turnkey systems has generally improved over the years, but one need only to have followed the recent public exchanges between the Chicago Public Library and DataPhase to realize that problems can still occur and be rather severe.

Vendors have complained that librarians often do not say what they really mean and do not have a realistic understanding of the expenses involved in developing automation systems, in introducing enhancements, and so on. Librarians have tended to view vendors as having an obsessive interest in profits and as being prone to promising anything and everything to realize a sale.

Such antagonism is unfortunate. Libraries are the livelihood of vendors specializing in automated library systems, and vendors are able to design and install generalized systems far less expensive than a library could develop on its own. Minor misunderstandings can occur in even the best of library/vendor relationships. Miscommunication can happen in discussing or documenting such matters as exactly what features a system does or does not have, in defining the respective responsibilities in installing a system—especially in site preparation—and at just about any other juncture in selecting, purchasing, implementing, and using a system. The best defense against misunderstanding is for the relationship between the two to be kept formal and businesslike. When a Request for Proposal is let, and later when signing a contract, the contents and any subsequent clarification concerning costs, capabilities, responsibilities, and so on, should be clearly articulated and formally documented. This will not insure against all possible mishaps and misunderstandings, but it will establish what each party expects of the other and will create a framework for dealing with any subsequent problems in a responsible manner.

4. *Some vendors go out of business.* There can be nothing more frustrating than purchasing a system or service from a vendor only to have the vendor go out of business at a later date. The commercial library automation market has grown extremely competitive in recent years, and substantial capital and a certain level of continuing success is required for a vendor to stay in business. Some do not succeed. Especially in the case of major purchases such as minicomputer-based integrated systems, the failure of a vendor in the marketplace means that those libraries that have purchased a system may be left with expensive hardware that is difficult to maintain and software that has no prospect of future support and enhancement outside the library.

Some consultants strongly urge that the best way to guard against the problems that arise when a vendor goes out of business is simply to purchase a system from a well-established vendor and to avoid purchasing from less tested vendors. The other side of this coin, however, is that even well-established vendors had to start someplace and that new entries in the marketplace are not doomed to failure simply because they are new. Because they realize the importance of attaining a critical mass of customers and therefore credibility in the marketplace, new vendors are often willing to give substantial price reductions and almost go overboard on individual and customized attention to a library's needs and requirements. Such enthusiasm can itself be a double-edged sword, especially with very new systems, but the point here is that the matter of selecting established versus new vendors is not cut and dried. Whether established or new, a library should strongly consider the financial soundness of a vendor before purchasing a system, although this falls far short of a guarantee. Even if the vendor is on a firm financial footing when the system is purchased, it is impossible to predict with certainty how the vendor's financial circumstances will fare in the future.

The library should always try to protect itself in advance against some of the most devastating effects should its vendor go out of business at a later date. If the vendor uses hardware supplied by a major computer manufacturer, equipment maintenance will be less of a problem than support and enhancement to the software, which most likely will have been developed by the vendor. In the case of hardware, it is important that a library clearly establish rights of ownership in its purchase contract and guard against the possibility of receiving equipment the vendor has purchased through a lien. Contractual arrangements should also be made at the time of purchase to allow the library access to software source codes and rights to modify software in the event that a vendor does go out of business. These represent only partial solutions since subsequent development by the library itself can be an expensive venture. But these measures will allow at least some possibility for future development.

5. *Development plans, delivery schedules, and implementation dates tend to be delayed.* Whether an automated system is being supplied by a vendor, designed by a local computer center, or developed within the library itself, one of the longstanding lessons of library automation is that systems tend not to be up and running by the date originally targeted. In the case of vendor-supplied turnkey systems, delivery is more reliable now than it was at one time, but installation of enhancements still frequently falls behind schedule. In recent years, at least two major vendors of large-scale turnkey systems have run into serious difficulties by overextending themselves in the area of promised development and delivery. In at least one of these cases, the final product for a statewide circulation system never was delivered and the contract was cancelled after two years of repeated postponements.

It is, therefore, important in the selection of an automated system that the library clearly distinguish between what is currently available and what is promised as a forthcoming enhancement. Some libraries are influenced in their selection of an automated system by future developments that the vendor has announced. This can be risky. The library considering future development in its selection process should carefully examine the past record of the vendor with respect to promised enhancements, and should be prepared to face the possibility that projected changes might be delayed, or, worse yet, never realized. If a decision is made to purchase a system that is not yet fully operational anywhere or one to which a major developmental overhaul is necessary to meet the library's particular needs, it is crucial for the library to protect itself financially in its contract against nondelivery.

Even when hardware and software are delivered on time, a phase of debugging or of tracing difficult-to-identify "gremlins" causing some sort of malfunction is sometimes necessary, resulting in a delay before the system can actually be implemented for full use. In more than a few cases, the library itself has been responsible for a delay by failing to adequately prepare the installation site, by having to go through a great deal of administrative red tape, or by severely underestimating the time required to convert manual bibliographic or other records to machine-readable form.

Whatever the reason, delays in delivery implementation or enhancements can result in considerable frustration for everyone involved. Relations between the library and its vendor or computer center can become strained to their upper limits, and anxiety levels can increase among library staff who already might have some trepidation about the installation of the new system. Contractual clauses provide the strongest incentive against late delivery and postponement on the part of a vendor, but such provisions are not absolute assurance. And they should not be seen as an immediate solution to all problems associated with delays. Although the library may have the ultimate "right" to withdraw from a contract or assess damages on the basis of contractual provisions regarding vendor delays or postponements, such action should always be viewed as a last resort; both the vendor and the library will already have invested a tremendous amount of time and expense in a purchase. And if a system or enhancement is not implemented on time, all the contractual provisions in the world will not relieve the added stress for staff members already anxious about the new system, nor will it diminish the disappointment of others on the staff who are eagerly awaiting it. The way in which an automated project is presented to staff between the time of initial decision and the time of actual implementation is one of the most important factors in determining how smooth the transition to automation will be, and an important part of that preparation is dealing with the possibility of delays and initial problems in getting the system up and running.

6. *What is retrieved from a system must first be put in.* Among the most consistently underestimated factors in implementing an automated system are the time and effort required to convert manual data to machine-readable form. Whether for a mailing list maintained on a microcomputer or for a large-scale online catalog, appropriate data must be input before the system will be of any functional value. The conversion of manual records to machine-readable form is one of the most crucial aspects of library automation, and it is important that a library realistically assess the amount of time, effort, and coordination required for a conversion project and its associated costs. (Chapter 10 deals in greater detail with retrospective conversion of manual bibliographic records to machine-readable form.)

Depending on the approach to conversion and the type of automated system for which records will be created, another often unanticipated aspect of automation is the amount of effort required to clean up the machine-readable database after it has been loaded into a system or used to generate another product. This is particularly the case where a library has created its machine-readable database over the course of several years, such as many libraries using a bibliographic utility have done. Countless libraries have been horrified when they examine their records for the first time in a tangible product, such as a COM catalog or online in a circulation system or public-access catalog. Typographical errors, incorrect call numbers, obsolete forms of name and subject headings coexisting with current forms, records that did not accurately match any item in the library's collection, and items in the collection for which there were no records in the database are all maladies that can be expected when first examining the results of a large-scale conversion effort.

Because conventions of bibliographic description do change and because a library collection is dynamic rather than static, maintaining a database entails more than simply adding new records to it. Once the database has been created, and even after it has been cleaned up, it is still necessary to delete, modify, and otherwise maintain existing records to preserve integrity and consistency. The utility of an automated system will somewhat depend on the quality of the data in it, and quality can be maintained only through constant and careful attention.

7. *Machines do not work all the time.* Whether an automated system is used exclusively by library staff or in public service, a source of frustration will be unscheduled downtime, those periods when the system should be working but is not. Regardless of the type of system, its level of sophistication, or its costs, there will be such periods. A specification that libraries are often able to incorporate into contracts with turnkey system vendors is "guaranteed" 98 percent system uptime. This percentage may seem extremely high, but it is important for the library to realize the meaning of even as little as 2 percent downtime. If the library is open 80 hours per week, as an example, 2 percent downtime means that the system will not be functioning an average of 6 to 7 hours per month. Also, "downtime" as defined in many contracts refers only to periods during which the central processing unit is down. In addition to these periods, more localized downtime will occur when individual terminals are malfunctioning or when there are problems with telecommunications lines.

Whether a system is being used for technical or public service, a library should always have contingency plans for periods of unscheduled downtime. For strictly technical-services systems, terminal operators should have other duties that can be carried out when a system is down. Unfortunately, the tendency in many libraries has been to devise reserve activities that are either pure drudgery or whose sole purpose is to keep staff busy until the system comes back up. When that happens, the staff may actually come to resent the computer for being down. Tasks scheduled during downtime should be meaningful and necessary. When users are directly affected, the library should have a backup system or at least clearly established manual procedures that inconvenience patrons as little as possible. Some libraries with large-scale circulation systems frequently have microcomputer-based systems as a partial backup. Others rely on manual procedures. Some libraries with online public access catalogs periodically spin off COM versions for use in the event of long periods of downtime.

8. *Automated systems do not do everything that the library would like them to do.* When a library is investigating turnkey systems for automating any of its operations or services, it usually finds that no system on the market can do everything or has every feature that the library wants. Also, certain desirable features may be available but at additional costs beyond the library's resources. If a library is working with a local computer center on a project or design of a system, sacrifices may have to be made for the sake of saving time or costs.

Even though a system may not include everything that the library wanted at the outset, there will still be a certain excitement and enthusiasm upon installation. Staff members and library users without previous automation experience will be amazed at what the system can do and how quickly it improves operations or services. As the novelty wears off and the system is used more, staff and patrons will become increasingly aware not only of what the system can do, but of what it cannot do, and of additional features that could be added to improve it. Although still appreciated, the system that was first viewed as able to do so much becomes subject to more critical examination.

The realization that there is no ideal system and a growing awareness of shortcomings can lead to a certain amount of frustration for staff and/or patrons. If there is a positive side, it is that the ability to articulate inadequacies is an indication that users have progressed beyond the starry-eyed phase to a more realistic and critically evaluative grasp of automation in libraries. In the long run, this understanding may lead to improvements in system design.

In the case of vendor-supplied systems, the most glaring shortcomings as seen by one library will probably be similarly viewed by others using the same system. Most utilities and vendors have formal or informal user groups to suggest enhancements to their systems. Although actually instigating changes in a system can seem to be a hopelessly slow process, disenchantment can best be confronted if problems are dealt with openly, both within the library and in relating to users and to the library's vendor, utility, or computer center.

9. *There will always be a new or improved system available that is bigger, better, or less expensive than the one just purchased.* Because computer technology changes so quickly, the best value or state-of-the-art system at a given time is not likely to remain so for long. This is particularly true for newer technologies and in commercial environments that are still growing rapidly. The net effect of development and competition is

beneficial for the library as a consumer, but it does mean that there is always likely to be another system or service that is more sophisticated or a better per-dollar value than the one currently in place.

There is a natural reluctance to make a major investment in something that may seem outdated or of lesser value by comparison only a short time later. However, this reluctance should not be allowed to become the guiding consideration in a library's automation plans. In the first place, if anticipation of later developments is allowed to play too great a role, the result will be a continuous state of indecision. To be certain, better systems will become available. But as they do, expectations will likely increase proportionally, and the library may continue to find itself in the same predicament: There will always be something better just around the corner. Also, although the acquired system or service may be surpassed in the marketplace, it is still likely to be a significant improvement for several years over the manual or less sophisticated automated system it replaces. If not, the library should seriously consider why it wants to acquire a new system anyway.

In purchasing an automated system, libraries should indeed exercise caution and carefully assess the state of the applied art and changes that are likely to occur in the near future. This is particularly true with a new technology, major advance, or innovative application. Often the earliest systems or applications of a particular type will be dramatically improved on soon after as competition intensifies. But once a technology and market have reached a certain level of reliability and sophistication, it is important that planning and decision making not be indefinitely postponed in constant anticipation of possible new developments.

10. *Some people do not like computers.* In fact, some people passionately hate computers. For some, dislike is based on philosophical grounds, but for most these negative feelings stem from a lack of familiarity with the machines. Either way, such feelings are very real and usually very strong. The problems of computer fear and lack of familiarity are declining rapidly as a greater proportion of the population becomes knowledgeable about, or has grown up with, computers. But computer "literacy" is by no means universal, and libraries in the mid-1980s still have to deal with people who mistrust these machines and who seem almost to seek out computer mishaps to support their biases.

Although libraries certainly cannot overcome all mistrust and fear of computers among staff and users, it is important to avoid establishing policies and procedures that merely reinforce negative feelings. For library staff, preimplementation educational sessions and continuing training activities are crucial. As already noted, careful plans must be worked out for allocating meaningful staff work during periods of unscheduled computer downtime.

When library users are involved, friendly and adequate levels of assistance and effective backup systems or procedures can help to offset some of the frustration that patrons may experience when a system is not working properly. It is also very important that library staff not make the computer a scapegoat. A common phrase in libraries and elsewhere in responding to errors, for example, is that "the computer must have made a mistake." System malfunctions can, indeed, cause errors or loss of data, but a large proportion of what are commonly cited as computer mistakes are in fact the result of human errors in programming or in inputting or manipulating data. Not only is the responsibility misplaced in such cases, but in blaming everything on the computer, patrons can be even further alienated. For some library users, it will merely reinforce what may already be negative feelings. Other users who are more familiar with computers are likely to know better, and will see through the explanation as an attempt to foist blame on an innocent machine. In either case, the library is not doing itself or its patrons any favors in the area of public relations.

In addition to being straightforward about the source of mistakes when they occur, libraries should also establish policies that emphasize immediate resolution of errors that are in any way connected to a system, be they of human or machine origin. To explain to a library patron who has already had one bad experience with the computer that an error cannot be corrected until the end of the week or the end of the month because of updating procedures is merely adding insult to injury. Nearly all systems have override capabilities and other exception procedures, and these should be used when they can help to clear up problems expeditiously.

The issues raised here are some of the recurring themes that libraries commonly face in automation. In most cases, the problems they raise cannot altogether be avoided, but an awareness of their existence during the planning process can at least help to reduce the magnitude of their impact. Dealing with them in an open and straightforward manner can make the transition to an automated system or service much smoother for everyone involved.

Current Trends

The themes described so far have remained fairly constant over the past quarter-century. Some have changed more than others in degree of appropriateness, but all are still pertinent to library automation in the mid-1980s and should be kept in mind. Yet a library must also be aware of conditions and trends more specific to a present environment at a given time. An appreciation of these is crucial in developing a sound approach to automation and in exploring available options.

The current environment of library automation is extremely complex, the product of a whole range of interacting and constantly changing influences. Although it is impossible to isolate all of them, several of the more prevalent are examined below. Since so many libraries are turning to the commercial sector to meet their automation needs, the primary focus here is on trends within or in approaching that area.

The Funding Context

Whether venturing into the commercial marketplace or following another course, a most crucial hurdle for a library in pursuit of automation is to obtain the necessary funds. The cost of automating library operations varies widely, depending on application and scale. In many instances the development or purchase of a system or service means substantial capital outlay. In today's economic climate, large sums of money are not easily obtained by libraries. During the 1960s and part of the 1970s, many automation ventures were financed by grants, endowments, and comparatively generous allocations from parent bodies. Not that funding was ever easy to get, but the allocation of funds is even more competitive and closely scrutinized today, and it is likely to remain so through the decade.

Yet despite tighter funding, more libraries are automating now, with even larger scale systems, than ever before. One reason is that automation is more cost effective today. The costs of certain types of automation have not increased as rapidly as other goods and services, and for some applications have actually been decreasing. But large-scale automation of many library operations and services is still an expensive venture.

A less tangible but important factor behind the increased levels of funding is the increasing level of awareness and acceptance of computers throughout society in general. The 1960s and 1970s, although characterized by a more favorable financial climate, were a period of much more limited computer application in society at large, when computers were seen as the playthings of large corporations or institutions and the government. Libraries seeking funding for automation during those decades frequently had to first introduce their boards or other governing bodies to the basic concept of computerization, and only then move on to the next challenge of convincing them that the library actually needed such expensive and complex technology.

In the 1980s, when computers have come to be accepted much more as part of everyday life in so many endeavors, libraries are in a stronger position to lobby for automation. Just as librarians themselves have become more familiar with the actual and potential uses of computer technology, so have people on library boards and other governing bodies. There is no longer as great a need to educate nonlibrarian decision makers about the general concept of computerization, and bringing up the possibility of automating library operations or services is not likely to raise as many eyebrows as it used to. Boards and administrations still want justification, usually in financial terms, but they are likely to be initially more receptive than they would have been in the past. Given the economic climate, a library has to present its request convincingly, and there is still resistance from some quarters even about the basic concept of automating the library. But overall, the state of the technology, the number of available options, and the greater degree of familiarity with and acceptance of computerization have all combined to create a more favorable setting in the mid-1980s for obtaining funding for library automation than has ever existed before.

Commercial Market Expansion, Competition, and Choice

For all practical purposes, the commercial library automation market has existed only since the early 1970s. Before that, libraries were generally on their own in developing computer-based systems or services. Through the late 1970s and even later for many types of applications, commercial options were few, and many libraries continued to rely on local computer centers for development of automated systems.

But the situation has changed dramatically in the 1980s. As automation has come within realistic grasp of more libraries, the commercial market has expanded and competition has increased. In addition to more libraries automating, there has been constant advance in microcomputer technology. Library systems used to need large mainframe computers or minicomputers, making automation an expensive venture primarily open to larger institutions. With the advent of the microcomputer and the ever-increasing development of micro-based library applications and software packages, automation is now feasible for small libraries as well. With minicomputers for larger libraries and microcomputers for much smaller ones, probably the least served market right now is the medium-size library, such as on most four-year college campuses. This is the size of library that—on an individual basis at least—still cannot easily afford the bigger minicomputer-based systems, but whose collection or circulation activity is too much for most microcomputer-based systems. In some cases this void has been filled through joint ventures involving the sharing of a larger system among several libraries, and it is likely to be further overcome in the near future by more powerful micro-based systems. The implications of these two trends and their interaction are discussed in greater detail later.

Among vendors of all sizes of systems, the source of products and services currently available is an interesting blend of commercial and library development. Some vendors have developed their own systems from the start. But among others, the development of a system for, or even by, an individual library has played a key role. The entry of several vendors has been predicated on the generalization of a system they developed under contract for a single library. This was the basis for the entry of Data Research Associates into the broader turnkey market, and more recently for the Sedna Corporation and Sirsi Corporation with its UNICORN turnkey system.

In other instances, a commercial vendor has arranged for marketing rights to a system whose applications software was initially designed by the library or its local computer center. The VTLS system, developed at Virginia Tech, is an example. After spending a couple of years marketing VTLS, Virginia Tech transferred marketing rights to Hewlett Packard, on whose equipment the system was originally designed to run. A similar situation is Sperry's marketing of the online public access catalog developed by the Minnesota State University System Project for Automated Library Systems (sometimes referred to as the Mankato State System). The hardware manufacturer link exemplifying both of these examples is not characteristic of all such vendor/library arrangements. The UNIFACE system developed at the Tacoma Public Library, for instance, is now being marketed by Midwest Library Service, a company traditionally more involved in providing library services. Yet another variation is the emergence of new commercial firms founded by former employees of a library who were responsible for designing an in-house system. The systems offered commercially by the new firms differ from those designed at the library, but the expertise is clearly carried over from one location to another, and there is sometimes a marked resemblance among the features of the two. An example is Carlyle Systems, formed by some of the principals in the design of the University of California's MELVYL system.

In contrast to these examples, several libraries have opted to vend their systems themselves rather than through an arrangement with a commercial firm. This is particularly so for a number of library-designed microcomputer software packages, but it applies to some much larger systems as well, including software developed for large-scale systems at Northwestern University, Pennsylvania State University, the Georgetown University Medical Center Library, the Washington University School of Medicine Library, and Pueblo Library District in Colorado. In some of these cases, marketing efforts have been highly organized; in others they have been far less formal.

The number of specific systems mentioned here could easily be doubled or tripled even in terms of just the larger scale systems commercially available. They are noted simply as examples of the many sources from which, and arrangements through which, automated library systems have emerged on the market.

Overall, the very active marketplace resulting from these types of ventures and arrangements works strongly to the advantage of libraries. There is a broader range of products from which to chose. The greater level of competition helps to keep down prices and leads to development of better systems, more sophisticated features, and greater attention on the part of vendors to enhancing their systems. Against this background, expansion of the market also makes it imperative that a library develop a well-organized approach to evaluating its general options for automation and the specific products available. Without such care, the library will fail to take the fullest possible advantage of the opportunities brought on by increased competition and choice. The library must have a clear idea of what is needed and why, and then examine the available products within the framework of these criteria. Establishing evaluative and comparative criteria for a variety of applications is examined in detail in later chapters. But, in general, libraries have more opportunities and a broader range of options for automation than ever before. Careful planning and a well-organized evaluation effort are essential to making the most of a favorable environment.

Single-purpose/Multipurpose Systems: Integration and Interfacing

In the late 1970s, the following scenario was typical of a library with an extensive level of automation. The library used a bibliographic utility as its automated cataloging system. Its online circulation system was supplied by a turnkey vendor, running on a minicomputer housed in the library. The automated serials control system was locally developed and running on the parent institution's mainframe computer. The acquisitions system might have been automated in a similar fashion, although the library might instead have been using a batch processing system provided through its major book jobber. In the public services area, the library may have replaced or supplemented its card catalog with a COM catalog. It was performing online reference database searches for patrons through such services as DIALOG, BRS, and SDC. For interlibrary loan, it used computer-generated union lists of serials and its bibliographic utility to determine locations for items not held in its own collection. Requests to borrow at least some of these materials were probably being sent to other libraries via TWX.

Even by today's standards, this "typical" library had a wide range of automated operations and services. It used at least half a dozen, most requiring separate and distinct pieces of equipment. Other than possibly having an interface connected between its bibliographic utility and turnkey circulation system, and using the tapes from its utility as a basis for production of a COM catalog, the various systems would operate entirely independently of one another and with a separate database for each system. With those two exceptions, it would be necessary to rekey data for any materials for which information was needed in different databases.

Even today, some libraries have continued to pursue the course of using different systems for different sets of operations, although some of the specifics have changed. The library may have begun to use an online serials control system, either by purchasing a single-purpose, stand-alone system or by using a system available through a serials subscription agent. Its acquisitions system is also likely to be online, either through its book jobber, bibliographic utility, or on a single-purpose, stand-alone acquisitions system. The COM catalog may have been replaced by an online catalog developed through the library's computer center, and interlibrary loan requests are most likely transmitted via an electronic mail service or through the interlibrary loan communications subsystem of its bibliographic utility.

But in addition to this approach to automation, there has been another significant trend in recent years: The evolution, as an option in commercially available products, of multipurpose integrated systems. Integrated systems attempt to address two of the main problems in using a series of single-purpose systems: the need for many different types of equipment and the necessity of re-entering much of the same data for the same items into different databases.

Integrated systems have long been a popular goal in library automation. There were a few automated systems developed by libraries even in the 1960s that achieved a certain level of integration, especially in technical processing applications, but these were generally locally designed and not commercially available. During the 1970s, the realization of one goal—reducing data-entry duplication—expanded a bit further. Much of the progress centered on the use of the library's machine-readable records created through its cataloging activity on a bibliographic utility. These institution-specific records, provided on tape, could be loaded into an automated circulation system, used to generate a COM catalog, contributed to a union list project, and used for other purposes. Some enterprising companies developed electronic interfaces that allowed on-line direct transfer of data from a bibliographic utility to systems, thus bypassing the need for tapeloading. Although these developments did help to incorporate use of the same data into more than one system, the systems themselves and their functional aspects remained largely separate for most libraries. Direct transfer of data from one system to another was, at best, an example of the interfacing of systems rather than truly the integration of their functions into a single system.

During the 1980s, there has been a greater move toward integrating a variety of library functions into a single system. In some cases, this has focused on a broad category of operations, such as technical services. Each bibliographic utility has an acquisitions module to complement its cataloging component, and OCLC has continued to maintain a serials control capability first introduced during the mid-1970s. Many well-established vendors of circulation systems have also taken this direction. Some newer vendors have introduced smaller systems designed to handle combinations of cataloging, acquisitions, serials control, and circulation.

If we include circulation, the above examples demonstrate a trend toward integration of activities having to do with technical services. Equally important in this regard has been incorporation of capabilities that obscure traditional divisions between technical operations and the public services. This was one of the most important consequences of the interactive interlibrary loan subsystems developed by several bibliographic utilities during the late 1970s and early 1980s. No longer were these utilities simply technical processing systems with interlibrary loan locations as a passive by-product. With the introduction of communications subsystems, interactive data manipulation on the utilities extended beyond technical services applications.

Most commercial vendors, in addition to integrating circulation, acquisitions, a cataloging capability, and sometimes serials control, have also added a public-access-catalog module to their systems. In shared arrangements among several libraries, some systems allow a librarian or patron in one facility to charge out an item in another library, thus becoming an enhanced version of an interlibrary communications system. At least a few of the systems also allow dial-up access to services such as DIALOG and BRS on the same terminals that are used for internal operations.

Both multipurpose systems, which have been much in vogue, and single-purpose systems have strengths and weaknesses. A multipurpose system will generally be less expensive than a series of separate single-purpose systems performing the same functions. There will probably be additional savings in time and cost, and an overall increase in efficiency, because a single database rather than several is maintained. An integrated multipurpose system becomes a tool around which many traditional but somewhat artificial distinctions between various operations within a library can be broken down a bit.

Favorable as these points may be, a library takes some risks with the multipurpose approach. Most of them involve being locked into a single system developed by a single vendor. This is particularly risky when not all appropriate modules are fully operational on a system that the library buys. For example, many commercially available integrated systems do not yet have an operational serials check-in-module. By making a commitment to automate on a multipurpose system, a library in such a case must simply wait and hope that the check-in component will suit its needs.

Even if a purchased system already includes a module for just about every desired routine application, the library is still locking itself in. As discussed later in detail, at some time the library may want or need to replace one automated system with another—difficult to do with a single multipurpose system.

Another problem involves the design of a system that tries to do so many things at once. With a multipurpose system, the vendor may not give all modules the same priority. As a result, some modules may receive less attention in design and development even to the point that they are not as adequate and far less sophisticated than single-purpose systems designed to perform roughly the same operations.

Although designers of integrated systems may argue that point, it is interesting that some vendors are now seeking alternatives to the "one source, one system, all functions" goal. Geac, for example, announced an agreement with Faxon, allowing users to access Faxon's serial's check-in system through their Geac terminals and to download serials holdings from Faxon into the Geac system. In a somewhat different arrangement, UTLAS and CLSI now have a joint marketing agreement. It gives CLSI a more direct association with a large shared cataloging database than it has ever had. UTLAS gains an association with a vendor of a system that includes circulation and an online public access catalog module, functions that UTLAS itself never developed. For UTLAS, such agreements are not new. The Canadian utility had much earlier agreed to market portions of the acquisitions and serials control systems of Innovative Interfaces.

These examples mainly concern integrated multipurpose systems, but they also point up the trend toward "intervendor" agreements and projects. There are others. For example, Carrollton Press and Blackwell/North America (BNA) announced that records from Carrollton's REMARC database can now be run through BNA's authority control system less expensively than if the library went to BNA independently. And OCLC has made agreements with other vendors as an alternative to strictly internal development in some areas. The most important of these has been in abandoning development of OCLC's ill-fated "Local

Library System" in favor of agreements with two firms for already developed systems.

All of these examples demonstrate a certain flexibility in direction of development and something of a backing off from the general commercial philosophy of the early 1980s that a single vendor could develop a virtually complete system offering the best components for all applications. Libraries might want to take note of this trend and its implications for their own approach to automation.

The separate single-purpose system has remained a viable approach to automation in the 1980s, but it is still plagued by some of the same obstacles of the past. In particular, it is unlikely that the library can fully interface all of the separate systems. It might be able to interface a bibliographic utility with all or some of the other systems, but interfacing the other systems with one another is less likely. This means that some amount of duplicate keying will be necessary, and that will mean some degree of inconsistency between records for the same items in different databases. Until this obstacle is overcome, single-purpose systems will remain somewhat inefficient in terms of a library's overall automation plan.

In today's environment, then, the library that wants to automate several of its operations with commercial systems has three major options. It can implement a single system to handle all operations, recognizing the pros—financial savings and database management efficiency—and the cons—unavailability of some modules at present, locking into one vendor and one system, and possible uneven sophistication among modules. Or, the library can use different single-purpose systems, a more expensive option and less efficient regarding data entry and database management. These shortcomings may be overcome by interface devices, but the library should be careful to consider the extent to which interface is practically feasible. The third option is that a library need not necessarily consider multipurpose versus single-purpose systems as an either/or decision. For certain applications, all or some of the modules of a multipurpose system might be used. For others, a separate single-purpose system might be used with the further possibility that it might be interfaced with the multipurpose system. As with the second option, the library must be careful to determine the extent to which interface will be possible.

There is no one approach that will be best for all libraries in all circumstances. For this crucial decision, however, the library must examine all possibilities with regard to its own conditions, opportunities, and limits. Particularly in evaluating integrated systems, the library must not only examine a given system as an overall unit, but must also scrutinize each module to see how well it will handle the particular operations for which it was designed.

Shared Systems

One of the most visible trends during the 1980s has been the sharing of automated systems by libraries. To greater or lesser extent, libraries have entered into multi-institutional projects in automation since the 1960s. During the 1970s, such projects took on a more concrete aspect in the formation and growth of the online bibliographic utilities, in the publication of computer-generated union lists and statewide COM catalogs, and in joint purchase and use of online circulation systems. The trend has accelerated during the 1980s, with a rapid area of growth in the sharing of circulation systems, many of which are doubling as online public-access catalogs.

In 1983, Joe Matthews estimated that as many as 65 percent of the operating large-scale commercial turnkey systems were being used by more than one library.[2] Through that year and into 1984, the joint purchase and use of these systems continued. Perhaps the most significant recent example is the issuance of a Request for Proposal by the New York Public Library, Brooklyn Public Library, and Queens Borough Public Library for the joint purchase of an integrated system; at the estimated cost of $10 million, this exceeds the annual income of all but about two or three of the largest turnkey library automation vendors! The size of the New York project may be exceptional, but there are other current examples of groups of libraries jointly purchasing minicomputer-based systems. Although there is no clearly defined optimum number of participants for sharing a system, limits are usually defined by capacity requirements and telecommunications costs.

For the library that chooses to enter into a group arrangement for the purchase and use of an automated system, the effort can require a different perspective on planning and decision making than in most other cooperative activities. For certain types of applications such as these, the sharing of larger scale systems usually enables the participating libraries to automate less expensively than if each were to purchase its own system. In the process, it also enables smaller libraries to automate those applications far sooner than would otherwise be the case.

Although libraries have long cooperated with one another, many of the traditional forms of cooperation could be carried out with fairly little impact on the individual library's internal policies, procedures, and decision-making processes. But sharing an automated system requires a far more formal approach. In some situations, a single library may develop or purchase a system and then seek additional libraries to tie into it, but in many other cases, there is mutual participation from the outset. Either way, the participants are likely to lose some of their individual autonomy in decision making. The selection of a system, for example, is not based on an individual library's choice, but on a consensus of a group of libraries. The participants may also feel that certain policies or procedures should be closely parallel in the libraries in order to make the sharing function more effective. There may also be an advantage to standardizing certain bibliographic and data-entry practices in creating machine-readable records so that the system can more easily merge or manipulate those records. All these factors and others imply that each participant may have to surrender a certain degree of individuality and local decision-making independence. Based on current evidence, many libraries are willing to do so in order to realize the financial and other benefits of joint ventures in library automation.

Will the trend toward shared systems continue as strongly as before? Technological developments are bound to complicate what have been some fairly clear economic advantages in sharing a system. As noted earlier, for certain sizes of libraries, sharing has been the only financially realistic option for automating such functions as circulation and the public catalog. But during the next few years, advances in microcomputer development and reductions in computing power-per-dollar costs may make micro-based systems powerful and affordable enough to interest single libraries of this intermediate size. That possibility, combined with likely increases in ground data transmission costs, may unseat the shared system as the only or even most appropriate solution for intermediate-size libraries to automate certain functions. Other developments such as the optical disk might also affect this option.

Besides the option of shared systems as the most cost-effective solution, additional considerations such as resource sharing will be important in deciding on an approach to automation. Because of resource sharing, as well as the general uncertainty about the direction of technological developments and how they will interact with one another, it is premature to write off shared large-scale systems as a viable approach, but libraries should be aware of the trends that in the not-too-distant future may change the picture considerably.

Localization of Shared Cataloging Databases

A curious aspect of the trend toward the shared multipurpose system is that, while broadening the geographic scope of a library's participation in most types of automated activities, it may eventually narrow it in others. For functions like circulation control and the public catalog, shared systems clearly result in a broader level of networking. But for one other function at least, the sharing of multipurpose systems may eventually narrow the scope of some libraries' participation in cooperative automation. This function is the sharing of basic bibliographic records, what might be called a "shared cataloging database."

Since the 1970s, the predominant way to share basic bibliographic records has been through participation in bibliographic utilities—OCLC, RLIN, WLN, and UTLAS. Outside of circulation control and the public catalog, there has been rather widespread commitment to these systems as the most appropriate way to create, share, and obtain basic bibliographic information.

The bibliographic utilities, in general, are alive, relatively well, and still growing, but there have been increasing signs that the overall commitment to these systems is no longer so solid. Formal reports at statewide and smaller group levels have been recommending that cooperating libraries turn to locally shared, multipurpose systems as the highest level at which to share a basic bibliographic database, rather than participate in the more broadly based utilities.

To date, libraries in most of the groups that have turned to the more localized approach were never members of a utility anyway. But even among those groups whose members have participated in a utility, there are indications of a rethinking about the most economical and most efficient level at which to venture into a shared cataloging database. Few libraries or groups have as yet actually abandoned participation in a utility for a shared multipurpose system, but the mere fact that the possibility is being more openly and seriously examined is itself significant. And unlike a few years ago, large multipurpose systems are now in place in a number of locations that easily have the technological capability to serve as regional, state, and local alternatives to the utilities.

Although this issue has practical implications for libraries investigating automation, it has a more philosophical side as well. If a strong trend toward more localized "highest level" shared cataloging databases does take hold, it could eventually have significant repercussions for bibliographic control, documentation, and resource sharing on a broader scale. It is still too early to determine whether a concrete trend will develop away from participation in the utilities as a consequence of the use of more localized shared multipurpose systems. But for libraries examining the locally shared system, the short-term benefits should be weighed against participation in resource and bibliographic sharing on a broader level.

Remote Processing

Whether in systems used in a single library or in those shared among several libraries, an important trend in automated library system development is the remote processing function.With this capability, a library has access to a centrally stored database, housed in a computer either within or outside the library, but performing at least part of its data processing activity on local terminals rather than entirely through the central system. The result is a reduction in message traffic going through the central system, and this can have positive consequences for response time in carrying out other types of transactions that must interact directly with the central system. In addition, sometimes a reduction in telecommunications expense is possible.

Remote processing capabilities have already been incorporated into some commercially available integrated systems, as well as into some of the bibliographic utilities. CLSI, for example, has a terminal that allows certain basic record maintenance functions to be carried out on it rather than interactively through the central computer. Records are downloaded from the central database onto disk, modified in a local terminal mode, and then batch-transmitted in their revised form back to the central system. Record editing can consume considerable resources when carried out interactively on the central unit, and reallocating much of this work to a local terminal can reduce total message traffic and can therefore result in improved response time for carrying out other functions, such as circulation and public access, through the main computer.

The CLSI capability has implications even for a system used in a single library, but another example of remote processing draws on a bibliographic utility whose main computers are used by virtually thousands of libraries. Since early 1984, OCLC has been introducing a series of "microenhancer" software packages for use on its M300 workstation, a modified IBM Personal Computer. These packages serve much the same purpose as CLSI's remote processing capability. With the cataloging microenhancer, for example, an OCLC library is able to key numerical search keys—such as Library of Congress Card Numbers—onto a disk on its M300 workstation and then batch-transmit the search keys to the main OCLC computers. The OCLC database is then automatically searched, and bibliographic records matching the numerical search keys are batch-transmitted back to the library and downloaded onto disk. The library then edits the records—adding specific locations, modifying call numbers, subject headings, and the like—and then batch-transmits the modified records back to the main computers for card and tape production. Response time is much faster in the local mode than through OCLC's main computers. The use of the microenhancer packages also enables a library to spend less overall time in direct online connection to the main computers, and for some OCLC libraries, that reduction is enough to replace their leased-line connection with dial-access participation through a packet-switching network and actually realize a savings in telecommunications expense.

By removing certain data manipulation tasks from a central to a local unit, this approach to processing can improve overall efficiency and system performance and at the same time reduce expenses, at least in some cases. Remote processing is likely to be incorporated into more commercially available systems in the near future. It may eventually provide a critical bridge linking participation in broader nationwide systems with use of more localized shared and strictly local single-library systems.

System Obsolescence and Replacement

Something that very few libraries consider when purchasing a system is the possibility of eventually having to replace it with another. In the commercial marketplace, vendors of automated systems have made concerted efforts to continually upgrade equipment and introduce software enhancements, a competitive necessity. They have also been careful to revise their systems to build on previously existing hardware and software, rather than totally revamping a system to the point where it is incompatible with what has already been installed. This approach makes a great deal of sense for both vendors and libraries. The library is able to upgrade its system so that it does not become competitively outdated in hardware or software capabilities, and the vendor is able to retain a customer base through the years.

Large-scale automated turnkey systems are simply too recent a phenomenon, however, to project how long this strategy can continue to be viable. There may come a point, for example, when drastic changes in hardware are warranted by the state of the technology. With software that had its origins several years in the past, each revision becomes increasingly complex. And the growing complexity of the programs just serves to limit the direction and magnitude in which still further changes can be made.[3]

In time, continual revision of systems now in place may no longer be cost effective or competitively viable. If so, a vendor will have to design and introduce a new system that might differ significantly from the old. That might mean a cutback on equipment upgrades and software enhancement for the older systems. Commercial library automation vendors have thus far very strongly resisted an obsolescence approach to system design, but will this stance hold up through probable significant advances in technology during the last half of the decade?

It may be too early to tell about obsolescence, but other factors for some libraries may dictate replacing one system with another. To date, most replacements have been motivated by extremely strained library/vendor relations or by other exceptional circumstances. Whatever the motivating factor, libraries need to recognize the possibility that they may wish to, or need to, replace even a very large system someday. When viewed in this perspective, the planning process for library automation becomes not a one-time event, but a long-range continuing process.

Especially for the library looking toward the commercial market as its likely source of automated products and services, the mid-1980s promises complex and sometimes almost contradictory trends. The marketplace is clearly more competitive than at any time in the past and there are certainly more options, but there are no simple answers to such questions as single-purpose versus multipurpose systems, shared versus single-library systems, and level of participation in sharing basic bibliographic information. Remote processing and linking of systems developments may be important in finding the most effective solutions to these questions, but no one yet can tell exactly how great or in what form the impact of these trends will be. A significant influence is bound to involve the directions in which certain key technologies develop. The rest of this chapter examines three of the most significant of these technologies: microcomputers, optical disk, and telecommunications.

Microcomputers in the Library

Microcomputers are a comparatively recent phenomenon. The first fully assembled models became commercially available in 1977 and were aimed primarily at hobbyist and entertainment markets. Processing capabilities were limited and storage capacity extremely low, insufficient for any serious business application. But even at that time, the implications were apparent, and developments in the technology have been greatly pronounced ever since.

As with most new technologies, microcomputers had their share of early growing pains. Lack of standards in an extremely competitive and fast-moving industry has resulted in compatibility problems, and the microcomputer industry in its earliest years was characterized by some of the same software problems encountered in the early stages of the minicomputer industry, namely, lack of adequate commercial software in terms of quantity and quality. For most microcomputer applications, the situation with respect to quantity of software has certainly changed, but the growth in the number of packages available has been accompanied by a wide range in quality.

Also characteristic of most new technologies, early expectations about microcomputers often exceeded actual capabilities. However, microcomputer technology has advanced so rapidly that general improvements and increased capabilities have not lagged far behind the early expectations. The earliest commercial microcomputers were based around a 4-bit microprocessor. This quickly gave way to 8-bit architecture, followed by 16-bit, and in 1984 the 32-bit microprocessor was found in a number of models. These major advances have translated into increased capability and speed. Within the library field, there was a time when visions of microcomputer applications for large-scale bibliographic database management and processing operations were premature and lacking in appreciation of the then limited capabilities of low-priced, popularly advertised machines. Secondary storage capacity for microcomputers was, not too long ago, so limited that one could not really talk in terms of bibliographic file applications except for very, very small libraries. And unless a library wrote its own applications programs, there were very few library-specific software packages available anyway.

All this has been changing rapidly during the past few years. Librarians have come to a clearer understanding of the relationship between bibliographic database requirements, microcomputer capabilities, and costs, but the technology itself has been making such quantum advances that some of the original expectations may have only been slightly ahead of their time. And the pace of development in microcomputer technology is not likely to slacken in the very near future. Such prefixes as "micro" and "mini" are already extremely ambiguous when applied to computers, and they are likely to become even more so in the next few years, at least by today's standards.

Libraries have generally kept pace with the rest of society in cradling microcomputers to assist in a wide variety of purposes. It is not a question of whether micros will come into common use in libraries, for they already have. The question, rather, is the breadth of purpose for which they will be used and the impact they will have on the total environment of library automation and on trends in the library automation marketplace. There is already a large body of library-oriented literature devoted to microcomputers, ranging from articles, to books, even to several periodicals devoted specifically to microcomputer developments and applications in libraries. The content of this literature ranges from announcements and discussion of technical developments and new models of equipment, to strategies for purchasing hardware and software, to descriptions of various types of applications and reviews of specific software packages.

The discussion cannot deal even cursorily with all of the many aspects of microcomputers that are pertinent to libraries. Rather, what follows is a brief overview of some of the major categories of applications for which libraries have been using microcomputers. Advances in the technology will have profound implications for the exact manner and scale of applicability in the future, but these areas are likely to remain among the most important types of microcomputer applications in libraries.

General Administrative Uses

Librarians have long been accustomed to viewing computerization in terms of its implications for handling bibliographic data. With the microcomputer, this has been changing. There are a number of administrative functions, for example, that can be streamlined with the use of a microcomputer. One of the most popular is in conjunction with word processing applications. Although the word processing software packages available for microcomputers are not generally as sophisticated as those used in dedicated word processing machines, an important advantage of the microcomputer is its versatility. Word processing is only one of many functions that a microcomputer can perform, whereas dedicated word processing systems are usually more singular in purpose. For word processing applications in most libraries, microcomputers suffice quite well.

At its most elementary level, word processing on a microcomputer can replace just about any administrative function for which a typewriter has traditionally been used. This includes correspondence, internal memoranda, staff reports, and library newsletters. The main difference between word processing on a microcomputer and using a typewriter is in the text-editing capabilities of the former. Text can be stored on disk and when corrections or other revisions are required, only the affected portion need be modified and a new copy of the page or document printed. This saves considerable time by eliminating the need to retype a page entirely because of minor typographical errors, omission of words, or subsequent revision to text. The use of a microcomputer for word processing is especially appropriate in this regard for preparing drafts of documents that are almost certain to need revision. The file for a document can also be built nonsequentially, rather than having to type it in the order that it will appear in its final form as is usually necessary using a conventional typewriter. This is a handy feature for formal reports, library newsletters, and other applications in which different individuals may be responsible for submitting different parts of a document.

An application related to and sometimes used in conjunction with word processing is the creation and maintenance of various kinds of patron and specialized mailing lists. These lists often require constant additions, deletions, and changes, and are therefore well suited to handling on a microcomputer. There are software packages available that allow these lists to be used along with word processing functions to provide personalized correspondence to library users, potential supporters, and so on.

In addition to word processing and mailing lists, there are a number of administrative operations that can take advantage of computational and accounting software packages for use with microcomputers. One is the electronic spreadsheet, ideal for work such as budgeting that is likely to undergo constant computational changes before it is in final form. The spreadsheet can reduce the time spent in making revisions and analyzing their overall impact on a budget by instantaneously recalculating the entire budget after even a single change is made in the raw data.

The range of applications of microcomputers for general administrative purposes in a library is probably about as broad as the range of those purposes themselves. The number-handling capabilities of a microcomputer make it a convenient tool for sorting, manipulating, and helping to analyze a wide range of library statistics, including circulation, interlibrary loan, and reference queries. Libraries have developed programs ranging in purpose from staff scheduling, to inventory control for equipment and supplies, to personnel records and payroll. A microcomputer is thus a valuable tool in libraries for a much broader set of applications than just those pertaining to manipulating bibliographic data. There are many types of administrative operations in a library that are similar to those in other organizations, and it is in relation to these that some of the most outstanding benefits of a microcomputer may be realized in a library.

Public-Services Applications

A number of libraries are putting microcomputers to work in their public-services departments. Some focus on building databases containing information that may have been previously maintained in manual form. Public libraries in particular have used microcomputers to maintain a wide variety of community information databases, public events calendars, career information files, and employment listings. Some libraries circulate microcomputer software packages to patrons much as any other media, and there are a number of public libraries that even circulate the microcomputers themselves. More common, however, has been simply for libraries to provide public-access microcomputers for on-site use, on which patrons can schedule time and use their own software programs or those made available by the library. Because of the level of demand, many libraries do find it necessary to schedule access time very carefully, often imposing a maximum length of time a user may reserve during one session or collectively during a week. Restrictions are sometimes put on certain uses, such as videogames. These practices differ among libraries but are usually a response to the level of demand.

Widely varying levels of service are offered in support of public-access microcomputers. Some libraries have installed public-access machines with minimum staff support available, an approach much the same as when a new photocopy machine is introduced. This has not always proved entirely satisfactory, as the library patrons who might be most interested in using the machines are also the ones least likely to be knowledgeable about them. At the other end of the spectrum, some libraries have initiated rather extensive projects to foster computer literacy. Special classes are offered, taught either by library staff or others. These libraries also try to ensure that some of their public-services personnel are knowledgeable enough about microcomputers to assist users for at least certain types of queries.

A library that plans to initiate such services, and especially to develop in-house expertise among a number of staff, should not underestimate the magnitude of this undertaking. It will require time to train the staff and thereafter to assist users. If these extra activities are incorporated into an already too busy schedule, what can only follow is frustration on the part of both library staff and users. Careful planning is extremely important if an extensive level of support service is to be provided.

One of the decisions involved in providing public-access microcomputers is whether to charge for use. Some libraries do not levy any rental fees, feeling that access to microcomputers is a public service function like many others. Many libraries do, however, charge a rental fee for use of a machine. Some very simple coin-operated devices for attachment to microcomputers can be purchased for under $100; more elaborate models cost from several hundred dollars and up into the thousands. In most cases, libraries charge a rate equivalent to $2 to $3 per hour, with access usually available in increments ranging from 10 minutes to an hour. The fees collected are often earmarked to help defer the cost of equipment, to be applied toward purchase of additional microcomputers or software packages, or to support collection development in the area of microcomputing.

Terminals and Communication Devices

One of the clearest examples of the versatility of microcomputers is that, in addition to many strictly local applications, they can be used to communicate with larger computers and with other microcomputers for a wide variety of purposes. One use of microcomputers as terminals connected to larger systems is described in the section on remote processing earlier in this chapter. By using micros in this fashion, some of the processing burden can be removed from a larger central unit, potentially resulting in better response time and lower telecommunications costs. Most of the bibliographic utilities have begun to use microcomputers for this purpose, as have some of the vendors of larger turnkey integrated systems.

Libraries are also employing micros to access databases available through retrieval services like DIALOG, BRS, and SDC. By using appropriate software, libraries can upload searches and download, reformat, and print results in a form that might be more attractive to the end user, and in the process realize at least nominal savings in telecommunications expense. Although downloading from such services may seem to open up a variety of interesting possibilities, it is important to realize that there is much more at issue here than simply the technological capability. Downloading and the end use of captured data may in some cases be in violation of contractual agreements or applicable copyright law, and libraries wishing to download data from these services should verify that such practices are permitted, under what conditions, and for what purposes.

In addition to interacting with larger computers, libraries can use microcomputers to communicate with one another for such purposes as transmission of interlibrary loan requests and other messages. Colorado, Kansas, Montana, and New York are among several states that have begun to replace other types of equipment with microcomputers in formal state interlibrary loan networks. While such use in this application does not differ appreciably from the way in which earlier equipment—such as teletype machines and teleprinters with cassette recorders—was used, the advantage of microcomputers is their versatility. When not being used in networking, they may be employed in other ways, as described earlier.

Bibliographic Processing and Catalog Applications

Administration, public access, and networking are important applications of microcomputers in libraries, but one of the major concerns is their suitability for handling bibliographic processing and catalog functions. Library files generally require a rather significant amount of storage space, up to several hundred bytes per record, depending on the application. Early microcomputers were simply not powerful enough to accommodate bibliographic files of more than a few hundred or, at most, a few thousand records. Some libraries forged ahead anyway, concentrating on limited applications, such as reserve room circulation, film bookings, and catalogs of small special collections. Commercial bibliographic applications software was scarce, and libraries generally had to write their own programs. Although the paucity of readily available software had its down side, it also had some positive consequences in serving as an impetus for librarians to learn to write computer code and apply it in the context of everyday activities.

As storage capacity and processing speed improved, microcomputers can now effectively handle much larger files of bibliographic data compared with even two to three years ago. Along with this increasing sophistication has come a proliferation of software designed to handle such applications as cataloging, acquisitions, serials control, circulation, and the public catalog.

The multitude of software packages available and their prices can seem confusing. For example, a "circulation" software package can be purchased for under $100, but some sell for $20,000 and up. Adding hardware requirements to the cost of the software, microcomputer-based systems for conventional bibliographic processing operations can range in price from a few thousand dollars to more than $100,000. A closer look shows that these so differently priced packages are, not surprisingly, much different in terms of functional capabilities and size of library for which they are designed. Some are appropriate for the very small library and are predicated on the use of floppy disks and a single terminal to handle a few hundred or few thousand records; others have the capacity to host many terminals and to process tens of thousands, and even hundreds of thousands, of records.

The most compelling consideration for the library investigating microcomputer potential for technical processing or public catalog applications is capacity, for this will essentially determine availability and overall cost of a system. In addition, and regardless of projected use for a very small library or a much larger one, microcomputer packages for library processing should be scrutinized according to the same criteria for evaluating software, whether it is to run on a mainframe, minicomputer, or microcomputer. Many of the microcomputer packages designed for very small libraries are nowhere nearly as functionally sophisticated as those intended for larger systems, but even the small packages show considerable variation. As a basis for comparison, the library requiring even a very small package should be aware of the range of functional characteristics useful for a particular application.

What types of packages are available for bibliographic processing and catalog applications on microcomputers and what are the general range of costs? With the exception of a few larger turnkey microcomputer-based systems, most bibliographic applications software is appropriate for smaller libraries of up to about 30,000 volumes, and many of the packages have been designed specifically with school and special libraries in mind. Although the distinctions are vague, most micro-based bibliographic processing software currently available can be grouped into three categories: packages designed for collections of only a few thousand volumes, those aimed at libraries of between about 10,000 and 30,000 volumes, and those designed for use in systems up to 100,000 or more volumes.

The focus for the small facilities has primarily been on packages to assist in producing catalog cards and in circulation. Card production is facilitated by enabling a full set of cards for a title to be generated on a printer on the basis of a unit catalog entry keyed onto disk. Although very simple, these programs obviate the need to photocopy unit cards and individually type headings onto them. A number of these also include routines for producing spine labels, book pockets, and book cards. These packages are generally priced between $100 and $250, with some less than $100 and a few as high as $500 to $600. Some recent examples of microcomputer-based card production packages include Catalog Card Maker (Winnebago), Quick Card (Library Software Company), Card (Capital Systems Group), Cardpro, Ultracard (Small Library Computing), Cardmaker (Hugh Starke), TeleMARC III (Catalog Card Corporation), and Booktrak (Follett). A micro-based service unlike any of these is LSSI's Micro-MARC. Using a microcomputer, the library enters search keys onto disk and batch-transmits them to a host computer housed at LSSI, whereupon matching full bibliographic records are found in the LC MARC database. Cards are then produced for the matching titles and mailed to the library.

Probably the greatest diversity of available software is for circulation functions. A number of elementary packages designed for small libraries use floppy disks. The primary purpose is to facilitate detection of overdues and preparation of overdue notices. These packages invariably use an absence-based approach to circulation, meaning that no bibliographic or patron records are kept permanently on file. Rather, the circulation attendant must key in abbreviated item and patron identification for each charge. When an item is returned, both elements of the transaction record—patron ID and item ID—are purged from the file. Few of these smaller packages can accept or monitor holds; some have a fine calculation function. They are generally designed for libraries with about 500 to 2,000 items in circulation at any one time and may range in price from less than $100 up to $250 for software only. Most vendors of these packages do not sell the hardware on which the software is used. It is up to the library to acquire the appropriate configuration. Examples of circulation software packages in this category include Bookworm (J. C. Hammett Company), Circulation Management System (Orchard Systems), Date Due (William L. Brown), Library (Gerald Noser), Overdue Materials Record (Minnesota Computer), and Overdue Writer (Library Software Company).

A number of circulation programs are aimed at slightly larger libraries, in about the 10,000- to 30,000-volume range. Many are significantly more sophisticated than the packages for small facilities. Usually requiring the use of at least a 5 Megabyte (Mb) or 10 Mb hard disk, they are generally inventory-based systems, meaning that bibliographic and patron records are created and permanently stored in the system. Most employ barcodes and light pens rather than requiring the actual keying of data for each transaction. Although this approach requires more time in bringing a system up since an initial conversion must be made, it will result in far quicker charging once the system is operational. In addition to routine checkout, return, and overdue detection functions, many of these packages are able to handle holds and automatically calculate fines.

The software packages even with these more sophisticated capabilities are relatively inexpensive, ranging from about $600 to $2,000. Some examples include Booktrak (Follett), CIRCA I (Highsmith), Circulation Plus (Library Software Company), the EASTWIND circulation package (DataPhase), the INMAGIC circulation package, Library Circulation System (Micro Library Software), and Micro CIRC (Micro Library Software). Highsmith also offers CIRCA II for somewhat larger libraries of between 20,000 and 50,000 volumes for about $3,500. Vendors of some of these packages will also supply hardware on request. An adequate configuration to run the software effectively will usually cost between $3,000 and $5,000, and sometimes more.

A number of software packages are aimed at libraries of less than 30,000 volumes and priced at less than $2,000, but far fewer standalone acquisitions, serials control, or online public access packages are available for these size facilities. Follett markets extremely low-priced packages for acquisitions and serials control for very small libraries. Little software for acquisitions and serials control is aimed specifically at libraries in the 10,000- to 30,000-volume range. A few packages—like Small Library Computer's BIB-BASE/ACQ, the INMAGIC acquisitions and serials control packages, and a serials control package available from Read-More Publications—that are designed to handle somewhat larger libraries but are priced at or below $1,000 are still inexpensive enough to attract libraries with under 30,000 volumes. For online public access catalogs, some packages for very small libraries are priced at under $2,000, among them Computer Cat (Micro Library) and the INMAGIC online catalog software. For libraries with up to 25,000 volumes, UTLAS markets an online catalog package, INFOQUEST, priced about $4,500.

Some of the vendors noted above provide packages for more than one application. Several packages offered under one series name, however, does not always mean that the series as a whole represents an integrated set of software, or that all packages act on a single database of bibliographic records. More often than not for smaller packages, each applications program runs separately from the others in the series and requires its own database. There are some exceptions, one being DTI's Card Datalog, a series of packages designed to handle cataloging and public access, acquisitions, serials control, and circulation. Each module, priced at about $2,000, can be purchased and operated separately, or several of the packages may be purchased, used in conjunction with one another, and operated off a single database. Still relatively inexpensive, the DTI software has been written to run on a broader variety of equipment than most smaller packages and was designed with somewhat larger libraries in mind than many comparably priced or only slightly less expensive packages.

A few micro-based systems have been designed for considerably larger libraries. Some are fully integrated, multipurpose systems aimed principally at libraries with between 50,000 and 100,000 or more volumes. Examples include CLSI's System 23, versions of OCLC's LS/2000, and a version of Advanced Library Concepts' ADLIB. Ringgold also markets a circulation package, Nonesuch, in this general category. For the most part, these systems are sold as a total hardware and software package. The price generally exceeds $50,000 and may even run above $100,000 for libraries with high capacity and terminal requirements. The vendors of some of these systems do, however, occasionally agree to sell software only to libraries that already have suitable hardware, but the price is still far greater than for any of the smaller packages noted earlier. For circulation alone, for example, the software for at least two of the systems mentioned here is priced above $15,000.

Apart from a handful of circulation and multipurpose systems, a few micro-based software packages are designed to handle acquisitions and serials control in medium and larger libraries. Because of the nature of the applications and their single-purpose function, some of the middle and even lower-priced acquisitions and serials control packages are suitable for medium-size libraries, such as the INMAGIC acquisitions and serials control packages and Small Library Computer's BIB-BASE/ACQ. In a more expensive and somewhat larger capacity range, CLASS markets a multiuser version of its Checkmate serials control software, which can handle up to 6,000 current subscriptions at a price of about $4,500, and a single-user version for about $2,500. Gaylord's GS-500 acquisitions package can also handle fairly large libraries and is priced at about $5,000. Hardware on which to run the package, including a 20-megabyte hard disk, is available from Gaylord for about an additional $10,000. For even larger libraries, Innovative Interfaces markets microcomputer-based acquisitions and serials control systems that can handle libraries of just about any size. Two Association of Research Libraries members—the University of Michigan and the University of Kansas—have purchased the acquisitions system. The ability to handle such large requirements, however, runs the cost of hardware and software into the tens of thousands of dollars.

Either for single or multipurpose systems, distinctions between minicomputers and microcomputers become particularly blurred at the upper end of the micro-based scale, not just in terms of complexity but also in price. It is a very large leap from a $500 micro package operable on hardware costing a few thousand dollars to a micro hardware/software system costing in the tens of thousands of dollars and even upward of $100,000. Unfortunately, not many micro-based systems and software packages are aimed at libraries between these extremes. Especially for circulation and integrated systems, a considerable number of libraries remain too large for the smaller packages but cannot yet afford the larger and more expensive systems. Right now, small libraries are realizing the greatest benefit of microcomputers in terms of being able to automate their bibliographic processing operations. But greater balance among sophistication, capacity, and price should certainly be realized, and possibly in the rather near future. As it does, the role of microcomputers in bibliographic processing operations in libraries will continue to increase in importance. Although microcomputers are not yet the solution for automating bibliographic processing in all libraries, their versatility and inexpensiveness make them an affordable and extremely useful tool in any library, large or small.

Optical Disk Storage of Text

Even in the early 1970s, some predicted that optical disk would soon become the foundation for a major revolution in the storage and delivery of textual information. Development was subsequently hampered by technological and economic obstacles, but by the mid-1980s, many of the problems seemed to have been solved. The heightened interest in optical disk as a text storage medium no longer stems from speculation and potential, but from intensifying activity in the commercial marketplace.

Optical disk for data storage serves much the same role in computerization as magnetic tape and disk. The revolutionary implications of optical disk are not so much in its basic purpose as in how it is accomplished. In the form of what looks like a simple phonograph record, a single one-sided, 12-inch disk can store as many as one billion bytes (1 GB) of data, equivalent to several reels of 6250 bpi magnetic tape, or nearly 3,000 360 KB floppy disks. Put another way, a 1 GB optical disk can store more than 20,000 full-length pages of printed text, or the equivalent of several hundred books.

In addition to storage capacity, optical disk has other promising characteristics. Whereas producing multiple copies of most types of computer storage media containing data is a rather slow process, a recorded master of at least one type of optical disk can be rapidly copied in large quantities using a stamping technique similar to that used in the manufacture of phonograph albums. And given a certain quantity, the copies may be produced for a cost of a few dollars each.

The physical qualities of optical disk also afford many advantages over magnetic media: disk is less prone to damage from handling; data is far better protected from dust particles; disk cannot be erased by magnetic fields; and disk is easily removable from disk drives. Also, optical disk is no longer viewed as appropriate storage only for large mainframe computers or even minicomputers, but for microcomputers as well. Perhaps most encouraging for librarians, optical disk is not limited to the domain of corporate or other applications outside the immediate environment of libraries. Several vendors of automated library systems and services began demonstrating the use of optical disk during 1984, with a few planning to incorporate its use as a routine part of their system or service in a short time.

There are two kinds of optical disk: optical digital and optical video. Data is recorded onto both forms through a production process involving the burning of microscopic pits onto the disk surface. But there are differences in the specific techniques used and in the applications emphasized. As text storage devices, the emphasis in optical digital disk development has been oriented toward the storage of digital data for direct computer processing; optical videodisk makes use of analog as well as digital technology to record and access data.

One of the chief obstacles in the use of optical digital disk for direct computer access has been the permanency of the records. Once information has been burned onto the disk surface, it cannot be rewritten, an obvious limitation if frequent updating of files is required. Experiments with alternative types of materials and recording techniques, however, have enabled some firms to develop prototype erasable disks. To date, the optical digital disk has been an expensive technology with limited application. But with advances such as this, the market is expected to expand and costs should decrease in the near future. Storage capacity on these disks is far greater, and per-kilobyte storage costs will be far less than for their magnetic counterparts.

As a text storage medium, optical videodisk is likely to have the most immediate consequences for libraries. Although data are also represented in the form of microscopic pits burned onto the surface, this technique uses analog as well as digital technology. After text has been captured in digital form on some magnetic medium, for example, images of the encoded data are copied onto standard analog videotape. The videotape is then run through a laser process in which analog signals from the tape are read and used as the basis for burning the microscopic pits into the surface of a disk. The premastering and mastering procedures are expensive and require highly sophisticated equipment to produce this first copy of a recorded disk. But once the master is obtained, copies can be made very inexpensively through a stamping process. In a 1983 article in *Computer Technology Review*, a vice-president of Reference Technology (a firm involved in optical disk technology in Boulder, Colorado) reported that a set of data can be produced for as little as $10 per disk when ordered in quantities of 1,000 or more.[4]

Economy of scale, then, is a crucial element in the current trend of the optical videodisk industry, along with the emphasis on equipment that is affordable to a mass market. This goal has been realized in most cases by providing an inexpensive control device that interfaces a microcomputer with standard commercial videodisk players serving as storage devices. At least one company has taken this a step further by developing a control unit that contains a microprocessor. The result of all this is that the equipment capable of accessing a 1 GB disk of prerecorded data costs only a few thousand dollars.

The emphasis in optical videodisk development has concentrated on mass distribution of inexpensive copies of prerecorded disks that can be accessed on low-cost equipment. Although it is too early to ascertain the magnitude or exact direction, this technology is likely to have profound implications for libraries. One area concerns access to large bibliographic files such as those maintained by the utilities and information retrieval services. Because of the enormous capacity and low cost of disk mass production, distribution of periodically updated disks containing the contents of these databases for local access represents a possible alternative to current operations in which libraries dial into the databases remotely stored on centralized computers. The entire OCLC bibliographic database of more than 11 million records, even given a liberal proportion of disk space to store indexes, for example, could be written onto about a dozen or so disks. For the utilities, there would be a logistical but not insurmountable problem in that the growth of the databases is dependent to some degree on decentralized, rather than centralized, input of new records. But of even greater concern, both the bibliographic utilities and the information retrieval services have substantial capital invested in centralized online technology; a shift to distribution of optical disk for decentralized local access would require a major reallocation of resources. It will be particularly interesting to follow the interaction between the principal partners in the library-oriented information retrieval services industry: the actual producers of the databases and the vendors like DIALOG and BRS who mount them and provide online access to them. Database vendors may have enormous investments in online technology, but database producers generally do not, and some are looking very closely at the possibility of themselves distributing copies of their databases on optical disk directly to libraries and other users.

Optical disk also has enormous potential as a medium on which to distribute databases containing the full text of books, periodicals, and other media. An especially useful characteristic is the ability to interleave text and visual images on a single disk. But with full-text databases as with bibliographic databases, there is a great difference between what is technologically attractive and what is realistic, given the environment into which this application would be introduced. Although it may be technologically possible to mass-produce disks containing hundreds of books or thousands of articles for a few dollars apiece, no publisher or group of publishers can recover expenses in this manner, and no other agency can act as a third-party producer until copyright and royalty issues are resolved.

Despite these uncertainties, optical disk is making an impact in the library world. One of the first projects to capture the interest of librarians was the announcement of the ADONIS program in the early 1980s. Although this project never really got off the ground, it did at least raise the consciousness of many librarians with regard to the enormous capacity of and the role that optical disk technology might play in the storage and delivery of text in the future.

The ADONIS project, to be launched by six major publishers of medical, scientific, and technical materials, proposed to record the full text of each article in some 1,500 periodicals onto optical disks housed at a central facility in Great Britain. Each disk would contain the text of about 25,000 journal pages, or the equivalent of between 2,500 and 3,000 articles. The consortium planned to use the MEGADOC system developed by the Philips Research Labs in the Netherlands, on which it would be possible to mount as many as 64 disks on a single "jukebox" configuration. The mass-storage potential was projected to exceed 1.5 million pages, or the equivalent of more than 150,000 articles. ADONIS did not aim to mass distribute disk copies, but to provide a document delivery service, with articles copied from the disks onto paper and mailed to requestors. There was also talk about the possibility of transmitting the digitized articles via satellite and telefacsimile. In 1983, however, three of the publishers dropped out of the program, marking the end to what would have been an exciting application of a new technology.

Library of Congress activity with optical disk systems has also captured the interest not only of the library community, but of other potential users. Although libraries generally tend not to be among the first or early users of emerging technology, LC's involvement is an exception. Its earliest involvement with any form of optical disk was in the implementation of its DEMAND system in 1982. Working with the Xerox Electro-Optical Systems division, the DEMAND project called for the storage of images of 5.5 million LC unit entry cards on optical disk. When card sets are requested through LC's Card Distribution Service, the image of the appropriate unit card can be retrieved and a set printed. The capacity of a single disk is 200,000 card images.

During the year that DEMAND was implemented, LC let two further contracts for development of optical disk systems. One was with Sony Corporation for the implementation of a system to store a variety of nonprint media on optical disk. The other was with Integrated Automation (formerly Teknakron) to develop a system to store text of printed materials. Beginning in 1983, about 500,000 pages of printed matter would be copied annually onto optical disk until the end of the pilot program in late 1986. As presented by LC, a major purpose of the project is to examine optical disk storage as a means to carry out "prospective preservation." The project focuses mainly on recording the full text of current issues of selected serials onto disk. When an issue of a designated title arrives at LC, each page is electronically scanned and its image recorded onto disk. As applied in this project, a single disk stores between 10,000 and 15,000 pages of text. Although the stored data may also be retrieved from disk, there is limited flexibility concerning avenues through which data can be accessed. Because of the conversion techniques used in the scanning and recording process, the text cannot be automatically indexed for searching. At present, LC does employ an intervening manual step that identifies text as to title and issue of the serial in which it appears. Thus, with these known items, a user can retrieve the first page of the issue and then browse through it or even skip directly to a desired page.[5]

With the launching of the LC projects, optical disk has come onto the library scene. Its emerging role was further accentuated by the demonstration of applications by several library automation vendors during 1984, some of whom planned to introduce optical disk into routine use with their systems or services late in the year or in early 1985. Library Systems and Services, Inc. (LSSI), for instance, vendor of the Mini-MARC cataloging system, is converting the LC MARC database to optical videodisk. The LC MARC file is to be supplemented on disk by the Library Corporation's Any-Book database, containing bibliographic information on more than one million in-print, English-language titles along with name/address records for more than 20,000 publishers. Bibliographic records in this combined database, called BiblioFile, should be accessible by author, title, title keyword, LCCN, and ISBN, and the entire database is to be updated and new disks distributed monthly to subscribers. The hardware configuration for the system consists of an IBM Personal Computer and a videodisk player and control unit available through LSSI.

During 1984, Carrollton Press also demonstrated optical videodisk with its MARC and REMARC Videodisk Library System (MARVLS), containing LC MARC records and REMARC records created by Carrollton. (The REMARC database and Carrollton's batch-searching and retrospective conversion service are discussed in Chapter 10.) In terms of the MARVLS service, it is expected that storage of the entire database of several million LC MARC and REMARC records will require only about four disks. Like LSSI's service, MARVLS will employ an IBM Personal Computer, a videodisk player, and a control unit. Also in 1984, CLSI demonstrated its LaserCat, a system for accessing a database of LC MARC records recorded on optical disk, which can be used as a source of cataloging information for CLSI users.

The exciting prospects of storing more than one million bibliographic records on a single disk accessible using a microcomputer and of storing the full text of 20,000 pages of books or periodicals per disk clearly have tremendous implications for libraries. The commercial applications noted above have centered on the distribution either of data in the public domain (LC MARC records), of data over which the distributor has proprietary rights (Carrollton Press with REMARC records), or of data for which arrangements have been made between two information suppliers (LSSI's inclusion of the Any-Book database). Furthermore, each involves the distribution of bibliographic data. Especially when looking toward full-text applications, the relationships between providers of technology and one or more layers of data suppliers are almost certain to become more complex, raising issues such as copyright and royalty that must be worked out before optical disk can carve its niche in the storage and distribution of text. But such matters will surely be resolved, and although the form may be as yet uncertain, optical disk has a role in libraries.

Telecommunications

Distribution of information on optical disk may have important consequences for the manner and extent to which telecommunications is used to convey data from one location to another. But even if such distribution flourishes, it will by no means replace the need to transmit certain types of information from one point to another using telecommunications. Libraries have already come to rely heavily on telecommunications technology in automation. Because telecommunications does permeate so many of the automated activities in the library today, its uses in relation to library systems and services are discussed throughout this book. Since libraries generally do not have the opportunity to influence technological development in the area of telecommunications, it is necessary for most librarians to have expertise in the technology itself. But because libraries do rely on telecommunications, and because there are options available when its use is required, this section provides an overview of two of the more important technical aspects of telecommunications—transmission modes and transmission media. Advancements in these areas will influence the manner in which, and perhaps even the purposes for which, libraries will transmit and receive electronic data in the future.

The telecommunications technologies described here are not restricted to those carrying textual information. They are multipurpose and in varying combinations are able to carry voice communications, text, and many types of visual images. The primary emphasis here, however, is on communication of textual data.

Textual Data and Transmission Modes

One of the problems in the transmission of textual data from one location to another during the past quarter-century has been that the channels over which data are sent were generally designed to carry other types of messages. Most specifically, normal telephone lines—the medium through which most data communication still occurs—were engineered principally for the transmission of voice. Normal telephone lines operate in an analog mode, meaning that information is carried in continuous wave patterns. Information coming out of a computer, on the other hand, is arranged in discrete units, and in signal patterns that are not suitable for transmission over channels operating in an analog mode. This incompatibility led to development of the device known as a modem (modulator-demodulator), whose function is to translate digital information—such as the 0's and 1's of the computer—into continuous wave cycles and back again so that it can be sent over analog channels.

A present trend in many countries is the construction of digital communications networks that will replace or supplement the existing analog networks. Digital networks can carry voice communications, although in different technical fashion than in analog transmission, and are much better suited to handling digital information being sent remotely to and from computers. They can carry data faster, more efficiently, and less expensively than analog networks. In the United States, long-range plans call for converting much of the public switched network—what we think of as the regular telephone network—from analog to digital mode. This will occur very slowly, however, and will be a patchwork process. It is unlikely that the conversion, even if undertaken in earnest, will be proportionately significant by the end of this century.

Transmission Media

The matter of analog versus digital has to do with the form in which signal patterns are sent from one point to another. A somewhat different aspect of telecommunications is the nature of the medium over which the signals are sent. There are several basic types of transmission media in present use. Three are ground, or line, media: twisted wire pair, coaxial cable, and optical fiber. Two others—microwave and satellite—are free space media and carry signals through the air rather than over physical lines. Another transmission medium involves the use of lasers, but as a communications technology it is still in a comparatively early stage of development.

Twisted wire pairs are what we commonly associate with traditional copper wire telephone lines. In library applications involving access to remote computers, most data transmission occurs over this type of line, sometimes in the form of enhanced lines that allow faster transmission speeds at reduced costs. Although use of these lines seems adequate for many purposes, transmission of data over wire pair media is considerably less effective than over some of the other types of media described below. The amount of information and the speed with which it can be transmitted over a particular type of medium has to do in large part with the frequency range at which signals are carried, and the bandwidth that the medium supports. Since wire pair transmission uses a lower frequency and supports a smaller bandwidth than other media, its information carrying capacity is lower. The necessity to communicate with many information retrieval services at the rather slow speed of 1200 baud, for example, has much to do with the limitations of the twisted wire pair medium over which the data are carried.

Coaxial cable is generally installed for transmission of data over relatively short distances and is used for some telephone trunk lines and widely for cable television broadcasting. Because they occupy higher frequency ranges and a broader bandwidth, cables of this type are able to carry considerably more information at faster speeds than wire pairs.

The implications of optical fiber technology for data communication are enormously promising. The speed with which data can be transmitted over optical fiber far exceeds the maximum speed attainable over copper wire. While libraries are accustomed to transmitting and receiving data at a speed of 1200 bits per seconds when using services like BRS and DIALOG, transmission over optical fiber generally occurs at a rate of 90 million bits per second or greater. At this speed, the full text of a 30-volume encyclopedia could be transmitted over a distance of 25 miles in less than six seconds!

Signals are transmitted over optical fiber in a way fundamentally different from the way they are transmitted over wire pair and coaxial cable. The latter two are metallic and transmit signals that carry an electrical current. Optical fibers are made of glass and transmit signals in the form of light; they do not conduct an electrical current. Although research and experimental use of optical fiber as a transmission medium was being conducted even during the late 1950s, it was not until well into the 1970s that the technology was refined to a point where it could be brought into commercial use. The first installation of optical fiber for regular use in the United States was the construction, in 1977, of a 2.5-mile path in Las Vegas between a hotel and the local telephone system headquarters.[6]

In addition to handling transmissions at higher speeds, the advantages that optical fiber has over metallic line media are numerous. Optical fiber has a lower transmission error rate, and because it does not conduct an electrical current, it is immune from electromagnetic interference. It is also smaller, lighter, more flexible, and generally more resilient to weather and wear.

For the most part, optical fiber has been used as a transmission medium over only very short distances and most commonly for telephone trunk lines. When a 150-mile path was constructed in the United Kingdom linking Birmingham and London in mid-1982, it was hailed as the world's longest operational fiber optic link.[7] This is a record that has been surpassed often since then. In the United States, AT&T has estimated that it should have more than 10,000 miles of optical fiber routes in domestic use by 1995.[8] The Federal Communications Commission has approved U.S. participation in laying an optical fiber submarine cable between the United States and Japan, and AT&T plans to have operational a similar transatlantic link by 1988.

Microwave and satellite as transmission media for communication between points on earth have in common the fact that they transmit signals over the air rather than through physical lines. Invariably, they are used in conjunction with line media that provide the final link. Signals from a point of origin, such as a broadcast studio or a computer, are sent through some form of line medium to a microwave or satellite earth station, transmitted over the air, received at another earth station, and conveyed again through line media to their final point of destination.

While microwave and satellite both send signals over the air, there is a fundamental difference between them. Signals transmitted using satellite communications are literally sent into space and reflected back. Since the satellites that reflect the signals are located so far above the earth, transmission between two distant points on earth can be achieved with a single relay function performed by the satellite. Signals sent by microwave, on the other hand, do not travel through outer space, but rather along a line of sight between microwave stations. The curvature of the earth imposes severe restrictions on the distance over which it is possible to retain this line of sight. To transmit information by microwave over any considerable distance, the signals can travel only at about 25- to 30-mile intervals before they must be received by another station and relayed to the next.

Communications satellites travel in geostationary orbit about 23,000 miles above the equator. The first communications satellite, the Intelsat I or "Early Bird," was launched in 1965. Intelsat I and other early communications satellites simply received signals and reflected them back to earth. Later satellites supplemented this with a capability for amplifying the signals received before transmitting them back to earth. Amplification reduced the problems caused by loss of signal strength over the great distance involved. This improvement enabled smaller and less expensive earth receiving stations to be used.

It is likely that all five of these communications transmission media will remain in use for some time. However, the proportion of their use with respect to each other will change; some will increase in use and others will decline. The use of microwave transmission, for example, may eventually be supplanted by optical fibers on one hand and satellites on the other. Optical fiber may eventually even alter the scope of purposes for which satellite transmission is used, making the latter cost-effective only in transoceanic or transcontinental communications. However, the capital investment involved in developing and putting into place new transmission media is high, and conversion of an already extensive communications network, such as the public switched network in the United States, is an enormous task. By the time it can be carried out, it will not be surprising if there are even newer transmission media that will make the more recent ones appear as outdated then as copper twisted pair wire seems now.

Because libraries represent a very small fraction of the users of communications technology and are thus in a primarily reactive position, they will have little opportunity to exercise any direct influence over developments in the technology itself. For the most part, the concern of libraries will continue to be on the end result of the communication rather than with how it is transmitted or over what type of medium. But libraries do need to be aware of developments in the technology and of the options for tapping into it. An overview of some of these options appears in Chapter 8.

Notes

1. Carlton Rochell, "Telematics—2001 a.d.," *Library Journal* 107 (October 1, 1982): 1810.
2. Joseph R. Matthews, "The Automated Library System Marketplace 1982: Change and More Change!" *Library Journal* 108 (March 15, 1983): 547.
3. For further discussion of this topic, see S. Michael Malinconico, "Planning for Obsolescence," *Library Journal* 109 (February 15, 1984): 333–335.
4. Patrick J. Call, "Optical Video Disks Provide Multigigabyte Storage at Low Cost," *Computer Technology Review* (Winter 1983).
5. For a review of this project, see Linda Beth Criswell, "Serials on Optical Disks: A Library of Congress Pilot Program," *Library Hi Tech* 1 (Winter 1983): 17–21. For a description of some of the recording technology used in optical disk storage in general, see Larry Fujitani, "Laser Optical Disk: The Coming Revolution in On-Line Storage," in *Communications of the ACM* 27 (June 1984): 546–554.
6. For a description of optical fiber technology, see Michael Koenig, "Fiber Optics and Library Technology," *Library Hi Tech* 2, no. 1 (1984): 9–15.
7. "204 K Optical Fibre," *Telecommunication Journal* 49, no. 10 (1982): 717.
8. "Long Lines Announces Routes for Single-Mode Installations," *Fiberoptic Technology* (June 1983): 129.

8

Basic Approaches:
Options and Resources

Implementing an automated system or service requires careful and systematic planning. It is still often necessary to justify automation to boards or administrators of parent institutions. It is also important to have a general understanding of possible approaches and to have a clear idea of the roles various agencies and individuals will play in planning and implementation.

Deciding to Automate

The most important question for any library considering the automation of a specific operation or the design of a more comprehensive overall plan is "why automate?" By the time the library is ready to look at specific alternatives, those involved should know exactly why automation is taking place and specifically what it should accomplish. In the mid-1980s, justification for automation hardly seems necessary to most librarians. But in approaching those who fund or otherwise ultimately approve automation, the library must be able to convincingly present its rationale from a number of different perspectives. In so doing, the library will be establishing the initial framework within which further plans can be drawn and decisions made. The library can identify what it hopes to accomplish through automation and will have concrete objectives against which later to judge whether those ends have been achieved.

Of the many reasons given to justify automation, the following are the most frequent:

To increase technical processing efficiency

To realize financial savings or to contain costs

To improve library service

To improve library administration and management

As a basis for reorganization

As a response to a breakdown of crisis proportion in the existing manual system

To facilitate the sharing of resources

Automation for its own sake

Not all of the above are equally valid, but each is legitimate in that it has been used at one time or another as a primary spoken or unspoken rationale for automating. Most projects are undertaken with more than one of these purposes in mind. But for the purposes mentioned above, it is important in establishing a basis for planning that a library sort out and articulate the relative importance of each reason for which it is automating.

Increased Processing Efficiency

Particularly for technical services applications, an automated system almost always improves processing efficiency over a manual system. Increased efficiency is realized when the same tasks are performed with fewer staff or in less time than was possible under the manual system, or when different or additional tasks are performed to provide supplementary benefits considered worth the extra effort or costs.

Increased efficiency is so characteristic of automated technical processing systems that if a library cannot foresee this occurring through automation, it may not have closely enough analyzed its manual system or evaluated the available automated alternatives.

Saving Money and Containing Costs

All libraries would like to justify automation on the grounds that it will immediately lower operating costs. There certainly are cases where cost savings have been realized through automation, but the overall evidence suggests that the financial benefits of automation are not as sweeping as once anticipated. How valid a rationale financial savings is for automation depends on the specific situation and on circumstances such as type of application and system involved, level of staffing required for the automated system versus the replaced manual system, and local decisions about how the new system or service will be used.

More than an absolute lowering of operating costs, the library may hope that the new system will better contain the rate of increase in per-unit operating costs over time. If a library collection and its use are expanding rapidly, an automated system should decrease the rate at which it is necessary to add staff and the rate of increase in other costs due to the additional work load. This can also be true for libraries with more moderate growth rates, although on a correspondingly less dramatic level.

Although cost containment is certainly a potential advantage of automation, it has too often been presented as an established fact rather than what it truly is—a possibility. Like actual lowering of costs through automation, containing costs depends on the specific situation, on such variables as the growth rate of local activity and trends in salary and wage rates. The library should weigh these as realistically as possible in any cost projections and should not automatically assume that considerable financial benefit will materialize in the form of cost containment.

In cases where the amortized and continuing costs of an automated system are in fact lower than the costs of the manual system it replaced, savings are almost inevitably realized through staff layoffs or transfers to other departments in the library. If at all possible, most libraries opt for the latter. Once the new system is up and running, even these kinds of savings are often not realized to the extent that was originally anticipated. The automated system indeed should be able to reduce the time spent in carrying out exactly the same tasks that were performed under the old manual system, but the automated system will also likely introduce new time demands to carry out tasks that were previously impossible or neglected. For example, the circulation files in many manual operations are arranged in only one sequence, by due date, call number, or transaction number, and thus the staff time devoted to patron inquiries is limited to one point of access. Most automated circulation systems offer file inquiry through many access points, including author, title, and patron name. As soon as library users become aware of this, the staff can expect to spend a certain amount of additional time on the types of queries that were impossible to answer under the old system. The principle of spending additional time with an automated system to perform tasks that were not possible or practical with a manual system will apply to just about any set of library operations—cataloging, circulation, acquisitions, serials control, and so on.

When the staff time spent in taking advantage of all the additional capabilities of an automated system is added up, it may be as substantial as the time required to perform fewer tasks under the old system. But herein lies an important point. If the library is able either to transfer some of its personnel to other departments in the library or to perform a greater variety of tasks in a department with the same level of staffing, the library as a whole may not be saving money, but in all likelihood it will be improving the level of service to users.

Improved Service to the User

There is little doubt that improvement of service to library users is one of the most concrete benefits to be gained through automation. In technical processing operations, automation often leads to acquiring and processing materials—and therefore getting them onto the shelf—faster than was possible under the previous manual system. In public services, these benefits are no less pronounced. With online circulation systems, improvement in inventory control capabilities and expansion of access points leads to better service for the user population as a whole. Online searches through information retrieval services often enable bibliographies to be compiled for patrons in a fraction of the time it would have taken to conduct an equivalent search manually. COM catalogs, even if their content is little more than pictures of catalog cards, have the advantage of being easily placed in many locations. Online public-access catalogs also have this benefit; in addition, they usually allow for more up-to-date data and also provide for greater flexibility in searching than do card and even COM catalogs.

The most persistent obstacle in justifying automation for the sake of improved service is the difficulty of assigning a quantitative or dollar value to the benefits derived. If an automated system provides better service, but costs more than a not so service-effective manual system, at what point is the added value worth or not worth the additional cost? There are no steadfast answers to that question, and unfortunately, governing and funding authorities sometimes have a tendency to place a lower cost-equivalent value on enhanced service than the library staff might deem appropriate. Under such circumstances, the library administration must simply persevere in presenting as convincing a case as possible, for improved service to library users is the most legitimate of all possible reasons for automation.

Improved Administrative and Management Information

Seldom do libraries view improved administrative and management information as a primary goal in converting an operation to an automated system. Improved administration and management can be a convincing argument for purchasing a microcomputer, but by itself it seldom justifies the purchase of a quarter-million-dollar integrated library system. However, its importance as a strong supporting role, even in the case of large systems, should not be underestimated. For a great many applications, automated systems can generate a variety of statistical compilations that are too time consuming to undertake under a manual system. If used effectively, these reports can provide valuable assistance for administrative and management purposes, ranging from budgeting to collection analysis and development to staff scheduling. In presenting the case for automation to governing and funding authorities, a library may find that the potential for improved management information can be a persuasive supplementary selling point.

As a Basis for Reorganization

Introducing an automated system or service into a department will inevitably have an impact on the organization of staff duties and interaction and on overall policies and procedures. If the department has achieved a relatively comfortable balance among these factors, one of the greatest challenges of introducing automation is to do so in a way that will preserve the positive atmosphere of staff relations and organization. Under less satisfactory circumstances, the introduction of an automated system and its disruptive influence have sometimes been viewed as a convenient excuse for forcing change in organizational structure. But automation undertaken for this purpose seldom achieves the desired end. Unless current problems can be traced almost exclusively to inability of an existing manual system to handle the volume of work, introducing a new system along with changes in policy and procedures generally compounds the magnitude of organizational problems rather than reducing it. If the problems are interpersonal and organizational, rather than attributable to the manual system itself, they should be recognized as such and dealt with on that level rather than at the system level.

In automating an operation, a library should certainly take advantage of the opportunity to incorporate changes in organizational structure, policy, and procedures where needed, but reorganization should never be anticipated as a catch-all solution to problems that may require attention at another level.

As a Response to Breakdown of a Manual System

Sometimes the chief impetus for automating is that an existing manual system in a library is simply no longer able to handle the work load. The results of a system taxed beyond limits are usually very visible: enormous backlogs in cataloging, lack of accurate or timely fund-account reports in acquisitions, disorganized circulation files, or sprawling and internally inconsistent card catalogs. In spite of a host of very positive reasons for introducing automation into a library under calmer circumstances, the visible effects of a manual system that is breaking down have probably been a more persuasive selling point for automation than any other. Because of the toll on staff and users, it is unfortunate that a breakdown of crisis proportion often has to occur before the library can finally convince its governing authority that an automated system may be a necessity rather than a luxury. It is best not to have to prove so tangibly why the library needs to replace its manual system, but given the economic reality of automation, libraries for some time to come may find themselves having to draw heavily on this justification.

Sharing Resources

Each rationale discussed so far has presented automation in terms of library-specific needs. As information continues to be generated on such a prolific level, the sharing of resources becomes a viable strategy that libraries can use to alleviate the need for each facility to collect all documents that might be requested by clientele.

Theoretically, the question of resource sharing can be viewed as somewhat independent from the question of automation itself. In practical terms, however, the two are very closely intertwined in today's environment. Depending on the application, automated systems can facilitate the sharing of resources by making communications and dissemination of holdings information a faster, more efficient, and less expensive task than is possible through manual channels. This is not always an easy point to sell to governing and funding authorities, who may see resource sharing simply as an activity by which the library will serve an even broader community than it already does, and hence as a potential drain on its resources. If this is the perception, the library must convincingly present the other side of the argument: that participation will also enable the library to draw upon a much broader pool of resources than it ever could before.

Automation for Its Own Sake

Traditionally, automation simply as an end in itself has been greeted with some measure of disdain within librarianship. Libraries have been cautioned that financial savings, cost containment, improved service, or some other clearly demonstrable goal must be achieved in order to justify an automated system.

Such advice still deserves respect. But the question of "automation for its own sake" can also be put into another quite different and equally valid perspective. This broader view was summarized by Waters and Kralisz in a paper on financing the electronic library: "We do not any longer decide to put telephones in our libraries. Our libraries would be absurd without them. It would be a sad commentary if some day we were still debating the computer, videotext, and other electronic information delivery formats when they had become an essential element of the way society communicates."[1]

Viewed from that perspective, what has sometimes been labeled automation for its own sake in fact becomes automation for a purpose—a purpose defined by the library's role as a collector of and provider of information. Society at large is constantly becoming more accustomed to computers and to information that is processed and delivered through electronic means. If the library is unable to keep pace with the rest of society in the way it processes, uses, and presents information, the perception of its role in an information society may change, but not for the better. Computers and electronic information are no longer extravagances; they are part of everyday life. A library should not automate an operation simply for appearance's sake, but neither should it be oblivious to the importance of how that appearance will influence the perception of the library in a computerized and dynamic information society.

Hardware and Software: Major Options

As a library begins to investigate alternatives for automating, its level of direct involvement with hardware and software may take on many different forms. The predominant arrangement varies in libraries from one application to another. For some applications, there is relatively little choice in the hardware/software arrangement, but for others, the library may have far greater latitude, and a library with fairly extensive automation will probably rely on more than one type of arrangement among the totality of its efforts. But one important element in the planning and selection process should be the library's awareness of the general advantages and disadvantages of the types of arrangements that might be available.

Arrangements and Evaluation Criteria

Table 8-1 identifies most of the types of arrangements possible between a library and the computer hardware and software used in automated systems. The vertical columns identify three alternative computer hardware arrangements. In any online system, the library will be required to have some type of equipment in-house, such as terminals,

TABLE 8-1 COMMON HARDWARE/SOFTWARE ARRANGEMENTS IN LIBRARY AUTOMATION

| | Main Computer Location | | |
Applications Software Source	Central Site of Library Automation Vendor	Computer Center of Library's Parent Institution	In the Library
System developed remotely	Remote access; e.g., bibliographic utilities, information retrieval services, serials subscription agents, acquisitions book jobbers	Purchase of software from vendor or another library to run on large mainframe or minicomputer	Turnkey system; hardware and software purchased from one source Purchase of hardware and software from different sources
Software developed through local computer center	—	Local system; software developed by local computer center and run on its equipment	—
Software developed by library	—	—	Strictly in-house system; most commonly found with microcomputer applications

but the alternatives in Table 8-1 more specifically concern the location of the actual central processing unit itself.

The horizontal rows in the table distinguish among different approaches to the development of applications software. In a few instances, libraries may have hardware or software arrangements slightly different from those shown in the table, but they are indeed rare. The matrix that constitutes Table 8-1 results in a number of possible hardware/software combinations, but a couple are almost contradictory by definition, and others are extremely unlikely. However, several are fairly common in library automation. Again, the predominant arrangement in libraries varies according to application. It should also be noted that an important and rather common variation does not show up as a separate type of arrangement in the table: namely, the sharing of an automated system by several institutions. As it pertains to the group as a whole, however, the sharing of a system will involve hardware/software configurations in Table 8-1.

Especially in those cases where it is possible to approach automation of a particular function from a variety of options, several criteria are useful for evaluating the advantages and disadvantages of each. The most important criteria are:

Initial costs

Continuing costs

Degree to which software can initially be customized to meet library-specific needs

Level of computer expertise required on the part of the library

Control over system performance

Control over hardware upgrade

Control over software enhancements

These criteria may be applied in evaluating any of the hardware arrangements shown in Table 8-1. In the remainder of this section, several of the major hardware/software arrangements identified in Table 8-1 are discussed in terms of their major uses in libraries and their advantages and disadvantages according to the criteria outlined above.

Remote Access to Online Services

This hardware/software arrangement is one of the most common for certain types of automated library applications. Under this arrangement, the central computer hardware is located at the central site of the online vendor. The vendor also maintains, and usually develops from the outset, the applications software that is mounted on the computer.

Probably the most familiar examples of this type are the bibliographic utilities and the reference-based information retrieval services. A number of commercial library processing systems also operate under this arrangement. Autographics AGILE II is an example of a system that can be used for, among other applications, cataloging and online maintenance of bibliographic records. Both Ebsco and FAXON offer online serials subscription services through remote access to a centrally maintained system. Some of the major book jobbers provide similar capabilities for online ordering and acquisitions control, and at least one vendor of automated circulation systems offers the remote access option.

One of the most immediate advantages of using an online service of this type is that it seldom requires a substantial initial investment on the part of the library. There may be costs associated with the purchase and installation of terminals, and in some cases an initial implementation and training fee, but the investment involved will be far less than the cost of purchasing a turnkey system or of developing applications software locally.

As a library continues to use an online service for a longer period, the advantage of low initial expense may be fully or partially offset by telecommunications costs and system use charges. Projection of continuing costs is one of the most crucial points for comparison when examining the hardware/software arrangements available, particularly when considering the costs of using an online service. While several online services have supplemented access to centralized computers with local processing capabilities, the main emphasis is still on interaction with a remote, centrally located computer, and of the three options described in this section, the telecommunications costs will almost invariably be higher in using an online service than in using either a locally developed and maintained system or a turnkey system. These costs are, of course, only one factor among many that should be considered, but the library using an online service should be prepared for significant telecommunications costs.

The method of levying continuing system use fees exclusive of telecommunications charges (and sometimes incorporating them) varies according to the application and from one vendor to another. System use charges are sometimes levied on a per-transaction basis, sometimes at a fixed monthly rate, and often in some combination of the two. Income from these charges is used by the service to pay for administrative overhead, operational support, marketing, and development. Expenses associated with hardware upgrades and software enhancements are usually not recovered through a specially designated fee, but rather are incorporated into regular transaction and monthly charges. Since expenses for upgrades and enhancements are distributed to some extent among all users, each library is paying part of the initial cost of developing any new feature, even if it does not plan to use that capability. Still, the per-library contribution is comparatively low since the total cost of development is distributed among what is often a large number of users. For system features that are special-purpose rather than systemwide, most online services make an attempt to break out system use charges on a feature-specific basis, so that continuing operations costs can be recovered as much as possible directly from those who most benefit from the feature.

For certain types of applications or in some libraries, the continuing use charges and telecommunications costs incurred in using an online service may offset the advantage of low initial investment after a rather short period of time. In other cases, the online service may be the most cost-effective option over the long run. To emphasize an earlier point, it is crucial to take continuing costs into account when comparing various approaches to automation. And these should include not only direct system use expenses, but also staff costs. For some applications, such as cataloging, the use of an online service may require considerably less staff time, and therefore less staff costs, than options with lower direct expenses, such as a strictly local system.

Use of an online service does not require the library to have any in-house computer expertise. While advantageous for the library in terms of savings in personnel costs, another consequence is that since hardware and software decisions are made elsewhere, the library has no direct control over system performance or enhancement. When the central computer is unexpectedly down or response time is slow, the library has little immediate recourse other than to complain. There is no control over decisions pertaining to upgrade of computer hardware. In most cases, this does not pose a problem, since the service coordinates the introduction of new hardware with the measures necessary to adapt its existing software. The result usually either is transparent to the user or actually improves system performance. Problems occur only when the upgrade yields unanticipated negative results, or if the service procrastinates upgrading of hardware when such action would lead to noticeable improvement. In either instance, there is really very little an individual library can do to remedy the situation.

There is also a compromise of control with respect to software applications. The online services must try to offer a satisfactory complement of system features to maintain a competitive position, but their systems are still generalized and not customized to the needs of each and every user. In the selection process, a library cannot expect the features available through an online service to meet every criterion of what it would consider ideal for its own purposes. Online services do have to be responsive to their clients, and many sponsor user groups and provide other mechanisms for suggesting software enhancements. The introduction of new features is a slow process, and will still be generalized, but in the long run a library should see a gradual evolution in the sophistication of the system.

Turnkey Systems

Another major approach to automation is the turnkey system, which involves locating a computer in the library and mounting software that is supplied by the vendor from whom the system is purchased or leased. Probably the most common examples of turnkey systems at present are minicomputer-based integrated library systems. The advent of microcomputers has also made an impact on the turnkey market for circulation, public access, and cataloging systems and has given rise to a number of lower priced acquisitions and serials control systems as well.

In contrast to online services, a turnkey system usually requires a more substantial initial capital outlay. Minicomputer-based integrated systems normally start at around $150,000 and may run above one million dollars for very large libraries. At the other end, some microcomputer-based turnkey systems can be purchased by very small libraries for only a few thousand dollars.

There is seldom a per-transaction charge associated with use of a turnkey system. Once the system is installed, most of the continuing costs are incurred for hardware and software maintenance. If terminals are located in remote branches, there are recurring telecommunications costs, although they are far lower than if an online utility or commercial service was being used for the same purpose. There are different approaches used by vendors to charge for hardware and software maintenance. In some cases, charges are levied separately; other vendors combine the two. Either a combined charge or a software-specific charge usually covers the cost of receiving routine enhancements to the generalized software supplied by the vendor, but in most cases there is an additional charge for major modifications or major new modules that the vendor introduces. Although maintenance charges for hardware should be fairly straightforward when a system is purchased, the possibility of eventual upgrade expense is sometimes overlooked by libraries. If growth in the size of a library's files or in the number of transactions exceeds the capacity of the system to handle the increased volume, the library may need to acquire new or additional equipment. During the early 1980s, in a disturbing number of instances, libraries installing turnkey circulation systems purchased hardware with the understanding that it was sufficient to allow for considerable growth, only to find that the system's capacity was reached at a much earlier point than anticipated.

Turnkey systems, like remote access online services, are generalized. There is sometimes more flexibility in the degree to which a vendor will consider customizing its system to meet an individual library's needs than is the case with a bibliographic utility, but not all vendors are willing to customize. Even if a vendor does agree, customization is expensive. If the vendor modifies its generalized software, the library is charged accordingly.

In using a turnkey system, there is little need for hardware or software expertise on the part of the library staff. Some must know a bit more about operating a computer than is necessary for an online service, but that can easily be learned by individuals totally unfamiliar with computer architecture and programming.

One advantage of the turnkey system over online, remote-access services is that the library may be able to exercise a greater amount of control over certain types of decisions relating to hardware performance and upgrade. The system still goes down on occasion and there still are periods when response time is unacceptably slow. But when the library owns the computer, at least it will usually be able to deal more directly with the appropriate maintenance agency, rather than having to simply notify an online service or a computer center, only perhaps to then be left in the dark about the nature of the problem, what is being done about it, or how soon it will be corrected. Being better informed does not necessarily solve the problem more quickly, but it does at least enable the library to have a more direct grasp on the situation.

A library that has a turnkey system also generally has more direct control over decisions about switching to new equipment or upgrading existing configurations than is possible with online services or local computer centers. The degree of control over software enhancements is about on par with an online service, with similar opportunities to those available for users of online services: namely, through participation in channels that forward user groups and other advisory suggestions to the vendor.

System Development through Local Computer Centers

A third option prevalent in library automation combines the use of a central computer housed in a university, municipal, or corporate facility with the design and maintenance of software applications by personnel employed by that facility. For any given application, this approach is usually predominant in pioneering efforts, but becomes less common once a turnkey market begins to evolve. This was noted most recently with respect to online public-access catalogs, where the pioneering OPACs of the early 1980s were almost invariably developed through parent computer centers at major research libraries, a few public libraries, and some corporate libraries. But apart from such pioneering efforts, the development of a system with the aid of a local computer center is still an option being pursued by a number of libraries for a wide range of applications.

Of the approaches to library automation described here, this is most sensitive to local circumstances. For the library itself, it may be the least or the most expensive alternative. The local system may be brought up smoothly and fit the library's needs more satisfactorily than could be hoped for with any other option, or the entire effort could degenerate into a nightmare for everyone concerned.

There are three chief reasons why a library might choose development through a local computer center. First, the library's governing authority might insist on it, not wanting to divert funds to outside sources when it feels that there are sufficient institutional and human resources on site to design and maintain a system. Second, this option may be the least expensive for the library if the host institution is willing to absorb development and maintenance costs out of a general fund. Third, the library may feel that a locally designed system can better fulfill its concept of the ideal system than anything available through an online service or from a turnkey vendor. If the design and implementation are successful, this assumption is often valid.

Although local systems offer a great deal of potential flexibility, the degree to which this advantage is actually realized depends on a number of factors. Computer center personnel must be able and willing to design the system in accordance with the library's requirements, and once the system is operational, the library's needs must be treated as high priorities. Adequate hardware capacity must be ensured not only when the system becomes operational, but over the long run as well. During the design phase, the parent institution must be willing to allocate substantial human and financial resources toward development. Especially for a complex application such as circulation or an online catalog in a large library, the development of applications software will require several "staff years" to complete. Even with a team of programmers working on the project, the library will have a considerable wait between the time the project is approved and the time a system is actually up and running.

Local development is initially a very expensive approach to automation of large-scale library applications. Although development costs are perhaps not coming directly out of the library's budget, someone is paying for them, and most likely in greater amounts than if the funds had been used to purchase a turnkey system. During the 1960s and 1970s, recurring expenses associated with hardware maintenance, software enhancement, and telecommunications for a locally developed and operated system were often absorbed by the parent institution. In a growing number of instances over the years, though, at least part of these expenses have started to be charged back to libraries and other departments that are using the computer facilities and personnel.

If computer center personnel are responsible for programming library applications and monitoring hardware, the library does not really need to have in-house computer expertise. What it does need, however, is one or more staff members who can articulate functional requirements in such a way that they are clearly understood by the programming personnel who must then translate them into computer code.

It would seem on first impression that a library with a locally developed system should be able to have more direct control over system performance and enhancement in this arrangement than it would under most other alternatives. But this differs from one specific setting to another, and under some circumstances, the library may in fact have less control. More so than online utilities and commercial services, for example, local computer centers have been known to change hardware or introduce a new operating system with little attention to promptly and thoroughly adapting and debugging all applications software. If library applications are rather low on the computer center's list of priorities, the library may have to suffer for a while until the computer center gets around to fully converting the library programs. In terms of software enhancement, it should be possible with a local system to tailor modifications more to the specific needs of the library than would normally be the case with an online service or a turnkey system. But this also depends on specific circumstances and on computer center priorities and policies. Customized change is certainly more feasible in a locally developed system, but this in itself is no guarantee as to if or when requested changes will actually be made.

As emphasized here, the success in locally developing and maintaining an automated system through a parent institution's computer center is almost entirely dependent on the specific circumstances of each situation. There may be important advantages to be gained through local development, but the risks are high. The arrangement between a library and a computer center has worked extremely well in many cases and has yielded some of the most sophisticated systems in use in libraries today. But unless a library can be assured that it will receive a high level of continuing support from its computer center, the development and maintenance of a local system in this fashion is an unpredictable venture.

In-Library System Development

Although system development through a local computer center has been fairly common over the years, libraries have rarely given their own staff the job of developing a large-scale system. In some cases, computer center staff members have been assigned to work exclusively with the library, and some libraries employ programmers to work with the center. But the entire responsibility for designing system software does not generally rest with library staff, except perhaps in a multi-library project where resources are pooled.

Of the automation options noted in Table 8-1, designing an original system would generally accommodate a library's needs most closely and would allow maximum control over such aspects as system performance, hardware upgrade, and software enhancement. But all these benefits are countered by just one obstacle—cost of development. Few libraries can afford to pay staff and other expenses required to design original software for a large-scale system when far less expensive options are available. In terms of real costs, the price for local computer center or original software development of a library system may be about the same, but in many such cases, at least part of the costs are subsidized by the parent institution as a centralized service.

In-house development may be rare for the large-scale system, but the microcomputer has allowed libraries to develop their own programs for smaller, specialized applications. In some small and medium-sized libraries, staff has designed software to handle acquisitions or serials control on a microcomputer, and, in some very small libraries, even circulation and public access. But usually the application has involved more specialized files, such as for interlibrary loan records, staff scheduling, film rental, community services, and so on. For many libraries, in-house software development in those areas is an excellent use of readily available technological and human resources, and as long as their scope is clearly defined and not overly ambitious, such programs can be written by staff without any major reallocation of resources.

Independent Software Purchases

Generally in an automated turnkey library system, the hardware and software are purchased together, supplied through a single source. The turnkey vendor is usually not the actual manufacturer of the hardware, but, acting as a third party, sells equipment to the library as part of an overall hardware/software package. In some arrangements (see Table 8-1), the library purchases software from a source other than the hardware supplier. For large-scale applications, this option is most often exercised in one of two ways. The most common is when the library has access to a mainframe or minicomputer already located in the computer center of the parent institution. Less commonly, the library itself already has a minicomputer, perhaps initially purchased as part of a turnkey system, and now wishes to replace the original software supplied with that system with completely different software from another source. But far more common than either of these two large-scale circumstances is the use of microcomputers for which libraries purchase a great deal of third-party software to assist in a variety of tasks.

Regardless of how it is applied—on a parent institution's mainframe or minicomputer, on a library's own minicomputer, or even on a microcomputer—purchasing software and hardware separately for bibliographic processing applications has certain advantages and disadvantages over the other options cited in Table 8-1. If a computer is already in place, the initial costs of getting a system up and running will certainly be less than for a comparably sized turnkey package, since only software, not hardware, will have to be purchased. One disadvantage, however, is that if there already is hardware in place, the number of specific packages that can be run on it may be severely limited. This is particularly so regarding large-scale systems to be run on mainframes or minicomputers. At one time, very few library applications packages were available on a software-only basis for use on the larger computers. Fortunately, there has been a modest increase in recent years in availability. More libraries that have developed local systems for their own use are offering to sell or lease their applications software. The library itself may make the software available; in other cases, marketing rights have been awarded to a commercial interest. Turnkey vendors are also now more willing to license their software for use on equipment already available to a library, something they adamantly resisted in the past.

But despite the constant increase in the number of packages available on a software-only basis, a library may still find the selection too limited. Most available large-scale packages are intended for use on one of only a handful of different computer types. The library with access to a computer not included in this handful will have a difficult, if not impossible, task in finding an appropriate software package. And the selection is not extensive even for libraries that do have access to the more popular models. Libraries small enough to run an applications package on a microcomputer have more packages available than those that use a mainframe or minicomputer, but they still have hardware limitations. Most microcomputer library applications packages have been written for use either on Apple or IBM equipment.

The initial costs of independently purchased software vary enormously. Very simple microcomputer-based packages for various applications can be purchased for less than $100; commercial packages to run on mainframes or minicomputers can run into the tens of thousands of dollars. The continuing expenses associated with this option also vary greatly. One of the important dependent cost factors is the way in which enhancements can be added to the original software package. With most smaller microcomputer arrangements, continuing enhancement is neither provided by the vendor nor possible for the library to undertake. The package is sold as a one-time product; any subsequent version must be purchased as a new package. In some cases, however, the owner of an earlier version may purchase a revision at a considerably reduced price. With larger-scale packages for use on mainframes or minicomputers, most commercial vendors offer software maintenance arrangements not unlike those available for most turnkey systems. Routine enhancements to existing modules are provided as part of the maintenance agreement, while major reconfigurations or new modules are likely to carry an additional charge outside the regular maintenance fee. Some libraries that license their software to other libraries follow a similar practice, but some sell the software on essentially a one-time basis with no further enhancements. With the one-time arrangement, the purchasing library is usually given access to the source code and programs so that it may, if it chooses, enhance the programs itself. This right to modify, however, is rarely an option in purchasing software from a commercial vendor. If such an arrangement is worked out, access to the source code and the right to modify programs will invariably carry stringent provisions governing distribution to third parties. In any event, local enhancement will always be an expensive route for the purchasing library simply due to the amount of programmer time required.

Concerning the required level of in-house computer expertise and control over system performance, hardware upgrade, and software enhancement, many advantages and disadvantages of the software-only approach to automation are the same as those found with turnkey options or development of a system through a local computer center. They will vary according to where the computer is located and to the specific arrangements regarding software enhancement. But there is a very special need for caution with this option. When there is a problem with an automated system, it is sometimes difficult to determine whether the source is in the hardware or software. In the case of online services, turnkey systems, and those developed through a local computer center, there is one primary agency to whom the library can turn when system problems occur. In the case of independently acquired software packages mounted on a local or in-house computer supplied from a different source, the library is far more likely to encounter finger-pointing back and forth when there is a system problem. Software providers may insist that the problem source must be in the hardware, and hardware suppliers might be equally adamant that it must be in the software. It may take real persistence on the part of the library to get either side to consider the possibility that the source may rest in one product over the other.

A library's level of direct involvement with hardware and software depends on a number of factors, including governing and funding circumstances, type of application, capacity of the system, and specific alternatives available in the marketplace. In most cases, a library that has automated several of its operations has different levels of involvement for different applications. When a library selects a specific system for an application, the level of direct involvement with hardware and software is only one consideration. The ultimate keys to successful automation, as a process rather than a machine, seldom lie in hardware or software at all, but rather rest with the human beings involved.

Planning and Implementation Participants

The human element is the difference between implementing an automated system and simply installing one. Among the most crucial components in any phase of automation is the interaction between the agencies and individuals who play a role in the project.

At the most general level, the library needs to identify who will be involved, when, and for what purpose. As self-evident as this may sound, a lack of clear understanding of the range of participants and the roles they play is still at the heart of many of the difficulties encountered in library automation projects today.

Several types of agencies and individuals with which a library may interact during the implementation of an automated system or service are listed below:

Library staff

Administrative and governing authorities

Regulatory agencies and purchasing departments

Computer center personnel

Vendors

Consultants and attorneys

Other libraries

Telephone companies and other agencies

Library users

Not all of these parties will be involved in every type of automation project, but it is important not to prematurely exclude the possible relevance of any of them, no matter how large or small the project. An oversight can lead to misunderstandings or last-minute surprises, with the result almost always unanticipated delay, inconvenience, or additional expense.

Role of Library and Staff

The library and its staff is the focal point relating to all other agencies and individuals that might play a role in an automation project. During the course of the project, it may be necessary and desirable for some of the other parties to interact with each other, but it is crucial for the library to assume a coordinating role and to be aware of what is going on at all times.

One of the more difficult balances to achieve in planning and implementing an automated system or service is the level of staff involvement in various phases of the project. Staff awareness and participation before installation are crucial to the success of the new system or service. If all planning activities are shrouded in secrecy, there is likely to be so much defensiveness, rumor, and resentment built up among the staff that even the best of systems will have difficulty in succeeding once it is brought up. On the other hand, the opposite extreme can also lead to problems: democratic involvement carried too far can easily turn into anarchy in the case of planning for automation.

Various levels of involvement should be established. One level will be "supreme authority," most likely the library director or a high-level designate, who will make decisions when the participation process is deadlocked or administrative approval is needed.

If the automation project requires a substantial financial investment and several specific systems are available, many libraries establish a project team to draft functional requirements, evaluate alternatives, and select a specific system. The core membership of the team is usually comprised of individuals from the library department or departments that will be most affected by the new system or service. In selecting a multipurpose system, the representation should be as diverse as the sets of operations that the system will address. In many cases, the impact of a new system reaches beyond the confines of just the department or departments most directly involved. Inclusion of a staff member or two from outside the primary department or departments can add an important perspective to the project team. It may also be valuable to include one or two individuals from outside the library, such as a high-level administrator from the parent institution or a member of the local computer center staff. Apart from the project team, other formal or informal committees may also be established for specific purposes. For example, a public relations committee can play a crucial role if the new system or service will directly affect library patrons.

There are additional levels at which library staff should be involved. During the needs assessment phase, interviews should be conducted with as many staff members as possible who will be affected by the new system. After a system has been selected, but before it is installed, efforts must be made to educate different levels of staff. This point is examined in greater detail in Chapter 9, but it should be noted here that preinstallation information sessions are vitally important to the success of any automated project.

When a library is planning to implement a large-scale system, it is almost imperative to appoint a project coordinator. Often a member of the project team from its inception, the coordinator will need to devote full-time attention to the many phases of the project. It is the coordinator who sees to technical and many administrative details, makes certain that the scheduling of various activities falls into a complementary pattern, and often is the person responsible for carrying out training and other educational activities. Even after the system is up and running and has been successfully tested, the coordinator position is often retained on full-time status.

Selecting a project coordinator is one of the most critical decisions that upper management makes during the course of planning and implementation. That person, by virtue of the position and its responsibilities, will become the most knowledgeable staff member in the library about the progress of the project and its ins and outs. The coordinator must be communicative and be able to relate easily to the rest of the staff and to the other parties involved. The coordinator must be able to exercise discretion with the information he or she holds, but should not be the kind of person who is overly possessive of or secretive about the information at his or her disposal.

With small-scale systems or small libraries, the situation is somewhat different and often less formal. Even in these instances, however, involvement of staff who will be affected at all levels by a new system or service is a requisite to successful implementation.

Administrative and Governing Authorities

One of the first groups a library usually deals with in planning for automation is its administrative or governing authority. Especially if the proposed level of automation requires substantial capital investment, presentation of the library's needs and the garnering of support can be major tasks in themselves.

Once the library has received approval to initiate more formal planning, the relationship between a library and its parent authority remains important. From very early on, the library must be fully aware of any conditions or restrictions that will affect planning, such as policies governing disbursement of funds. For example, the governing authority may be able or willing to approve funding only for local development of a system or, conversely, may be predisposed toward purchasing a system from a commercial source. Whatever the limitations or reasons, the library should be aware of them before it gets too far along in the planning process. During the course of a project, the administrative or governing authority should be kept informed of general progress, of any major snags encountered, and of the action being taken to overcome them. Some libraries have asked a high-level administrator from the parent agency to serve on the project team. If that person takes an active interest, his or her knowledge of the priorities and inner workings of the university, municipality, or corporation can add an important perspective to the planning effort.

Regulatory Agencies and Purchasing Departments

Two other authorities that may have bearing on a library's plans and procedures for automating are regulatory agencies and purchasing departments. Pertinent regulatory limitations or requirements are all too often discovered at the last minute or even after the fact. Progress grinds to a halt and the library may even have to backtrack a few steps.

Particularly when equipment installation is required, state or local codes should be examined. Most often, these codes apply to electrical wiring and the like, but they may also pertain to less obvious elements such as telephone cables. For example, when a library in Nevada was preparing to install an OCLC terminal in 1982, the local telephone company had to postpone its part of the site preparation work after it arrived on the scene and found that the appropriate conduit for the telephone cabling had not yet been laid. A regulation regarding conduit for new telephone lines had only recently been introduced, and the library had not otherwise required any telephone work since the regulation had come into effect. The situation was easily resolved, but it is typical of the range of matters that can be affected by regulations.

Misunderstandings can also arise as a result of stipulations in labor union contracts. In using a parent institution's computer to run a circulation system, for example, the hours of employment specified in the union contract for computer personnel may not correspond to all the hours the library is open and needs its system up and running. Even a minicomputer in the library may have to be turned on each day slightly before normal working hours. If library employees belong to a union, there may be a problem unless early scheduling is covered in the union contract. Often such conflicts are not discovered until the local software has been developed or a turnkey system installed. They can usually be worked out, but only after last-minute negotiations.

University, municipal, and corporate purchasing departments usually have regulations and procedures to which the library is bound. For example, many libraries are required to seek competitive bids from a variety of vendors unless the condition of "sole supplier" can be clearly established, which is not often the case in purchasing an automated library system. In purchasing a system, the library should also have a clear understanding, in advance, of the extent to which the policy of its parent agency is to award contracts solely on the basis of lowest-cost bid versus allowing flexibility to consider nonfinancial evaluative criteria as well. In preparing a bid document or contract, the library will want to state payment or other conditions, and it must be certain that these terms conform to purchasing department policy.

The examples cited here have had to do mainly with the purchase and installation of the more obviously major components of an automated system. But the library should be aware that similar conditions might also apply to even minor peripheral purchases required for the system. In the installation of an automated circulation system at the Houston Public Library, for example, a delay was introduced into site preparation arrangements when the library was informed that it could not even purchase additional electrical outlets without going through a formal bid process.[2] Another concern, discussed more fully in the next chapter, is whether the vendor will be required to post a "performance bond"; this often is regarded to be a routine requirement of municipal purchasing departments but it rarely is a routine matter for library automation vendors.

Computer Center Personnel

If a library is part of a university, municipality, or corporation that has a central computer facility, varying levels of participation can be solicited from computer center personnel. If a system is being designed or software transferred to run on the central computer facilities, the level of involvement will obviously be very high. Even when purchasing a turnkey system, though, some libraries have successfully drawn on local computer expertise during various stages of planning and implementation. Computer center personnel may be able to assist the library in translating capacity and performance claims into language that the library staff can better understand in terms of its own requirements, and some libraries have enlisted a staff member from the computer center to participate on the project team to help in writing systems specifications and in evaluating vendor proposals. There are still problems in communication between librarians and computer center personnel, but a local expert willing to take an active interest and learn about libraries as well as teach about computers can be a valuable asset to a library's automation project.

Vendors

A library purchasing a turnkey system must maintain a delicate balance when interacting with its vendor. An atmosphere of mutual trust must be established, at the same time backed by formal documentation of expectations and responsibilities. Implementation will be a much smoother process if this balance can be achieved than if the relationship is marred by informality, mutual distrust, or ambiguous definition of responsibilities.

During a library's selection process, the qualitative and quantitative evaluation of system features and costs is paramount, but the reputation and past performance of the vendors involved should not be altogether discounted. Once a system has been selected, patience and clear understanding are essential ingredients in the negotiation of a final contract between the library and the vendor. The library must remain firm in its most important demands during contract negotiations, but it must also be certain that those demands are realistic. This is an area where the library might benefit in engaging the advice of outside consultants, attorneys, and even local computer center personnel.

After a contract has been signed, the library will invariably have further questions about site preparation and other details as installation draws nearer. The library may be inclined to rely on local resource people for advice on some of these matters, but it should keep in mind that the vendor has probably answered most of the same questions many times before, and the library should not hesitate to take advantage of its vendor's experience.

Consultants and Attorneys

An outside consultant with special expertise in library automation is commonly brought into a project. The cost of the proposed system or service usually determines the extent to which formal consulting is warranted. When a library is purchasing a large-scale system or creating a multi-institutional network, experienced consultants can often provide a degree of insight and skill that is worth their fees. Libraries investigating possibilities for cooperation among a number of institutions often engage consultants very early on to outline the widely varying alternatives available and the advantages and disadvantages of each. In single-institution projects, involvement of the consultant usually comes later, often focusing on the preparation of bid documents, evaluation of responses, and negotiation of contracts.

For projects on a smaller scale, such as the purchase of a microcomputer or a decision about which information retrieval services to subscribe to, the initial investment is seldom sufficient to justify the price of formal consulting. Many state libraries and regional networks have attempted to fill this void by developing staff expertise in these areas and offering assistance to libraries for nominal or no fees. In many locations, local user groups also sponsor programs or provide informal assistance that can be helpful to the library in evaluating and selecting equipment or services.

Many libraries are required to send all contracts through their university, municipal, or corporate legal departments for approval. This is a valuable check when contracting for an automated system or service. Libraries and library boards that are not required to get formal approval from legal counsel might consider enlisting the advice of an attorney anyway. Under either circumstance, it is important to bear in mind that specifications for data-processing equipment and services are not familiar to all attorneys. If a major purchase is involved, it may be worthwhile to seek an attorney with previous experience in data-processing contracts.

As an alternative to specialized legal advice, a number of library automation consultants have considerable experience in evaluating contracts for automated library systems. The use of a consultant for this purpose will not negate the value of an attorney's involvement, but it may eliminate the need to find an attorney with special experience in the area of automated systems and services. Under this type of arrangement, the library, the consultant, and the attorney with general background should work together closely through the contract negotiation stage of a project.

Other Libraries

A valuable source of information for any type of automation project is other libraries. Institutions that have already undertaken a similar project can lend valuable insight into the general planning process, and a great deal can be learned about specific systems or services from libraries already using them.

Some important qualifications must be kept in mind when seeking comments and advice from other libraries. First, when a specific turnkey system is being examined in another library, it is important to know when the system was purchased and how it differs from the version currently being offered by the same vendor. A library may have purchased the system several years before when the automation market and the system itself were quite different, and it may not have taken advantage of all upgrades or enhancements made available since the initial purchase. Second, it is advisable to talk with a number of librarians rather than just one or two. Every good vendor has at least a few dissatisfied customers, and every not so reliable vendor has a few perfectly happy clients somewhere. It is better to draw on the experiences of several libraries using a system than risk the possibility of contacting a library that has had an atypical experience. Third, and most important, specific circumstances and needs vary from one library to another. Even when a turnkey system is purchased, its introduction into yet another new setting carries with it a certain uniqueness because of the library's own organizational structure, the pattern of interaction among its staff, and the policies and procedures in effect. The machinery may be the same, but the requirements and conditions into which it is introduced may not be. As long as these qualifications are kept in mind, a great deal of insight can be gained from the automation experiences of other libraries.

Telephone Companies and Other Participants

With everything else that is going on during the course of an automation project, it is very easy to overlook any of a host of other agencies and individuals that may need to be called in at some point. One of the foremost of these is the local telephone company.

In a recent networking project in the West, a group of libraries, after years of planning, had finally reached a stage where hardware had been selected and a contract signed. Upon arrival of the computer at the central site, a request was made for the telephone company to install the necessary dedicated lines into the host computer. The group was then informed about a moratorium in that part of the city on installation of new lines. The problem was quickly resolved and turned out to be more of a nuisance than a real obstacle, but this example is indicative of the pivotal role that telephone companies can play in the installation of an automated system.

Even advance dealings with telephone companies is a double-edged sword. Especially in large urban areas, telephone companies usually require a period of lead time for installation of dedicated lines that is convenient for their own scheduling. Estimating the appropriate time at which to schedule telephone work is difficult in projects like the installation of an automated library system, where the overall scheduling is sensitive to a multitude of factors right up to the last minute. On the other hand, it is important to adhere as closely as possible to a telephone company's announced schedule, since these companies very much dislike postponing their part of the work because of delays caused by circumstances outside their control.

Other agencies or individuals may also be involved, especially during site preparation. Electrical upgrading may be needed, special flooring may have to be installed, or perhaps wall carpeting in the room housing a computer needs to be installed in order to reduce noise flow to the outside. These activities are likely to require the assistance of outside personnel.

Library Users

Automated circulation systems, COM and online catalogs, and reference-based information retrieval services directly affect the way people use a library. Too often libraries have viewed the impact of new technology on users as beginning on the day a system or service becomes operational. One day there is no online search service, for example, and the next day there is. Crucial changes such as the introduction of a COM catalog or COM supplement to a card catalog are sometimes sprung upon users with little or no advance warning. Where a library is preparing for an online catalog or circulation system, nonfunctioning or staff-only terminals are often installed well in advance without users being given the slightest clue as to their eventual purpose. Although library staff may have been engaged in planning the end product for months or even years, the average library user is unaware of this and may be struck by the apparent suddenness of it all.

For a new system or service that will affect users directly, a public relations campaign should begin well in advance of the operational stage. To some extent, the library will already have begun this process when it lobbied its case before the funding authority, and on an even larger scale if it undertook bond issues or other public-funding drives. Once a firm decision has been made and the library is well on its way, it is crucial to accelerate the public relations campaign. Newspaper articles, public announcements, brochures and displays, and even demonstrations during the advance stage of the project help to ease conversion to the new system or service.

The library must time its public relations efforts carefully. An awareness campaign should begin early, but the library must be sensitive to the possibility of delays in implementation, which could work to the detriment of the campaign if users have been led to expect an operational system on a certain day or during a specific week or month and the system or service is not ready then. No matter how elaborate and well thought out the advance campaign, there will still be many users with no awareness of the new system or service until they are directly confronted by it. But the more people who know that a change is coming and are aware of the benefits to be derived by them as library users, the smoother the transition will be.

Identifying the various agencies and individuals who will be involved in an automation project will not ensure against all possible problems, but it may help to avoid major snags and long delays. Automation seldom follows an easy step-by-step procedure, but certain phases are characteristic of most projects. Once a decision has been made to consider automation, and depending on the nature and scope of the system or service, subsequent planning may call for any or all of the following activities: analysis of current procedures and definition of requirements for the new system or service; preparation of requests for proposals and evaluation of vendor responses; negotiation of contracts and site preparation; installation; acceptance testing; and training. These aspects of automation planning are discussed in the following chapter.

Notes

1. Richard L. Waters and V. F. Kralisz, "Financing the Electronic Library: Models and Options," *Drexel Library Quarterly* 17 (Fall 1981): 110.
2. Jay B. Clark, "DataPhase at the Houston Area Library System," in *Library Automation: Five Case Studies,* Maurice J. Freedman, ed., *LJ* Special Report, no. 22 (New York: R. R. Bowker, 1982), p. 31.

9

Selecting, Procuring, and Introducing an Automated System

This chapter examines procedures in selecting and procuring an automated library system, including preparing and training staff for its implementation. Library automation is too complex a process to list procedures in a step-by-step formula that will fit all institutions under all circumstances. The level of formal procedure in planning and implementing an automation project varies widely according to library preference and the nature of the application. Subscribing to a reference-based information retrieval service or buying a microcomputer is quite different from purchasing a quarter-million-dollar minicomputer-based turnkey circulation system. An information retrieval service or a retail microcomputer outlet would be rather perplexed to receive a lengthy bid document from a library wishing to use a few hours of search service per month or seeking to purchase a microcomputer or two. Turnkey circulation vendors, on the other hand, are accustomed to receiving such documents.

The discussion here focuses primarily on the purchase of larger automated turnkey systems by libraries with a fairly large staff. This emphasis provides the broadest possible framework for treating a wide range of issues in the procurement of an automated system. It does not, however, negate the importance of taking many of these same concerns into account in automation projects of lesser scope.

Analyzing Operations and Requirements

When libraries begin to investigate the possibility of automating a set of operations, they usually do so in response to existing conditions.

There is a notion, sometimes clearly conceived, sometimes vague, that certain problems with the current system, manual or automated, could be alleviated if a new system were introduced.

One of the first activities in seriously considering automation is to carefully analyze the current operations of the department or function involved. This means more than simply stating the general impressions that may have led to exploring automation in the first place. Acquiring a system based solely on general impressions will probably solve the more outstanding problems, but the library may miss out on an opportunity to take this one step further and improve on other procedures as well. General impressions are just that—summary observations, usually of visible results and not necessarily of causes, and the problems identified are often viewed in isolation from their broader context. A more systematic analysis of current operations can help pinpoint the source of the problems and help one to view them in relation to their broader context. It will confirm the more obvious problems and will uncover others that may be less dramatic or visible, but that might still deserve attention. The results of the analysis should help to articulate the features desired in a new system and to assign a comparative degree of importance to each.

Analyzing Current Operations

Analyzing current operations and formulating a concept of what is desired in a new system are closely intertwined. As the current organization and procedures are examined, it will become obvious which tasks are most in need of streamlining or clarifying. It is important to distinguish between problem areas that can be addressed directly by automation and those that might simply be a result of inefficiencies in organization or ambiguities in procedure under the current system. In many cases, the ineffectiveness of a manual system is not due to the fact that it is manual, but rather to the way in which work flow is organized and tasks are defined.

When current operations are analyzed and ways explored in which automation may lead to improvement, five general considerations and comparisons surface over and over again—time, money, control, relationship, and service. An analysis of current operations should determine for each task or set of tasks involved:

How much staff time is being spent on it

How much money it is costing (including staff)

How much control is being exercised over the items or records handled

How it relates to other tasks

How it translates into level of service for the library user

These same questions should be asked when exploring the implications of a new system and defining the requirements for it.

The library should not enter into an examination of current operations with strongly preconceived notions about what it expects to find, but it is necessary to clearly establish what to look for. Using criteria such as those above, the library should examine as many tasks and as many results as possible. Without bias, the library should pay particular attention to those areas where a manual system seems to have become bogged down. Almost regardless of the bibliographic operation or library service being considered, certain elements common to manual systems are especially vulnerable to problems and breakdown if overloaded. Some of these manifest themselves as symptoms of a problem and others as a cause, but in any case they provide valuable yardsticks to measure the effectiveness of a manual system and compare it with expectations about an automated system.

The following list and examples are not meant to be comprehensive, but will identify some of the elements common to library operations and services that are most likely to be problem areas, and that can point directions for expectations about a new system and any reorganization that might ease its incorporation into library routines.

Backlogs. Any bibliographic processing operation can experience backlogs: materials waiting to be ordered or cataloged; periodical issues waiting to be checked in; items waiting to be shelved after circulation; catalog cards waiting to be filed in the public catalog; and so on. If backlogs are increasing, and not of a temporary or seasonal nature, they are the most visible signs that a processing system is either operating inefficiently or is simply unable to handle the volume of work being placed on it. An analysis should take special note of backlogs and attempt to identify all the reasons contributing to them.

Filing. Filing of paper forms and records is common to manual systems used for almost every type of bibliographic operation. If there is no filing backlog, it means that the resources allocated are at least keeping pace with the activities that are generating the material to be filed. If there is a filing backlog, it usually indicates an imbalance in the allocation of resources. Especially if the size of the backlog is growing, a contributing factor may be that the per-unit amount of time required in filing is increasing. This is especially characteristic of large files, such as public catalogs, into which cards are constantly being added but seldom removed. An analysis of current operations should not only calculate the amount of time required and staff costs incurred for filing, but should also sample existing files to estimate their level of accuracy.

General processing routines. In addition to filing, each bibliographic operation in a library involves staff time devoted to a variety of processing tasks. In analyzing current operations, it is important to examine these as individually as possible in terms of the effectiveness with which they are being carried out, the amount of time required, and the manner in which problems in performance affect other processing routines.

Control over records and items being handled. This is an essential part of analyzing current operations. In circulation, for example, can overdue materials be easily identified? In serials control, is it possible to determine that an issue is past due before the following one arrives? Is it possible to readily identify titles to which the library has subscribed but for which no issues are being received at all? In acquisitions, what is the procedure for identifying items on order for more than six months but not yet received? Can one determine where in the processing stage an item is currently located? The list could go on and on. In almost every type of bibliographic operation, there are one or more particularly crucial points of vulnerability: blind spots, a "twilight zone" of sorts, into which records or even the items themselves can temporarily or permanently disappear. In analyzing current operations, the library should attempt to gauge the degree to which records or items are exposed to such vulnerabilities and to pinpoint the junctures at which they are most likely to occur.

Access to records. The vulnerabilities described above are frequently the result of a limited range of access points to records. In planning for automation, bear in mind that flexibility of access is one of the strongest attributes of automated systems. Thus, when the library is analyzing current operations, it is crucial not only to identify the access points available in the present system, but also to ascertain which additional ones would help to bring a greater degree of control over the records and items being handled.

Consistency of records and duplication of efforts. If bibliographic operations in a library are highly compartmentalized, there is likely to be some degree of inconsistency between departments in the bibliographic practices they employ. For example, the most appropriate form of filing entry for a journal title might be viewed quite differently by the departments responsible for acquiring, cataloging, and checking-in issues. Particularly in manual systems that often have only one access point to records in departmental files, these inconsistencies can lead to confusion when departments have to cross-check. At the same time, there can be a considerable degree of redundancy in the information being recorded and filed for each title. The analysis of current operations should determine the extent to which departments keep their own records for items and how much of the information is or could be common to all. It should also identify the types of problems that arise because of inconsistencies between records and how often they occur.

Statistical information. Cataloging statistics, acquisitions fund reports, and circulation statistics are examples of compilations that provide valuable management information if used effectively. Compilation of statistics under a manual system is often too time-consuming at all but the most cursory levels of detail. Automated systems, on the other hand, can generate statistical information so easily and prolifically that the major problem is usually to decide what types of compilations really are important and what types are mere excess. In analyzing current operations, the library should identify the types of data being gathered and their use. It is also important to discover the types of data not being collected now that would be useful in the future.

Financial loss and unnecessary expenditures. Libraries lose a certain amount of time and money because of such things as duplicate orders, serials subscriptions that are paid for but for which no issues are ever received, items that are charged out and never returned, and so on. Some degree of this is inevitable. But it is necessary in analyzing current operations to determine the extent to which financial losses or unintentional expenditures are caused by limitations of procedural constraints. The examples cited above can usually be attributed to a lack of sufficient access points. The analysis should focus on where money is being lost, why, and how much. If part of the loss is due to limited flexibility in the current operations, this represents a very real dollars-and-cents cost of the manual or automated system itself.

Patron service. Patron dissatisfaction is analogous in some ways to processing backlogs. It is a problem that can manifest itself in a very visible, or in this case vocal, manner. Observation of patron complaints and examination of misunderstandings between the library and user can be valuable techniques in analyzing current operations. Patrons may not be able to identify the causes of a problem, but they can definitely articulate the results. By tracing backward, it may be possible to discover the source of the problem and determine if it might have been the result of vulnerability in the current system or procedures.

The analysis of current operations should not focus just on the tasks involved or on the problem areas identified. This will be a major part of the study, but it will also be necessary to examine the volume of activity particular to the operation under investigation: this includes the number of items acquired or cataloged, the number of circulations per unit of time, the maximum level attained during peak periods, temporal patterns of use of the public catalog, and so on.

The analysis of current operations should not be carried out so as to appear threatening to staff. If staff members feel confident that the purpose of identifying problems, analyzing procedures, and measuring quantities is to improve operations with a new system rather than to point blame for existing inadequacies, their observations and opinions can be among the most valuable sources of information in studying the current system and in helping to define requirements for a new one.

Requirements for a New System

Another purpose of an analysis of current operations is to formulate ideas about what is desired in a new automated system. Here is where information from staff interviews can prove particularly useful. The general goal of a new system will be to assist staff, and patrons if appropriate, to do their work faster, better, and more efficiently. During the examination of current operations, ideas will begin to crystallize with respect to which tasks can most be aided or replaced and which problem areas or points of vulnerability most need to be addressed. The library should begin to put together a list of specifically what, in functional terms, the new system should be able to do.

During staff interviews conducted at the analysis stage, the initial tally of desirable features will most likely emerge as a wish list, rather loosely organized and even containing some contradictions. It is an inventory of what everyone involved would like in the best of all possible worlds. However, it is important to take a cautious approach to expectations, even during the discussion stage, for no automated system will be able to do everything that everyone would like it to. In practical terms, there is a significant difference between features that are desired, features that are needed, and features that are even possible. Especially if one is purchasing a turnkey system, there will have to be compromise.

At some point it will be necessary to begin to scrutinize the list of desired features more closely. This is frequently done by a project team, but additional input should come from other staff through individual or small group interviews. The first step is to resolve any contradictions and remove any impossibilities or impracticalities. If suggestions made by staff during earlier interviews are discarded, it is a good public relations gesture to carefully explain the reasons for doing so to the staff members who had originally tendered them.

The next stage of refinement is to assess the relative importance of the remaining features. These will most likely fall into three categories: (1) those that, after closer examination and further discussion, are found not really to be of much importance after all, (2) those that are deemed absolutely essential, and (3) those that fall somewhere in between. The features that fall into the first category can be removed from the list. Those in the second category are functional requirements for any new system. Those in the third category are features that are desired but not required. It is critical to carefully distinguish between the second and third categories. Required features should be just that: required, leaving no room for debate when it comes to evaluating specific systems. A system not providing all features included in this category should not be considered for selection.

However, a system should not be ruled out if it does not provide all of the functions stipulated as desired but not required. Since different systems offer a different mix of these, the library must decide how it will judge the relative importance of each optional feature. One approach is to consider them all to be of equal value, but this will seldom correspond to reality. If several optional features are stipulated, there will probably be a consensus among the project team or staff that certain of them are more desirable than others. A second approach, then, is to rank the optional features in order of desirability. This is certainly more discriminating, but the problem occurs in how to assign equal units of gradation between each ranking. For example, the library may feel that the second and third highest ranking features are extremely close in desirability level, but there may be a large degree of difference between these two and the most highly rated feature. A simple ranking procedure does not recognize these differences in magnitude of desirability.

A third approach that does recognize magnitude is a weighting procedure. The desirability of each feature is measured according to an arbitrary but common scale, such as 10 or 100. The major problem here is in deciphering exactly what the values mean relative to each other. For example, is a feature assigned a value of 60 on a scale of 100 really three times more desirable than a feature assigned a value of 20? Despite some drawbacks, the weighting procedure is often the most viable approach.

A fourth alternative, something of a hybrid between the second and third approaches, is to group features according to general levels of desirability. In examining optional features in detail, the library may discover that there are certain natural breaks in degree of desirability. Two or three functions might emerge as clearly the most desirable, followed by another cluster of features that are desirable but not at the same level as the first grouping, and finally by some additional features that are decisively less important than those in even the second grouping. The resulting clusters can then be ranked or weighted accordingly, with each individual feature assuming the value assigned to the cluster of which it is a part.

Regardless of the method, it is best to make some kind of qualitative or quantitative distinction between optional features when several are being considered. This will provide the key to compare the functional capabilities of different systems that have each met the minimum requirements.

In addition to functional requirements, the library must also establish system capacity and performance requirements. (Performance requirements are discussed later in this chapter.) For capacity requirements, the library must determine the quantity of data that a new system will need to handle. It is imperative that the library not only be able to accurately state current needs, but also to estimate requirements during the course of the next five to seven years at least. Too many libraries have developed or purchased systems adequate for current needs, only to encounter major obstacles soon after when expanding files or increasing levels of activity reached system capacity.

The library should be careful at this point to express its capacity requirements in library terms rather than computer terms. It is more meaningful, and less ambiguous, to state that a system must be able to process a certain number of transactions per unit of time or accommodate a certain number of bibliographic records of certain length than it is to say that a system must have a main memory or secondary storage capacity of a certain number of bytes. Because there are other requirements, bytes of main memory or secondary storage and characters of bibliographic data will not correspond on a one-to-one basis, and the exact ratio will differ from one system to another.

After functional and capacity requirements have been defined, the next step will differ according to the situation. Libraries developing a completely in-house system will probably go shopping for hardware. Those developing a system through a local computer center will begin to negotiate their requirements with center personnel. Some libraries purchasing a turnkey system will begin to evaluate systems and make a selection. Many libraries purchasing a turnkey system, however, will be required or will want to go through a more formal intermediate procedure. This involves the preparation of a Request for Proposal. The proposal process, when used effectively, is far more than an exercise in paper shuffling. It can establish an analytical framework within which different systems are evaluated and a selection is made, and can further serve as the groundwork for negotiating the final contract with the vendor whose system is chosen.

Request for Proposal

The Request for Proposal (RFP) document in library automation is most common in projects involving the selection and purchase of a fairly large-scale system from among two or more distinct alternatives. RFPs can also be useful, and are often required by the library's parent organization, even for a smaller scale purchase, even when there is only one alternative available, or even when the library has already decided which system it will purchase. In the latter two cases, the primary value of the RFP is to serve as the beginning of a formal, documented understanding between the library and the vendor. Conditions set forth in the RFP and the response will be further elaborated and refined during contract negotiations.

Although the RFP is useful for these latter purposes, libraries should be sensitive to the position of vendors in those cases where the library has already arrived at a decision and must send RFPs to several different vendors simply to satisfy the requirements of internal purchasing departments. Drawing up a response to an RFP requires time and effort, and therefore expense. Vendors can frequently tell when an RFP has been written to overwhelmingly favor a response from one particular vendor in the field. For example, the RFP might specify, as absolute requirements for the system, a feature or combination of relatively minor features that are available only through one particular system. Where this is obviously the case, many vendors will not even attempt to respond to the RFP. For the library that is approaching selection from a much more open position, a lesson can be learned from this: exercise caution in specifying absolute requirements. If functional and other requirements are too stringent, the library may find that it has narrowed its options beyond what it intended. For libraries that have not already selected a system, the RFP should be presented in a form that will allow a certain degree of flexibility for response, especially with regard to hardware configurations and applications software.

Preparing the RFP

A detailed discussion of all elements commonly included in elaborate RFPs is beyond the scope here. At this stage many libraries involve a consultant, especially when large-scale systems are being purchased.

Well-written RFPs from other libraries can serve as a further source of information, although it is important when examining them to carefully distinguish between form and content. Even for the same type of application, specific requirements will vary from one library to another, and therefore it is necessary to differentiate between general stipulations and institution-specific requirements or preferences. The primary value of drawing on RFPs written by other libraries is in establishing the structure of the document and in determining general areas of coverage to be included.[1]

RFPs generally include introductory matter, details pertinent to the process vendors must follow in responding to requests, a description of what is required and desired in an automated system, identification of contract-related matters and levels of support that should be addressed in vendor proposals, and the manner in which cost information should be presented. Each of these major areas is briefly reviewed below.

Introductory matter. The RFP should include a general statement as to the type of operation for which automation is being considered, a general description of the library, and some of the parameters that are particularly relevant to the operation for which an automated system is being sought. Either here or elsewhere in the RFP, it is important to include a section in which definitions are stated for the principal terminology used in the request. A vendor's interpretation of a term may not be exactly the same as the library's, and a clear definition of terminology can help to avert misunderstandings that might otherwise arise between a library and a vendor.

Setting up vendor responses. The library determines the conditions and procedures to be followed by vendors in responding to the RFP. A specific address, along with the name of a specific person, department, committee, or other type of heading, should be included to avoid the possibility of a vendor's proposal being misplaced or delayed within the library as a result of the routine shuffle of the mail. A specific deadline for proposals, including date and time of day, should be stated, along with a description of policies and procedures regarding extension of deadlines and late arrival of proposals. There should also be a statement of policy and procedures for issuing amendments to the proposal if necessary.

The RFP should request a description of vendor qualifications and a list of current customers. Lists of selected customers are not of uniform value and often amount to little more than a vendor-selected list of satisfied clients. In addition to names and addresses of current customers, the vendor should identify the basic configuration being used by each and the size of the files and volume of activity being handled. This will enable the library to determine whether the vendor has experience in providing systems to libraries of a size and with a volume of activity similar to its own. Such libraries can serve as a valuable source of information and comment about the system and the vendor's quality of service.

In many cases, vendors will have questions concerning the RFP, relating both to general conditions and specific content. The RFP should include a statement of the procedure for requesting and receiving clarification. In the past some libraries have held a bidder's conference for this purpose, attended by all vendors interested in answering the RFP. But because of the expense involved and the logistical difficulties of arranging such a meeting of all interested parties, libraries now generally opt to handle vendor questions by mail. Even so, formal procedures should be spelled out in the RFP. The library should also include a general description of how it will evaluate proposals and should indicate the anticipated time frame for making a selection.

Required and desired capabilities. One of the most crucial purposes of the RFP is to outline what the library expects an automated system to do. One set of stipulations will be concerned with system capacity requirements. The library should be able to state its file size needs in terms of the number of records and characters that the system must be able to handle, along with the volume of each type of pertinent transaction over a unit of time and the maximum required during peak periods. If known, the number of terminals a library plans to use and their locations should be provided. It is important in stating these requirements to take into account the possibility of growth during the next several years and to distinguish between present needs and anticipated incremental future needs.

Another type of requirement is performance criteria: how reliably and how quickly the system must perform its assigned tasks. Two particularly important criteria are downtime and response-time measurements. The library should state the maximum percentage of unscheduled downtime allowable and maximum response-time levels for the types of transactions that will be performed. The library should also state the functional capabilities that are absolutely required in a system and those that are desirable but not required. The two sets of features, required and desired, should be very clearly separated and labeled accordingly. The RFP should also include suggested, and in some cases required, parameters for testing the entire system as a prerequisite to final acceptance and payment. Acceptance testing is discussed in more detail later in this chapter.

Contract-related matters and levels of support. The RFP should serve as a foundation for contract negotiations between a library and the selected vendor. A vast array of items can be included in an RFP to help establish this foundation. These items may be treated in considerable detail and stated either as preferences of the library or, in other cases, as non-negotiable requirements of the library, its purchasing department, or its governing authority. In still other RFPs, these items are stated simply as points of consideration that vendors must address in their proposals.

Regardless of the approach, the list of items for inclusion can be quite extensive. Some of the more common include policies and procedures relating to performance bonds, terms of payment, hardware and software maintenance, site preparation and installation responsibilities and requirements, delivery and scheduling guidelines, and so on. It is also important to ask vendors to detail their support services, including training, documentation, and general assistance, both in preparing for implementation and on a continuing basis after the system has been accepted.

Costs of the system. An RFP should describe the framework within which costs are expected to be presented by vendors. It is to the library's advantage to stipulate that both initial and continuing costs be broken down by the vendor as specifically as possible. In the initial purchase price, vendors should state the hardware that will be supplied and the price assigned to each major component.

The feasibility of delineating costs for applications software will vary depending on the application and the vendor's pricing policy. Where applicable, vendors should be asked to stipulate costs for the required functional capabilities, followed by separate pricing additions for modules or features that the library has identified as desired but not required. This will assist the library in evaluating the relative worth of desirable features and comparing costs of various combinations of features both within and across systems. Stipulation of all other charges, such as for delivery and installation of equipment, should also be requested.

In addition to initial costs, it is important for the library to require a complete delineation of costs that will be incurred on a continuing basis after the system has been installed. Types of continuing costs include those for hardware and software maintenance, additional equipment, per-unit transaction fees if applicable, supplies, and any other direct expenses that will be paid to the vendor on an ongoing basis. The library should request that these continuing costs also be broken down as individually as possible. It is not always possible to separate cost units as distinctly or unambiguously as described here, but vendors should be asked to do so to the fullest extent possible. Libraries will have a better idea of what they are paying for and will be better able to compare costs among alternative systems.

Evaluation and Selection

When an RFP is issued, vendors should be allowed at least six to eight weeks to respond with a final proposal. Once all proposals have been received, the library is ready to begin the evaluation phase. There are three things to be evaluated: (1) the proposals themselves, (2) the systems being proposed, and (3) the vendors presenting them. These three are closely interrelated, and excluding any one may lead to a decision that is not in the best long-range interests of the library.

Several criteria should be considered when evaluating the various combinations of proposal, system, and vendor. Even if a library does not have to go through a formal proposal process, several of these criteria can still be applied when evaluating available systems and their vendors.

Does the proposal answer the request? If the library does let an RFP, one of the first tasks in evaluating responses is to determine whether each proposal has adequately addressed the concerns raised in the RFP. Allowing for a certain degree of flexibility in format and content, the library has the right to expect each proposal to cover the points outlined in its RFP. This step in evaluation is generally a de-selection process. A positive final selection should not be made merely on the basis of a proposal that is carefully prepared, but some systems might be eliminated from consideration if presented in proposals that do not adequately address the library's RFP. A well-written proposal does not necessarily ensure that a system or vendor support will be of equally high quality, but a poorly written proposal, or one that seems to be generalized or possibly addressing another library's RFP, should be taken as a warning. If a vendor has not taken the time and effort to reply adequately to an RFP, it is unlikely that the vendor's subsequent support services will be much better.

Contract-related conditions. In addition to the basic adequacy of proposals, libraries often evaluate conditions regarding such matters as performance bonds, terms of payment, liability, and so on. In some cases, a vendor's policy toward certain aspects of sale and implementation can be quite different from those the library wants. It is a mistake, however, to regard contract-related matters too strictly during the initial evaluation, since they are often subject to negotiation and are areas in which a vendor may be willing to make concessions. The library must, therefore, be careful not to eliminate a proposal on the basis of what might be negotiable points. Selection should be based on other criteria and contractual matters left to be negotiated with the chosen vendor. If the library and vendor are later unable or unwilling to come to terms on certain conditions, the library can then reverse its selection and opt for a different system.

Is the system adequately matched to the library's capacity requirements? One of the first priorities in evaluating proposed systems is to determine whether each is, in fact, adequate to handle the library's files and level of activity. A system must be large enough to effectively handle the library's capacity requirements—this is imperative. A less considered aspect, but an equally important one, is the possibility that the system as proposed is too large. Growth potential should be considered within reasonable limits—limits that the library should already have determined and stated in its RFP. But some libraries have inadvertently purchased a much larger—and more expensive—system than they would ever need in the foreseeable future, and it is crucial that a library be certain it is not purchasing overkill in system configuration and capacity.

Functional capabilities and general requirements. Part of the evaluation process is to determine the extent to which different systems meet the required and desired functional features outlined in the RFP. Systems that do not provide all of the capabilities indicated as required should be eliminated. If the RFP included a number of features desired but not required in a system, it is possible that no system will be able to provide all of them, or that any two systems will offer exactly the same combination of such features. Approaches for assessing the relative value of desired but not required features are discussed earlier in this chapter. With any of the methods described there, the value of different combinations of features can be compared across systems. After proposals have been received, considerable attention should be devoted to this part of the evaluation process, since functional capabilities are among the most important considerations in selecting an automated system.

In examining the capabilities of various systems, the library should draw a strong distinction between those that are currently available and those that are forthcoming. Capabilities not yet actually operational should be considered very cautiously. If they are taken into account at all, they must be rigorously judged according to the likelihood of their realization and the cost implications. A vendor's past record of promise versus performance should be closely scrutinized before taking any forthcoming capabilities into account. The library must also be certain that the systems being considered meet all other requirements specified in the RFP, including those pertaining to performance.

System reliability and support channels. The purchase and installation of a system are only the beginning of a venture into automation. Once the system has been installed, there will be a variety of continuing support needs. These, along with the proven reliability of a system in the field, should be taken into consideration in the initial selection process.

One type of continuing support concerns hardware and software components. The library should be informed in vendor proposals of the basic arrangement for equipment repair, routine maintenance, and any necessary debugging of software. Certain types of equipment may lend themselves to locally available support services more readily than others. This can be a significant factor when a system is down and an on-site visit is necessary to correct the problem. Since the library will be using the new system for several years hence, its proven reliability in the field and the level of continuing hardware and software support should be important considerations in the initial evaluation process.

Upgrade and enhancement. The level of sophistication and capacity of automated systems change fairly rapidly. So do library needs and activities. One area of great hesitation in purchasing an automated system is the fear that it will not remain sufficient or that it will become antiquated in comparison with state-of-the-art standards after a very brief period. If the library feels that it may need to add more terminals, increase storage capacity, or otherwise augment its hardware configuration at a later date, expansion potential of various systems should be considered during the initial evaluation process. At this level, the potential for expansion of each system should be judged according to what is *currently* possible, not according to as yet undeveloped upgrade capabilities that *might* (or might *not*) be introduced by the vendor at some point in the future.

On a longer range basis, most library automation vendors attempt to remain competitive in the ever changing environment by introducing new equipment or software enhancements to their systems. A vendor's future performance in this area cannot be predicted with absolute certainty, but past performance can sometimes serve as a general guideline. In evaluating this aspect during the initial evaluation process, the library should be aware that new developments and innovations by vendors are not in themselves the most critical factor. More pertinent points are how well new equipment and software enhancements can be incorporated into older versions of the system and at what cost. A new development will be of little value to a library if it is not compatible with the system in place, or if it requires such a major overhaul that it is likely to be too expensive. Some vendors have better records than others in pursuing a course of change that emphasizes integration of new developments into existing systems.

Vendors. Libraries sometimes go to either of two extremes in the amount of importance they attach to a vendor as opposed to a system in the evaluation and selection process. In some cases, a particular system is selected primarily because the vendor stands out as particularly friendly or helpful in demonstrating and answering questions about its system. This is not an appropriate chief criterion on which a system should be selected. However, it is just as inappropriate to completely disregard records of vendor performance and even subjective impressions. If, for some reason, the library is convinced that it has legitimate cause for distrusting a particular vendor or has found previous dealings to be uncomfortable, these factors should definitely be taken into account. Distrust or ill will is not a good foundation on which to initiate the purchase of an automated system. The vendor's record of support and the relationship between promises and performance should also be weighed, and this is where interviews with other libraries can be particularly instructive.

Benchmark tests and demonstrations. It is important to study a prospective system in actual operation. One way of doing so, usually after a system has been selected but before a contract is signed, is to require a benchmark test, having the vendor demonstrate the system under actual conditions and levels of activity that match the library's needs. Such tests can be enormously time-consuming and are seldom required by libraries unless the system in question is new or has not before been placed in a library of comparable size or with an equivalent volume of activity.

During the evaluation process, participating staff should have the opportunity to see each system being considered in actual operation. Vendors are usually willing to schedule private demonstrations at conference exhibits and the like. These are, however, only of the most general value, since the capabilities are often demonstrated using either vendor-selected files or very small test databases. These conditions are sufficient for demonstrating the basic features, but actual system performance has very much to do with the size of the database, and an artificially composed or carefully chosen database may not give an accurate picture of performance under the library's own conditions. If a system is already in place in a variety of settings, the most reliable demonstration is for library representatives to observe the proposed system in actual operation in other libraries.

Delivery date and scheduling. Scheduling and the time frame for delivery of a system are sometimes relevant in the evaluation process, but their principal value should be as de-selection criteria in extreme cases. For turnkey systems, there is seldom much variability from one system to another in the time frame for installation, unless a vendor is tremendously backlogged or has projected new models or software enhancements as part of the proposed package.

If the expected delivery date seems sooner than the library prefers, a more satisfactory time frame can usually be negotiated before signing the contract. In any case, a system should be eliminated from consideration on the basis of delivery date and scheduling only if the time frame is clearly unacceptable and there seems to be no room for negotiation.

Costs. A critical part of a vendor proposal is the presentation of costs. A system should not be selected strictly on the basis of lowest cost bid unless the library is required to do so. As long as the cost of a proposed system is below what the library establishes as a maximum limit, it should be evaluated according to all other criteria before considering cost.

In calculating the cost of each system, the library should consider all costs that will be incurred for the initial implementation and for continuing use several years into the future, not just the initial purchase price listed on the proposal. Not all systems will necessarily require the same level of staffing; differences in site preparation requirements or conversion techniques may have financial implications; the pricing strategy for continuing hardware and software maintenance may be quite different from one system to another, and so on. As many of these variables as possible should be taken into account, including even those such as staffing that are not part of the direct costs of the system itself.

The most difficult part of comparing costs between systems is in determining how to relate cost factors to other factors, such as functional capabilities, reputation of vendor, and so on. Each system has different features and its own strengths and weaknesses, and each has a different cost associated with it. The problem confronting the library is how to relate all of these differences and come up with a standard measure for determining the comparative value of each system in relation to the others. It is possible to calculate a cost-benefit ratio, but even this is a somewhat subjective approach since the comparative value of each system feature and every other nonfinancial criteria would have to be assigned with a certain degree of subjectivity in the first place.

If a library has rigorously examined responses to RFPs, the systems proposed, and the vendors, often one alternative will emerge as the clear preference for the library's own circumstances. If this is not the case—if two or more alternatives are rated very closely—the selection will obviously be more difficult. There is no steadfast formula to make the decision easier in such cases. Cost-benefit ratios, criterion-by-criterion numerical rankings, weighting techniques, and other quantitative methods can assist greatly in evaluation, but they cannot ensure that one alternative will emerge as the clear preference. After the quantitative measures are weighed, two or more systems may still be so closely rated that minor overall differences are nearly irrelevant. Under such circumstances, it is necessary to step back, collect thoughts, and try again to arrive at a consensus.

Contracting

Once a selection has been made, the library is ready to enter another stage: the negotiation of a contract with the vendor whose system has been selected. Especially in the purchase of a large-scale system, contract negotiation is particularly crucial.

Sometimes, a starting point for negotiation can be the library's RFP, in which certain contract-related expectations or requirements may have been stated and addressed by vendors. But upon notification that its system has been selected, some vendors will routinely tender a standard version of their contract. If a library receives this standard contract, it must keep three things in mind when examining the contents. One, the contract must be viewed as the vendor's concept of an ideal statement of conditions within realistically attainable limits. It is written from the vendor's point of view. This is not a deceitful practice; it is the standard philosophy behind the writing of any contracts, in librarianship or in any other field. Unfortunately, what are defined as "realistically attainable limits" vary a great deal from one vendor to another. In some cases, they are fairly reasonable; in others, merely hopeful. Two, any contract written to ensure maximum protection for one party is likely to result in a certain degree of vulnerability for the other party. In this case, that other party is the library. Three, the library has a responsibility to itself to closely scrutinize the contract and to negotiate for changes in any area where it is exposed to such vulnerability. Especially in the purchase of a large-scale system, vendor-supplied contracts are not cast in stone. They are not offered to libraries as a "take it or leave it" proposition. They can and should be negotiated, and vendors are accustomed to libraries requiring negotiation. This is such an accepted practice that if a library or its legal counsel is uncomfortable with any part of a standard contract, but the vendor insists that no part of the contract can be altered under any circumstances, the library may be well advised to look elsewhere for a system.

Some libraries use the vendor's standard contract as a starting point for negotiation; others elect to initiate a contract version themselves. In either case, there will be certain points on which vendors are unlikely to bend and certain points on which libraries should refuse to yield. Many provisions will fall somewhere in between. Negotiation is a compromise, and neither the vendor nor the library should expect the other to sign its own idealized version of a contract.

The library should work with its attorney, and consultant if one is used during contract negotiations, to determine at each step where it can accept a vendor stipulation, where it must demand its own conditions, where there is room for compromise, and the implications of each proposal and counterproposal if accepted. If many or major changes are required, contract negotiation can be a very tedious process and can require considerable time and a great deal of communication between a library and the prospective vendor.

One of the first rules of contracting is that every aspect of the negotiations be carefully documented, in writing, and even appended as part of the contract if necessary. Verbal agreements and explanations are convenient, but they can also be ambiguous, can lead to confusion, and are of questionable legality. Therefore, it is crucial not only that the contract be fully written in its final version, but also that there be an exhaustively documented written record of all negotiations and changes leading up to the final version.

Contract Purposes: Negotiation Philosophy

In negotiating a contract, the library should consider all provisions from the perspective of what it hopes to accomplish with a system, how it can best ensure success in achieving those ends, and how it can best protect itself in the event that the ends cannot be realized. The most immediate purpose of a contract is to serve as a legal document defining the relationship between the parties involved, but within this framework, the library has an obligation for its own best interests to negotiate a contract that will adequately serve several broad purposes. First and foremost is an assurance that the system does, and will continue to do, what the library expects it to do. As a prerequisite, the library should have a very clear idea of what it wants from a system in terms of function, capacity, and performance. The library should require that these or other mutually agreed on expectations be articulated in the contract in the form of a guarantee by the vendor, along with a definition of the courses of action open to the library in the event that the system does not meet the stated expectations.

Another purpose of the contract from the library's point of view is to gain a complete delineation of the initial costs of a system and the cost ranges that will be incurred on a continuing basis. Insofar as possible, the contract should not leave any room for hidden or unanticipated cost factors associated with the purchase, maintenance, or upgrade of a system. Although it obviously will not be possible to state exact costs for as yet undeveloped upgrade capabilities or enhancements, the vendor should be willing to state general conditions governing pricing for the library in relation to pricing that will apply to other libraries at the time a new development is made available.

One of the main purposes of a contract is to define the areas of responsibility for each of the parties involved. For an automated library system, the most immediate provisions will address procedures required between the time a contract has been signed and the time the system has been installed and accepted by the library as satisfactorily meeting stated expectations. Specific areas of concern include site preparation, delivery and installation, training and documentation, and acceptance testing. In addition, the contract must also cover postacceptance responsibilities such as maintenance and continuing vendor support services.

From the library's perspective, a contract must also define the future relationship between the library and the system and its vendor. Some aspects of this relationship, such as pricing and maintenance responsibilities, have already been identified. In addition, the library must be aware of contractual provisions governing such matters as software modification privileges and rights of resale. The vendor will rightfully demand certain limitations on what the library may do with the system it purchases, but the library should also try to ensure that the flexibility of future efforts will not be stymied by vendor exclusivity clauses, hardware or software restrictions, or any other requirement that might hamper the library's decision-making options for planning in the future.

A contract defines conditions of liability and unsatisfactory performance by either party. For many libraries, this is one of the least comfortable parts of negotiating a contract, for in most cases the provisions implicitly have to do with circumstances in which something has gone wrong. It is tempting merely to hope that none of the conditions involving liability or unsatisfactory performance will ever occur, or to anticipate that such matters could be resolved through calm verbal negotiations, but wishful thinking is no basis for the conclusion of a contract. If areas of liability and unsatisfactory performance are difficult to deal with before a system is installed, they are nearly impossible to resolve after installation unless their treatment has been spelled out in the original contract.

Under most circumstances, a vendor will want to transfer liability to a library as soon and as fully as possible and will want to avoid any conditions in the contract pertaining to vendor nonperformance, partial performance, or delay of fulfillment of responsibilities. This is understandable from the vendor's point of view, but unacceptable from the library's viewpoint. Since these are areas where a vendor will want to ensure maximum protection, the library must approach negotiations with an equally strong commitment to protect its own interests. The library must be prepared for hard negotiation on questions of liability and unsatisfactory performance, and it must also be willing to accept its own share of responsibility. Hopefully for the library and vendor alike, provisions in the contract relating to potential negative events or circumstances will in the end simply take up space on paper and will never have to be invoked, but the possibilities and their implications are too critical not to be a major focus of attention during contract negotiation.

Finally, the contract should provide a framework within which any future conflicts, disagreements, or misunderstandings can be resolved. The adage about prevention being the best cure is applicable to contracts, and the library and vendor should strive to conclude a contract that minimizes the possibility of problems and misunderstandings ever arising. But no matter how carefully a contract has been drawn up, there always seem to be one or more contingencies that have escaped precise delineation or are not interpreted in the same way by each party. Although the contract may not provide a specific solution under these circumstances, it will still serve as the framework within which such problems and ambiguities can be examined and resolved. If the original contract has been carefully thought out and written, disagreements or misunderstandings will often be minor and can be resolved without threat of legal recourse by either party.

The negotiation and conclusion of a contract will in some cases be fairly expedient and straightforward, but it can also be very complex and demanding. Treatment of all aspects of negotiation and contract content for automated library systems is beyond the scope of this book. The following discussion, therefore, focuses on some of the most important general considerations and specific concerns in contracting for automated library systems. Although by no means exhaustive, these are among the most frequently encountered provisions, and often require the greatest fortitude on the part of libraries in negotiating favorable conditions with vendors.

Purchase Price

A number of provisions in a contract relate to various financial aspects of acquiring and maintaining a system. Some have to do with the initial purchase and others with continuing costs. Some provisions are clearly financial in content; others do not deal quite so obviously with costs but have important financial consequences nevertheless.

One category has to do with the hardware and software of the system. A list of all hardware should be supplied in an exhibit to the contract. A simple list is not enough, however. It is crucial that the contract guarantee that the total configuration of the various components will work and will perform according to acceptance standards stated elsewhere in the contract. This is a fundamental point in purchasing an automated system. The signing of a contract should never, in and of itself, constitute purchase. Rather, it should indicate a firm commitment to purchase if, and only if, the system satisfactorily meets the functional and performance expectations stated in the contract. The key to final purchase approval is acceptance testing, described later in this chapter.

In an industry that changes as rapidly as computerization, a concern that must be dealt with in contract negotiation is the possibility of changes to a system between the time a library signs a contract and the time when the system is installed and has passed all acceptance tests. Two points are particularly important in this regard. The first concerns substitution. The library should try to secure the right to substitute, if it wishes, any new hardware or software that becomes available from the vendor between the time a contract has been awarded and the time at which a system has been formally accepted. The contract should stipulate that if the new components are less expensive than those originally listed in the exhibit, the library will be awarded the lower price. If the new components are more expensive, the library must expect to pay the difference if it chooses to exercise this right of substitution. The contract should include a stipulation that the price to the library in that case will be no greater than the standard price announced by the vendor.

The right of substitution should be expressed solely as an option of the library. The contract should guard against any opportunity for the vendor to change equipment without the library's written consent. Any statements allowing for the supply of "comparable equipment" to that stated in the exhibit should not be accepted; "comparable" can often translate into refurbished, less expensive, or less sophisticated than what the library originally agreed to pay for.

The second point concerns price changes for the same system components for which the library has contracted. Between the signing of a contract and acceptance of a system, such changes can go in either direction: The vendor may raise or lower the price of certain components. Just as with the introduction of new components, the library should seek conditions of most favorable pricing under either circumstance. Contractual provisions should guarantee the original price in the event that price increases are announced by the vendor, and at the same time the library should be assured that new prices will apply if price reductions are announced before the system has been accepted. In this manner, the library is assured that the original price in the contract represents a maximum, but that it will receive the benefit of lower costs should the vendor announce reductions. Most vendors are willing to accept these conditions.

It is to the library's advantage to extend these guarantees for as long a period as possible. The vendor may wish to terminate them on delivery or installation, but the library should try to retain them at least through acceptance testing and, if at all possible, through the warranty period. The latter may be difficult to attain, but there is precedent for it in data processing contracts.

Performance Bonds

After a contract for a large-scale system has been signed, one of the first financial transactions is frequently the furnishing of a performance bond by the vendor. The performance bond is essentially an affirmation that the vendor intends to supply the library with a system that meets the acceptance standards stated in the contract. The bond is usually in the amount of the purchase price of the system and will revert to the vendor when the system has passed all acceptance tests. If a library plans to require a vendor to furnish a performance bond, it is important to insist that a single bond be issued and that it be tied with full acceptance of the entire system. Several bonds in smaller amounts, each tied to a different phase of implementation, should not be permitted, since their total amount would not be tied to realizing the end product—a system in full and acceptable working order.

Payment Schedule

The contract should clearly state the procedures and schedule to be followed by the library in paying for the system. Payment must always be contingent on fulfillment of certain implementation activities, never simply according to specific calendar dates.

The payment schedule is usually tied to three different phases of implementation: signing the contract, certificate of installation, and final acceptance by the library. From the library's point of view, the greater the percentage of total payment that is contingent upon acceptance, the better. Optimally, the library would have the greatest protection if the total amount were payable upon final acceptance, but a vendor will seldom agree to this. It is reasonable, however, for the library to insist that at least one-third of the total payment be contingent on completion of all acceptance tests, and that as little as 10 to 20 percent be payable on signing the contract, with the remaining 40 to 60 percent being paid when the system is installed and certified by the vendor as in full working condition.

Site Preparation

The contract should delineate the responsibilities of each of the parties involved, and one of the duties usually falling on the library is preparing for installation of equipment. The time and work involved should not be underestimated. If the equipment includes a central computer, a separate room may have to be prepared for housing it. Computers need certain temperature and humidity conditions, which may require the library to add or reconfigure some components of its existing heating and cooling system. The room may need new flooring, a change in lighting, installation of wall coverings, fire protection apparatus, and so on. Additional electrical outlets will probably be needed, as might a separate circuit breaker or voltage regulator. Cabling for computer to terminal connection may mean some careful planning, and physical locations at which terminals will be placed may need some remodeling.[2]

The library normally pays all expenses associated with site preparation, but it should demand clear explanation from the vendor as to exactly what is expected. Unfortunately, in some instances vague instructions have either resulted in unnecessary expense or have allowed vendors to justify delay in installation on the grounds of inadequate site preparation by the library, when in fact the real reasons for the delay may have had nothing to do with the conditions of preparation. Since requirements will vary from one vendor or system to another, the best way to insure against either of these possibilities is to insist on clear, system-specific site preparation details in the contract.

Some purchasers of data processing systems have been able to negotiate a provision that the supplier will reimburse any site preparation expenses that might be incurred due to instructions that later prove erroneous. In any event, the contract should stipulate that, as a final measure, the vendor will inspect the site and issue written approval when preparation requirements have been fulfilled.

The reverse side of all this is that, having provided sufficient instruction, the vendor has a right to expect the library to fulfill its part of the obligation within the time frame mutually agreed on. Site preparation often does require more time and effort than originally anticipated, and it is essential that, before the contract is signed, the library have a realistic notion of what will be involved and how long it will take.

Delivery and Installation

In most contracts for turnkey library systems, delivery is scheduled within about 90 days after the signing of the contract. This can vary, and agreement to a time frame for delivery is one of the reasons why a library must have a clear idea of how much time will be required for its preliminary work, such as site preparation and, if necessary, barcoding of items in its collection or conversion of all or part of its bibliographic records to machine-readable form.

Another contract concern is to determine which party will pay for delivery. The vendor will most likely want shipping charges to be assumed by the library, but the library should attempt to have the vendor assume responsibility. One of the reasons for this is that the direct cost of shipping is not the only financial consideration involved. There are also questions of insurance and liability. Most common carriers do incorporate a certain amount of insurance coverage into their shipping charges, but in the case of expensive electronic equipment, the amount of coverage and maximum liability is often far from adequate, and additional insurance may be necessary.

After delivery, it should be the vendor's full responsibility to unpack and install the system. A contract should also require the vendor to provide written certification when the system has been installed and is considered to be in proper working order. Normally, installation and certification take place within one to two weeks after delivery. Whether this or another time frame is mutually agreed on, the contract should state a definite time after delivery by which the system must be installed and certified as operational.

Transfer of Liability

The conditions for the transfer of system liability from a vendor are often overlooked by libraries during contract negotiations. The vendor usually wants liability to transfer on delivery or installation of the system, certainly logical from the vendor's point of view, since the system is housed at and operating in the library. But there is also justification for a library to negotiate for transfer only after completion of all acceptance tests. If a contract has been properly negotiated, a library does not actually own the system until final acceptance, and hence it should not have to assume liability for something that is technically still owned by the vendor. Not without some justification, vendors frequently balk at granting this concession, but a library should carefully weigh the implications and additional costs before assuming liability prior to formal acceptance of the system.

Training and Documentation

Vendors generally include provisions in the contract for training and documentation on the system. Particularly in the case of training, it is to the vendor's benefit to provide adequate levels of support, as this will reduce the need for continuing assistance during the first few months a library is using the system.

The need for initial training when the system is newly installed is self-evident. For this purpose, the library must make sure that the contract states what will be covered in training and that provisions ensure certain levels of operational proficiency rather than just providing for a specific number of days of instruction. In turn, the library should recognize its obligation to make staff members available on mutually agreed on training dates and to ensure that those sessions receive the undivided attention of trainees.

Less obvious than during the initial implementation is the need to state conditions for training on a continuing basis. After the library has developed a certain level of in-house expertise, new staff members can frequently be trained by a designated member of the library's own staff. Libraries also often develop their own training aids and support materials for this purpose. But while the library may develop sufficient in-house expertise to train on the system as it is initially configured, there may be a need for further vendor-supplied training when upgrades or enhancements are added to the system. The contract should clearly state the conditions under which update training will be provided and at what cost to the library.

Documentation pertaining to the system and its operation is frequently something more of a problem. Whether in librarianship or any other field, automated systems have a notorious reputation for being accompanied by inadequate documentation. Although it is not always possible to completely circumvent this problem, it is important that the

contract ensure, both for the initial phase and for upgrades and enhancements, the library receives as much documentation as is available,
in sufficient quantities, and preferably at no additional charge.

Acceptance Tests

A crucial part of any contract for an automated library system is the
statement of conditions under which the library will approve final acceptance. Conditions should not include the signing of a contract, delivery of the system, certificate of installation, or completion of training. There should be no stipulation in the contract that any use of the
system for processing by the purchaser constitutes acceptance. The
only satisfactory conditions for acceptance should be successful completion of a series of formal tests demonstrating performance according to
the expectations stated in the contract. The library should propose the
specifics of these tests and the standards that must be met. They should
be stringent, and a tough stance should be taken in negotiations. Three
types of system performance should be tested: function, reliability, and
response time. Testing should begin only after the staff has received
adequate training from the vendor. This will reduce the possibility that
any problems in performance might be attributable to staff mistakes
rather than system failure.

The functional tests should aim to verify that the system can indeed
perform all functions promised by the vendor and stated in the contract. But the fact of functional performance is not enough in itself.
The system must also be able to execute each function within a reasonable, per-transaction time period, and the system as a whole must perform reliably for an extended period, and this is where reliability and
response-time tests come into play. Obviously, terms such as "reasonable" and "reliably" are vague at best, and that is why the contract must
describe in detail the measures that will be applied and the standards of
performance that will be acceptable.

The reliability test determines the amount of time a system is not
functioning properly in relation to the total amount of time the system
is scheduled to be functioning. The result is a measure of system
downtime. In contracts for automated library systems, it is reasonable
to stipulate a maximum of 2 percent downtime as the required standard of performance. In addition to straight downtime percentage,
some data processing contracts also define requirements for intervals
between periods of downtime, although this is not common in library
contracts.

The contract should clearly identify the procedures to be used for
measuring downtime and should also define the measurements in

terms of each system component. A failure in some parts of the total system, such as the central processing unit, is more severe than failure in other parts, such as a single terminal or peripheral device, and reliability tests often take this into account by assigning downtime coefficients to each part of the total system.

The reliability test usually requires that a system meet the stated performance standard over a 30- or 60-day period. The system should not be required to meet this on a daily basis, but rather on an average over 30 or 60 consecutive days. In order to attain the acceptable level of performance, the test may have to be restarted one or more times. The total amount of time usually allowed for a system to pass the reliability test is 90 days for a 30-day requirement or 180 days for a 60-day requirement.

A response-time test is of much shorter duration, often as little as an hour or two. The purpose is to ensure that all system functions can be carried out under peak conditions within the range of acceptable response time specified in the contract. The procedure for measuring response time must be precisely stated in the contract, along with the types of transactions that will be carried out during the test, the number of terminals that will be performing each type of transaction, and the maximum allowable average response time broken down by type of transaction. The level of activity carried out during the test should be at least equal to the maximum load that the library ever plans to experience with the present system configuration. As many of the library's terminals and remote locations as possible should be included in the test. In essence, the goal of the response-time test is to try to make the system collapse. Hopefully, this goal will not be achieved, but rather, the system will withstand the onslaught of activity and perform according to the standards set forth in the contract.

If the system passes all requirements of each test, the library accepts the system and approves final payment. In some cases, purchasers of data processing systems have been able to negotiate contract provisions assuring continuing performance levels based on the same standards used for acceptance tests, but this has not been common in contracts for automated library systems.

If the system passes the acceptance tests in almost every respect, but falls slightly short in one or two areas, the library may be tempted to release payment on verbal agreement that the vendor will take appropriate corrective action. This should not be done, as final payment may in and of itself be legally construed as formal acceptance. If all acceptance tests are not fully passed, in whatever degree, the contract should specify a number of alternatives open to, and at the discretion of, the library. A discussion of these options follows.

Performance, Remedial Action, and Damages

At various junctures during the term of a contract, either party may fail to fully execute its stated responsibilities. Apart from maintenance, which is discussed later, the most vulnerable areas of performance are during the period between the signing of a contract through the formal acceptance of a system. It is absolutely essential to the library that conditions constituting vendor nonperformance, delay, and partial and otherwise unacceptable performance be stated in the contract, supported by provisions identifying the library's options under any of these circumstances. The provisions may be drawn together in a separate section of the contract, or they may be placed in the sections to which they apply.

In cases of unsatisfactory vendor performance—such as delay in delivery or failure of the system to meet acceptance standards—the contract should delineate the possible courses of remedial action. The most extreme is termination of the contract by the library, a drastic move and, under most circumstances, of benefit to neither party, but provision must be included for this eventuality since in extreme circumstances termination may be the library's only viable option. The library should reserve, as its primary alternative to termination, the right to extend the agreed-on dates on a continuing short-term basis until it either deems the performance acceptable or it opts for termination.

In the specific case of potential failure of a system to pass acceptance tests, the contract should also specify a number of other options for the library. These should include the possibility of accepting modifications to the system, the right to permit extension of the test period, the right to accept the system as is, and the right to revise the acceptance requirements and re-initiate the tests under the less stringent standards.[3] It is important in all cases that the library retain absolute control over selecting which of these options it wishes to exercise. Especially with alternatives that allow for extension of the test period, a definite period of time should be stated for the duration of the extension. In any instance of unsatisfactory performance, the library should formally notify the vendor in writing. If written notification is not given, the library may not be able to demand the necessary remedial action.

Many libraries negotiate provisions for payment of damages in the event of unsatisfactory performance by a vendor. These are generally of two types: actual and liquidated damages. Actual damages are designed to recover the purchaser's direct expenses resulting from unsatisfactory performance by the supplier. If a vendor fails to deliver a system, for example, the contract might allow award of actual damages in the amount spent by the library for site preparation. Liquidated damages are most commonly, but mistakenly, referred to as penalties. A contract can include provisions allowing for payment of liquidated damages but should never refer to these as penalties, since they would probably be unenforceable if construed as such. For delays caused by the vendor, liquidated damages are usually expressed in terms of an amount of money per day for each day of delay. A standard amount in contracts for large-scale automated library systems usually ranges between $100 and $200 per day. There must be a maximum number of days, usually between 90 and 180, over which liquidated damages can accrue. Anything much beyond this range might be construed as a penalty, in which case the entire provision could be found invalid. The exact amount and duration of liquidated damages must be weighed against the magnitude of the purchase, with the cumulative amount being kept to a fairly small percentage of the total cost of the system.

In formulating a stance for negotiating provisions for damages, the library should carefully identify each juncture in implementation where the vendor has an obligation to perform, outline the consequences for the library in the event of unsatisfactory performance, and wherever possible, calculate the cost to the library of inadequate performance. The reverse side to unsatisfactory vendor performance, of course, is failure by the library to fulfill some part of its obligation. This can happen, for example, if the library has not adequately made site preparation arrangements by the agreed-on date. The library should seek maximum protection for itself by negotiating for damage-free provisions, and should negotiate for stipulations that, if there are any delays caused by the library, the delay in the overall timetable will be no greater than the period of delay caused by the library itself. This is important as there have been instances in which vendors have taken advantage of a brief delay caused by the library to delay their own obligations for much longer periods.

Force Majeure

Vendor-supplied contracts will include a force majeure provision stating that the vendor cannot be held liable for delays or other failure to perform caused by acts of God, riots, strikes, insurrection, war, fire, or any other event beyond its control. The substance of these provisions is basically reasonable. However, the library should insist on two qualifications. First, the contract should specify an upper time limit to the extent of delay or other failure to perform, after which the library is free to terminate the contract. Otherwise, the library could be tied indefinitely to a contract for which there might be little hope for fulfillment for several years. Second, the library should require that force majeure provisions be mutually applicable in the event that delays are caused by the library owing to similar unfortunate circumstances.

Warranty

An automated system should be under warranty for a period of time mutually agreed on by the library and the vendor. The warranty should be expressed as a guarantee that the system will be free of defects during the established period and that replacement of parts or any other repairs will be at the expense of the vendor. The warranty should cover all critical and, especially, all electronic components of the system. Warranties for computerized systems frequently exclude some items, such as ribbons and other expendables. A list of excluded items should be explicitly stated in the contract and checked carefully by the library to ensure that no major components are listed among the exclusions.

Standard vendor-supplied contracts almost invariably include a provision that all warranties other than those expressly stated are excluded from the contract. The library should review such statements carefully. In all but one state in the United States, products sold commercially are covered by the Uniform Commercial Code (UCC), which imposes implied warranties of merchantability and fitness for purpose. These implied warranties can, however, be limited or excluded by specific provision in any contract, and that is the purpose of blanket statements that exclude all warranties not expressly stated in the contract in hand. Many vendors are adamant that such an exclusionary provision remain in the contract, often on the grounds that the UCC requirement of fitness for purpose is too vague and leaves the seller in too vulnerable a position. The vendor's position is not without some justification here. But if the vendor categorically insists on provisions excluding implied warranties, it is all the more important for the contract to precisely spell out what is and what is not covered by the expressed warranty. Furthermore, if the library successfully negotiates for very explicit conditions governing functional, reliability, and response-time requirements in the contract, it will essentially have secured a guarantee of fitness for purpose anyway.

A point of contention in contract negotiations for automated systems often revolves around two temporal aspects of the warranty: when it will begin and how long it will last. Some standard form contracts stipulate a warranty of 90 days or less commencing on installation. For a large-scale automated library system, neither of these conditions should be readily accepted. The warranty period should definitely not begin until completion of acceptance tests, since ownership should not transfer before that time. The library should also negotiate strongly for a one-year warranty period, although this will not always be possible to obtain.

Hardware Maintenance Agreements

The hardware maintenance agreement is an important aspect of contracting for an automated system. Maintenance agreements should be carefully scrutinized and clearly understood, for the library will normally have to live with them for the duration of the system. Maintenance of system hardware by the vendor is often arranged through manufacturers of the equipment or through third party maintenance firms. Provisions for routine preventive maintenance should be included in the agreement, along with a detailed description of the conditions, procedures, and allowable time frames for remedial maintenance in the event of system failure or degradation of performance. The duration of the agreement should be specified, along with provisions for automatic renewal and with a clear statement of the conditions under which either party may terminate the agreement. The annual amount that a library can expect to pay for maintenance charges varies according to system and other factors such as the timeliness of service guaranteed in the agreement. Overall, annual hardware maintenance charges for hardware and software combined usually range between 10 and 15 percent of the purchase price of the system.

In many standard contracts furnished by suppliers of automated systems, the maintenance agreement and all associated charges become effective on installation of the system. From the library's perspective, it would seem more appropriate for the agreement, and especially the charges, to take effect much later, after acceptance and only at the close of the warranty period. As logical as this may sound, it is often not the case with large-scale automated systems. Maintenance payments frequently begin with installation, and must be made even during the warranty period. But these can be a point for negotiation. The most favorable position for the library is for the maintenance agreement to take effect on transfer of liability, with the maintenance charges waived until completion of the warranty period. Such arrangements have been successfully negotiated in other types of data processing contracts, but have been less common for large-scale library systems.

Since a serious malfunction in hardware is so disruptive of operations, some libraries have been able to negotiate provisions for awarding credit against charges when a service call is not provided according to the standards or within the time frame specified in the agreement. In monitoring maintenance agreements, the library must carefully document all events pertaining to the execution of the agreement, including a description of any problems with the system and the course and timeliness of action taken to remedy them. Another concern that should be part of the hardware maintenance agreement is the availability of spare parts. Ready access should be guaranteed. For certain types of equipment, including additional terminals, on-site storage in the library is a fairly standard procedure in the purchase of large-scale automated library systems.

The hardware maintenance agreement is often a very lengthy document, and the discussion here focuses only on a few of the broader concerns in such agreements. A model that is useful in establishing guidelines for maintenance agreements was put together by the Mountain West CLSI Users' Group in 1982, and that and other sources illustrate considerable detail and provide examples of actual wording of provisions.[4]

Software Arrangements

Just as with hardware, system software should be covered by warranty and maintenance agreement. Provisions for software maintenance are usually less complex than those for hardware. One of the most important sets of software-related provisions concerns the distribution of enhancements. For some turnkey systems, the cost of software enhancement is included as part of the annual combined hardware/software maintenance fee. More recently, however, some vendors adopted a two-prong approach to pricing of software enhancements. When a new major module is introduced—such as acquisitions or serials control—the software must be purchased at additional cost. But once a module is purchased, the cost of subsequent minor enhancements is included as part of an annual maintenance fee associated with that module. There are still some vendors that separately price each new release, but the cost is usually less than the full purchase price to those libraries that already own the system. In any event, the vendor's approach to the supply and pricing of software enhancements should be clearly spelled out in the contract.

Another major area of concern regarding software is the right of access to the software source code, which is the key to gaining access to, and making modifications in, the programming detail. For their own protection, some vendors understandably object strenuously to granting a library access to its source code. If the library is certain that it has no immediate need to modify the vendor's software, it can go halfway on this issue, but it should never agree to complete barring of access to the source code under any and all circumstances.

Although the library may foresee no immediate need to modify the vendor's software, the following possibilities should be considered:

The vendor may go out of business

The vendor may discontinue involvement in the field of automated library systems

The vendor may discontinue support of the particular system that the library has purchased

The vendor may not provide sufficient enhancement to the system in the future

The vendor's support of the software may be abysmally poor

Under any of these circumstances, the library could be in a difficult position if it has surrendered any and all rights to software modification and to the source code. If the vendor refuses to supply a copy of the source code directly, the library must at least insist on some form of escrow arrangement, meaning that the vendor will deposit a copy of the source code at a neutral site, and the contract should then state the conditions, covering eventualities such as those above, under which the library can gain access to the code. In this way, the library can partially protect itself against being "left in the lurch" if a vendor goes out of business or discontinues a system or inadequately supports it. Even when dealing with well-established vendors, and even if the library does not see a need for it in the immediate future, some form of right of access to the software source code is a necessary contractual safeguard.

Apart from these more drastic circumstances, some libraries attempt to negotiate for immediate right to modify the vendor's software. If the vendor is willing to consider granting such permission, the library can expect very stringent contractual provisions. There will be, quite reasonably, provisions prohibiting the library from commercial sale or other transfer to third parties. Some libraries and vendors have worked out amicable arrangements whereby software modifications may be made by the library, and are then generalized by the vendor and offered to other users of the system, sometimes with financial compensation being awarded to the library. If such arrangements are made, the terms should be incorporated into the licensing provisions. Libraries that want to negotiate a licensing agreement that will allow modification should pay careful attention to contractual provisions regarding the implications of modification for warranty and maintenance agreements.

Future Prices

Earlier sections touched on the question of pricing changes between the signing of a contract and the acceptance of a system. Since the library will probably own a system for at least several years, the pricing question is likely to be even more important over the long term than in this shorter interval. As a goal in negotiating, the library must try not to leave itself open to a situation where pricing for additional and spare components escalate far beyond the original expectations when the system was purchased. For replacement parts and upgrades that were available at the time the system was purchased, the library should be especially aware of terminology such as "availability at then current prices," which refers to costs at time of subsequent purchase and has no guaranteed relationship to prices when the system is first acquired. One way for libraries to safeguard against exorbitant increases for such components is to seek assurance of a maximum allowable percentage increase in prices for those components. At the same time, the library should try to secure the advantage of lower costs in the event that standard prices for components are reduced. In essence, then, the library should try to put itself in a position where "then current prices" apply in the future only to price decreases, not increases.

The contract should also cover pricing for components and enhancements that are not yet available when the system is purchased. Obviously, specific amounts cannot be attached to future products, but the library should reserve an option to purchase them at a price no greater than the vendor's standard prices to new customers. The library may try to negotiate for a "most favored nation" provision, enabling it to purchase products at the lowest price charged by the vendor to any of its other customers.

Right of Resale

The library should seek provisions allowing it to sell the entire system at some future point if it so chooses. There is likely to be some resistance to this by the vendor, but it will probably be accepted if resale is limited to another library. In negotiating such a provision, the library must be certain that the entire system is covered, including hardware, software, documentation, transfer of liability, and so on.

Modification and Termination

The contract should state the procedures to be followed for making any additions or modifications to the contract itself and should specify conditions under which either party may terminate the agreement. Modification is a formal process and should always require written amendment. Provisions for termination can be mixed blessings. The library must try to secure maximum flexibility for itself. At the same time, it should require precisely stated conditions under which the vendor may terminate. Failure to take this latter stance can leave the library open to problems, particularly in areas such as maintenance provisions. Although the library may be able to gain concession of a fixed annual charge for maintenance, or at least a maximum allowable annual percentage increase, this is not complete protection if other provisions do not limit the conditions under which the vendor may terminate the agreement. A vendor could conceivably terminate the agreement simply in order to negotiate a new agreement with much higher charges. While this strategy has been used in data processing in some areas, it fortunately is not at all common in the automated library systems market. But the mere possibility does point out the vulnerability that can occur if conditions in a contract are not adequately protective.

All of the points discussed in this section on contracting are important to the library. There are many other matters to be considered, covering such diverse areas as limitations of liability, liability for infringement, duration of the contract, and so on. The contract is a document that the library should approach with the most businesslike candor. Some of the safeguards for libraries noted here will be fairly readily agreed to by vendors, others will not, and a few are already included in some of the standard form contracts tended by vendors.

The library cannot expect to successfully negotiate all provisions according to its own concept of what the contract should be. It will have to forego some concessions to gain others. In all cases, negotiations should keep in sight the ultimate goals of the library and of the vendor. The library wants a system that fills its needs, works well, and will continue to do so without any surprises along the way. And contrary to the beliefs of some, the primary goal of any respectable vendor is not "to take its customers to the cleaners." Its chief goal, rather, is to stay in business and if possible to increase its share in the competitive marketplace and this can seldom be achieved by deceiving its customers and providing poor service.

Staff Preparation and Training

Of all the stages involved in implementation of an automated system, the one that may ultimately be the most crucial determinant of success—but the one most often sacrificed in the midst of all the other activities—is the preparation and training of staff. The vendor will provide some amount of formal training on the system, but this should be viewed as only one phase in the process. Like the whole question of implementation, staff preparation and training should not be narrowly defined or seen as one temporally distinct element in the implementation process. It should begin early and be a continuing effort. The formal process of system-specific staff preparation obviously cannot begin until a system has been selected. But once a contract has been negotiated, staff preparation geared specifically to the new system should begin immediately.

Preliminary Preparation

The preinstallation phase of staff preparation should focus on familiarizing staff with basic facts about the system and making them aware of what will happen over the next several months. Staff should also be informed how the new system will affect departmental and library operations, policies, and procedures, as well as how it will relate to their own particular jobs. The most general of these concerns can be discussed in large group sessions. But as more specific information is presented, smaller sessions should be arranged according to levels and types of participation that will be required once the system is installed.

In focusing on levels and types of participation, several categories of involvement can be distinguished. Specifically, the library might wish to identify as many as eight different groups, depending on the size of the staff and the nature of the system involved. They would include staff members:

With general administrative responsibility for the system

With direct supervisory responsibility for operation and use of the system

In the department whose operations are being automated and who will be using the system on a day-to-day basis (such as terminal operators)

In the same department who will not be using the system on as regular a basis, but who will use it for limited purposes, and whose routines will be altered by the system

In the same department who will not be using the system at all and whose routine will not be altered by it

In other departments or branches who may have occasion to use the system for certain limited purposes

In other departments or branches who will not have occasion to use the system but whose routines may be affected by it

In other departments or branches who will not use the system and whose routines will not be affected by it

Distinctions can be made within each of these groups, and some groups may be combined for some purposes. The approach and amount of time spent with each group in preliminary preparation will obviously differ, as well they should. Staff whose duties will be little affected by the system certainly do not need the same focus or depth of presentation as those whose primary job responsibilities will include using the system during the better part of their working day. Nevertheless, it is important not to exclude any group from an opportunity to learn something about the system and the changes it may entail as it relates, however remotely, to their own responsibilities and duties.

At the higher levels of staffing are those individuals whose primary participation will be administrative responsibility for the system. In general, these are the people who approve the bills, talk to governing authorities, and oversee the general administration of the library or one of its departments. These individuals are ultimately responsible for day-to-day operations, but their involvement is often quite far removed from the routine tasks that comprise a large part of those operations. These individuals will usually have such broad responsibility that it will be difficult to interest them in the finer points of screen scrolling techniques or the implications of distinguishing between a 440 and a 490 field on a MARC record. But since administrators will have final approval over the time allowed for preparing other staff for a new system, it is crucial for them to at least appreciate that such matters will be relevant for some personnel.

Staff members with direct supervisory responsibility over the operation of the system will need to familiarize themselves with many of the system's finer details. This is particularly important during the earlier stages of implementation. Until the system is installed and terminal operators and others in the department have a chance to develop skill in using it, the supervisor is the person to whom staff will turn, sometimes with specific questions and sometimes just to have anxieties alleviated. This is a very important role, and the individuals supervising operations when the system is eventually installed will need to instill a sense of confidence and calmness about the forthcoming changes. They will be viewed by other staff as authorities about the new system, and as such, they must remain at least one step ahead of everyone else in their knowledge of the system if they are to provide the needed support.

Once the system is installed, operations staff will likely become rapidly acquainted with the ins and outs of using it, to the point where their logistical knowledge will probably soon exceed the supervisor's. The need for bolstering the confidence of the staff will be replaced with a confidence based in newly acquired knowledge and skills. This transition should not be viewed as a threat to the authority of the supervisor as long as levels of responsibility and decision making remain clearly defined. The supervisor does not have to remain the most expert authority about the operational ins and outs of the system, but he or she does need to remain the person to whom the staff should turn for a decision when needed.

Different people will be differently affected by the introduction of a new system. For some, it may mean a new set of everyday responsibilities and duties, in essence a much different job. Others will see a less pronounced impact, but may still experience some degree of change in job-related duties, in procedure if not in substance. There will be still others who will not be directly involved with use of the system, but who will nonetheless be working in an environment with obvious change going on all around them. And in this sense, they too will be affected by the introduction of the new system.

In preliminary preparation, staff members whose duties will be affected should be made aware of the basic nature of the system and what it will do. General information sessions should be conducted by appropriate supervisors, perhaps involving a project coordinator if one has been appointed. Each staff member should be told how his or her duties can be expected to change under the new system, and how work flow and responsibilities among staff members will be organized. Since it will probably be necessary to introduce further changes and refinements in organization once the system is actually up and running, the likelihood of such alterations should also be pointed out well ahead of time. Otherwise, future adjustments may be viewed negatively by staff, rather than from a positive perspective of refinement and improvement.

There are differing views on conducting training sessions for staff before installation. Obviously, such sessions cannot include hands-on experience since the system is not yet installed, but there are other approaches, such as written and computer-assisted instruction. Written instruction can have merit, if it focuses on general content rather than detailed operation. When a library is implementing a MARC-based cataloging system, for example, preliminary training is best focused on the general structure and major fields of the MARC format, and perhaps an overview of basic search retrieval strategies available on the system. Procedures associated with actual terminal operation cannot easily be simulated on paper, and efforts to do so often lead more to confusion and increased anxiety than anything else. Computer simulation is more promising, but there is still a great deal of room for development here, especially on a system-specific level. The library must use considerable caution, then, in any preliminary efforts that focus on what can be called training rather than more general instruction and information.

Apart from preparing departmental staff directly affected by the introduction of a new system, it is also important to devote attention to staff elsewhere in the library. The consequences of most operations in a department of a library are not entirely self-contained. They extend into other areas of the library as well. Similarly, any changes in those operations, such as are likely to occur with the introduction of an automated system, will probably have some degree of impact on other departments and branches as well. The introduction of an automated circulation system, for example, often requires modification of certain procedures in technical processing departments. The use of a bibliographic utility for cataloging may require certain changes in the appearance of catalog cards, and this may have at least some implications for reference librarians who assist patrons in the use of the card catalog. These less direct consequences should not be overlooked in preparing library staff for the introduction of a new system. Under some circumstances, it may be necessary for staff in other departments to actually learn how to use the new system, at least for certain purposes. In other cases, staff will not need to learn how to use the system, but they should at least be aware of its existence and any implications it may have for the performance of their duties.

The approach advocated here attaches much importance to carefully preparing and training staff in conjunction with the introduction and use of an automated system. If such a systematic program is perused, it will cost the library in terms of time, having staff attend in-house informational meetings and training sessions rather than performing other important duties. Even without such detailed preinstallation preparation, the system will sooner or later probably be incorporated quite comfortably into library routines and will be accepted and even appreciated by most of the staff. So, the value that accrues from a careful program of education and preparation sometimes seems temporary and intangible when viewed in retrospect, after the system has been up and running for a while. Nevertheless, the weeks and months preceding installation can be trying for staff and a period of real agony if anxiety and uncertainty are allowed to become the reigning attitudes toward the forthcoming changes. The library owes it to its staff to try to alleviate these doubts and make the transition as positive an experience as possible.

In-house Training and Problem Trainees

Once a turnkey system is installed, vendors should provide hands-on training for system and terminal operators to be able to do their jobs successfully. After initial training by the vendor, the library may wish to develop in-house expertise to conduct training for new terminal operators hired as a result of staff turnover or expansion. A great deal more flexibility can be built into the design of in-house training than is normally possible in training by the vendor. For the vendor, training may mean travel from one city to another, and given the costs involved, neither library nor vendor can afford to have each new terminal operator trained by vendor personnel.

If the library develops an in-house training program, it should be a formal, well-organized activity. Assigning training duties to whoever on the staff happens to be most available at a particular time will not suffice. There should be one staff member who is responsible for training on a particular system or module. The proportion of an individual's time devoted specifically to conducting training sessions will depend on the size of the operation and the rate of staff turnover.

Whatever approach is taken in the way of in-house training, there are some general principles to any complex automated system: (1) especially in training staff for whom terminal operation will be a major part of their job, keep the number of participants in a session very small, to allow a more relaxed, less pressured atmosphere in which trainees can exchange information and ask questions; (2) training should be an even balance of hands-on experience and offline presentation and discussion wherever possible; (3) depending on circumstances, try to conduct training in a series of brief sessions rather than in a one- or two-day marathon; learning a multitude of commands and techniques, especially when combined with learning library policies and procedures, can be an exhausting experience and too much information presented in long sessions will not be retained well; (4) each session should focus on a specific set of related functions or techniques; (5) leave enough time between sessions to enable trainees to practice, review, and provide feedback; (6) when in session, allow, and in fact require, trainees to give full attention to the task at hand; employees should not be running in and out of sessions trying to take care of a dozen other things at the same time.

A few problem situations are common to in-house training on automated systems in libraries. One is that there will inevitably be problem trainees, who are most likely to fall into any one of four categories: those who are afraid of the system, those who resent having to learn to use it, those who approach it with reckless abandon, and those who have such a strong mental block that they simply cannot learn to use it effectively. Those most likely to fall into at least some of these categories will be staff members who were employed in the library since before the system was purchased, and whose duties are being redefined without a great deal of choice on their part. The library can exercise some control over employees hired after the system is up and running by hiring individuals who at least show a willingness to learn, but this kind of control will not necessarily be possible in selecting the initial corps of staff from within the department to learn to use the system.

Of problem trainees, the easiest to deal with are sometimes those who simply have an initial fear about learning to use the system. Usually, such fear is based on lack of previous experience with any type of computerized system. These individuals can often be identified immediately by observing the way they approach the keyboard for the first time. They either tap a key as quickly and lightly as possible and then draw their finger away as rapidly and as far back as possible, as though fearing that the keyboard might bite back, or they press a key and hold it down forever, as though by doing so the key will not be able to bounce up and retaliate. If the situation is handled properly, any fears can be alleviated very quickly. This type of fear is usually so exaggerated by the time a trainee actually sits down at a terminal that it often disappears with the first successful retrieval of a record or editing of a line on a screen, and it is all downhill from there. Nevertheless, until these staff members do feel more comfortable with a system, the trainer should work as individually as possible with them, and avoid having several other staff members staring over the shoulder of these trainees.

Other employees resent having to learn to use the system. This is usually more difficult to deal with than fear, since resentment often cannot be overcome as easily. These trainees are usually also very obvious. They consistently fail to do any required preparatory work, act totally disinterested during group sessions, and refuse to actively participate. Management and training staff must be careful before making immediate judgments, for these are also symptoms that can be manifested by fast learners who are simply bored with the seemingly slow pace at which the training is being conducted. If such is thought to be the case, the trainer should speak to the individual to effect some sort of compromise, because such behavior, regardless of origin, can be very disruptive in a group training session.

If, on the other hand, the individual really does have a strong resentment toward having to use the system, and is not learning how as a result, it is important to confront the person to try to determine the nature of the resentment. If there is no improvement in attitude or performance thereafter and if he or she is an otherwise satisfactory worker, one option is to reassign the person to another activity or department. If that is not possible or if the library chooses not to do so, another possibility is termination of employment. Confronted very directly with such a possibility, the trainee may develop a sudden interest in learning to use the system. If not, the library may have to follow through on the option of release.

The third type of problem employee has all of the opposite qualities of the first two types: nothing is feared, and the major problem in dealing with attitude is sometimes simply in trying to hold the trainee's enthusiasm at least partly in check for the benefit of others being trained at the same time. Overly enthusiastic trainees seldom pose a really serious problem, but if team terminal practice is included as part of the training, there are a couple of possibilities that must be guarded against. These trainees tend to want more than a fair share of their allocated terminal time, and they also overzealously instruct other trainees on the basis of their real or imagined expertise. If any of this reaches a disruptive level, the trainer should privately convince the overly enthusiastic employee to allow others to participate as well and explain that the training has been organized and paced to accommodate a variety of backgrounds and levels of expertise among the various participants. Public scolding or embarrassment should never be used as a strategy for quieting these employees, for if their energy can be properly channeled, they often turn out to be among the best and most reliable workers.

For the staff member who just cannot seem to learn to use the system, the trainer should exercise maximum patience and should allow for as much individual time, practice, and attention as possible. Even given special attention, however, there may be a few employees who simply will not be able to master the system. If the employee makes an earnest attempt, this is a far different situation from the trainee who refuses to learn. If at all possible, the individual who cannot learn to use the system but seems otherwise competent should be assigned other duties or even, if necessary, assigned to another department. Most of all, such employees should not be made to feel stupid or incompetent. They have not failed as an employee, but only in the specific task of mastering a system that makes up one small part of the library's total operation, and they should be given a chance to demonstrate competency elsewhere in the department or library.

Some difficulties in dealing with problem trainees can be greatly reduced if training can be conducted on a one-to-one basis, but this is not practical in all situations. In some cases, such as with automated circulation systems in academic libraries, group training sessions will almost be a necessity at least at those times of the year heavily affected by seasonal cycles in student staff turnover. In any group training session, one of the major challenges is to effectively deal with widely varying levels of competence, aptitude, and attitude. Even if there are no problem trainees, some individuals in the group will have had more experience in using computers or libraries than others, and some will simply learn faster than others. It may not be convenient, or even advisable, to try to arrange groups according to level of experience or on the basis of general impressions about aptitude or attitude. In these circumstances, holding several brief sessions, interspersed with hands-on experience, can help to minimize the impact of differences among trainees. Training can be somewhat more indivdualized and learning more self-paced.

Much of the training on automated systems in libraries takes place on the job. Although the instructional value of on-the-job experience must be recognized, the better prepared the staff are when they are placed in the actual working environment, the less likely they are to be inse-cure, make mistakes, and need assistance from supervisors and more experienced staff. But even with such preparation, it is important not simply to turn new staff members loose on the terminals without close supervision at first. No matter how much practice and preparation are involved, the actual use of a system in a real environment will introduce additional factors and a different atmosphere for the terminal operator than during the training sessions. It is important, therefore, that new terminal operators always have immediate access to assistance from more experienced operators and, whenever possible, from supervisors.

With a system that requires a large number of terminal operators, even a moderate rate of staff turnover will result in a steady demand for training. If the system incorporates changes on a fairly regular basis, the demand will be even more constant, since all staff will need to be instructed in how to use the new or modified features. In deciding on a training approach, the library will have to gauge, under its own circumstances, how much time will be required and exactly how system-atic a program can be afforded.

Notes
1.   A source that still serves as a valuable guide to preparation of RFPs and contracts is Kevan Hegarty, *More Joy of Contracts* (Tacoma, Wash.: Tacoma Public Library, 1981).
2.   For a description of some of the parameters of site preparation, see "Physi-cal Planning Guidelines for Housing Library Systems," *Library Systems News-letter* IV (January 1984): 4–8.

3. For a more detailed outline of acceptance tests, see Hegarty, *More Joy*, pp. 2–7 and 40–48.

4. The document that has been used by a number of libraries in the Rocky Mountain Region purchasing CLSI systems is the "Model Maintenance Contract Developed by the Mountain West CLSI Users' Group." The model contract is indeed an ideal; few if any vendors are likely to grant virtually all provisions suggested in this or any other model contract.

10

Bibliographic Records to Machine-Readable Form

When a library decides to install an automated circulation system, to implement a COM or online public-access catalog, or even just to have its holdings identified in a local, state, or regional union catalog, one of the tasks that must be faced is the conversion of manual bibliographic records to machine-readable form. In many instances, the library has already begun to cumulate a machine-readable file through its present cataloging service, be it a bibliographic utility, a book jobber, or a commercially available or locally designed stand-alone system. For all practical purposes, such services and systems have been available to libraries for little more than a decade, a few years longer if one counts some earlier batch-processing systems. As a result, if a library has been creating machine-readable records only for new items as acquired, a very large percentage of its collection—virtually everything cataloged up until the time it began to use an automated service or system—will still be represented by bibliographic records that exist only in non-machine-readable, or manual, form. If the library wants to put these manual records into a form that can be read and manipulated by a computer, it is faced with the major and sometimes awesome task of converting them. This process of recording older manual records into machine-readable form is called retrospective conversion, sometimes referred to as recon, retrocon, or retroconversion.[1]

What distinguishes this conversion from the entry of new records into an automated system is the magnitude of the undertaking, often the procedures used, and the options available. A library acquiring several thousand items per year and entering records for those new acquisitions into a machine-readable database will have 10, 20, 50, or even many times more that number of older bibliographic records that do not yet exist in machine-readable form. Whether the library catalogs a few hundred titles per year, a few thousand, or tens of thousands, the proportion of nonmachine-readable to machine-readable records is likely to be extremely large.

The conversion of manual records that have been cumulated over decades and even centuries can be such a huge undertaking and so expensive that some libraries have consciously decided not even to attempt it. Some that have already implemented online catalogs, for example, have avoided retrospective conversion by establishing a dual-catalog: the card catalog serves as the closed or frozen record of all materials in the library published or acquired before a certain date, and the automated catalog serves as the active record for everything published or acquired after that date. The date of division is usually the date that the library first began creating machine-readable records for its current acquisitions.

With certain types of applications, however, a dual system is not very practical, and with most others, not very desirable. A financial argument might be made in favor of establishing a dual public catalog, but it would be extremely awkward to maintain two circulation systems side by side, one for materials with machine-readable records and one for those without. For an automated circulation system, at least the major portion of a library's older holdings will have to be converted to machine-readable form. Even in the case of public catalogs, many libraries have felt that a single unified catalog, containing records for all items in the collection, is worth the expense of conversion. Some libraries have also viewed a complete conversion as an opportunity to clean up the inconsistencies in their catalog that have arisen as a result of decades of changing cataloging rules, reversals in library policies and procedures, and less than adequate filing maintenance and authority work.

A favorite cartoon in the professional literature depicts an idealized view of retrospective conversion as a librarian emptying a catalog card drawer into a large funnel placed atop a computer terminal. If only it were really that easy! Unfortunately, retrocon still takes an enormous amount of time and labor. There are some machines in existence that can scan, and convert into machine-readable form, the text of a document that has been printed or typed. A pioneering example of machines that can convert almost any text into other forms of communication is the text-to-speech Kurzweil Reading Machine, already familiar to many librarians. Other machines can convert printed or typed text into digitized data for computer storage, but these are still expensive and not in wide distribution. Even if the price were lower or if machines were cooperatively purchased by libraries, there is still the problem, in dealing with catalog cards, of differentiating between, and appropriately coding, the various bibliographic elements contained on them. Machines may be able to handle this in the future, but right now libraries are left with more difficult alternatives.

Purposes of Retrospective Conversion

One of the major selling points of creating a machine-readable database of a library's holdings used to be to serve as a security backup file for the card catalog. If a flood or vandalism or other disaster destroyed some portion of the catalog, but not the collection, the machine-readable file could serve as an inventory and even to create new sets of catalog cards. This may still be a valid use of a machine-readable database describing the library's holdings, but it is seldom the chief reason for retrospective conversion, and it probably never really was.

Most libraries enter into a retrospective conversion project for one or more of the following purposes:

1. To add locational information to a local, state, or regional union catalog of holdings used by participants primarily in conjunction with interlibrary loan.
2. To create a machine-readable database to be used as the basis for a library-specific COM catalog.
3. To create a machine-readable database to be loaded into a circulation system, online public-access catalog, or integrated system that the library has just purchased or developed.
4. To create a machine-readable database for an as-yet undetermined purpose, or at least without having yet selected or developed a specific system into which the database will be loaded.

The first purpose is unique among the four, in that in many cases the individual library is not provided with a machine-readable database of its own holdings as a final product. When a large union catalog already exists, the initial phase of participation by a library may simply involve submitting Library of Congress Card Numbers (LCCNs), International Standard Book Numbers (ISBNs), union catalog control numbers, or brief author/title/date of publication entries. These are matched against the union catalog database and the library's location identifier is added to records for titles that are already represented in the database. There is often an automated authority protocol used by the group as a whole, so even the library's specific forms of names and subject headings may not appear in the catalog, since in the case of discrepancies, they would be subsumed under the group standard anyway. After the matching phase is completed, only then might the library be requested to provide more complete bibliographic information, and only for those titles that did not match a record already in the database.

When the library has purchased or developed an automated circulation system, integrated system, online catalog, or is preparing to generate a COM catalog, the purpose of the conversion is for the library to obtain an institution-specific database to be used in very specific and known ways. Many libraries undertake retrospective conversion, however, long before they purchase or develop a system, and without really knowing exactly how their machine-readable database will be used in the future or even if it will ever be. At first glance, this approach without immediate application may seem somewhat shortsighted, but this is not necessarily so. For one thing, the institution-specific database may be created almost as a by-product of a conversion for a different, more immediate purpose, such as contributing locational information to a union database or catalog. Also, retrospective conversion is indeed an expensive process, and its costs over time have been increasing. As salaries and other costs have risen, so has the cost of a retrospective conversion project. In some cases, grants or other funding opportunities have also been made available. For example, many OCLC libraries carried out retrospective conversion during the 1970s using work-study students as staff, at a time when only a small percentage of those students' salaries was paid directly by the library or even by the parent institution. In addition, this was during a time, unlike the present, when OCLC did not apply any system-use fees for retrospective conversion. While these specific conditions are now a thing of the past, the costs for retrospective conversion will probably continue to escalate, and the longer a library waits, the more expensive the project is likely to be when finally undertaken.

Data Elements and Format

Various options for, and approaches to, retrospective conversion are discussed in the following sections of this chapter. First, however, it is important to review some fundamental questions pertaining to the philosophy with which a library enters a retrospective conversion project. These center around the data elements and format in which a library elects to record bibliographic information for the titles it is converting.

Emphasis on Full Bibliographic Records

At one time, many libraries recorded only minimum amounts of information on their retrospectively converted records, such as author, brief title, date of publication, call number and specific location, and perhaps subject headings, depending on the application. There were at least two very practical reasons for minimizing the amount of information for each item. First, it reduced the time and effort required for conversion, since less information had to be keyed. Second, computer storage space was expensive, and the storage capacity of most systems required frugality in the amount of space devoted to each record.

In the past few years, there has been a shift of emphasis in retrospective conversion toward including more comprehensive levels of description, even when the full range of data may not be immediately relevant. One reason for this has to do with advances in computer storage technology accompanied by decreases in storage costs. At one time, it did make a significant financial difference whether the average length of machine-stored records was 100, 250, or 500 characters, but this is no longer such a vital consideration. A second and perhaps more important reason is that, even when there is a clear idea of the immediate purpose for a retrospective conversion project, there may be future, presently unanticipated uses that will require additional types of data. To consciously exclude some bibliographic detail in a conversion now may be inviting problems later. To upgrade an existing database so that it will incorporate information not included in the original conversion can be an expensive process and may entail essentially a second conversion requiring almost as much effort as the first. With full bibliographic records from the start, on the other hand, the library may still want to extract only certain elements to use in certain applications, but the availability of the full record may save considerable effort and expense in other applications in the future.

Partly as an impetus and partly in response to the trend among libraries toward preserving detailed bibliographic records in machine-readable form, there are a number of systems and services that facilitate retrospective conversion by making large generalized databases of full bibliographic source records accessible to libraries. By matching titles in its own collection against the source records in these databases and adding its own call numbers, locations, and other institution-specific data, a library does not have to key virtually all bibliographic information in order to obtain full records. It can simply accept most of the information appearing on the source records, and add, delete, and modify the source data selectively, hence requiring little additional effort to obtain full records over what would be necessary to obtain more abbreviated records.

MARC Format and Categorization of Data Elements

The amount or types of information that constitute a "full bibliographic record" is certainly open to debate, but since the late 1960s the accepted standard has been the MARC format. This is the format in which records are stored in the databases of the bibliographic utilities and in those maintained by most other vendors, upon which libraries may draw as sources of information to facilitate retrospective conversion. MARC has become such a widely accepted standard that if a library creating a machine-readable database might want to participate in a joint automation effort, contribute its holdings records to a union automated catalog, or purchase a commercially available automated system without incurring special programming charges—and most libraries will want to keep as many of these options open as possible—it is almost imperative that the library's machine-readable records be recorded in MARC format.

The data that can be contained in a MARC record include the entire spectrum of information normally represented on catalog cards—authorship, title, edition, physical description, series statements, notes, subject headings, added entries, call numbers, and various control numbers—plus a great deal of other potentially valuable categorizing information that can be encoded in fixed field elements and elsewhere on record.

"MARC format" is a term that applies to the composite of what are actually eight different formats, each defining a structural coding scheme for a particular type of material, including monographs, serials, scores, sound recordings, manuscripts, maps, audiovisual materials, and machine-readable data files. In each format, a number of field tags, as many as 100, may be used to identify different types of bibliographic information, and most fields are divided into several subfields to identify even more discrete elements of information. Each of the eight formats has some uniquely defined fields and subfields, and although there is occasional ambiguity across the formats, the coding scheme is generally consistent from one to the next when similar types of information are represented.[2] The use of the generic term "MARC format" has grown out of this overall consistency and the logic imposed on the collective structure of the formats.

With eight different types of material categorized, and well over 100 defined fields of information and hundreds of subfields defined, the number of discrete types of data that may be included on records conforming to the MARC format is enormous. In retrospective conversion as in the cataloging of current acquisitions, many libraries will be using a service that makes available a database of generalized source records, and the accuracy and completeness of these records can vary tremendously between, and even within, the various databases that can be used for such a purpose. In the cataloging of current acquisitions, most libraries examine the bibliographic information on source records rather closely and make any modifications that might be deemed appropriate to local practice and procedure. But in retrospective conversion, most libraries feel that the magnitude of the task is simply too great to enable them to be as meticulous about examining every subfield of every field on every source record. Whether keying original records or verifying and modifying source records in large generalized databases, then, one of the most important decisions a library will make in a retrospective conversion project is in defining exactly which fields and subfields are most crucial for its own purposes in each format. The library must insure as much accuracy and completeness as possible in creating or in accepting and modifying records, but it must also adopt a strategy that will allow a conversion to be carried out in a period of months or years rather than decades.

A detailed discussion of all the individual fields and subfields of bibliographic information is not possible here, but shown below is a general structure for categorizing such elements for purposes of retrospective conversion, regardless of the option chosen or the approach used to carry out a project. When examined along with the library's purposes for carrying out a conversion project, this categorization can provide a framework for evaluating the need to verify and edit various types of information that may be available on, or absent from, machine-readable source records encountered in a library's retrospective conversion project. The specific types of information are shown here only with reference to monographs, along with their numerical MARC field tags.

Traditional access points: These fields of information are used to identify name, title, series, and subject entries. Accuracy and completeness is crucial. The following are the most important:

100	Personal name main entry
110	Corporate name main entry
111	Conference or meeting name main entry
130	Uniform title main entry
240	Uniform title
245	Title
440	Title of series
600	Personal name subject heading
610	Corporate name subject heading
611	Conference or meeting name subject heading
650	Topical subject heading
651	Geographic subject heading
700	Personal name added entry
710	Corporate name added entry

711 Conference or meeting name added entry
740 Title traced differently

Unique item bibliographic identifiers: These fields are used to identify information that may be useful in specifically identifying a work and in distinguishing between different editions of the same work. Accuracy in these fields is also important, especially for projects in which records from several different libraries will be merged.

250 Edition statement
260 Imprint

Descriptive information: These fields do not affect traditional access points; while sometimes used to assist in bibliographic identification, they are more often simply descriptive of the contents of a work. In a large conversion project, absolute accuracy and completeness are probably not as crucial in these fields as for access points and unique item identifier fields. Most of the MARC 500 fields for monographs fall into this category. Certain subfields within other fields also fall into this category, such as field 300 subfield c, "Other physical details" (illustration statement).

Coded categorizing information: Of all bibliographic information, this is unique to machine-readable, as opposed to manual, records. These fields contain a potentially powerful source of information that can be used to automatically select certain categories of records for preparation of special catalogs, to serve as the basis for search qualifiers in online catalogs, and so on.

008 Fixed field elements. The 008 field for monographs consists of 17 subfields. Examples of subfields include government publication code, conference level, language of publication, date of publication, type of illustrative material, biographical content, fiction indicated, and so on.

041 Language codes

043 Geographic area codes

045 Chronological codes

Although data, especially in the fixed fields, have enormous potential application, treatment in a retrospective conversion project is problematic. The origin of the difficulty is that these fields are often incomplete in source records other than in those created by the Library of Congress. Thus, a library will have to examine these fields quite consistently and may have to add appropriate data rather frequently in order to insure accuracy and completeness. Complicating the task, however, is the fact that modification of the fixed fields is probably more diffi-cult and time-consuming than modifying just about any other part of a MARC record. The information is coded rather than in descriptive text; its verification and modification generally require more interpre-tive cataloging expertise than most retrocon staff are likely to have; and for some items, may require examining the physical piece itself rather than simply a bibliographic surrogate such as a shelflist card. Some libraries adopt a compromise approach to treating these elements, se-lecting certain of them for verification and modification as appropriate, while ignoring the remainder.

Standard control numbers: Although these are not generally types of information relevant to library users, they are often crucial in library automation projects, both in terms of selecting source records and in automation efforts that require merging of several different libraries' machine-readable databases. Dewey and LC call numbers supplied on records by national agencies and other libraries are not included in this list.

010   Library of Congress Card Number (LCCN)
020   International Standard Book Number (ISBN)
027   Standard Technical Report Number
069   National Library of Medicine CATLINE Citation Number
074   Government Printing Office Item Number
086   Superintendent of Documents Number

The two most commonly used numbers in automated record process-ing, extraction, and merging are the LCCN and the ISBN.

Peripheral information: These data do not generally have an obvious value to the library user or often to the library staff. Perhaps the most commonly cited example is field 300 subfield c, "Physical dimension" (size). In some cases, peripheral data are part of a field in which other subfields are extremely important. An example is in the field 245 "Title" field, where subfield a, "Title proper" is crucial, but subfield c "Remainder of title page transcription" is less likely to be so.

Accuracy and Completeness

The amount and types of bibliographic information that a library includes on its machine-readable records—and that it verifies and modifies on source records on a generalized database if one is used—should be decided on the basis of several considerations. Foremost among these should be the anticipated most immediate uses of the database, the time and effort the library is willing or able to spend in the conversion effort, the financial resources available, and the degree to which the library tries to ensure database flexibility for future applications.

As already mentioned, the source records contained in the generalized databases that most libraries use for retrospective conversion are of uneven quality. Many are complete and extremely accurate. But others, although qualifying as "full bibliographic records," are far less complete and can contain typographical errors and various other types of inaccuracies. Compounding this problem in a conversion project is the fact that a certain portion of the library's manual records that it is converting are also likely to be incomplete, contain inaccuracies, or reflect older cataloging practices and procedures that the library no longer follows. In comparing library-specific manual records with generalized source records, it is not always easy to tell which of the two are in error or are less adequate than the other.

For the library using a generalized database of source records as the foundation for its conversion project, then, one part of the decision concerning the extent to which source records are verified and edited for accuracy and completeness will be to define a policy for resolving discrepancies between manual records and source records. There are three general strategies available to the library. First, it can always simply accept all bibliographic information appearing on source records. Second, it can always edit source records to precisely reflect the bibliographic information on the library's manual records. Third, it can more closely examine each discrepancy on a case-by-case basis and make a decision accordingly. Although the last of these strategies may be optimum from a perspective of quality control, it is also far more time-consuming than either of the other two alternatives. Whichever strategy the library adopts, it is important that the policy and procedures be made very clear to those on the conversion staff. The proportion of items for which such discrepancies will occur should not be underestimated; differences will be detected for at least an irritating minority. Such discrepancies can be extremely confusing to the terminal operators and offline editing staff who are responsible for resolving them, and this—in addition to broader considerations of accuracy and completeness—makes it imperative that the library define rather precisely which fields and subfields on source records will be examined, and how any discrepancies between the source records and the library's manual records should be handled.

Major Options

Three primary options are available to a library for converting retrospective bibliographic records to machine-readable form: full keying of all information at the library or by an outside agency, online conversion using source bibliographic records, and offline conversion that combines keying of brief data with automated matching against a database of source records. Many libraries use an approach or service similar to one of these for current cataloging, and may or may not wish to use that same service for retrospective conversion. As long as the records are generated in compatible formats, however, there is no "absolute" reason for a library to use the same system or service for retrospective conversion that it uses for current cataloging. Additional factors may influence a decision to use the same system or service, but a library does not have to ignore other options for retrospective conversion simply because it is using a particular system or service for current cataloging.

Full Keying

When converting manual bibliographic records to machine-readable form, a library, or an agency it hires, may key all of the desired information for each record onto a terminal and into some form of computer or computer-readable storage. Of all the options, this is by far the most labor intensive and probably most costly. At one time, it was quite commonly used, but now its primary application in retrospective conversion is in smaller libraries, in libraries with systems not using the MARC format, and in libraries that want to enter very brief records into an automated circulation system. For libraries that want the end product to be a file of bibliographic records in the MARC format and containing more than very abbreviated information, full keying of each record is not likely to be a suitable alternative. For any of the options discussed here, there will be a need to fully key all information for a certain proportion of the retrospective records, but that proportion can be greatly reduced if the library opts for either of the options described.

Online Conversion

Many libraries carry out their conversion project online. There are two general alternatives for online conversion. One is through access to a remote online database containing source records. For the most part, this option involves the use of one of the four bibliographic utilities —

OCLC, RLIN, UTLAS, or WLN. There are, however, other online services that may be used in a similar fashion. Though not generally thought of as bibliographic utilities, they serve much the same function insofar as providing access to large files of source records. One example of a commercial service of this type is Autographics' AGILE-II system, an online, interactive system that allows access to an LC MARC file and to the records of other libraries when appropriate arrangements are made.

The second alternative for online conversion is to borrow, purchase, or lease a database of source records and load them onto a computer located in the library or local computer center. This technique has been most commonly employed when a library is converting records to be used in its new circulation system. One form of this arrangement involves directly borrowing, purchasing, or leasing the machine-readable bibliographic database of another library. The other library's records, then, serve as the source records for the conversion. Another type of arrangement involves obtaining such a database directly from the vendor whose system has been purchased.

Online conversion allows a library to exercise maximum internal control over the way a conversion project is carried out. To create a machine-readable record for a title using OCLC, for example, a terminal operator first checks to see if an OCLC master record for that title already exists in the database. If a record is retrieved, the operator keys in the library's own call number (if different from that available on the master record), adds other local data if necessary, and may make changes in the bibliographic data contained in the master record to conform to the library's own authority structure if necessary. After this editing, the terminal operator enters a command that will copy the modified record onto an institution-specific computer tape at OCLC. For titles for which there is no corresponding master record already available, the library must key a full bibliographic record into the online database in order to have a record appear on its tapes. Some libraries, rather than having a tape subscription, transfer records from their online utility directly into a local system. Retrospective conversion using this approach is available through each of the bibliographic utilities. However, if a library is examining a bibliographic utility as a conversion option, it should be aware that most utilities allow use of their online databases for retrospective conversion only if the library agrees to also perform all of its current cataloging on the system. A library cannot generally become an online participant in a bibliographic utility simply to carry out a retrospective conversion project. The reason for this guarded policy is that the system-use fees the utilities charge for retrospective conversion are usually below or near actual operating and support costs. Therefore, the utilities cannot afford to extend retrospective conversion use to libraries that do not participate in more substantive revenue-generating activities, most specifically ongoing current cataloging. The notable exception is the Washington Library Network, which offers an offline batch-processing option to nonmember libraries in a few western states.

The online procedures for conversion using a locally loaded database are somewhat different, but the premise is similar to the use of a bibliographic utility or other remote access service. By retrieving records created by other libraries, a library is able to generate its own machine-readable database with minimal keying required. For each title in a collection, the library searches the database to see if there is a record for that title. If so, the library adds its own call number and location information and can modify any of the bibliographic information it so chooses. At the end of the conversion, records are purged of items in the externally supplied database that are not in the library. For the titles that the library owns but for which no matching record can be found in the database, the library must fully key new records into the system.

Although the definitive criteria of "online conversion" as described here is that it is carried out online in the library itself rather than at a remote site, some libraries do not use their own staff for this project, instead hiring independent firms to provide employees who come into the library and work. Even under such an arrangement, however, the library is able to maintain fairly close control since the project is still being carried out on site.

Offline Conversion

The third major option available to libraries for retrospective conversion consists of a number of services collectively referred to here as providing offline conversion services, or batch searching and record extraction. The typical scenario for this method begins with the library supplying one of these services with a list, in machine-readable form, that includes the library's local call number, location, and holdings plus such information as LCCN, ISBN, abbreviated entry (for example, author, title, and year of publication), or brief bibliographic search key (for example, a specified portion of the author's name and part of the title) for each item in its collection. These lists are generally created in one of two ways—using a standard IBM Selectric typewriter equipped with an Optical Character Recognition (OCR) typing ball or by keying the data onto a magnetic tape or disk. Some vendors will accept lists or shelflist records in nonmachine-readable form, but in such cases the vendor will have to key this type of information at its own facilities, at additional cost.

The information supplied by the library is then processed against a large bibliographic file maintained on the vendor's computers. In nearly all cases, these files include records issued on LC MARC tapes, and usually they also include additional records contributed by, created for, or purchased from other libraries that have conducted retrospective conversion projects. The records in the file are almost invariably in the MARC format. The amount of information they contain can vary considerably, ranging from quite detailed, such as those issued by the Library of Congress, to quite a bit less detailed in the case of some non-LC records.

In processing the information supplied by the library, the numbers and/or brief bibliographic records are matched against corresponding records in the vendor's general bibliographic file. When there is a hit—that is, a match between the data supplied by the library with a record in the vendor's general file—a copy of the full bibliographic record is extracted from the general file and placed onto an institution-specific tape. After each title for which the library has supplied information is processed against the vendor file and the appropriate full records extracted, the leftover titles—for which no record was found—can be dealt with in a variety of ways. Depending on the specific vendor and the library's decision, the library will usually have the option of keying a full bibliographic record for each of the leftover titles itself and submitting it to the vendor for addition to the institution-specific tape, or of having the vendor key the full record and add it to the library's tape.

Any automated matching and record-extraction technique will normally require some amount of postmatching and postextraction editorial work. Especially for items for which bibliographic search keys rather than unique numbers are submitted by the library, there are likely to be multiple matches for some and inappropriate matches for others. Multiple records for a match must be examined manually to select the one that corresponds to the title owned by the library, and some libraries selectively or completely check one-to-one matches to verify accuracy or to assess the quality of information in the extracted full bibliographic record. Even in the case of supposedly unique numbers like LCCNs or ISBNs, there are likely to be some instances in which multiple matches and inappropriate matches are retrieved.

To whatever extent the library chooses to verify and edit records, it has two major ways to go about it. The database of extracted records can be loaded onto a local computer for online verification and editing, or the library or vendor can generate computer printouts from the file.

The first method is a sort of hybrid approach to conversion, whereby the database is created offline, but verification and editing are performed online. The second method, using computer printouts, is more strictly offline. Corrections are made on the printouts or compiled on disk or tape and then run in batch against the database. In either case, the amount of editorial work involved in any batch-searching and record-extraction project will depend on the number of multiple matches and on the library's view on verification and quality control checks for one-to-one matches. Some libraries perform this latter task for virtually every record, while at the other extreme some do not perform any post-extraction verification at all.

One of the features of batch searching and record extraction is the degree of flexibility concerning the distribution of work load between the services and contracting libraries. A library may locally create the lists or numbers or abbreviated bibliographic entries to be used as input, but an option of most services is that portions of the shelflist or microfilmed copies may be sent for keying by the vendor itself. Some services perform editing as well, resolving multiple matches and providing spot or complete verification of one-to-one matches to ensure accuracy. Some services will also key full bibliographic records for those titles where no match is found. Such options do, of course, have a price associated with them, but some libraries feel that certain steps can be performed less expensively by the service than by its own staff, and others simply cannot take on the additional work internally, regardless of the cost. The important thing here is that many of the vendors are flexible, offering the library the option to define the balance of involvement between the library and the vendor in input creation, postmatch verification and editing, and full entry of records for nonmatches.

Currently, the batch-searching and record-extraction option is offered by only one of the U.S. bibliographic utilities, the Washington Library Network, though OCLC was planning to have such a service operational by late 1984. The WLN service is available to online participants in the Pacific Northwest and to libraries in several other western states through an arrangement with CLASS. Libraries can key brief search entries either into an online file or onto magnetic tapes or disks, and the entries are then batch processed against the main WLN bibliographic database. When a match is found for a search entry, the full bibliographic record is copied onto an institution-specific tape. In general, the WLN service is less flexible in the arrangements available for work load distribution than are most commercial vendors offering retrospective conversion services. WLN's own staff does not key in search records for libraries or perform any of the postmatching editorial work. Full records for nonmatches can be entered only by WLN online participants, and must be keyed by the library and go through normal procedures for adding new records to the WLN database.

A number of commercial vendors offer batch-searching and record-extraction services for retrospective conversion. Among them are several of the major book jobbers and COM vendors. In the case of COM vendors, a prevalent form of retrospective conversion activity has been in conjunction with maintaining statewide databases. At least one such project, the maintenance of a database for the state of Wisconsin, spawned a microcomputer-based retrospective conversion software package that is now available on the broader market for libraries that wish to add their holdings to, and extract records from, large bibliographic databases. This software package, MITINET, was developed by Information Transform, with the support of the Wisconsin Department of Public Instruction, for use with Apple microcomputers to assist Wisconsin libraries in providing data about their retrospective holdings. Brief search keys, usually just an LCCN or a control number from the Wisconsin COM catalog, are entered onto disks, along with the library's local call number and location data, and the disks are then sent to Brodart for matching against the statewide database. Locational information is added to the full master record in the statewide file, and the full record is copied onto an institution-specific tape if the library chooses to generate such a product. LCCNs for which no record is found in the statewide database are then searched against a more comprehensive bibliographic file maintained by Brodart, and full records for matches found there are added to the Wisconsin database and, if appropriate, to the institution-specific file as well. Independently of the Wisconsin project and Brodart's service, the MITINET software package is available to libraries outside the state with the price ranging between $85 and $250, depending on the size of the library.[3] Also apart from this particular arrangement, Brodart offers other batch-searching and record-extraction options, and a number of other COM vendors also maintain large databases and will accept brief input records on floppy disks, magnetic tapes, and OCR for matching against their files.

Of the commercial retrospective conversion services, probably the largest and the one that has certainly received the most publicity is the Carrollton Press REMARC database and batch-searching/record-extraction service. Since 1980, Carrollton has been involved in a project to convert more than 5 million Library of Congress records included in the REMARC database to machine-readable form. The records included in the REMARC database are for titles cataloged by LC between 1897 and 1968, and for those cataloged since 1968 but not included on

LC's own MARC subscription tapes. As of mid-1984, about 4 million records had been converted by Carrollton.

Confusion exists among some regarding the relationship between the Library of Congress and the Carrollton Press and its REMARC database. The relationship is mainly contractual; Carrollton is converting the manual records and supplying LC with the machine-readable product. Staff at the Library of Congress is not keying the records; that is being done under Carrollton's auspices, primarily at facilities in Scotland. The machine-readable records are in the MARC format, although some of the MARC-defined fields and subfields are not included on REMARC records. More specifically, the exclusions are: Dewey class numbers, ISBNs, untraced series, notes fields, and Superintendent of Documents numbers. Also, the title proper is included, but the subtitle is not, and fixed field elements are included only when they can be determined on the basis of tagged information already appearing in variable fields, hence excluding some fixed fields like government publication status and fiction indicator.

Carrollton offers a batch-searching and record-extraction service to libraries that matches brief search keys on a variety of input media against a master database consisting of records created both as part of the REMARC project and of those supplied on LC MARC tapes. Libraries key LCCNs, local call number, location, holdings, other local data, and brief title search keys in some cases onto machine-readable input media. These records are then sent to Carrollton where they are searched against the combined MARC/REMARC data. Matching records are copied onto tape and sent to the library. To assist contracting libraries in creating their machine-readable search records, Carrollton often loans Apple microcomputers to the facilities for the duration of the project without additional charge. As of mid-1984, there were about 50 libraries under contract with Carrollton for use of the REMARC service; several were large research libraries.

One approach to the batch-searching and record-extraction option that has gained in popularity is the use of multiple vendor databases for searching and extracting. This arrangement is often the result of agreements between vendors themselves. One example is an option offered through MARCIVE, a service that supplies machine-readable records and other products primarily to special libraries. The general bibliographic file maintained by MARCIVE consists strictly of records supplied on LC MARC tapes, National Library of Medicine tapes, and U.S. Government Printing Office tapes. Hence, it cannot supply records for most pre-1968 titles. MARCIVE has an arrangement whereby LCCNs for which no matching records are found in its own database can be searched against Carrollton's REMARC database. Another ex-

ample of multiple database arrangements is an option offered by
CLASS, whereby records are first searched against the WLN database.
For titles for which no matches are found, the search keys are reformatted by WLN and sent to Carrollton for searching against the RE-
MARC file. The advisability of searching against multiple databases,
whether through vendor options or arrangements made by the library
on its own, will depend on several factors, including the degree of
exclusivity of coverage between the databases involved, the amount of
work or costs in reformatting the search keys to conform to each vendor's requirements, and the pricing structure used for searching on
each service.

In addition to vendors that provide batch-searching and record-
extraction services, another type of organization that can be involved in
at least one part of the process is an independent data-entry business.
The library planning to use a searching/extraction service, but not
wishing to key any search data on its own, has two alternatives. One,
mentioned earlier, is to contract for data entry by the vendor whose
database will be searched. This is usually an option, although not always, as demonstrated by WLN's requirement that brief search data
must be keyed elsewhere. The other option is to contract with an
agency that specializes in data entry, although not offering a database
searching service of its own. One California-based company that has
done some of this work for libraries is Saztec, which will contract to key
information in the format required by any of the database-extraction
services. Another is Electronic Keyboarding, which has considerable
experience in library data entry for some very large customers. The
business of these companies is data entry, and they usually guarantee a
high degree of accuracy, proofreading, and input data correction as
part of the standard arrangement. Sometimes these quality control
measures are priced separately, but often they are incorporated into
the basic pricing unit. Although these services may be obtained regardless of which vendor database is to be used in matching and record
extraction, it is crucial that the data-entry service be extremely familiar
with the search format required by the specific vendor that the library
plans to use, since each searching/extraction vendor has a distinct preferred format in which they would like data to be submitted. Some
vendors will agree to process search records in formats other than their
own, but there may be an additional programming fee for this option.

Another conversion alternative that is offline at least in terms of
results is OCLC's Retrospective Conversion Service and similar services
offered by some of the OCLC affiliate networks. With this option, the
library sends actual or microfilmed copies of portions of its shelflist or
other catalog source to OCLC or a network for conversion. In the case

of the OCLC service, conversion staff match the library's manual records against the online OCLC database much as the library would if it were conducting the work itself. In the case of networks, some use the OCLC online database, while others—such as AMIGOS and SOLINET—have also mounted their own database. In addition to OCLC and some networks, there are some commercial services that provide off-site conversion using the bibliographic utility of which the contracting library is a member. Conversion is actually performed online under all of these arrangements, but since it is carried out remotely rather than in the library, the resulting product is equivalent in form to that provided by batch-searching and record-extraction services: namely, an offline product that has been created outside the library and without direct online involvement by library staff.

Comparing the Options

The decision to undertake a retrospective conversion project is one of the most important that a library will make in planning for automation. The characteristics and quality of the end product—an institution-specific, machine-readable database of a library's holdings—will in large part determine the flexibility with which the database may be used, and may even define the limits of the systems or products in which it can be employed. Therefore, it is crucial that a library contemplating retrospective conversion carefully assess the major options, and different systems and services available.

Criteria that should be considered by a library when selecting an option for retrospective conversion are discussed in this section. The primary concern here focuses on the decision of whether to use an online, in-house approach or a batch-searching and record-extraction service, and within that framework, on the major criteria for evaluating the products and services available through different vendors.

Allocation of Financial Resources

No matter how a library carries out retrospective conversion, it is an expensive venture and can consume a considerable amount of staff effort and salaries. Whichever option the library pursues, extra funding beyond the normal operating budget is likely to be required. Evaluating the costs involved in different options and services will be discussed later; the important issue here is first to realize that comparing the real costs of different alternatives may be of secondary importance if other constraints are imposed on how funding may be disbursed.

Knowledge of possible restrictions on the disbursement of funds is particularly important when considering the amount or type of work that can be carried out internally versus what can be contracted to an outside source. For example, in some academic facilities, salaries paid to student staff to carry out activities in-house may be subsidized through federal or state financial assistance programs, with the institution contributing a certain percentage of the total hourly salary. In such cases, the library's parent organization may be willing to fund part or all of the activities in-house that it cannot fund through an outside service, even if the real costs of using the outside service are in fact less than those of doing the work internally. Other libraries may find themselves in quite the opposite situation. There may be a total freeze on staff hiring, for example, that prevents the library from carrying out conversion activities in-house, but funds may be available elsewhere that can be used to contract for outside services, even if the real costs in doing so are greater than if the library were able to hire additional staff and perform the activities internally.

Disbursement of public funds not always follow what some would call rational patterns of costing behavior. Nonetheless, these practices are often a very real part of the environment in which decisions must be made. For any library seeking additional funding for a retrospective conversion project, it is important to have a clear idea of any externally imposed or peculiarly local conditions that may dictate how and to whom the funds may be disbursed.

General Impact on Staff and Facilities

Certain "less financial" factors may impose limitations on carrying out some or all of the activities involved in retrospective conversion in-house. These have to do with staffing and facilities. If the library is to hire extra personnel for the project, there must be a sufficient local labor pool on which to draw. Also, to what extent can additional workers and new procedures be integrated into the available facilities, existing work flow, and patterns of staff interaction. An in-house retrospective conversion is likely to require at least some amount of space and possibly new or reallocated equipment. In addition, an in-house project may mean some degree of modification in overall work patterns and will introduce new duties and responsibilities that must be incorporated into the overall staff organization. The psychological impact of all these changes should not be underestimated.

The other side of this question, of course, is how the existing staff might view a retrospective conversion project being carried out by an outside service and, to a greater or lesser extent, beyond their supervision and direct participation. In deciding whether to conduct a project completely in-house, completely through an outside service, or in some combination, the library must assess the availability of additional staff, consider the adequacy of existing facilities and space in the library, and take into account the impact that the decision will make on current personnel. The importance of these factors will vary according to each library's specific circumstances, but they should not be overlooked in any case.

Completeness and Accuracy of Data

After taking into account possible restrictions on the allocation of resources and limitations on staffing and facilities, it is important for the library, if it is still in a position to look at all options and approaches, to consider the anticipated quality of the final product—the machine-readable records. Although the final product cannot be fully evaluated until completion, certain considerations can serve as guidelines in anticipating the qualitative results.

One important point of comparison in evaluating online conversion and the various batch-searching and record-extraction and other services is the completeness and accuracy of records in the supplier's general file. It is significant that all major utilities and commercial retrospective conversion services share a common set of records in the form of LC MARC records generated since 1968.

LC MARC records for a title will not differ significantly from one utility or vendor to the next. And although there are occasional inaccuracies and omissions of pertinent data on LC MARC records, the overall information quality is high. Since cataloging records have been created in machine-readable form by LC only since 1968, however, a library using an online service, another library's database, or a batch-searching and record-extraction service for retrospective conversion will have to rely heavily on non-LC records as a source of information for older materials. All utilities and commercial services have such non-LC records in their databases, recorded in MARC format and supplied by member or customer libraries that have used or are using the service. Although most utilities and vendors are likely to have a nearly equivalent number of LC MARC records in their databases, the number of non-LC records can vary greatly from one to the next. The database maintained by MARCIVE, for example, includes only records created by the National Library of Medicine and the U.S. Government Printing Office in addition to those by LC. The database of the Washington Library Network contains only about a million non-LC records contributed by member libraries. The REMARC file includes nearly 4 million records—a number continually growing—that were not created by the Library of Congress but are based on information that Carroll-ton has converted from LC's manual shelflist. The largest number of unique non-LC titles in a single database can be found in OCLC, which contains about 9 million non-LC records input by member libraries, at least 2 million of which are based on LC cataloging copy provided in the *National Union Catalog* and other print sources.

The number of non-LC records will be important in determining the hit rate of a library's retrospective records against a database, but quantity is only part of the concern. The other part is quality. What is the degree of completeness and accuracy of information appearing on non-LC records in a utility's or vendor's general database? Non-LC records in these databases are almost invariably represented in the MARC format, but they may not always contain as much comprehensive data as is typically found on LC MARC records. It is important to stress here that the level of completeness, accuracy, and overall quality of many non-LC records in various databases is just as high as that of LC MARC records, and some would argue that in certain cases it may even be higher, depending on the original source of the records and the extent to which they have been upgraded. It is also important to realize, however, that there is more overall variation in quality of non-LC records, and since different utilities and vendors usually draw on different sources for non-LC records, comparing the completeness and accuracy of these records among the databases of the various services can be extremely important.

One way to evaluate the general quality of non-LC records in the databases of various batch-searching and record-extraction services is simply to ask the opinions of other libraries that have used those services in retrospective conversion projects. But a more systematic approach is advisable. The first step is for the library to decide which types of information in a bibliographic record will be most crucial for its own purposes. The second step is to approach other libraries that have used a service and ask to borrow or purchase copies of full-record editing lists or other forms supplied by the vendor to evaluate their accuracy and completeness in terms of the library's own data criteria. An even more straightforward approach is for the library to seek an arrangement to submit a small sample of LCCNs or brief records to vendors to match against their database, with the library then receiving full-record printouts of matches for examination. For current users of a bibliographic utility, the procedure is somewhat simpler and does not require any outside assistance. The library can simply search a sample of its titles online, print out the records retrieved, and examine them to determine completeness and accuracy of bibliographic information in terms of the types of data it considers most important.

The library's concern with completeness and accuracy of information on non-LC records will depend on a number of factors. Perhaps first and foremost, it should be recognized that even an incomplete record or one that requires correction may still be better than no record at all, in which case full keying would have to be performed. Nevertheless, since verification and editing do represent a substantial investment in time and effort, it is desirable to start off with records that have as high a level of quality as possible. The quality of non-LC records that are used or extracted is determined by the utility's or vendor's approach to its database, including such considerations as original sources of non-LC records, amount of upgrading, and level of completeness and accuracy required of new records being entered into the database.

Record Verification and Editing

When a library's manual records are searched against an online database or against a vendor file, a number of ambiguous situations can arise. Multiple source records may be retrieved for some titles, a single but inappropriate source record can be retrieved for others, and source records containing inaccuracies or information not precisely the same as in the library's corresponding manual records can be retrieved for still others. If the library wants its institution-specific database to be relatively complete and accurate, it must establish procedures to verify and edit the records examined in an online conversion or extracted from a vendor file.

Some librarians have questioned whether verification and editing really merit as much attention as they are sometimes given in a retrospective conversion project. Experience has shown, however, that neglect of quality control during a conversion can lead to a great many problems and to a very expensive cleanup later when the database is put to a definite use. It is important to strike a proper balance that will result in a highly satisfactory database while minimizing the amount of time and effort expended in achieving this goal.

In terms of procedures used for resolving multiple matches, for identifying inappropriate matches and typographical and other errors, and for handling information discrepancies between local manual records and database source records, there is a fundamental difference between online conversion and the use of a batch-searching and record-extraction service. With online conversion, these procedures are usually carried out before the record is entered into an institution-specific file or onto tape. Most of the verification and editorial work can thus be performed on an ongoing, record-by-record basis at the same time that the machine-readable database is actually being created.

With batch searching and record extraction, on the other hand, these tasks are performed only after all or a large number of records have been extracted and supplied in machine-readable form. Record verification and editing are thus on a postextraction and batched basis.

The procedures for either of these methods are not inherently better than for the other, but their differences are great and do require different types of staff involvement and work flow. In online conversion, for example, the individuals involved are often required to have some degree of proficiency in a variety of tasks, including searching the database, selecting appropriate records from among multiple matches, verifying the completeness and accuracy of information in the records retrieved, and editing records as necessary. With batch searching and record extraction, a greater degree of task specialization is possible if the library so desires. The duties of some staff members may be limited to keying search codes or abbreviated entries for matching against the vendor's database, while other staff may be assigned to multiple-match resolution, and still others to verifying and editing one-to-one matches.

One of the strongest features of online conversion is its interactive nature. A library may add to, delete, or otherwise modify virtually any part of a source record for its own file for whatever reason it so chooses. A library planning to use a batch-searching and record-extraction service should query each vendor being considered as to policy concerning postextraction editing. Some vendors offer essentially a "one-shot" effort. In such cases, any modifications to records extracted and supplied in machine-readable form to the library must be made by mounting the file onto a computer available locally or through another vendor. This is not a negative or inadequate approach, and may be well-suited for some needs, as long as the library is aware of the nature of the service and has access to other computer facilities that have adequate software to allow inspection and modification of records. Other services offer more extensive postextraction editing options, such as providing paper printouts of records and then performing modifications as noted by the library. This option is most common when the vendor is maintaining the library's database on an ongoing basis for production of a COM catalog or for other purposes.

Time and Costs

Regardless of the option chosen, a retrospective conversion project will consume a great deal of time and expense. Sometimes part of the staff-related costs may be assigned to existing staff and absorbed into the normal operating budget, but few libraries are in a position to re-allocate enough time and money from other operations to completely cover the additional work and expense required.

Allocation of human and financial resources for specific tasks will differ under each of the major options available for retrocon. But whether the options include full keying of all records, online conversion, or contracting for a batch-searching and record-extraction service, there are certain common factors that will affect how time and money are spent. The mix of these factors will vary in proportion from one option to another and from one service to another within a major option. Some time and cost factors may be inconsequential for one service or option but quite significant for another; for other factors the situation may be reversed.

The major factors relating to time and cost in a retrospective conversion project are:

> Importance of hit rate on the source database
> Nonstaff expenses
> > System use charges for hits against the source database
> > Offline products: the machine-readable database and hard copy edit lists
> > Additional facilities
> > Additional equipment
> Staff expenses and time requirements
> > Administrative tasks
> > Project tasks
> > > Searching or search key input
> > > Multiple-match resolution
> > > Verification of matches
> > > Editing of records
> > > Keying of full or abbreviated records for nonmatches

As throughout most of this chapter, the following discussion relates primarily to two of the three general options available to libraries: online conversion and batch-searching and record-extraction services. Full keying of all records is an option that will mean a substantially greater amount of staff time than the other two and will be more costly owing to its exclusively labor-intensive approach.

Hit Rate

If a library plans to convert all its manual bibliographic records to machine-readable form online or using a record-extraction service, one of the most important considerations affecting the total cost of the project is the hit rate of the library's manual records against the vendor's or utility's database. The higher the hit rate, the fewer the records that will have to be converted by full keying, which is invariably the most expensive per-unit task involved in retrospective conversion. In general, the greater the number of unique-title records in a source database, the higher a library's hit rate will be.

The importance of the hit-rate factor is sometimes glossed over by vendors with smaller databases in an effort to show how the cost of using their service is less than others because of their low per-hit charges. In reality, any such savings may be more than offset by the greater expense required for full keying of records for which no matches are found. The variation in hit rate between small source databases and much larger ones depends on the nature of a library's collection. For a collection comprised mainly of recently published, common English-language titles, the hit rate against a database consisting almost solely of the LC MARC records will probably not be significantly lower than the hit rate against a much larger database that has supplemented LC MARC with several million non-LC records. For libraries with a substantial proportion of older (pre-1968) or foreign-language titles, the difference between the hit rate on a small database and a much larger one is likely to be much greater.

Nonstaff Expenses

Some important cost considerations mentioned above fall under the broad heading of nonstaff expenses. Probably the most obvious of these is the charge by a utility or vendor for each library record successfully matched to a source record in its database. These charges usually range anywhere from 20 to 50 cents per record used or extracted. With use of another library's database, there are seldom per-unit pricing arrangements, but the source library may choose to request some form of one-time payment. Once again, an important thing to keep in mind in comparing per-hit charges is the cost of full keying of those records for which there is no hit. It may be well worth paying a somewhat higher per-unit charge if the hit rate is also likely to be higher, as the additional expense may be offset by the savings realized in having to fully key fewer records.

In addition to per-hit charges, another category of expense is the cost of offline products provided by the vendor or utility. With a batch-searching and record-extraction service, there are generally two types of offline products: magnetic tapes or other machine-readable media containing the extracted records, and edit lists, usually in paper form, to be consulted for resolving multiple matches and for verification and editing. Some libraries receive edit lists containing only problems, such as multiple-match records. Others request printouts of a portion of the total number of records extracted to spot-check for accuracy; still others receive printouts containing virtually every record extracted in order to carry out record-by-record verification and editing for the entire database.

Some vendors offer other options, too, such as printouts of all subject headings appearing on records extracted as a means to assist the library in authority work. Some incorporate the cost of the machine-readable tapes and of certain types of edit lists into the per-hit charges; others price the offline products separately. The library comparing costs of batch-searching and record-extraction services should be aware of the different types of offline products offered and how they are priced.

With regard to online conversion through bibliographic utility, magnetic tapes containing the library's edited machine-readable records are invariably priced separately from any per-unit online fees for retrospective conversion. The utilities generally do not offer hard copy edit lists. Part of the reasoning is that in some utilities the library's record is permanently retained online and any verification and editing can also be performed online. Even in the case of OCLC, where library-specific records are not retained online, many libraries consider edit lists unnecessary as long as careful attention is given to online verification and editing when the records are being converted. Libraries using a bibliographic utility have two options if they do wish to generate hard copy batch printouts of their machine-readable records. Printouts can be generated from the tapes by a commercial vendor, or they can be produced on a local computer capable of processing the tapes, for which there may be a charge depending on the financial relationship between the library and the computer facility.

The library may require additional facilities or equipment for retrospective conversion. With online conversion, this may mean purchasing or leasing one or more extra terminals and perhaps peripheral printer equipment. For a batch-searching and record-extraction service, equipment costs are likely to involve purchase of typewriters, OCR typing balls, or microcomputers for use in preparing search key input. For use with some services, the search input may be keyed onto a local mainframe or minicomputer and copied onto magnetic tape.

Both with online conversion and preparing input for batch-searching and record-extraction services, many libraries have been able to avoid purchasing additional equipment. Retrospective conversion projects using a bibliographic utility are often carried out by special staff during evenings and weekends when existing terminals are not otherwise in use. Record-extraction services often loan input equipment for the duration of a project at no additional charge. Even when such an arrangement is not possible, the equipment that a library may have to purchase, such as a typewriter or microcomputer, will be multipurpose and will have other applications beyond the retrospective conversion project.

Staffing Cost Factors

Staffing will involve participation at different levels, and salaries will range from minimum hourly wages at some levels to professional wages at others. A mistake commonly made in planning for retrospective conversion is to underestimate the amount of administrative and supervisory time that will be required. Responsibilities such as budgeting, accounting, and negotiating contracts for service do take some time. Much more pronounced, however, will be the time required of upper-level staff for training and supervising project personnel, for determining policies and procedures, and for resolving general and even item-specific problems having to do with ambiguous record matches, editing requirements, and so on. These responsibilities are sometimes initially assigned to regular staff members simply as additional duties. After the project has started, however, many libraries discover that the amount of supervisory attention required is greater than originally anticipated. If the library's in-house involvement is extensive and a number of full- or part-time clerical staff are employed, it may be worthwhile to assign a staff member full-time responsibility for coordinating the project, training clerical staff, which has a tendency toward continual turnover in retrospective conversion work, and making decisions involving bibliographic problems.

Major nonsupervisory project tasks comprise the core of a retrospective conversion project. In online conversion, the first four tasks identified on page 304 are usually combined into a single operation. Terminal operators search the database, resolve multiple matches, verify accuracy of information in a record, and make modifications if necessary. Manual records for which source database matches are particularly ambiguous and records for which no match can be found are usually flagged for later consideration by upper-level staff. The number of records that can be searched, verified, and edited per hour will depend mainly on three factors. One is response time. Especially with a bibliographic utility or other remote access service, the library has little control over this other than scheduling terminal work at off-peak hours when response time is likely to be fastest. The second factor is the proportion of the library's records that can be searched by means of unique numbers, such as Library of Congress Card Numbers. Numerical searches are generally more specific and require fewer keystrokes than searches based on bibliographic text such as titles and name entries. The third factor is the amount of verification and editing that must be performed. This will depend on how stringently the library has defined its policies for blanket acceptance of information on source records versus verifying and modifying those records to conform to the library's manual records.

Some libraries involved in online conversion report conversion rates of from 30 to 40 records per hour. In these cases, the library invariably cannot be performing any extensive editing of bibliographic information. Local call numbers and holdings information might be added to the source record, but few changes other than these can be made at that rate. When bibliographic information is edited to conform to the library's manual records, the rate of conversion is lower. An important factor here is the extent to which information on the library's shelflist or other bibliographic record being used for conversion can be accepted as official, and the source record modified accordingly without further checking elsewhere. If this can be done, a terminal operator will probably be able to convert from 15 to 30 records per hour. If other sources of information, such as an authority file, have to be consulted for very many records, the overall rate can fall to as low as 6 to 10 records per hour.

In using a batch-searching and record-extraction service, the first four project tasks listed previously can be performed more exclusively of one another than in online conversion. The rate at which each of the tasks can be performed, however, will vary according to some of the same criteria described above, such as the extent to which the extracted records are verified and edited. In the initial keying of search strategies, the variable most affecting the rate of keying is the nature of the search statement. This can be as brief as an LCCN and local call number and location for some services. It can be of intermediate length, including the aforementioned elements plus a few characters from the name of the author, the title, and the date of publication. It can be even more extensive, requiring keying of complete titles, author names, and publication data.

Even in comparing rates for the same type of search statement, claims about the rate of keying vary widely. Some cite keying of LCCNs and local data at 30 to 40 per hour; others claim rates in excess of 100 per hour. A project at Old Dominion University noted 152 entries per hour keyed using OCR when the search data consisted only of LCCNs. When also entering call numbers and copy or location information along with the LCCN, the rate dropped to 64 per hour.[4] Although these rates are considerably higher than online conversion rates, it should be remembered that the tasks involved are not comparable. The rates cited here are only for keying input. They do not include resolving multiple matches nor verifying and editing records. These tasks must be performed only after records are extracted, and the amount of time spent can vary enormously according to how closely the library chooses to examine those records.

Some record-extraction services will contract to perform certain of the project tasks. The costs vary according to task and amount of work involved. The charge for keying of search entries usually ranges from 5 cents to 20 cents per entry, depending on how much information is to be included. The prices for keying full bibliographic records for items for which no match was found can range anywhere from $1.25 to $10 per record. At the lower end of this range, it is usually the library's responsibility to prepare coded worksheets or to label information on its shelflist cards with appropriate MARC tags. At the higher end, the service will accept uncoded information and will have its own staff assign MARC tags. Not all batch-searching and record-extraction services offer these options, and some offer a more limited venue than others.

There are so many project-specific variables in retrospective conversion work that the overall per-unit cost for a library will very much depend on individual circumstances. In cases where an attempt has been made to include all the cost factors involved—direct and indirect—the figure almost always comes out between $1 and $2 per title, exclusive of the costs of full keying of bibliographic records for which no match is found. Libraries in the initial stages of investigating retrospective conversion options frequently view the per-hit system charges of vendors and utilities as the most important unit of cost comparison and as the main indicator of the overall costs of a project. Regardless of the option or service chosen, however, this per-unit system charge is in fact only one element in the total cost of a project, and in many cases is one of the least expensive parts. In examining options for retrospective conversion, a library should take a far broader view of factors that will contribute to the time and expense required to carry out a successful project.[5]

Restrictions on Use of Records

In selecting a system or service for retrospective conversion, the library should understand any contractual restrictions regarding the use of the derived or extracted records. It might seem that by paying a utility or vendor, a library is essentially "purchasing" copies of the records to do with as it pleases. This is not necessarily the case. From any system or service, the derived or extracted records can almost always be used within the library itself without restriction. Just as inevitably, however, the library will probably be contractually prohibited from selling or giving copies of the records to competitive vendors for permanent addition to their generalized databases. This is a reasonable restriction. But in between strictly local use and transfer to competitors, there is a very large grey area concerning the use of records in what might include statewide union catalogs, regional union lists of serials, circulation or public access catalogs shared locally among a few libraries, and so on. The contracts of some retrospective conversion services explicitly prohibit use of derived or extracted records in such projects without express written permission of the vendor and payment of additional royalty fees. The contractual provisions of other services are vague or ambiguous on this point. By readily accepting such restrictions or unclear provisions, the library may be yielding some degree of the flexibility with which it can enter into cooperative automation efforts in the future. Thus, a library should examine contractual provisions regarding the use of derived or extracted records very closely when it selects a retrospective conversion service. There may be some latitude for negotiating these points with a vendor before the library begins, and flexibility for use is certainly worth taking the time and making the effort to negotiate.

Shelflist Conversion and Alternate Strategies

A major decision in planning retrospective conversion is to define the approach to take in regard to determining which set of manual records to use as the basis for conversion, what proportion of the collection to convert, and in what order. Many libraries assume that a de facto purpose of retrospective conversion is to convert virtually all of their retrospective titles to machine-readable form. To achieve this, the library's shelflist is generally used as a basis for the project and titles are converted in strict shelflist call-number order from "A through Z," or "0 through 999," or similar sequential fashion with other classification schemes. With this approach, the physical items represented by shelflist records are generally not themselves inspected as records are converted.

Despite reasonable arguments in favor of shelflist conversion, it is not the only option. Some libraries convert from bibliographic records other than the shelflist. Some libraries require inspection of each physical item as its corresponding manual shelflist or other bibliographic record is converted. Others take a more selective approach, converting items only as they circulate or in conjunction with a reclassification project. Still others carry out retrospective conversion in conjunction with the barcoding of a collection for an automated circulation system. These approaches along with shelflist conversion are discussed below. In evaluating them and selecting the approach or combination best suited for its own particular circumstances, a library should examine a variety of questions, including:

1. For what type of automated application will the library's machine-readable bibliographic database be used?
2. What bibliographic elements are considered crucial to include in the machine-readable record, and can these be determined solely on the basis of information contained on shelflist or other bibliographic records without inspecting the actual items they represent?
3. When is the last time a library carried out an inventory of its collection?
4. Will the library convert records to machine-readable form for virtually all items in its collection or for only a portion of them?
5. Will the retrospective conversion project be completed in its entirety before the resulting machine-readable records are loaded into an automated system or are used to generate other products by computer?
6. Will the library be engaged in a reclassification project at any time in the near future?
7. Are the machine-readable records likely to be used in an automated circulation system, and if so, has a specific system been firmly selected?
8. Do the library's shelflist records contain complete or only partial holdings and bibliographic information? What proportion contain universal identification numbers such as LCCNs or ISBNs?
9. If the library's shelflist records are incomplete, abbreviated, or lack such numbers as LCCNs, are there more detailed records available in the library, such as in the public catalog?

Shelflist Conversion

The most common approach to retrospective conversion is still based on sequential conversion of manual shelflist records to machine-readable form without physically inspecting the actual items represented by those records. Preparing input through a batch-searching and record-extraction service with this approach normally involves a typist or terminal operator working with a drawer of shelflist cards, entering a predefined search key for each card that might include LCCN if available, the library's call number and holdings information, and sometimes brief bibliographic data. The typist or terminal operator constructs a search key for each card in the drawer, moves on to the next drawer, and so on through the entire shelflist.

With online conversion, the procedure may be somewhat more complex, since it usually involves immediate comparison of each shelflist card with one or more online source records, and will require interactive modification of at least some information on a record-by-record basis.

The advantages of this approach are that it is fast, comparatively orderly, and less disruptive of regular library operations and services than other options. Shelflist drawers may be easily removed and put back in place. Furthermore, if the shelflist is converted in strict sequential call-number order from beginning to end, it will always be easy to determine which part of the collection has been converted and which has not. There will be some inconvenience when other staff members want to examine a shelflist card in a drawer that has been removed and taken to a terminal or typewriter for data entry, but this is a fairly minor nuisance given the magnitude of a retrospective conversion project.

There are, however, some potential problems with the strictly sequential shelflist conversion approach. In general, it is indiscriminate. Each item in the collection is assigned a value of equal importance for representation in machine-readable form. This includes even items that may not have been used by patrons for years or possibly decades, as well as items that may have been lost or stolen and thus are no longer in the collection at all.

Concerning the time and effort spent in converting items that are seldom or never used, this is not a major problem if the library has decided to convert its entire collection. But for libraries that plan to use their machine-readable database in an automated system before the conversion project is completed, the nondiscriminating, strictly sequential shelflist approach is not the most time-effective alternative. It would be better first to convert the items that are most likely to be used when the automated system is implemented.

What can be done about this problem without abandoning the general approach of shelflist-based conversion? Probably the most common solution is to convert those portions of the shelflist representing the most heavily used sections of the library collection as expressed by the proportion of total circulation to total items available for circulation. If, for example, circulation statistics show that psychology is the most heavily used part of the collection in terms of circulations per number of items available, the library may convert its Dewey class 150-159 shelflist records or LC class BF records first. In this way, records for the most heavily used sections will be in machine-readable form by the time an automated system is implemented. This is still an imperfect approach, of course, in that no matter how broadly or narrowly the class ranges are defined, discrimination between items is still lacking within those ranges. Despite this limitation, it is more discriminant than a strictly "0 through 999" or "A through Z" approach, and does not introduce a great deal more complexity into the work flow as long as the library carefully monitors which parts of the shelflist have been converted and which have not.

Another solution that is at least partially discriminating is to convert records only for items published after a certain date. This approach also focuses on gross collection use patterns in that more recently published materials are generally used more frequently than older materials. And there is also a certain advantage in that this method clearly distinguishes, by date of publication, which items in the collection have been converted. This can be especially useful for the library that will be producing a COM catalog for public use or implementing an online public-access catalog before all items have been converted. It will be possible to define inclusion in the automated catalog according to date of publication.

Although this approach does have these advantages, it is not very practical for the library that plans eventually to convert its entire collection. In the first part of the project, during which only items published after the cut-off date are converted, terminal operators or OCR typists will still have to examine each card in the shelflist to ascertain date of publication. In the second part of the project to convert the remainder of the collection, the staff will again have to examine date of publication for virtually each record, this time to determine whether it was converted during the earlier phase. For the project as a whole, this double handling will lengthen the time and increase the effort.

For the problem of converting records for lost or missing items very little can be done other than conducting a collection inventory in conjunction with the shelflist conversion. If the library can afford such an undertaking and feels that it is in order anyway, an inventory immediately preceding or along with the conversion can be of real benefit. The savings in time realized in conversion, however, will not totally compensate for the amount of time spent in taking the inventory. Furthermore, if the library does not use its machine-readable database until some time after beginning the conversion, the value of the inventory will be diminished: items will be lost or stolen between the time of the inventory, the end of conversion, and the implementation of an automated system. If the loss is high, still another full inventory may be required to identify records that should be removed from the database. So, all in all, a preconversion or coinciding inventory can be useful but since it will be a time-consuming and partial measure, it should be justified in its own right rather than solely on the grounds of the retrospective conversion project.

For the library that plans to use its shelflist as the basis for a retrospective conversion project, certain problems may crop up because of specific shelflisting practices over the years. It is important to address as many of them as possible before a project begins. For example, any or all of the following may be present in a shelflist, for which clear policies and procedures will have to be defined:

1. Some locational stamps may represent subsumed branches or locations that are no longer valid.
2. LC cards may have been purchased in the past for editions different from the library's copy, with the LC data having been crossed out and replaced with the library's own.
3. Different editions of a work may be listed on a single shelflist entry.
4. Practices for cataloging supplements and indicating dashed-on entries may have varied over time, and in some cases may represent items that the library may now wish to consider as separate entities.
5. Practices for indicating locational or other copy-specific data on shelflist entries may have varied in the past.[6]

These and other practices may not seem overwhelmingly difficult to professionally trained catalogers, but they are very likely to be cryptic and confusing to terminal operators and OCR typists who perform much of the actual conversion work and have no formal experience in dealing with them. The important point is to identify potential problem areas, define appropriate policies and procedures for dealing with them, and be certain that terminal operators and OCR typists are sufficiently versed in how to treat them.

An important decision in online conversion will be to determine what to do about shelflist records for which ambiguous matches or no matches are found in the source database. Most libraries use a strategy in which one level of conversion staff is assigned responsibility only for handling the unambiguous online matches. The common procedure is for the operator to place a raised marker in front of, or to attach a paperclip to, any shelflist card for which an unambiguous match cannot easily be determined. Some libraries even use several different types or colors of markers to flag different types of problems—no matches, near matches to a different edition of the same work, and ambiguous matches, which are in some cases even more clearly identified according to a specific type of ambiguity, such as the date of publication or slight variations in title statements. Upper-level staff is then responsible for going back through the shelflist, examining the flagged cards, and deciding on the appropriate action. With a batch-searching and record-extraction service, these verification, editing, and multiple-match resolution procedures are carried out only after records have been supplied, but they will still be necessary to the extent that a library chooses to exercise quality control.

Most difficulties in shelflist conversion can be avoided by careful planning and by adequate training of staff. Even with the lack of discrimination between entries being converted, the shelflist approach is generally much faster and more convenient than other alternatives. The most serious limitation, and the one that prevents some libraries from using the shelflist, occurs when the library's shelflist records are too abbreviated to provide adequate holdings or bibliographic information about the physical items they represent. Under these circumstances, the library may have to turn to other bibliographic records, or even the items themselves, as a basis for its conversion project.

Other Bibliographic Catalog Records

Some libraries have always maintained their shelflists as an official record of both bibliographic information and local data, detailing locations, holdings, and various types of copy-specific information. For these libraries, the shelflist is an excellent source from which to convert records to machine-readable form. But other libraries have chosen to ignore or de-emphasize one of these categories of information in their shelflist. In some cases, this has taken the form of minimizing bibliographic data. The shelflist has served primarily as the authoritative record of location, holdings, and copy-specific data for each title, accompanied by the other brief bibliographic identification. In other libraries, the opposite has been the case; the shelflist has served as a record of bibliographic detail, while locations, holdings, and copy-specific information have been recorded elsewhere, usually on the main entry card in the public catalog. In still other libraries, the shelflist does not contain the most complete information either for bibliographic purposes or in terms of local data. In these cases, again, the most detailed records in the library are usually the main entry cards in the public catalog.

There are strong advantages in retrospective conversion to using the most detailed manual records available as the basis for conversion. And in the cases described above, the shelflist may be inadequate as a source from which to convert. Under such circumstances, the library may have to use cards in its public catalog as the record for conversion.

Using entries in the public catalog as the basis for conversion may be almost a necessity in some cases, but there are some very obvious problems with this approach. For one, it will be an inconvenience to library users. In shelflist conversion, careful planning can reduce potential conflicts caused by having one or more drawers of cards out of their cabinets and at a terminal. But the public catalog cannot quite as easily be redirected.

Besides the impact on library patrons, using the public catalog for retrospective conversion will result in some waste of time and some special types of difficulties. If the library has a separate main entry or title catalog, the procedure is relatively straightforward. Most libraries, however, have either dictionary catalogs or catalogs divided into two parts, one for subject entries and the other including both name and title entries. In using such catalogs for conversion, the library will encounter problems because of multiple entries for each item being converted. Clear procedures will have to be established to avoid duplicate keying or searching. The most effective way to avoid these problems is to signify one type of entry as the sole unit of conversion, in most cases, the main entry card. Terminal operators and OCR typists will have to be able to distinguish these cards from other types. This may not be a difficult skill for professionally trained librarians, but few terminal operators or OCR typists in conversion projects already have this expertise and will have to acquire it. Even when this is achieved, the procedure will still be more time-consuming than shelflist conversion.

Overall, then, conversion based on records in the public catalog will result in a longer project and in more inconvenience than when using the shelflist. But for some libraries, this approach will be necessary. And some have even found themselves in the unfortunate position of having to draw on both the shelflist and the public catalog to garner adequate data to convert records. When this happens, a conversion project will require very careful planning and clearly defined procedures, and will be even more time-consuming than projects that can draw on a single set of manual records.[7]

Bibliographic Record/Item-in-Hand Conversion

Whether using shelflist or public-catalog cards as bibliographic records for conversion, some libraries choose to examine each physical item as its record is being converted. One advantage to this approach is that it serves as an inventory check. Also, in many cases neither the library's bibliographic record nor the source records retrieved online or extracted from a vendor database contain all information that might be appropriate for inclusion in a full MARC record, and examining the item itself can enable the library to be more confident that complete information is being recorded. In other cases, having the item in hand will make it easier to resolve discrepancies between the library's manual records and corresponding source records.

The item-in-hand approach has strong arguments in its favor, but there are some logistical complications when it is used in conjunction with a sequential conversion effort, whether based on shelflist records or public-catalog entries. With online conversion, the procedure normally involves removing items from the collection, bringing them to the terminal to be available as their corresponding bibliographic records are being converted, and reshelving them. For shelflist conversion, materials can be removed in sequential blocks, since conversion order is by call number. In conversion from a public catalog, removing items is a more random process since the conversion order is alphabetical. In either case, the temporary removal of items from their shelving location can be an inconvenience for technical services staff and library users alike. Truckloads of materials might have to be brought into what may already be an overly crowded workroom, and considerable staff time and effort will be added to the project simply in removing and reshelving materials. Unless turnaround time is very quick, this approach will be a disservice to patrons who might be trying to find materials that are, in fact, in the process of being converted. Furthermore, some items will be in circulation at the time that their shelflist or public catalog card is encountered for conversion.

In using a batch-searching and record-extraction service, some of these problems may be less pronounced since postextraction editing lists can be taken into the bookstacks for comparing records with items in the collection, rather than having to remove the materials themselves for any length of time. Still, the physical inspection of each item will be an inconvenience to library users in the open stacks and will consume a great deal of staff time.

As an overall strategy, examining every item as its record is being converted or verified and edited will require much additional time and will cause clutter and inconvenience. Even with other approaches there will still be a need to inspect some of the items as their bibliographic records are being converted in order to resolve some of the multiple matches or to verify and modify source records in particularly ambiguous matches. But this will cause far less upheaval than if examining virtually every item when its record is converted.

Conversion of Materials as They Circulate

Most libraries cannot afford the time and effort required to examine each item if they are carrying out a full conversion of their entire collection. But some conversion strategies allow item-in-hand inspection to be more readily incorporated into a retrospective conversion project. The most common of these options is to convert items only as they circulate to library users. If the library is still using a manual circulation system, the conversion procedure normally involves gathering materials that have been returned by library patrons and, after discharge, routing them through the conversion staff before reshelving. If the library already has an automated circulation system up and running, somewhat different procedures are used, and these are discussed in a later section on barcoding.

Even before a library has purchased or developed an automated circulation system, conversion of materials as they circulate has a number of plusses. It allows physical inspection of items as they are being converted to ensure accuracy and completeness of the machine-readable record. It has a built-in inventory function; time and effort will not be spent converting items that are already lost or missing from the collection. Perhaps most important in some circumstances, this approach discriminates between items in the collection on a more functional basis than do approaches based strictly on sequential conversion of shelflist or other bibliographic records. Rather than assigning each bibliographic entity an equal value for conversion, it places a higher priority on items that circulate and, therefore, will probably be in higher demand for subsequent use as well. This may be of secondary importance to libraries planning to complete full conversion before their machine-readable records are actually needed for any automated system, but it will be a primary consideration for libraries putting their databases to practical use before completing full conversion. Finally, conversion of items as they circulate offers still another advantage to those libraries which may have to weed their collection because of space or as part of routine policy: items not converted as the project proceeds are those that have not circulated, and that might, therefore, be the most likely candidates for removal.

It is extremely important for a library converting on the basis of circulation to effectively coordinate activities between the circulation department and the conversion unit and to emphasize expediency in all phases of the work flow. A primary reason is that the most heavily used items in the collection are also the ones most likely to be in demand by other library users. It is therefore imperative, from a public services point of view, that returned items be converted and reshelved with as little delay as possible.

If the circulation rate of unconverted items exceeds the rate at which they can expeditiously be converted on return, it will be necessary to establish certain procedures to avoid backlogs and time delays. For example, if an average of 200 previously unconverted items circulates per day, but the conversion staff can process only 50 items per day, then only the first 50 items returned in a day might be sent to the conversion unit. A more systematic procedure is to establish a "next previous" circulation cut-off date. When examining returned items, only those that had a "next previous" circulation after the cut-off date are sent through conversion. This requires that circulation history can be readily determined from date-due slips or by other means that will not add a great deal of extra work. As the project continues, the average number of unconverted items being circulated is likely to decrease, and the "next previous" circulation cut-off date will have to be adjusted accordingly.

Procedures must also be established to make sure that once an item has been converted, it is not sent back through the conversion unit after subsequent circulations. This can be handled rather easily by stamping or otherwise marking items in a predetermined location, such as inside the back cover for books, when they are first converted. The circulation staff can then be instructed that items so marked do not need to go through the conversion unit on discharge, but may be reshelved immediately.

With clearly established policies and high priority placed on rapid turnaround, conversion of materials as they circulate is a viable approach that overcomes some of the limitations of strictly sequential conversion. It is also more systematic in discriminating between heavily used, little used, and never used items in the collection, which can be of particular importance to libraries that either choose not to carry out a full conversion of the entire collection, or at least cannot do so before an automated system is installed.

Combining Retrospective Conversion with Reclassification

Another approach is to combine the retrospective conversion project with partial or complete reclassification of a library collection. Reclassification is in itself a considerable undertaking and requires, at the minimum, handling each item to add a new spine label and changing the call number on all bibliographic records. With this much handling of materials and their bibliographic records, conversion of the manual records to machine-readable form can be incorporated into the routine without requiring very much additional effort. Particularly in an online conversion, the library will find that the work in retrospective conversion and reclassification is fairly similar. It is also possible to combine this approach with conversion of materials as they circulate. By doing so, the distinction between used and unused older items in the collection becomes particularly pronounced as they will be physically separated according to classification scheme.

Reclassification of materials from one scheme into another is a project in its own right and should be evaluated on its own merits. It should not be undertaken as an incidental by-product of retrospective conversion. To the contrary, the relationship should be viewed in the other direction, with the conversion of manual records to machine-readable form being an important by-product of a reclassification project undertaken on its own merits.

Barcoding

Most online circulation systems today use light pens or other scanning devices to read and record information as items are charged out to library patrons. This requires each item to have at least one special light-sensitive label. The labels commonly used are barcode and OCR. The barcode label, which contains a numerical identifier coded according to the thickness of and distance between a series of parallel bars, is the type most commonly seen on consumer products. The OCR, or Optical Character Recognition, label has machine-readable information printed in the form of characters that are also eye-readable.[8]

Generally, the data on either label are simply for the purpose of unique identification and do not contain coding that is descriptive of any characteristic of the item in question. In library terms, the information is equivalent in purpose to a strictly sequentially assigned accession number that does not have any content-related meaning. The National Library of Medicine developed an intelligent coding scheme for use with its Integrated Library System in which barcode numbers did reflect certain qualities of the item, such as volume and copy numbers. Most systems have not yet adopted an intelligent coding scheme and may not do so anytime in the near future.

When implementing an online circulation system, one of the most labor-intensive tasks is affixing a barcode or OCR label to each item in the circulating collection. This task can be incorporated into a retrospective conversion project. Unfortunately, even with barcode labels alone, there have been at least three different major types of labels that have been used in libraries and that are not strictly compatible with one another. Since each commercial circulation system vendor has traditionally used a preferred label, it has been risky for a library to incorporate labeling into a retrospective conversion project unless it has already contracted for or is very certain of the specific circulation system it will implement. On the more encouraging side, some major vendors can now modify their systems to handle more than one type of label. But affixing labels without very specific implementation plans is still risky, and it may limit or complicate the library's options for selecting a system.

If the library is carrying out a retrospective conversion project in conjunction with impending implementation of an online circulation system, it can include labeling as a step in any of the options described above. Each item will have to be handled sometime during the project, but there are different ways of going about this. One is to combine labeling with conversion of materials as they circulate. This will not ensure that all items in the collection will be labeled before the circulation system is implemented, but the library is at least able to prepare items that are more likely to circulate once the system is operational.

It is possible, however, to use other approaches to barcoding. In conducting a shelflist conversion online, for example, one option is to enter a barcode or OCR number into the online record, affix a label to the shelflist card, and then take the shelflist into the stacks with a corresponding set of labels, which are then affixed to the corresponding items. With online conversion, the most helpful device for entering barcode numbers into machine-readable records is a light pen that can be attached to a terminal. The barcode can be scanned and its number will be automatically entered into the record.

For libraries that have already completed a retrospective conversion project without assigning barcode or OCR numbers to their machine-readable records, one way to assign numbers is through the online circulation system once the library's database has been loaded. Numbers can be entered through scanning, and items can be labeled either as they circulate or in shelving order. In the latter case, some circulation system vendors have portable devices that can be taken into the stacks for recording numbers as items are labeled.

In addition to options in which barcode or OCR numbers are read directly online into machine-readable records, services are available with the ability to mount a library's database on a computer, automatically insert barcode numbers into records, and supply libraries with sets of labels and printouts identifying which labels should be affixed to which items in the collection. The library can often specify that call numbers and very brief bibliographic information be included on the labels; then the labels themselves suffice for identification and no separate printouts are necessary. With this approach to assigning barcode or OCR numbers, the library should require that the labels be provided in call-number sequence. A service should be able to do this rather easily when it mounts the library's database simply by sorting the records into collection units and then call-number order before inserting numbers and printing labels. Having the label sequence correspond to shelving order greatly expedites labeling. Even with this sequential correspondence, some form of data that provides sight verification is helpful, either on the labels themselves or on printouts, since some items will be misshelved, missing, in circulation, or will have been overlooked in the conversion. In libraries that already have an automated circulation system up and running before conversion is complete, a matter that must be dealt with is how and when to convert previously unconverted materials that are presented at the circulation desk for checkout. The typical way is to affix a barcode label to the unconverted item, charge it out, and key brief item identification data—often just the call number—into the system to establish a link between the item and the new barcode. The brief online item information is then retrieved and upgraded to a full bibliographic record.

Database Maintenance

The primary purpose of retrospective conversion is to create a machine-readable database of a library's bibliographic records to use in an automated system, or from which to generate other products through processing on a computer. There are limited exceptions, such as when a library carries out a project solely for the purpose of supplying general holdings information to a union catalog. In the more common instances where libraries will be using their machine-readable records for other applications, the broad parameters that should define any approach to retrospective conversion include the specific purposes for which the database will be used, the quality of records desired, and the costs involved.

Regardless of the attention given to the creation of machine-readable records during the conversion project, it should be realized that a bibliographic database is not a fixed product. Once created, the machine-readable records will continue to need modification to accommodate changes in cataloging rules and practices, in subject heading terminology, and so on. For the library that is already using its records in an automated system, the procedure for carrying out these modifications is primarily a design issue, defined by the capabilities of the system into which the records have been loaded.

For the library whose database is not being actively used in other applications, modification is more difficult. The longer a database is inactively stored, the more out of date the information becomes. If the database created during a retrospective conversion project is supplemented by tapes containing records of current cataloging activity, there is likely to be even less consistency in format and content among the library's complete set of records over time.

When a library that has inactively stored its machine-readable records does get to the point of actually loading the database into an active system, discrepancies will be found resulting from minor changes in format, and even greater discrepancies will be found owing to changes in cataloging rules and subject heading terminology. Plain and simple mistakes will also crop up in some of the machine-readable records resulting from miskeying and other human error.

Given the problems caused by inactivity over time, some libraries that are not using their databases for applications like circulation or public access have nevertheless brought them online strictly for purposes of ongoing maintenance. Some libraries are able to load their records onto a locally available computer to perform at least some database maintenance functions. Some commercial vendors, such as Autographics and Brodart, also provide online database maintenance services.

For libraries not yet using their database for specific applications and not having the computer or financial resources to maintain it online on an ongoing basis, some vendors offer one-time processing options that can be useful when the library is getting ready to load its records into a system that has been purchased or developed. AMIGOS, Blackwell North America, and Library Systems & Services, Inc., are three of the organizations offering such services. Commonly available options include the ability to consolidate a library's records and to process them against the *Library of Congress* Name Authority File and against subject authority lists. The use of such services may be helpful in reducing the number of older records that will require authority work once the database is brought online, but it will not obviate the need for performing catch-up maintenance altogether.

Since a bibliographic database will require ongoing attention sooner or later, a retrospective conversion project is just the beginning of the process of creating and maintaining machine-readable records for older titles in a library collection. It is, however, the most crucial part of the process. It is the most time-consuming and labor intensive, and the nature of the project and the library's approach to it will determine the flexibility with which the database can be used for subsequent applications.

Notes

1. For a detailed treatment of retrospective conversion, see Ruth C. Carter and Scott Bruntjen, *Data Conversion* (White Plains, N.Y.:Knowledge Industry Publications, 1983).
2. For a more detailed discussion of the MARC formats and the relationship between them, see John C. Attig, "The Concept of a MARC Format," *Information Technology and Libraries* 2 (March 1983): 7–17.

3. For a description of MITINET, see Hank Epstein, "MITINET/Retro: Retrospective Conversion on an Apple," *Information Technology and Libraries* 2 (June 1983): 166–173.
4. Walton, Terrence, "Retrospective Conversion Project at Old Dominion University," *Journal of Library Automation* 12 (September 1979): 281–282.
5. For further discussion of analyzing costs of retrospective conversion, see Stephen H. Peters and Douglas J. Butler, "A Cost Model for Retrospective Conversion Alternatives," *Library Resources & Technical Services* 28 (April/June 1984): 149–162.
6. For a discussion of some of these types of problems and how one library handled them, see "The Texas A&M University Project Description," prepared by Barbara Lucido, reprinted in *Retrospective Conversion*, Spec Kit #65, Washington, D.C., Association of Research Libraries, 1980, pp. 43–58.
7. For a description of the procedures used at one library confronted with this problem, see Phyllis Rearden and John A. Whisler, "Retrospective Conversion at Eastern Illinois University," *Illinois Libraries* 64 (May 1983): 343–346.
8. For a general overview of barcoding, see Ann de Clerk, "Barcoding a Collection—Why, When, and How," *Library Resources & Technical Services* 25 (January/March 1981): 81–87. 1983):129.

III

Applications

11

The Role of Bibliographic Utilities

It has long been recognized among libraries that, for certain endeavors, cooperation can result in a reduction of expenses at each participating institution and at the same time can mean better overall service to all involved library clientele. Although this idea and examples illustrating it certainly predated the use of automated systems in libraries, it is a principle that has had particularly profound implications for large numbers of libraries in their ventures into automation. This chapter focuses on cooperative activities involving systems that have come to be known as the bibliographic utilities.

The term "bibliographic utility" has become accepted parlance for identifying cooperatively based online systems whose origins were in the sharing of cataloging data. In North America, there are currently four major bibliographic utilities: the Online Computer Library Center (OCLC), the Research Libraries Information Network (RLIN), the Washington Library Network (WLN), and the University of Toronto Library Automated Systems (UTLAS). Although different in many respects, these four share certain similarities. Each entered into a networking environment as primarily a shared cataloging system. That focus has remained important, but each has introduced capabilities that extend beyond the sharing of cataloging data. Each of the four systems is maintained on central computer facilities with remote access provided through video display terminals or teleprinters located in libraries communicating with the central computers over leased telephone lines and packet-switching networks. Each utility is legally defined as a not-for-profit organization. The case can be made for the bibliographic utilities as cooperative ventures existing solely for the use of their participating libraries. The number of users and technological require-

327

ments of these systems, however, have as a general rule necessitated some form of management and governance other than direct and equal participation by virtually all users of the system. The exception is RLIN for which the full members are actually "owner-operators" organized in a board of governors in which a "one library, one vote" rule applies.

It is impossible to even approximate the number of North American libraries whose daily operations are influenced one way or another by the bibliographic utilities. The nature of that influence takes on a wide variety of forms. Some libraries are direct participants, with terminals located on their premises; others are indirect participants through processing centers or special arrangements; still others have no formal status as users of any of the systems but still gain access to one or more of the databases and rely on their information.

By late 1984, about 5,000 libraries in North America were participating in the shared cataloging aspect of the utilities by contributing original records or by assigning locational identifiers to existing records. This figure, however, is deceptively low owing to problems of formally defining a contributing library. For example, a single participant for purposes of OCLC membership is defined as a library with a unique three-character locational identifier, yet there are numerous instances in which a single identifier is assigned to a processing center that contributes cataloging for scores and even hundreds of administratively separate libraries. If these are taken into account, then the total number of libraries in North America that are participating in shared cataloging through the utilities is probably at least double the 5,000 figure. In addition to direct participation in shared cataloging, some of the utilities have formal arrangements whereby libraries can use cataloging information contained in their databases without necessarily contributing original records or assigning identifier symbols to existing records. RLIN, for example, has a "search only" user status that allows libraries to access the database without being a cataloging user.

The number of users of bibliographic utilities falling into the categories described above can more or less be documented at any given time, but far more elusive is the number of libraries searching the databases and extracting cataloging or other information without having any contract to do so. This type of use comprises a major problem for some of the utilities, since it does not generate revenue for use of the same information that authorized users pay for, but it still competes with those authorized users for computer access time and resources.

In terms of number of libraries participating, number of unique titles in its database, and number of locations for those titles, OCLC is by far the largest bibliographic utility in North America. Of the approximately 5,000 libraries directly participating in the shared cataloging component of any of the four utilities, more than 4,000 use the OCLC system.

The size of the bibliographic databases is somewhat more difficult to state since the utilities do not calculate this in the same way and some of the utilities, such as RLIN, have special databases which the others do not. OCLC and WLN, for example, express the number of bibliographic records in their databases in terms of master records, with each one theoretically representing a distinct bibliographic entity. Late in 1984, the OCLC database contained about 12 million bibliographic master records, with perhaps as many as 500,000 to 1 million being duplicate or purged records. The number of locations for the 12 million records—that is, the number of three-character library identifier symbols attached to all master records—exceeded 150 million.

The WLN database contained close to 3 million master records in that same period. A number were Library of Congress MARC records for which there were no recorded locations among the WLN membership. On records for those titles held by at least one WLN member, there were about 3 million library locations recorded.

The RLIN database is not organized in the same manner as those of OCLC and WLN. For each bibliographic entity, there is a "primary cluster member" similar to a "master record." This record is the one with the highest level of compliance with network cataloging standards. Other cluster members express variations in the cataloging practices of member libraries. Over 10 million records were included in early 1983, and this figure covers both distinct bibliographic entities and those that differ only in the manner in which they are cataloged.

UTLAS reports the number of records in its databases in terms of individual library records rather than master records. As a result, for purposes of numerical comparison UTLAS figures equate more closely to the number of holdings available on OCLC, WLN, and RLIN than to the number of master records. For that same period, the number of individual library records on UTLAS was about 22 million.

The numerical dominance of the OCLC membership and the historical dominance of its database among the bibliographic utilities are attributable to a variety of factors. Not the least was OCLC's head start by several years over the others in a broad, multijurisdictional networking environment. At least among the bibliographic utilities based in the United States, a factor of equal importance was the difference in the way each utility evolved with respect to focus of membership. Since it opened its doors to nonacademic libraries and to libraries outside the state of Ohio in the early 1970s, OCLC has marketed its system to libraries of all sizes and all types. When the Stanford (California) BALLOTS system was adopted by the Research Libraries Group (RLG) and transformed into RLIN, on the other hand, it became by definition a utility of far more limited membership. Although allowing a broader spectrum of libraries to participate as users of the shared cataloging system, the marketing efforts, and in fact the definition of full membership, became explicitly linked to the membership of the Association of Research Libraries, consistent with RLG's orientation toward major research libraries. The WLN membership base is likewise limited, not by type or size of library, but by a self-imposed geographic emphasis. Participation was initially restricted to libraries in the state of Washington, thereafter broadened to include libraries in other states in the Pacific Northwest.

Certainly not all libraries in the United States are users of a bibliographic utility, and in fact when considering all types and sizes of libraries, more are not users than are. But a significant proportion— probably a clear majority—of the nation's library resources are held in libraries that do use a bibliographic utility. As such, the decisions, philosophies, and policies governing the utilities and the way in which they meet internal and external challenges have an important bearing on a large segment of the American library community.

General System Capabilities

Just as the bibliographic utilities differ in their approaches to membership, so they differ in their approaches to developing and maintaining an online system. These differences underscore the unique character of each and in some cases the divergent interests of their respective memberships. With their initial focus on the sharing of cataloging information by libraries, each utility has continually enhanced features of its system to support that function and has added new capabilities. Table 11-1 illustrates the extent to which each of the utilities implemented certain general features and capabilities by the mid-1980s. It is important to emphasize that the comparisons shown are general features only; in instances where two or more of the utilities offer a similar feature, the specific details of its application can vary greatly from one to another. Furthermore, constant refinements and expansion of capabilities are characteristic of each of the utilities; some of the features listed as unavailable through a particular utility were at the time in advanced stages of development or testing, and work on many others was in the planning stages.

TABLE 11-1   GENERAL FEATURES OF BIBLIOGRAPHIC UTILITIES

	OCLC	RLIN	UTLAS	WLN
Cataloging				
Use of MARC format	Yes	Yes	Yes	Yes
Online display of local bibliographic information	No	Yes	Yes	Yes
Online display of local non-bibliographic information	No	Yes	Yes	Yes
Required review of new member input records	No	No	No	Yes
Online error reporting	No	Yes	No	Yes
Automatic periodic batch searching	No	Yes	No	Yes
Batch retrospective conversion	No*	No	No	Yes
Authority Files and Authority Control				
Online name authority file	Yes	Yes	Yes	Yes
Online subject authority file	No	Yes	Yes	Yes
Online series authority file	Yes	Yes	Yes	Yes
Online validation of headings	No	No*	Yes	Yes
Local authority files maintained online	No	No	Yes	No
Cataloging and Catalog-Related Products				
Catalog cards	Yes	Yes	Yes	Yes
Label sets	No	No	Yes	Yes
Accessions lists	Yes	Yes	Yes	Yes
Magnetic tapes of cataloging activity	Yes	Yes	Yes	Yes
Book and/or COM catalogs	No	No	Yes	Yes
Individualized bibliographies	No	No	Yes	Yes
Acquisitions				
Order creation	Yes	Yes	Yes	Yes
Central batch mailing of orders to vendors	Yes	No	No	No
Central batch mailing of orders to libraries	Yes	Yes	No	Yes
Online transmission of orders to selected vendors	Yes	Yes	Yes	Yes
Claiming capability	Yes	Yes	Yes	Yes
Online fund accounting	Yes	No	—	Yes
Serials Control				
Check-in capability	Yes	No	—	No
Claiming capability	Yes	No	—	No
Interlibrary Loan				
Unified holdings display	Yes	Yes	Yes	Yes
Serials union listing holdings display	Yes	No	No	Yes
Interface with bibliographic subsystem	Yes	Yes	No*	No*
Communications capability	Yes	Yes	Yes	No*
Online and/or offline performance and statistical reports	Yes	Yes	No	No*

TABLE 11-1 (cont.)

	OCLC	RLIN	UTLAS	WLN
Circulation Control				
Network-developed system	No	No	No	No
Vended systems or discount arrangements	Yes	No	No	No
Searching				
LCCN, ISBN, ISSN	Yes	Yes	Yes	Yes
Name, title, series	Yes	Yes	Yes	Yes
Title keywords	No	Yes	—	Yes
Subject headings	No	Yes	Yes	Yes
Boolean searching	No	Yes	—	Yes
Term truncation	No	Yes	—	Yes
Name and Address File	Yes	Yes	Yes	Yes

* High priority development in late 1984.

Cataloging Systems

Although bibliographic utilities have broadened their offerings to libraries, shared cataloging remains the cornerstone of their services. Bibliographic records are added to each of their databases through two principal methods. The first is the batch loading of machine-readable records, such as those supplied by the Library of Congress or other national agencies. The second method is direct online member input of records.

The major premise on which shared cataloging databases are founded is that all libraries cataloging a particular item will do so in a fairly similar manner, arriving at approximately the same conclusions in determining choice and form of entry, assigning subject headings, and otherwise describing the item at hand. Each of the bibliographic utilities recognizes, however, that not all libraries choose to describe an item in exactly the same fashion as other libraries in every case, and each system provides capabilities that allow libraries to modify records in the database to suit local interpretations and requirements.

One of the most fundamental aspects of the utilities is the way these local modifications are handled and especially the form in which they are preserved. RLIN and UTLAS preserve the full extent of local cataloging information online by creating a separate record for each title cataloged by each library, even when a newly created record is based on or identical to the information in a record that is already in the database. WLN, although using a master record concept and stressing conformity in accepting bibliographic information to appear on those records, does make provisions for the online maintenance and institutional access to local modifications of bibliographic data appearing in the master records. In contrast to the other three, OCLC does not preserve any local cataloging information online for member libraries. Any changes or additions to a master record by a participating library are reflected on the library's offline products, such as catalog cards or institution-specific magnetic tapes of cataloging activity, but they are not retained for future online display when the master record is retrieved by the library at a later date.

These differing approaches by OCLC on the one hand and RLIN, UTLAS, and WLN on the other represent fundamentally divergent paths to the nature and purpose of the online database. In the case of OCLC, the database is strictly a collective source of generalized cataloging information. In the case of the other utilities, the system accommodates this purpose, but in addition provides member libraries with online institution-specific detail of their cataloging activity, and it can therefore be used by libraries as an online localized bibliographic database management system. The availability of localized data allows the networks to be used for cooperative purposes that go beyond those of cataloging or even interlibrary loan. RLG, for instance, views RLIN as but a technical infrastructure by which such common problems as collection development, preservation, and expensive purchases can be addressed by its membership acting together rather than separately.

Original cataloging is time consuming, and many members of the utilities establish an internal waiting period before entering original cataloging on the database. During that time the cataloging staff occasionally searches the database to see if a record for the item has been entered by another participant or supplied by a national agency. Repeated searching can in itself be time consuming, and RLIN and WLN each have a capability that automates this procedure; a library can key in brief bibliographic information for a title once, and this record is automatically searched against all new records subsequently entering the database. Such a capability enables RLIN and WLN members to establish a temporary and brief online record in the database and to reduce in some instances the original cataloging required at a library. This feature is most appropriate for titles likely to be cataloged by a national agency, and both utilities emphasize that it should be used judiciously, and not to avoid the effort of contributing a new record to the database.

One of the primary concerns of any shared automated system to which participants contribute records that in turn will be used as source records by other participants is the extent to which control is exercised over record quality in the database. Even with a high degree of conscientiousness on the part of contributing libraries and an acceptable level of quality in cataloging records emanating from the national agencies, errors will inevitably occur in at least some of the records entering the databases. Some errors may be typographical, others inappropriate coding, and others interpretive, but in all cases they are an inconvenience to all members of the cooperative. Each library using an existing record as a source of cataloging information for its own purposes must correct any errors before or after accepting information on the existing record, and in a shared database this represents a duplication of effort.

Quality control in a shared database can be exercised on two levels: preventive and corrective. Each of the utilities stresses the importance of the preventive aspect by encouraging members to conduct their own quality reviews before adding records to the database. The most rigorous preventive measures among any of the utilities, however, are taken by WLN. The entire file system through which all cataloging is performed emphasizes procedural checks and balances at the member library even for local adaptation of an existing master record, and this review process is extended to the network level for all new member input master records entering the database. Although LC-supplied records are loaded into the database without central review, virtually all new records entered by member libraries are sent through a final quality review by central network staff before being added to the database. OCLC is a master record-based system like WLN, but a central review process is not deemed feasible owing to the enormous rate at which new master records are being input by member libraries—approximately 8,000 per week. For RLIN and UTLAS, the creation of individual records for each title cataloged by a library also makes central review impractical.

For corrective maintenance, three of the bibliographic utilities have prescribed procedures for member libraries to report errors detected on source records in the database. On RLIN, a library may correct errors in its own local cataloging records directly online, but errors on records supplied by a national agency must be reported to network headquarters for correction. On OCLC and WLN, errors detected in any master record must be reported to and corrected at network headquarters. UTLAS users may correct their own records online, but there is no significant attempt at the network level to correct errors in any records supplied by national agencies.

WLN and RLIN have sophisticated capabilities enabling libraries to report errors through the online system; OCLC still requires manual reporting. By 1983, OCLC was still reviewing the possibility of expanding its enhance capability to allow selected libraries the ability to permanently modify master records in the database. That capability has been in use for some time in conjunction with the CONSER (conversion of serials) project, but the only records affected are those for serials. An expansion of the capability to other formats would distribute the workload for error correction to a small number of participants, although error reporting by libraries other than these would remain a manual procedure.

Both as a measure to assist in quality control and as a service to expedite cataloging by member libraries, some type of online authority file is maintained by each bibliographic utility. The records contained in it may be consulted by member libraries to determine standard forms of headings. As such the capability serves a dual purpose in promoting conformity among headings in the database as well as making authority work in the creation of new bibliographic records at the member library less time consuming. The coverage in authority files maintained by RLIN, WLN, and UTLAS includes name, series, and subject headings. Only name and series authority files are available on OCLC. The files maintained by OCLC, RLIN, and WLN are generalized and systemwide; only UTLAS supplements its generalized file with the capability of storing institution-specific authority files online.

Among the U.S.-based utilities, WLN has developed the most sophisticated capabilities for integrating online authority work with online cataloging procedures. When creating a bibliographic record, a terminal operator using WLN can issue a command that prompts the system to automatically check all headings in the record against the appropriate generalized WLN authority files. If a heading on the bibliographic record matches an authorized form of authority heading, the system displays a coded response beside the heading on the bibliographic record, indicating that it is an approved heading. When a heading on the bibliographic record matches a cross-reference in the authority file, the system supplies a coded response beside the heading on the bibliographic record, indicating that it is an unauthorized heading. The approved form is automatically supplied on the bibliographic record immediately above the unauthorized heading. If a heading on the bibliographic record matches neither an approved form nor a cross-reference, a coded message indicates that the heading is new to the system. In that case the cataloger may wish to search the online authority file to see if a suitable alternative to the heading might exist. Among the other utilities, only UTLAS has a capability for online authority validation of headings similar to WLN's. Implementing such a feature is high on the list of RLIN's priorities.

The utilities offer member libraries a range of offline products generated on the basis of a library's online cataloging activity. All four utilities provide centrally produced catalog cards, accessions or new titles lists, and institution-specific magnetic tapes containing machine-readable records of a library's cataloging activity, which can be used in producing COM (Computer Output Microform) catalogs or for loading into online circulation systems, public-access catalogs, or other local systems. The form of these products and their distribution may vary. For example, WLN ships catalog cards arranged in sets to member libraries once a week. UTLAS ships cards once a week but offers the option of having cards arranged in sets or in filing order. Both OCLC and RLIN ship cards daily, arranged only in catalog filing order. Beyond these offerings, UTLAS and WLN also provide label sets and have arrangements to produce book and COM catalogs for member libraries.

Other Technical Processing Operations

To offer participants a more comprehensive system, each of the utilities broadened its capabilities to include technical processing in addition to cataloging. The most common effort has been the development of acquisitions subsystems. All four offer libraries a capability for creating an online order record. Although the display and content of the online form differ among the utilities, each system incorporates a feature whereby essential bibliographic information is automatically transferred onto the online order record from a bibliographic record in the database, if such a record already exists. After the online order form has been completed by entering additional pertinent data, it is sent to the specified book jobber or publisher in a variety of ways. On any of the four systems, libraries can print hard-copy order forms locally, based on the online record, and then mail them to the appropriate publisher or book jobber. OCLC, RLIN, and WLN offer an additional option; the printed copies of orders can be centrally produced at network headquarters and mailed to the library; the library in turn mails them to the appropriate jobber or publisher.

These are rather cumbersome scenarios that contradict two of the main advantages of online systems—speed of activity and reduction in paper shuffling. OCLC has expedited the process somewhat in that libraries may request that printed orders be sent from network headquarters directly to jobbers and publishers, bypassing the step of routing the forms back through libraries. RLIN, UTLAS, and WLN offer a different option, which takes full advantage of online capabilities; selected jobbers and publishers have access to a central network file containing the online orders created by libraries but only a relatively small number of publishers and jobbers are taking part. OCLC is almost certain to implement a similar capability. More publishers and jobbers are also likely to take part if the number of libraries using the acquisitions subsystems available through the utilities is sufficient.

The acquisitions subsystems offered through the bibliographic utilities differ with respect to availability of some general features. One feature that differs is the relationship between an order record for an item and the bibliographic record, and the extent to which ordering information is retained upon completion of the acquisitions cycle. As a separate bibliographic record is created for each title in each library on RLIN and UTLAS, there is a higher degree of continuity in these systems between a library's online order record and the final form of its full bibliographic record. The same online record is used and built on from the creation of an order, through the acquisitions cycle, to the completion of the final full cataloging record. Essential ordering information can be permanently retained in the completed online bibliographic record. This is not the case on OCLC and WLN, which use the bibliographic master record concept. A library's local information is retained online in its order record, but that record is distinct from the master bibliographic record in the database. Once the acquisitions cycle is completed for an item, the order record is purged from the online files. These order records in WLN are copied onto magnetic tape so that a machine-readable file of a library's order records is available. This is not done on OCLC; the only permanent records of a library's orders are those supplied on periodic paper or microfiche activity reports.

An important component of an acquisitions system that distinguishes it from a simple ordering system is a fund-accounting capability. OCLC and WLN have online fund-accounting systems and accompanying offline reports as a regular feature of their subsystems. UTLAS has approached development of a fund-accounting capability somewhat differently. Rather than developing the component itself, UTLAS concluded an agreement in mid-1982 with Innovative Interfaces to market that company's INNOVACQ system as a microcomputer-based interface that handles fund accounting and other functions to complement the UTLAS online ordering capability. After considerable analysis and member discussion, RLIN decided not to develop this capability, the lack of workable mechanisms for linkage to local check-writing and other accounting systems being a major obstacle. As a result, a number of RLIN members also have begun using INNOVACQ in a manner directly analogous to that being made by UTLAS users.

In contrast to acquisitions, development in serials and circulation control among the utilities has been rather sparse. Only OCLC has attempted to develop capabilities internally in both areas. OCLC's serials control subsystem, first implemented during the mid-1970s, enables libraries to create institution-specific control records for serials titles. In contrast to full bibliographic records on OCLC, local data are stored online on serials control records. A check-in capability is operational, but it has suffered from lack of an automated claiming function, problematic retrieval procedures, and a general lack of enhancement. The most successful application of the OCLC subsystem has been in connection with the union listing capability introduced in 1981. The success of this component is due to its implications for interlibrary loans rather than technical processing.

OCLC's efforts to develop circulation control have focused concurrently on two areas: generalization of the software of the Claremont College Total Library System and in-house design and development of the Local Library System, both to be operational during 1983 at least on a test basis. Each will be a stand-alone system using equipment other than the terminals used by libraries for other OCLC operations, and each system will eventually incorporate capabilities other than circulation.

OCLC's entry into the local systems market is a significant step, for it marks a departure from the approach the bibliographic utilities have traditionally taken to their role in the library community. Some of the other utilities have shown an interest in local control systems, but their approach has generally focused on development of interfaces to existing systems rather than development of their own. In particular, the Research Libraries Group, RLIN's parent organization, has sponsored development capabilities to interface RLIN with existing automated systems used by its member libraries for circulation and other purposes. The first such link was developed by the Pennsylvania State University and implemented there in early 1982.

Reference and Interlibrary Loan Applications

Certain features developed to assist libraries in technical processing, the primary application of the bibliographic utilities, have also had important implications for reference services. Put simply, the databases of these utilities are one of the most powerful reference tools available to libraries. The bibliographic records in the databases constitute an enormous resource, whose use sometimes seems limited only by the imagination of the librarian or patron using them. The following account, from an OCLC library in Illinois, is an example of how reference librarians have learned to apply the utilities for their own purposes.

> One of the fascinating things about browsing through OCLC's computerized catalog, which contains information on books and other materials from the year 1000 A.D. to the present, is its versatility. A case in point is the discovery in the computerized catalog of a concise history of *The Jazz Singer*, which was a hit movie in 1927 when Al Jolson starred in it, and a not-so-hit in 1980

when Neil Diamond resurrected it. From a listing of the entries retrieved from the OCLC computerized catalog in response to the search key for *The Jazz Singer*, a librarian can easily piece together the following information: *The Jazz Singer*, a 1927 film starring Al Jolson, was based on a play that was based on a short story that appeared in 1922 in *Everybody's* magazine. The play was called *Prayboy*, the story from whence it sprang, "Day of Atonement." Author of both play and short story was Samson Raphaelson. Also, way back in 1927, the Warner Brothers movie was novelized, with Arline De Haas spinning off the novel based on the movie based on the play based on the short story.[1]

In addition to bibliographic records, there are other files that are valuable in reference work. A name authority file, for a reference librarian, is a combined dictionary of pseudonyms and a handbook of brief biographical information. Each of the utilities has created a name and address directory file of libraries, publishers, and other library-related agencies as part of their acquisitions subsystems. Fortunately, the definition of a "library-related agency" is often extremely broad, and the name and address file available on some of the utilities is beginning to take on the appearance of a rather broadly based online directory of organizations and institutions, much to the appreciation of reference departments that have access to a terminal.

The range of flexibility in reference work to which the bibliographic utilities can be applied depends on many characteristics, such as size of database, types of files maintained, display formats available, whether institution-specific data are stored online, and so on. (RLIN, for instance, in addition to providing access to conventional cataloging data, provides access to "special databases" such as the *Avery Index to Art and Architecture Periodicals* and the *Eighteenth-Century Short Title Catalog*.) One of the most important characteristics is the range of access points available for searching the database. Each of the utilities offers access to bibliographic records through a variety of control numbers, such as Library of Congress Card Number (LCCN), International Standard Book Number (ISBN), and International Standard Serial Number (ISSN), and each offers some form of access by personal names, corporate and conference names, titles, and series titles. The flexibility by which the latter access points may be searched varies depending on the utility, the greatest level of distinction being between OCLC and the other three. OCLC users must follow a prescribed truncated search key strategy. RLIN, UTLAS, and WLN have greater flexibility, allowing for searching on full words, complete entries, and keywords in some types of entries regardless of position. RLIN, UTLAS, and WLN also have varying capabilities for retrieval of bibliographic records by subject heading and capabilities allowing for Boolean searching and term truncation. As an added service, UTLAS and WLN offer options whereby online search results can be printed offline at the network headquarters and mailed to the requesting library.

In addition to their application in general reference work, these databases have been extremely important to interlibrary loan operations. At the bibliographic level, they are reliable sources for verification, and the locational data on bibliographic records place them among the most valuable tools available to interlibrary loan. Drawing upon the value of these built-in features, which were a result of cataloging subsystems, each utility has implemented or is developing a facility to allow online transmission of interlibrary loan requests among participants.

OCLC was the first utility to introduce a sophisticated interlibrary loan subsystem in 1979. The subsystem permits a member to send an online request to as many as five different libraries in the order it specifies, with automatic referral from one potential lender to the next in the event that the item cannot be supplied by a particular lender. When a request can be filled, the borrowing and lending libraries each have access to the online request form and continually update it to show the current status of the loan.

RLIN introduced an electronic messaging facility in 1980 that enabled users to communicate interlibrary loan requests to each other, but it was not until 1982 that a more complete interlibrary loan subsystem was implemented. Although differing in some details from the OCLC system, it includes several of the same essential features: automatic transferral of selected information from a bibliographic record onto an online interlibrary loan request form; ability to select and specify the order of contacting several potential lenders; automatic referral from one potential lender to the next; and status updating procedures. In addition, the RLIN subsystem and the OCLC system include an online performance reporting file.

Of the four bibliographic utilities in late 1984, only WLN did not have some form of operational electronic capability to allow members to communicate interlibrary loan requests, although installation is among the highest of its developmental priorities.

UTLAS has never developed a sophisticated interlibrary loan subsystem in the sense of what is available or planned by the others. Rather, it has provided its users with a general all-purpose online communications facility over which interlibrary loan requests may be sent along with other types of messages. UTLAS plans to enhance the facility to include automatic transfer of bibliographic information from a bibliographic record to a standard online interlibrary loan request form, but it is not likely that features beyond this will be added in the near future.

General Approaches

In terms of options offered, there are essential similarities and significant differences between the bibliographic utilities. At the very broad level, each utility offers an online cataloging subsystem, at least some form of authority file, offline cataloging and catalog-related products, an acquisitions subsystem, features pertinent to reference work and interlibrary loan, and searching capabilities for accessing records in the various online files. When the general features within each of these broad categories are examined, however, variances show up in the extent to which they have been developed by each utility, and it is at that level that differences between the utilities become even more pronounced.

Regardless of the level at which differences occur, they are the outcome of conscious decisions and priorities established by each utility in the direction of its development. As a result, each of the utilities has certain features or characteristics that are more sophisticated or advantageous to libraries than those offered by the other utilities. Conversely, each has certain areas in which it offers less, at least at present, to libraries than do the other utilities.

OCLC's approach to development emphasized breadth of membership, size of database, and informal resource sharing among its users. In terms of online cataloging and search retrieval, the OCLC system has the least sophisticated capabilities and is the least oriented toward institution-specific detail. On the other hand, it has had by far the largest number of unique titles in its database on which to draw for cataloging information. Among the three utilities based in the United States, it has most widely opened its doors to membership. With OCLC's extensive membership, large database, and enormous number of holdings, it is hardly surprising that OCLC placed such a comparatively early emphasis on developing a sophisticated interlibrary loan subsystem.

The WLN system, in its initial design and since its implementation in the mid-1970s, placed its highest priorities on use of the database as a closely scrutinized cataloging system, perhaps best exemplified by its authority control system, the most sophisticated available through any of the utilities. Although all of the bibliographic utilities lay claim to placing a high priority on quality control over the online database, only WLN has formalized it to the extent of centrally reviewing virtually every new record input by members into the shared database. This procedure is feasible only because the number of new records being added by members is comparatively small owing to its smaller resource base. The fact that WLN has had fewer library resources on which to draw than the other utilities is due to the decision to limit direct participation on a regional basis. With its comparatively strong emphasis on technical processing applications, its smaller bibliographic database, and fewer numbers of members and locations in the database, the fact that WLN is the last of the four utilities to develop an interlibrary loan messaging subsystem is no more surprising than the fact that OCLC was the first.

The institution-specific structure of Stanford's BALLOTS has been preserved and further enhanced since its adoption by the Research Libraries Group and its subsequent renaming as RLIN. It was so institution-oriented, as a matter of fact, that until 1981, the use of RLIN for purposes of interlibrary loan was cumbersome, requiring retrieval of a listing of brief individual institution-by-institution records in order to determine the full range of locations for an item. This was resolved by reconfiguration of the bibliographic database, which included, among other things, a clustering of locations. At the same time, however, the separate institutional records were preserved.

RLIN has generally not been the first utility to bring up any auxiliary capability, such as a systemwide acquisitions or interlibrary loan subsystem, but when these capabilities are introduced by RLIN, they are sophisticated and their features reiterate this utility's emphasis on balancing institution-specific detail with maintenance of a shared database. More than the other utilities, RLIN has been incorporated into a comprehensive range of cooperative programs of its full members, those libraries participating in RLG. This is sometimes reflected in features available through RLIN, such as an online cooperative purchasing file.

Like RLIN, UTLAS places a premium on the retention of institution-specific detail for its users. There is a fundamental difference, however, between not only UTLAS and RLIN, but more generally between UTLAS and the other three. UTLAS is, in the stricter sense of the term, more a utility than a cooperative organization; its users are referred to as clients rather than members. Within this framework, UTLAS attempts to provide users with a wide selection of services targeted toward the individual needs of libraries. Some UTLAS features are distinct among the utilities, such as its capability for maintaining institution-specific authority files online and its approach to storing the full text of little-used records offline. Although it is unlikely that UTLAS will aggressively market online participation in its system in the United States, the utility has become involved in offering certain auxiliary services, such as its conversion of the New York Public Library's authority file to fully MARC-compatible format.

Major Issues Facing the Utilities

Each bibliographic utility is distinctive in some of the general features it offers, in the specific form of those features that are also provided by other utilities, and in its approach to membership. At their foundation, the utilities are cooperative ventures in library automation, whose existence and welfare are fully dependent on the participation and support of member libraries. But to view these utilities as purely collective efforts of groups of libraries bonded by a spirit of cooperation is a severe oversimplification. Because of their size and technological requirements, they are also complex organizations existing in a competitive, highly fluid, and sometimes divisive environment.

Because each utility exists in the same highly volatile environment, there is a certain commonality in the types of challenges with which they are confronted. There is a multiplicity of closely intertwined pressures that influence the welfare and direction of the bibliographic utilities. The success with which these pressures are handled by each one is likely to have considerable bearing on its further role in American libraries. The specific challenges, and their relative importance, change over time, but there are several broad categories of issues that are a constant part of the environment of the bibliographic utilities. These issues are detailed in this section.

Financing, Development, and Growth

One of the most persistent pressures facing the utilities is financing of their operations. Maintaining sufficient hardware and software to support the users of systems as large as these is an enormously expensive venture. But to remain technologically viable to libraries, just maintaining an existing system is not enough; there must be carefully planned enhancements and, when necessary, major expansions. There usually are substantial overhead expenses for simply housing the central computer facilities and for retaining a staff of technical experts. In addition to computer-related personnel, the utility must have at its disposal a cadre of staff knowledgeable about the content of the information available through the system.

One of the major premises of a bibliographic utility is that information in the database is shared by users; therefore, the value of that information and the ease and convenience of its use by libraries are to some extent dependent on the timeliness, accuracy, and overall quality of that data. Recognizing the role that users play in contributing information to the shared database and given the uninterrupted flow of changes in cataloging rules, MARC formats, and system features, utilities must have adequate human resources to train librarians, generate appropriate documentation, and respond to user requests for interpretation and guidance in use of the system. If the utility sees itself as existing in a competitive environment, whatever the source of that competition may be, it will also have staff and other expenses associated with planning and programs to market its products and services.

Although all four North American utilities drew heavily on external grant funding or other appropriations during their inception, each has strived since that time to establish financial self-sufficiency through system-use fees charged to libraries subscribing to services. The bulk of these fees consists of per-unit product charges. For example, a library is charged a set amount each time it uses an existing bibliographic record in the database for its own cataloging, another amount for each catalog card ordered through the system or for each magnetic tape of its cataloging activity generated at the central facilities, and so on. There is some variation among the utilities in the finer points of per-unit product charging schemes, and certainly in the amounts charged, but their basic pricing structures are essentially similar.

The degree to which financial self-sufficiency has been attained varies. Until recently only OCLC had achieved complete self-sufficiency in the sense of full cost recovery from payments for products and services by participant libraries. WLN continues to be subsidized in part by the state of Washington, and UTLAS, after a $400,000 operating deficit in 1981, received an $8.9 million loan from the University of Toronto to make some necessary changes in the system and alleviate an immediate financial crisis. The operation of RLIN has been a continual financial challenge for the Research Libraries Group. Particularly in the late 1970s and into the early 1980s, RLG programs were heavily subsidized by grants from private foundations, including monies delegated for the support of RLIN as the group's cataloging utility. In 1980–1981, 24 RLG members pledged $4 million in long-term loans to support program activity. Although not all grants, loans, and appropriations to RLG have been used to support RLIN, until recently the continuing operation of the utility has had to rely on part of these funds. Now it is fair to say that the operational aspects of RLIN and the development aspects of RLG are largely separate although necessarily closely related.

The bibliographic utilities walk a philosophical and financial tightrope with regard to pricing. On the one hand, the uncertain nature of external funding makes it almost imperative for a utility to work toward financial self-sufficiency. On the other hand, the reality of competition with each other and with the commercial sector imposes limitations on the level of pricing for services. Perhaps even more important than competition, however, is that the utilities are perceived by their memberships as institutions that exist primarily for the good of their constituency and only secondarily, if at all, in and of themselves. According to this sentiment, the utilities are not supposed to be profit-making businesses; their purpose is to provide desired services to libraries at the lowest possible cost. The specific forms in which this sentiment is expressed are sometimes fraught with inconsistencies, disagreements as to the scope of desired services, and failure to recognize certain accepted principles of financial management. But at the base level, this sentiment is properly the cornerstone of the bibliographic utilities and one that governing and management personnel must heed, even when there are problems with its form of expression.

One continuing challenge confronting the bibliographic utilities is the allocation of resources to system development. The combination of narrow financial margins and high costs of development makes it important for a utility to select very carefully the areas in which enhancements to the system will be made. The development of an entirely new component, or even a relatively minor modification of an existing one, is an expensive investment. Particularly when introducing a new subsystem, the decision must be based on sound judgment that there is a real need and that it will be used by a sufficient number of participants to justify the development cost. When the capability already has well-developed competition in the marketplace, such as an acquisitions system, it must also be of competitively high quality and low cost.

At least in the case of OCLC, perhaps because it has ventured into more areas than have the other utilities, the allocation of resources does not always seem to have followed the philosophy of weighing need against cost. In the mid-1970s, OCLC introduced an online serials check-in capability that had virtually no existing competition in the marketplace. But whether because there was not yet a strong enough perceived need, or more likely because of its lack of sophistication, the subsystem failed rather miserably. Only in the early 1980s, through the addition of a union listing feature, did any part of the investment of that initial effort show any promise of recovery. The extent of use of OCLC's acquisitions subsystem has also been disappointingly low in relation to original expectations. Many OCLC libraries have pointed to its per-unit price as a major deterrent, and others have indicated its lack of certain features. It will be interesting in light of past experiences to see how well the local library systems to be offered by OCLC will fare in a growingly competitive and sophisticated marketplace.

A concern related to the scope of system offerings is the size of a utility, both in terms of its database and its membership. A rather common philosophy among shared automation ventures of any type seems to be that the bigger the database, the better. There is certainly justification for this in a shared cataloging system, in that the larger the database, the more likely that a record for any given item will already exist, and therefore the less original cataloging any participant will have to perform. At least among the utilities in the United States, however, the expression of this philosophy assigns an identical value to each record in the database and assumes the necessity for storing all records online in their entirety.

The number and size of libraries using a system also have ramifications for a utility, financial and otherwise. In the United States, RLIN and WLN have imposed some limitations on membership growth, but OCLC has essentially followed a philosophy of "the more, the merrier." Although this approach has enabled OCLC to build a commanding superiority in numbers over the others and to avoid charges of elitism, which have been levied especially against RLIN, it is a tradition that is potentially, and in some cases already, the cause of a dilemma at OCLC and some of its affiliate networks. Most of the larger and medium-sized libraries in the United States are already members of a bibliographic utility. Hence, the majority of inquiries about, and new memberships in, OCLC are now coming from comparatively small libraries. Although the revenue base of these libraries is also smaller, their service demands are not necessarily less than the larger users. Smaller libraries require the same base of documentation, training, and ongoing assistance as do larger ones, and in some cases more, since the larger institutions frequently have a staff coordinator responsible for training and assisting other staff members in matters pertaining to the use of OCLC.

The financial implications of adding smaller and smaller libraries are that staff and other expenses at OCLC and affiliate networks will rise in proportion to revenues at a rate greater than when larger libraries comprised a greater percentage of the total membership. This is likely, over the long run, to have pricing ramifications for all members of the system, new and old.

There are no tangible signs that OCLC or any of its affiliate networks is turning away new members on the basis of size alone, nor is there any pressure to do so being brought to bear by larger libraries. But the permanence of open membership is dependent to some extent on the continued willingness of larger libraries to accept the responsibility of subsidizing service to smaller ones, and this attitude is in turn dependent on the image of OCLC's role and purpose as viewed by its membership.

The technology of the systems operated by the utilities is extremely complex, and decisions regarding development efforts and size have important technological consequences. Although slow response time and downtime complaints have been rather persistently voiced by users of some utilities through the years, there was never a more serious crisis at either OCLC or RLIN than during late 1981 and early 1982. The lessons learned during that experience have important implications for the pace at which new features are added presently and will be in the future. From the point of view of many users of OCLC and RLIN during the crisis, the systems simply were not working for a period of several months. That was not quite the case in a literal sense, but performance was so impaired that libraries could not count on the availability of the system for their own staff scheduling and work flow. The results were severe disruptions of work patterns in libraries, decreased revenues for the utilities, and a high degree of frustration for all involved.

Some of the problems of the 1981/1982 crisis were related to hardware; OCLC had just completed the physical move of its central computers into a new facility and had added some new pieces of major equipment, and RLIN had recently switched its operation to a new computer at Stanford. A compounding set of problems, however, was that each utility had also been implementing software enhancements of major magnitude. Between September 1980 and late 1981, OCLC installed a series of new system features and modified a number of existing ones, including improvements to its search retrieval capabilities and interlibrary loan subsystem, the introduction of an online name and address directory, an acquisitions subsystem, and a union listing capability, and carried out a machine conversion of records in its database to *AACR2* form. RLIN had also been working on a variety of enhancements, the most dramatic being the reconfiguration of its database, successfully implemented in September 1981. These changes sometimes affected other parts of the system in unforeseen ways, and the magnitude and pace with which they were implemented took their toll on both OCLC and RLIN in the form of overall system performance. The changes had been motivated by a response to expressed member needs and a desire to make the systems more attractive to present and potential users, but the most immediate results were a great many problems.

Underlying the whole matter of system development and size is a very fundamental question concerning the role of the bibliographic utilities in automation in American libraries. Are the utilities primarily systems to support the sharing of bibliographic data, or should they try to be all things to all libraries in the way of automation? The degree to which each utility perceives its role as falling somewhere between these extremes has a great deal to do with the priorities assigned to development and marketing efforts. At various times the utilities appear to have taken different approaches to this question. Some degree of flexibility in defining the scope of their role is necessary given the competitive and technological nature of the environment in which they exist, but that flexibility can be expensive if coupled with hasty action or, at the other end of the spectrum, indecision.

Competition, Cooperation, and Accommodation

Distinctions among the bibliographic utilities in terms of competition, cooperation, and accommodation remain important, but there is evidence of gradual lessening. In some areas, the result is increased competition, in other cases, increased cooperation, and in still others a delicate blend of the two. Some of the developments exemplifying this trend are examined here, with particular reference to the three utilities based in the United States.

Despite the availability of noncataloging subsystems, the primary tour de force of each of the bibliographic utilities remains their use as shared cataloging systems and, in a broader sense, as shared databases of bibliographic information. Even the system capabilities offered by each to assist libraries in other operations such as acquisitions and interlibrary loan ultimately rely on this sense of purpose of shared bibliographic information. It is only natural, then, that the focus of both competition and cooperation among the utilities has centered on features related to the cataloging function, on the quantity and quality of bibliographic data available, and on the pool of libraries to supply that information.

In the late 1970s, the balance between competition and cooperation among the utilities was skewed almost entirely in the direction of competition, particularly in regard to relations between OCLC and RLIN. The Research Libraries Group had defined full membership status for RLIN use quite narrowly (basing its definition on that of the Association of Research Libraries), and although the competition between it and OCLC, therefore, focused on a relatively small number of libraries, those at the center of attention were the largest in the United States. Competitive strategies were intense and, at least according to some versions, not always in the spirit of dignified competition. Although seldom offered in a public forum, reports stated that several private foundations contributing grant funding to universities, and to university libraries through the Council on Library Resources (CLR), were applying pressure on university presidents to bring their libraries into the fold of RLG and RLIN, even if that meant discontinuing membership in OCLC.[2]

OCLC's official stance during this period was that libraries could hold membership in OCLC and gain access to its database only if they agreed to perform all of their current cataloging on the system. This requirement made it financially impractical for an RLIN library to have legitimate access to the OCLC database. Although this represented OCLC's formal posture, a number of RLIN libraries continued to use OCLC for special projects with OCLC's approval.

The value of online shared cataloging systems had become well established by the end of the 1970s, but there was concern in many quarters that the degree of competition then characterizing the major utilities might not be in the ultimate best interests of American libraries or of the utilities themselves. Since the 1960s, there had been speculation about the eventual emergence of a national bibliographic network in the United States. Earlier projections foresaw the existence of a single nationwide system as the most efficient means of providing online shared bibliographic information. These speculations were sound in assuming the likelihood of a centralized national system, but in the United States, a centralized "top down" nationwide system remained only a topic of discussion during the 1970s, and by the end of the decade it was apparent that the concept of a single shared database had been supplanted in reality by the existence of not one but three major databases designed to provide such information.

The obvious redundancy in effort in providing shared cataloging data through three mutually exclusive systems was recognized, but given the reality of the situation, it was apparent that a single database accessible to all libraries could evolve only on a basis quite different from the centralized model. Further, given the relationship between the bibliographic utilities at that time, and particularly the form of competition then existing between OCLC and RLIN, there were indeed real doubts as to whether any developments at all were likely to occur in a cooperative direction.

Against this background, the Council on Library Resources commissioned the Battelle Institute to conduct a study of the comparative benefits, technical options, and costs that would be involved in establishing mechanisms to allow interutility database access among users of OCLC, RLIN, and WLN. Battelle examined a number of pertinent questions and issued a final report in September 1980.

After comparing certain characteristics of the databases and the benefits that would accrue to users had they access to one or both of the other utilities in addition to their own, the Battelle report presented three alternatives for interutility access. One option focused on offline batch processing of search requests, whereby unsuccessful online searches on one utility could be transferred onto magnetic tape at network headquarters and shipped to the other utilities for batch searching against their databases. The other two options allowed each utility direct online access to the other databases; a library could in essence search each of the three distinct databases on a single terminal. The difference between the two online options was in how they proposed to handle the differences in the search retrieval languages used by the utilities. The report further compared the three access alternatives with respect to timeliness of data, convenience for libraries, ease of implementation, and costs of development and maintenance.

The Battelle report[3] was the subject of some controversy for awhile. There were certain methodological problems with the quantitative aspects of the study,[4] although these were overshadowed in the library press by the reporting of OCLC's objections to the failure of the report (in OCLC's opinion) to address some of the crucial economic questions raised by the alternatives presented for the sharing of access to bibliographic data.

The Battelle study was neither initiated nor sanctioned by the bibliographic utilities, and the final report left a number of important questions unanswered. But despite its flaws, the project was significant, ultimately not so much in terms of its findings or recommendations, as in the simple fact that it represented a formal attempt to address the question of closer cooperation between the utilities in the exchange of bibliographic information. Policies have changed and projects have been initiated that are bringing about closer cooperation in very concrete ways and allowing libraries access to a broader range of information. At the same time, it is not yet entirely clear the extent to which some of these activities are cooperative or ultimately competitive, or what the long-range impact on libraries and on the utilities themselves will be. In the immediate future, however, the impact will be to broaden the amount of information available to users of the bibliographic utilities.

Changes in the direction of more available data have all required a certain degree of technological modification of the systems involved, but many are the result more of shifts in management policy than of complex technological changes. This is best exemplified in the case of magnetic tapeload projects undertaken by each of the utilities. One of the clearest policy shifts in this regard was OCLC's introduction of partial user and tapeload membership categories in 1982. In essence, these new categories allow users of other utilities or other automated cataloging systems to become users of the OCLC system as well. In the case of partial user status, this represents a reversal of OCLC's earlier insistence that only libraries contributing all of their current cataloging to OCLC could access the database for any purpose. The partial user category provides a pricing mechanism whereby libraries may use OCLC for searching, determining interlibrary loan locations, using noncataloging subsystems, and capturing bibliographic information from the database without actually cataloging items through the system.

The tapeload membership is somewhat different; in this category, a locational identifier of a tapeload member is affixed to the OCLC master record for each title cataloged by the library. Rather than being done online, however, it is performed by running an institution's magnetic tapes, containing machine-readable records of its cataloging activity generated on another system, against the OCLC database. This allows a library's holdings to be reflected on both the primary system used by the library and on OCLC without requiring dual online entry of data by library staff. OCLC offers this option at a reduced price that makes dual membership in OCLC and another utility financially feasible, and the library by virtue of its tapeloading is granted full rights of access to the OCLC database.

In many states or regions where RLIN members had felt ostracized as uncooperative for not making their holdings information known to the broader segment of libraries in the area using OCLC, the tapeload option provides a way for a library to accommodate these concerns without having to abandon its commitment to RLG and RLIN. By late 1984, nearly all of RLG's full members had become, or were seriously considering becoming, either tapeload members or partial users of OCLC.

RLIN engaged in a similar venture with respect to OCLC tapes. A number of RLIN members were previously members of OCLC and had significant numbers of machine-readable bibliographic records stored on OCLC tapes that were not available for access through RLIN. The RLIN tapeload capability enabled these records to be added to the RLIN database.

These developments at OCLC and RLIN have had a positive impact on individual libraries using either utility by expanding the amount of information available in both databases. The tapeloading programs are too recent, however, to gauge their impact on the utilities themselves and on the positions of OCLC and RLIN relative to each other. On the surface, these changes appear to promote cooperation, or at least accommodation, but there is an element of competition that could surface.

The impact of OCLC's tapeload and partial user policies could show itself in any number of quite different directions. One possibility is that RLIN full membership will remain relatively stable and that a number of present members, although continuing to use RLIN as their primary utility, will choose to become tapeload or partial users of OCLC, which would increase OCLC's revenue base and perhaps enhance its position relative to the other utilities. The reverse side of the coin is that the policies open the door for some very large OCLC member libraries to switch to RLIN as their primary cataloging database without having to give up the benefits of access to the OCLC database. Even if these libraries were to retain tapeload membership in OCLC, the price difference between tapeloading and online cataloging on the system is large enough so that a significant quantity of such membership changes could have important financial repercussions for OCLC. The impact of RLIN's success with a sophisticated tapeload capability could also be in any of several directions, but the long-range impact of these developments will depend on many factors yet to emerge. In the meantime, their most immediate result is benefit to the primary users of both utilities.

Like OCLC and RLIN, WLN has also developed capabilities for the loading of bibliographic and locational information from tapes containing machine-readable records of individual libraries. WLN strategies, however, differ from those of OCLC and RLIN and follow two main avenues. One is in connection with arrangements for duplicating WLN software in other libraries. A general condition of WLN's licensing agreement that allows other libraries to duplicate WLN software for local purposes is that the library's machine-readable records must be run against the WLN database and be added to it when there are not already corresponding WLN master records. Under this arrangement, the contracting library's locational information is not added to the database, just its bibliographic records. Tapeloading has not been fully implemented as yet for all current duplication agreements, but the implications for growth of the WLN database are substantial when one considers some of the libraries with which such agreements have been made—either directly (as with the University of Illinois, the University of Missouri, and the National Library of Australia,[5] for instance), or indirectly through Biblio-Techniques, Inc. (as with Columbia University, Johns Hopkins University, and the University of California at San Diego, for instance).

The second type of arrangement WLN offers is through its retrospective conversion batch-processing service. Previously available only to WLN members, this service is now available to non-WLN libraries in Arizona, California, Nevada, and Utah through an agreement with the California Library Authority for Systems and Services (CLASS). A library in any of those states can contract to send magnetic tapes to WLN containing very brief bibliographic information, whereupon the tapes are run against the WLN database. In cases where the brief library records match a WLN master record, the full-length MARC records are spun off onto a tape and sent back to the library. The implications of this service for the growth of the WLN database are just the opposite of the software duplication agreements: new bibliographic records are not added to the database, but for matching records, locational identifiers are added.

In the library press and elsewhere, most of the coverage about expansion of the bibliographic utilities has focused on OCLC and RLIN. The less frequent attention to WLN may have to do with its narrower geographic scope of direct online participation; WLN does not market itself as a nationwide online bibliographic utility. Yet the possibilities for the increase of bibliographic and locational information in the WLN database through duplication agreements and broader marketing of its retrospective conversion service may have important implications if these programs are successful and expanded. Given this possibility combined with WLN's interest and participation in work on the online exchange of information between different automated systems, the impact of WLN on the sharing of bibliographic data among libraries in the United States is likely to be far more prominent than its current geographic limits might suggest.

At a far more complex level than the tape processing capabilities described above, one of the most important developments that will affect the relationship between the bibliographic utilities is work on the online exchange of information between systems. Since 1980, RLIN, WLN, and the Library of Congress have been working on a series of projects to enable data to be exchanged between the three in an online mode rather than having to rely on tapeloading. In 1980, the Council on Library Resources awarded a grant to the three organizations to develop a link that would allow the online exchange of authority information. A second phase of the Linked Authority Systems Project was also funded by CLR, as was a related project, a standard network interconnection (SNI), which was to focus on the exchange of a broader range of information than just authority data.

The actual link to allow online exchange between RLIN, WLN, and LC was scheduled for implementation in 1983, but development delays have resulted in a 1984 target date for LC and RLIN and a 1985 date for WLN joining the other two. If successful, SNI may be the most significant development to date affecting relationships among the bibliographic utilities. The RLG announcement about the grant to develop the link proclaimed that "the long range implication of the use of the SNI is that any computer system will be able to connect with any other computer system to create a nationwide bibliographic database."[6] This eventuality became all the more realistic in 1984 with the signing of letters of intent to use SNI by a number of library system vendors

including Biblio-Techniques (BLIS), Northwestern University (NOTIS/
LUIS), and Geac.

The interconnection will unquestionably have important consequences for the relationship between RLIN and WLN and their
method of interaction with the Library of Congress. A major question
will be OCLC's reaction to the final project and subsequent involvement, if any. OCLC was not one of the original participants in the
project, but it soon after became involved to the extent of offering, at
its own expense, any staff expertise that could be helpful to the principal participants. Although this was a cooperative gesture, OCLC made
it known that it was not yet ready to commit itself to actual linking, at
least "until the economic benefit has been demonstrated."[7]

The latest relationship among the utilities appears to be characterized primarily by cooperative effort and coexistence. The standard network interconnection is certainly a cooperative effort in terms of the
relationship between RLIN and WLN, and the tapeloading projects
allow each utility to broaden the amount of information in its database,
but not to the detriment of the other utilities. The relationship among
the utilities has been delicate in recent years, however, so the end of
competition is not at all certain.

Viability: External/Internal Competition,
Image, and Identity

The bibliographic utilities have held a collectively secure position in
the American library community for the past several years. There has
been some challenge from the commercial sector, particularly since the
advent of the microcomputer, but by and large competition has focused on activity that is marginal to the utilities, such as in acquisitions,
serials control, and circulation systems. The main sources of commercial competition in cataloging systems are two stand-alone automated
systems and a few of the larger book jobbers and COM vendors that
have built substantial machine-readable bibliographic files. However,
these services can hardly be compared, since features such as locational
information and interlibrary communications capabilities make the
utilities far more than cataloging services. Unless there are some dramatic changes in form, the commercial cataloging services are not likely
to lure many current users of bibliographic utilities.

One of the ironies in the potential challenge posed by vendors with
large machine-readable bibliographic databases is that, in many cases,
those databases have been built partially with records supplied from
the databases of the utilities themselves. The conveyance has been indi-

rect, drawing on records of individual library cataloging activity performed on a utility and supplied to the vendor on magnetic tape for further processing and product generation. The problem for the utilities is that the cataloging information on these individual library records is being provided to other libraries that are potentially but not currently users of a utility.

In 1980, OCLC announced its intention to more fully examine the implications of third party use of such machine-readable records. The issue was complex, involving some very fundamental questions concerning ownership of the database, the information in it, and the relations between OCLC as a corporation and its constituent membership. The general sentiment in the library community was that once a library had paid a fee for a machine-readable copy of an OCLC record, that copy became the property of the library to do with as it pleased—even if that meant allowing the record to be loaded into a vendor's general bibliographic file for use in providing cataloging information to other libraries.

Although regarding this practice as a competitive threat, OCLC had backed off by early 1981 and adopted what was termed a "liberal" stance with respect to third party use. The library press in particular interpreted this position as a resolution of the issue. But the issue was not at all resolved; its consideration was merely postponed.

On January 1, 1983, OCLC copyrighted its database. In practical terms, the issue of copyright and third party use is not an effort to restrict a library from loading its OCLC records onto a computer for its own use or even to supply them to a vendor for generating other products. What it is intended to do, however, is to challenge the rights of anyone involved to use those records for providing competitive services without making royalty payments to OCLC and its membership.

The greatest source of competition for the bibliographic utilities in the near future may not come from the commercial sector per se, but rather from efforts at the state and local level, in some cases involving current users of the utilities. In a number of states, there is discussion about the possibility of creating statewide online networks as alternatives to the utilities, and in several locations, systems are already in place that could serve that purpose.

Several states have been maintaining statewide bibliographic databases for several years already, although the form usually does not yet constitute significant competition for the utilities. Such databases have been built by merging the machine-readable records provided by libraries in the state on magnetic tapes of their cataloging activity on a bibliographic utility. These databases are being used in most cases as the basis for a commercially produced statewide COM catalog distributed to libraries as a tool for determining interlibrary loan locations. These catalogs sometimes serve as sources of cataloging information, but by and large such use is limited to smaller libraries and is not organized into formal service.

Statewide databases of this sort do not represent substantial competition for the bibliographic utilities, and in fact their value in many cases largely depends on continued library participation in the utilities. A critical distinction between the presently existing statewide databases and those that may represent a closer step toward actual competition with the utilities is likely to be marked by the shift of statewide database maintenance from external commercial services to in-state facilities. It may also be marked by the greater use of these databases as sources of cataloging information for libraries that are not members of the utilities, especially in their efforts to convert retrospective holdings to machine-readable form and to add locational information to the database. This is a popular scenario proposed in a variety of consultant reports over the past several years.

Most states that are examining the possibility of a statewide database would continue to rely on library participation in the bibliographic utilities as a primary source of records. The extent of competition would be primarily for the activity of smaller libraries, which may be unable to afford the services of a utility anyway, and for retrospective conversion work. Although the retrospective conversion procedure would deflect some activity from the utilities, it would not substantively impair their value and would not have major financial consequences.

The maintenance of a statewide database for the purposes just described could exist, in fact, quite compatibly with the bibliographic utilities. Real competition would surface only when, and if, statewide databases are brought online accompanied by sophisticated retrieval capabilities, an online cataloging component, and the availability of a major source of current cataloging data such as that supplied on LC MARC tapes. The expense of creating what in essence would be a new online bibliographic utility would be enormous and, at first glance, perhaps out of reach of most groups of libraries. But it is a very real possibility, and some states and local groups have been seriously examining just such undertakings as possible alternatives to the existing utilities.

The creation of statewide utilities or adoption of other automated systems to serve the same function as the major utilities has by no means reached a stage where either could be called an inevitability. On the other hand, such databases have become more widespread. There are some who feel that state-based or local systems may be less expensive, although this remains to be demonstrated; that they will be more accessible to a wider variety of libraries; and that greater control over costs and development priorities can be exercised by participating libraries than is now possible with the major utilities. All these justifications have an underlying theme, however—a sentiment that at least some of the utilities are simply no longer responsive to their membership and have grown away from identity with some libraries. Under these circumstances, the utilities are being evaluated by some libraries strictly as technical systems in and of themselves and removed from their original cooperative purpose. As technical systems, there are more sophisticated alternatives available to at least some of the utilities, and as a basis for cooperative efforts, there are more tangibly defined groups with which to identify.

Although at their foundation the bibliographic utilities are cooperative library organizations, the complexity of their operations and the environment in which they exist require that they also function as fiscally and administratively astute organizations. To achieve success on an ongoing basis in such an environment requires effective governing, sound management, and careful planning in financial administration and technological development.

As any cooperative venture grows in magnitude and membership, the mechanisms for its governing, management, and planning are bound to become further removed from the everyday involvement of individual users and from the responsibility of a central organization staff, or of representatives drawn from the user population, or both. Each of the utilities has come to be seen by its membership as an entity worth perpetuating, and the most direct responsibility for carrying out this mission falls to its governing and management structure. The distinction between the mission and the apparatus created to carry it out sometimes becomes vague, with the result that a utility can take on an appearance of an entity in itself, separate from the libraries that constitute its membership. There is certainly variation among the bibliographic utilities in the degree to which any centralization of decision making has occurred and in the extent to which each has come to take on a life of its own, but some amount of standardization is necessary owing to the complexity of the organizations.

The dual roles of the bibliographic utilities as cooperative organizations of not-for-profit social institutions and effectively run not-for-profit business entities sometimes come into conflict with one another and appear at times, at least to some members, to operate at cross purposes or to be imbalanced. Perhaps the most important single factor that will determine the future role of the bibliographic utilities in the American library community rests in the ability of each one to reconcile this dual role to the satisfaction of its membership.

Although libraries in the not-for-profit sector are consistently becoming more sophisticated in a business sense, this leaning has remained tempered by a perception of libraries as primarily social institutions guided by a motivation other than financial return. Part of the broad support for the bibliographic utilities over the years has been tied to a perception that they have a similar social purpose; cooperative organizations first and businesses second. With this perception, libraries have endured periods of slow response time and downtime, questionable development investments, and less sophisticated features than desirable and than might be available elsewhere because the utilities were ultimately part of the same broader picture.

To satisfy the goals of their users, the utilities do have to act and survive as businesses. But if they are perceived simply as businesses and lose the force of their support as a cooperative social venture, they will begin to be judged by libraries in just those terms—as businesses, and their services evaluated in a very businesslike fashion. Under such circumstances, system performance problems, financial investments in development areas that are less than successful, and comparatively less sophisticated system features may not be quite so widely tolerated as they have been in the past.

When the possibility of state-based systems as alternatives to the existing utilities is examined, the reality is that the alternatives being considered are not to RLIN or to WLN but to OCLC. RLIN and WLN are already systems with a focused membership, and as a result have a greater likelihood of preserving a close identity in an environment currently characterized by a strong element, although maybe not yet predominant, leaning toward more localized control. OCLC's membership approach has, since the mid-1970s, emphasized a sense of large-scale identity, of bigness. This sense has been, and still is, responsible for eliciting strong support from many of its members, who feel that a utility should not be restricted by state, regional, or type-of-library boundaries. Nevertheless, more than in the other utilities, there is a segment of the OCLC membership that feels a sense of alienation brought about by a remoteness of participation in decision making and a feeling that the utility has grown so large that it is no longer responsive to its individual members or even its collective membership.

There are activities now underway and likely to increase that will have an important bearing on the role of the utilities in the American library community. These activities are not necessarily headed in the same direction. Some developments and philosophies tend toward the formation of an online national bibliographic database, or at least toward interfacing different systems, exemplified by the standard network interconnection project. Other developments and philosophies suggest the possibility of forming far more localized online bibliographic databases than now exist. The proliferation of regional, local, or statewide bibliographic systems would not exclude the possibility of their eventual interconnection, but would undoubtedly complicate it.

Such is the environment in which the bibliographic utilities of today must operate, a fluid and unpredictable one. The ultimate success of the utilities in meeting the divergent challenges will depend on their ability to provide systems that are technologically and economically competitive, on how successfully they are able to balance the image of cooperative organization with the necessity to perform as a business, and how well they are able to retain a sense of purpose and identity among their memberships.

Notes

1. Personal communication.
2. One of the few places noting this aspect of competition at the time between OCLC and RLIN was in an essay by Michael Gorman, "NETWORK! or I'm Rational as Hell and I'm Not Going to Take It Anymore," *American Libraries* 11 (January 1980): 48, 50.
3. Donald A. Smalley, William G. Griffith, Ann M. Walker, and Michael B. Wessells, *Technical Report on Linking the Bibliographic Utilities: Benefits and Costs* (Columbus, Ohio: Battelle Columbus Laboratories, 1980). For a summary and discussion of the Battelle study, see C. Lee Jones, *Linking Bibliographic Data Bases: A Discussion of the Battelle Technical Report* (Washington, D.C.: Council on Library Resources, 1980).
4. For example, the sample of titles used for comparing cataloging "hit rates" among the databases ". . . was restricted to current monographs" (*Technical Report . . .* , p. 16), thus excluding older titles pertinent to retrospective conversion because it was felt that ". . . titles from retrospective conversion projects would only represent the small number of libraries involved in the study" (*Technical Report . . .* , p. 16). This restriction arbitrarily minimized the importance of one of the primary uses of bibliographic utilities in libraries and one of the major distinctions in the comparative composition of the databases. The LC MARC database itself had matching records for 86 percent of the titles in the sample, and since all these utilities load LC MARC monograph records into their databases, the result was a far smaller range of comparative hit rates among the three than would have been the case had the sample included some pre-MARC titles. Also in the section on comparative cataloging hit rates, the report recognized its own limitations, explaining at one point that ". . . the 258 titles contributed by OCLC members do not constitute a proportion of all OCLC titles that is large enough to support statistically valid inferences about the hit rates experienced by OCLC libraries in general" (*Technical Report . . .* , p. 18). Several other problems were discussed in an unpublished 1980 paper by Ronald E. Diener and Carl A. Anderson, "The Battelle and CLR Reports on Linking."

5. For a description of some of the early WLN arrangements, see Thomas P. Brown and Raymond DeBuse, "Replicating the Washington Library Network Computer Software System," *Journal of Library Automation* 14 (September 1980): 202–205.

6. Quoted in "Standard Network Project Undertaken by RLG," *Advanced Technology Libraries* 11 (April 1982): 2. For descriptions and progress reports on the Linked Systems Project, see the following articles: Wayne E. Davison, "The WLN/RLG/LC Linked Systems Project," *Information Technology and Libraries* 2 (March 1983): 34–46; and Ray Denenberg and Sally H. McCallum, "RLG/WLN/LC Computers Ready to 'Talk,'" *American Libraries* 15 (June 1984): 400–404.

7. W. David Penniman quoted in "OCLC to Be in Design of Network Protocol," *OCLC Newsletter* 141 (May 1982): 2.

12

Characteristics of Technical Support Systems

One of the primary evaluation criteria in the design or purchase of an automated system should focus on what the system does and how conveniently and efficiently it does it. Some characteristics will be common to almost every automated system that addresses a particular type of library operation, but beyond a certain level, no two independently developed systems are likely to provide exactly the same capabilities in even the general functions they perform. The distinctions become even greater when very specific features are compared. All acquisitions systems with fund-accounting capabilities, for example, allow for the actual cost of an item to be entered on an order record when the item and invoice are received. Not all such systems, however, can divide the cost of the item among two or more funds, and very few are programmed to automatically point out instances where the actual price of a received item is considerably higher than the expected price.

The needs of libraries are diverse enough, their operations complex enough, and automation imperfect enough that even for a defined set of operations, there is a great deal of room for interpretation about what the important features in a system are. These differences of opinion manifest themselves concretely in the form of differences between systems that have been designed to handle essentially the same set of operations. With turnkey systems, the complexity of interpretation is compounded by another factor: the need in a commercial market to offer a unique product, one that does at least a few things competitive systems do not, and that does some parallel things in a different enough manner to somehow distinguish them as "better."

One result of all these forces is that systems frequently include a number of "bells and whistles" features that go beyond the most basic functional capabilities. Some may seem superfluous; the impression can be gained that some vendors go to great lengths to provide long lists of system features that simply differentiate their system from others, rather than necessarily performing something useful. There is a reverse side to this picture, however. Although striving to give the product a unique identity, vendors of automated library systems are not so financially independent that they can afford to invest the enormous amounts of money required to develop software unless they are convinced it is a strong selling point for the system. Any vendor who has been in the library business for any length of time has learned what the most crucial needs of libraries are, and these are the needs that are generally addressed in the development of their systems.

Many would argue that, if anything, most of the turnkey systems available are too similar and do not offer enough diversity, rather than too much. Nevertheless, there *are* differences. Taking into account systems that have been locally developed by libraries, there is a wide range of features that have been included in automated systems for any given set of operations. This chapter examines some of the characteristics that apply to automated technical support systems, first in terms of several that are important regardless of the application, and then in terms of special considerations for more specific sets of operations: cataloging, acquisitions, serials control, and circulation. The approach is not to describe specific systems that are available for each of these applications. In the present environment of library automation, the list of specific features provided by a particular system can change rapidly; new systems are constantly appearing on the market and existing ones disappearing. The approach is rather to describe a range of functional capabilities, some of which are fairly standard on a number of systems, with some less common. The emphasis is on online systems, and characteristics are drawn from both turnkey systems and locally developed ones.

It has long been a goal in library automation to develop systems that are multipurpose, being able to handle more than just one set of operations. The degree to which this is actually being achieved is greater now than at any time in the past. For example, one can rarely find a vendor today who claims to be selling a "circulation system." CLSI, DataPhase, Geac, and practically all other vendors of minicomputer-based systems now market "integrated library systems," "library information systems," "library management systems," and so on. The distinction is not just a matter of semantics. While these systems may not have achieved the status of a "fully integrated library system," they have indeed incorporated such operations as acquisitions, serials control, and others into what used to be strictly circulation systems.

Notwithstanding the continual movement toward multipurpose systems, each of the four applications examined in this chapter—cataloging, acquisitions, serials control, and circulation—still constitutes a distinguishable set of operations in terms of the functions performed. There are certain features of automated circulation systems, for example, that are really not pertinent to specific chores performed on an acquisitions system, and vice versa. Each set of operations, then, entails certain procedures or functions that are most relevant to those operations specifically.[1]

General Characteristics

There are certain requirements that systems designed to handle any of the four different sets of operations described here have in common: bibliographic and other data must be recorded in them, records must be accessed, and items must be differentiated according to their status within the context of the particular set of operations. The specifics will vary from one application to another, but general characteristics relating to these requirements provide an important framework for evaluating an automated system for any application, and several of the more important of these are examined below.

Searching Strategies

There are considerable differences among systems in the avenues through which they permit access to records in a library's file. Four major approaches to retrieval are used in automated library systems: a menu approach, use of abbreviated search keys, entry of full-term exact order search statements, and a fourth approach that allows for much greater flexibility than the other three.

A menu-based system prearranges access points of records according to a treelike structure through which the searcher progresses until the choices are narrowed to the single record being sought. The searcher does not enter search terms, but rather selects from among a series of system-presented alphabetical groupings of titles, subjects, authors' names, and so on. The broad category selected is then broken down into a narrower list of alphabetical subgroupings, and so on through as many steps as necessary until a single record is found. This can be time consuming and gives the searcher very little flexibility.

In the other three approaches, the user will often have to use a menu at some point during the course of a dialog, but the search is initiated by keying an alphabetical or numeric search statement. Some systems require the user to enter a derived search key: in other words, to abbreviate search terms. One of the most commonly used systems employing this approach is the Online Computer Library Center (OCLC). A title search, for example, consists of entry of the first three characters of the first significant word in a title, two characters of the second word, two of the third, and one of the fourth (fewer abbreviated terms are entered if the title consists of fewer terms). This approach has some strong points in that it requires few keystrokes for the initial search, but it can also be very cumbersome if the resulting search argument fits a large number of records in the system. For example, a search constructed as "jou, of, th, a" will retrieve an enormous number of records. After the system has displayed a group listing of all records that fit this key, a specific record is pursued by a menu approach, constantly narrowing the groupings by line selection until the single desired record is displayed.

Another approach involving keying of an alphabetical or numeric statement requires the user to enter characters in search terms exactly as they appear in the indexed field of a record or records. Few systems using this approach require it for virtually all types of searches. It is most common for searches involving numerical record identifiers such as the Library of Congress Card Number (LCCN) or International Standard Book Number (ISBN). The "exact term" approach is less commonly associated with searching author or title bibliographic fields, although several systems in the past have required full-term precise order statements for searching subject heading fields.

An approach far more flexible than any of the above allows for use of keywords and has very lax requirements about the number or order of terms in a search argument. The BALLOTS (now RLIN) system developed at Stanford is one of the most long-standing examples of flexibility in searching on an online library system. In addition to keyword searching, such systems frequently allow for truncation of search terms and for full expression of author names, titles, and so on, thus in fact incorporating the other two keying approaches described above. In searching for the title *Journal of the American Speleological Society*, for example, the user could construct a truncated search key such as "jou, of, the, a," could input the entire title in exact order, or could simply search on the term "speleological" or even a truncated form of it.

Most of the systems employing these more sophisticated techniques also allow for Boolean searching, so that in the above case, the user might combine the terms "journal" and "speleological" in a search statement. Many systems allow for combinations of terms from different indexed fields, such as allowing author, title, and subject heading terms to be combined in a single search statement.

This fourth approach is by far the most flexible and comprehensive of those described here. Its value may be much more important for some applications than others, but, in general, the greater the flexibility in search strategy construction, the less time staff will spend in searching, and the more time they can spend doing whatever is necessary once the appropriate records are retrieved.

Access Points

Another concern with search strategy formulation is the range of elements within records that can be used as access points. Each application will have certain access points that are more crucial than others. In general, however, access points can be broken down into two major categories: unique identifier (usually numeric) and bibliographic (usually alphabetical). Common numerical access points include locally assigned accession, purchase order, barcode or exact call numbers, and "universal numbers," such as LCCN, ISBN, Superintendent of Documents Number, International Standard Serial Number (ISSN), CODEN, and national bibliography number. For purposes of retrieval, the advantage of unique numerical identifiers is that searching is usually much faster, since at least in theory each of the above is a unique number and a search will retrieve one and only one bibliographic record from the database.

The most common bibliographic access points are author, title, series, and subject, although others may also be appropriate. In general, access by author and title is almost essential regardless of whether the system supports cataloging, acquisitions, serials control, or circulation functions. Being able to combine terms from the author and title fields is also advantageous regardless of application. Online access by subject may be less important for strictly technical applications, although an ability for the system to at least collate records by subject and print listings may be extremely useful. Some libraries or vendors that have chosen to incorporate subject access in technical operations systems allow, in addition to term searching, for access by truncated classification numbers as a supplementary approach to subject retrieval.

In addition to unique number and bibliographic access points, some systems allow for the qualification of search statements by parameters such as language and date of publication. When combined with a term search, such qualifiers can be powerful in refining the scope of the search and narrowing the number of records retrieved.

Listing and Compilation Parameters

Online systems usually have the capability to produce a wide range of offline listings and statistical compilations. This compilation feature is not altogether different from the principles involved in online retrieval and display; namely, the ability of the system to collate records according to various criteria. There may be functions that the library thinks need not be incorporated in online retrieval but might be useful for offline reporting. For example, a library might not consider online subject access to on-order records a necessary feature of an acquisitions system, but the capability to print offline listings of on-order items by subject to distribute as part of a current-awareness service might be useful.

The types of compilations and listings that can be produced by an automated library system are almost infinite from the standpoint of technical possibility. When the library has control over deciding what types of compilations and listings to generate, the main problem is usually where to stop rather than where to start. Experience has shown that the most useful reports are those that focus on summary and exception rather than totality and routine. In a circulation system, for example, a listing of every item that was circulated, returned on time, and routinely reshelved is simply unmanageable and serves little purpose. More useful are summaries of circulation by classification groupings, listings of lost or missing items, and listings of titles that have not circulated in the past year or two. The most appropriate types of listings are fairly specific to the particular type of application involved and are discussed in greater detail later in this chapter.

Assistance, Simplicity, and Ease of Operation

For too long there seemed to be a feeling among many librarians that staff training in use of a system was an adequate substitution for clarity of screen displays, ease of terminal operation, and simplicity of commands. Primarily since the advent of online public-access catalogs—which do not easily allow the opportunity for advanced or extensive training of system users—clarity, ease of use, and simplicity have begun to receive attention on a wider scale for automated systems in libraries, even for those that support exclusively technical processing operations. Online "help" screens and other instructional displays can be very useful, although there is still a great deal of room for improvement. Unfortunately, online access to and use of such displays is still so complex in some systems that those who know the system well enough to be able to figure out how to retrieve and use them probably will not need to. In terms of input and retrieval, commands should be unambiguous and relatively simple and should require minimum keystroking. Terminal keyboards should be easy to use and control keys should be properly identified as to the function they perform. If possible, staff should not have to perform such gyrations as having to depress two keys at once or three keys in sequence just to generate a single character.

Range of Record Statuses

Within any given set of operations, there is usually a need to establish a variety of record statuses. Any given item described in a circulation system may be charged out, on hold, missing, and so on, while any item described in an acquisitions system may be on order, claimed, received but not invoiced, received and invoiced, and so on. The specific types of statuses will vary according to application, but on the general level it is important in designing or purchasing an automated system to carefully examine the range of statuses available to be certain that it will accommodate the library's requirements. The degree to which statuses can be differentiated usually has implications for the diversity of the types of automatic activity performed by a system.

Input Screens

Two primary approaches are used by automated library systems for inputting data into records. One is the use of system-supplied prompts, which ask the terminal operator to enter appropriate information for each prompted field or subfield. After one prompt has been answered by keying in data, the system asks for the next type of information; the terminal operator keys an appropriate response, and so on through the record until all prompts have appeared in sequence and have been answered.

The other approach uses a template, or "mask" or workform, a display that shows, all at once, the basic fields and subfields into which data can be entered. The terminal operator moves the screen cursor from field to field and keys in information where appropriate. Some systems using this approach allow for protection of certain fields and subfields so that data either cannot be input because it will be system-supplied, or because it can be input only by certain levels of authorized personnel. Routinely used fields are sometimes only the ones displayed, but provision is made for the terminal operator to add more ephemeral fields and subfields of information when necessary. It is most convenient for input if systems allow for insert and editing capabilities so that minor corrections or additions to information can be subsequently made without having to retype the entire text of the field or subfield in which the changes are required. It is also best if all input and editing changes to a record can be communicated to the main computer by a single transmission of the entire record rather than on a field-by-field basis.

Coding Input

Automated systems for various applications frequently require the same piece of data to be entered on many different records. In an acquisitions system, for example, the same name and address of a book jobber or publisher from whom an item is being purchased may have to be keyed into hundreds or even thousands of online records each year. In claiming a book or an issue of a periodical, the same general message, accompanied by more specific detail, may have to be input on a significant number of online records so that offline notices may be prepared. Many systems have simplified input of such repetitive information by establishing coding schemes. For example, a two- to four-character numeric code or alphabetical abbreviation might be established for each jobber or publisher from whom the library regularly orders materials. On the online record, the terminal operator needs only to supply this abbreviated code, and the system will automatically print the vendor's full name and address when it prepares purchase orders offline. Similar coding schemes have been developed to trigger the printing of standard messages on correspondence to vendors, publishers, and library patrons, and on internal reports and memos. This greatly simplifies the input procedure. While many systems have this capability, some libraries will also deem it important to consider what happens in the online record after a code has been entered. Specifically, does the code remain or does the system automatically translate it into more complete text in the online record itself? For being able to determine information about an item, the latter approach is preferable. The trade-off is that if there is very much coded information entered, its translation into full text may clutter a screen display or even mean that an online record may have to be automatically expanded to several screens.

Review-File Capabilities

Many automated systems allow new or revised records to be placed in a special temporary file prior to their addition to the main file and prior to their activating subsequent system activity such as fund adjustment, production of catalog cards, or printing of various forms. Especially with new staff members, the availability of an interim review file can be a useful feature. After records are entered into the interim file, more experienced staff can retrieve and review them and make any necessary changes before adding them to the permanent file and triggering subsequent system activity.

Multivolume Sets, Multiple and Added Copies, and Partial Activity

Often the acid test of an automated system is how well it deals with multivolume sets, multiple and added copies, and partial activity. For some systems, these transactions represent exceptions to what they are best designed to handle. In other cases, systems are designed presupposing that such transactions will constitute a significant portion of the library's activity.

In a sense, serials control subsystems have as their primary aim the management of materials that are *all* exceptions to the one-volume, one-copy, one-time processing routine. But in addition to serials control, other operations such as cataloging, acquisitions, and circulation will usually have to handle at least a certain number of multiple copies, multivolume sets, and so on. In the case of multiple copies, some systems create completely separate records for each copy of an item; others indicate copy-specific information in separate fields on a single record; others have a hierarchical treatment of records or pages of records containing copy-specific information tied to a "higher level" page or record that contains general bibliographic and other information applying to all copies of the item.

For any of the applications discussed in this chapter, not all systems are equally sophisticated in handling multivolume sets, multiple copies, and partial activity. For libraries whose collection patterns focus on single copies of single volume works, the approach used by a system for handling these more complex types of transactions will be of minimal importance. But for libraries that purchase very many multivolume sets, or that have many branch libraries and collections for which multiple copies are acquired and from which they circulate, the ease with which these materials can be handled should be a primary consideration in designing or purchasing a system.

File Updating

While the term *online* connotes instantaneity, not all online systems meet such expectations in virtually every function they perform. In designing or purchasing an automated system, the library should consider the timeliness of file updating by the system once a decision is made to permanently add or modify a record, or when a transaction is carried out. For example, an online circulation system with overnight updating of all transaction files defeats part of the purpose for the system being online in the first place. Immediate updating of files is critical for certain types of activities, although it is true that others can be left to overnight updating without posing too serious a problem. In general, the more immediately all files are updated for all types of online transactions, the less likelihood of duplicate effort or of other activities being carried out by staff that work at cross-purposes with one another.

Case-Specific Override

To reduce the amount of manual work, automated systems are designed to trigger certain actions based on generalized policy, procedure, and guidelines. In most acquisitions and serials control systems, for example, claiming is automatically generated after an order has been outstanding for a certain period of time. In circulation systems, return of an overdue item triggers the calculation and recording of fines. The ability of a system to execute these logical next steps is extremely useful, as it eliminates the need to do such things manually. However, there will be extenuating circumstances for individual cases in which the library may wish to alter the routine action carried out by a system. In the acquisitions example, a publisher may report that an ordered item will not be available for several months. In that case, it will be annoying for both the library and the vendor if claiming forms are generated and sent every 30 or 60 days during the interim. It should be possible to defer claiming action by simply modifying the expected arrival date on the appropriate online order record. In the circulation example, a system should allow a library the option to waive fines and therefore override the calculation and automatic recording of fines in individual cases. Without these override capabilities, the library surrenders too much policy control to the system, sacrificing its prerogative for making exceptions under extenuating circumstances.

Integrated Systems

If the library is exploring the possibility of designing or acquiring an "integrated system," it is important to find out exactly what that will mean. An integrated system should allow for each record to be built on from the order stage through its use for circulation and, if appropriate, for public-access functions. The same information about an item should not have to be keyed more than once. This does not necessarily mean, however, that exactly the same content or format of a record must be displayed in each component of the system. For example, it is useful to have bibliographic information and the status of on-order items displayed in an online public-access catalog module, but it may not be advisable for all financial information in those records to be displayed to the public.

In addition to build-on records and flexibility in content and format display, retrieval in an integrated system should be possible both from the entire database and from selected portions of it. It should be possible, for example, to retrieve records from the entire database regardless of whether they represent items on order or already in the collection. For some purposes, it will be useful to be able to retrieve on smaller sets of records, such as only those for items on order or in process or only those used for serials check-in. This can reduce the amount of time spent searching since irrelevant records will not be retrieved. It is desirable to have both capabilities: retrieval on the entire database and retrieval on selected portions defined by application.

Institutionally Defined Parameters

Especially in evaluating generalized turnkey systems, an important characteristic is the degree of flexibility for the library to define some of its own parameters. For circulation, for example, a system should be able to allow the library to define its own categories of borrowers and items and its own loan periods and should permit the library to decide what types of offline listings and statistical compilations it wishes to have generated. It is also important that once the library-defined parameters have been profiled, they can be easily modified. Most turnkey systems do allow some local definition of parameters, but certain systems allow more flexibility than others.

With these general characteristics of online systems in mind, the rest of this chapter focuses more specifically on each of four sets of operations: cataloging, acquisitions, serials control, and circulation. The general options for automating each set of operations, concentrating mainly on the turnkey market, are reviewed, along with some of the more important functional characteristics of systems pertinent to each set of operations.

Cataloging

An automated cataloging system generates products that will make up the public-access catalog. These products may be catalog cards or machine-readable records that serve as a basis for the production of COM or book catalogs or are loaded into an online public-access catalog. Machine-readable cataloging records may also be used for other purposes, such as producing accessions lists and special bibliographies, loading into a circulation system, compiling library collection data, contributing to union catalogs, and so on.

The content of a cataloging record consists of bibliographic description and local copy, holdings, and call-number information. Other types of information may be appended to the same record, such as acquisitions or serials check-in or circulation data, but the primary focus of the "cataloging" record as described here is the content of the record concerning bibliographic description and the types of local data referred to above.

Apart from local development and transfer of software, there are four major options available to libraries for automating cataloging activities: (1) participation in a bibliographic utility, the most widely used option in terms of direct online access; (2) various commercially available systems, such as Mini-MARC, or software packages used primarily for cataloging; (3) systems that very clearly serve to automate other library operations as well, such as online circulation systems; and (4) a book jobber or COM vendor, which has in the past been rather indirect: although use of one of these services' catalog cards has been an option for receiving library-specific file of machine-readable cataloging records, online interaction with the library's full file was rarely possible. A major exception has been the AGILE-II system offered by Autographics, a COM vendor, which allows a library online access to its file and provides a capability for adding records and modifying existing ones. More recently, Brodart has begun to offer a similar service.

Most of the features described in the first part of this chapter are relevant in considering the design or selection of a cataloging system or module. In addition, there are several others that are specific to cataloging functions.

MARC Format

Online cataloging systems generally permit storage of bibliographic records online and allow a library also to produce offline machine-readable versions of those records. In addition, they provide a format and structure into which data is entered and stored. Increasingly since 1968, the MARC II format has become the predominant basis for the representation of machine-readable bibliographic information in cataloging systems.

Developed and refined by the Library of Congress (LC) and others during the mid- and late 1960s, the MARC format actually consists of several different formats, each addressing a particular type of material: There is a format for books, for serials, for maps, and so on through eight different types of material, plus one for authority records. As much consistency as possible and as many common fields across the formats as possible are retained. The term *MARC format* is used here to refer generically to the total of the individual formats. (The creation and early evolution of the format are described in Chapter 2, and several of the fields and subfields are outlined in the discussion of retrospective conversion in Chapter 10.)

There are three primary reasons why most libraries now use the MARC format. The first and major reason has to do with the very rationale behind its development: the recognition that a common record structure and format would greatly facilitate the exchange of bibliographic information between libraries, groups of libraries, and systems. A second factor has been the use of the MARC format by the bibliographic utilities. The systems of all four of the utilities in North America have used the MARC format at least since their application in an online networking environment. The third factor, based on the first two, is that there came a point at which commercial vendors widely recognized that, as more libraries began to insist on maintaining records in the MARC format, their systems had to be able to do so if they were to remain viable in the marketplace. For the most part, any automated cataloging system being designed today without representing records in the MARC format is either being locally developed or is targetted for use in very small libraries.

Certainly no "law" dictates that a library should use MARC format, but multi-institutional automation projects are more commonplace now among all types of libraries than ever before, which makes it all the more crucial for libraries to have their records in a format that can be easily exchanged and merged with records of other libraries and from other systems. At one time during the 1970s there was some degree of confusion as various systems claimed to represent records in MARC format, while others were said to represent records in either "MARC-compatible" or "MARC-like" formats. Fortunately, some of the ambiguity has cleared up as more systems have adopted formats that rigorously conform to the standard used by LC itself. Nevertheless, some systems still do not use MARC. Especially if purchasing a cataloging system, module, or software package of the smaller turnkey variety, libraries wishing to have their records represented in MARC or MARC-compatible format must exercise caution, and the use of MARC format should be stated as a requirement in an RFP or in a contract for purchase. Terms such as MARC-compatible remain ambiguous and are used in any number of different ways. Vendors that use such phrases should be asked to explain exactly what is meant, and specifically how their format differs from that used by LC. Libraries should be especially wary of statements that records can be "easily converted" or upgraded to full MARC. Ease of conversion is a matter of interpretation and in many cases it is not easy at all. There are ways to upgrade records, such as through the use of some conversion services, but this can involve considerable additional expense and will result in the extraction of very generalized records, at least some portion of which will have to be reviewed and edited.

A fairly common sentiment among some types and sizes of libraries is that the MARC format is too complex to be applicable to their situation. The format is indeed quite detailed, but it is important for a library to realize that for its own internal purposes and catalogs, it does not have to "fill in all the blanks" and accept or input all details that appear or could appear on a record. A higher level of completeness will be mandatory only if the library is inputting original records into a shared database such as a bibliographic utility, and libraries that are smaller or have very general collections are likely to have very few titles that are not already in the database anyway. In this sense, the degree of complexity is partly a myth, and even if there is somewhat greater complexity than with non-MARC-based systems, the added attention required may well be worth it if the library ever intends to enter into a joint automation effort with other libraries.

Availability of Source Records

The creation of cataloging records on automated systems involves two major stages: intellectual work to determine the content of a record and keying that content into the system. In both processes, cataloging can be expedited tremendously if the system provides ready access to a large number of generalized source records, such as MARC records created by the Library of Congress or those created by other libraries. The availability of source records reduces the amount of intellectual time that library staff will have to spend in original cataloging and will also cut down on the amount of information that must be keyed to adopt a source record and generate a library-specific, machine-readable copy of the record. When source records are available through a system, many libraries choose not to accept the content exactly "as is" until verifying that the information corresponds to their own authority structure and is accurate and complete. Even in such cases, any revisions are usually fairly minor and a great deal of time is saved.

Availability of source records has always been a cornerstone of the bibliographic utilities. Each of their databases contains LC MARC records as well as others, in the MARC format, contributed by participating libraries. In contrast, many of the systems and software packages commercially available for in-house use do not provide a database of generalized source records. Mini-MARC and AGILE-II are the major exceptions. The Mini-MARC system is accompanied by a backfile of, and a continuing subscription to, LC MARC records provided on floppy diskettes or, more recently, videodisk. Unlike the utilities, Mini-MARC provides only records created by the Library of Congress. AGILE-II is more similar to the utilities in the provision of source records, in that records created both by LC and by other libraries (those also using AGILE-II) can be accessed as sources of cataloging information. Major book jobbers also have databases containing LC records and others created by or for customer libraries that can be used to generate cataloging products.

The systems that provide source records vary considerably in terms of quality and especially quantity of records available. Nearly all major systems providing source records include either the full extent or at least a major portion of the LC MARC database. The largest differences occur in records created by other member or customer libraries. Databases of book jobbers and COM vendors have had a rather notorious reputation over the years for containing large numbers of contradictory, incomplete, or inaccurate records. OCLC has also had a long-standing reputation for having a "dirty database." During the first few years of operation, this description was somewhat accurate, but in terms of records input by member libraries over the past several years, continuing claims about low quality of member records are more rhetoric than fact.

The number of source records available ranges from a few hundred thousand in the databases of some book jobbers to more than eleven million in OCLC. The importance of the size of a database of external source records depends on an individual library's circumstances. In general, the larger the database, the higher the "hit rate" will be, that is, the higher the percentage of source records will be that a library finds for the titles it is cataloging. This may vary if certain databases are particularly strong in a special area that corresponds to the library's collection strength. In any event, the comparative numbers of source records in different databases should not be construed as reflecting the proportion of difference in the hit rates that a particular library may expect to find. While the OCLC database may be more than four times as large as that available through Mini-MARC, for example, the hit rate will be nowhere near four times as great on OCLC as on Mini-MARC for current cataloging activity. The hit rate will be at least as high on OCLC for any library, since the LC MARC records provided by Mini-MARC are also contained in the OCLC database, and in just about every instance the hit rate will be higher on OCLC because of the additional member input records. However, for the library with a general collection consisting predominantly of commercially published, English-language titles, the difference in hit rates for current cataloging may be negligible since most of its titles will be covered by LC MARC records common to both systems. The situation with respect to retrospective conversion of older bibliographic records can be quite a different story, as most of a library's records will predate LC MARC. This special situation is examined in detail in Chapter 10.

Entry and Preservation of Local Data

Even with an automated cataloging system or service that provides access to source records, the library may find it necessary to add to, delete from, or modify the bibliographic information appearing on some source records so that the derived copy will reflect the library's own cataloging practices or interpretations. There will also be some titles for which source records are not available, and the library will have to create original records for these.

In addition to bibliographic information, the library will have to enter a variety of local data when using a source record as a basis for its own cataloging. At the most basic level, the library must enter its own call number or at least ascertain that a call number on a source record is acceptable for its own use. The materials of most libraries are organized into more than one collection, and the library will want to indicate the specific collection into which an item is placed—main collection, reference collection, and so on. If the library owns more than one copy of an item, it will want to be certain that all appropriate local information is entered about each copy. In addition to call number, location, and provision of data at the copy level, there are numerous other types of local information that can be pertinent to include in cataloging records: accession numbers or barcode numbers in some circumstances, extent of holdings of a multivolume set, ordering information, local notes, and so on. The range of such data deemed important to include on cataloging records varies tremendously from one library to another.

The method of recording, storing, and retrieving local copy-specific cataloging information will be of fairly minor consequence to some libraries, most likely those that are organized into only a couple of different collections and generally purchase only one copy of an item. At the other extreme, this can be a fundamental concern when a library has several branches, each with several collections, and when multiple copies of a title are frequently purchased and distributed among various branches. There is a great deal of variation in the way that cataloging systems and modules are designed to handle such circumstances. Records should be structured or linked in such a way that the library does not have to rekey information, such as bibliographic detail, that is common to all copies of an item in all locations. It should be possible to enter information that is different, such as location or copy number or accession or barcode number, easily and distinctively. With locational information, the system should allow both general location, such as a branch, and the collection within that location, such as reference, to be entered in coded form consisting of only a few characters.

The reverse side of copy-specific-information input is the retrieval of that information. If the automated cataloging system is to serve essentially as an online record of copy-specific data and as an authority for bibliographic information about each title in the library's various branches and collections, the records that are retrieved must reflect the full range of information that was input. Nearly all cataloging systems allow for this, although there are differences among them in the ease with which such data may be retrieved, consulted, and modified when necessary. The clearly outstanding exception is OCLC. It cannot be used as an online record of local data or local bibliographic information. Although any local additions, deletions, or other modifications made to source records in the OCLC database are reflected on catalog cards and offline machine-readable tapes that the library may purchase, they are not preserved online. Thus, after a library has used and revised a source record for its own purposes, the next time the record is retrieved by that library it will not show the earlier local revisions. This characteristic is OCLC's greatest drawback for some types of libraries. Recognizing this limitation, some OCLC members have pursued various schemes to enable them to have online access to their own cataloging records for purposes of ongoing record maintenance. For libraries not yet using an online circulation system or public access catalog, the most prevalent options are to load tapes containing a library's derived copies of OCLC records onto a local computer or the host computer of a commercial service like Autographics or Brodart. Once a library has actually implemented another system for circulation or public access, continuing maintenance of their derived copies of OCLC records is usually carried out on that system.

Authority Control

Part of the intellectual work in determining cataloging information about an item involves fitting bibliographic description into as consistent an overall structure as possible. For this purpose, many libraries maintain separate authority files for names of persons and corporations, titles of series, and subject headings. Many try to follow Library of Congress practice as closely as possible, but even in these cases, there is often a greater or lesser degree of local departure from strict LC practice, and there will be certain names and series for which LC has not established headings.

For those libraries maintaining tight control over the forms of name, series, and subject headings under which entries are grouped in their catalogs, authority work requires a substantial amount of attention. In using an automated system, the amount of time and effort expended in authority work can be reduced if authority files are maintained online on the same system that is used for cataloging. Some cataloging systems provide online authority-file capabilities; others do not. Even among those systems that do, there is considerable variation in what is maintained. The online authority files can be either local and specific to the individual library, or they can be strictly external and generalized. Some systems allow for both, providing access to an external file, such as Library of Congress machine-readable authority files, while also allowing the library to maintain its local forms of headings on the system.

There is also an important distinction between simple access to authority files and the broader concept of "authority control." Some systems that provide online access to local or external authority files like to promote this feature as authority control, but in fact, merely providing access to files is a very weak form of "control." A truer form of authority control is provided on a few systems, among them the Washington Library Network (WLN). Under the WLN system, headings in master bibliographic records in the database are automatically updated on a continuing basis to reflect changes in authority-file headings. The WLN system also provides for online verification of each heading recorded on new records being input into the database by member libraries. If a heading on a new bibliographic record does not conform to an authorized form of heading in the authority file, the system will automatically inform the terminal operator. An authorized heading must then be selected or a new one created before the bibliographic record can be entered into the system. For some libraries, this level of sophistication is not crucial, but for others, a sophisticated authority-control capability can result in significant savings in time and will help to ensure consistency among headings in bibliographic records.

Rights of Use of Records

In Chapter 10, one of the criteria noted for comparing options for retrospective conversion is the flexibility a library retains for using the records it derives or extracts from a source database. This is also relevant in the selection of a system or service for the cataloging of current acquisitions. As with retrospective conversion, it is specifically relevant in the selection of a service that provides access to a database containing generalized source records.

None of the cataloging services providing access to a database of source records presently imposes any restriction on a library's use of derived or extracted records in strictly internal applications. But when it comes to a library contributing those records to a database shared with other libraries, or supplying them to the source database of another vendor, the issue takes on an entirely different character. Most services impose contractual restrictions on such uses, at the minimum requiring the library to obtain the service's permission before contributing records derived or extracted from its database to other, "third party" databases. Sometimes a service may contractually reserve a right to deny permission altogether, or to assess a royalty fee when permission is granted.

In still other instances, the contractual obligation, if any, is unclear. This has been especially the case with regard to use of derived records by OCLC libraries. Since 1983, a great deal of controversy has surrounded the question of the extent to which OCLC, as a corporate entity, is able or should be able to impose restrictions on how a library can use the records it derives from the OCLC database. The existing contracts between OCLC and its affiliate networks—most of which were signed in the late 1970s—and those between the networks and individual OCLC libraries do not really address the issue adequately. In general, OCLC management takes the position that it has a right to impose certain restrictions on how member libraries can use their records derived from source records in the database. On a variety of philosophical and even legal grounds, opponents assert that OCLC, as a corporate entity, neither has nor should have the right to restrict member use of records derived from the database. Such control is seen as counter to OCLC's tradition and public mission as a not-for-profit, membership-based organization, and there are serious reservations about its right to exercise central control over records derived from source information that has been created and entered into the database by member libraries and by the Library of Congress rather than by OCLC as a corporate body.

By late 1984, the question of restrictions on the use of records derived from the OCLC database was still very much up in the air, comprising a major obstacle in contract negotiations between OCLC and its affiliate networks. Regardless of the solution reached in this situation, however, the controversy has highlighted the importance of restrictions on use of derived or extracted records as a major criteria in evaluating and comparing cataloging alternatives. A library cannot expect carte blanche in terms of the rights to use the records it derives or extracts from a source database for virtually any purpose whatsoever, nor should it allow its future options to be severely limited. If a cataloging service with source records does impose limitations on the use of derived records, a library should insist on precise contractual statements defining the restrictions and an exact statement of any royalty fees that would apply. Most services will want the right to defer stating any exact conditions and fees until the time at which the library actually needs to request permission. Although this approach is certainly understandable from the service's point of view, it does mean a degree of uncertainty and vulnerability for the library and for its participation in any cooperative automation project in the future.

These characteristics—record format, source record availability, local data entry and preservation, authority control, and ownership of records—are important factors to take into consideration when purchasing or locally designing an online cataloging support system or module. Especially when combined with other considerations, such as the general characteristics of automated systems outlined earlier, no one system presently in use or economically feasible is likely to be "the best" in all categories. Different systems have different strengths and weaknesses. The individual library must take into account its own requirements and financial circumstances, and, often among the most important criteria in selecting an automated cataloging system, the way in which it may wish to interact with other libraries locally, regionally, and nationally.

Acquisitions

Acquisitions systems are designed to facilitate ordering and receiving library materials and monitoring expenditures of funds for those materials. The acquisition of library materials is a complex process involving a number of variations on the general theme. Some materials may arrive damaged and have to be returned, others may not arrive within a reasonable period of time, actual prices will differ from expected prices, expensive purchases may have to be distributed across several different funds, and so on through a variety of contingencies that do not conform to the simple procedures of order, receive, pay for, and charge against a particular fund.

Manual acquisitions systems are extremely labor intensive and paper intensive, and usually allow for only a limited range of management information to be compiled. Automated acquisitions systems, on the other hand, can substantially reduce the amount of paper shuffling and can perform a number of monitoring activities and generate reports that escape most manual systems. It is often difficult to draw a line even in manual systems between where one set of operations such as acquisitions stops and another such as cataloging begins. With many automated library systems, the distinctions are even less clear. For our purposes here, focus on the technical process of acquisitions begins at the point when a decision has been made to order an item and ends at the point when the final disposition of the order has been concluded, be it payment for receipt, return without replacement, or cancellation.

Apart from local development and transfer of software from another library, there are four principal sources of acquisitions systems on the market today: bibliographic utilities, book jobbers, vendors of major circulation systems, and vendors offering single-purpose turnkey acquisitions systems or software packages. Each has certain general advantages and disadvantages, and within each category there are differences in orientation and types of features offered.

A major strength of the acquisitions systems offered by the utilities is the large databases of bibliographic records on which a library can draw. All four of the major North American utilities offer acquisitions components that are tied in with their bibliographic databases, allowing for the transfer of certain types of information from existing bibliographic records directly onto the order records being created by individual libraries. Each utility also has a substantial online file containing names, addresses, and other pertinent information about vendors.

Among the larger book jobbers, both Baker & Taylor and Brodart offer an online acquisitions system to their customers. Neither provides access to nearly as large a bibliographic database as do the utilities, but their systems have other advantages. Although not as large as those of the bibliographic utilities, Baker & Taylor and Brodart each maintain a bibliographic database large enough to yield a high rate of fulfillment for many of their customers. In addition, certain levels of each vendor's system provide access to information about the warehouse availability of items supplied through the jobber, a capability that can reduce the level of uncertainty about at least a portion of the titles customers wish to order. Titles in stock can be ordered online through each system, a feature that can expedite the receipt of materials, often by several days, since the amount of time required for the initial order to get from the library to the jobber is reduced through the online capability. Although one of the primary purposes of the systems offered by book jobbers is to promote their book-jobbing services, the systems offered both by Baker & Taylor and by Brodart also allow for local production of hard copy purchase orders by libraries to send directly to publishers, which will be necessary for those titles the jobber does not maintain in stock.

There are a number of integrated library systems on the market that include acquisitions modules. Several, such as CLSI, DataPhase, and Geac, were traditionally associated with turnkey circulation systems and have since added acquisitions modules. Many of the newer integrated systems have included acquisitions capabilities from the start. These systems do not provide direct access to large generalized bibliographic files as do the utilities or book jobbers; however, at least with regard to the utilities, this limitation can be rather easily overcome by attaching an interface device that enables online transfer of bibliographic records directly from the utilities into the local integrated system. The records taken from the utility databases in this way can serve as the bibliographic foundation for the creation of order records on the systems. Online transfer of bibliographic records from the databases of the utilities into other systems for such purposes is fairly common, but libraries should be aware of how this practice may relate to their contractual obligations with the utility.

One of the chief strengths of the acquisitions components available on integrated systems is their interaction with other system modules. Acquisitions records are stored in the same database as records for items already in the collection, and, especially if an online public-access component is also being used, this can be an attractive feature. The records for on-order items can be included in the catalog, and most systems that offer the combination of acquisitions, circulation, and public access allow not only for on-order records to be retrieved in the public-access module, but also permit patrons to place holds for the on-order or in-process items.

In addition to the three alternatives described, there are several single-purpose acquisitions systems and software packages available on the commercial library automation market today. Some are identified in Chapter 7 in the section on bibliographic processing application on microcomputers. Although these systems do not provide direct access to book-jobber files, to databases of a bibliographic utility, or to library-specific circulation or public-access databases, a certain degree of integration can sometimes be achieved through attachment of interface equipment. Because their design emphasis focuses specifically on one set of library operations, rather than serving as just one of several modules of a larger system, some of these single-purpose systems are, in fact, among the most sophisticated acquisitions options available. Especially with an interface capability, these systems constitute a competitive alternative to the acquisitions systems offered by the utilities, jobbers, and major circulation vendors.

Whether a library is designing or purchasing an acquisitions system, a broad range of functional criteria is instrumental in facilitating the acquisitions process. Some of the more important are examined below.

Handling Different Types of Orders

For purposes of acquiring library materials, a number of order-related distinctions are important to larger and even to many smaller libraries. An automated acquisitions system should be able to handle and distinguish between the full range of types of orders appropriate to the library.

Some of the more commonly defined types of orders include:

One-time order to be invoiced

Prepaid

Rush

Cash purchase (such as from a local bookstore)

Phone order

Free publication

Gift

Exchange

Items received as a consequence of membership

Standing orders

Items received through approval plans

Continuations

Depository items

Items received through participation in special programs

The number of distinctions that should be made between types of orders will depend to a large extent on the library's purchasing patterns and on the purposes for which the acquisitions system will be used. In terms of automated processing, the main purpose of making distinctions between types of orders is so that the system can treat each type somewhat differently. For example, while automatic printing of purchase orders is characteristic of online acquisitions systems, some can be programmed not to print purchase orders for any items with an order type specified as "gift." Another example of differential treatment by order type is to establish different claim cycles for different types of orders—for rush orders as opposed to normal orders, as opposed to exchanges, and so on. Most online acquisitions systems allow the library flexibility in defining order types. But equally important is to also compare how various automatic processes—such as the printing of purchase orders or initiation of claim cycles—can be differentiated on the basis of order type.

Status of Orders

An important feature of automated acquisitions systems is their ability to identify the stage of the acquisitions cycle at which an item or items may be located at any given time. Following are some of the statuses commonly used in acquisitions systems to differentiate between stages of the cycle for any given order:

Outstanding

Shipped

Received but not paid

Received and paid

Returned

Claimed

Canceled

In-process

On hold (for later ordering)

Like differentiation by type of order, distinction by status of order is associated with specific system-monitoring activities or capabilities. For an outstanding order, for example, the system should monitor the passage of time in relation to a predefined claim cycle established for a particular jobber, publisher, or order type, and should notify the library when an order has not been received within the allotted period. The CLSI acquisitions module has an interesting monitoring feature whereby an item, once received, can be tracked through different stages of subsequent processing, and if the item is held at any stage for longer than a library-defined amount of time, an "internal claim" notification is issued by the system. Although system-triggered actions and reports tied to status can be extremely helpful, it is important that order-specific override capabilities also be available. These can be useful, for example, when a normal claim cycle needs to be adjusted to take account of notification by a publisher or book jobber that a particular item will not be available for several months. By adjusting the claim cycle for such an order, the system will not generate claim notices at regular intervals during the time that the library knows the item to be not available.

Creating Online Acquisitions Records
and Generating Orders

An online acquisitions record should be able to include a variety of types of information, including bibliographic, financial, and order-related. Each record should indicate order type, jobber or publisher to which the order is being sent, number of copies ordered, final destination of each copy after receipt and processing, fund or funds to which the purchase is being charged, encumbered and expended prices, invoice numbers, copy-specific information, details and chronology relating to order status, and there should be space somewhere in the record for entering explanatory notes or messages. These are essential types of information on acquisitions records, but there may also be others depending on the system, the library's preferences, and the relationship of the order record to other automated components of the system.

Some fields of information on an order record will not be completed until after the order has been sent and further information becomes available. However, a substantial portion of the data for an order will be entered when the record is first created. Different systems have incorporated various automatic processing capabilities that facilitate the initial creation of a record and preparation of offline forms when necessary. The number of such system-driven features continues to increase as more sophisticated systems are developed and as existing systems are enhanced, but some of the more helpful that are already available include:

Automatic transfer of essential bibliographic data from another source (such as a source record on bibliographic utility) directly onto the online order record.

Provision for library selection of the jobber or publisher to which the order is to be sent.

Provision for coded input of book jobber or publisher onto the online record with automatic expansion into full name and address on purchase orders printed offline.

Allowance for coded location-specific and/or type-of-order-specific shipping instructions, which will be expanded to their full text on offline forms.

Automatic calculation of jobber or publisher discounts for an order.

Automatic calculation of total encumbrance when multiple copies of a title are ordered.

Automatic duplicate-order warning if the library attempts to create a record for an item that is already on order. In some circumstances, the library may wish to create an additional order for an item already on order, so the system should not altogether prevent duplication of orders. But it should allow them only after a clear warning has been issued and, as added security, should even require a slightly different command to be entered to finalize an additional order for a title already on order.

Automatic display of a warning message and/or prevention of an order if the encumbered price exceeds or nearly depletes the remaining balance of the fund against which it is being charged. The library should be able to determine the point at which a fund should be considered "near depletion" for purposes of displaying a warning message or preventing an order.

Automatic display of a message and/or requirement of different procedures or special authorization to finalize an order if the price of an item exceeds a certain amount.

Provision for easily creating a new order record from a record for a canceled order for the same title.

Capability to accept and store "on-hold" orders for release at a later date.

Provision for offline purchase orders to be printed either immediately from the online record or in a batch mode. For batch printing, the system should arrange purchase orders by jobber or publisher or any library-specified parameter.

Provision for printing of purchase orders in different formats according to jobber or publisher requirements.

With the exception of the last, most of these features are fairly standard in automated acquisitions systems and are usually supplemented by additional ones that facilitate creating online records and sending orders. For some libraries, an important concern will be the ease with which acquisitions records can be created when an order is being placed for multiple copies of a title with different final destinations for each. Some acquisitions systems handle this through tiered or linked records so that each copy can be treated individually, while representing information common to all or a portion of the copies on a more general-level record.

Subsequent Action on Orders

After an order has been sent, subsequent action may follow any of a variety of courses. If all goes well, the next step requiring use of the online order record will occur when the material arrives, accompanied by an accurate invoice. The date of receipt, exact price, and other details can be entered onto a record and a check or payment voucher generated. There will be variations on this theme for other types of orders. For orders that were prepaid, some of the payment information will have been entered earlier. For items such as gifts or materials received as a result of approval plans, no item-specific order records will have been created prior to receipt, and therefore such records will have to be created on receipt. Outside the normal cycle, a whole range of other circumstances can arise: a jobber or publisher may reply that an item is either temporarily or permanently out of stock; materials may fail to arrive for months with no correspondence as to why they have not yet been shipped; items that are received may have been damaged in transit; shipments may arrive but not exactly match the item or items on order. An automated acquisitions system must make provisions for handling all such contingencies.

Acquisitions systems can perform several types of automatic monitoring activities between the time an item is ordered and the time it is received, and can also facilitate subsequent updating of records and files through a variety of interactive processing features. As in the initial creation of orders, the list of such capabilities can be quite lengthy. Following are some of the more common or useful:

On receipt of an item, automatic notification by the system if the actual price exceeds the encumbered price by a specified percentage.

On receipt, immediate updating of all files, including fund accounts.

On receipt, display of system-supplied instructions or options for disposition of items. The CLSI acquisitions module, for example, differentiates for the terminal operator three possible routes for disposition, according to whether previous copies of the same title have already been cataloged by the library, are in process, or neither.

When multiple copies of a title are issued on the same order, there should be a "batch receipt" updating capability. Each copy should not require individual treatment for updating of its status to received.

When partial shipments are received, received and missing portions should be able to be treated according to the respective procedures for receipt and non-receipt; the library should not have to await receipt of the missing portions before processing the first part of the shipment.

The system should monitor claim cycles established for each jobber or publisher and/or type of order. When a claim date has been reached, the system should either automatically generate a claim form or list the item for claim review online or offline. The system should allow the normal claim cycle established by any parameter to be overridden on an order-specific basis.

Some systems automatically adjust jobber or publisher-specific claim cycles based on previous jobber and publisher performance as monitored by the system. This may be a useful feature in an automated acquisitions system, but it is not a common one. While most systems monitor vendor performance and allow for changing jobber and publisher-specific claim cycles, it is rare for these two features to be interactive in the automatic manner described here.

A system should be flexible in offering the library the option of automatic claim form generation or printing of offline claim candidate review lists. Some libraries will prefer to review a list of overdue orders and decide whether to claim rather than giving the system a free rein to print claim notices first. If this is the case, it is useful if the system allows the library to then claim selected items simply by entering order numbers from the review lists, rather than having to call up each record individually.

Balancing of jobber and publisher invoices.

Another matter concerns the final disposition of an order record once it is completed. There are three possibilities. In a multipurpose system, an order record for an item is likely to serve as the foundation for the cataloging record, which in turn will be used as the basis for a record in a circulation module and/or online public catalog. In such a case, order records or at least certain of their elements are retained online permanently. The second alternative is for the entire order record to be copied onto tape or disk. In addition to providing a machine-readable historical file for acquisitions-related purposes, the records so stored may eventually serve as the database for other systems brought up at a later date, such as a circulation system or online catalog. The third possible disposition is purge from the online system without copying onto tape or disk. With this option, the library will have no machine-readable file of its order records. Under either of the latter two options, completed records are seldom deleted from the online files immediately, but rather after a waiting period that in some systems is as long as 180 days.

Online Fund Accounting

A fund accounting capability is what distinguishes an acquisitions system from a simple ordering system. Some aspects of the interaction between order records and financial records have already been cited. For example, an acquisitions system should issue a warning or prevent ordering when the fund account designated on the record will be over-drawn or nearly depleted as the result of a purchase.

The accounting practice of some libraries is to minimize the number of different funds against which purchases are charged; in other cases the number of established accounts is quite large. Most online acquisitions systems are able to accommodate just about any number of separate funds. Financial information about each fund at any given time should include at least the following:

Current allocation

Encumbered amount

Expended amount

Balance

Some systems provide further distinctions within these categories, such as free balance versus cash balance, and others provide additional types of summary information, such as initial fund allocation, average price per item purchased out of each fund, and separate tracking of funds involved in returns for credit and the like. Online financial information is usually presented for each fund in summary year-to-date totals with monthly or other periodic breakdowns. While preserving figures by individual funds, many systems also allow several tiers to be established for which amounts from various funds are combined. In a multibranch environment, for example, the library might wish to summarize financial data for each branch, for various regional or other groupings of branches, for particular collections (such as reference) across branches, and for the library as a whole. An online acquisitions system should allow this degree of flexibility in its fund accounting component.

Among other fund accounting features, most systems allow online transfer of funds from one account to another but restrict the ability to make any such modifications to financial records to special high-level passwords secured for selected personnel. Nearly all online acquisitions systems provide for different levels of authorization, with the highest and most guarded reserved for online modification of financial records. Since the entire acquisitions cycle for an order is not always completed during a single fiscal year, it is important that a system be able to handle at least two years' worth of financial data online at one time and make appropriate distinction for each fund between the fiscal years involved.

A fund accounting component should also be able to make provisions for accommodating shipping and handling charges in a manner appropriate to the library's accounting practices. This can usually be done in essentially one of two ways: by creating one or more separate accounts specifically for handling and shipping charges, or by including such charges in the fund against which the order itself was charged. If the latter approach is taken and several copies of an item charged to different funds are placed on a single order, the system should be able automatically to compute the proportional amount to be charged against each fund.

The ability to divide a single cost across different funds is useful, not only as it applies to shipping and handling charges but also to the cost of the item itself. Some libraries may wish to divide the cost of an especially expensive item among several funds. If this has been a common practice under a manual system and the library wishes to continue it under an automated system, it should be advised that fund cost-sharing capabilities are not common to all commercially available acquisitions systems. Another feature not common to all systems, but useful for some libraries, is automatic conversion of foreign currency exchange for purposes of payment and fund accounting.

Online Access Points

Of the general access points described in the introduction to this chapter, acquisitions records should be retrievable by as many control numbers (LCCN, ISBN, and such) as possible. This will require, of course, that such numbers be input into indexed fields on the acquisitions record when the initial order is created. Insofar as bibliographic access is concerned, acquisitions order records should be retrievable at least by the author and title of the items on order. In addition to these more general access points, the system should allow for access by points specific to the acquisitions function. At the minimum, these should include purchase order number, fund account name or number, and jobber and publisher name or number.

These access points will generally be used for retrieving single records, be they order records, fund records, or vendor records, rather than groupings of records. In addition to single-record retrieval, however, computerized systems have a tremendous capacity for grouping records, and acquisitions systems are no exceptions. The list of possibilities is almost endless. It would be possible, for example, to retrieve all order records according to order status, type of order, name of requestor, final collection destination of items on order, and so on through the entire list of elements that can be distinctly identified on online records. Many acquisitions systems, however, are limited in what they offer in terms of grouping for purposes of online display. Detailed listings by characteristics such as those identified previously are more standardly provided in the form of offline reports.

Offline Products

Online acquisitions systems can generate two types of offline products: forms and listings. A system should be able to generate any item-specific forms either directly from the online order record or in a batch mode along with forms for other orders. Following are some of the more usual or useful types generated by online acquisitions systems:

Forms:

Purchase orders, single-sheet or multipart

Claim and cancellation notices

Requestor notification cards

Checks or vouchers for payment

In-process worksheets and forms

Internal form advising when an item has remained in a particular stage of processing for more than a specified length of time

Listings:

Selection lists for branch ordering

Lists of gifts by donor

Lists of titles by characteristics such as final destination, type of order, status of order, or any combination thereof

New titles lists

Lists of potential claim candidates

Lists of orders that have been claimed more than a specified number of times

Lists of orders not invoiced within 30 days after receipt

Fund activity summary and detail reports

Lists of funds overexpended or near depletion

Vendor performance reports

Offline forms are necessary or desirable in many settings, and listings can serve as effective management tools if used properly. Whatever types of listings are provided, two important considerations are the types of information included for each entry and the criteria by which entries on the listing can be arranged. As an example, a list of potential claim candidates might best be arranged by vendor and then by title or purchase order number. However, there are other first-order group-ings for claim candidates that might also be useful for certain purposes, such as by fund or final destination of items. Most commercially avail-able acquisitions systems offer a fairly broad range of offline listing possibilities, but not all systems offer as much flexibility for defining arrangement patterns within listings as some libraries might like.

Vendor Records and Performance Reports

Most online acquisitions systems allow for the creation and mainte-nance of a file of records containing relevant information about jobbers or publishers from whom the library orders materials. The number of vendor records in such a file may be quite large and include records not only for jobbers and publishers, but also for other vendors and for libraries and library-related agencies and organizations. These more expansive files are especially characteristic of the bibliographic utilities, each of which maintains a name-and-address directory for shared use by its participants. Vendor files that are not shared among a number of libraries, but are institution-specific, are usually quite a bit smaller. In these cases, libraries frequently do not create records for virtually every jobber or publisher from whom they order, but only for more com-monly used sources.

The amount and types of information included in vendor records will depend on how the library may wish to use those records and on the level of interaction and monitoring to be performed by the system. At the minimum, a record should include the vendor's name, address, and telephone number, and a record number and/or alphabetic mne-monic if these are to be used as access points or as coded input into order records. If the system is to perform more sophisticated interac-tion and monitoring than just translating a vendor number or mne-monic into full name and address on offline forms and reports, the vendor record must also contain information appropriate to the addi-tional functions that are performed. The more common additional fields include vendor-specific claim cycles, discount rates, and various financial data on which the system draws for such purposes as auto-matically computing discounts and claim dates.

In addition to online interaction between vendor and order records, many acquisitions systems monitor vendor performance and produce reports tracing that performance. The reports usually show, for each jobber or publisher, the total dollar amount spent, the number of orders sent, the number and percentage of orders filled, and the aver-age time for fulfillment, usually measured as the period between re-lease of an order and receipt of the material. While these are fairly standard, some systems provide additional types of information about each vendor, such as analyses relating to the issuance and disposition of claims or tracing the pattern of encumbered versus actual prices.

Serials Control

The main distinction between most automated acquisitions systems and serials control systems is more in the form of the materials with which they deal than in the functions they perform. The range of operations that automated serials control systems are designed to facilitate includes:

Initial ordering

Check-in

Claiming

Routing

Binding control

Subscription monitoring

Payment and invoice control

Fund accounting

Production of offline lists and forms

As can be seen from this list, there is a great deal of overlap in function between acquisitions and serials control systems. Central to both are the ordering, receipt, and claiming of materials and mechanisms to assist in payment and fund accounting. Yet there are only a few—mostly locally developed—systems that even attempt to incorporate acquisitions and serials control into a single component. The most frequently cited reason for a system to handle serials apart from other types of materials has to do with the nature and complexity of the publications themselves. Although many of the functions overlap, most "acquisitions systems" in use are designed to handle the full complement of operations only for firm orders. Some are quite capable of addressing certain aspects of serials subscriptions, most particularly ordering and renewing, payment and invoice control, and fund accounting, but rarely do they allow for check-in, claiming, routing, and binding of issues.

The content of a serial is, by definition, not contained within a single unit nor published within a single set, but rather is contained in multiple units arriving over a period of time. In a practical sense, this quality of continuation distinguishes serials from items that can be treated as distinct pieces. A monograph has a nonchanging title, is received once, and is paid for once. Several claims may be issued for it, but they are all for the same single physical piece. A serial has quite different characteristics. Although in one sense a serial can be considered a bibliographic entity, the title associated with the whole can change, the parts that make up the whole are received on a continuing basis—any of which may or may not have to be claimed—and payment has to be made over and over again as long as the serial continues to be published and subscribed to by the library. To make matters even more complicated, there are many different ways in which the parts of serials are issued in terms of frequency, regularity, and the levels of hierarchy by which the parts relate to the whole.

Of the four applications discussed here—cataloging, acquisitions, serials control, and circulation—automation has been applied less extensively in American libraries to serials control than to the other three. There has also been the most skepticism about the very appropriateness of automation in serials control in the first place.[2] The primary source of this reluctance can probably be attributed to the same factors responsible for the design and use of separate systems when applying automation to serials control, namely, the nature and complexity of the publications themselves. Computers are best equipped to handle regularity and predictability, which serials are known all too well to defy.

Computers simply cannot deal with serials in as efficient and tidy a manner as any library would like, but automation is not, as some claim, entirely useless for purposes of serials control. Even a relatively unsophisticated automated serials control system can do things just about as fast and as well as a manual system, and a well-designed and more elaborate automated system can improve on many aspects of serials control. The speed with which some tasks can be carried out in a manual system, such as basic check-in, has not really been improved on very much, if at all, by even the more sophisticated automated systems, but other functions such as claiming, subscription control, and fund accounting can be enhanced.

Prior to the mid-1970s, the only online serials control systems in libraries were locally developed and maintained. Even into the 1980s, the OCLC Serials Control subsystem was about the only online alternative to local development. Since then, the number of systems has expanded appreciably, although still not to the extent that one can see with acquisitions systems.

Among the bibliographic utilities, OCLC is still the only one that is attempting to offer a distinct serials control subsystem through a centralized computer facility. UTLAS has been involved in providing serials control capabilities, but in the form of distributed interfaced systems rather than through a centralized approach. While not yet entirely abandoning its centralized serials control subsystem, OCLC scheduled the introduction, for late 1984, of a microcomputer-based serials control software package for distributed use on its M300 workstation terminal.

In addition to the utilities, there are at least two other serials control systems that are in one way or another tied with cooperative library networks. One is PHILSOM, developed at the Washington University School of Medicine Library and used in a networking environment by a number of medical libraries for both serials check-in and union listing. The second system is CHECKMATE, a microcomputer-based software package marketed by CLASS.

In the commercial sector, serials subscription agents have played a leading role in making online serials controls accessible to more libraries. The most widely used of these in the United States are Ebsco's EBSCONET and Faxon's LINX. The advantages of using a subscription agent's system are not entirely unlike those afforded by the use of acquisitions systems offered through book jobbers. Although the agents do not generally warehouse serial issues in the manner that book jobbers hold an inventory of monographs, there are still benefits in being connected online with the agency responsible for seeing that materials are supplied to the library. Orders and claims may be transmitted online, and current pricing and a great deal of financial and other information can now be accessed through these systems. In addition, both Ebsco and Faxon maintain large bibliographic files accessible to customers and provide online information about title and other bibliographic changes. While some serials routines can be facilitated through use of either of these systems, only Faxon has developed what can be called a more comprehensive "control" component of its own in terms of providing capabilities for check-in and a number of associated local control functions. In 1984, Ebsco began to market CLASS' CHECKMATE as a package for handling these more strictly local functions.

While Ebsco and Faxon have been the leaders in the United States among serials subscription agents, the Blackwell firm has assumed a similar role in Great Britain with its development of PERLINE, a system based on a distributed processing approach. As configured for British libraries, most functions on PERLINE are performed in the library on microcomputers or minicomputers that are sold as part of the system, with remote communications capabilities for times when there is need to access more generalized files stored on Blackwell's main computers. In 1983, Blackwell began marketing PERLINE as a stand-alone system in the United States, and by late 1984 had sold the system to several very large research libraries among others.

Other commercial sources of automated serials control include a few single-purpose systems and software packages, and components available on several of the larger multipurpose integrated systems. Several single-purpose systems and packages are identified in Chapter 7 in the section on library processing applications of microcomputers. In general, there are fewer single-purpose systems and packages available for serials control than for any of the other traditional sets of operations discussed in this chapter. The same is true for larger multipurpose systems, for which serials control is usually the last module to be developed. Although nearly all vendors of integrated systems have serials control modules at least in a planning stage, comparatively few actually have them operational as yet.

The general characteristics of automated systems outlined earlier in this chapter are important for evaluating serials control systems just as they are for evaluating cataloging and acquisitions systems. Several features more specific to serials control are examined below. Capabilities that are part of the initial ordering and financial monitoring process are not reviewed here, however, since these functions as performed on serials control systems are usually rather similar to those performed by acquisitions systems.

Elements of Serials Control Records

Depending on the complexity of the system, fields for any of the following types of information may be included in the online record for each title in a serials control system.

Control numbers (LCCN, ISSN, local control number, etc.)

Basic bibliographic data

Alternate titles

Cross-references

Country of publication

Language of publication

Publication status

Frequency

Issues per volume, volumes per year, etc.

Collection and shelving location

Retention code

Holdings

Issues expected to be received next

Claim cycle

Claim date for issue expected to be received next

Listing of claimed issues

Routing information

Binding information

Subscription status (i.e., active or inactive)

Source of subscription

Subscription interval

Subscription renewal date

Subscription price

Postage and other charges

Payment and invoice information

Fund information

Notes

Depending on the file structure and interaction of the system, full detail for some of this information need not be included on the title record itself. For example, much of the routing information is frequently kept in a separate file and interacts with a title record to produce offline routing slips. Not all serials control systems allow for coverage of all of the types of information listed above, but even in less comprehensive systems, the amount of data included can easily exceed the capacity of a single terminal page display. Most systems organize page displays according to general categories, such as check-in information, financial and subscription information, and detailed holdings, and usually display different amounts of information according to the function being performed, such as check-in or public access.

Online Access

Serials control title records, hereafter referred to as check-in records, should be retrievable by as many control numbers as possible, in addition to author and title elements. Many systems allow for the library to specify more than one retrievable version of a title on each record. Subscription agents find this to be particularly necessary, since customers sometimes follow cataloging practices or have preferences that result in forms of entry different from those appearing on bibliographic records in the agent's generalized file. Blackwell's PERLINE allows for as many as five indexed alternative titles to be designated in each check-in record. This number may amount to overkill, but it is beneficial if at least one or two alternate title fields be available, especially if the library is using a system that draws on records from a generalized bibliographic file for creation of local check-in records.

In addition to bibliographic access by author and title, some systems permit retrieval by subject. The value of subject access depends on how the system is to be used. If it is used strictly for check-in and associated purposes, retrieval by subject is not crucial. But it is a most useful capability if online public searching of serials records is allowed.

For access to check-in records apart from general control numbers and bibliographic elements, the situation is rather analogous to that with acquisitions systems, in that there is a host of groupings for which online retrieval or offline listings can be useful: by country or language of publication, by source of subscription, by subscription renewal dates, by fund, and so on. Even when there is considerable flexibility for online retrieval, many libraries prefer to rely most heavily on offline listings to inspect their serials titles according to broad groupings such as those identified above.

Additional access points will be necessary to retrieve other types of records that might be maintained. If the system includes sophisticated routing capabilities, it will make use of a separate file containing a list of all employees to which any materials are routed, and records in this file must be accessible by employee name or number. If available, vendor files will also require access by vendor name or number.

Arrival Prediction

Three features central to any even moderately sophisticated serials control system are check-in, claiming, and automatic prediction of arrival of serial issues. The latter capability is the crucial connection between the other two and is particularly instrumental in the claiming function. Systems that forgo arrival prediction and claim notification have been designed and used in libraries, but they really represent more of a simple electronic inventory of holdings than an actual "control" system.

The purposes of an arrival-prediction capability are twofold. One is to monitor the sequence in which issues of a serial can be expected to arrive. This will allow the system, prompted by previous check-in activity, to predict the number or date of the next issue that will need to be checked in. The second purpose is to establish a date by which the next issue should arrive. This date should not be thought of as a "prediction" in the sense of an estimated time of arrival, but rather as an upper limit beyond which there may be cause for concern if the issue has not yet arrived. This date, then, is the point at which the connection is made between the "predictive" and claiming capabilities of a system.

Serials control systems designed to predict arrival and establish claiming dates draw on such things as frequency patterns, regularity of publication, and historical performance. The level of sophistication with which a variety of publication parameters can be handled has considerable bearing on the overall utility of the system for check-in especially for claiming operations.

Some serials control systems base their calculation of claiming dates almost entirely on frequency of publication, and do so in a very generalized sense. For example, all issues of all quarterly publications are expected to arrive within a certain number of days after the receipt of the previous issue of a title, or in some systems within a certain number of days after the regularly established cover or publication date of the issue. Other serials control systems allow for somewhat greater title-specific flexibility. For example, if tied to cover dates, a three-week overdue claiming cycle might be established by the library for one title published on a monthly basis, while a four-week cycle might be established for another. A few systems take this one step further and can automatically adjust claiming dates on the basis of title-specific and even issue-specific past performance. For example, the issues of a quarterly with cover dates of March, June, and September might consistently arrive, year after year, within the month following their respective cover dates, while the December issue might just as consistently be published late and never be received before the second month following the cover date. Systems with a capability to establish claiming dates based on title-specific historical patterns can help to reduce the number of claims by recognizing a pattern of predictability that might not be obvious if performance were viewed on a strictly linear scale.

One of the greatest obstacles for claiming capabilities is the diversity of publishing patterns for serials. It is one thing for a serials control system to be able to establish claiming dates for serials that are published daily, weekly, biweekly, quarterly, semiannually, or annually, but quite another matter to handle less neatly defined publication patterns. Some serials, for example, are published monthly for ten months out of the year, with the other two months combined into a single issue. One of these titles may choose June and July to combine; another may choose December and January, and so on through a long list of possible combinations. Some "weeklies" take holiday breaks and are actually published only 50 times per year, others may be only 49. The variety is endless. One need only examine the publication patterns of *American Libraries, Library Journal, Library Journal Hotline,* and some recent Haworth Press library-oriented journals to see the level of complexity that arises when attempting to define frequency of publication.

Less sophisticated serials control systems simply cannot handle even subtle variations on standard frequency patterns. Fortunately, there are other systems that can, especially if the pattern is predictable on a long-term basis, as with *American Libraries,* for example, whose combined issue is always for the months of July and August. These more sophisticated systems often base arrival prediction on a publication pattern table established for each title in which it is possible to indicate exactly on which days or during which weeks or months issues of the title are published. This allows a system to effectively handle just about any frequency pattern, no matter how peculiar, as long as it is predictable and consistent from one year to the next. Even with the more complex systems, there will always be a certain number of serials with frequency patterns that cannot be programmed simply because the serial is published with such varying and unpredictable frequency. In these cases, claiming intervals are established only on a very general level, if at all.

The sophistication level with which a system can handle different publication patterns is extremely important to the library, because it directly affects the efficiency of the check-in and especially the claiming function of the system.

Check-in and Claiming

When an issue of a serial is received by a library, the first routine in using an online serials control system is for a terminal operator to call up the online check-in record and verify that the issue is, in fact, the one that is expected to arrive. If so, the next procedure is very simple. Receipt is recorded, a routing slip is printed if applicable, and the transaction is complete.

The format in which information about the issue is presented on a display varies from one system to another. In some systems, there is a single-screen record for each title, one field that contains details like the volume, number, and date of the issue that is supposed to arrive next, or even of the next several expected issues. In several systems, there is a multipage record for each title. One page is a check-in screen, which includes only the most essential bibliographic data elements plus the details about the expected issue or, in some cases, about the next several expected issues. Other fields, such as detailed holdings and financial and subscription information, are presented on subsequent pages of the record. These other pages can easily be accessed from the check-in display, but it is seldom necessary to do so if the issue in hand matches the one that is predicted to arrive. This type of record arrangement is convenient for the terminal operator (and for his or her eyesight) and allows a more rapid check-in, since it is not necessary to stare at a cluttered screen to zero in on a few lines of pertinent infor-

mation. With either of these approaches, however, the terminal operator generally has to key in only one or two characters and a control
command at the top or bottom of the display to record receipt when
the issue in hand corresponds to the expected issue. The system automatically transfers the number or date of the received issue into a
detailed holdings field, calculates the number or date of the next expected issue, and places it into the expected-issue field. No further
action is required of the terminal operator.

These are the most common techniques used on serials control systems, but there are variations. In at least one locally developed large-
scale system using an expected-issue field, the number or date of the
issue received must actually be keyed into the detailed holdings field
rather than being automatically transferred, even if the issue in hand
corresponds to the issue expected. The system still automatically calculates the details about the next expected issue, but given the capabilities
of the system to perform this function automatically, the requirement
to actually key data into the detailed holdings field first is cumbersome.
While most systems present data about expected issues and holdings in
line fields, there are at least two systems that provide an optional check-
in matrix display, a sort of electronic Kardex. Receipt is relatively
simple and may be indicated with only a couple of keystrokes. Date of
receipt does not have to be keyed into the appropriate box in the
matrix if the issue received is the expected one. Such data is automatically recorded into the appropriate box when the receipt command is
entered.

So far, this description has focused on procedures used when the
issue received corresponds to the issue expected. A second—and, one
hopes, not so common—possibility is that the issue received has a
higher number and/or later issue date than the issue expected. This
implies that one or more issues were not received and that it may be
appropriate to generate a claim for the missing or "skipped" issue(s).
To handle such a situation, the system must allow two things to occur at
the terminal. The later issue that is received must be checked in, and
claiming action must be generated for the missing issue(s). Different
systems will allow receipt of the later issue in different ways. In some,
the terminal operator may first have to enter an appropriate command
to indicate that the expected issue is missing. The system will then
update the expected-issue field to indicate the number or date of the
following expected issue. If the new expected issue matches the item in
hand, the terminal operator can then enter the receipt command. If
two or more issues have been skipped, the terminal operator continues
to enter missing commands until the receipt command can be entered
because the expected-issue field finally corresponds to the issue in

hand. Other systems allow the terminal operator simply to key the appropriate data about the received issue over the existing data in the expected-issue field and then enter the receipt command. The system is then able to determine which issues have been skipped, a procedure that can save time if several issues are missing. In systems that list the next several expected issues on a check-in screen, there are procedures that allow issues anywhere in the list to be received quite easily. Some systems accommodate more than one of these approaches.

Regardless of the exact procedures used to record receipt of the issue in hand, any system with a claiming capability must also then be able to record issues that are missing and mark them to consider as claim candidates. The manner in which this is done varies from one system to another, but centers around two major options. One is to allow a claim notice for the missing issue(s) to be printed offline immediately from each online record as receipt and missing issues are being recorded. The other is to automatically record details about missing issues in a special file from which claim notices for all missing issues recorded during one or more sessions can be printed offline in a batch mode. Most systems provide for both options, allow the library to exercise one or the other at its own discretion.

Some libraries will not want to follow as automatic a procedure as either of these claiming options implies, and will prefer instead to review claim candidates before actually printing the notices. Most serials control systems easily accommodate a review procedure. Details about all missing issues are placed in a special review file when originally recorded, and the contents may either be examined online or printed offline. If a system provides claim candidates listings, online, offline, or both, an important consideration is the procedure that is then used to tell the system which candidates should indeed be claimed. The library should not have to individually retrieve the full check-in record for each title for which it wishes to claim an issue. Rather, it should be possible to conduct a general claim session and simply enter record numbers from an offline list or line numbers from an online menu to update all appropriate records and to initiate the printing of notices for all issues being claimed.

The circumstances and procedures described above assume that missing issues have been detected at time of check-in. This is only one of two ways that most systems facilitate claim control. The second is automatic detection of overdue issues. The foundation of this capability is the calculation and system monitoring of arrival dates by which each issue of a serial should arrive.

With automatic detection of overdue issues, the system constantly monitors check-in records to spot titles for which an upper-limit arrival date of the next issue has lapsed. Once a candidate has been thus identified, the procedures for claiming usually parallel those for skipped issues. Pertinent details about the title and the overdue issue are placed into a claim file for online review, offline listing, or automatic printing of claim forms without review. Because it does not depend on arrival of subsequent issues, automatic detection can mean fairly early identification of potential claim candidates.

Nearly all serials control systems incorporate mechanisms both for claiming missing issues observed at time of check-in and for automatic detection of overdue issues. If the automatic detection capability of a system is adequately sophisticated, it will minimize the number of claim candidates that have to be identified for the first time only when later issues are received. However, the ability of a system to calculate claiming dates and monitor them does presuppose some predictability about the frequency with which particular issues should arrive. If a serial is published on a completely irregular basis, the system cannot impose predictability.

Most serials control systems deal with totally irregular publication patterns in one of two ways. Serials with no predictable frequency may be treated simply on an acceptance basis. Potential claiming dates are not established, and since it is impossible to know even approximately when to expect the next issue, there is no attempt to automatically determine when that issue would be overdue. The only way that claim candidates can be identified is if the next issue received has a higher volume or issue number than the expected issue. A variation on this theme is for the library to establish an arbitrary claim cycle. This measure will at least ensure that the title will periodically appear in a review file. Some systems attempt to introduce a measure of automatic detection for irregular publications by establishing claiming intervals based on historical performance. The claiming interval for the next issue is established as the interval between the dates on which the two most recent issues were received. If the expected issue is not received during this projected interval, details about the title and next expected issue are automatically transferred into the claim review file for online or offline consideration.

Most systems allow for a missing or overdue issue to be claimed several times. The interval between each claim generation or review is generalized in some systems according to frequency. Other systems allow for more flexible definition of intervals on a title-by-title basis. Most systems further provide a capability for generating lists of all outstanding issues that have been claimed at least three, four, or some other specified number of times for special review and disposition. In preparation of claim notices, some systems are able to store and generate differently worded messages to an agent or publisher depending on whether an issue is being claimed for the first, second, or third time, as well as according to whether the serial is a free or paid subscription, whether its frequency is regular or irregular, and so on.

At the opposite end of the spectrum from the routine check-in and claiming functions is the situation in which back issues or claimed issues of a serial are received. In the case of a back order, receipt is recorded on most serials control systems simply by entering the appropriate data into a detailed holdings field on the check-in record. In the case of claimed issues, some systems require the receipt to be indicated through the online claim file rather than on the check-in record itself. In these systems, the receipt action in the claim file both deletes the claim file listing and updates the check-in record automatically. In other systems, the procedure is reversed. The check-in record may be retrieved, on which there is a list of claimed issues of the title, and an abbreviated procedure indicating which issues have been received will automatically update the holdings statement and will delete the claim listing from both the check-in record and the claim file. Some systems permit either of these approaches.

Check-in and claiming are the essential features of a serials control system. Largely because publication and the arrival of many serial issues is irregular and unpredictable, libraries with an automated serials control system will find that a substantial amount of manual monitoring and decision making may still be necessary. This will be particularly true if the system is not sophisticated in being able to handle a wide variety of frequency patterns and in permitting claim cycles to be established on a title-specific basis. But realizing the inherent limitations in automating serials control, the systems that permit greater flexibility in these areas will help to keep problems requiring manual attention to a minimum, and will indeed improve the degree of control that libraries can exercise over their serials operations.

Routing Capabilities

Besides check-in and claiming, many systems provide additional features. Three of the more common are routing, binding control, and subscription monitoring.

Not all libraries need sophisticated routing capabilities, especially if most current issues are simply received, processed as necessary, and shelved for general use. But for a number of organizations, especially in the corporate area, this is not the case. Issues of periodicals and other serials are routed to employees within the organization, and it is often the library's responsibility to receive the issues, maintain a file of which employees want to see which titles, and prepare a routing slip on receipt of each issue. In large organizations especially, this can be a major task. Employees leave and their names must be deleted from the routing lists for each title they had received. A list of all titles must be given to any new employee to whom issues might be routed, and the routing lists updated as necessary. Besides maintaining employees' names for each title, the library will usually have to arrange each list in a particular routing order, alphabetical or other. In some cases, it may be necessary to route certain "theme" issues of a serial in a different order or to additional employees depending on contents.

Under these circumstances, a sophisticated routing capability is an essential feature of an automated serials control system. Routing capability is usually based on interaction between check-in records and employee files that are maintained in the system. Merely having a field on each check-in record containing the names of employees to whom that title will be routed is seldom sufficient in itself, except in very small organizations or those with very few subscriptions. If individual check-in records are not tied to special routing files, maintenance of routing information on the automated system will be as time consuming as with a manual system. Each affected check-in record will have to be individually retrieved and modified every time an employee leaves or a new one begins.

Serials control systems with sophisticated routing capabilities have at least one and usually two files specific to routing that interact with check-in records. One is an employee file; the other can be a routing file containing a record for each title and a list of employees to whom issues are routed. When a check-in record is updated to indicate receipt of an issue, the system should immediately print the appropriate routing list either automatically or with a very simple additional command. A most critical aspect is the interaction between the employee file and online routing lists. If an employee leaves and his or her name must be deleted from each title-specific routing list on which the name appears, this should be able to be done globally by simply deleting the name from the employee file.

Binding Control

Binding control will have wider application in more public and academic libraries than will routing capabilities. The purpose of a binding control feature is to automatically signal which issues of a serial should be bound and when, to keep track of the progress of issues through the binding process, and to print appropriate forms both for internal use and for sending to outside binderies along with the materials to be bound.

There are principally three alternative time frames used among automated serials control systems for informing the library when issues should be bound. The first is on receipt of the last issue of the volume or other unit. Another is to inform the library, through a special online file or offline listing, after a specified amount of time has passed since receipt of the last issue to be included in the bound piece. The third is to trigger a binding notification when the first issue of the next volume is received.

Most binding operations require several different forms or lists to be used to carry out the process of retrieving issues, sending them to an in-house or external binding unit, and receiving and shelving the returned bound units. The types of offline products, and requirements for system tracing features, can be illustrated by describing the basic work flow associated with a particular in-house system presently in use at Brigham Young University (BYU) in Provo, Utah.[3] The BYU system is based on one developed during the early 1970s at the UCLA Biomedical Library, and also served as a model for the serials control module of Computer Translations Inc.'s (CTI) commercially available integrated library system.

To identify titles whose issues should be bound, the BYU system automatically notifies the library after a specified period of time following receipt of the last issue that comprises a binding unit. Each week a list of all such titles is printed, along with instructions as to where materials such as volume table of contents and indexes are supposed to be located. For any serials control operation, this information is crucial; since there can be a number of variations, it is useful for records in a system to include information relating to table of contents and index location whenever possible.

The next step in the BYU system is to produce hard copy bindery pick-up slips for each title, indicating which issues should be retrieved from the stacks. If all issues are not there, replacement action is taken or binding activity is put on hold pending further decision. If all issues are present, the issues are taken to bindery preparation and a code is entered into the system, which triggers the printing of a three-part title-specific bindery instruction ticket. The types of information included on these tickets vary from one system to another, but may include title-specific instructions relating to such matters as binding color and type; style, color, size, and placement of lettering on the spine; instructions for handling volume table of contents, title pages, and indexes; and verification details as to the issues to be bound.[4]

At BYU, two parts of the bindery ticket are retained for internal use and one goes with the issues to a commercial binder. When the materials are ready for shipment, a code is entered into the system, whereupon a packing slip is printed. When the materials are shipped to or picked up by a commercial binder, a further code is entered into the system indicating that the issues are at the bindery. When the bound volumes are returned, a final code is entered indicating receipt, and appropriate holdings fields on serials records are updated.

This particular binding-control capability is only one of many that have been developed by libraries or are available commercially, and there are certainly variations from one system to another. BYU's system, however, does illustrate the basic requirements of a binding control component. The system should be able to generate offline slips or general lists indicating which issues of which titles should be bound, as well as packing slips and title-specific binding instructions. There should be a way to update records so that issues can be traced through the binding process. Many systems also include a "bindery claim" feature to notify the library when issues have been at a bindery longer than a predetermined amount of time. Some libraries, alternatively, handle bindery claiming control through their manual or automated circulation systems, charging the issues out to the bindery much as materials are charged out to patrons.

Subscription Monitoring

Another feature for serials control systems is subscription monitoring for the purpose of informing the library when it is time to renew a subscription. Notification should be made far enough in advance by the system to allow the library ample time to make any decisions or inquiries necessary, and to secure authorization for and processing of payment if a subscription must be prepaid. Especially during a time when subscription prices continue to escalate faster than library budgets, an important by-product of subscription monitoring can be the generation of lists of renewal candidates along departmental or other customized lines. These lists can then be circulated for renewal consideration.

Considering the characteristics of the materials they are designed to handle, automated serials control systems are likely to remain a long way from perfect. Nevertheless, a well-designed system can permit a library to exercise more effective control over serials than is possible in a manual system. In particular, the operations having to do with claiming, routing, binding, and subscription monitoring can be handled more effectively for a larger proportion of titles. But it is important in purchasing or designing a system for a library to also recognize the likelihood that some portion of titles and issue-specific problems will always require manual treatment.

Circulation

Circulation systems and circulation modules on multipurpose systems are primarily an inventory control for monitoring the whereabouts and flow of individual items in a library collection, once they have been processed and made available for public use. Notwithstanding extensions of this purpose, such as monitoring of items before they are fully processed and the inclusion even of items that are not intended for use outside the library, the primary focus of circulation control is on that part of the collection that is readily accessible to the public and from which materials may be borrowed. There are several aspects to handling circulation transactions, and an automated system should be able to allow for all of the following functions:

Checkout of materials to patrons (charging)

Renewal of loans

Return of materials from patrons (discharging)

Placement of holds on materials charged out

Identification of overdue materials

Issuing of recalls for materials on loan

Reserve collection circulation

Handling of fines payment and accounting

Preparation of offline notices

Statistical compilation and generation of reports

In terms of the number of different approaches available, libraries may actually have a somewhat narrower range of choice for automating their circulation operations than for automating cataloging, acquisitions, or serials control. With the latter three operations, there are usually several broad approaches available, each having its own strengths and weaknesses. Included among these are usually systems available through one or more of the bibliographic utilities, from book jobbers or subscription agents, from vendors offering multipurpose systems, and those offering single-purpose systems.

Other than local development, the option that has evolved for circulation has been far more uniform, in the form of turnkey systems and software packages. The only bibliographic utility presently active in marketing a circulation component in the United States is OCLC, and the approach used is virtually indistinguishable from that associated with systems in the commercial sector. And the commercial market exhibits less diversity in approaches to circulation than in the options for automating cataloging, acquisitions, or serials control. There is nothing in the circulation system market, for example, that quite parallels the "system/materials" connection of book-jobber acquisitions systems or subscription-agent serials control systems. There is also less opportunity for drawing a distinction based on multipurpose versus single-purpose system approaches. Nearly all commercially available minicomputer-based circulation systems handle other technical operations as well, most particularly acquisitions. Although a library may not wish to purchase or use the noncirculation modules that are available with these systems, it is becoming more and more difficult to find what could be called a strictly single-purpose circulation system on the market.

Excluding local development and transfer of software from one library to another, what has evolved for online circulation systems then is a fairly uniform option consisting of multipurpose turnkey systems. Whichever system is purchased, computer equipment will be installed and will operate locally. There are some exceptions to this, most notably in regard to some of the processing functions performed on Gaylord's system and in various other time-sharing arrangements offered by a couple of vendors. With these exceptions, circulation systems will be run entirely on equipment housed in the library. There may be a need for "remote access" in terms of branch locations or several independent libraries sharing a single system, but in these instances the central computer will still be housed at one of the sharing sites rather than at a vendor's facility.

What may be lacking in terms of many distinctive approaches and different categories of sources for online circulation systems is more than made up for by the number of specific systems available. As of 1984, there were more than 15 commercial vendors promoting circulation systems or software packages in the United States. There are also a number of microcomputer-based systems and packages available for smaller libraries.

Because of the diversity of operations they are designed to handle, many of the systems that perform circulation control can no longer be evaluated simply as "circulation" systems. But no matter how many different sets of library operations a multipurpose system might be designed to handle, certain functions will be specific to circulation control, and some of the more important are discussed in detail in the remainder of this chapter.

Patron and Item Records

A sophisticated online circulation system will contain at least two types of records essential to the circulation process. One is a patron record and the other an item record. There will be a separate record for each registered patron in the patron file and a separate record for each item in the item file. The item file is, in fact, often broken down into two interrelated files or subfiles, one containing general bibliographic records and the other containing records with copy-specific local and circulation-related data. For libraries that frequently purchase multiple copies of titles and have several branch locations, the ease and sophistication with which a circulation system can distinguish items at the copy-specific level is a crucial concern. Item records containing copy-specific details can be linked to a more general-level bibliographic record, but there should also be unambiguous information for each copy, and the system should allow different circulation limits to be set for each copy and location. Fortunately, most of the large-scale turnkey systems are designed to handle multiple copies and locations fairly well.

The amount of information included in a patron record will vary from one system to another. The range of basic information in a patron record includes such elements as name, registration number and expiration date, address, telephone number, alternate address and telephone number (such as place of work), and demographic data such as date of birth, primary language, and residential/geographic location code or census tract. In order to interact with other parts of the circulation system, records should also include fields in which patron type and status are indicated. Coded data in these fields can serve an important purpose in enabling the system to distinguish between different categories of patrons when performing such functions, such as determining loan periods, blocking subsequent charges because of overdue materials or outstanding fines, and so on.

The patron record should also be a link whereby certain types of circulation-related data can be displayed online or printed offline on a patron-by-patron basis. Following are examples of types of information commonly accessible in connection with an individual patron:

List of all items currently charged out

List of overdue materials currently charged out

List of all items on which a patron has placed a hold

List of patron's current outstanding fines or other financial obligations, also identifying the items for which the obligations were incurred

Complete history of a patron's financial obligations and payments

Reasons for blocking further charges to a patron

Indicator as to whether the patron has been notified of outstanding delinquencies

Date of patron's last circulation transaction

Number of circulation transactions for a patron over a given period

Access to this type of data can be extremely useful, not only to the library, but to the patron as well. An overriding concern with the collection and availability of such information is confidentiality and security. Any type of patron records showing a connection with specific items is usually retained only for current charges and for past charges associated with a fine or other delinquency that is still outstanding. Most systems also try to provide protection through the use of a multi-level authorization structure, in which the ability to display or print more sensitive types of patron-related data is reserved for the higher-level authorization codes.

Many of the earlier automated circulation systems in use in libraries were "absence" systems in which item-specific information was retained actively online only for materials that were actually in circulation at any given time. This approach is confined today primarily to smaller micro-computer-based systems. In larger systems, the emphasis is on maintaining records in the online file for every item in the collection, or at least for every item that is not permanently restricted as noncirculating. Another change in emphasis is that nearly all systems now permit on-line storage of full-length MARC records instead of requiring use of far more abbreviated records. Not all of the information contained in a full record needs to be displayed or acted on for all circulation functions, but its availability can be useful in certain circulation-related activities as well as in other applications if the system is multipurpose.

As mentioned earlier, some systems establish a two-tier approach for representing bibliographic and local information. Item records contain copy-specific and circulation-related data, which are linked to bibliographic records that contain more general descriptive data common to all or several copies of the same title. The data contained in item-level records establishes a unique identity for each item, and usually includes information relating to location, sublocation, call number, volume number if part of a multivolume set, copy number, and barcode number. There are also fields containing data related specifically to the circulation function. Category or type of item or circulation status code can serve as a variable in loan period calculation, and such data as date of last transaction and number of charges over a given period can serve as a basis upon which certain statistical and management information can be generated.

Loan Period Calculation

While much of the system interaction characteristic of online circula-tion systems takes place at time of checkout, return, placement of holds, and so on, one of the most fundamental interactions between patron records and item records is in the procedure used for determin-ing loan periods. Few libraries have a single loan period that applies uniformly to all transactions. Some establish differential loan periods based on categories of borrowers; others make distinctions according to types of library materials; still others take both variables into account.

Almost any online circulation system will allow the library to have different loan periods based on either borrower categories or types of material, but a real strength of many systems is how easily they allow both of these variables to be taken into consideration in determining loan periods. The key elements in this capability are the designated fields on patron records and item records specifying the type or cate-gory of each. An online loan period "matrix" is created, matching each patron category with each item type. A standard loan period is then profiled into the system specific to each patron category/item type com-bination. This allows the library a great deal of flexibility in establishing different loan periods. Since the calculation of due dates is performed automatically by the system on the basis of this matrix, the use of several different loan periods will not pose the types of problems that it does under a manual system.

Charging

The charging, or checkout, of materials to library patrons is the most basic function of an automated circulation system. Nearly every large-scale system now uses barcode or OCR labels as a basis for charging and related functions. A label is attached to each patron identification card and to each item in the circulating collection. A charge is recorded simply by "reading" the patron and item labels with a light wand. This action establishes a link between the patron identification and the unique identification of the item(s) charged. In the simplest (and, it is hoped, most frequent) scenario, a borrower merely presents his or her patron registration card along with the materials to be checked out; the circulation attendant scans the patron and item labels with the light pen; the system calculates the appropriate due date for each item and acknowledges the charge. A due date is stamped or otherwise indicated on each item, and the patron is on his or her way.

That sequence may apply in the majority of cases, but not every charge should be quite so routine if the system is at all sophisticated.

During the short amount of time that it takes to read the labels and approve a charge, the system should be instantaneously performing a number of verifications and checks on patron records and on item records and should include:

Verification that the patron's registration has not expired or is otherwise invalid.

Confirmation that the patron record has not been "flagged" as containing incomplete or inaccurate information (for example, the library may have determined that an address on file was incomplete if the postal service had returned an overdue notice for a previous charge due to insufficient address).

Determination that the patron should not be blocked from further borrowing due to any of a variety of library-specified circumstances: excessive unpaid fines or replacement bills, current loans overdue, current loans equal in number to the maximum allowed by the library at any one time, and so on.

Verification that each item presented is on file and not shown to be currently checked out.

Determination that an item is not on recall, or on hold for another patron or for other action, such as mending, binding, or immediate placement in a reserve book collection.

Confirmation that an item is not in any other way blocked for charging, such as if its item status is noncirculating or if its current status is lost or missing.

Verification that the borrower is eligible to charge each item presented according to patron category and item category definition.

In other words, the system should verify that a patron is eligible to borrow materials, confirm that each item presented is cleared for circulation, and determine that the combination of patron and item categories constitutes an allowable charge. If any of the above conditions are not met, the system should block the charge and display the reason for doing so.

What happens at that point will depend on library policy. The system itself should provide a mechanism whereby blocked charges can be overridden on a case-by-case basis and the materials checked out in spite of the preventive conditions. In providing a blocking capability, a system should also allow a library some degree of flexibility in defining the limits that will trigger a block. For example, some libraries may wish to block further charges to patrons with any outstanding fines regardless of the amount, while others may allow further charges as long as the total amount of fines owed does not exceed a certain level. A system should be able to handle either of these conditions and allow the library to specify the exact amount at which further charges will be blocked.

While these clearing checks are the basic interactive capabilities that an online circulation system should invoke during the charging process, some libraries may consider other checkout features important under certain circumstances. One concerns the ease and immediacy with which a system can handle charging of materials that are unlabeled and for which item records have not yet been entered into the system. This is a crucial consideration in settings where a system will be up and running before the entire collection has been converted for circulation purposes. If a full record must be entered into the system before an item can circulate, there are bound to be serious problems at the circulation desk and long lines of impatient patrons. Fortunately, most systems accommodate circulation of not fully converted items by requiring only a skeletal amount of information in an item record before the item can be charged out through the system. This enables the library to circulate unconverted materials immediately and enter complete information later, when more time and attention can be given to creating a full item record.

Renewal

Closely related to the charging function of an online circulation system is its capabilities for handling renewals. In essence, a renewal is simply a special type of charge, and the system should perform all the same kinds of control checks that it does for a charge. It should verify patron eligibility, check the patron's record to determine if any blocks have been imposed since the original charge was made, and should determine whether any holds have been placed against the item and if it is otherwise cleared for charging.

In addition to the routine checks that should be performed for any type of charge, others will be especially pertinent in the case of renewals. The system should confirm that an item presented for renewal is in fact already charged out, and that the patron number presented is the same number to which the original charge was made. The system should also check to see whether the due date for the original charge has already been surpassed. If so, the system should display a message to that effect. The decision to permit or block renewals of overdue items should be a matter of library policy, and a system should be able to accommodate either option. If renewal is permitted, the system should automatically calculate and record any overdue fines for the original charge as soon as the renewal is issued. If renewal is not permitted, fines should be automatically calculated and recorded on return of the item.

Many systems permit renewal policies to be profiled differently for each branch location or each item category, taking location or item category into account to determine whether an item may be generally renewed, and if so, how many times and for how long each time. A number of systems also allow different limits on the loan period for a renewal, usually of shorter duration than the period for the original charge. Remote renewal is another fairly common capability. Rather than having to appear in person and present materials for renewal, a patron can simply call in and renew items over the telephone. This requires a terminal operator to key in certain data that would otherwise be read with a light pen, and there are differences among systems in the ease with which renewals may be made with neither patron badges nor items being physically present.

Discharging

When an item is returned to the library by a borrower, it is necessary to complete the transaction and disengage the connection between the borrower and the item. With most online systems, this is accomplished by reading item labels on returned materials with a light pen in the same manner used for charging materials. The status of the item is automatically altered to indicate that it is once again available for circulation. Certain types of data are recorded for statistical purposes, but item-specific information as it corresponds directly with a patron should be removed from the system unless there is a delinquency associated with the transaction.

If there is a delinquency, the system should record the pertinent information on a patron record, perform any necessary financial calculations, and print notices or other documents used in monitoring or trying to clear the delinquency. The most common delinquency that will trigger such action at discharge is in connection with the return of overdue materials for which a fine will be assessed. The system should calculate the amount of the fine, note these details on the patron record, generate a fine notice (either immediately or later in batch mode, at the library's discretion), and adjust the patron's borrowing status if the fine causes a block against further charges. These actions will be invoked when an overdue item is returned without immediate payment of fines. The system should also allow for the circumstance in which a patron returns an overdue item and wishes to immediately clear all financial obligations associated with the transaction.

Another important activity that a system should perform as part of the discharge process is to determine whether any holds have been placed against an item. If so, the system should display a message instructing the terminal operator to place the item on a holds shelf or send it to another appropriate destination. It is important that the notification to the terminal operator be prominent, and even require the operator to acknowledge the message with a special command. A number of systems supplement screen messages with audible signals from the terminal when a hold is detected, and some immediately generate a holds-shelf slip for the item, showing the name of the patron who has placed the hold and the pick-up location, if at a branch other than the one to which the item was returned. When an item on hold is discharged, the system should also at the time initiate action that will result in the printing of a holds-available notification ready for mailing to the patron who had placed the hold. Preparation of these notices is usually in batch mode. In addition to identifying returned items for which holds have been placed on behalf of patrons, a system should also be able to trap returns according to any of a variety of other reasons dictating nonroutine disposition. Library-initiated holds can be placed, for example, on items that have been recalled for any reason, on those needed for binding or mending, or on materials to be sent to a cataloging or conversion unit for entry of full-item records if they were circulated on the basis of abbreviated records.

For multibranch libraries, one of the primary concerns insofar as discharging is the ability of a system to handle materials returned to a location other than their home branch. Fortunately, most turnkey systems are designed to accommodate this inevitability fairly easily. Generally, items may be discharged at any branch, not just at the one from which they were charged. To discharge an item at other than its home location, most turnkey systems will trigger the display of a message indicating to which branch the item must be returned, and some will simultaneously print a transit slip to accompany the material back to its home site.

In order to provide a sophisticated level of monitoring and control, a circulation system requires constant interaction between various files, records, and functions. Several examples have been described in terms of their bearing on charging, renewals, and discharging. Each time an item is charged, renewed, or discharged through a sophisticated system, it should be subjected to numerous checks before being cleared for that part of the circulation transaction. In the next several sections, a discussion of charging, renewal, and discharging is recast in terms of some of the more important of these verification and check functions that typify online circulation systems.

Overdues

One vantage point of control from which a circulation system can be viewed is its activity pertaining to overdue materials. There should be three distinct points in the circulation cycle at which a system should be able to identify overdue materials and prompt further action. The first relates to the charging function, whether for a new charge or a renewal. If the system detects an overdue status when processing a new charge on an item that has simply been retrieved from the stacks and presented for checkout by a patron, it is a clear indication that a problem exists. For an item to have a primary status of overdue, there has to be an active charge on it. This implies that, for one reason or another, the item did not make it through the discharging process after its most recent charge. Exactly what will happen at this point will depend on library policy, but the system itself should at least allow for the possibility of immediately discharging the item as it relates to its previous circulation and then charging the item to the patron who has presented it without further delay. In doing so, the system should automatically calculate any fines associated with the previous transaction, as though the item were just returned, and should allow for noting the problem on the previous patron's record. Some libraries may wish simply to cancel any fines associated with overdues of this nature rather than pursue the matter further, in which case the fines capability should be able to be overridden and the amounts and accompanying details not recorded.

The decision of whether to allow renewal of overdue items should be a matter of library policy, and a system should be able to accommodate either option. If renewal is permitted, the system should, at the time of renewal, immediately calculate and record any fines associated with the original charge. If normal policy is not to permit renewal of overdue materials, the system should automatically prevent any attempt to renew, but it should also provide a capability for overriding a block on a discretionary, case-by-case basis. When renewal is refused, fines should be calculated and recorded at the time of discharge.

The second point at which a circulation system should act on overdue materials is through automatic identification of charged items that have not been returned by the date they were due. The automatic detection of overdues by circulation systems is a feature somewhat analogous to the claim identification capabilities of acquisitions and serials control systems. When a due date has been passed, the system should automatically flag an item as overdue and generate an offline notice ready for mailing to the patron. This step is usually done in a batch mode on a daily or sometimes less frequent basis. The library should be able to profile into the system its standard policy regarding the number of overdue notices that will be sent and the intervals between each before an item is considered lost and a replacement bill issued.

The third point at which a system should take action on overdue materials is on discharge. When a returned item is identified by the system as overdue, all applicable fines should automatically be calculated and the amounts and other appropriate details about the transaction recorded. Fine notices should be prepared, usually in a batch mode but with a capability for immediate printing if so desired.

Holds

Most systems check to determine whether holds have been placed against an item. The most frequent points at which detection will occur is on renewal attempt and discharge. As described earlier, the system should automatically notify the terminal operator, prepare a holds-shelf slip, and generate a holds-waiting notice for any item identified as having a current hold against it. In addition to detection at time of renewal and discharge, all new charges should be checked for possible holds on the item. In the case of new charges, identification of an existing hold usually signifies that an item was either lost or misshelved, overlooked by the patron who had placed the hold, or not handled properly when returned after its previous circulation. Under any of these circumstances, it should be the system's responsibility to detect the hold placed on the item and prevent a new charge. Final disposition—whether to observe the system block and retain the item, or to override the block and approve a new charge to the patron who found the item on the shelf—should be a matter of library policy, and a system should allow for either option to be exercised.

Many early online circulation systems were limited in their flexibility for handling the placement of holds against titles of which the library owned multiple copies, housed in a variety of locations. Most systems today are more sophisticated in their ability to deal with these circumstances, although some still are more flexible than others. In the case of holds placed against multiple-copy titles housed at various locations, most major turnkey systems provide for at least three alternatives. A hold may be placed against the first copy that becomes available system-wide, against the first copy available at a specified location, or against a specific copy. At least one system interjects edition as another variable, permitting holds to be placed against a specific edition or against a title regardless of edition.

Although some of the early online circulation systems allowed only one hold to be recorded against an item at any given time, most systems now allow for queuing of multiple-hold requests. A number of systems complement this capability with the automatic generation of "purchase alerts" for any item where the number of active holds exceeds a library-specified limit. This feature can be very useful as a purchasing aid, as it is a way to identify titles for which demand very clearly exceeds the library's existing supply.

The multiple-holds capabilities in the major turnkey systems are fairly uniform in their approach to establishing queuing sequences. Holds are automatically added to a queue for an item simply in the order in which they are submitted. While the basic automated process is chronological, there is more variation among systems in the ease and degree of flexibility with which a holds queue can be manually adjusted or overridden. Some all but prevent the reordering of a queue that has been established by the system and allow insertion of new names only in the last position. Others allow for certain positions in the queue to be changed, usually the first. More and more, however, the library is allowed greater flexibility in being able to adjust system-supplied queues and insert new names into any position within a queue.

Another type of holds-processing activity has to do with cancellation of hold requests. Most systems recognize three different circumstances under which hold requests may be canceled. One is request by the patron, either before or after an item has become available and a pick-up notification issued. Another is failure by the patron to pick up an item within a specified period of time after having been notified that it is available. In such cases, the system should automatically cancel the hold and issue a notice or place the item on a list, informing the library that the hold has been canceled. Some systems will also generate a holds-cancellation notice for mailing to the patron. If other patrons have placed a hold against the same item or title, a system should, on cancellation of one hold, automatically generate a pick-up notice for mailing to the next person in the queue. The third cancellation circumstance occurs when the library has to cancel holds when the only copy of an item has been lost or withdrawn. In the case of a lost or missing item, some systems will automatically cancel all holds when the library changes the item's status to lost or missing and will generate explanatory cancellation notices for mailing to each patron whose name was in the queue at the time of cancellation.

A useful feature for some libraries will be the ability to place a future-date hold on an item. For example, if an academic library knows that a particular item will be needed for a reserve collection at a certain time in the future, placing a future-date hold will allow the item to circulate freely until that time; then the hold, and often a recall, will automatically be activated.

Recalls

Most online circulation systems recognize recall as a distinct status and invoke certain types of action based on it. Items that have been recalled are blocked against further charging and renewal and are trapped at discharge. In addition, most systems enhance their recall function with other special features. Some will automatically generate recall notices in lieu of, or along with, overdue notices for overdue items on which there are holds. Some systems also permit fine rates higher than for normal overdue rates to be set for recalled items. Another capability is future-date recall. Similar to the future-date hold capability described earlier, this feature enables an item to circulate routinely until the specified date is reached; at that time a recall notice is automatically generated. For libraries that frequently own multiple copies of titles in several locations, an important feature will be the degree to which a system allows a library to exercise control over determining which copy will be recalled.

Fines and Replacement Billing

A function common to most online circulation systems is the calculation and recording of financial data related to overdue and lost materials. Whenever an overdue item is renewed or returned, the system should automatically calculate any fines associated with the charge, record the appropriate amounts and item-identification details on the appropriate patron record, and trigger immediate or later printing of a fines notice ready for mailing to the patron. The fines notice should provide adequate identification of the item as well as instructions for payment. Since the mailing of fines notices for very small amounts of money can be a nuisance and can be expensive simply in terms of postage costs, some systems allow small fines to cumulate until the total reaches a specified dollar amount before a notification to the patron is issued. If applicable to library policy, a system should also allow maximum per-item fine amounts to be established.

Most systems are able to generate replacement billings for items that are lost by a patron. Two circumstances can lead to the use of this feature. One is when a patron voluntarily reports the loss of an item that was charged out. The other is initiated by the library, usually because an item has not been returned within a specified period after the due date. It should be possible to profile parameters into the system to specify the point at which an item will be considered lost rather than simply overdue, defined either in terms of a specified period of time following the due date or after a specified number of overdue notices have been sent.

Under either of the above circumstances, a replacement-billing capability allows a system to calculate and record the amount to be billed for a lost item and then to generate a replacement bill for mailing to the patron. The usefulness of the calculation feature depends entirely on whether the system is able to determine the replacement cost for an item based on the information at its disposal. To do so, one of two conditions must be present. Either the library will have to charge a single standard amount for replacement, or there will have to be information in each item record that can be used as a basis for calculating replacement cost, usually an original purchase price or a replacement-cost category indicator. If the library neither charges a standard amount nor records replacement price ahead of time, then a replacement cost will have to be input by a terminal operator when the item is reported lost. At that point, however, the system should take over and complete the automatic processes, recording the amount and item-related data on a patron record and generating a fines notice, either immediately or later in a batch mode at the library's discretion.

Even when one of the above conditions is present, some libraries still prefer to interject a manual step into the process, usually to make a final check that the item is in fact not on the shelf or to verify the replacement cost. Online systems generally accommodate this step by generating offline listings of items that are reported to be lost and are awaiting final verification by the library.

As a part of the fines accounting process, a system should be able to permit immediate payment of fines upon renewal or discharge in the case of overdues and, insofar as possible, of replacement charges in the case of items reported lost by patrons. The library must decide whether charges and renewals to patrons with outstanding financial obligations will be permitted, blocked, or blocked only if the total exceeds a specified amount. A system should be able to accommodate any of these options.

Reserve Collection Circulation

Academic libraries often maintain one or more reserve collections for the purpose of circulating materials that have been designated by instructors as required or recommended course readings. In principle, circulation of reserve materials does not differ dramatically from the more routine types. The distinguishing characteristics, however, are the expected frequency and especially duration of circulation. For many of the materials placed on reserve, expected use will be high and often very concentrated, and instead of being checked out for days, weeks, or even months, reserve materials are likely to be circulated in terms of hours.

The time factor alone necessitates special design for handling reserve circulation. Many of the earlier systems were not designed to handle circulation involving fractions of days or multiple charges and discharges for a single item on a single day. And there are still online circulation systems in use today that cannot readily accommodate the circulation time frame required for a reserve collection; most of these systems were brought up several years ago without a reserve circulation capability. Most minicomputer-based turnkey circulation systems now include a reserve circulation capability. While the need for reserve circulation is most commonly found in academic settings, other types of libraries may have comparable requirements for circulating items on a very short-term basis.

A reserve circulation capability generally permits the same types of functions to be carried out as for general circulation: charging, renewal, discharging, placement of holds, detection of overdues, issuing of recalls, and calculation and recording of fines and replacement costs. The capability must make special allowances, however, for the shortened time frames. Loan periods must be defined in units at least as small as hours and must accommodate special periods such as overnight loan. A reserve component should also be able to calculate fines in terms of very small time units and generate various types of notices on a frequent standard basis as well as on demand.

Almost invariably, library materials in a reserve collection will have shorter loan periods and different fine rates than when part of the normal circulating collection. Especially for materials placed on reserve for a few weeks or months on an annual basis, the constant re-definition of circulation parameters each time an item is transferred in or out of the reserve collection can be extremely time consuming. Therefore, some systems allow two sets of parameters to be stored in an item record: one for reserve, and the other for general circulation. While materials are on reserve, circulation is dictated by the reserve parameters; when they are removed from reserve, the general parameters are reactivated. Not all systems have this capability, and it is a feature that will not be particularly important for many libraries. But for libraries that do have a very active reserve collection, comprised largely of the same library materials that are constantly being shuffled in and out of reserve, the ability to store two sets of circulation parameters in an item record can be helpful.

Some special types of listings and reports can be very useful in a reserve component. Probably the most common is the generation of offline listings of reserve materials arranged by instructor and course.

Some systems also allow online access to titles by these elements. Another common capability is the compilation of use-related statistics showing circulation data for each title and even for broader groupings of titles by course or instructor. A special reporting feature available in some systems is an alerting capability identifying titles that have extremely high demand based on use or holds activity. This is comparable to the purchase-alert feature often provided for general circulation and triggered on the basis of hold queues. For reserves, an alerting feature can be useful in suggesting when it might be advisable to increase the number of reserve copies of a particular item.

Offline Notices and Reports

A characteristic common to nearly all online circulation systems is the ability to generate a wide variety of offline notices and reports. Several types of patron notices were identified earlier, including:

Overdue notices

Holds pick-up notices

Holds-cancellation notices

Recall notices

Fines notices

Replacement bills

Receipts for payment

In addition to patron notification forms, most systems generate internal notices, such as holds-shelf slips and transit slips to accompany items to their home location if returned at a different branch. The most important thing about all of these notices is that their preparation should be prompted automatically on the basis of relevant online activities. It should be possible to generate them either on demand or in a batch mode. The library should also have some degree of flexibility in being able to specify the standard format and wording of each type of patron notice, including an ability, if there is a need, to prepare bilingual notices. In specifying the amount and types of information to appear on notices, a primary goal should be to include sufficient information for the patron to easily identify the item or items to which the notice refers.

Other offline products produced by circulation systems are of two basic types: listings of patron, item, or transaction detail and results of statistical compilations. A turnkey system will generally offer a standard package of listings and statistical reports that can be generated on a periodic basis. The library is often permitted some degree of latitude in designating other parameters on which it wishes to have statistics compiled and reports produced, although the amount of flexibility varies from one system to another.

For listings of patron, item, and transaction details, the possibilities are broad in terms of technical feasibility. Following are some of the listings commonly provided as a standard feature of major turnkey systems:

Items in a specific branch or collection in call-number order, useful for purposes of general inventory

Items that have circulated more than a specified number of times during a specified period of time

Items that have not circulated at all, or less than a specified number of times, during a specified period of time

Items that have been reported lost

Items that have been reported missing

Items that are overdue, sometimes used for purposes of shelf-checking prior to generation of overdue notices

Items on hold

Items on which there are more than a specified number of holds ("purchase alerts")

Items in a reserve collection, arranged by course number, professor, author, title, etc.

Items to be removed from a reserve collection at a specified time, such as at the end of an academic term

Delinquent borrowers arranged by patron name and/or type of delinquency, and showing essential details of the delinquency

Borrowers blocked from further charges, with reasons for the blocks

The technical range of statistics that can be gleaned from circulation systems is almost infinite. Some reports focus simply on tabulations of items in a collection, number of patrons registered, and so on, independent of circulation-related activity. A few of the more common include:

Total number of items in a collection, branch, or librarywide

Number of items by type of material

Number of items by status, such as lost or missing

Distribution of items by classification-number groupings

Total number of patrons registered

Number of new patrons registered during a given time period

Number of patrons registered by patron status, age, geographic location, etc.

Most systems cumulate statistics for circulation activity according to several parameters. Compiled and reported for a specified time period, examples of circulation-related tabulations include:

Total number of charges, renewals, and discharges

Number of transactions by type of material; classification-number grouping; patron category, age, or residential location; and so on

Number of overdues

Number of holds placed, picked up, and canceled

Number and amounts of fines calculated, collected, and forgiven

Number of charges and renewals blocked, reason for block, and number of blocks overridden

Number of reserve collection items circulated by item, instructor, and course

Number of patron notices generated by type

For any of the types of compilations referred to in these two lists, it is important for multicollection and multibranch libraries that a system be able to provide information librarywide, for each branch or collection separately, and for any combination of collections or branches that the library wishes.

The number of possibilities for single-parameter listings and statistical compilations is quite large, and the range increases dramatically when cross-parameter listings and compilations are considered. For example, it would be technically feasible to compile a report showing the total number of items of a particular type and within a certain classification-number grouping that have been reported lost or missing from a specific branch location. While this may be technically feasible, most systems are far more limited in what they actually provide than in what is technically feasible. The library may desire a certain level of sophistication and flexibility in specifying the combination of parameters for which listings and reports will be generated, but it is equally important to carefully consider the actual usefulness of what may appear to be some quite intriguing possibilities. The example cited above may help to identify collection areas prone to a high rate of theft or may be of general interest from a research perspective, but in day-to-day operations a periodic report showing this level of detail may be of little practical use. A full complement of listings and compilations, no matter how useful individually, will be of little collective value if the staff has neither the time nor the inclination to plow through them on a regular basis and obtain information that will lead to more effective library policies, procedures, and service. If, on the other hand, listings and reports can be kept to a manageable quantity and their purpose defined, they can be a valuable product of an online circulation system.

Notes

1. For the past decade, a periodic source of information about specific technical processing systems and their functional capabilities has been *Library Technology Reports,* published quarterly by the American Library Association. See also the series *Library Systems Evaluation Guides,* published by James E. Rush Associates, Inc.
2. See, for example, the essay by Huibert Paul, "Automation of Serials Check-in: Like Growing Bananas in Greenland?" *Serials Librarian* 6 (Winter 1981/Spring 1982): 3–16, and 6 (Summer 1982): 39–62.
3. See H. Kirk Memmott, K. Paul Jordan, and John R. Taylor, "On-line Serials at Brigham Young University," in *The Management of Serials Automation* (New York: Haworth Press, 1982), pp. 61–70.
4. Susan L. Miller, "Inventory and Holding Features," in *Serials Automation for Acquisitions and Inventory Control,* William G. Potter and Arlene F. Sirkin (Chicago: ALA, 1981), p. 48.

13

Online Catalogs:
The User Interface

One of the most exciting aspects of library automation today is the transition to online public-access catalogs (OPACs). This is not to minimize the importance of automation in other applications, such as those described in Chapter 12. To the contrary, as more libraries continue to automate various parts of their technical processing operations, the issues pertaining to the selection and use of systems specific to those operations are crucial. But the design of such systems has attained at least a certain degree of functional maturity. There may be differences of opinion about the utility of certain features, or about how best to incorporate a particular processing capability within the overall system, but such debates are usually conducted at a rather specific level of detail. At a broader level, there is general consensus about what a cataloging, acquisitions, serials control, or circulation system should do as far as function is concerned.

The development of online catalogs, on the other hand, has not reached a comparable stage of maturity. There is no common agreement even about the major features or basic approach that should be provided, much less about how the major functions should be performed in relation to one another or how much and what types of information should be provided to the system user. Some OPACs stress simplicity of operation above all else, even if the resulting product is little more than an electronic card catalog. Others are highly sophisticated retrieval systems that allow the user far greater flexibility than is available through other forms of the library catalog. This level of sophistication, however, is often achieved at the expense of simplicity of

n. The sophisticated systems may require catalog users to
techniques to which they have had little or no previous expo-
ther in the library or elsewhere.

Most OPACs attempt to draw a balance between extremes, striving
for simplicity of operation and, at the same time, attempting to provide
benefits that are lacking in other forms of the library catalog. This
compromise may be the prevailing philosophy in the design of OPACs,
but there is a great deal of room for interpretation as to what constitutes the limits of "simplicity" of operation or "sophisticated" retrieval
capabilities. Compounding this problem are very basic differences of
opinion as to what library users need in a catalog, and how sophisticated a system most people can handle effectively or even want to use.

Sources of Development

The online catalog in libraries is mainly a phenomenon of the 1980s.
Only a few academic and some special libraries had implemented them
earlier. (Some of these, as well as those emerging in the early 1980s, are
noted in Chapter 4.)

In mid-1983, Hildreth reported that OPACs were in use in more than
100 libraries in the United States.[1] These and subsequent systems have
evolved from several different directions and a variety of sources. For
example, of 34 OPACs described by Matthews in 1982, about half had
been developed by libraries; the other half were developed commercially.[2] OPACs developed by libraries generally are in use only at the
originating institution, although an increasing number of libraries have
sold or leased their software to other libraries. Commercially developed
systems are already in use in a substantial number of libraries.

Some OPACs in use today emerged from online circulation systems.
Probably the best example of a long-standing library-developed OPAC
with origins in an online circulation system is LCS at the Ohio State
University. In the commercial area, all of the largest- and longest-estab-
lished online circulation system vendors have developed OPAC modules, including such firms as CLSI, DataPhase, Geac, and Universal Library Systems.

The evolution from a circulation system into a system that incorporates a public-access component has been fairly common in the commercial area, but a number of OPACs developed by libraries were designed
first and foremost as online catalogs, independent of circulation functions. The University of California's MELVYL system and the Catalog
Access System of the Minnesota State University System Project for Automated Library Systems (MSUS/PALS) are two examples. Whichever
component of a large-scale, in-house automated system is developed—

circulation or OPAC—development of the other may follow. Some of the systems developed by libraries, such as VTLS designed by Virginia Polytechnic Institute, also incorporate functions in addition to circulation and public access; acquisition capabilities are the most common, and some provide serials control capabilities.

Locally designed OPACs are found in many types of libraries, although the most widespread development has occurred in the academic library. Some of the better known include systems developed by Ohio State, the University of California, Northwestern University, the Minnesota State University System, Virginia Polytechnic Institute, Dartmouth College, the Claremont Colleges, Washington State University, and Pennsylvania State University. OPACs have also been developed in medical libraries, such as systems at the National Library of Medicine (NLM), the Washington University School of Medicine in St. Louis, and the Beth Israel Hospital in Philadelphia. OPACs developed by public libraries have not been as numerous, although the Pikes Peak Library District in Colorado and the Dallas Public Library are examples of public libraries that have developed and currently use their own online catalog systems. In addition to academic, medical, and public libraries, some smaller special libraries, especially in corporations, use locally developed online catalogs.

In the commercial field, the almost universal tendency has been to offer OPAC capabilities as only one of several system components. Earlier we noted various vendors initially offering online circulation systems; large-scale multipurpose systems with public-access modules are also available from a number of other commercial vendors, such as Advanced Library Concepts, Biblio-Techniques, Data Research Associates, Dynix, Easy Data, Electronic Memory, Inc., and OCLC. Carlyle, Inc., founded by some of the individuals involved with the development of the University of California's MELVYL system, was for a long time unique in the commercial sector in offering a large-scale system that is exclusively an OPAC, without capabilities for circulation or other applications. As more libraries can afford online catalogs, activity in the commercial marketplace is likely to intensify. New vendors will appear, and some of the existing ones will undoubtedly go out of business.

Among the bibliographic utilities in North America, at least three can be said to be involved in OPAC development in one way or another. The University of Toronto Library Automated Systems (UTLAS) markets INFOQUEST, a microcomputer-based OPAC software package. OCLC is vending modified versions of the NLM Integrated Library System. The Washington Library Network's (WLN) involvement has been in the form of licensing its software, which has been used by the

Southeastern Library Network (SOLINET) in its LAMBDA system, is in several other library projects, and is also the basis of the commercially available Biblio-Techniques Library and Information System (BLIS), which includes a public-access component.

Focus on the User

Online catalogs can be looked at from several perspectives. Many issues pertain to their design and use in libraries, ranging from the number of terminals required to service a given number of users, to the ergonomics of terminal placement, to the types and amount of information to be included in a catalog, as well as its arrangement on a screen display. But in examining any form of library catalog, online or other, the distinction between its implications for the internal operations of the library and its implications for library users must be kept in mind. Even though these two perspectives do act on one another in the creation and use of the final product, the distinction is important. The internal-operations perspective has to do primarily with the production and maintenance of a catalog; the library-user perspective has to do with the presentation and use of it.

The introduction of offline, computer-produced book and Computer Output Microform (COM) catalogs was a significant step in the evolution of the library catalog, but almost exclusively in terms of production and maintenance. Computer-produced, offline catalogs addressed many of the problems inherent in card catalog production and maintenance, and many labor-intensive tasks that were fundamental to card catalogs were eliminated with the use of computers and machine-readable records. With offline computerized catalogs, only one unit entry record had to be created for each item; the computer expanded this record into as many individual catalog entries as necessary and performed all alphabetization and filing tasks to maintain the catalog. It was also much easier, at least in theory, to change a major catalog heading; the change could be made once and applied to all affected entries by the computer—quite a difference from manually typing a new heading onto each card to which a change applied.

However, as far as the library user was concerned, the benefits of computer-generated offline catalogs were far less pronounced. The actual format of the catalog certainly changed in some instances, but the basic content, and the basic avenues through which records in the catalog could be found, really did not. The principles used for access to entries in computer-generated book and COM catalogs mirrored those of the card catalog, and the information was often identical and sometimes even less in amount. From the user's standpoint, computer-produced book catalogs were little more than card catalogs in bound volumes, and COM catalogs little more than card catalogs in a box. Given such frustrations as dealing with multiple parts of a catalog issued in editions and supplements, and equipment breakdowns with COM catalogs, most advantages of computer-produced offline catalogs were not noticeable to the user and, at any rate, could often be overshadowed by the logistical difficulties in using them.

In contrast, many OPACs represent a radical departure both from card catalogs and from offline computerized catalogs in their implications for the user. As described later in this chapter, access to records can be enormously broadened in an online catalog over what has typically been provided in other forms, but these benefits are accompanied by a new set of requirements and demands on the catalog user. The relationship between user and online catalog is fundamentally different from that in use of other catalog forms. The online catalog is interactive, not passive, and requires the user to engage in a dialogue quite uncharacteristic of card, book, and COM catalogs. Just to look into the catalog requires new procedures on the part of the user. A search must be physically, not just mentally, initiated by typing onto a keyboard or issuing a command through some other means. The system will respond according to the very specific action initiated by the user. In many instances, the user will then have to initiate further action based on the system's response, and so on back and forth until the user arrives at the desired end of the search or otherwise terminates the dialogue. This interaction and the nature of system responses represent a significant departure for the user from simply thumbing through catalog cards or pressing a button, turning a knob, or sliding a handle on a microfilm or microfiche reader.

The fact that an OPAC is intended for users of library materials is perhaps the fundamental distinction between this application of automation and those which serve strictly internal processing functions. Such matters as simplicity of operation or sophistication of retrieval capabilities should be important considerations in the design and selection of any automated system regardless of application, but self-evidence in operation may be less important in a technical processing system in which the library is able to exercise a certain degree of control over the selection, training, and monitoring of system users.

The design of an online catalog must take into account a quite different set of circumstances. Considerable diversity exists among users in their level of knowledge about library catalogs and in the extent to which they are familiar with the use of computerized systems. The library will usually have little opportunity to balance this diversity through a planned program of controlled instruction and monitoring. Most people will not use the OPAC as part of everyday routine, and hence their knowledge and skills will not be constantly reinforced.

An example of the well-placed emphasis in discussions of OPACs on users and their interaction with the catalog is the series of studies sponsored by the Council on Library Resources (CLR) during the early 1980s, aimed at gaining a better understanding of what users want and need in online catalogs, their likes and dislikes, and the dynamics of their interaction with catalogs. Despite the vast array of differences among existing OPACs and lack of specific guidelines for development, at the base of these differences is a common goal: to design online catalogs that will allow the user maximum flexibility and yet will be easy to use. Investigations like those sponsored by CLR should help to establish a stronger foundation for realizing such a goal. Phrases such as "user friendly" have become almost meaningless because of their sometimes indiscriminate use to describe systems or features that commonsense observation shows are "anything but." Yet the overuse, and even misuse, of well-worn phrases does not negate the relevance of the concepts they represent. The degree to which OPACs are willingly accepted by library users will indeed depend in large part on just how user friendly these systems are.

Technical processing systems can be evaluated largely in terms of functional capabilities, or what a system can do. But the circumstances in which OPACs are still used are too different for such a simple evaluation. Equally and perhaps more important is the question of how easily system functions can be learned, understood, and applied to the fullest extent by a diverse group of users. For any given characteristics in their operation, OPACs are still simply too new, and their use still too little understood, to be able to state categorically that one approach is somehow "better" than the other. The next chapter and the remainder of this one focus on certain operational features of online catalogs and some alternative ways in which they have been made available. Fundamental to all of the features described is the most basic improvement that OPACs have made on other forms of the library catalog: the expansion of avenues of access to catalog records. Some of the techniques used to accomplish this are reviewed in the next section.

Access to Bibliographic Records

The usefulness of different forms of library catalogs can be compared in a variety of ways. One of the most important criteria is simply the extent to which a catalog fulfills its basic purposes. Although the purposes of the library catalog are not cast in stone and depend on one's perspective, one set of standards by which library catalog functions have been measured throughout the twentieth century is the principles of Charles Ammi Cutter as noted in his *Rules for a Dictionary Catalog.*

Cutter enumerated three major "objects" of a library catalog.

A catalog should allow someone to find a book if its author, title, or topic is known.

A catalog should fulfill a gathering function, showing what a library owns by a given author, on a given subject, or in a given type of literature.

A catalog should provide assistance in the choice of a book, either as to its edition or its literary or topical character.

A fourth commonly recognized catalog function, although not explicitly noted by Cutter, is collocation, having to do with the arrangement and relationship of headings within the catalog.[3]

Underlying most of these functions is the fundamental matter of access to bibliographic records in the catalog: the points of entry through which a record for an item may be found. Cutter's first object—the finding function—is the essential basis for access, but the gathering and collocation functions also have to do with accessibility to records. The function least directly related to access is assistance in the choice of material, which has more to do with content of a bibliographic record than access to it.

Whether Cutter's objects still provide the most viable criteria for defining the purposes of a library catalog in an online era is debatable, and some have questioned the degree of completeness to which these objects have ever actually been realized in libraries.[4] Cutter's principles stem from a time quite different from the 1980s. New factors—including but not limited to those of a technological nature—should not be disregarded in defining the purposes of a library catalog. Nevertheless, Cutter's principles serve as a point of departure in many discussions of online catalogs, and concerning access to bibliographic records they still provide a convenient framework for comparing online catalogs with one another and with other forms of the library catalog.

Access to bibliographic records in library catalogs has traditionally been marked by a high degree of rigidity, requiring considerable knowledge and exactitude on the part of the user.[5] Generally, access is gained through four types of bibliographic elements: author, title, series, and subject. Multiple author and subject headings are assigned to an item as rules or judgment dictates, but the number is usually kept to a minimum. The terminology selected for headings is also tightly controlled, with the library usually trying to establish a one-to-one correspondence between headings and the persons, corporate bodies, or concepts they represent.

These practices may be understandable from a practical point of view, but they do impose certain limits on accessibility to records. The user can indeed locate an item in the collection for which the author, title, or subject is known, but only under some rather inflexible conditions. To find a record under the title, the user must know the full and exact wording of the title—not some or most of the words, but all of the words, and in their correct order. For access by author, because of the pre-AACR 2 practice of establishing full and singularly valid forms of names, it has not always been enough to know the form of an author's name as it appears on publications or by which the person is popularly known. It has been necessary for the user somehow to know the exact form of a person's or corporation's name as it has been established by the library, often on the basis of considerable research. Where there are discrepancies in name form, it has been up to the user to figure out the form selected by the library. Access by subject is even more problematic. Singularly valid forms of headings are selected from among all possible equivalents, but because of the greater conceptual complexity involved, there is even greater likelihood in subject searching that discrepancies will arise between the terminology selected by the library and the vocabulary chosen by the user. The problem is further compounded by the general conservatism in libraries toward changing the vocabulary used in headings and by complicated subject heading formation and filing sequences.

Such practices, which result in a lack of flexibility, are all but dictated by necessity in card catalogs; however, they were also carried over generally intact to offline versions of computerized catalogs as well. Given the capabilities of computers and the elimination of the need for manual filing, there is no strictly technological reason for some of these practices to have been retained so uniformly. Additional access points, such as by keywords appearing anywhere in titles or assigned subject headings, could have been provided with little or no appreciable increase in human labor. Similarly, duplicate listings under variant forms of names could have been supplied in the catalog. These expansions would have required greater sophistication in indexing and would have resulted in a far greater number of entries, and thus larger catalogs, but whether for economic reasons, ties to tradition, or something else, expansions of this type were never characteristic of offline computerized catalogs. Only with the introduction of online catalogs have such expansions taken firm hold, and they are changing the very concept of access to records in the library catalog.

Some OPACs adhere quite closely to other forms of the catalog in the ways in which access to records may be gained, requiring just as much exactitude and exhibiting just as little flexibility. These are essentially electronic card catalogs. Other OPACs significantly broaden, and even fundamentally change, the traditional concept of access. An overview of several techniques by which this is accomplished is presented in the following pages. There is considerable variation among OPACs in the specific procedures required in applying these techniques; some of the more specific procedures are examined in detail in Chapter 14.

Keyword Searching

One technique that many OPACs use to allow greater flexibility of access to records in the catalog is keyword, or term, searching. This feature enables a user to retrieve records on the basis of single terms or combinations of terms appearing anywhere within specified fields of a bibliographic record, such as author, title, or subject heading. In finding an item by title, for example, a user can retrieve a record simply by entering one or more words in the title, regardless of sequence or position. A user can find a record for *The Peoples of the Soviet Far East*, for instance, by entering the title-search terms "Soviet," "East," and "Peoples." The record can also be retrieved simply by entering the term "Peoples," or any other single term or combination of terms in the title. A number of OPACs also allow keyword searching on author fields (especially useful in the case of corporate author names) and on fields containing assigned subject headings, and some permit retrieval on the basis of terms appearing within a variety of other bibliographic fields.

Keyword searching has certain advantages over the exact order, full-phrase searching required in other forms of the library catalog. In corporate author searches, the keyword capability means that the user does not have to know the exact hierarchy and order in which a corporate author name appears in the records. For title searches, the user does not have to know the full and exact wording of the title to be able to find it in the catalog. A keyword search capability expands, and actually alters, the traditional concept of locating an item for which, in Cutter's terms, "the author or title is known." In searches for single titles or single names, although the entry of selected keywords is certainly less precise than a full title or author's name and can result in retrieving extraneous records, among those retrieved will be the desired item.

Keyword capabilities are particularly useful in subject searching. When a catalog permits retrieval of terms appearing anywhere within assigned subject headings, the user does not have to know the full and precise wording and filing sequences of assigned subject headings and subdivisions as they appear in the records themselves. Many OPACs allow a broadened view of the subject elements in a bibliographic record; for instance, by allowing keyword searching on title fields. Given the usually high level of correlation between the subject content of works and the terms appearing in their titles, a keyword title search composed of one or two terms can be a viable form of subject searching in online catalogs. Some OPACs, in fact, automatically retrieve from title fields when subject searches are initiated. When the user carries out a subject search, records are retrieved for items in which the search terms appear either in assigned subject headings or in the title field of a record. Whether or not this combination is provided automatically by the system, the ability to search assigned subject headings by keyword, supplemented with term searching on other fields of the bibliographic record, makes subject access generally far more expansive in an OPAC than in other forms of the library catalog.

Truncation

Some OPACs allow a user to truncate, or abbreviate, search terms. For example, many online catalogs allow retrieval of records with an author's surname and first initial. Even though the full forename may be stored on the bibliographic records, the use of an initial is sufficient for retrieval.

In addition to truncation or even omission of forenames and middle names, some OPACs permit retrieval on truncated forms of surnames. Others allow truncation of keywords in titles and assigned subject headings. Entry of the term "prehist" in a title search, for example, will retrieve records containing the terms "prehistoric," "prehistory," or any other derivative in the title. This facility often applies to phrases as well, especially in the case of searching on assigned subject heading fields. Entry of the phrase "Moving Pictures," for example, will retrieve records assigned subject headings "Moving Pictures, Talking," or "Moving Pictures—History," and so on.

In a search on assigned subject headings, truncation on most OPACs requires an explicit expression by the user. A special character must be keyed to indicate that a term or phrase is being entered in truncated rather than in complete form. In title searches, some OPACs require the user to supply a special truncation designator; others provide an implicit form of truncation whereby the system automatically truncates a search term or phrase for retrieval according to an internally prescribed number of characters or words, regardless of how many the user has entered. This distinction between explicit and implicit trunca-tion—user-initiated and system-initiated—is important and is discussed again in Chapter 14. By either means, the net effect of truncation is to broaden the set of records retrieved over what is possible in a search requiring complete and exact terms or phrases.

Boolean Operators

Most OPACs allow the user to combine two or more search terms through the use of Boolean operators, such as "and," "or," and "not." In most OPACs, a Boolean "and" is assumed when two or more terms are entered in a search statement, especially if the search is conducted on a single field or type of information, such as author, title, or subject. Only records containing all specified search terms will be retrieved. In the earlier example of entering the terms "Soviet," "East," and "Peoples" in a title search, only records for works containing all three words in the title would be retrieved.

Some OPACs allow the combination of terms from different fields or serving different functions, such as an author's surname and a title word, in which case the user is generally required to enter a mnemonic code preceding each term indicating the field or function to which it applies and then linking the terms with an explicitly stated "and." OPACs with fuller Boolean capabilities allow the user to construct search statements with other operators as well, the most common being "or" and "not." Depending on which operator is used, the result of Boolean search capabilities is to allow a user to either broaden or nar-row the set of records retrieved.

Additional Access Points and Indexed Fields

Capabilities such as keyword searching expand access to records through traditional avenues like author, title, and subject. Some OPACs index other fields of bibliographic description as well. In a few OPACs, virtually every term in every field of a bibliographic record is indexed. Taken to the extreme, author, title, and subject access are replaced by an all-encompassing concept of access by "bib-liographic description"; the more specific elements of author, title, and subject headings become simply qualifiers for refining the scope of a search. OPACs generally have not taken quite this broad an approach, although some have indexed certain additional elements, such as names of publishers, for retrieval on term searches that act upon several different fields simultaneously.

Bibliographic Qualifiers

A number of OPACs offer a more restricted idea of nontraditional access points in the form of bibliographic qualifiers that the user can employ to limit the results of a search. The two most common are language and date of publication. By including a language code or publication date or range of dates in a specified manner as part of a search statement, a user can block the retrieval of records for items that would otherwise qualify but are considered too old or too new to be useful or are in languages that the user does not read.

Other bibliographic elements could be incorporated into OPACs for purposes of qualifying search statements. The possibilities depend largely on the types of information discretely identified and consistently entered into records in the bibliographic database. For libraries with records in the MARC format, one likely source of qualifiers is from the elements constituting the fixed fields. Based on these elements, an OPAC could provide the ability to limit retrieval according to government publication, conference publication, fiction, juvenile literature, and a host of other categories. Few existing OPACs, however, currently offer a range of qualifiers beyond the elements of language and date of publication.

Treatment of Alternative Terminology

In a somewhat different but not unrelated category, OPACs have attempted to address traditional limitations of access in library catalogs in the treatment of alternative forms of name headings and subject terminology. The most frequent method used by card and offline catalogs has been to provide cross-references guiding the user from variants in the form of a name or subject term to the authorized, library-established heading under which full bibliographic entries are listed. As noted earlier, this technique is not altogether service-effective, since cross-reference cards can be "buried" within long lists of entries or complex headings.

Online catalogs generally fall into two categories in attempting to deal with likely alternatives in the terminology through which users might seek access. One technique essentially mirrors the approach commonly used in card catalogs, namely, by cross-references guiding the user to the authorized terminology. When an online cross-reference is displayed in response to a search, the user must then key in or otherwise instruct the system to search under the authorized term or phrase. Although this approach is similar to that used in most other forms of the library catalog, the presentation is usually more distinctive because the cross-reference message will be displayed prominently on a single screen instead of being buried among other information.

Other OPACs have taken a different approach with respect to cross-references by essentially dispensing with them from the user's point of view, using instead a recognition of equivalent terms as valid for retrieval. If the library has assigned "Women" and "Females" as equivalent subject terms in an online authority file, for example, the user will retrieve the same full listing of records in a search on assigned subject headings regardless of which of these two terms is entered in the search statement. This approach still requires the creation and use of an authority file, but the linking of terms is strictly internal and visible to the user.

Other features, such as the use of word proximity in term searching, have been incorporated into some OPACs to further expand the accessibility to records in the catalog, but those described here are the most common, and they significantly broaden the ways in which library users can approach the catalog. None of these features is new to online information retrieval systems used in the library environment in general; they have been standard in such systems as DIALOG and BRS for many years. What is new is their incorporation into the public catalog. Librarians have long assumed that systems such as DIALOG and BRS require special expertise and training for effective use. What is most challenging about OPACs is that at least some of these same sophisticated features are intended for people without formal training and with only limited need to use them. Taking these factors into account is perhaps the most crucial element in the successful design of online public-access catalogs and their implementation in the library environment.

The User Interface

Because they are interactive and can offer far broader approaches to access, OPACs are a fundamentally different form of catalog than their predecessors. The overall difference can result in greater value for the library user, but not without costs in human terms. Interaction with computerized systems and the use of such techniques as keyword searching, truncation, Boolean combinations, and so on, involve skills that many users do not have, especially within the context of application in a library catalog. For many, lack of familiarity with computers and retrieval techniques extends well beyond use in an online library catalog. There are still many library users for whom interaction with a computer for any purpose remains an alien experience. This situation is changing rapidly as more and more of the population become educated in computer use, but for some time to come, unfamiliarity is a condition that must be taken into account in the design of online catalogs.

User/System/Catalog Interaction

Using an OPAC requires the interaction of three primary participants: a library user, a computerized system, and a library catalog. With an OPAC as both a system and a catalog, the rules governing behavior can be fairly mechanically and consistently structured, even if at times they are complex. As an online computerized system, an OPAC incorporates certain rules that dictate how a user must enter commands and how the system will react to them. In the library catalog function, certain aspects of interaction will be governed primarily by rules and conventions adopted by the library regarding descriptive cataloging, summation of subject content, and so on.

Rather than distinguishing between an OPAC as a library catalog and as the mechanical means of conveyance, some discussions blend the two functions together. However, it is important to recognize such a distinction on at least a conceptual level, for each purpose has characteristics that can independently contribute to success or failure in using an OPAC. Some patrons may be well versed in the use of computerized systems and their retrieval techniques, but may be almost totally unfamiliar with the library's cataloging and other bibliographic practices that do, in fact, influence the degree of success in using the system. Other patrons may have a fairly comprehensive understanding of the structure and organization of library catalogs, even in online form, but may be unskilled in the mechanics of using computerized systems and unfamiliar with retrieval techniques. Any advantages gained by introducing clarity, ease of use, and greater flexibility at one of these levels can be offset by undue complexity or lack of clarity at the other. By taking advantage of the power of the computer, an OPAC can be more flexible than conventional catalog forms, but it must be so in a way that allows these new methods to be easily learned and understood.

Although the rules that govern the behavior of an OPAC as a system and as a catalog can be fairly mechanical and consistent, the rules that govern the behavior of the library user are not. First and always, "the library user" is an elusive entity. Human factors that influence online catalog use, such as levels of knowledge, skill, and motivation, vary widely from one user to another, and even within the same user at different times. Complicating matters is the user's perception of how an OPAC works. It is one thing to say that an online system performs a certain way or that certain rules govern the structure and organization of a library catalog, but the more important consideration is the user's own perception about how the system works or how the catalog is structured and organized.

The design features of an OPAC can either facilitate or inhibit interaction between user and system. As noted earlier, libraries are not always able to provide the desired level of guidance and assistance when making as significant a change as introducing a sophisticated online public-access catalog. Therefore, an OPAC must be designed to minimize the need for offline guidance, taking on some of the instructional responsibilities and burden of assistance itself. An OPAC must be easy to use and its features easy to learn, and it must be as free as possible from cryptic language, confusing conventions, and complex rules that are meaningful only to the system. The term "user friendly" may be ambiguous and trite, but the concepts it represents are perhaps the most crucial criteria for evaluating systems designed to handle the interaction between a computer, a library catalog, and a diverse group of library users.

General Sequence of Dialogue

There are certain similarities from one online catalog to another in terms of the sequence of stages in which dialogue occurs. For most OPACs that are not entirely menu-driven, dialogue between a user and the online catalog generally conforms to the following:

USER: Enters a command to begin session.
OPAC: Acknowledges user's command.
(At this point, some multipurpose automated systems require the user to indicate a wish to search the library catalog, as opposed to some other file on the system, such as a community information file or library events calendar. When the user initiates the appropriate action to select the library catalog file, the OPAC will acknowledge the selection.)
USER: Enters a search statement.
OPAC: Provides "first-level retrieval" of records conforming to the user's search statement.
USER: Manipulates and refines results of first-level retrieval in order to eventually display record(s) desired.
OPAC: Responds accordingly to manipulation and refinement until the user terminates the session or enters a new search statement.
USER: Enters command to terminate session.
OPAC: Acknowledges user's command.

OPACs vary in the extent to which each stage in this general sequence is explicitly necessary, especially in the earliest and latest steps—the begin-session, file-selection, and terminate-session procedures. Many OPACs do not require the user to instruct the system that a new search session is about to begin or to explicitly select the catalog file. Instead, the OPAC is constantly set for a bibliographic search, enabling the user to begin searching immediately on arrival at the terminal. Similarly, many OPACs do not require the user to explicitly inform the system when a session is completed. The user terminates the session simply by walking away from the terminal, and the display remains on the screen until a new search statement is entered.

Even when specific begin-session or end-session procedures are required or available, their execution is normally simple and straightforward. The real substance of interaction occurs between the time a user enters a search statement and the time at which he or she feels the search is completed. The end of a search may be the display of a single bibliographic record for an item, a list of abbreviated bibliographic records containing one or more of the desired items, or a response or display that leads the user to conclude that the item or items are not in the catalog.

The dialogue from entry of a search statement through final resolution may require any number of user-initiated actions and system responses. The more specific manner in which various OPACs handle the stages outlined above is examined in the next chapter. But in terms of the general nature of the user interface, it is important here to comment on two of the stages in particular. The first involves entry of a valid search statement and the initial system retrieval of appropriate records. In some OPACs, this stage consists of a single step by the user and a single response by the system. In others, there are two or more interactive steps involved. For example, the user may first be required to indicate the type of search being conducted—author, title, subject, whatever—to which the system responds by acknowledging the type and issuing instructions to enter search terms. The user then keys in the appropriate term or terms, and the system responds by providing first-level retrieval of all records in the database matching the two-step search statement. Some OPACs, depending on the complexity of the search statement, require even more than two interactive steps before the statement is complete and records are retrieved.

The second major stage of interaction involves the manipulation and refinement of the search results provided by the system at the first level of retrieval. If the search is satisfied at the first level, this will be unnecessary. In many cases, however, the search is not satisfied at the first stage, and final resolution may require several steps in manipulating and refining the initial results. For example, a user may seek full bibliographic detail about a specific work, but can remember only one or two words in the title. If the words are very general, for example, "History" or "Education," a keyword title search will retrieve a large number of records at the first level. To identify the specific work and arrive at a full bibliographic display, the user may have to wade through a rather lengthy discourse with the system.

These two crucial stages of interaction—entry of a search statement and manipulation and refinement of first-level results—are, in fact, part of a continuum in interaction with an online catalog. The distinction between them is made partly on the basis of convenience for purposes of discussion, but also partly on the basis of the crucial role that first-level retrieval plays in establishing the context for subsequent interaction.

There are few areas in OPAC design that exhibit as much diversity as does presentation of the initial system response to a search statement. First-level retrieval in some OPACs involves simply an indication of the number of records retrieved, even if there is only one. The user must then enter another command to actually see any bibliographic information at all. Another approach indicates the number of records retrieved, but immediately displays bibliographic information if only one record is retrieved. Other OPACs display at least some bibliographic detail at the first level, even if a number of records are retrieved. The way in which this is done, however, can vary considerably. For searches where very large numbers of records are retrieved, some OPACs group individual records at a general level if necessary so that everything can be summarized on a single screen display. In others, the first level consists of brief bibliographic information about each item, regardless of the number retrieved or the number of screens required for brief display, so long as a system limit is not exceeded. In some OPACs, the system automatically scrolls through the entire list of entries until the user initiates some action to freeze the display. In others, a single "page" of entries is fixed, and the user must then enter a command in order to see subsequent pages of information, one at a time. A variable in this approach is the criterion used for arranging individual entries in the list. The basis for arrangement of records in such a listing can vary from one OPAC to another. Entries are displayed in some online catalogs alphabetically according to author, title, or subject heading. The primary basis in others is reverse chronological order by date of publication. In still others, the basis is by some principle strictly internal to the system or something that may not be immediately apparent to the user, such as sequentially by system-supplied bibliographic record control number.

These examples underscore the diversity among OPACs at this crucial stage of interaction. Whatever method is employed, the first level of retrieval is the starting point from which interaction between user and online catalog will progress.

For any of the stages of dialogue outlined previously, there are specific issues that have a direct bearing on the degree to which an OPAC can clarify and assist interaction between a user and the catalog. Some of these are examined in the next chapter. But underlying the specific issues are more general concerns that are pertinent to the user/system/catalog interactive process regardless of the stage at which interaction is occurring. Among the more important of these general concerns are the explicit features designed to assist the user in conducting dialogue with the system, the language and related conventions employed in OPACs, the nature of the progression of dialogue, and the extent to which a system accommodates different levels of users. These are discussed below.

User-Assistance Features

Earlier we divided the sequence of dialogue between a user and an OPAC into general stages. The length and complexity of dialogue can vary from one OPAC to another and from one search session to another on the same system, but a requirement of any OPAC is that the dialogue must be carried out according to a specific set of rules and within the range of options designed into the system itself. At least at this time, conversation with any OPAC is not entirely free-form. An OPAC will understand only certain instructions expressed in a prescribed way, and often only at certain points within the course of the dialogue. A command that is valid at one step in the dialogue may not be valid at another. Thus, the range of commands available, the manner in which they must be expressed, and the timing with which they may be used are all strictly defined by the system. For meaningful dialogue to occur, the burden of adjusting to all those limits is on the user. It is the user who must learn, understand, and conform to the syntax and semantics of the system, not the other way around.

Despite occasional protests to the contrary by some OPAC designers, the rules of operation and conventions of dialogue are not self-evident in most OPACs. A user does not simply intuit the available commands or how and when they are to be entered. They must either be learned and remembered at some point, or the various requirements must be obviously presented to the user on a step-by-step basis during each search session.

In response to these needs, OPAC designers have tried to build in various online mechanisms to assist a user in carrying out his or her portion of the dialogue. Some of these address short-term and very specific needs, informing the user at any particular moment in a dialogue about the options available at that point and how they may be exercised. Others are more general or long term. The form in which, and the extent to which, such features are provided vary tremendously among OPACs, but they can be grouped into six general categories:

1. General explanatory messages.
2. Search history: messages indicating what has been done at a previous step or steps during a search.
3. Options and prompts: messages indicating what options are available for the user's next action and how they may be exercised.
4. Error detection: messages displayed in response to an invalid command entered by the user.
5. HELP screens.
6. Online tutorials.

User assistance features do not always fall distinctly into one and only one of these categories. For example, a message explaining a user error might also outline the options available for the user's next action; a message in response to a valid command that outlines the options available at that point might also explain what was just done. More often than not, however, these different types of messages and the user-assistance features they signify are independently identifiable, even when two or more are represented on a single screen display.

General explanatory messages. Most OPACs provide messages outlining the general limits of using the system. Frequently, these messages are concentrated on an introductory screen displayed at the beginning of a search session. They commonly carry the following types of information:

General library data: name of library, hours the system is available, and so on.

Files available on the system (library catalog, community calendar, and the like).

Scope of coverage of the bibliographic database.

List of commands or features that may be used during a search session.

Options available for searching (author, title, subject, etc.).

How to enter a search statement.

How to retrieve detailed online HELP screens.

Where to obtain offline assistance.

No existing OPAC can provide all of these types of information on a single screen display, and some types are less commonly included than others. A list of files available on the system, for example, is necessary only on multipurpose systems in which the user must select the library catalog file as opposed to some other. A complete list of all commands that may be used at any point during a search is sometimes presented on a separate HELP screen, or not in summary fashion at all. Figures 13-1 through 13-3 illustrate some introductory screen displays used in OPACs.

Although general explanatory messages are usually emphasized on introductory displays or outlined in fuller detail on separate HELP screens, some may be included on displays at stages of the dialogue as well. This is most often in the form of messages reminding the user of the major options available for searching, the procedures required to enter a new search statement, or the command required to retrieve a HELP screen either general in content or specific to the step that has been reached in the dialogue. An example of this type is shown in Figure 13-4.

Search history. Some OPACs can keep track and inform the user of dialogue that has occurred up through any given point in a search. Few, however, have this capability beyond repeating, as part of a system response, the single most recent command entered by the user; for an example, see Figure 13-4.

A number of OPACs, in fact, do not even go so far as to repeat the most recent command; instead, they simply display a response without repeating the command or terms that led to that response. Not sur-

---

```
LUIS:  ' LIBRARY USER INFORMATION SERVICE                                L9QA

         LUIS can be used to find BIBLIOGRAPHIC, CALL NUMBER and LOCATION
information for materials held by Northwestern University Libraries and by
the Garrett/Seabury Library.  (Use the card catalog for materials not in the
LUIS database.)  CIRCULATION information for materials charged out through
the computerized system is also available.

TYPES OF SEARCHES:                              COMMANDS:
- FOR INTRODUCTORY SCREEN FOR TITLE SEARCHES:   Type t
                         AUTHOR SEARCHES:        Type a
                         SUBJECT SEARCHES:       Type s

- FOR USERS ALREADY FAMILIAR WITH LUIS:         Type t=, a=, s=, st=, or sm=,
  (To start a search from any screen)           followed by a SEARCH TERM
                                                 (title, author, or subject)

- FOR CIRCULATION INFORMATION SCREEN:           Type d
  (Available for the Evanston Campus main       (call no. must be known)
  and Science-Engineering libraries only)

TO CORRECT A MISTAKE, type over the error or clear screen to start over.

TYPE COMMAND AND PRESS ENTER
```

Figure 13-1 Northwestern University's LUIS, introductory screen. From this (or any) screen, a user may select a more detailed author, title, or subject introductory screen.

Welcome to TOMUS
The On-Line Multiple User System

TOMUS contains records for books in many libraries in this geographic area.

To look for a particular subject, type FIND SUBJECT (or just F S), then the
subject, for example, FIND SUBJECT SOLAR ENERGY, or F S MUSHROOMS.

To look for an author, type FIND AUTHOR (or just F A), then the author,
for example, FIND AUTHOR MARK TWAIN, or F A JOSEPH CONRAD.

To look for a title, type FIND TITLE (or just F T), then the title, for
example, FIND TITLE LIFE ON THE MISSISSIPPI, or F T VICTORY.

To look for a book by author and title, type FIND AUTHOR, the author
AND TITLE, then the title, for example, FIND AUTHOR CONRAD AND TITLE VICTORY.

After you have typed one of the above commands, press the key marked RETURN to
start the search. After TOMUS completes the search and reports, type DIPLAY
and press the RETURN key to see information on the books TOMUS has found.

There are many other ways to use the system to look for books. For more
information, type HELP and press the RETURN key.

>

Figure 13-2 Carlyle Systems' TOMUS, initial screen display.

```
      ***** WELCOME TO THE PHOENIX SYSTEM *****
      FOR THE LATEST DEVELOPMENTS IN PHOENIX, TYPE    NEWS

To learn how to use the PHOENIX system, press the key marked CLEAR and then
press the key marked LESSON. (On terminals outside the Library, type  LESSON.)

If you do not understand a response, type a question mark
If you need help, type  HELP

For information on available databases, type   ?BASES

You are now connected to the LIBRARY data base.
ENTER COMMAND
```

Figure 13-3 University of New Brunswick's PHOENIX, initial screen display.

```
LUIS SEARCH REQUEST:   A=COMMONER
  AUTHOR/TITLE INDEX -- 7 ENTRIES FOUND
   1  NU:COMMONER BARRY +ALTERNATIVE TECHNOLOGIES FOR POWER PRODUCTION PREP <1975
   2  NU:COMMONER BARRY +BALANCE AND BIOSPHERE A RADIO SYMPOSIUM ON THE ENV <1971
   3  NU:COMMONER BARRY +CLOSING CIRCLE NATURE MAN AND TECHNOLOGY <1971
   4  NU:COMMONER BARRY +HUMAN WELFARE THE END USE FOR POWER PREPARED FOR T <1975
   5  NU:COMMONER BARRY +POLITICS OF ENERGY <1979
   6  NU:COMMONER BARRY +POVERTY OF POWER ENERGY AND THE ECONOMIC CRISIS <1976
   7  NU:COMMONER BARRY +SOCIAL COSTS OF POWER PRODUCTION PREPARED FOR THE <1975


TYPE LINE NO. FOR BIBLIOGRAPHIC RECORD WITH CALL NO.
TYPE e TO START OVER.   TYPE h FOR HELP.
TYPE COMMAND AND PRESS ENTER
```

Figure 13-4 Northwestern University's LUIS. Message on this display informs user that a HELP screen may be retrieved at this point in a dialogue. Included in the top line of display is a repeat of search strategy to which the system has responded.

prisingly this can lead to confusion, especially if the user has made an error in entering a search term. For example, if in Figure 13-4 the user had mistakenly keyed in "Comoner" as an author term rather than "Commoner," the system would probably have replied that there were no such entries in the catalog. If the search term was not repeated as part of the system response, the user would probably surmise either that he or she misspelled the term or that the library did not own any materials by an author whose surname was Commoner. One cannot assume that the user would conclude the former over the latter. Even in OPACs that do repeat the user's previous command as part of the response, there is always the possibility that the user will not read the screen thoroughly enough to realize that a term was misspelled or that a command was entered inappropriately, but such a feature at least attempts to give clearer explanations of system responses to user commands.

Options and prompts.   Along with each response to a valid user command, some OPACs display messages that can assist in selecting and executing the next step in the dialogue. In some cases, these messages only inform the user of which options may be exercised at that point. In others, the actual procedures required to exercise each option are also explicitly stated. The types of messages that provide either or both levels of assistance generally fall into one of three major categories.

1. Questions prompting the user to answer yes or no.
2. Lists of alternative actions that can be taken at that point, sometimes including how to exercise each.
3. Textual or other prompts that indicate where a command is to be entered.

There are several variations within each category, and some OPACs incorporate all three approaches at one point or another during a dialogue. Figures 13-5 through 13-8 illustrate messages in Geac's online public-access module to inform users of optional courses of action available at various points in a dialogue. In Figure 13-5, the user is presented a number of options for the next step, in addition to a textual prompt indicating where to enter the command to initiate that step. If the user enters the letter "T," indicating a title search, the system responds by displaying the screen illustrated in Figure 13-6. There is another textual message demonstrated here, indicating where to key in the desired title.

The options available to a user may differ according to the specific point that has been reached in a dialogue. As a result, not all commands will be equally valid under all circumstances. Compare the display screens in Figures 13-5, 13-7, and 13-8; each lists options available at a specific

---

023 DEVELOPMENT SYSTEM   - GEAC LIBRARY SYSTEM-   *CHOOSE SEARCH

WHAT TYPE OF SEARCH DO YOU WISH TO DO?

    1. TIL - TITLE, JOURNAL TITLE, SERIES TITLE, ETC.

    2. AUT - AUTHOR, ILLUSTRATOR, EDITOR, ORGANIZATION, CONFERENCE, ETC.

    3. A-T - COMBINATION OF AUTHOR AND TITLE.

    4. SUB - SUBJECT HEADING ASSIGNED BY LIBRARY.

    5. NUM - CALL NUMBER, ISBN, ISSN, ETC.

    6. KEY - ONE WORD TAKEN FROM A TITLE, AUTHOR OR SUBJECT.

ENTER NUMBER OR CODE: ¶¶   THEN PRESS SEND

Figure 13-5 Geac's Online Public Catalog Module. Initial screen display outlining search options and instructions for entering next command.

023 DEVELOPMENT SYSTEM   -GEAC LIBRARY SYSTEM-   *TITLE SEARCH

START AT THE BEGINNING OF THE TITLE AND ENTER AS MANY
WORDS OF THE TITLE AS YOU KNOW BELOW.

Ex: WUTHERING HEIGHTS

Ex: HOW TO SUCCEED IN BUSINESS WITHOUT

ENTER TITLE: ¶¶   THEN PRESS SEND

Figure 13-6 Geac's Online Public Catalog Module. Screen display on which search terms are to be entered.

023 DEVELOPMENT SYSTEM   -GEAC LIBRARY SYSTEM-   *TITLE SEARCH

YOUR TITLE: ACID   MATCHES 2 TITLES

                                              NO. OF
CITATIONS IN ENTIRE CATALOG
  1 ACID-HOSE/   1
  2 ACID RAIN : THE NORTH AMERCIAN FORECAST/   1

TYPE A NUMBER TO SEE MORE INFORMATION -OR-
    FOR - MOVE FORWARD IN THIS LIST   BAC - MOVE BACKWARD IN THIS LIST
    CAT - BEGIN A NEW SEARCH
ENTER NUMBER OR CODE: ¶¶   THEN PRESS SEND

Figure 13-7 Geac's Online Public Catalog Module. List of brief records retrieved on basis of search terms entered.

step in a search on the Geac system. For example, entry of the command "FUL" presented as an option in Figure 13-8 to examine the full bibliographic record for this particular title presupposes that the user has conducted and refined a search to the point where a brief record for a single title has been displayed. This command would be meaningless if entered at the point represented in any of the preceding three figures, since the required condition for the command had not yet been met.

```
023 DEVELOPMENT SYSTEM        -GEAC LIBRARY SYSTEM-        *TITLE SEARCH
   AUTHOR: HOWARD, ROSS, 1946-
   TITLE: ACID RAIN : THE NORTH AMERICAN FORECAST/
   IMPRINT:TORONTO, ONT. : ANANSI, c1980.

                    LOAN    CALL                CPY
   LOCATION         TYPE    NUMBER              #    STATUS
   BMAIN                    TD885.5.S85H68      1



   FUL - SEE COMPLETE CITATION           IND - SEE LIST OF HEADINGS
   HLD - PLACE A HOLD ON THIS ITEM       CAT - BEGIN A NEW SEARCH

   ENTER CODE: ¶¶                               THEN PRESS SEND
```

Figure 13-8 Geac's Online Public Catalog Module. Copy level and status information display of single bibliographic record.

Not all OPACs are this comprehensive in informing the user at each point in a dialogue about the options available as the next step. In Figure 13-9, for example, the user is instructed how to carry out either of two options, that of displaying more of the titles retrieved for a search or that of checking on availability, but there is no mention that other courses of action are in fact open at that point, nor are there instructions as to what those other options are or how to exercise them. In Figure 13-10, the user is not given any online guidance about how to display more complete information about the title, how to begin a new search, or how to exercise any other option that might be available at that point, and in fact, there is no mention at all of which options are available at this point.

The examples in Figures 13-9 and 13-10 may seem somewhat extreme in the dearth of online guidance they provide, but they are not really so exceptional. To the contrary, some of the examples cited earlier are exemplary in the degree to which they explicitly inform the user of options available and how to exercise them. Some OPACs lacking in online point of progress guidance sometimes rely primarily on such features as separate online HELP screens and offline guide cards, instructional pamphlets, and so on, to provide assistance to the user.

Error detection. When unfamiliarity with computerized systems in general, and online catalogs in particular, is combined with the stringency of rules and conventions required for dialogue with an OPAC,

```
        BENSON, E. F.  (EDWARD FREDERIC),  1867-1940                      (107 TITLES)
    01                              ALAN
    02                              ALL ABOUT LUCIA                      1940
    03                              ARUNDEL                             1915
    04                              AS WE ARE
    05                              AS WE WERE* A VICTORIAN PEEP SHOW    1934
    06                              AS WE WERE; A VICTORIAN PEEP SHOW    1937
    07                              THE BABE, B. A.; BEING THE UNEVENTFUL 1897
    08                              THE BLOTTING BOOK                    1908
    09                              The blotting book /                 1976 FBR
    10                              THE CHALLONERS                      1904
    PAGE 1   FOR MORE TITLES ENTER PG2; FOR AVAILABILITY ENTER DSL/ AND LINE NO.
```

Figure 13-9 Ohio State University's LCS. User is instructed how to display more brief records retrieved by the search and how to check availability status, but is not advised as to other options available at this point in the dialogue.

```
PPL> A/MICHENER,JAMES
Barcode:101127777          Patron:000000000        DueDate:None
F           MICHENER,J                              LastUse:27-May-82
            CENTENNIAL
MICH        LCCN:74-005164                          InvDate:20-Feb-79
Broadmkt Branch                                     TotCirc:15
```

Figure 13-10 Pikes Peak Library District's Maggie's Place. Default format for display of bibliographic record. Screen display does not inform user of dialogue options available at this point.

one result is that there is bound to be a certain amount of miscommunication and misunderstanding between the user and the system. The ways in which a user contributes to a breakdown in dialogue vary in degree and kind. So do the ways in which the system responds.

In terms of system response, the primary distinction is whether the system can detect that the user has made a mistake. If not, the request will be processed as though correct: for instance, when a user simply misspells a search term. If the command itself was structured correctly, an OPAC cannot tell that the search term was misspelled, and it will attempt to retrieve records and display a response on the basis of the misspelled term.

For certain types of mistakes, however, the system may be able to recognize that the user has made an error. This usually occurs when a user has misspelled the command name itself (as opposed to just the search term), has tried to use a particular command at a point in the dialogue where it is not allowed, or has entered more search terms than are permitted in a single statement. These and other possibilities have a common source: The user has made a request that the system recognizes as contradictory to the basic set of rules and conventions required for dialogue. The system does not fully understand what the user is trying to do. It cannot process the request in a normal fashion, but it can detect the fact that miscommunication has occurred.

The exact forms of system response under such circumstances vary, but they generally fall somewhere within the following four levels. The system

1. recognizes that an error has been made and responds in a prescribed manner;
2. responds by including an explicit acknowledgment that an error has been detected;
3. attempts to explain why it considers the user's request to have been an error;
4. suggests what corrective action should be taken.

The relationship among these levels is usually hierarchical. It would be possible, of course, for an OPAC to respond to an error only by suggesting corrective action, without explicitly stating that an error had been made and without any attempt to explain why the user's action was considered an error, but this is unusual. In practice, a response at one of the four levels almost always includes action or explanation pertinent not only to that level, but also to each level preceding it.

In general, assistance to online users in response to errors is not well developed in OPACs. A number of OPACs do not interact at even the second level of response. One OPAC, for example, merely displays the "begin-session" screen when an error is detected, regardless of the point to which the search has progressed, and without any explicit statement that an error has been made. Others respond simply by redisplaying whatever was on the screen at the time that the erroneous command was entered, again without explicit acknowledgment of an error or statement explaining why the system responded in that manner.

Most OPACs, however, do respond at least at the second level of error detection, displaying a new screen that includes an explicit statement noting an input error. Some stop at this level, with no further elaboration about why the command was in error or how it could be corrected, thus giving the user only minimal assistance. The language in which the acknowledgment is stated is often cryptic if not downright unsettling for an inexperienced user. Messages such as "Error Type 23" or "You have entered an Illegal Command" are likely to be discouraging to the novice, whose level of confidence in approaching the catalog may not have been very high in the first place.

More and more, efforts are being made in OPAC design to provide error messages that are meaningful in content and positive in tone, explaining the nature of an error or indicating why the system is unable to process a command, and in some cases even suggesting what corrective action should be taken. In earlier OPAC designs, however, cryptic statements predominated even at these levels, as illustrated by the following examples cited by Salmon:[6]

> You have attempted to change the TYPRUN OPTION, whose value is fixed for your terminal and cannot be changed. The value of the TYPRUN OPTION for the terminal is "$TYPRUN."

> The format requested was unclear. The command should be entered:
> Format: D Set#/Format/Display Option
> Example: D 1/LTTL/ABST

The first example does in a way attempt to explain why the system considers the user's command to be in error, but its content is about as comforting, and as useful, as an "Illegal Command" message. The second example has detected the nature of an error and has even shown the user how to format the command properly, but the corrective action is still offered in summary OPAC language rather than being explained in easily understandable language. Contrast these examples with the display in Figure 13-11, which explains an error and suggests corrective action in terms that are likely to be easily understandable even to novice users.

Regardless of the clarity and comprehensiveness with which OPAC messages explain errors detected by the system, there is still the question of miscommunication that is not automatically detectable. A user may enter a command or terms in a search statement that are perfectly valid from the system's point of view, but that do not really represent the action the user wishes to take. Because a system cannot provide

---

```
Your last search command did not include any terms, or
keywords, to search.  When you retype your command,
please be sure it includes at least one word to search.

For related information, type

    HELP KEYWORD      HELP FIND      HELP AND       HELP OR
    HELP COMMAND      HELP BROWSE    HELP AND NOT
```

Figure 13-11 Carlyle Systems' TOMUS explanatory message received after an error has been detected and a request for help entered.

information about, or suggest corrective action to, mistakes that it cannot detect, these sorts of errors are potentially the most damaging to a dialogue. Some techniques, such as repeating the user's command as part of the system response, can provide some help, but they still rely solely on the user and not the system to recognize the mistake.

A rather exceptional feature has been incorporated into the OPAC at the Washington University School of Medicine Library, which attempts to provide at least some level of error detection beyond the fundamental rules and conventions required for dialogue. In the event that no records are retrieved on a search term, the system automatically modifies the user's term by omitting vowels, double consonants, and final s's, and then searches the modified term against index terms that have been created similarly. The result is that, under certain conditions, appropriate records can be retrieved even when a search term has been misspelled.[7] This feature, while certainly not foolproof, goes one step further than most OPACs in attempting to incorporate greater tolerance of user errors into the system. No matter what sophisticated features are included, OPACs will not automatically detect all types of user mistakes, but this problem is certainly not unique to online forms of library catalogs. And, in fact, OPACs have a far greater capacity for recognizing user errors than do any other forms of the library catalog.

HELP screens. Most OPACs provide some degree of online assistance in the form of special HELP screens, which contain information describing various aspects of using the system. Their function is not unlike that sometimes provided on general "begin-session" displays or in informative error messages, but these screens are usually displayed in response to a specific, user-initiated request for aid.

The available number of HELP screens ranges from only one or a few on some OPACs, to 30 to 40 on others, to more than 150 on the University of California's MELVYL system. On OPACs that provide comparatively few, the instructional data are usually quite general and related to major stages of a dialogue. The HELP screen in Figure 13-12 is retrieved on the ULISYS system when a user keys in the command "Help" prior to a search. It summarizes the types of searches that may be made and how they must be constructed.

On OPACs with a greater number of HELP screens, explanation is usually offered on several levels ranging from the very general to the more specific. The more specific levels of detail may provide guidance related to the use of particular commands, access points, or system features such as Boolean searching or truncation, and they sometimes pertain to specific points that have been reached in a dialogue.

A detailed HELP screen available on Northwestern University's LUIS system is illustrated in Figure 13-13. It is displayed on request after the

```
UNIVERSAL LIBRARY SYSTEM
ULISYS CONTROL PROGRAM
PLEASE ENTER FUNCTION CODE? O


                     UNIVERSAL LIBRARY SYSTEMS
                  Welcome to our automated catalogue

               Please follow these simple instructions

To search by, Enter, Followed by,          Example,

AUTHOR         AU=    Author's name         AU=HOFFMAN STANLEY
TITLE          TI=    Title of work         TI=PRIMACY OR WORLD ORDER
AUTHOR/TITLE   AT=    Author/title          AT=HOFFMAN / PRIMACY
SUBJECT        SU=    Subj, heading         SU=UNITED STATES

For RESERVE BOOK ROOM items you may also search by .........

COURSE         CO=    Course name           CO=ARTS
INSTRUCTOR     IN=    Instructor name       IN=BROWN A
COURSE/INSTR   CI=    Course/instr,         CI=ARTS 101/BROWN A

Then press the RETURN key to send the message to the computer,
For more detailed HELP instructions type MORE HELP and press
the RETURN key,
?
```

Figure 13-12 Universal Library Systems' ULISYS. General HELP screen outlining search options available and providing instructions on how to carry them out.

```
LUIS SEARCH REQUEST:  S=UNIONS
          Possible reasons for the message NO SUBJECT HEADINGS FOUND:

1.  Your request is not in the subject heading form used in one of the three
    subject headings lists used in LUIS.  To learn more about subject searching:
    a)  Type s -- for all materials in LUIS except:
    b)  Type st -- for most materials in the Transportation Library
    c)  Type sm -- for most materials in the Medical Library

2.  No materials are in the LUIS database under the subject heading you have
    used.  Consult the appropriate subject headings list for related subject
    headings, or check the card catalog for materials not in LUIS.
    (Type s or st or sm for information on the subject headings lists.)

3.  A typographic or spelling error was made in search term.

4.  An inappropriate command code was used (e.g., s= used for searching
    a medical subject).
IMPORTANT:  When unsure of spelling or form, try shortening search term.
FOR INTRODUCTION TO LUIS, type e

IF YOU NEED MORE INFORMATION, ask a library staff member.

TYPE COMMAND AND PRESS ENTER
```

Figure 13-13 Northwestern University's LUIS. HELP screen displayed in response to user-initiated HELP command after system has retrieved no records for subject search term entered by user.

system has informed a user that no records were retrieved after a subject search. The HELP screen repeats the entered subject term and suggests possible reasons why no records were retrieved. If the user concludes that the first reason was the source of the problem, he or she might take the OPAC's advice and enter the command "s" to see a more complete explanation about subject searching for materials in the main library. The system would then display the subject introductory screen shown in Figure 13-14. A user may, however, request that screen without first retrieving the screen in Figure 13-13.

Of all existing OPACs, the MELVYL system on the University of California campuses has the most extensive array of HELP screens. Many pertain to specific circumstances and are most relevant at certain points of progress in a dialogue. When requested in reaction to a system-supplied error message, the data on some HELP screens are somewhat diagnostic. If, for example, a list of six entries has been retrieved and the user requests fuller bibliographic information about a seventh record, the following error message is shown:

You have asked to display record numbers that do not exist.

If the user then enters a HELP command, the system's response is:

You have asked for a display of record number 7, but your search result contains only 6 records.

```
TO SEARCH BY SUBJECT:                              EXAMPLES:

- TYPE s= followed by a subject term or portion    s=television  s=shakesp
  of subject.                                      s=symbolism in art

To determine the subject headings used in LUIS,
you may wish to consult the Library of Congress
Subject Headings (LCSH) list. This two-volume
red book is available near library terminals.
EXAMPLE: LCSH indicates that materials on labor
         unions will be found under "Trade-unions"
         but not under "Labor-unions", "Unions",
         or "Labor, organized". ,
FOR MORE INFORMATION ABOUT USING LCSH, TYPE m

NOTE: Most Transportation Library subjects must      EXAMPLES:
      be searched by st= and Medical Library         st=urban transit
      subjects by sm= ; type st or sm for details.   sm=vestibular nuclei


TYPE t FOR INTRODUCTION TO TITLE SEARCHES, OR a FOR AUTHOR.
TYPE e TO START OVER.
TYPE COMMAND AND PRESS ENTER
```

Figure 13-14 Northwestern University's LUIS. Subject HELP screen explaining general parameters of subject searching on the system.

You may not ask for a display of a record number greater than 6. To read more about the DISPLAY command, type HELP DISPLAY.

It is extremely important that, after display of either a user-requested HELP screen or a system-initiated error message, the point of progress in a dialogue is not lost. The user should be able either to return immediately to the point in the dialogue reached before a HELP screen or error message was displayed, or even to proceed from the HELP or error display directly to the next logical step. Although this capability is fairly common to OPACs, in some a request for HELP or a system-detected error will mean that the user has to begin the search all over again.

Online tutorials. Probably the most elaborate form of online assistance that an OPAC can offer is programmed tutorial instruction. Rather than being problem- or situation-specific, an online tutorial is more a teaching facility than a "moment-of-need" reminder. Few existing OPACs currently provide a fully developed online instructional package. Although such a feature might be useful, it does presume two conditions. First, it implies that the rules and conventions required for dialogue are too complex, or at least not self-evident enough, for effective communication without formal instruction. Second, its value would ultimately depend on the inclination of users to take advantage of it.

Both of those conditions run counter to trends detected in most OPAC-use studies. Users generally prefer to be led through a dialogue on a step-by-step basis, getting point-of-progress assistance only when necessary. They do not want to spend a great deal of time and energy reading about how to use the system and memorizing rules and conventions. Some users might indeed welcome such features and would be glad to use them, but OPAC designers should never view online tutorials as a substitute for clarity and completeness provided as part of routine system responses during interactive dialogue. Such a shifting of priorities would ultimately detract from the overall suitability of an online catalog. An online tutorial can be of value, but only if intended as additional to, not in lieu of, other types of online user assistance.

Language of the Dialogue

Each of the system features already described can play a crucial role in determining the ease with which a user can carry out a dialogue with an online catalog. But merely incorporating any or all of these features into an OPAC does not ensure their usefulness. The manner in which they are presented is equally important, and one of the most critical elements in this is language: the terminology used to convey messages, to prompt commands, to explain options, and so on. The difference between a feature itself and its mode of expression can be illustrated by an example cited earlier. An error message was displayed informing the user that he or she had attempted to change the TYPRUN OPTION, whose value was fixed and could not be altered. The user probably had not the faintest idea of what a TYPRUN OPTION was, much less wanting to change it. From the message displayed, the user may have been able to surmise that the intended command had been entered incorrectly, but that conclusion was not part of the actual language used in the error message.

That example may be extreme, but in fact most OPACs do use a great deal of specialized system and other jargon. Generally, the language carries a certain degree of ambivalence in basic approach. There is a commitment to employ "natural-language" vocabulary, both expressed by the OPAC and required of the user, that as closely as possible resembles everyday conversational language. At the same time, there is also a strong and visible reliance on language that is not natural in any common conversational sense. It is, rather, "inside" language, specific either to the OPAC itself or in some cases to computerized systems or library catalogs in general. To understand inside language, the user must be familiar with it or clever enough to figure it out. In either case, at some point the user must learn new vocabulary that may have little or no application outside the specific context of the OPAC itself.

The two emphases in language—specialized and natural—are frequently interwoven into a single statement displayed by an OPAC or required of its users. In the following examples of system messages prompting the user's next action or stating one or more options available, the balance of emphasis is on specialized language.

ENTER (#, [ESC], CR, 'T', 'B', Un, Dn, +XX):

[ESC]-> START AGAIN

ENTER ENTRY # TO DISPLAY, F2 TO VIEW OVERHEAD, F4 TO VIEW BACK, F1 TO EXIT

VALID COMMANDS FROM THIS DISPLAY: a= t= e i b

These instructions and explanations are specific to the rules and conventions for dialogue in the OPAC in which they occur; even given that context, they are by no means self-evident. At some point, a user will have to learn the function of the codes on that particular OPAC. Compare those system messages with the following, in which a greater balance of emphasis is on natural language.

For more information, type HELP and depress the RETURN key

If you want to see the full bibliographic description, press RETURN

Choose from this list, enter here:

Enter the letter that corresponds to what you want, then press SEND

    T-Look for a book using a TITLE

    A-Look for a book using an AUTHOR

    C-Look for a book using a CALL NUMBER

    S-Look for a book using a SUBJECT

    X-Go back to Main selection menu

ENTER:

To determine the location and availability of a specific title, type ST=
followed by the line number. EXAMPLE: ST=2 and RETURN.

The language used in these messages far more clearly instructs the user
what to do or what options are available. The last expression does
require entry of rather cryptic language— ST=—to exercise an option,
but its use is at least explained in natural-language terms and an example is provided.

There is yet another, more subtle level at which OPAC language can
be specialized. It consists of terminology that may be natural in the
sense that users are likely to be familiar with it even outside the OPAC
environment, but that can still have specialized and very specific meaning within the OPAC environment. For example, instructions such as
ENTER, EXIT, press RETURN, and *SEND* are common English-language terms, but their meaning must be understood in the context of
the OPAC itself. Such instructions may be clear to those experienced in
using some type of computerized system, but not all users will have that
experience.

The specialized meanings of natural-language terminology in OPACs
apply not only to "system" vocabulary, but also to the vocabulary of
librarianship. Phrases such as "main entry," "copy number," "full bibliographic record," "Library of Congress Subject Heading," and many
others displayed on OPACs all use fairly common terminology, but the
way in which the words are combined produces a special meaning in
the context of the library catalog that is probably not obvious to most
users. Even such an innocuous term as "author" can cause confusion
under some circumstances. In OPACs with the traditional distinctions
of author, title, and subject for searching, for example, a user who
wishes to see a list of books *about* rather than *by* an author must treat
the author's name as a subject term rather than as the name of an

author. This may be an easy distinction for librarians, but it may not be self-evident to all OPAC users. In judging the appropriateness of terminology for presentation in OPACs, librarians should not only be wary of vocabulary that seems somewhat "computerese," but should take into account the effects of using their own jargon as well.

The language used in some OPACs draws appreciably on nonalphabetic characters, both in the presentation of information and in the command structure used in dialogue. In searching an online catalog, users may have to treat certain characters differently from the method that is usual in searching other forms of library catalogs. Most online systems, for example, recognize some nonalphabetic characters, particularly numerals, as valid in themselves. Thus, in searching for the title *50 Houses of Charleston, South Carolina,* users of some OPACs may have to enter the first word as *50,* not *fifty.* This runs exactly counter to the standard procedure in searching in card catalogs.

Punctuation within search terms can be another problem, and some OPACs have strict rules governing its use. In dealing with words, phrases, or abbreviations such as *O'Hara, Al-Hardalo, I/O,* or *I.W.W.* as search terms, some OPACs retrieve records only when the punctuation within the term has been entered in the search statement exactly as it appears in the appropriate field of the machine-stored bibliographic record or records. This places something of a burden on the user; he or she may not know the exact punctuation, and is certainly unlikely to know how it appears in the record until the record is actually retrieved. In contrast, some OPACs do not allow any punctuation within search terms, even though the punctuation will be displayed on the retrieved records. Still others are flexible, retrieving records whether the user includes or omits the appropriate punctuation within search terms.

Some OPACs rely heavily on the use of punctuation to separate major elements of information in search statements and bibliographic displays. Users frequently must separate elements of a search statement—for example, the command name or functional qualifier from the actual search terms—by some form of punctuation, most commonly a diagonal slash (/) or equals sign (=). In OPACs that permit Boolean searching, special provisions—sometimes in the form of punctuation—must be made for the user to differentiate between the function of certain words as Boolean operators and as normal search terms. In one OPAC, for example, the words *and, or, not* in a search statement are automatically assumed to represent Boolean operators separating the search terms on either side of the operator. If the user wants any of those words to function as a normal search term, he or she must place quotation marks around the word in the search statement (as "and").

In some OPACs, forms of punctuation are used to separate elements in bibliographic displays. In one OPAC, for example, imprint data are enclosed between a less-than sign (<) and a greater-than sign (>), and subject headings are separated by a diagonal slash followed by a number sign (/#). Although this practice tends to clutter the display with nondescriptive characters when used in excess, this use of punctuation does separate discrete pieces of information and is not really a problem unless the user infers that the characters signify something more than simply demarcation.

Most OPACs attempt to use natural, easy-to-understand language in explanatory messages, descriptions of options, bibliographic displays, and so on, but they have not broken entirely free of cryptic codes, computerese, and technical library jargon. In fact, it is doubtful that they could, or should even try to, free themselves entirely of specialized language. Terms such as *enter, entry, exit, record, index,* and so on, will always have different meanings and connotations depending on the context in which they are used. An OPAC is as legitimate a context as any other, and specificity of meaning in that context asks no more of catalog users than might be required when applying the terms in other contexts. Clear and understandable language should be part of the pursuit of user-friendly OPACs, but individuals will always have to learn certain precise meanings to carry on dialogue with an OPAC. This is not to say that OPAC languages should not be refined; on the contrary, there is still a great deal of room for improvement. The language used in OPACs must be balanced between the need for precision in a specialized context on the one hand, and the ease with which it can be learned, understood, and applied on the other.

Progression of Dialogue and Accommodation of Diversity

Many of the features already described relate to the clarity with which an OPAC can assist a user in progressing from one point in a dialogue to another. A related but somewhat broader question concerns the ease and speed with which a user may move around among various points or change the direction of a dialogue.

In general, OPACs impose fairly stringent limitations on the number of directions that a dialogue may take from a given point. At any juncture, the user will usually have two or more immediate options, but these will not necessarily include all the options that a user might see as the next logical step for his or her own purposes. The user will always be able to move the dialogue to a point where that desired option may be exercised, but it may require several separate steps to do so. For instance, an OPAC may contain the holdings of several different libraries. A user may complete an author search in one library's catalog, but find no records under the author's name. If the user wishes to search the same author in one of the other library's catalogs, several steps might be required just to get to the point where the same name can be searched in the other catalog.

The speed and ease with which an OPAC allows a user to move in various directions during a dialogue are dictated by design. In the example just given, greater complexity in progression is caused in part by the fact that the OPAC is multi-institutional, containing the catalogs of several different libraries. In a multi-institutional OPAC in which so many steps are required to execute the same search in different libraries' catalogs, a design assumption would have to had been made that a user was much more likely to want to search a single library's catalog for different items than different libraries' catalogs for the same item.

But even in OPACs where dialogue does not have to take into account such factors as switching from one library's catalog to another's, the progression through which dialogue must occur is usually rather inflexible and often requires several steps if the user wishes to change directions or otherwise exercise an option that is not immediately available at a given point of progress. One of the more common circumstances is when a user has begun or completed one search and decides to begin a new one. In a number of OPACs, three separate steps are required to enter the new search statement under these circumstances. First, the user must return to the main menu. He or she must then select the type of search desired: author, title, subject, and so on. When the OPAC acknowledges this second step, the user enters the search term or terms, the third step.

The limitation of options at any given juncture in a dialogue and the segmenting of dialogue into separate and distinct steps can actually be quite helpful for novice OPAC users, minimizing ambiguity and reducing the risk of a user's becoming overwhelmed and confused by a plethora of alternatives and different rules and conventions. Such actions emphasize simple and logical progression, proceeding one step at a time. For users who have little or no experience with computerized retrieval systems, who are unfamiliar with library catalogs, or who have very straightforward needs, such an approach can help them understand what is happening and gain greater confidence and skill in the use of an OPAC.

For the user who has greater experience or more complex needs in using an online catalog, the degree to which an OPAC tends to segment the progression of a dialogue can be something of a nuisance. The necessity of carrying out two or three or even more interactive steps to get to a logical nearby point in a dialogue can come to be seen as overly rigid, simplistic, and time consuming, leading to impatience and frustration on the part of the user.

Thus, OPAC design is faced with the formidable task of attempting to accommodate both novice and experienced users, and both simple and sophisticated needs. Some OPACs have tried to minimize this problem by building in at least a few optional capabilities that allow dialogue to be expedited, or more sophisticated features to be used, without compromising the availability of the simpler actions for those who are less experienced or who have less complex searching needs.

Among some of the features designed to expedite dialogue, one is to allow the user to "stack" commands, that is, to enter two or more commands in a single statement. For example, in an OPAC that normally requires two separate steps to enter search terms in a combined author/title search—one to enter an author's name and the other to enter the title—there might also be an optional procedure that enables the user to construct a single search statement containing both elements.

Another example of stacking commands, this one pertaining to commands for displaying bibliographic records, can be drawn from the MSUS/PALS online catalog. Like many OPACs, MSUS/PALS can display individual records in several different formats, each containing a different amount and arrangement of information about the same item. Although there is a "default" format that normally displays, a user also has the option of requesting a longer, more detailed version. When a search statement has retrieved several records, the user can select any one of them to display in the default format by entering the command DI for display, followed by the set number assigned to the record: for example, DI 3 for the third record in the set. When the default format displays, the user can then enter another command to display the long version of the record. But there is also an option for these two steps to be combined in a single statement, DI 3 L, which will immediately display the third record in a set in its longer format.

Although stacking commands enables a user to expedite dialogue by combining two or more steps that may otherwise be carried out separately, there are other, usually less powerful features available in many OPACs that can also reduce the amount of time and effort required of the user. The most common is simply to allow a user to abbreviate some of the language required in entering commands. For example, one OPAC allows the command name FIND to be entered in either its complete form or abbreviated as F. A number of OPACs offer similar options; they do not really affect the course of progression, but they do give a user the opportunity to reduce the amount of keying effort required.

The realized and potential ways in which OPACs can accommodate both novice and experienced users, frequent and infrequent users, and simple and complex needs all at the same time are important, but greatly complicated by two additional factors. First, the user population does not include simply novice and experienced users, or simply frequent and infrequent users. The overwhelming majority of OPAC users are occasional users who defy the simplistic dichotomy of novice versus experienced in any matter pertaining to OPAC use, whether it is familiarity with computerized systems, knowledge about library catalogs, or the complexity of their needs. A second and related factor is that these limits cannot always be stated even with respect to a single user. Each user will have his or her own mix of expertise and levels of retention when it comes to specific features and rules and conventions, and one person's strengths can be another's weaknesses.

The complexity and nonuniformity of the library-user population pose a tremendous challenge in the development and refinement of online catalogs. It is not a condition, however, that is unique or new to online versions of the library catalog. The same diversity influences catalog use whether one is dealing with card, COM, or online catalogs. The latter certainly brings in new elements in the form of computer terminals, interactive dialogue, and the possibility of more flexible retrieval techniques, but it also provides the opportunity to introduce mechanisms that can at least begin to address the question of diversity by enabling a single catalog to accommodate different levels of expertise, knowledge, and need without prejudice toward one group of users. Other forms of the library catalog have never been able to make this claim. OPACs have only just begun to address this issue, and there is no way of knowing how far it will be possible or desirable to go in developing hierarchically structured features that accommodate different levels of user need and even take into account such matters as increasing familiarity on the part of individual users.

The Limits of Online User Assistance

Assisting patrons and conducting formal instruction in the use of library catalogs are recognized functions of public service librarians. If carefully designed, the library catalog in its online form can assume some of these responsibilities, but it is unlikely that online user-assistance features will ever altogether obviate the librarians' role in providing aid and instruction in the use of the catalog. As Anne Lipow has noted with regard to online catalog use, "If there is a way to make a mistake, to misinterpret instructions, there will be a large number of users who find that way."[8]

There is a growing and already sizable oral history of miscommunication between OPACs and their users. The range of incidents is itself staggering, but two examples can illustrate a common type of misinterpretation and miscommunication. In describing online catalog use in four different libraries, Carole Weiss Moore noted that a common experience was for users, realizing that they had made a spelling or other error before transmitting a command, to try to delete the command from the screen by depressing seemingly logical keys marked "Clear," "Erase," "Rub Out," and so on—the results were never those desired, and such attempts often threw a search into near total collapse.[9] Lipow relates another experience at the University of California at Berkeley, also having to do with the use of the terminal keyboard: "I found a man the other day typing 'return' because my catalog instructs you to press return after keying your side of the transaction. He was indeed pressing R-E-T-U-R-N; he didn't realize there was a return key."[10] Some such problems could perhaps be at least partially alleviated through better system design and more user-friendly equipment or instructions. Especially in the first case, it is difficult to fault novice users for depressing inappropriate keys when the language on them seems to express exactly the action that they want at that point. But there is only so far that care in design can be expected to go in solving the multitude of problems that some users experience with online catalogs. In the second example, the misinterpretation might have been avoided if an instruction had elaborately informed the user to "depress the blue RETURN key located on the right-hand side of the keyboard" or some such statement. For each situation for which the more detailed message would add clarity, however, it would probably lead to confusion in another.

Especially given the contemporary environment into which online catalogs are being introduced, there will always be users, inexperienced with computerized retrieval systems or library catalogs or both, whose problems would not be avoided regardless of the clarity of instructions, the explicitness of error messages, or the number of HELP screens available. Explicitness and clarity of explanation should be guiding principles in the design of OPACs, but they are still not likely to eliminate the need for offline guidance materials and human assistance. If anything, the present state of OPAC design and the current environment in which online catalogs are being introduced argue for more, not less, offline assistance and formal instruction in the use of the library catalog. This need must be tempered, however, by a willingness to accept one of the long-term goals that should dictate the design of online catalogs: to make their effective use as free of reliance on outside assistance as possible. It is a goal that librarians should perceive as desirable, not threatening.

Notes

1. Charles R. Hildreth, "Pursuing the Ideal: First and Second Generation Online Public Access Catalogs" (paper presented at the ALA LITA/RTSD Preconference: Online Catalogs, Online Reference, June 23–24, 1983).

2. Joseph R. Matthews, *Public Access to Online Catalogs* (Weston, Conn.: Online, Inc., 1982), p. 113.

3. Charles Ammi Cutter, *Rules for a Dictionary Catalog*, 4th ed. (Washington, D.C.: Government Printing Office, 1904).

4. D. Kathryn Weintraub, "The Essentials or Desiderata of the Bibliographic Record as Discovered by Research," *Library Resources and Technical Services* 23 (Fall 1979): 392.

5. See Patrick Wilson, "The Catalog as Access Mechanism: Background and Concepts," *Library Resources and Technical Services* 27 (January/March 1983): 4–17.

6. Stephen R. Salmon, "Characteristics of Online Public Catalogs," *Library Resources and Technical Services* 27 (January/March 1983): 59.

7. *Ibid.*, p. 53.

8. Anne Grodzins Lipow, "Practical Considerations of the Current Capabilities of Subject Access in Online Public Catalogs," *Library Resources and Technical Services* 27 (January/March 1983): 85.

9. Carole Weiss Moore, "User Reactions to Online Catalogs: An Exploratory Study," *College and Research Libraries* 42 (July 1981): 301.

10. Lipow, "Practical Considerations," p. 85.

14

The Online Catalog: Dialogue, Searching, Bibliographic Display

The language in which dialogue occurs, the progression from one step to another, and the range of user assistance features are all crucial to the framework that makes up the interface between a user and an online catalog. They are important to all steps in a dialogue, not just to one particular stage or feature. This chapter focuses on interaction at several generalized stages of dialogue outlined earlier, concentrating on certain characteristics as they pertain to the retrieval and the presentation of bibliographic information. For many of these stages, there is considerable diversity in the approaches taken by existing OPACs.

Begin-Session Protocols

Some OPACs allow a user to directly enter a new search statement at almost any stage of a dialogue. Most, however, require a preliminary step in which the user must return to some type of initial screen display each time a search is begun. Whether the user has just approached a terminal or has already been conducting a search and wishes to start a new one, a command or set of commands must be entered to retrieve the "begin-session" screen, which is the point of departure for entering the search statement.

In some online catalogs, however, additional begin-session procedures are either required or available as options. They usually establish certain boundaries for the subsequent dialogue. In a few OPACs, an added preliminary procedure is the selection of one of two or more optional major command modes—for example, beginner or advanced. Another preliminary action on some OPACs is file selection, which usually occurs in two circumstances: in multipurpose systems in which the public catalog is only one of several files accessible to the user, or in multi-institutional OPACs in which several libraries' catalogs are independently accessible. In either case, the user may have to enter a command to activate the appropriate file or to switch from one file to another before a search statement can be entered.

Related to but less comprehensive than specifying entirely different command modes, another preliminary begin-session procedure found in some OPACs enables the user to specify certain limits related to the language or form in which dialogue will occur, most often having to do with system response. These options dictate such characteristics as the length of system messages or the format in which single bibliographic records are displayed. For example, the system might allow the user to specify in advance whether certain types of system messages displayed will be brief in content or more fully explanatory.

Additional begin-session procedures are usually options, not requirements. For each, there is almost always a "default value," a single option under which the system operates unless explicitly told by the user to do otherwise. Public-access terminals in multipurpose systems, for example, are normally preset for searching the public-catalog file. As long as the user does indeed wish to search that file, no explicit action is required to select it. In multi-institutional OPACs maintaining a separate file for each library, the terminals in each library are usually set for searching that particular library's catalog. Only if the user wishes to search a catalog of one of the other libraries is it necessary to use file-selection procedures. OPACs that provide different message lengths or bibliographic record formats usually operate the same way. One message length or record format serves as the default value, and a user must make a preliminary selection only if an option other than the default value is desired. In general, OPACs keep preliminary steps to a minimum, and additional procedures cater to the more experienced users or to those wishing to exercise an option that is different from the one judged to be of most use to the majority.

Access Points, Indexed Fields, and Search Types

The relationship between search statements and retrieval characteristics is perhaps the single most crucial link in a dialogue between a user and an OPAC. Although this relationship may at first seem self-evident and straightforward, that is not always the case. Many characteristics differ in application from one OPAC to another, and not necessarily in the most obvious ways.

After carrying out the necessary begin-session procedures, the next stage entails the entry of a search statement. In constructing such a statement, the user is often required to explicitly key in or select "search type" qualifiers, which identify the function of each term entered in the statement.

Before noting the variations for construction of search statements, it is necessary to see how search types relate to two other concepts: access points and indexed fields. The relationships among these three are crucial in considering the formulation of search statements and in determining how those statements interact with the retrieval characteristics of a system.

The three terms—access points, indexed fields, and search types— can be confusing. They are sometimes used almost interchangeably, and one source of confusion is that, in some OPACs, the concepts they represent do in fact rather closely coincide. In others there are very important distinctions among them.

Table 14-1 shows three examples of relationships among access

Table 14-1. RELATIONSHIPS AMONG ACCESS POINTS, INDEXED FIELDS, AND SEARCH TYPES

	Search Types	Indexed Fields (and MARC Tags)	Access Points
Example 1	Author	Author main entry, author added entry (100, 110, 111, 700, 710, 711)	Author
	Title	Title, uniform title, title added entry (245, 240, 740)	Title
	Subject	Personal name, corporate name, conference, topical, and geographic subject headings (600, 610, 611, 650, 651)	Subject
Example 2	Name	Author main entry, author added entry, personal name subject heading, corporate name subject heading, conference name subject heading (100, 110, 111, 700, 710, 711, 600, 610, 611)	Author, some subjects
	Term	Title fields, topical and geographic subject headings; sometimes notes and other fields (245, 240, 740, 650, 651; sometimes 520, 500, etc.)	Title, most subjects
Example 3	Term	All indexed fields	Author, title, subject

points as defined in the traditional sense of the term, indexed fields as applied within the context of machine-readable bibliographic records, and search types as employed in some online catalogs. These examples do not cover all the ways that the three concepts relate to one another in all OPACs, nor do they address the question of numeric search types (LCCN, ISBN, and so on). However, each example does represent a relationship found in at least one OPAC now in use.

In the first example in Table 14-1, there is essentially a one-to-one correspondence among access points, indexed fields, and search types in an OPAC. An author search allows access by name, retrieving records based on a match between the author-search terms entered by the user and terms appearing in designated author fields on machine-readable records. The same correlation applies to title and subject searches. In some OPACs, the search statement must include the full author's name, exact title, or a complete form of subject heading as it appears in machine-readable records. Other OPACs are more flexible, allowing for retrieval on keyword and truncated term searching. But even with greater flexibility, there is a strict correspondence among access points, indexed fields, and search types.

Example 2 in Table 14-1 represents an important departure in the relationships among these three concepts. Access by author is broadened to the concept of access by name. This is not always simply a change in nomenclature, for there might be a somewhat different set of indexed fields that serve as the basis for retrieval. As suggested in Example 2, for instance, personal and corporate name subject headings might be added to the list of author fields indexed for searching by name.

The term search in Example 2, like the name search, is an important departure from Example 1. Most visibly, it eliminates title and subject searches as distinctive types, encompassing them both. In addition, some OPACs that use this more comprehensive term-search approach index fields other than title and subject for retrieval. Usually, this means the addition of notes fields, but some OPACs include others as well. The system will retrieve all bibliographic records in which search terms entered by a user appear in the title of a work, in an assigned subject heading, or in any other field that might be indexed for term searching in that particular OPAC.

The third example in Table 14-1 points up the most radical approach to the relationships among access points, indexed fields, and search types. It revolves around the designation of only one search type, thereby virtually eliminating traditional distinctions among author, title, and subject searching, and it does not even recognize the distinction between names and other terms that characterize Example 2. In the third example, each term is treated the same for purposes of access and retrieval, regardless of the function it may serve in any bibliographic record. When a user enters a search term, all records will be retrieved that contain that term in any indexed field.

These three examples represent different approaches, but a number of online catalogs incorporate more than one approach. Several OPACs that provide distinct author, title, and subject search types, for example, also have a more comprehensive term search that acts on various combinations of these fields as well as perhaps on other indexed fields. An interesting and somewhat unusual approach to this whole matter is used in the online catalog of the Beth Israel Hospital Library in Philadelphia. Search terms can be entered on this system without search type designators, and the system will retrieve records in which the terms appear in any indexed field on the record. If, however, the search retrieves a large number of records, the user can then qualify whether the entered terms should apply only to author, title, or subject fields.[1]

Constructing the Search Statement

There are a number of different approaches used in OPACs for constructing a search statement. After the required begin-session procedures have been carried out, the system is prepared to accept and process a search statement, which generally consists of a search command name, a search type qualifier, and one or more search terms. There are significant differences among OPACs in the specific procedures required to enter a search statement, and these differences can be viewed in terms of three important implications:

The extent to which all three components of a search statement— search command name, search type qualifier, and search terms— must be explicitly keyed by the user.

The number of steps required to enter the search statement.

The flexibility with which a new search statement may be entered at various points during a dialogue.

A considerable number of variations in constructing a search statement can result, but by far the greatest number of OPACs use one of four basic approaches described below (see Table 14-2 for a summary of each approach according to the three characteristics outlined above).

One approach to constructing a search statement requires a user to explicitly enter all three components of the statement: search command name, search type qualifier, and one or more search terms. For instance, with the MELVYL system at the University of California, a

TABLE 14-2. CONSTRUCTING SEARCH STATEMENTS IN OPACS:
BASIC APPROACHES

Inquiry
Which of the following components of a search statement must be explicitly stated by
user: search command name, search type, search terms?

Approach 1: All three
Approach 2: All three, but search command name and search type designator are
combined
Approach 3: Search terms only, search command assumed from begin-search display and
search type dictated by where search terms are keyed in begin-search display
Approach 4: Search type and search terms only; search command assumed from
begin-search display

Inquiry
At what point(s) in a dialogue may a new search statement be entered?

Approach 1: Usually at about any point
Approach 2: Usually at about any point
Approach 3: Only from an initial begin-search screen display
Approach 4: Only from an initial begin-search screen display

Inquiry
How many steps are required to enter a search statement?

Approach 1: One
Approach 2: One
Approach 3: One if from an initial begin-search screen display; two or more from other
points in a dialogue
Approach 4: Two if from an initial begin-search display; three or more if from other
points in a dialogue

typical search statement by author would appear as shown (with the
components of the statement labeled accordingly):

FIND	PA	MURL SMITH
Command name	Search type qualifier (function qualifier)	Search terms

In this single statement, the user has issued a command to retrieve
records for all items written by an author whose name is Murl Smith.

A second basic approach is a variation on the first. The user explicitly
enters all three components of the search statement, but the command
name and search type qualifier are combined into a single element. A

search for author Murl Smith, using Northwestern University's LUIS, would appear as

A=Smith, Murl

and using Pikes Peak Library District's Maggie's Place, as

A/Smith, Murl

The elements A= and A/ indicate that the command being entered is a search command, and at the same time they define the type of search as an author search.

Both of these approaches allow an OPAC user to enter a search statement in a single step. Since all three components are explicitly entered in a statement, a new search can be initiated at almost any point during a dialogue in most OPACs that use either of these approaches. The user does not have to return first to a main menu or other initial screen display.

In contrast, OPACs using either of the two other basic approaches to constructing a search statement (identified as Approaches 3 and 4 in Table 14-2) do require the user to return to some initial point, usually the introductory screen display before a new search can be entered. In most OPACs using these methods, after the required return commands have been executed, the system is then prepared to accept a search statement. Thus, once the point is reached where a search statement can be entered, it is not necessary to explicitly key in a search command name, as in the first two approaches. But remember that the user must execute one or more preliminary steps before reaching that point.

The third approach to constructing a search statement, illustrated in Figure 14-1, relies on a fill-in-the-blank technique. From the introductory screen display, a user can enter a search statement in a single step. OPACs using this approach generally do not even require the user to explicitly state the search type. It is designated simply on the basis of where, in a range of options, the search terms are entered. In the example in Figure 14-1, after the user carried out any necessary procedures to retrieve the display, he or she could enter a search statement for the author, Murl Smith, simply by keying the search terms following the system-supplied "Author:" search type designator.

With the fourth basic approach, the user must carry out two separate steps in constructing a search statement once preliminary procedures are completed. In the first step, the user selects the search type from available options. In some OPACs, a mnemonic value is entered (a for author, t for title, n for name, and so on); others use a numerical value corresponding to each search type. The system responds to this selection by displaying a new screen, and the search terms are entered on

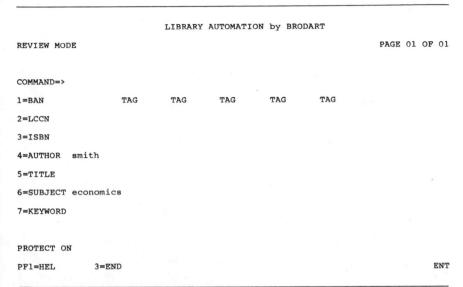

Figure 14-1 Brodart's online public-access catalog module. Display screen on which search terms are entered.

that screen as the second step in the process. This two-step approach, as has been used in the Geac Library System, is shown in Figures 14-2 and 14-3.

All four approaches described here require the user to explicitly key in at least the search terms for which an OPAC will retrieve records. But some OPACs do not require explicit keying of even these elements. In the touch-sensitive version of CLSI's Public Access Catalog, for example, the user virtually never keys any commands or terms onto a keyboard. Instead, the user continually selects alternative commands or terms from a list of options presented on a screen simply by touching the screen at the place where the desired option appears. Although this may seem to be radically different, it is essentially a variation on the fourth approach described above. A user begins a search from a designated initial display and must first select the desired search type. The next display divides the entire alphabet into several groupings. Once the grouping that contains the desired term is selected, a new display breaks that alphabetical grouping into subgroupings. This narrowing process continues until the desired search term appears as a category in itself. As is readily apparent, this single "step" for selecting a search term can easily consist of a rather large number of narrowing sequences and can be quite time consuming.

In the construction of a search statement, all but a very few OPACs

---

023 DEVELOPMENT SYSTEM   -GEAC LIBRARY SYSTEM-   *CHOOSE SEARCH

WHAT TYPE OF SEARCH DO YOU WISH TO DO?

1. TIL - TITLE, JOURNAL TITLE, SERIES TITLE, ETC.

2. AUT - AUTHOR, ILLUSTRATOR, EDITOR, ORGANIZATION, CONFERENCE, ETC.

3. A-T - COMBINATION OF AUTHOR AND TITLE.

4. SUB - SUBJECT HEADING ASSIGNED BY LIBRARY.

5. NUM - CALL NUMBER, ISBN, ISSN, ETC.

6. KEY - ONE WORD TAKEN FROM A TITLE, AUTHOR OR SUBJECT.

ENTER NUMBER OR CODE: AUT¶¶   THEN PRESS SEND

Figure 14-2 Geac Library System. Selection of search type.

---

023 DEVELOPMENT SYSTEM   -GEAC LIBRARY SYSTEM-   *AUTHOR SEARCH

FOR PEOPLE, ENTER LAST NAME FIRST.
     EX: BRONTE, EMILY
     EX: MONDRIAN, PIET

FOR OTHER AUTHORS, USE NORMAL WORD ORDER.
     EX: NATIONAL RESEARCH COUNCIL
     EX: UNITED STATES GENERAL ACCOUNTING OFFICE.

ENTER AUTHOR: ¶¶   THEN PRESS SEND

Figure 14-3 Geac Library System. System responds by supplying screen for entry of search terms.

follow one of the four basic approaches described above. The "best" one for any particular library will depend on a number of variables, for the entry of a search statement is just one aspect of dialogue between user and OPAC. For the novice, or in instances where only one search is needed, Approaches 3 and 4 are convenient, usually the most self-explanatory, and require the least amount of explicit keying. For the experienced user, or when several different searches must be conducted, Approaches 1 and 2 are likely to be more expedient. They necessitate only one step for each search and do not require maneuvering the system back to an initial screen display before each new search is entered.

Combining Search Types

Many OPACs allow different distinct search types—such as author, title, subject, or name, term, and so on—to be combined by the user in a single search of the database. In the last chapter, it was noted that a Boolean searching capability enhanced access to bibliographic records in online versions of the library catalog. The ability to combine search types is a form of this capability.

OPACs use several approaches to allow the combination of different search types in a search statement. One technique requires the user to enter all elements of the search in a single progression such as:

FIND PA SMITH AND SU ECONOMICS

Here, the user has identified each search term according to type— personal author and subject—and has linked them with the explicit Boolean operator "and."

A second approach uses a fill-in-the-blank technique to allow combination of distinct search types in a single statement. One OPAC that has used this approach is Brodart's online catalog illustrated in Figure 14-1. The same screen display can be used to enter either a single-type search statement or one in which two or more search types are combined. In combining search types, the user merely enters each term in the space adjacent to the system-supplied search type labels.

A third general technique requires the separate entry, in one or more steps, of each search type qualifier/search term pair being combined, in obvious contrast to the first two approaches, in which pairs are entered in a single step. The user must execute two separate steps for each search type qualifier/search term pair: the first to indicate the search type, and the second to enter the actual terms themselves. This procedure is repeated for each search type qualifier/search term pair being combined, and thus will require several steps simply to combine two search types and the desired search terms.

A fourth technique for combining search types is quite different from any of the above. In the first three approaches, the user must take an explicit action to combine two distinct search types. In the fourth approach, a combination essentially is made available by the system as a separate, single search type in and of itself. The most common example is a designated author/title search. The two examples shown below represent author/title search statements using this technique, the first on the ULISYS online catalog module and the second on Ohio State University's LCS.

AT=Smith/industry

ATS/Smitindus

The elements AT= and ATS/ each represent a single combined search type, which obviates the need for a user to enter author and title elements in two distinct steps. In LCS (the second example), the author and title terms are entered as a derived search key consisting of the first four characters of an author's name and the first five characters of the first significant word of a title. ULISYS allows the user to enter the author's complete surname and the complete first word of a title.

When available, this fourth approach is frequently offered in OPACs only with respect to a combined author/title search. A few do provide additional combined search types. MSUS/PALS, which offers discrete author, title, title keyword, and subject search types, as well as a combined author/title search, also provides a term-search type which essentially combines title and subject searches. Several OPACs offer a term-search capability in lieu of distinct title and subject search types, but only a handful such as MSUS/PALS offers it in addition to the other two.

Though there are variations on each, the four techniques described here constitute the major approaches used by OPACs to allow a combination of distinct search types in a single search of the catalog. Each technique has advantages and disadvantages depending on user needs related to simplicity, clarity, and expediency. All are fairly straightforward in execution, and only the third approach requires a substantially greater number of steps than those needed for entering single-type search statements.

Subject Access

Although enhancement to all traditional channels of access in library catalogs is an important attribute of OPACs, the broad concept of subject access merits particular attention. Prior to the 1980s, it was generally held that known-item author and title searches were far more prevalent in library catalogs than were subject searches, a contention supported by numerous studies of card catalog use. But in the early 1980s, studies of use patterns in a number of OPACs revealed a different picture. Subject searches, at least in these online versions of the catalog, were the predominant type of search conducted by users.

As described in the last chapter, subject access in card and offline, computer-generated catalogs is usually hampered by:

rigidity and complexity of headings

need for the user to know complete and exact form of headings

minimal number of headings assigned to items cataloged into the collection

Many features have been introduced into online catalogs to broaden subject access and expand the flexibility with which records may be searched by subject. Different OPACs employ these features to varying extents. The general usefulness of each of the subject-access features outlined below varies, but the quantity in which they are available in any given OPAC is likely to have at least some bearing on the quality of subject access provided by that OPAC. Some of these avenues of subject access were noted in the last chapter, but they are summarized here.

Character-by-Character Exact-Match Searching on Assigned Subject Headings

1. User must know and key in exact, full form of assigned subject heading.
2. Assigned subject headings are usually drawn, with local variations, from standard lists such as Library of Congress Subject Headings, Sears, and so on.
3. Has no greater flexibility for subject searching than card or COM catalogs.

Keyword Searching and Truncation on Assigned Subject Headings

1. Both features, although not interdependent, introduce greater flexibility and can result in broader access than the character-by-character exact-match approach described above.
2. The following examples for the single subject heading "Learning, psychology of—Congresses" compare how records must be retrieved using character-by-character exact-match searching with how the same records may be retrieved using keyword searching, subject heading phrase truncation, and combination of keyword and term truncation (punctuation rules may vary, and examples assume the capability to enter more than one keyword in search statement, allowed on some but not all OPACs that offer keyword searching).

   Character-by-character exact match:
      learning, psychology of—congresses
   Keyword:
      learning
      psychology

psychology learning
learning congresses
congresses psychology
etc.
Phrase truncation:
learning
learning, psychology
learning, psychology of
Keyword searching combined with term truncation:
psychol
learn
psychol learning
congress psycholog
psych learn con
etc.

Increased Number of Bibliographic Elements Indexed for Subject Retrieval

1. Subject access expanded through concept of "term" searches (see Table 14-1).
2. Records retrieved when search terms appear not only within assigned subject headings, but also within other designated elements—titles, contents notes, and so forth.
3. Some OPACs offer both subject search and term-search types; former usually applies to assigned subject headings specifically; the latter is more comprehensive, and includes other bibliographic elements, such as title fields, as well.

Keyword Searching on Title Fields

1. More restrictive than multiple-field term searching described above.
2. This "backdoor" approach to subject searching draws on the principle that vocabulary in title of a work, especially nonfiction, normally is descriptive of work's basic subject content.

Shelflist Browsing

1. Openly available browsing feature allows user to enter full or truncated call number and view records in shelflist order (in card or COM form, shelflist files are maintained almost exclusively for internal bibliographic control, housed apart from public catalog, and seldom readily available to users).
2. Allows review of works in shelf order (including titles in circulation or otherwise not on shelf) without physically going to stacks.

Online Lists of Subject Headings

1. In some OPACs, the first level of retrieval in response to subject search.
2. Contains subject heading entered and subdivisions and/or alphabetically proximate headings.
3. User selects heading initially entered or otherwise listed; system displays bibliographic records assigned that heading (see the sequence illustrated in Figures 14-4 through 14-6 for an example of this approach).
4. In some OPACs, retrieval of a subject heading list is a distinct operation from retrieval of bibliographic records assigned a particular heading; one search type for entering heading to retrieve list of headings, another for entering it as search term to retrieve bibliographic records containing that heading.
5. Currently, primary emphasis for OPACs offering this feature is simply on providing alphabetical lists of approved headings and subdivisions; a few OPACs are attempting to incorporate more information about nonalphabetical relationships between terms, such as through see-also cross-references and explanatory notes.

```
HELP

                    UNIVERSAL LIBRARY SYSTEMS
                Welcome to our automated catalogue

              Please follow these simple instructions

To search by. Enter. Followed by.          Example.

AUTHOR         AU=    Author's name        AU=HOFFMAN STANLEY
TITLE          TI=    Title of work        TI=PRIMACY OR WORLD ORDER
AUTHOR/TITLE   AT=    Author/title         AT=HOFFMAN / PRIMACY
SUBJECT        SU=    Subj. heading        SU=UNITED STATES

For RESERVE BOOK ROOM items you may also search by .........

COURSE         CO=    Course name          CO=ARTS
INSTRUCTOR     IN=    Instructor name      IN=BROWN A
COURSE/INSTR   CI=    Course/instr.        CI=ARTS 101/BROWN A

Then press the RETURN key to send the message to the computer.
For more detailed HELP instructions type MORE HELP and press
the RETURN key.
? SU= ECONOMICS
```

Figure 14-4 Universal Library Systems' ULISYS. Initial search screen. User enters a subject search under the term "Economics."

```
 SU=ECONOMICS
?                                                      SU=ECONOMICS
Line    Subject heading or terms
1       Economics (203)
2       Economics. (1)
3       Economics--1965- (2)
4       Economics--Addresses, essays, lectures (19)
5       Economics--Anecdotes, facetiae, satire, etc. (1)
6       Economics--Bibliography. (4)
7       Economics--Biography. (1)
8       Economics--Collected works. (1)
9       Economics--Collections. (4)
10      Economics--Dictionaries. (13)
11      Economic security--United States. (6)
12      Economic security--United States--Congresses. (1)
13      Economics--Examinations, questions, etc. (4)
14      Economics--France--History. (1)


To display next screen type 'NS'
TO SEE THOSE TITLES IN THE CATALOG UNDER THE SUBJECT HEADING YOU'VE CHOSEN
TYPE 'DT=' FOLLOWED BY THE LINE NUMBER
? DT= 11
```

Figure 14-5 Universal Library Systems' ULISYS. System responds to request for search by displaying list of subject heading derivatives. User selects one of the specific headings to view bibliographic records.

```
 DT=11
?                                                      DT=11
SELECTION:  Economic security--United States. (6)
      Call number         Author          Title
1     338.973 W643t       Wilcox, Clair, 1 Toward social welfare; an analysis of
2     338.973 T342f       Theobald, Robert Free men and free markets.
3     368.4 T849e         Turnbull, John G Economic and social security [by] Joh
4     320.05 R494                          Risks and its treatment : changing so
5     368.4 T849e4        Turnbull, John G Economic and social security [by] Joh
6     338.973 R825q       Rubinow, Isaac M The quest for security / Isaac M. Rub


To display previous screen type 'PS'
TO DETERMINE THE LOCATION AND AVAILABILITY OF A SPECIFIC TITLE,
TYPE 'ST=' FOLLOWED BY THE LINE NUMBER EXAMPLE:   ST=2  AND  'RETURN'
FOR MORE DETAILED INFORMATION ON A SPECIFIC TITLE, TYPE 'BI='
FOLLOWED BY THE LINE NUMBER EXAMPLE:   BI=5  AND  'RETURN'
?
```

Figure 14-6 Universal Library Systems' ULISYS. System displays list of brief bibliographic records containing specific subject heading selected.

Display of Only Subject Headings from Bibliographic Records

1. In the University of California's MELVYL system, a user may specify that only subject heading fields be displayed for a set of records retrieved in response to search. (See Figure 14-7.)
2. All bibliographic data other than the subject headings assigned to each record are suppressed in the display.
3. This feature may be useful in guiding a user to subject headings closely related to a topic on which some records have been retrieved.

<u>User's command</u>:   Find Subject Art Impression# France

<u>MELVYL's response</u>:

Search request: FIND SUBJECT ART IMPRESSION# FRANCE
Search result: 43 records at UC libraries

<u>User's command</u>:   Display Subjects

<u>MELVYL's response</u>:

Search request: FIND SUBJECT ART IMPRESSION# FRANCE
Search result: 43 books at UC libraries

1.
Subjects: Prints, French -- Exhibitions.
                     Post-impressionism (Art) -- France -- Exhibitions.

2.
Subjects: Impressionism (Art) -- France.
                     Painting, French.
                     Painting, Modern -- 19th century -- France.

3.
Subjects: Matisse, Henri, 1869-1954.
                     Neo-impressionism (Art) -- France.

4.
Subjects: Water-color painting, French.
                     Water-color painting -- 19th century -- France.
                     Drawing, French.
                     Drawing -- 19th century -- France.
                     Impressionism (Art) -- France.

Figure 14-7 University of California's MELVYL. Subject headings only display for records retrieved.

4. In Biblio-Techniques's BLIS System, this approach also allows for the extraction of all access points, including subject headings, for use in additional searches.

Because OPACs are such a comparatively recent phenomenon, the actual worth of many of these features for enhancing subject searching is still uncertain. Although equivalents of some of these features have long been offered in other forms of the catalog, they have seldom been so readily available to catalog users. Libraries have long maintained card files in call-number order; many have displayed authorized lists, such as Library of Congress Subject Headings, near the catalog to aid in determining appropriate subject headings for a search; and many libraries include all subject tracings on all catalog entries for a particular item, giving clues to other headings where similar works might be found. But such features of card and COM catalogs have seldom been very actively promoted as aids to the library user. In the online catalog, such features are all available in one place, through a single terminal, and their presence is far more apparent.

Character-by-Character versus Keyword Searching

Character-by-character and keyword searching were compared earlier in relation to subject access in online catalogs. But the contrasts between them are also applicable to access by title and corporate name and, to a somewhat lesser extent, by personal name. With a character-by-character approach, a search by subject, title, corporate name, or personal name, or any other parameter, will retrieve only records in which the text in the appropriate indexed fields matches exactly the string of terms entered in a search statement. Keyword searching does not require such a level of precision. Records will be retrieved as long as the search term or terms appear anywhere within the appropriate indexed fields, regardless of position and regardless of what additional words might also appear in those fields.

For any type of search, each approach has certain advantages and disadvantages. The character-by-character method has some of the disadvantages found in requirements for searching in a typical card catalog. The user must have complete information about a title or a form of name or subject heading as represented in the catalog. Keyword searching is not so rigid, in that it enables a user to find records even if only a word or a few words in a title, name, or assigned subject heading are known.

However, keyword searching is not without limitations. Its flexibility is advantageous under many circumstances, but in some situations its impreciseness can be a problem. An example of such a situation was described by Stephen Salmon as it applied to the prototype design of the University of California's MELVYL system. Although modifications were later introduced, in the original version of MELVYL all alphabetical searches were essentially keyword; there were no provisions for carrying out character-by-character, exact-match searches. As a result, a search of the database under "war and peace" in an effort to find records for Tolstoy's 1866 work reportedly retrieved nearly 500 records, including not only those for *War and Peace,* but also for all others in which the search terms appeared anywhere in the title.[2] The problem of imprecision can be especially profound when using a broad term-search type that retrieves records based on the appearance of search terms in any of a variety of indexed fields.

Although a number of OPACs incorporate both the character-by-character and keyword approaches, quite a few provide only one, and there is still an inclination in some cases to promote one or the other as being more effective or otherwise "better." In actuality, the greatest liability of either approach is when it is provided exclusively of the other. Neither method is always the most suitable, for their strengths and weaknesses vary according to circumstances. For broadening the concept of subject access and for allowing users to find records when they possess only partial bibliographic information, a keyword search capability is indispensable. But especially for known-item searches in which a user does have complete bibliographic knowledge—an exact title or author's name as it appears in the catalog—a character-by-character search capability can be clearly superior. A keyword-only search, when full bibliographic data are known, probably means that an inordinate amount of time and effort will be spent by the user in sifting through a long list of records that he or she knows to be irrelevant to the purpose of that search.

An OPAC should provide both character-by-character *and* keyword search capabilities, and a number already do. With both approaches, the user is given maximum flexibility for selecting the search strategy that will be most suitable and most economical for his or her specific circumstances.

Truncation

Like keyword searching, truncation opens the possibility of broader retrieval than does character-by-character, exact-match searching. The basic questions concerning truncation in an OPAC are whether it is available at all, and if so, whether it applies to terms, phrases, or both, and whether it must be explicitly stated by a user or is implicitly assumed by the system.

The clearest example of truncation is in the use of derived search keys, whereby a user is *required* to truncate each search term according to a prescribed formula and is restricted to a maximum number of such terms that can be entered. Derived search keys, not common in OPACs, have long been used for some types of searches in Ohio State University's LCS. A user conducting a title search on this system has had to enter the first four characters of the first significant word of a title, and the first five characters of the second word. Fewer characters could be entered if either of the first two words in a title contains fewer than the prescribed maximum, or if the title consisted of a single word, but a greater number of characters from the first or second words could not be entered, nor could characters from subsequent words in the title. So, a title search for *Quantitative Techniques for Business Decisions* would have to be entered as

TLS/quantechn

If the desired item is in the database, it will be retrieved by using the above search key, but so will records for any other titles that have "quan" as the first four characters of the first significant word and "techn" as the first five characters of the second. LCS has also used derived search keys for author searches and for combined author/title searches.

The derived search key example in LCS is very explicit in terms of user action: It is the user who must perform the truncation. Some OPACs, however, have internal truncation; it is the system, and not the user, that formulates the derived search key. A user may enter more complete search terms—for example, the complete title *Quantitative Techniques for Business Decisions*—but before processing the search, the system will internally truncate the phrase and each term according to a formula that is not apparent to the user. It is this truncated search statement, rather than the user's more complete statement, that serves as the basis for retrieval. The desired record will be retrieved in the database, but so will any others for which there is a match with the internally truncated statement.

A certain amount of imprecision is inherent in derived search keys. The search key algorithms can be designed to maximize precision, but there are bound to be some searches that retrieve a large number of records that are not relevant to the user's needs. Perhaps even more of a problem with internally derived search keys, where the user cannot see the truncation that occurs, is that he or she may be confused about why the system is responding the way it is.

Derived search keys, which demonstrate both term truncation (searching on less than complete words) and phrase truncation (searching on fewer words than might be included in complete bibliographic data), are extreme examples of truncation in OPACs. In systems that do not use such keys, term and phrase truncation are often approached somewhat differently. Term truncation, when available, is usually associated with keyword searching and almost invariably requires explicit action on the part of the user, generally in the form of keying a designated nonalphabetical character—a number sign (#), asterisk (*), or hyphen (-), for example—as the last element of a search term. Here are examples of truncated keyword title searches in the MSUS/PALS system:

TT electric#
TT psycholog#

In the first example, records will be retrieved for any items in which the terms *electric, electrical, electricity*, or any other derivative of *electric* appear in the title. In the second example, records will be retrieved for items in which the terms *psychology, psychological*, or any other derivative of *psycholog* appear in the title. If the special truncation designator is not stated, the system treats a string of characters as a complete word. In the first example, but without the # designator, at least some records would probably be retrieved since the term *electric* is likely to appear in exactly that form in a certain number of titles. However, if the special designator is not entered in the second example, there will almost certainly be no retrievals, since the term *psycholog* is not likely to appear as a complete word in any title.

Although explicit entry of a truncation designator by the user is the general rule for term truncation, a few OPACs do implicitly treat search terms as truncated forms. In these systems, entry of the term *electric* would always retrieve records in which derivative words such as *electrical* and *electricity* appear in the title. There is no mechanism in this approach for the user to specify whether a search term is being entered in truncated or complete form; it is always treated as a truncated term.

Term truncation is most commonly associated with keyword searching, but phrase truncation is sometimes linked with character-by-character searching. Some OPACs do not use phrase truncation in any form. Records are retrieved only from an exact match between terms as entered in a search statement and terms appearing in the designated indexed fields of records. A title search consisting of the two terms *social statistics* will retrieve only records in which those terms make up the full and exact title. Records will not be retrieved for such a title as *Social Statistics in the Eighties*. A character-by-character subject heading search under the phrase *clocks and watches* will retrieve only records in which those three words are the exact and full form of a subject heading. It will not act on subject headings in which *clocks and watches* is followed by subdivisions or other terms.

In OPACs that do incorporate phrase truncation, the same two basic approaches are available as for term truncation: explicit, in which the user must specify truncation, and implicit, in which the system automatically assumes it. With an explicit approach, the user normally designates truncation by entering, as the last element in a phrase, a designated nonalphabetical character, similar to those often used for term truncation. If the special designator is not included, the system will treat the string of search terms as a full expression and will retrieve only records for which it finds an exact match in the appropriate indexed fields. With either explicit or implicit phrase truncation, the result is to expand the scope of retrieval. For a title search containing the phrase *social statistics,* phrase truncation will retrieve records not only for those works whose full title is *Social Statistics,* but also for such titles as *Social Statistics in the Eighties.* A truncated subject heading phrase search under the phrase *clocks and watches* will retrieve not only records in which that is the complete heading, but also records for such headings as *Clocks and watches—adjusting; Clocks and watches, electric;* and *Clocks and watches in art,* or any other headings in which clocks and watches are the first three terms.

As with term truncation, an explicit approach to phrase truncation is more flexible for the user because he or she has the option of entering a string of search terms as either a complete expression or as a truncated phrase. The implicit approach leaves the user no option: The sequence of terms will always be treated as a truncated phrase. As described earlier, this can lead to frustration for a user who knows the precise title desired or the full form of an author's name or subject heading, especially if only one or two words are involved. The desired records will be retrieved, but probably so will a long list of others that have little or no relevance to the user.

Truncation can be a valuable enhancement to searching in an online catalog. Like keyword searching, however, it is suitable in certain situations, and can be a deterrent in others. And it should be provided, not instead of character-by-character, exact-match searching, but as an additional option. Its use should remain at the discretion of the user, not as a mandate of the system.

Alternative Terminology

In any OPAC, some proportion of searches will result in no records being retrieved. This proportion can be significant. For example, in studies in the early 1980s, Northwestern University reported no retrievals for 39 percent of all subject searches in its LUIS system; the University of California noted 35 percent; and Syracuse University gave 53 percent for no retrievals in the online catalog.[3]

Many factors contribute to these high numbers, but obviously a main one must be the discrepancies between user and catalog terminology to represent the same concepts. Character-by-character, exact-match searches on names and assigned subject headings are especially prone to such discrepancies, where the user must enter terms in the exact form as the library has chosen to represent them in the catalog. Some OPACs have not yet addressed this problem through any online mechanisms. In these OPACs, discrepancies between user and catalog vocabulary simply result in no retrievals, and it is up to the user to guess what other terms might be appropriate or to seek offline guidance in determining the proper terminology.

Some OPACs have tried to tackle this problem online. The two primary methods were noted in Chapter 13 and are only summarized here. Both require online authority files in place, and both require the system to recognize some alternative terminology and then route the user to the proper vocabulary.

The first method focuses on online display of cross-references. When the user enters a search term contained as a cross-reference in the authority file, the system refers the user to the library-established term or form of heading used for that name or concept in the catalog. An example, cited by Charles Hildreth, is as follows:[4]

> The name you entered, Holt, Victoria, is entered in this catalog under Plaidy, Jean.
> Do you wish to continue this search? (If "YES" press the RETURN key.)

The user must then either key in the proper form or, as in the example above, simply enter a designated command to search under the correct form.

The second method is to provide a strictly internal link from an unauthorized heading to an authorized form, displaying the correct bibliographic records with no further action by the user. This eliminates some of the user's work, but can be confusing; if a user enters one name or subject heading and retrieves records displaying a different name or subject heading, he or she may conclude that the system misunderstood the search terms.

The way in which an OPAC treats alternative terminology is especially important because it deals with a very complex situation. The quantity of alternative terminology that can be used to express a single concept, especially for a subject, can be significant. One of the more promising techniques developed to help reduce this problem is to program an OPAC to record the terminology used in searches that retrieve no records, and then to analyze that terminology in order to add new cross-references to the authority file.

Displaying Bibliographic Data

The previous sections discussed procedures for searching the online catalog, the desired conclusion being the retrieval of bibliographic records matching the search terms entered. When that occurs, the next major concerns in the dialogue between user and OPAC are the manipulation of results and the presentation of bibliographic information. Manipulation of results includes procedures to broaden the set of records retrieved, narrow the set, or display one or more specific records within the set. Rather than discussing in detail the various techniques for manipulating results, the primary focus in the remainder of this chapter is on the presentation of individual bibliographic records in terms of the information they contain.

Just as there are differences among OPACs in the procedures required for searching, so there is variety in the presentation of bibliographic information retrieved in response to searches. This section focuses on two levels of presentation: a first level for those instances in which a search has retrieved multiple records, and a second level focusing on the display of single bibliographic records.

First-Level Retrieval for Multiple Matches

A search in an OPAC has one of three results: No records are retrieved, only one record is retrieved, or more than one record is retrieved. If no records match the search statement, most OPACs display a message to that effect, and the user may enter a new search statement. If only one record is retrieved, the majority of OPACs will display a short, medium, or long version of the record. This section focuses on the third result.

More than one record is almost certain to be retrieved in searches on assigned subject headings, in keyword searches of various types, often in author searches, and sometimes even in title searches. When multiple records are retrieved, the first level of presentation in most OPACs consists of a list containing one or up to a few lines of brief bibliographic data about each record matching the search statement. If the number of records is relatively small, the list will fit on a single screen. For a large number, several screens may be required, in which case the user can page or scroll to subsequent screens until the desired record or records are identified.

Almost all OPACs use the brief-listing approach to multiple retrievals, but there are alternatives. In at least two systems, a search will always result in the display of a single bibliographic record, even when more than one matches the search statement. The user pages through subsequent records one at a time. This is essentially the online equivalent of thumbing through a set of catalog cards in a drawer, one card at a time.

Several OPACs, instead of displaying the brief list, require an intermediate step between the search statement and the display of any item-specific bibliographic information. The two most common intermediate steps are a display indicating simply the number of records retrieved in response to a search (Figure 14-8) and a display containing a list of author names, terms, or subject headings that match or nearly match the search terms entered. In Figure 14-8, the user entered an author search for George Hoffman, and the system responded that eight records were retrieved. At this point the user may instruct the system to display brief bibliographic information about all or selected records.

In Figure 14-9, the user entered a search for an author, surname Miller, and the system responded by displaying a list of names conforming to those terms. In Figure 14-10, the user entered a subject heading search, to which the system responded by displaying variations of the search term. In each of these examples, the display indicates the number of records in which each term or phrase is contained. This can be very useful, but not all OPACs providing these types of lists also supply those data. In any event, the user's next step from a list will be to select one of the terms or phrases and key in the corresponding line number. The system will then respond by displaying a list of brief records containing that term or phrase.

```
AU HOFFMAN GEORGE
     8 RECORDS MATCHED THE SEARCH
TYPE DI 1-8  TO DISPLAY THE RECORDS
>
```

Figure 14-8 Minnesota State University System Project for Automated Library Systems (MSUS/PALS) Catalog Access System. Listing retrieved in response to author search for "Hoffman, George."

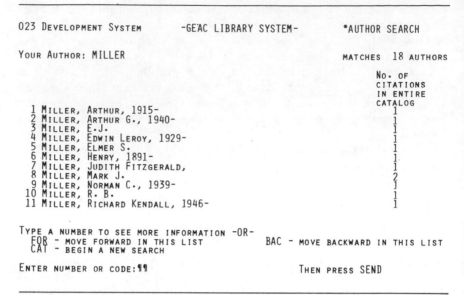

Figure 14-9 Geac Library System. Author headings list.

Figure 14-10 Ohio State University Library Control System (LCS). Subject headings list.

Whether in direct response to a search statement or as a result of an intermediate display, the first-level retrieval of bibliographic records gives the user concrete search results in the form of selected bibliographic elements from each matching record. At this first level, there are distinct differences among OPACs in the amount of data supplied for each item when multiple records are retrieved. The basic difference stems from the purposes for which this level of retrieval is intended. These purposes, and the degree of success in attaining them, can be assessed in terms of whether the information included about each item in a list is sufficient:

1. to distinguish it from other items in the list.
2. for the user to positively identify it as the one that is sought.
3. to ascertain the location at which it should be found in the library.
4. to determine its availability status.

The display at the first level of retrieval for multiple matches in many OPACs is intended to serve only the first purpose or perhaps the first two. To determine call number and other locational data—and sometimes even to make a positive identification of an item—the user must select a record from among the list and enter a command to view a longer version of it. Other OPACs try to circumvent that need by displaying, for each item, more data at the first level, including more complete bibliographic description, locational information, and sometimes even availability status.

In some OPACs, the data elements displayed for each item at the first level of retrieval are fairly extensive; including, for example, Library of Congress Card Number, author's full name, complete title, full imprint statement, physical description, and call number. This amount of data should always be sufficient for a user to clearly distinguish among records included in the list, to positively identify the items desired, and to determine the shelf location of any item listed. In order to include this much data for an item, its brief-listed record will have to be allotted between two and four lines of information on the screen display. But a far more predominant approach in OPACs is to restrict the description of each item in a multiple-record display to a single line. This approach is illustrated in Figures 14-11 and 14-12.

The "one-record, one-line" approach does allow a greater number of brief records to be displayed on a single screen, and with enough information in most cases to distinguish items and to positively identify desired items. There are, however, glaring exceptions. Limiting the item description to a single line means restricting the number of data elements that can be included, and it also restricts the number of characters allotted to each element; obviously, in some cases the data will not be sufficient for identification. In searches that involve lengthy names of prolific authors (such as the United States Congress House Committee on . . .) or long and general titles (such as Proceedings of the Conference on . . .), such severe truncation can result in a listing in which items cannot clearly be distinguished from one another or positively identified as the desired item. Limiting the number of data elements can have similar results. Some OPACs, for example, do not include such elements as an edition statement or date of publication in

```
PUBLIC CATALOG                                    Searching: DEMO


AUTHOR (BOOKS/SERIALS): KROEBER, A. L 1876-1960
FOUND: 4

REF  DATE   TITLES                           AUTHOR        CALL NUMBER
---  ----   ------                           ------        -----------
R1   1963   An anthropologist looks at histo Kroeber, A. L CB19 .K686 1963
R2   1963   Anthropology: biology & race.    Kroeber, A. L GN320 .K7 1963
R3   1953   Anthropology today:              International  GN4 .I52
R4   1948   Anthropology:                    Kroeber, A. L GN24 .K7 1948
(END)




CHOICE: R1
```

Figure 14-11 OCLC LS/2000. Response to author search retrieving multiple records.

```
Screen 001  of 001
NMBR DATE   --------------------TITLE-------------------- -------AUTHOR-------
0001 1973   Alfred Kroeber,                               Steward, Julian Hayn
0002 1963   An anthropologist looks at history.           Kroeber, A. L.
0003 1953   Anthropology today;   an encyclopedic inventor International Sympos
0004 1948   Anthropology:   race, language, culture, psych Kroeber, Alfred Loui
0005 1944   Configurations of culture growth,             Kroeber, Alfred Loui
0006 1947   Cultural and natural areas of native North Am Kroeber, Alfred Loui
0007 1963   Culture :  a critical review of concepts and  Kroeber, A. L.
0008 1968   Essays in anthropology presented to A. L. Kro
0009 1966   Fierabras, chanson de geste.
0010 1953   Handbook of the Indians of California.        Kroeber, Alfred Loui
0011 1952   The nature of culture.                        Kroeber, A. L.
0012 1950-  Papers.                                       Kroeber Anthropologi
0013 1931   The Seri,                                     Kroeber, A. L.
0014 1965   Source book in anthropology,                  Kroeber, A. L.
0015 1940   Three centuries of women's dress fashions:  a Richardson, Jane.
0016 1903   Traditions of the Arapaho /                   Dorsey, George Amos,
0017 1964   Walapai ethnography /                         Kroeber, A. L.
0018 1942   Yurok narratives,                             Spott, Robert,
0019 1917   Zuni kin and clan,                            Kroeber, A. L.
----Type DI NMBR(s) to display specific records
>
```

Figure 14-12 Minnesota State University System Project for Automated Library Systems (MSUS/PALS). Response to author search retrieving multiple records.

single-line lists at the first level of retrieval. For a user seeking a record for a particular edition of a work that has gone through several editions, this limited first-level display will be inadequate to positively identify a desired item or even to distinguish items in the list from one another. In that and similar cases, the user's only approach is to select and view records in the list in their more complete version until the correct one is found. In some OPACs, users can, through a single command, request the system to scroll longer versions of several different records, but in most systems, they must select and display the longer versions one record at a time. So, although the single-line approach does have some advantages, it can also be a real inconvenience.

The data elements included at the first level of retrieval for multiple matches vary according to space restrictions and, more broadly, according to the purposes intended for this level of retrieval. The two elements most consistently displayed in nearly all OPACs are title and author. Invariably, the title or some part of it will be included for each item in the list. If appropriate, an author's name is either included in each record or, specifically in response to author searches in some OPACs, listed once at the top of a list of items by that author. The next most common elements are date of publication and call number. Other elements are far less frequent and are generally included only in those OPACs that devote two or more lines of description to each item. In some OPACs, especially those using the one-record, one-line approach, the data elements included depend on the type of search. The CTI online catalog, for example, includes call numbers on brief records retrieved in response to author or title searches, but not subject searches. The Ohio State University's LCS treats call numbers in exactly the opposite way: They are included on each record retrieved in response to a subject search, but excluded in response to author, title, or combined author/title searches. Other OPACs include the same data elements in all lists but arrange them differently according to the type of search conducted. In one system, for example, brief records retrieved from a title search give the title first, followed by date of publication, author, and call number. For subject searches, the order of the first two data elements is reversed: the date of publication appears first and the title second. But in most OPACs, data elements and their arrangement do not vary from one type of search to another.

Concerning the arrangement of brief records in a list with respect to one another, in most OPACs, the items appear in alphabetical or numerical order according to the first element displayed—author, title, subject, or call number, and so on. Ideally, the first order of arrangement should be defined by the search type: alphabetically by author for author searches, by title for title searches, and so on.

Full Bibliographic Record Displays

As emphasized in the preceding section, few OPACs include data elements beyond author, title, publication date, and call number at the first level of retrieval for multiple matches. This means that a rather long list of elements, such as edition statements, imprint, physical description, series statements, notes, subject headings, and added entries, is left out. Because these elements can be crucial for distinguishing between bibliographically similar works, for making positive item identification, or for helping to evaluate an item's relevance for a particular need, there are many instances in which users may want and need to see this more detailed information.

All OPACs offer access to more detailed individual records. In fact, most OPACs have at least two different versions or formats available for each item in the catalog, ranging from a short record with a few elements of description to a fully tagged MARC record containing even more data than are traditionally associated with full catalog entries.

Most OPACs provide access to these individual records in one of two ways—automatic system response and user-initiated action. If a search statement is so specific as to retrieve a single record, most OPACs will bypass the one- or two-line version and immediately display a more detailed form. Or, from the brief-listing display when a search statement has retrieved multiple matches, the user may initiate the action by selecting an item in the list and requesting a more detailed record of it. In OPACs that provide multiple versions of a record for each item in the database, one format is usually established as the default value, and individual records for all items will display in that format unless the user explicitly requests a shorter or longer version.

Of all format options available in all existing OPACs, probably no two are *exactly* alike. There are so many data elements and so many ways to present the material that the precise form is highly specific to an individual system. Even so, some of the differences are relatively minor, and at least at a general level of comparison, there are many similarities. The bibliographic record displays in Figures 14-13 through 14-18 demonstrate some of these differences and similarities. Each of these examples is roughly comparable to what might be called a "long" or "full" version in the respective OPAC. Two of the systems (TLS and LCS) have more abbreviated individual bibliographic record display formats available, and several allow an option whereby a user may explicitly request an even more detailed, numerically tagged MARC version of a record.

In the display formats used by these and other OPACs, four variables are most pronounced in determining the makeup and style of presentation:

1. data elements included
2. whether data elements are labeled; if so, the terminology used

```
   BI=1
?                                                    BI=1
          Kissinger, Henry, 1923-
973.924
K643y     Years of upheaval / Henry Kissinger..

          Boston : Little, Brown, 1982.

          xxi, 1283 p. : ill. ; 24 cm.

          Includes bibliographical references and index.

          1.   Kissinger, Henry, 1923-
          2.   Nixon, Richard M. (Richard Milhous), 1913-
          3.   Statesmen--United States--Biography
          4.   United States--Foreign relations--1969-1974.
          5.   United States--Foreign relations--1974-1977.


To display next screen type 'NS'      To display previous screen type 'PS'
TO DETERMINE THE LOCATION AND AVAILABILITY OF A SPECIFIC TITLE,
TYPE 'ST=' FOLLOWED BY THE LINE NUMBER EXAMPLE:   ST=2   AND   'RETURN'
?
```

Figure 14-13 Universal Library Systems' ULISYS. Bibliographic record display.

```
Author:      Kissinger, Henry, 1923-
Title:       Years of upheaval / Henry Kissinger. 1st ed. Boston : Little,
                Brown, c1982.
             xxi, 1283 p., [40] p. of plates : ill. ; 25 cm.

Notes:       Includes bibliographical references and index.

Subjects:    Kissinger, Henry, 1923-
             Statesmen -- United States -- Biography.
             United States -- Foreign relations -- 1969-1974.

Call numbers:  UCB   Main      E840.8.K58 A38 (CU-MAIN)
               UCB   Moffitt   E840.8.K58 A38 (CU-UNDE)
               UCD   Law Lib   E840.8.K58 A38 (CU-AL)
               UCD   Main Lib  E840.8.K58 A38 (CU-A)
               UCI   Main Lib  E840.8.K58 A38 (CU-I)
               UCLA  College   E 840.8 K58A38 (CLU-COL)
               UCLA  GSMgmt    E 840.8 K58 A38 (CLU-MGT)
               UCSB  Library   E840.8.K58 A38 (CU-SB)
               UCSC  McHenry   E840.8.K58 A38 (CU-SC)
               UCSD  Central   E840.8.K58 A38 (CU-SCu)
               UCSD  Cluster   E840.8.K58 A38 (CU-SCL)
```

Figure 14-14 University of California's MELVYL. Bibliographic record display.

@
KISSINGER, HENRY, 1923- /YEARS OF UPHEAVAL / HENRY KISSINGER. /1ST E
D. /BOSTON : LITTLE, BROWN, C1982. /XXI, 1283 P., [40] P. OF PLATES
: ILL. ; 25 CM. /# KISSINGER, HENRY, 1923- /# UNITED STATES - FOREI
GN RELATIONS 1969-1974. /# STATESMEN - UNITED STATES - BIOGRAPHY. /

Figure 14-15 Claremont Colleges' Total Library System (TLS). Bibliographic record display.

023 DEVELOPMENT SYSTEM   -GEAC LIBRARY SYSTEM-   *AUTHOR SEARCH

TITLE: EXCAVATING IN EGYPT : THE EGYPT EXPLORATION SOCIETY, 1882-1982/

IMPRINT: CHICAGO : UNIVERSITY OF CHICAGO PRESS, 1982.

PHYSICAL FEATURES: 192 P. : ILL., MAP ; 24 CM.

NOTES: INCLUDES BIBLIOGRAPHIC REFERENCES AND INDEX.

CONTENTS: THE EARLY YEARS/MARAGARET S. DROWER -- THE DELTA / A.J. SPENCER --
          THEBES / W.V. DAVIES -- ABYDOS / B.J. KEMP -- EL-AMARNAR / CYRIL
          ALDRED -- SAQQARA / GEOFFREY T. MARTIN -- NUBIA / H.S. SMITH -- THE
          ARCHEOLOGICAL SURVEY / T.G.H. JAMES -- THE GRECO-ROMAN BRANCH / SIR
          ERIC G. TURNER.

OTHER AUTHORS, ETC: JAMES, T.G.H.

SUBJECTS: EGYPT EXPLORATION SOCIETY -- ADDRESSES, ESSAYS, LECTURES.*
          EXCAVATIONS (ARCHAEOLOGY) -- EGYPT -- ADDRESSES, ESSAYS,
          LECTURES.
          EGYPT -- ANTIQUITIES -- ADDRESSES, ESSAYS, LECTURES.

LC CARD: 81021947

ISBN: 0226391914:

    BRF - SEE LOCATIONS AND CALL NUMBERS   CIT - RETURN TO YOUR CITATION LIST
    IND - SEE LIST OF HEADINGS   FOR - SEE NEXT CITATION IN LIST
    CAT - BEGIN A NEW SEARCH

ENTER CODE: ¶¶   THEN PRESS SEND

Figure 14-16 Geac Library System. Bibliographic record display.

3. sequence in which data elements are arranged
4. spacing between data elements

It is evident in Figures 14-13 through 14-18 that, although the displays are noticeably different in appearance, several contain a core of descriptive bibliographic data that very much mirror the types of information typically included on full-entry catalog cards. With some exceptions, OPACs generally have at least one display format—in addition to or other than a numerically tagged MARC format—that includes nearly all of the following types of descriptive data:

```
PUBLIC CATALOG                                    Searching: DEMO
QH308.2  .K55 1983

   Kimball, John W.
     Biology /  John W. Kimball.
     5th ed.
   Reading, Mass. Addison Wesley Pub. Co., c1983.
     xviii, 974, [31]p. :  ill. ; 26 cm.

     Biology.


LOCATION        CALL#/VOL/NO/COPY              STATUS

ORNL            QH308.2 .K55 1983              Available

(END)




     Press RETURN to continue or /ES to start a new search:
```

Figure 14-17 OCLC LS/2000. Bibliographic record display.

```
E855K55
Kissinger, Henry,  1923-
   Years of upheaval / Henry Kissinger.  1st ed.   Boston :  Little, Brown,
1982.  xxi, 1283 p. (40) p. of plates :   ill. ;   24 cm.
   Includes bibliographical references and index.
SUB: 1. NIXON, RICHARD M.  (RICHARD MILHOUS),  1913-  2. KISSINGER, HENRY,
1923-  3. STATESMEN--UNITED STATES--BIOGRAPHY  4. UNITED STATES--FOREIGN
RELATIONS--1969-1974  5. UNITED STATES--FOREIGN RELATIONS--1974-1977
LC CARD #:81-86320  TITLE #:2892904  OCLC #:08252644 820608   63q820608
PAGE 1   END
```

Figure 14-18 Ohio State University Library Control System (LCS). Bibliographic record display.

Author

Title, including:
  Title proper
  Subtitle
  Remainder of title page transcription

Edition statement

Imprint, including:
  Place of publication

Publisher
Date of publication

Physical description, including:
Pagination
Illustration statement
Physical dimension

Series statement

Notes

Subject headings

Added entries

These elements are essentially the 100 through 800 fields of the MARC format.

Locational details are also almost always included on full-record displays. In some cases, these consist simply of a call number. In OPACs that contain records of holdings in several different libraries, branches, or collections, the call number is normally accompanied by additional data that identify the specific holding location(s). There are some exceptions to the inclusion of locational data on full-record displays. Claremont Colleges' TLS (Figure 14-15), for example, does not provide this information on a full-record format, but only a shorter display format, which serves as the default option. If the user elects to view a full record after seeing the shorter version, it is necessary to either remember the locational details or return to the shorter version record.

Where there is a circulation component integrated with an online public-access catalog, the full-record formats often include circulation availability status. In other OPACs, such as ULISYS and TLS (Figures 14-13 and 14-15), circulation-related details are shown on a separate screen, which may be retrieved directly from the full-record display. Providing circulation information in any level of an OPAC display requires a link between a library's circulation system and its public catalog, but where there is such a link, circulation availability is a popular feature among catalog users.

In OPACs that have an additional shorter individual record display option, the amount of information included falls somewhere between the amount provided on a brief-listing entry and that on a full record. The abbreviation usually occurs at the expense of textual description; location details and circulation status are usually retained in the shorter formats. Most OPACs generally exclude certain major bibliographic fields from shorter formats—most commonly, series, notes, subject headings, and added entries—and retain only certain portions of other major elements. For example, only the title proper and subtitle might be included in the shorter format, while the remainder of title-page transcription appears only on the longer version. The number of data elements pertaining to imprint is also frequently reduced. Date of publication is usually provided in the shorter format, but the place of publication, publisher, or both are dropped. Pagination is often the only physical description appearing in a short-record format.

Debate continues over which traditional data elements—and possibly which nontraditional ones—are most useful in a bibliographic record in the library catalog. OPACs have not really made inroads into experimenting with nontraditional data elements (such as reviews or citations to reviews, an often-discussed possibility), but with more traditional elements, many OPACs have at least managed to change the focus of debate by providing different versions of the bibliographic record for each item in the catalog. The question is not so much which elements should be provided in the traditional sense, as at which format levels they should be provided. There are still no sure answers, but a hierarchy of display formats does at least attempt to address different levels of complexity in the needs and preferences of catalog users.

There are three additional factors that contribute to the makeup and presentation of a bibliographic record display format: the labeling of data elements, the sequence in which the elements appear, and the spacing between them. Some but not all OPACs precede each element in a full-record display with an identifying label. Those that do label selected or all data elements may use full terms or abbreviations. Labels can be useful but only to the extent that they are easily understood. Problems occur with labels that are greatly abbreviated, especially when representing library jargon. For example, "ME" for main entry and "CO" for collation provide little in the way of useful information for the one person who might otherwise find labels the most helpful—the inexperienced catalog user. Even among OPACs that provide full-term labeling, there is sometimes a tendency to use jargon rather than common language alternatives. Some systems, for example, have used "main entry" as a data element label; even though it is spelled out, it still represents jargon with which many users are not familiar.

In some OPACs, labels are distinguished very clearly from the bibliographic text that accompanies them, usually through one of two methods. One technique is to supply all labels in uppercase characters, while the bibliographic text uses both upper- and lowercase. The other is to use reverse video on a display so that the color of the background and characters of labels are directly the opposite of those in which the text appears.

In terms of sequence in which data elements appear in relation to one another in full-record formats, a fairly high degree of uniformity exists among OPACs, at least with respect to the arrangement of descriptive cataloging data. The arrangement usually follows the numerical sequence of MARC tags: author, title, edition, imprint, physical description, series, notes, subject headings, and added entries. On OPACs that supply circulation-related details on a full-record display, the information almost invariably appears as the last element or set of elements on the display.

There is less uniformity among OPACs in the placement of locational data. As seen in the screen display examples, locational information sometimes precedes the descriptive cataloging information (ULISYS, Figure 14-13), sometimes follows it (MELVYL, Figure 14-14), or may not even be provided at this level at all (TLS, Figure 14-15).

For the most part, call numbers are displayed on a single line, but there are some exceptions. In the ULISYS online catalog (Figure 14-15)—and in several other OPACs not shown here—the call number is presented on two or more lines in the upper left-hand corner of the display. This mirrors the practice generally followed in representing call numbers on catalog cards. More pertinent, however, it may also be easier to read than a call number on a single line, and it corresponds to the way in which call numbers are typically represented on the spine labels of the items themselves.

Two considerations of spacing have an impact on the presentation of information on bibliographic records. The first is with respect to how data elements are separated from one another. In many OPACs, this is done vertically: Almost every data element on a record appears on a separate line or set of lines. Examples are found in two of the figures in this section: ULISYS and Geac (Figures 14-13 and 14-16). Although certain elements in each are grouped on a single line, they are the less essential ones and are still distinctly labeled. In contrast, some OPACs adhere to a paragraph style that resembles the arrangement of information on a catalog card; see the MELVYL, OCLC LS/2000, and LCS examples (Figures 14-14, 14-17, and 14-18). In none of these three is the blocking arrangement exactly identical to the standard LC catalog card setup, but the similarities are strong. An arrangement that does not conform to either of these approaches is found in Claremont Colleges' TLS (Figure 14-15). Virtually all data elements in this full-record format are run together, with differentiation between them provided only by special characters and not at all by spacing.

The second spacing consideration concerns the use of vertical space between lines—as opposed to elements—of information. Whether representing the same or different data elements, some OPACs adhere to single spacing between lines of information in a full-record format (see Figures 14-15 and 14-18). Others use intervening blank lines as a method for more clearly demarcating between lines of information, and especially between data elements or blocks of data elements. The use of vertical space to delineate information on a display is primarily an aesthetic concern, but it can have important implications for readability.

Data elements in individual bibliographic record displays and the style of presentation do vary among OPACs, but various approaches can be grouped according to underlying similarities. This "different but similar" quality typifies many of the characteristics of OPACs described in this chapter. The approaches taken or features provided in conjunction with a particular characteristic may vary from one OPAC to another, but it is possible to find general similarities and group the approaches taken or features provided into major categories. It is when the total range of characteristics is considered and the minor differences in similar approaches are accounted for, however, that OPACs become the highly individualistic systems they are.

Concern has been expressed in some areas about the extent of individualism among OPACs, about the persistence of local design effects, and about the lack of agreed-upon standards around which to guide future development. Both the International Standards Organization Technical Committee 46 and the National Information Standards Organization (Z39) are actively working on a number of such standards. It would seem that OPACs are simply too recent a phenomenon to impose such rigidity on their evolution at this point. However, the value of technical standards is manifestly demonstrable and rigidity can be avoided by seeking consensus rather than uniformity. OPACs that have been developed thus far have already achieved a great deal of success in expanding the flexibility of the library catalog. But there are still many unanswered questions; there is still need for further experimentation and analysis; and there is still much room for improvement. Only after more questions are answered, more experimentation and analysis carried out, and further improvements made will the time be right to suggest sophisticated standards by which to guide future development of the Online Public Access Catalog.

Notes

1. For further discussion of this topic, see Dennis Reynolds, "Online Catalogs . . . Access Points, Indexed Fields, and Search Types," *Action for Libraries* 10 (April 1984): 3–4.
2. Stephen R. Salmon, "Characteristics of Online Public Catalogs," *Library Resources & Technical Services* 27 (January/March 1983): 49.
3. Reported by Neal K. Kaske and Karen Markey in "Online Public Access

Catalogs: Patron and Staff Experiences," Paper presented at the ALA LITA/RTSD Preconference: Online Catalogs, Online Reference, June 23–24, 1983.

4. Charles R. Hildreth, *Online Public Access Catalogs: The User Interface* (Dublin, Ohio: OCLC, 1982), p. 119.

15

Online Search Services:
The Context

The automated service offered most extensively to library users is on-line searching of remotely stored databases available from such government and commercial operations as the National Library of Medicine, DIALOG Information Retrieval Service, Bibliographic Retrieval Service (BRS), and SDC Information Service. These and a number of others have been around for several years and, in general, constitute the most sophisticated retrieval systems in library use today. Until fairly recently, these services and their systems generally have been intended for use only by those with sophisticated searching skills predicated on formal and extensive training. And except in some very technical environments, these services have not been viewed by libraries as appropriate for direct use by library patrons. But this pattern is shifting, as these and other operations place more and more emphasis on providing service directly to end users of information.

The end user emphasis is still in its early stages, however, insofar as a direct service is concerned, and online searching of bibliographic and other databases by librarians is likely to continue to grow rather than abate. It is that provision of searching as a library service that is the focus of this chapter and Chapter 16. The earlier chapters of Part III, Applications, examine automated systems in libraries primarily in terms of functional characteristics—what they do, supplemented, in the case of online catalogs, by a description of how these features work from the user's perspective. In this chapter and Chapter 16, the emphasis is on the state of the information retrieval industry, some basic issues confronting libraries in online search service operation, and the administration and organization of the service. This does not imply that the technical features of these systems are unimportant or simplistic; to the contrary, they are very sophisticated and their mastery is fundamental to the success of a library's online search service. But because this is a service to the library public performed by librarians, equally important to its success is the way in which it is financed, promoted, and administered.

For clarity, the phrases "information retrieval services" and "retrieval services" are used to describe vendors such as DIALOG, BRS, and SDC; the phrases "online searching" and "online search services" describe the public service function provided by librarians in searching the databases on DIALOG, BRS, SDC, and so on. The phrases "database producer" and "producer" identify those corporations and organizations that create machine-readable databases and lease them to the retrieval services, which in turn provide libraries and others with remote access to them.

Why an Online Search Service?

The benefits of online searching are obvious to libraries in which it is well established, but the library in the planning stages must be able to justify the expense of the service and the changes it can bring. Following are some of the major benefits of establishing an online service.

Access to a far greater number of bibliographic and other sources (especially for the smaller library, even with a subscription to just one online retrieval service).

A means of retrieval (perhaps the only one) in areas of interest outside the library's main collection.

Savings in user time and effort over manual search.

Public relations; employing computer technology enhances the library's image as a timely and sophisticated provider of information.

Expands the scope of the library's services.

Introducing online service in the library involves more than simply shifting a manual service to an automated operation. The nature of the relationship between user and librarian fundamentally changes when the sources, long available in print form, are introduced online, and the library must deal with several organizational matters that have not been applicable in the maintenance of equivalent manual sources for patron use. Matters pertaining specifically to the organization and administration of online searching as a library service are examined in detail in Chapter 16. This chapter examines several broader issues that play key roles in shaping the overall context in which this service is offered by libraries. An overview of the information retrieval industry and the major challenges confronting it follow, as well as an examination of two questions of particular importance in the provision of online searching as a library service: free versus fee-based services, and document delivery.

Information Retrieval and Online Databases

The growth in the number of available online databases and the services through which they are offered (traced in Chapter 5) continue into the mid-1980s. *The Directory of Online Databases,* compiled and published by Cuadra Associates, listed about 1,100 online databases and 189 information retrieval services in early 1982; by late 1983, it included nearly 1,900 online databases and 277 services.[1] In 1981, a report issued by Knowledge Industry Publications estimated about 200,000 users of online services in the United States spending around $680 million annually,[2] and these numbers have certainly increased since then. In a study surveying the use of 247 databases offered by 15 of these services, Martha Williams estimated spending at $129 million.[3] Early in 1983, among the services most familiar to libraries, DIALOG Information Retrieval Services counted its total subscribers at nearly 20,000, Bibliographic Retrieval Service (BRS) at about 8,000, and the New York Times Information Service (NYTIS) at around 5,000.[4] Not all, of course, but many of these users were libraries.

Library-oriented Information Retrieval Services

For practical purposes in establishing and operating an online search service for its users, a library need not worry that it will have to offer access to thousands of databases or learn hundreds of different retrieval systems. Although the number of databases and services that the library may wish to access will undoubtedly increase, a library's concern will be with the few that are most applicable to the traditional activities of a library.

The actual number of services used by libraries has remained fairly constant since the 1970s. Most used are DIALOG, SDC Information Service, BRS, and (until mid-1983) NYTIS; also, NLM (National Library of Medicine), Mead Data Central (MDC), and Westlaw. By the early 1980s, three new services had made a significant impression on the library market—CAS ONLINE, ISI (Institute of Scientific Information), and Pergamon INFOLINE. The ease with which they penetrated the library market—at least in comparison with other retrieval services—had largely to do with the fact that their online databases or print publications were already familiar to the online searching community. CAS (Chemical Abstracts Services) was the producer of chemistry-related databases that had been available through BRS, DIALOG, and SDC. ISI's *Science Citation Index* and *Social Science Citation Index* had also been accessible in online form through other services. For INFOLINE, Pergamon was able to rely on library familiarity with its established reputation as a publisher of scientific, technical, and medical titles.

Significantly, the decision by these publishers to establish their own services did not always mean withdrawal of their databases from other services. Although *Science Citation Index* and *Social Science Citation Index* are online through ISI's own retrieval services, both are also available through DIALOG, and the latter is available on BRS. Some databases produced by Chemical Abstracts are available on other services, although the full abstracts database is available only on the CAS service.

In the future, interest by libraries may extend to such possibilities as the NewsNet Service, which contains the full text of more than 100 newsletters produced by various organizations in the United States. During 1983, an interesting addition to NewsNet was *Wiley Book News*. Not only are the contents available online, but a subscriber may also establish an interest profile and be notified online whenever a new Wiley book that fits the particular profile is published.[5] Such a service really impacts more on a library's technical services operation than on its online search service, but it is a direction libraries will want to watch closely.

Within the group of database producers as information retrieval vendors, a recent development is the emergence of H. W. Wilson indexes online. A long-standing publisher of popular print indexes, Wilson has made a comparatively late entrance into the world of computerized database production. Since the early 1980s, Wilson has begun to convert some of its operations to computer, resulting in machine-readable databases for use in production of printed indexes and also serving as the raw material for online access. Wilson contracted for the creation of a retrieval language and by mid-1983 was able to demonstrate the BEACON system for retrieving citations from several of its indexes. Later known as WILSONLINE, the retrieval system is based on the ELHILL system used by NLM's retrieval service, and by association it shares a historical ancestry with SDC's ORBIT system. After a testing stage through the early part of 1984, at least some of the indexes became available later in the year through WILSONLINE.

Even among the small number of services that libraries tend to rely on, change occurs constantly. Both technologically and in the marketing arena, these services strive to enhance their systems to attract new users. CAS, for example, greatly expanded the content and searchability of its *Chemical Abstracts* database. Initially, bibliographic citations could be retrieved only in association with chemical substances or by

Chemical Abstracts citation number, and even then the citations were not accompanied by actual abstracts. By mid-1983, the abstracts had become available in the online *Chemical Abstracts* database, and in late 1983, bibliographic searching of citations by keyword and index terms was introduced. CAS is also involved in a major project to add to the online database substances that were covered in the print version of *Chemical Abstracts* between 1920 and 1964, but are still not online. DIALOG redesigned its software during 1984 to improve existing features and make new ones available, but in such a way that users will not be required to "relearn" the system. DIALOG also set up its own telecommunications network, which should be interesting to watch in terms of progress and eventual impact on telecommunications charges for libraries. BRS, among other things, was very active in loading full-test databases and stepped up the marketing campaign for its BRS Search software, which can be used for a variety of local information storage and retrieval applications. BRS also broadened the offerings within its "Colleague" series of subject-oriented database packages. Both DIALOG with its Knowledge Index and BRS with its After Dark have begun to approach the home microcomputer market.

An incident that clearly demonstrated the fluidity of the information retrieval service environment was the 1983 agreement between the *New York Times* and Mead Data Central. The *Times* announced that the rights for brokerage of its New York Times Information Service were being granted to MDC, whose visibility in the academic, public, and much of the special library market was not high. This transfer was not well received by many NYTIS users, a main complaint being that MDC databases were accessible only through Mead's own dedicated terminals; NYTIS and most other services used by libraries can be accessed through an extremely wide variety of equipment. There was also concern over the future standard of quality, since the number of staff responsible for creating and maintaining NYTIS databases had been drastically reduced. In addition, libraries were concerned about having to learn a new retrieval language, about MDC's pricing structure, and about its credit requirements.[6] By mid-1983, MDC had made a series of policy announcements partially addressing these concerns, including access through IBM personal computers among others. This sequence of events illustrates how organizational, technological, and market factors interact in the information retrieval service environment.

Databases

Like the information retrieval services, bibliographic and other databases used by libraries are constantly changing in scope, extent of coverage, and availability. Overall, the number is steadily increasing; in fact, just those services most heavily used by libraries cover a wide range of interests.

DIALOG offers online access to more than 180 databases; BRS and SDC exceed 70. Most other services used by libraries have fewer databases and smaller scope of coverage, but they do address certain disciplines and patron needs. Significant overlap occurs, especially among the larger and more popular databases. Some databases produced by Chemical Abstracts and available through their own service are also available through DIALOG, BRS, SDC, and Pergamon. Several others in science and technology are nearly as widely available, and a number in business, government, and the social sciences and humanities have broad exposure. (Management Contents, NTIS, ERIC, and PsychInfo are vended simultaneously through DIALOG, BRS, and SDC; many others are available through two of these three.)

The contents of online databases can be categorized in several ways, but perhaps the most visible distinction is between word-oriented and nonword-oriented. At present, nonword-oriented databases are primarily statistical, although some are taking on broader dimensions. For example, Pergamon's VIDEO PATSEARCH, although still word-oriented, allows users with a designated model of microcomputer to purchase videodisks from Pergamon containing graphic illustrations corresponding to patents described in the database. Thus, the service blends words and illustrations through two different modes of access, and the "contents" of the database take on greater diversity.

The predominant form of the word-oriented database is still "bibliographic," the online equivalent of printed indexes. Some include only citations; others include abstracts as well. A second level extends beyond simple bibliographic representation of documents to include the full document text. Such examples are becoming more frequent. Mead Data Central has been a long-time leader in full-text databases with its LEXIS and NEXIS and now with the New York Times Online. BRS has been at the forefront in loading full-text databases, including the 10-million-word *Academic American Encyclopedia*, the 25-volume *Kirk-Othmer Encyclopedia of Chemical Technology*, the *Harvard Business Review* since 1976, and a full-text database composed of 18 journals published by the American Chemical Society. DIALOG also offers the full text of the *Harvard Business Review* (since 1976), provides full-text databases of *Commerce Business Daily* and UPI News, and plans more activity in this area. Most recently, DIALOG and Information Access Corporation (IAC) announced that the full text of periodicals indexed in IAC's Magazine Index would be available on DIALOG, coverage dating back to early 1983. Another example of the trend toward full text is the availability of *Mental Measurements Yearbook* on SDC.

A third category of word-oriented databases is really an extension of the other two. The distinguishing characteristic is that these databases have no precise equivalents and are still very much in an emerging state. Those with the greatest initial visibility will be full text or directory, possibly drawing on a number of different printed sources to arrive at a unique collection of online information. At least at first, their content is likely to be applied, referencelike, and almost task-oriented. An example is the electronic Yellow Pages series on DIALOG. In each of seven different areas—construction, manufacturing, retailing, and so on—the database producer has compiled information from nearly 5,000 U.S. telephone directories and supplemented it with some demographic and financial data to provide a unique online database. As this "online only" trend gathers momentum, the databases are likely to focus more heavily on explanatory content rather than directorylike information.

When commercial retrieval services began to emerge in the early 1970s, the emphasis was almost entirely on scientific and technical databases. Among the services used by libraries in the mid-1980s, databases in science and technology still predominate, but not as extensively as they did. There has been growth in the number of databases in the social sciences, arts and humanities, and business and finance.

The library that is anticipating or already offering an online search service to a large group of users outside the areas of science and technology might find it useful to examine available databases according to the seven categories noted, which follow.

1. Bibliographic databases (corresponding to traditional academic-oriented indexing and abstracting print publications). DIALOG, traditionally offering the most extensive array in the social sciences, humanities, and arts, includes the MLA Bibliography, Philosopher's Index, PsychInfo (formerly Psychological Abstracts), RILM Abstracts, United States Political Science Documents, ERIC, PAIS, Religion Index, and Sociological Abstracts (the last four also available on BRS; ERIC on SDC as well). BRS leads in specialized databases in the education field, including Bilingual Education Bibliographic Abstracts, Exceptional Child Education Resources, School Practices Information File, and Resources in Vocational Education.

2. Business and financial databases (rivals science and technology). Some of these are bibliographic and cover standard periodical literature in the field, as ABI/INFORM and Management Contents. Some producers focus on coverage of financial reports, forecasts, and corporate news and statistics—Dun & Bradstreet, Standard & Poors, Arthur D. Little, Frost & Sullivan, Predicasts, Inc. These databases often include extensive financial data on U.S. and sometimes international cor-

porations. The Disclosure ^{tm} II database, for example, extracts financial and other reports submitted to the U.S. Securities and Exchange Commission by major corporations. Two databases produced by Economic Information Systems, Inc., available on DIALOG, gather information from a wide range of sources on virtually hundreds of thousands of manufacturing and nonmanufacturing establishments in the United States.

3. Legal databases. Westlaw and MDC have been the primary sources. There are also some law-related databases available on more familiar services. DIALOG has the Legal Resources Index, which indexes more than 700 law journals and newspapers, and LABORLAW and PATLAW, which document court decisions in the areas of labor and patents, respectively. Most library-oriented services also have one or more databases relating to proceedings of the federal legislature and courts.

4. News databases. There is considerable overlap in application here, particularly with business and finance. In an excellent overview, Nina Ross reported on some 21 news-related databases available through 1982.[7] Most, although not all, are based on coverage of major daily newspapers in the United States and abroad. The first and largest of the NYTIS databases, INFOBANK I, includes coverage not only of the *Times,* but also selectively of a number of other major U.S. newspapers and news-related magazines. NEXIS, a longtime staple of MDC, incorporates the full text of news stories from several major wire services and periodicals. DIALOG and SDC also have general news coverage databases. DIALOG's chief offering is the National Newspaper Index (NNI), produced by Information Access Company. The newspapers indexed in NNI include the *New York Times,* the *Wall Street Journal,* the *Washington Post,* the *Los Angeles Times,* and the *Christian Science Monitor.* DIALOG also offers a UPI News database, which contains the full text of all news stories carried over the UPI wire, and the World Affairs Report database, which primarily contains excerpts from a number of Soviet news publications. SDC's multisource general news database is NDEX, providing coverage of about 20 U.S. newspapers. SDC also offers the MONITOR database, which indexes articles from the various regional editions of the *Christian Science Monitor.*

5. Databases related to government activity, particularly at the federal level. Some are produced by the U.S. government; others are commercially produced, although many of the commercial ones are essentially a repackaging of information initially generated by government agencies. Some government-produced databases are well known and widely used: MEDLINE by the National Library of Medicine, AGRICOLA by the National Library of Agriculture, ERIC by the Na-

tional Institute of Education, MARC cataloging records by the Library of Congress, and the GPO Monthly Catalog by the Government Printing Office, to name a few.

In addition to bibliographic databases, the U.S. government also produces demographic, financial, and statistical databases. Several on DIALOG, for example, are produced by the U.S. Bureau of Labor Statistics and provide a range of statistics pertaining to labor and the economy. Three other databases on DIALOG are produced by the U.S. Department of Commerce with the intention of aiding the American business community. These are Foreign Traders Index, which contains information on business enterprises in more than 130 foreign countries; Trade Opportunities, to assist in identifying foreign markets for U.S. companies; and U.S. Exports, providing data on exports by the U.S. government and commercial enterprises. Another important set of databases produced by the U.S. government includes those reporting on research progress and opportunities, with the National Technical Information Service (NTIS) being a major supplier in this area. In addition, a number of commercial producers supply databases containing information about the activities of the U.S. government or based on government-supplied print sources. One of the major producers is Congressional Information Service, Inc., whose CIS database provides access to working papers of, and other information about, congressional committees and subcommittees. Another is Capitol Services, Inc., which produces *Congressional Record Abstracts* and *Federal Register Abstracts*. All three of these databases are available on both DIALOG and SDC.

6. Popular-interest publications. Services such as The Source and CompuServe have attempted to address the audience for these publications, but among the longer standing online services, the only appreciable example is the Magazine Index (MI) database produced by Information Access Corporation (IAC) and available on DIALOG. The launching of MI in an otherwise academic-, business-, and research-oriented online environment was a rather bold venture in 1980. The database now indexes almost 400 general-interest magazines, including, not incidentally, all of those indexed in H. W. Wilson's *Reader's Guide to Periodical Literature,* plus a couple hundred others.

7. General reference sources. Many of these are already familiar to libraries in hard copy. Three standard R. R. Bowker sources are available in online form, including *Books in Print, Ulrich's International Periodicals Directory,* and *American Men and Women of Science.* All are available on both BRS and DIALOG. Gale has two popular reference works online, *Biography Master Index* and *Encyclopedia of Associations,* as well as the more bibliographic-oriented *Book Review Index.* In early 1984, these

Gale publications were available online only on DIALOG. Other reference works available online include *Marquis Who's Who in America, Foundation Directory, Foundation Grants Index,* and two of Peterson's guides to colleges. Three encyclopedias have, at one time or another, been online in full-text version. The only one accessible to libraries in early 1984 was the *Academic American Encyclopedia,* offered on BRS. *Encyclopaedia Britannica III* is part of MDC's NEXIS, although the producer contractually required MDC not to allow libraries access to it. The third, *World Book Encyclopedia,* was online through the CompuServe service for a time, but has been withdrawn. Part of the problem with it appeared to be traceable to the exclusion of illustrations, maps, and other graphics, which have not historically lent themselves readily to online transmission. With the continuing emergence of videodisk and videotex technology in information retrieval, this limitation is being overcome. In the meantime, the reception of online encyclopedias and other materials that have traditionally relied on accompanying illustrations is likely to be lukewarm at best.

Online retrieval services and the databases they offer are certainly no longer bound exclusively to the province of science and technology. Scientific and technical research and application will remain a *tour de force* in online searching, but the library that does not recognize the ongoing expansion of service to other areas is likely to miss out on an opportunity to promote the value of library service to a far broader audience. The problem in handling some types of search requests in these areas may still be whether there is at least one appropriate database available, but it is more and more becoming a matter of which of several might be most appropriate.

The increasing number of retrieval services and the proliferation of databases are not the only ways in which changes in the online industry are affecting the way libraries view online searching as a service. The mid-1980s promise to be a time of change in the industry in many respects.

Challenges of the 1980s

The information retrieval industry is constantly confronted with new challenges—political, economic, and social, and those resulting from changes in the technology itself. Of the many influences giving rise to change, the interaction of four developments will be particularly important in shaping directions during the mid-1980s. One is the impact of the online database on the economy of its print version equivalent. Another is the proliferation of microcomputers and their impact on the way libraries use online databases offered by the retrieval services. A third development is in the area of pricing online services. The fourth is how extensively information retrieval services and database producers develop technological alternatives to the traditional ways in which their products have been disseminated. Trends in these four areas act on one another in ways that alter the structure of the relationship between information retrieval services, database producers, and libraries. Efforts to balance this interaction will have important consequences for the way in which libraries provide online search services to their users.

Impact on Print Subscriptions

Many of the online databases now used by libraries initially served as convenient by-products of the production process for generating hardcopy publications. Particularly in the area of indexing and abstracting publications, the creation of machine-readable databases was motivated mainly by the need to find a more efficient method for storing and manipulating information as the basis for the production of a printed publication. At the same time, it was apparent that with little additional effort on the part of the producer, the machine-readable databases could also be licensed to commercial retrieval services for online searching. For the producer, the licensing fee and any online royalty payments were additional revenue generated with little extra cost. It was also recognized quite early that this "best of both worlds" situation would not endure forever. Sooner or later, the database producer's print and online products would be competing with one another, and in all probability, the result would be an increase in online use and a decrease, or at least stagnation, in subscriptions to the print version.

The question of whether a producer's publication would be used online or in the print version might not be so crucial if the rewards had always been equivalent. However, the payments received by producers from retrieval services throughout the 1970s were proportionally quite low. The amount of online usage and the revenue realized were not sufficient to offset the threat of canceled subscriptions to the far more profitable print equivalents. Database royalty payments have increased appreciably during the past several years, but most producers still claim to be in a predicament. Online revenues are not yet an economically viable replacement for monies received from print subscriptions, and subscription cancellations are viewed by most producers as a real threat to their economic well-being.

It is difficult to accurately access the impact that online availability of databases has had on subscriptions to corresponding print publications. Some people have pointed out that, in a certain theoretical way, the impact should not be that great, and that the two modes are complementary rather than competitive. One argument points to known cases where online usage has resulted in a library's commencing, rather than canceling, a print subscription to a particular index. The online usage in these cases reportedly exposed the availability of certain indexes to which the library had never subscribed, and thus created a demand that was previously unknown or miscalculated, but was thereafter great enough to merit a print subscription. Another argument pointed out that in some libraries the choice is not, nor ever will be, an "either/or" situation; for reasons of affordability or institutional emphasis, the library never did nor would ever be likely to subscribe to the printed index regardless of whether it was online. Under these circumstances, any online usage by such a library represents clear revenue that would not otherwise be realized by the producer. In still other cases, it is argued that the print and online versions of the same publication represent two rather distinct sources despite their common genesis and that they address different types of needs and so are appropriate for different types of use. Hence, it is appropriate for many libraries to both subscribe to the print version and offer access to the online version; thus the two forms of the same publication can be seen as complementary rather than competitive.

Each of those arguments can list actual library evidence for support. But they also often focus on isolated cases or on certain categories of libraries. When viewed in the context of the library community on the whole, how valid are those positions? The relative paucity of data and the complexity of the economy over the past several years do make it difficult to establish the degree to which online availability has eroded the number of print subscriptions. Inez Speer surveyed 15 database producers in early 1983, reporting that, between 1977 and 1982, there was generally an annual attrition rate of between 2 and 5 percent to their printed indexing and abstracting publications. The producers were the first to admit, however, that the attrition could not be blamed only on availability of online services. The general state of the economy during these years, resulting in a tightening of library budgets, was also a major factor.[8]

Microcomputers and Downloading

The library's use of microcomputers in online searching can result in an improvement in service to users. The catalyst for realizing such benefits is the ability to download search results onto local disk, manipulate them, and print them out in a format different from that used by the retrieval service. If a search has involved the use of two or more databases, the results can be merged and any duplicate citation expurgated. In some circumstances, the library can also reduce the amount of time it spends online by using a microcomputer, resulting in at least a nominal savings in telecommunications expense.

From the library's point of view, downloading of search results carries these many advantages. At the same time, however, widespread downloading can have profound financial effects on information retrieval services and database producers. And these consequences are anything but advantageous.

Given the traditional context of pricing policy, there are two levels of concern for the services and producers. The most severe is the extent to which downloading could curtail search activity in general and could even represent potential competition. As noted earlier, information from an online database can be downloaded with great speed. This information is in machine-readable form. With the availability of appropriate software, it is possible to create one's own database from merged results for local searching, thereby obviating the need to use the service, or at least reducing the full search to an update when another user submits a request similar to one for which records had been downloaded. In the extreme case, a library or other agency could even download to the extent that it could repackage the cumulative results and offer a service in competition with the original one.

Such incidences in the use of downloaded data are probably few. It has been pointed out that each search request submitted by users, even if on the same topic, is unique in terms of individual needs. Therefore, using previous results again for a different user contradicts the library's purpose in offering an online search service in the first place. Repackaging and resale would become quite obvious if done on any appreciable scale, and probably, what with legal constraints, would not be successful. Because of these and other reasons, such applications of downloading are said not to be prevalent, do not noticeably affect the commercial services and producers, or, in the area of locally confined reuse, somehow fall under a principle of "fair use" of data that were already paid for.

Attempts to justify reuse or resale of machine-readable data are overshadowed by the fact that it is usually illegal and nearly always violates the contract with the retrieval service. Vendor contracts usually are very specific about what may and may not be done with retrieved data.

A somewhat "grayer" area of concern for services and producers is downloading for purposes of viewing results locally, eliminating duplicates, and reformatting citations. Libraries do this commonly and without any intent to reuse the data for other searches or repackage them for wider distribution. The complication occurs over the impact of these practices in the context of traditional pricing structures in the library-oriented information retrieval industry. As the commercial services emerged during the 1970s, their pricing plans revolved around two types of charges, the major one related to connect time—the amount of time a library spent online connected with the service's computer. This charge was levied by the service for access to and use of the system, independent of the costs for using the telecommunications network, such as TYMNET or TELENET, through which the link was made to the computer. The second type was a "per-hit" charge for each citation printed offline in response to a search. This was optional for the library in that it did not *have* to request a printout of the search results. The other alternatives were simply to view the results online, or to remain online and print them off locally on a teleprinter or on a slave printer attached to a cathode-ray tube (CRT). Given the rather slow speeds of such equipment, it was often less expensive to pay the per-hit charges.

This kind of pricing structure has posed serious complications in the 1980s, with the downloading capabilities of microcomputers perhaps the greatest potential challenge. From a retrieval service's or a producer's point of view, these capabilities strike at both components of pricing. By uploading search strategies and then downloading results and viewing and printing out citations locally, the savings in connect-time costs and offline printing costs for the library mean lost revenue for retrieval services and database producers. Given traditional pricing structures, the use of microcomputers presents a potential and real threat to their financial base.

Pricing Retrieval Services

Concern over downloading and print subscriptions has prompted cries for changes in the level and structure of pricing online services, although the traditional time-based approach has always had its problems. Library management has long been aware that the greatest share of the costs for online searching, on a minute-by-minute basis, stems from *access* to information rather than *results*. It is the attempt to get data, not the actual retrieval, that costs so much. This is particularly true when database royalty fees are charged on a connect-time basis. Most librarians might concede the fairness of time-dependent pricing for use of the service's computer resources, but most also think that additional charges should be based more on the results of a search than on the amount of time it took. From a library service perspective, a pricing structure balanced heavily toward connect time also introduces conflicts of quality versus economy. Searchers are discouraged from experimenting and using a number of approaches in a difficult search, when in fact another strategy might obtain results from a search that would otherwise be fruitless. This is particularly restrictive when the library charges fees for online searches; pursuing strategies that require additional time may not be a risk for which the user is willing to pay.

In addition to the problem for libraries, time-based pricing presents paradoxes for database producers and retrieval services. A well-indexed and efficiently constructed database, for example, obviously means less time online for searchers than one that is poorly indexed and sloppily organized. With time-based royalties, particularly if the database coverage is unique, a producer may be faced with the irony of being financially penalized for expending time and money to ensure a high-quality, well-indexed database. The more efficient the system, the better its response time, and the fewer the problems with telecommunications networks on any given day, the less revenues for the producer. Any investments to improve the system to provide more efficient searching will have similar consequences and will have to be offset by increases in connect-hour rates. Most libraries can appreciate this, but the retrieval service is still faced with a significant public relations challenge. And added to it is the sensitivity of time-based pricing to technology, such as when communication with the service's computers became feasible at a rate of 1200 baud, and 1200-baud equipment became less expensive. The connect-hour economy of the information retrieval services had been based on 300-baud communications speed; as more libraries made the transition to 1200 baud, the amount of time required to conduct a search decreased, as did revenues for the service. More recently, microcomputers with their downloading capabilities have posed other time-related challenges.

Despite all these problems, the time-based pricing structure has remained relatively intact. Major changes have stemmed from actions by the database producers. The initially low charge, combined with the possibility of increasing cancellations to corresponding print subscriptions, has prompted producers to change the level and even the structure of pricing for online access to their databases.

Database producers in cooperation with the retrieval services have implemented some very specific pricing plans in an effort to curb the long-range impact of cancellations of corresponding print publications. One is differential pricing of online access according to whether a user also subscribes to the print publication. Online users pay a higher rate if they do not, and this price difference can be substantial. Taken to the extreme, online access can be denied to nonsubscribers altogether. In 1982, a report of a survey in France found that subscription to the print version was a requirement for online access for nearly 25 percent of the 171 North American databases in use.[9] This surprisingly high percentage could well have been influenced disproportionately by the fact that the number of North American databases covered in the survey was relatively small compared with the total produced in the United States and Canada. Complete denial of online access to nonsubscribers is not characteristic of the databases available through the retrieval services most frequently used in libraries.

A more comprehensive approach used by producers has simply been to negotiate for higher all-around payments from retrieval services for use of their databases. This may mean higher licensing fees for the right to mount the databases, increased time-based royalty fees, and higher per-citation charges for offline prints. More recently, and in response largely to the downloading phenomenon, producers and services are also assessing charges for each citation displayed online. This fee is not yet universal among the databases used by libraries, but it has become a standard charge for many. In general, there has been a continuing trend among bibliographic databases toward shifting a greater proportion of producer royalties from time-related charges to per-citation charges, both online and offline. This can ameliorate at least some librarian concerns about paying royalty fees according to access rather than results, but by no means does it address all of them.

These approaches by producers are taken in part to achieve greater stability between print subscriptions and online use as potential revenue bases. At the same time, producers are employing still other strategies designed to maintain and increase their economic viability in a difficult environment that is still predominantly print, but moving more and more in an online direction. One of these strategies is to differentiate the content of online and offline versions of the same publication, so that they are not precisely equivalent and therefore may not be strictly competitive with one another. Most commonly, this has meant a greater amount of information in the print product than in the online database, usually including full abstracts only in the former. Another strategy is for producers to expand their line of hard-copy publications and online offerings by generating specialized publications from the same machine-readable database used in creating the more comprehensive product. Since much of the expense of creating these spin-offs will already have been incurred in compiling and maintaining the parent database, the specialized products are a relatively low-risk, high-return opportunity. Inez Speer, in her 1982 survey of database producers, discovered yet another type of response to the fluid environment: Producers have been forced to become more sophisticated in actively marketing both online and offline products."[10]

Some of these changes have affected the actual *structure* of pricing for online services, but their main impact has been more on the *level* of pricing. Connect-time and per-citation charges are still the framework within which most of these changes occur. Especially since 1982, however, other efforts have focused more directly on changing the actual structure, or at least introducing significant modifications to it. The I. P. Sharp retrieval service exemplifies one such modification. One component of pricing is a connect-hour charge, but it is a nominal amount. A second pricing component is based on the number of computer resources used during a search, in the form of a charge per central processing unit (CPU) used. The third component consists of a charge for each character displayed, a variation on the per-citation principle. Another variation can be seen in the pricing structure for searching the Excerpta Medica database on BRS, in which per-citation charging varies according to which bibliographic elements within citations are printed offline or displayed online.

Still another variation on the traditional pricing structure has been used for several years by CAS ONLINE, operated by Chemical Abstracts. The CAS structure incorporates the traditional pricing variables as well as some of the modifications described above, but it places the main emphasis on a per-search charge. There is an online connect-hour charge, but it is relatively low. There are online and offline per-citation charges, varying according to whether partial or complete records are printed or displayed. The primary component of pricing, however, is a fixed fee for each search conducted, regardless of the amount of time it takes or the number of records it retrieves.

Still another nontraditional pricing structure, and one that may be gathering momentum, is based on a flat monthly fee for using a service or particular databases on it. BRS uses this pricing strategy for its Executive Information Service, consisting of four specific databases. The service, which draws on two bibliographic databases—ABI/INFORM and Management Contents—and two full-text databases—the *Academic American Encyclopedia* and the *Harvard Business Review/Online,* can be accessed for $100 per month, regardless of the number of online connect hours of usage. Another example was CAS, which announced a flat-fee option for academic libraries; during 1984, they could use CAS ONLINE during off-peak hours at a fixed rate of $500 per month, regardless of the number of searches conducted or amount of time connected. The only variable billing is for offline prints, not included in the monthly fee. These two examples certainly do not indicate a major trend as yet, but it will be interesting to note if further instances appear. The flat-fee approach walks a financial tightrope between the ability of services and producers to realize an acceptable profit margin and the perception of users that such an approach is less costly than "pay-as-you-go" connect-hour pricing. There is indeed a narrow ground on which both of these requirements may be met, and the success of flat-fee pricing will depend upon how well the balance can be maintained.

To a more limited extent, some services have attempted to meet the challenge of downloading directly through pricing mechanisms. CAS, for example, offers an option whereby it will contractually sanction downloading of up to 50,000 records per year for a fixed annual assessment. Use of the records is limited to the contracting site, but allowance is made for remote access to the downloaded records by subsidiaries and branches of the central site. The assessment varies according to whether a user subscribes to the print version of *Chemical Abstracts*. During 1984, the annual downloading license for a print subscriber was $4,000; the assessment for a nonsubscriber was $8,000. BioSciences Information Service, producer of the BIOSIS database, available through a number of retrieval services, also provides for downloading through formal agreement and pricing arrangements.

Retrieval services and database producers are likely to continue these and other experiments with pricing for online retrieval. An even more rapidly evolving initiative, however, can be seen in the area of technology-related activities by services and producers alike, and some of these are described in the following text.

Technological Responses

After a period of concern, many services and database producers now view the advent of microcomputers and their downloading capabilities as the way to markets for new or additional products. One such avenue is in the development and sale of software packages to assist users in searching and in downloading results onto microcomputers. Retrieval services, database vendors, and others have developed a variety of packages, and the number is steadily increasing. Some examples are described below.

With SDC's ORBIT SearchMaster, users can create a search strategy on floppy disk prior to connection with SDC's computers, and then upload the strategy when the connection is made. After the search has been conducted and modified, if necessary, the results can be downloaded onto disk. SearchMaster also allows for storage and automatic execution of dial-up procedures and log-on. Another example is I. P. Sharp's MAGIC, which enables users to download and merge results from various numeric databases available through the service.

The comprehensive SCI-MATE software from ISI has two components, the Universal Online Searcher and the Personal Data Manager, which can be purchased separately or together. The Universal Online Searcher, for use on ISI's own retrieval service and competing services as well, facilitates use in such a way that the searcher need not even know the "native" retrieval language of each service. This versatility is achieved through a menu-driven approach to search strategy creation, with the software "translating" the user-supplied answers into the service-specific retrieval language. Although this feature can be useful in a search conducted on a service that is less frequently used, online searchers who are experienced on a particular service will usually find it preferable to search in that service's native language. The Universal Online Searcher allows a user to exercise this option. In any case, the results can be downloaded, either in their entirety or on a citation-by-citation basis. With the Personal Data Manager, the downloaded citations can be reformatted according to user-created specifications, merged with results of other searches if desired, and retrieved locally.

Some database producers have responded to the microcomputer environment with a different focus. Search Helper was developed by Information Access Company to facilitate the searching of its Magazine Index on DIALOG. It is designed for use by untrained searchers, thus enabling users to construct and execute their own searches rather than having to rely on a librarian intermediary. The user is guided through the formulation of a search strategy by a question-and-answer approach carried out prior to connection to DIALOG computers. The search strategy is internally translated and recorded onto disk in language appropriate for DIALOG. With automatic dial-up and log-on, the connection is made, the search strategy uploaded, and the search performed. Up to 20 citations are automatically downloaded, after which the online connection is broken and the user can view the results locally from disk. The pricing for this atypical service is quite low— $2.50 for each search. According to at least one reviewer, the 20-citation limit can be too restrictive and the search capabilities seem too simplistic. It was also noted, however, that Search Helper's capabilities were in fact more flexible than they might appear at first, but the more sophisticated features simply were not explained to the user.[11] Since Search Helper is intended for users—many of whom may not be familiar with or want to use sophisticated retrieval techniques—the simplification reduces the likelihood of user frustration caused by a myriad of options and detailed explanations.

A different approach is in the production and direct sale of "mini-databases" on floppy disk, for example, the ERIC Update series. As of early 1984, the series had 10 titles, each focusing on a particular subject interest. For each area of interest, ERIC extracts about 100 citations from its master ERIC database and distributes them on floppy disk to subscribers. Updated periodically, these disks are extremely inexpensive, at less than $5 per update per title.

BioSciences Information Service is taking a similar but more sophisticated approach through its BIOSIS Information Transfer System (BITS). Rather than defining generalized areas of interest like ERIC, the focus of the BITS program is on allowing each subscriber to establish his or her specific interest profile. BITS is thus essentially a producer-provided selective dissemination of information (SDI) service. With the distribution of updated disks containing up to 5,000 citations from *BIOSIS Previews,* the price for the BITS service in early 1984 was based on a sliding scale per-citation charge: 35¢ per citation for the first 1,000 supplied on an update, 25¢ per citation for the next 1,500, and 20¢ per citation for the next 2,500.

Still another interesting development, and one that is almost certain to grow, is the application of videodisk technology by retrieval services and by database producers. To date, most uses have been supplementary to, rather than in competition with, online searching of remotely stored databases. Two examples are in conjunction with Pergamon's PAT-SEARCH database and the BRS/College series. While the textual portion of the databases continues to be searched through a retrieval service, users can purchase videodisks containing accompanying graphic material for local display.

An interesting ongoing experiment with disk is a combined effort by Information Access Company (IAC) and Laser Data, Inc., with BRS also figuring into the project. The goal is to store all or some of IAC's word-oriented databases (Magazine Index, National Newspaper Index, and others) on locally searchable laser disk and be able to provide these to libraries and others as an option to remote access to the databases through online retrieval services. The exciting prospects here are the notion of the laser disks, which have an enormously greater storage capacity than conventional videodisk, and the potential for sophisticated searching of textual data on such disks. BRS enters the project by way of its BRS Search, a software program designed for local database management that would serve as the retrieval system for locally accessing IAC's databases on disk.

All these examples represent an important direction in the online information industry, one that is bound to lead to significant changes. Not least will be the relationship between database producers and the traditional online retrieval services. Prior to the advent of the microcomputer, remote access to a retrieval service's computer was a library's only economically feasible option for gaining access to these databases. For most database producers, offering access to their online publications through an independent retrieval service was a far more viable option than the prospect of setting up their own retrieval service. The symbiotic relationship between retrieval services, database producers, and libraries was appropriate to the technology of the times. But microcomputers and the prospect of such technology as optical disk have introduced new options and are unsettling traditional relationships and roles. Taken to its logical conclusion, the trend toward locally applied options such as the ERIC Update series and BioSciences' BITS could threaten the foundation on which online retrieval services have existed for more than a decade. ERIC Updates, BITS, and similar services that will follow represent a clear option to, and therefore competition with, services that continue to rely on remotely stored databases. The emergence of optical disk as an economically viable device for storage and retrieval would further accelerate developments in this direction.

As in all exciting developments in technology, one of the major pitfalls is the temptation to exaggerate the speed with which large-scale change is likely to occur. Most of the developments described here can still be called innovative rather than typical. As yet, only a handful of database producers have begun to disseminate any portion of their databases on locally searchable floppy disks, and among those who have, all are still specialized in approach. As for retrieval services such as BRS, DIALOG, SDC, and several others familiar to libraries, they are specialists in information and information technology and most will adapt to changes in the environment, incorporating new trends into their line of services or exploring new and different possibilities. It is important to watch developments and trends in this industry, for they will impact heavily on the way in which libraries view online searching as a service to users.

It will be some time before developments or trends reach the point where they overshadow the richness, variety, and economy of accessing databases through the existing retrieval services. In the meantime, remote access to these services will remain the standard option for most libraries.

Free versus Fee-based Service

Because the library is but one of a number of participants in the online search process, it can influence but not totally control the direction that future development will take. However, one aspect of the service over which the library does exercise much internal control is the way in which online searching is financed. The initial cost of establishing an online search service is almost invariably borne by the library. Some libraries meet this expense through additional appropriations to a regular budget, others through grants, gifts, or special endowments, and others by reallocating some portion of funds originally targeted for other services or other areas. This strategy sometimes includes cancellation of subscriptions to expensive and little-used print indexes and abstracts.

To meet the continuing costs of operation, many libraries introduce another source of funding—user-based fees. Rather than absorbing all the costs of online searching, the library recovers a portion of its continuing expense by charging users for each search conducted.

In Chapter 16, we examine some of the alternative pricing structures used by libraries. But underlying any of those plans is the broader concern, especially in publicly funded institutions, about the basic appropriateness of, and philosophy behind, charging users for library service. Some libraries view such fees as a necessity, without which online searching could not be provided. Others see fees for service as an aberration of the basic role and purpose of libraries in a free society. The "fee versus free" controversy has been a major issue with respect to online searching ever since libraries began to offer these services. Although the debate has toned down during the past several years, perhaps due to an acceptance of financial reality, the issue is still no more firmly decided on philosophical grounds than it ever has been. The controversy squarely brings into focus the question of whether the library's primary publicly supported purpose is to be a collector of hard goods or a provider of information. At one time, these purposes were mutually accommodating, but with electronic delivery of information, the matter is no longer quite so simple.

Most librarians philosophically have supported the idea that online searching should be a free service, that financing should come through generalized sources rather than user-specific fees on a search-by-search basis. During the height of this controversy during the mid- and late 1970s, the American Library Association (ALA) issued a fairly widely supported position statement expressing the view that

> . . . the charging of fees and levies for information services, including those services utilizing the latest information technology, is discriminatory in publicly supported institutions providing library and information services.[12]

Despite its rather broad support in principle, this statement contradicted the reality of what was being practiced in the majority of libraries then engaged in online searching.

The proportion of libraries that offer fee-based online services has always been difficult to estimate. One of the broadest surveys is the one undertaken by Mary Jo Lynch at ALA in 1981.[13] Of 985 usable responses by public, academic, and special libraries, 72 percent indicated a fee-based service and 28 percent a no-charge policy. Some significant differences appeared according to library type. Of 445 responses by larger university libraries, 93 percent indicated a fee-based service. The proportions for 53 public libraries and 137 four-year colleges were 72 percent and 68 percent, respectively, and other types of libraries ranged from 30 percent up. Although the years bring change, and the methodology used in the ALA study resulted in some imperfections in compiling the statistics, there is no reason to assume that the percentages are dramatically different on the issue today.

Financial Priorities

The reason most given for charging for online searching is simple—libraries can't afford not to. The service is expensive, and the only alternatives seem to be either not to offer it at all or to cut back funding in other areas of the library. Critics point out that there is an important distinction between willingness and ability to finance a service. At least among larger academic and public libraries, few are truly not able to absorb the cost of an online service within an existing budget. A library with a $500,000 materials budget could surely support a $10,000, $25,000, or even $50,000 or $75,000 online search service. It is thus, critics say, not a matter of financial affordability in the strict sense, but rather one of priority of allocation. And as two critics of fee-based service have observed, " . . . librarians seem to find it easier to justify expenditures for possession than for service."[14] But, as we will see later, the matter of financial affordability is much more complex than this.

Fee-based Searching as Precedent

Perhaps even more than the affordability argument, critics of fee-based service question the logic of charging for online searching while other library services are still free. The concern is that these fees establish a dangerous precedent. And as a precedent, critics argue, it could ultimately be a threat to the basic role of publicly funded libraries in a free society. If a commitment to no-charge library service is violated in one area, what is to prevent the charging of fees for manual reference assistance, circulation, or even basic access to the collection? (There is, in fact, precedent in publicly supported libraries for user-based fees for each of the services mentioned here. A few libraries provide a fee-based manual reference option to users who need extensive research. Some public libraries are now charging for circulation of paperback books. Under extenuating circumstances, and more as a political ploy to secure adequate funding, a few public libraries have imposed basic access fees on residential suburban users.)

There is fear that once the door to fees for service has been opened, there will be no way to close it, and what were once publicly funded institutions will become institutions whose funding in all areas of service relies more and more on cost-recovery through direct, user-specific fees. Not only is this seen as a threat to the concept of free and equal access, but as potentially debilitating to the library's basic role of neutrality. Services, and even the focus of a library collection—including the political and socioeconomic orientation of the materials it contains—will no longer be dictated by a commitment to objectivity and freedom of expression, but rather by the special interests of those individuals and groups who can most afford to pay. As such, publicly funded libraries as we know them could cease to exist, evolving essentially into information centers serving the needs and supporting only the opinions of the most financially persuasive groups in the community.

Uniqueness of Online Searching

Those who favor fee-based online searching disclaim the precedent argument on several grounds. Some discount its importance as an issue on the grounds that the services and collection orientation of publicly funded libraries are, even now, ultimately governed by the special interests of the most financially influential groups in the community anyway. Fee-based service, they say, would simply be more obvious recognition of this already established fact.

But most do not subscribe to this sentiment. Nor do they argue that charges should be levied on such services as manual reference assistance, circulation, and basic access to the collection. Rather, they justify charging on the grounds that online searching is somehow fundamentally different from nearly all other library services. They also point out that there are, in fact, precedents for charging for services available in or through the library, most notably photocopying.

To justify charging based on the nature of the service itself, several characteristics have been noted as more or less distinguishing online searching from such services as general reference, circulation, and general access. Sometimes a distinction is made on the basis of the technology used to deliver the service, but more frequently expressed are the nature and extent of the librarian's involvement. The librarian's responsibility in addressing general reference queries using manual sources is *usually* restricted to looking up quick answers or, in the case of bibliographic searches, to identifying appropriate sources and getting the user started. At this point, the primary responsibility for conducting the search shifts to the user. In an online search service, the librarian is, by definition, a far more active participant in the search itself. And even for a search that requires only a few minutes online, the time spent in conducting a presearch interview and in offline preparation of search strategy can add appreciably to the overall amount of time and effort devoted to each request.

Two other characteristics are sometimes cited as distinguishing online searching. One is that online searching represents a service for which the library incurs direct, out-of-pocket expenses imposed by an external source, in this case an information retrieval service. The other is that the results of online searching are most customized and user-specific than any other service provided by the library. Indeed, other than lender-imposed charges in interlibrary loan and the replacement cost of materials lost while circulating, online searching is probably unique in incurring user-specific, out-of-pocket, externally imposed costs to the library.

Critics counter these rationales for charging. Photocopy machines in libraries, they say, are a convenience not related to *access* to information. If a photocopy machine actually contained information, the analogy might be fair. But critics claim that to offer a free photocopy service is a convenience with no inherent bearing on access to library materials or services that makes only a little more sense than to dispense free sodas and candy bars if vending machines are available on the premises. What cannot be so lightly dismissed is the analogy with charges imposed in interlibrary loan transactions. These charges are, in fact, very directly analogous to fees for online service: An identifiable, out-of-pocket cost to the library is associated with each user-specific request. As such, a proponent of free search services, to maintain a strictly consistent philosophical point of view, must also advocate the absorption of all lending charges in interlibrary loan by the library. However, a library can restrict free access to those materials and services available on site—which would include locally provided access to remotely stored databases, but not to the actual materials in collections of other libraries. This rationale may be more an example of selective sidestepping than anything else.[15]

The argument that the technological devices used in online searching somehow distinguish those operations from other library services is seldom presented today as a rationale for fee-based service. This is fortunate, given all the evidence to the contrary. In the past, the technology, and especially the costs associated with it, were seen as a substantial enough issue to invoke the following response from Jan Egeland, then at BRS:

There are automated services elsewhere in the library, including circulation, cataloging, acquisitions—is there a charge for any of these services? Why, then, would libraries charge for automation in the reference department?[16]

Other arguments that single out online searching as an operation distinct from other library services also have inherent weaknesses. Justifying fees because of the greater time and effort required of a librarian has a major contradiction: Even those libraries that cite librarian involvement as a major reason to charge seldom include payment for the librarian's time. Rather, fees are based on full or partial reimbursement of the direct expenses of telecommunications, connect-hour, and per-citation charges assessed by the retrieval service.

There seems little evidence to support the uniqueness of online searching either on the grounds that it incurs direct, out-of-pocket expenses for the library or that it is a customized, user-specific service. Direct costs are imposed by external sources for the purchase of books and other materials, but users are not charged for borrowing or consulting them. Although online searching certainly focuses on the individual and on individual requests, so does general reference in most cases, and no user-specific charges are imposed for that service. But when those two justifications are combined, a case might be made that online searching represents a different set of circumstances from just about any other service the library may offer; it is a highly customized service for which the library incurs identifiable, user-specific expenses imposed by external sources. Even so, say the critics, that is no justification for charging fees.

Discriminatory Aspects

Critics of fee-based service see an immediate problem—inequality of access to information. Fee-based online searching is seen, here and now, to be discriminatory against those who cannot afford to pay, the objection voiced in the 1977 ALA statement noted earlier.

Proponents of fee-based service argue this issue in several ways. They say that libraries—in all the services they provide and in the collections they hold—are inherently discriminatory against some segments of users in one way or another anyway. The collection of an academic library, for example, is certainly less comprehensive in certain areas than in others, meaning that some faculty members and students are, in fact, being discriminated against. And public libraries cannot afford to collect comprehensively in all areas, so someone with offbeat or less common interests can also be said to be discriminated against. Valid or not, these arguments do not address the question of access to the service based on ability to pay. Collection development policies may indeed cater to the needs of some users more than others, but once a library does decide to purchase something or provide a particular service, access to that material or service is not based on user-specific fees.

A more valid argument against the charge of such discrimination is the provision of access to alternative sources of information, such as printed abstracts, indexes, and other hard-copy materials containing information equivalent to what is available in online databases. Several years ago, one author explained this solution as follows:

> Libraries can avoid discriminating against patrons who cannot afford to pay for computer searches. This "merely" entails subscribing to printed forms of computerized databases to which computer access is available in the library at extra cost. Patrons are thus able to obtain the information from those databases at no cost to them, or they can choose the more expensive computer-search option.[17]

This statement was written at a time when there were admittedly fewer online databases, but if that option was ever financially viable for any library since the late 1970s, few could afford it today. Apart from cost and the problem of online databases with no print equivalent, this argument assumes that the quality of alternative forms of access are equal. Yet, especially for users with relatively little sophistication in the use of library tools and for searches that are partially complex, this is not the case. In the first place, the user requesting an online search has the benefit of the librarian's direct participation, which the user of a manual index does not. Second, online is far more flexible and more likely to yield better results for a complex search than a manual source.

Some fee-based online services face the issue of financially based discrimination by waiving fees for those who cannot afford to pay. Even so, free searches are generally conducted only when a librarian determines that online is the only available source or is clearly superior to a manual search. This solution is difficult to implement. A great deal of judgment is required, both in evaluating the appropriateness of a request for online and in determining the definition of financial hardship and applying it to individual cases.

Both proponents and critics of fee-based service voice legitimate, practical, and philosophical arguments, with the critics probably having the philosophical edge. With the exception of interlibrary loans and penalties such as overdue fines and replacement charges, libraries have not traditionally been in the business of recovering any portion of their expenses directly from users on a use-by-use basis. If the main role of the publicly funded library is seen as a public provider of information, fees for services are inconsistent with that purpose and are indeed a dangerous precedent. Conversely, the strongest philosophical argument forwarded for charging would be the statement on the part of a library that it, indeed, perceives its primary mission to be a collector and possessor of information.

Expectations and Financial Reality

Libraries may look to philosophy or theory for overall guidelines, but they must function within the limits imposed by financial reality and by the political and social environment in which they exist. Online searching is an expensive service, especially when calculated on a cost-per-use basis. Although nearly all libraries could offer free online searching within their existing budget levels, few university administrators and faculties, local boards, or library users would look favorably on such a plan. Regardless of how librarians see their own present and emerging role in society, that role is also shaped by the needs and demands of those who use the library and by the perceptions and preferences of those who govern it. And in this context, many libraries cannot afford unilaterally to make even minor cutbacks in other areas to support a service that is likely to be used by fewer individuals and for which the cost is far higher on a per-use basis than for more traditional services.

If free online searching is to be provided, the financial reality is indeed that a library must either cut back in other service areas or secure what can be an appreciable amount of additional funding. Neither is an easy task. And so the library that does not want to cut back in other service areas, but cannot secure appropriations to cover additional costs, is left with only two options: charge for online searching or don't offer it. Most have chosen to charge. And as will become clear in the next chapter, the "fee versus free" debate cannot, in the end, be viewed as strictly "either/or" when one focuses on the extent to which libraries recover, as opposed to subsidize, the overall costs of their online operations.

Document Delivery and Digital Telefacsimile

By operating an online search service, the library provides access to a far broader range of sources than would otherwise be possible. Vast as this universe of information is, it has an important limitation, for it consists largely of citations and abstracts, rather than the full text of the requested documents. To make the service complete, the library must have a mechanism for completing the process. It should be able to deliver a document, or a photocopy, into the user's hands.

Computer technology has not only enhanced the ability of libraries to identify what documents are available on a given topic, but has created offline and online union catalogs to determine where those documents are. Electronic messaging capabilities provide the means instantaneously to convey a request to buy or borrow a particular document. Yet, there are still two crippling bottlenecks in the overall process of document delivery: the processing of a request at the site of the supplier and the means by which the document itself is conveyed to the requesting site. It is not unusual for libraries to have backlogs of several days or even weeks in processing requests, and postal service is still the primary means by which documents are sent from one location to another. So, no matter how rapidly processing and transmission are carried out by the requesting library, the overall process is likely to be bogged down by delays resulting from these two bottlenecks.

Present and Future

In the long run, the keys to more rapid document delivery will be the expansion of online databases to include full text of documents and the use of other technologies, such as optical disk, either in conjunction with or apart from online delivery. The trend toward online full-text databases is already in evidence.

But online full-text databases are not now, nor will they ever be, an all-encompassing solution to the need for document delivery in libraries. Even if the point is reached where most current publications are available online, there will still be retrospective materials that were published only in hard copy. It is highly unlikely that the majority of those will ever be converted to machine-readable form and permanently stored. Assuming that historical research continues to have value, libraries will still require a means for sending these older materials back and forth among each other.

The more immediate reality, however, is that many libraries are interested in more efficient and faster means of document delivery, at a time when full-text online databases and other advanced technologies are only beginning to address those needs. Two methods libraries are using to secure documents from remote locations are commercial document delivery services and digital telefacsimile technology. Each of these methods draws on technology to expedite the overall process, but at significantly differing levels. Both center around delivery of photocopies or facsimiles, not original documents. As a practical consequence, both focus on the delivery of brief documents, most particularly, copies of journal articles. (Many library consortia have established formal or informal courier services that quite effectively and rapidly answer most of the document delivery needs of the participating libraries. The value of such arrangements is not minimized here, but the focus of this section is on electronic aspects of document delivery, and as such, courier services are outside that scope.)

Commercial Document Delivery Services

During the past few years, a number of commercial firms have begun to offer document delivery services that boast a far lower turnaround time than is typical of library-to-library borrowing. Some operations have been set up specifically for this purpose; in other cases, the service is offered through a department or subsidiary of an established company, most often a publisher or database producer.

Most interesting about these ventures is that their main focus is not necessarily on reducing the amount of time a document spends in transit, but is rather on eliminating the processing delays so typical of library-to-library lending. Copies of documents are still delivered via postal services, usually at first-class rates or even overnight mail for a rush order. But the key factor in their success is that copies are routinely mailed within 24 to 48 hours after receipt of a request, and some services even offer a same-day option. The fees usually include royalty payments to publishers.

To locate and order a document from one of these services, libraries normally rely on bibliographic utilities, information retrieval services, and independent electronic mail systems. As an illustration of how this process works, let us look at UMI Article Clearinghouse service, a department within University Microfilms International. The holdings of UMI Article Clearinghouse are available in a hard-copy catalog, but they are also listed online on OCLC's union listing capability. Once the UMI location and holdings have been identified, a library can use the OCLC Interlibrary Loan subsystem to transmit the request electronically to UMI. Alternatively, whether from OCLC or non-OCLC libraries, the Article Clearinghouse can also accept requests transmitted on the ON-Tyme II electronic mail system or through DIALOG's DIALORDER online order service. Most information retrieval services used by libraries have some type of online messaging capabilities, and independent electronic mail systems are proliferating. The more active of the document delivery services are usually quick to embrace any such system if libraries are likely to use it as a means of communication.

This method of document delivery can indeed reduce the time required for a library to obtain a copy of an article, but the focus is on reducing the time spent in identifying an item, determining its location, transmitting a request, and processing the order at the site of supply.

Digital Telefacsimile

To date the most prevalent technology for transmitting documents electronically has been telefacsimile. (Some of the major projects and demonstrations are described in Chapter 5.) The numerous experiments with this method during the 1960s and 1970s all came to the same general conclusion: Telefacsimile transmission among libraries was an appealing idea, but there were simply too many practical problems with it. For one, the rate of transmission was too slow, generally requiring about six minutes for a single page to be sent or received. At that rate, the maximum number of pages a machine could send or receive in an eight-hour day was about 80. If transmission took place over an appreciable distance, the six-minute-per-page rate was also a financial drain, as the cost of sending each page was about equal to long-distance charges for a six-minute telephone call. Another drawback was that no machine could transmit directly from a bound volume, making it necessary first to make a photocopy of an article or portion of a book. This double-copying at the sending library meant extra time and effort. Also, complaints about the equipment and quality of reproduction were not uncommon. A high incidence of equipment failure was reported in several projects, and even when the equipment did work well, there were complaints about legibility, specifically concerning the smaller type in footnotes and on charts and graphs.

Many of the problems and complaints of the 1960s and 1970s have been overcome or dramatically reduced during the 1980s with the introduction of digital telefacsimile equipment. At least one digital telefax model was on the market as early as 1973, but it was not until the 1980s that the technology became refined and inexpensive enough to warrant a closer look by libraries.

From an operator's point of view, the procedure for transmitting copies on a digital machine is similar to that required for the older analog models. A page of a document is placed on a surface similar in appearance to the surface on a conventional photocopier. After a telephone connection has been established with the receiving site, the sending machine scans a page and converts the image into electronic signals, which are transmitted over the telephone line to the machine at the receiving site. A facsimile of the original is produced in hard-copy form based on the pattern of signals received. A number of options expedite this procedure—such as autodial, unattended answer, and automatic document feed—some of which are discussed later.

Digital machines and older analog models may seem similar, but the internal workings differ significantly. Digital machines are faster, less expensive on a per-page basis, and can produce clearer images of copies. There has also been considerable improvement in equipment reliability.

Digital telefacsimile machines are frequently called subminute machines because they can transmit an image of a page in less than 60 seconds. The speed of transmission depends on a number of factors, including the amount of text on a page, the quality of resolution desired, and the transmission baud rate selected, but the total turnaround time generally falls within a 30- to 90-second range; in any event, several times faster than the old 4- to 6-minute rate.

This faster transmission time is due to a number of factors. One is simply the technique used for signal generation. Analog machines generate a continuous electronic signal that varies in intensity at any point according to the value of the information represented. Signals generated by digital equipment are expressed in "0s and 1s," comparable to the form in which information in computers is represented. Although these digital signals have to be converted to analog form when transmitted over normal telephone lines and then reconverted by the receiving machine, the sequence is more compact than when the analog process is used throughout; and fewer signals translate into more rapid transmission.

Digital telefacsimile machines also reduce the transmission time by using data compression techniques. The machines record an image by dividing a page into hundreds of thousands of very small squares, or pixels, and assigning a representative value to the information appearing in each. With older analog machines, any pixel required the same amount of time to transmit as any other. Modern digital machines compress long sequences of pixels containing an identical value. Rather than transmitting the value of each pixel in such a sequence, the machine assigns the entire sequence a brief representational value and transmits it in that form. The receiver decodes the value so that the appropriate number of pixels in a sequence is reproduced when the facsimile copy is printed. This process can reduce the amount of information carried over the telephone line by as much as a factor of 5 to 10, which translates into faster per-page transmission time and lower per-page communication costs.

The quality of reproduction with digital machines has also been improved. Quality largely depends on the number of pixels into which a page is divided when an image is made. The maximum resolution on older analog machines was about 100 horizontal and vertical lines per inch (lpi), and the standard was more like 64 lpi. Most digital models provide both 100 lpi and 200 lpi capability. Transmission time about doubles at the higher resolution, but it is an important capability when transmitting very small print.

Although the focus today is mainly on digital telefacsimile technology, analog models are still being produced, and they are far superior to their counterparts of the 1960s and 1970s. The new models have white-space-skipping capabilities similar to the data compression and encoding techniques used in digital equipment. They are still not as fast as digital models, but can transmit a page in about two minutes. Few of these analog models offer a resolution higher than 100 lpi. However, these machines are less expensive and may be sufficient at sites that transmit or receive a low volume of materials.

Digital Telefacsimile in Libraries

With the appearance of digital equipment, libraries have once again begun to explore telefacsimile as a means of document delivery, although this trend is still in a testing phase. The following list is not comprehensive, but does identify some of the better-known ventures into digital telefax during the past few years.

In early 1982, the Denver Public Library began using Rapicom digital machines to transmit administrative messages and copies of brief documents between the central library and the branches.

During 1982, a number of health sciences libraries began using telefacsimile to transmit copies of documents requested through interlibrary loan; most of the machines were Rapicom, although at least one of the participants was using Panafax equipment.

Also during 1982, the law libraries at New York University and Columbia University purchased Rapicom equipment to transmit copies of documents between each other; Columbia also initiated a telefax document delivery service for law firms in the New York area that have equipment.

In early 1983, three state libraries and seven academic libraries in the Pacific Northwest launched a telefax pilot project using Rapicom equipment; the project was funded by the Alaska State Library and the Pacific Northwest Bibliographic Center board of directors.

In mid-1983, the Loan Division at the Library of Congress installed a Panafax MV-3000 digital telefacsimile machine.

In late 1983, six members of the Research Libraries Group (RLG) began a one-year trial project using digital machines; the project received $55,000 in foundation funding.

In late 1983, seven libraries in western Illinois received $59,000 in Library Services and Construction Act (LSCA) funding to establish an interlibrary loan telefax network; the participants include one community college library, one four-year college library, one university library, one public library, one regional library system headquarters, and two hospital libraries.

These examples illustrate some important trends in the adoption of telefacsimile in libraries. First, libraries installing telefacsimile equipment are not doing so on an individual basis, but rather as part of a cooperative venture. Too few machines are in place right now for a library to acquire telefax equipment without a fairly clear idea of with whom it will communicate, how often, and under what circumstances.

Another trend is that, by and large, the groups that have ventured into telefacsimile have been well-defined either in terms of type of library, similar subject interest, or geographic proximity. In some cases, all three conditions are present. Of the examples noted, the law libraries in New York probably provide the clearest examples. The venture in Illinois includes a wide variety of types of libraries, but six of the participants are within 20 miles of one another, and the seventh is only about 50 miles away. The RLG trial project is geographically expansive, with participants on both coasts and in between, but all six are large academic research libraries belonging to a well defined research library consortium. All things considered, the telefax network in the Pacific Northwest has probably included the greatest degree of diversity. Although a regional network, it extends over a wide territory and involves state as well as academic libraries.

Especially in those projects involving public and academic libraries, another general characteristic is the reliance on project-specific outside funding. The need for outside funding is not a strike against telefacsimile, nor is it necessarily a permanent condition. This means of financial support is quite typical of library automation in the early stages of adoption of a technology.

Costs of Digital Telefacsimile

There are three main categories of costs associated with digital telefacsimile—cost of the equipment itself, continuing equipment-related expenses, and telecommunications.

The cost of a telefacsimile unit depends on the sophistication of the equipment and the features it offers. Stripped-down digital models are priced below $4,000; fancier and more durable units can cost $8,000 or more. Equipment capable of meeting the needs of most libraries probably falls in the $3,500 to $6,000 price range. Most manufacturers offer three payment options: outright purchase, lease/purchase, and rental. Based on costs for a period even as brief as three or four years, outright purchase is the least expensive option. Some libraries, however, cannot afford an initial investment of several thousand dollars, or are otherwise restricted from outright purchase by institutional policies. If lease/purchase or rental is the only option, it is well to remember that, although the monthly payment for lease/purchase may be slightly higher than for term rental, the library has the option at the end of the period to own the equipment for a small additional buy-out fee. With straight rental, this option is not offered.

Some libraries may consider rental the best option in a technologically changing environment despite the cost, since the renter may have greater flexibility to change over to new or more sophisticated equipment. The catch is that most manufacturers require a fixed rental term rather than a month-to-month arrangement. The longer the term, the lower the per-month rental charge. But in agreeing to a term of even two or three years, the library may end up paying nearly as much as or more than it would have in just purchasing the equipment in the first place. Some rental agreements do include an option to upgrade to new equipment at any time during the term, but it would be restricted to the manufacturer's own line of equipment—something to consider.

Some libraries may also install an additional telephone for use exclusively with the telefax unit. If the library's regular telephone system operates through a switchboard, it is best to install a separate line for use with the telefax unit because the need to go through a switchboard to send or receive transmissions can create a problem.

Two major ongoing costs with a telefacsimile machine are maintenance and paper. The cost of a maintenance contract is usually a percentage of the original purchase price, normally between 8 and 15 percent per year, depending on manufacturer and model. The cost of paper averages between 5¢ and 10¢ per page, thermal paper being lower, and paper for machines using nonthermal technology priced higher. Remember that although thermal paper is the least expensive, it is also a lower grade, and more than a few libraries have received complaints from users about legibility.

Of all costs associated with telefacsimile, telecommunications may seem most prohibitive to libraries. Distance, time of day, and speed of transmission all influence the average telecommunications expense. Costs are negligible in strictly networking arrangements, but begin to mount whenever long-distance communication is involved. In general, the telecommunications cost for an intersystem transmission (at a resolution of 100 lpi) made during the middle of the day at standard phone rates is 40¢ to 50¢ per page, perhaps 25¢ to 35¢ per page if transmission occurs during evening hours, and 15¢ to 20¢ per page if the lowest possible rates are used. For libraries with a relatively high volume, the WATS service or other reduced-cost long-distance options can lower costs significantly.

The total per-page cost of using telefacsimile depends on so many factors that any suggested averages would be almost useless. Some libraries do not add in the cost of the equipment, for instance. Average cost can be influenced by volume of activity, especially if equipment costs are calculated, by relative proportion of local, intra-LATA, and inter-LATA transmissions, by the time of day during which a library normally transmits, and by particular telecommunications arrangements. In reporting on the Pacific Northwest project in 1983, for instance, Tracy and DeJohn calculated an average per-page cost of 85¢ for transmission from Washington State to Alaska. This took into account $440 per month for the lease of equipment transmitting a total of 2,000–3,000 copies per month and the use of a telecommunications network that was slightly less expensive than the public network daytime rates.[18]

With less expensive equipment and evening rate transmission, a library may be able to reduce the average cost of an inter-LATA transmission to as little as 50¢ per page, excluding staff costs and the expense associated with first making a photocopy of the original. If the price of equipment and maintenance are not included, the average cost is lower and really just amounts to telecommunications.

Telefacsimile Equipment Features

Telefacsimile machines have a number of features designed to minimize transmission expenses, provide convenient work flow, and offer greater flexibility in use. Some features are standard on most models; others are options at additional cost. Some features are essential for libraries; others would likely be used too seldom to justify the added expense.

One essential feature for libraries is automatic feed, standard on nearly all digital models. The importance of this feature is magnified by the fact that there is still no telefacsimile machine on the market that can transmit directly from a bound volume. Since the library must first photocopy the pages of such material, an automatic feed provides for more productive work flow than if an operator had to load a new page manually every 30 to 90 seconds. The total transmission time for a typical 10-page article is 7 to 10 minutes; with an automatic document feeder, the operator can turn attention elsewhere between transmissions. There is an even greater advantage when several articles are being transmitted to the same location. Continuous transmission of three 10-page articles, for example, frees the operator for up to half an hour. However, two notes of caution about the automatic feed. One, a staff member should always be near the machine—even if he or she is doing something else—in case the paper jams, the telephone disconnects, or some other problems arise. Two, be aware that some telefax machines have a capacity of only 30 or less pages, with 50 about the maximum.

Another fairly standard feature is unattended answer. This allows a transmission to be received without human intervention at that site. Without this feature, someone at the receiving site must manually acknowledge an incoming call before transmission can occur. Less standard is autodial, which, through use of a clocking mechanism, enables the sending site to load a document but defer transmission until a later programmed time. The principal advantage here is that transmission can take place during periods when phone rates are less expensive. The main limitation is that the number of pages sent in this way is limited to the capacity of the automatic document feeder. Furthermore, if transmission is set to occur after the staff leave for the day, failures due to paper jams or line problems will not be discovered until the next morning.

Technical standards for telefacsimile machines are overseen by a subcommittee of the Consultative Committee for International Telephone and Telegraph (CCITT), which to date has set standards for three machine categories. Group I pertains to older model (4- to 6-minute per page) analog machines, Group II to newer (2- to 4-minute per page) machines, and Group III to subminute digital machines. To conform to international standards, any machine in one group is supposed to be able to communicate with any other in the same group. Compatibility is thus ensured within each of the groups but not across groups. Group I machines are not necessarily compatible with Group II machines, and so on. Most manufacturers of telefax equipment, however, offer an option designed to achieve cross-compatibility. With the lower purchase price of analog machines, it may be most cost-effective for low-use participants in a telefax network to acquire Group II rather than digital equipment. The higher telecommunications expense for the slower equipment may be more than offset by the savings realized on the initial purchase and on a continuing maintenance contract. In mixing Group II and Group III equipment, however, a network must carefully examine the impact on the communications cost for the network as a whole, since any transmission between a Group II and Group III machine must always occur at the slower rate of the analog model. If a mix is determined cost-effective, a group of libraries must be certain to select machines that can be equipped for compatibility. This feature is almost always an option and therefore means additional cost.

Among the other numerous standard and optional features available on telefacsimile machines are a wide range of diagnostic capabilities, polling, automatic size reduction, and RS-232 interface, through which a unit can transmit data directly from a computer.

The Future of Telefacsimile in the Library

As noted earlier, no commercially available telefax machine provides the capability to transmit directly from bound volumes. Although many libraries have bemoaned this lack, in reality, the ability to transmit from bound material, without any other changes in technique, would not necessarily lead to greater productivity in library telefacsimile operations. The double-copying method does waste time and paper, but it is still more efficient in many ways than transmitting from bound material with existing technology. With 30- to 90-second per-page transmission by a machine that could copy directly from bound material, the operator would have to stay at the machine and manually flip pages, not having enough time between transmissions to do anything else.

The ideal solution is a capability to transmit from bound material in combination with a reduction in transmission time to a few seconds per page, or in conjunction with some other innovation that releases the operator during transmission. New types of "integrated services" photocopiers allow storage, transmission, and reception by a single unit, but they are designed for flat pages rather than bound volumes. Under the direction of J. Francis Reintjes, a research team at the Massachusetts Institute of Technology (MIT) has developed a prototype machine that may better address libraries' needs. The MIT machine can optically scan a page in a bound volume in not much more time than is required in conventional photocopying. Instead of the digitally encoded image being transmitted immediately to a receiving site, it is run onto a local computer and stored. The operator does not have to wait for this transfer before turning to the next page and copying it. This minimizes the time spent in copying and allows the computer-stored image to be transmitted unattended at a later time. The actual transmission time is not reduced, but because of the way the whole operation is designed, there is an overall reduction in staff time.[19] It may be some time before such a machine becomes commercially available, but it is a promising possibility.

Some other problems voiced by librarians with regard to digital telefacsimile are:

1. In light of the trend toward online full-text databases, telefacsimile is an outdated technology.

2. It is too expensive.
3. Not enough libraries use telefacsimile to make it worthwhile.
4. The quality of reproduction is still not adequate.
5. There is not really a need in most libraries to provide document delivery so rapidly.
6. The potential value of telefacsimile will always be undermined by delays in carrying out the basic processing steps at the sending site.

Some of these doubts have already been noted. The scarcity of telefacsimile in libraries, for example, may simply be a function of time; it is yet too early to tell. As for quality of reproduction, higher resolution machines can be developed, but the trade-off will be slower transmission. An interesting aspect of the MIT project was that the machine copied at a resolution of 300 lpi, considerably higher than the typical 200 lpi maximum on existing commercial machines. The higher the resolution, of course, the more time to transmit an image of a page and, therefore, the higher the telecommunications costs.

Although special libraries in general and medical libraries in particular might prove exceptions, there is indeed a real question as to the extent that most libraries and library users really need high-speed document delivery. One of the CLR-sponsored studies of telefacsimile during the 1960s found that the single greatest delay in the whole process of getting a document into a patron's hands occurred after the material had been received and the patron was notified that it could be picked up at the library.[20] To some extent, this may have been a matter of conditioned behavior on the part of patrons accustomed to waiting days or weeks for the interlibrary loan process to run its full course. But even if the majority of requests are less than urgent, for some, more rapid delivery would be valuable. The success of commercial document delivery services in recent years is evidence that such a need exists, maybe not for all transactions, but at least for some.

Perhaps the greatest obstacle to the successful incorporation of telefacsimile in libraries is the question of the whole broader process of which it is a part. A high-speed document delivery capability is of marginal use if processing backlogs impose a delay of several days or weeks into the handling of incoming requests. A decision to integrate telefacsimile into routine interlibrary loan operations does not simply involve a commitment to purchase a machine. It means carrying out all phases of an interlibrary loan operation in a timely and efficient manner. And there are many who believe that most libraries are not now ready, nor will be in the near future, to make that commitment.

The processing bottleneck typical in so many libraries is indeed an obstacle, but its impact on telefacsimile may actually be on how, not whether, telefacsimile is used. To date, most library use of and experimentation with telefacsimile have occurred within a context of library-to-library communication rather than commercial service to library document delivery. Whether this continues to be so may ultimately rest not so much on the technology itself or even costs, but on the ability and willingness of libraries to incorporate telefacsimile within a broader framework of priorities regarding interlibrary loan and resource sharing. If libraries are unable to resolve the last remaining manual bottleneck in the document delivery cycle—the processing of incoming requests—commercial services, and perhaps a few enterprising libraries, are likely to find their role in document delivery expanding to incorporate greater use of telefacsimile.

Notes

1. "Now More than 1000 Online Databases," *Online Review* 6 (August 1982): 349.
2. "Number of Databases Shows Record Jump," *American Libraries* 15 (February 1984): 118.
3. "Business Information Market Growth Will Be Lead by Online Database Services," *Online Review* 6 (December 1982): 482.
4. "Online Databases Grow in Number and Revenues," *Bulletin of the American Society for Information Science* 8 (August 1983): 6.
5. "Wiley Goes Online with NewsNet," *Online Review* 7 (December 1983): 455.
6. For a discussion of some of these concerns, see Maureen Corcoran, "Mead Data Central and 'All the News That's Fit to Print,' " *Online Review* 7 (July 1983): 32–35.
7. Nina M. Ross, "Newspaper Databases Update, 1982," *National Online Meeting Proceedings—1983,* New York, April 12–14, Martha E. Williams and Thomas H. Hogan, comps. (Medford, N.J.: Learned Information, 1983), pp. 463–473.
8. Inez L. Speer, "The Future of the Print Production in Relation to Online Searching," in *Proceedings of the ASIS Annual Meeting* 19 (1983) (White Plains, N.Y.: Knowledge Industry Publications, 1982), p. 286.
9. M. Wolff-Terroine, L. Ghiradi, and B. Marx, "Main Trends in Royalty Policy of Database Producers," *Online Review* 7 (April 1983): 106.
10. Speer, "Future of the Print Production," p. 287.
11. For descriptions of Search Helper, see Gretchen L. Johnson, "Search Helper," *RQ* 23 (Fall 1983): 96–97; and Pat Ensor and Richard A. Curtis, "Search Helper: Low-Cost Online Searching in an Academic Library, *RQ* 23 (Spring 1984): 327–331.
12. Quoted in Mary Jo Lynch, *Financing Online Search Services in Publicly Supported Libraries* (Chicago: American Library Association, 1981), p. 41.
13. *Ibid.*

14. Sara D. Knapp and C. James Schmidt, "Budgeting to Provide Computer-Based Reference Services: A Case Study," *Journal of Academic Librarianship* 5 (March 1979): 13.

15. For a presentation of this justification for charging for online searching, see John Linford, "To Charge or Not to Charge: A Rationale," *Library Journal* 102 (October 1, 1977): 2009–2010.

16. Quoted in James Rice, Jr., "Fees for Online Searches: A Review of the Issue and a Discussion of Alternatives," *Journal of Library Administration* 3 (Spring 1982): 26.

17. Linford, "To Charge," p. 2010.

18. Janet Tracy and William DeJohn, "Digital Facsimile: Columbia Law Library and Pacific Northwest Library Facsimile Network," *Library Hi Tech* 1 (Winter 1983): 12–13.

19. For a description of the MIT project, see J. Francis Reintjes, "Application of Modern Technologies to Interlibrary Resource-Sharing Networks," *Journal of the American Society for Information Science* 35 (January 1984): 45–52.

20. William D. Schieber and Ralph M. Shoffner, *Telefacsimile in Libraries: A Report of an Experiment in Facsimile Transmission and an Analysis of Implications for Interlibrary Loan Systems* (Berkeley, Calif.: Institute of Library Research, University of California, 1967).

16

Organizing and Administering the Search Service

Online searching of bibliographic and other databases is well established but hardly universal in the American library community. Any library considering this move should anticipate the scope, needs, and impact of the service, and prepare for the organization and administration, costs, promotion, and policy and procedures well ahead of time. The library already involved in online searching should constantly re-evaluate these factors to maintain quality of service.

Defining the Scope

All-important in the planning process to establish a search service is a clear definition of the scope in which retrieval services and databases will be used, the extent of searching that will be conducted, for whom, and under what circumstances. The library must be realistic about the extent of online searching it can provide based on the financial and human resources it is willing or able to commit. At the start of an online searching program, the temptation may be to offer the service on a wide basis, providing access to every interested user, and offering to search on any and all databases available through the retrieval service or services to which the library has subscribed.

However understandable, such a wide-open approach is unwise, especially at the start. Most libraries simply cannot afford to commit the many financial and human resources required to "go all out." Instead, a library may have to impose certain limitations on use of the service to ensure that the demand level does not exceed the library's ability to meet it. It is better to start off by providing a quality service on a limited basis than to be placed in a position where the library's resources cannot handle the level of demand created for them. If that occurs, there is likely to be either a breakdown of the service altogether or an unanticipated drain on the resources of other areas of the library, which in turn can lead to a lessening of quality in those activities as well.

Phasing in an Online Service

Financial and human resources often limit the scope of a newly introduced search service, but even if ample money and staff are available, it will take time for personnel to learn and feel comfortable with the retrieval system or systems and to familiarize themselves with the available databases. Regardless of the amount of training, practice, and study before formal initiation of service, an inexperienced searching staff will have to make adjustments when actually confronted by the first users. No matter how thoughtful the preplanning, the library is likely to discover that some rearrangements are necessary and that some policies and procedures have been overlooked or are ambiguous.

If online searching is widely promoted and immediately offered to a broad audience, the time required simply to keep up with the daily influx of search requests may make it impossible to deal with these other matters effectively. Crisis responses can become permanent solutions. But if the service is initiated on a more limited basis, all adjustments will be far easier. The staff will gain greater understanding of the needs and expectations of users and will have time to build confidence in their ability to use the system. Decisions can be made with deliberation rather than in response to a crisis. Policies and procedures can be carefully considered to arrive at permanent solutions.

Selecting a Retrieval Service

It is not difficult for a searcher experienced in one of the major library-oriented retrieval systems to learn another one, but it can be quite confusing to attempt to learn two, three, or more systems all at once if the staff has not had experience with at least one system. Care should be taken in selecting the initial service since searchers tend to prefer the first system they learn.

Cost and financial obligations are also important factors for some libraries. Cost comparison between retrieval services is not always easy. Pricing structures vary, and actual cost on a per-search basis is influenced by such variables as retrieval capabilities and performance features. In the past, many services required prepayment of an annually guaranteed usage deposit, meaning the library would have to commit to using the service at least a defined amount over the course of the year or forfeit the balance. Most services now offer at least one option with no guaranteed minimum usage, but many still provide discount incentives tied to annual guarantees and prepayment.

Perhaps the most important criterion in selecting a system is the breadth of databases available in relation to the interests of anticipated users, both in the immediate and long-term future. For a library that serves a community of users with generally little interest in scientific and technical research, for instance, it would obviously be inappropriate to select a service offering few databases other than science and technology.

Initial Users

To what group of users should the service initially be targeted? An online search service may be started in response to a request or proposal from a specific group of library users, and so, at least part of the initial user group is identified at the outset. If a library has decided to cancel a subscription to a particular index to help finance the online operation, it is especially important to consider the frequent users of the canceled print source as potential users of the new service. It may also be wise to include special-interest concerns in the university, city, or corporate administration, from a public relations perspective if nothing else. "Friends in high places" can be invaluable when the library needs financial and administrative support for expanding the service to additional groups.

All of these special users are important to consider as the initial target audience for online searching, but the library will probably be able to offer service, even initially, beyond these categories. It is still important, however, to clearly identify a coherent audience for a service that must be limited because of financial or staffing constraints. The library should have a clear idea of what segments of the user community will want the service and what segments presumably will not.

New programs are seldom introduced into libraries with the ultimate goal of making them available only to certain users, and for most libraries, online searching is no exception. The long-range goal is usually to make the service as widely available as possible, but this is rarely achieved all at once.

Regulating Demand Level

Whether a library is initiating an online search service or expanding the scope of an existing one, the level of demand must not exceed the library's ability to meet it. Demand level need not be left to fate or dictated entirely by the response of the user community. It can be regulated, at least to some extent, by library policy.

One of the most common ways to regulate demand is by providing service only to certain categories of users. In many academic libraries, online searching initially has been available only to faculty and administration. With additional resources, these libraries may open the service to graduate students, and eventually to undergraduates. This solution is much more difficult to implement in a public library where there is less precedent for differences in policy among the adult user population.

Another way to regulate demand is to make distinctions on the basis of individual requests. For example, some academic libraries that do not generally provide search services to undergraduates make exceptions when the library does not have a print index to fill a student's need. Some libraries make distinctions according to the complexity of requests. If a request involves a single concept corresponding to a major index term in a print source available in the library, the user is guided to that source. If, however, the search entails several concepts in combination, or if the best results can be obtained by searching on parameters indexed only in an online source, the request is referred to the online service. This "nature of the request" approach generally requires the reference or online searching staff to make judgments on a case-by-case basis. Obviously, such subjectivity can cause occasional problems, but in general this strategy serves the needs of users and the purpose of the service itself.

Libraries use two other methods to balance demand with available resources—user-based fees and promotion. In several ways, user-based fees help to maintain a balance between demand and resource availability. One, charging for searching deters some users altogether. Two, fees tend to discourage frivolous or spur-of-the-moment use—the user who must pay charges will presumably give more serious consideration to submitting a request than if the service were free. Three—and this is the most positive aspect of a fee-based service—the revenues can help to finance the service, even to the extent that online searching may not be possible without them. Recovery of at least some portion of the cost may also enable a library to provide a more extensive service and to accelerate the scope. Accordingly, it may not be necessary to impose as many restrictions based on user status or on the nature of search requests.

There is still much controversy surrounding fee-based service for online searching; for libraries that find it a necessary solution, a number of different charging structures may be adopted. The basic philosophical question of fee versus free is examined in Chapter 15, and some charging options are discussed later in this chapter.

Promotion (also discussed in detail later in this chapter) can be another tool in helping to regulate the level of demand for an online search service. A library with limited resources obviously should not launch an ambitious campaign to make its online service known to the entire user community. By limiting formal promotion and directing it toward well-defined audiences, the library can exercise some degree of control over the level of demand.

As already noted, libraries do not generally introduce a service with the intention of restricting availability. Yet each of the strategies just described limits use of an online search service. The key here is balance. A library simply cannot provide a level of service that it cannot support. Whatever techniques are used to achieve a balance, adjustments can be made as the library becomes more familiar with the retrieval system and the needs of users and as more resources can be devoted to them.

Anticipating Needs and Impact

In establishing or expanding the scope of an online search service, a library must consider several consequences if user demand is not to exceed the library's ability to meet it. Central among these are the internal needs of the service itself, the impact on the library as a whole, and the range of user response.

Needs of the Service

Three major elements related to internal needs must be considered— money, space, and time.

Money

Libraries without online search programs tend to oversimplify the financial aspects of such programs. It is tempting for a library that has purchased a microcomputer for other purposes or has just been offered "free" use of a communicating terminal by its computer center to conclude that online searching can now be provided at little or no additional cost. And it is easy to equate continuing expenses with telecommunications, connect-hour, and per-citation charges assessed by the retrieval service. Following that view, many libraries think they can easily absorb all initial and continuing costs into a budget with no special allocation for the online service.

But the cost factors in establishing and operating an online service (outlined later in detail) are far more numerous than simply the purchase price of equipment and monthly vendor invoices. Supplies must be bought on an ongoing basis. Manuals and searching aids have to be purchased both initially and as the service expands to include other databases and retrieval vendors. For effective promotion, or even to explain the service clearly, brochures must be printed and distributed. If quality service is to be provided, the staff members responsible for searching will have to attend training workshops and update sessions on vendor systems and databases. There usually are registration fees for such sessions, and unless the library is in a major urban area, there may also be travel expenses for staff.

Even with these additional costs, some libraries try to cover the expenses of an online search service from within the general budget. Equipment is purchased out of the budget line for general supplies; manuals and training aids out of the general materials budget; and training and continuing education expenses are covered by finding a few dollars here and there. This may work if the allocation in each of those areas increases proportionately, but that is not often the case. If increases in allocation lag behind increases in expenses to support online searching, the result can be a financial strain on the library budget as a whole. Absorbing expenses within an existing budget may be the only way that many libraries can initially finance an online search service, but it will mean sacrifice in other areas and will become particularly tenuous for financing beyond the introductory stages of a service. With this approach, there should also be a commitment to increase the overall budget to cover the expenses of the service as soon as possible. Any program to expand the service should increase the funding for new expenses. Failure to do so will place the quality of the service in jeopardy, or will again strain the funding allocated to other areas of the library.

Space

The amount of space needed for a search service depends on such things as the extent of the service to be offered, whether a formal presearch interview will be conducted between searcher and user, whether the user will be present at the actual online search session, whether drop-in requests will be accepted or appointments required, whether online searches will be conducted as a ready-reference service in addition to more formal searching, the extent to which staff members will have other duties in addition to searching, and so on.

If at all possible, dedicated space should be given to online searching rather than simply placing a terminal in whatever space happens to be available. The location and arrangement should allow the searcher to work without constant interruption by patrons or other staff. If presearch and/or postsearch interviews are to be conducted, a quiet place should be available. The terminal itself should be located where its use does not disturb other patrons or staff. Printers, in particular, tend to be noisy, and their constant clamoring can be a disturbance if they are placed in open space or other areas where patrons or staff are active.

Other needs concern visibility, ease of access, and comfort. The first two clearly have some practical advantages in increasing awareness of the service and making it easy for users to find. But especially in a service where the user is present during the online search, pleasant accommodations in the area are important. A terminal hidden in a corner of a storeroom may be least disturbing to other users and staff, but it is not likely to seem professional to users who must be led down a hallway and forced to sit amid stacks of extra shelving while their search is being conducted. As a practical matter and in keeping with the functional role of online searching, many libraries locate the search service as near as possible to the general reference department.

The amount of space devoted to the work area depends, in part, on the scope of the service and on the number of searchers involved. But even for a comparatively limited operation, there should be adequate space near the terminal(s) to house manuals and search aids and to allow the searcher to consult documentation conveniently while conducting a search. If users are to be present during the session, there must be enough room for searcher and user to sit together at the terminal. If extensive presearch and/or postsearch interviews will be conducted, will they take place in the same room as the one used for actual searching? With a one-person or otherwise limited service, interviewing and searching can be conducted in the same general work area. With a larger service in which several different interviews or online sessions might be occurring simultaneously, separate or well-partitioned rooms may be required. It will also be necessary to provide space for bookkeeping activities, including a desk or other area on which to do the work and file cabinets to store the papers.

All this means that the library may face conditions that are hard to meet in light of existing architecture: a place that is sufficiently large, quiet enough for private consultations, and one that is visible, easily accessible, and located near the most open areas in the library. Perhaps the best arrangement is a soundproof room, in or near a reference area, with windows looking out onto the larger area. Since such a setup is not always available, the library might anticipate some remodeling expenses, and as the scope of the service is expanded, the impact of increased activity on the space should be taken into account. To avoid overcrowding and makeshift arrangements, appropriate space plans should be made in advance.

Time

It is all too easy to underestimate the amount of time required to provide quality service. It involves much more than simply sitting down at a terminal and conducting a search. To learn and refine searching skills, staff must attend initial, update, and advance training sessions, and practice online before implementing the service. This cycle is repeated whenever the library expands its program to include an additional retrieval system, and when access is broadened to include a new or different database. To use the systems and databases most effectively, staff must study revisions to manuals and read vendor newsletters announcing changes and additions. This type of reading relates to the maintenance of skills required in performing everyday responsibilities.

Apart from the actual online portion of a search, time must be devoted to interaction with users to explain the service and to conduct presearch and sometimes postsearch interviews. Search strategy must be prepared before actually going online. If the service is to be promoted to any extent, the staff must have time to write promotional materials and prepare and deliver presentations before classes and other groups. Administrative matters need time and attention. Policy and procedures manuals must be written and revised. Whether done by online searchers or others, bookkeeping details, scheduling appointments, reading and perhaps further negotiating contracts with vendors, reconciling vendor invoices, and preparing reports for administrators all require time. Even in a fairly small operation, a significant amount of time is needed to keep up with changes in systems and databases, to explain and promote the service to potential users, and to carry out even cursory administrative tasks. As in the case of money and space, failure to allow for sufficient time can result in a breakdown in the quality of service.

Impact on Other Library Areas

Online searching will have an impact beyond the operation of the service itself. Some potentially negative aspects such as inadequate financial resources or pressures on space and staff time have already been noted. The paradox is that online searching, while competing for and possibly diverting money, space, and time from other services, can actually lead to an increase in the level of demand for those same services, which makes it all the more important that the library plan ahead to meet the internal needs of a search service in a way that will not rely on resources originally targeted for other activities. When drawing up a plan, the library should try to anticipate which other areas are likely to experience increased activity as a result of online searching and try to ensure that they are equipped to absorb the impact. The two main areas that will be directly influenced are general reference and interlibrary loan.

If the people who provide general reference will also be performing online searches, the most immediate impact of online searching on reference work will be on scheduling and division of responsibility. But apart from those, online searching is also likely to have an impact on the demand for general reference itself. If promoted widely, online searching will attract some patrons who have rarely or never used the library before. New users will affect the general reference department in terms of questions pertaining to catalog use, general information, and other areas. On a broader scale, online searching is a reference-type activity, and the more that patrons draw on one reference-related service, the more heavily they are likely to use the others as well.

Some reference librarians note a gradual difference in the questions and expectations with which patrons familiar with online searching approach traditional reference service. Patrons who have completed online search request forms, sat through presearch interviews, and been present at online sessions may acquire a slightly more sophisticated outlook on how information queries in general should be thought out and presented. Their requests at the general reference desk may be better articulated as a result. This change, although welcomed by reference librarians, can also be challenging. A user accustomed to online searching knows that information can be retrieved quickly and with minimum effort and, therefore, may be less patient in waiting for results to inquiries that require use of manual sources.

Another dramatic change due to an online service is the increased demand for interlibrary loans. Bibliographic searches will generate citations for materials not available on site. A library's online searching policy should be consistent with its interlibrary loan policy. For example, if online searching is to be promoted widely to undergraduate students in an academic setting, interlibrary loan should be available to them as well. If online searching is available to users without charge, so should interlibrary loan. Inconsistency between these two services results in frustration on the part of users. If citations to materials can be obtained openly or without charge, but access to the actual materials through interlibrary loan is either blocked or priced beyond the ability of some users to pay, patrons may be frustrated by the hint of valuable information beyond their reach.

Some libraries justify different policies for online searching and interlibrary loan on the grounds that the purpose of the online service is not necessarily to enable a user to gather all the materials cited and that an online search will still be of considerable value since at least some of the materials are likely to be available locally. However logical, this view will not make users any less frustrated if they cannot get what they want. The most important point to remember concerning the impact of online searching on interlibrary loan is that the demand will increase and that it may be necessary to allocate additional financial and human resources if the quality of service is to be maintained.

Another impact on interlibrary loan has to do with user perception of speed of service. Even if the loan and searching policies are consistent, and even if resources are allocated in anticipation of increased demand for service, there is still usually a delay in obtaining documents through interlibrary loan. The length of the delay, even in an efficiently run operation, is accentuated by contrast with the speed of online searching. Citations can be retrieved in a matter of minutes, but it can take days or even weeks to secure the actual materials—a sure source of frustration. In time, online delivery of full-text documents may speed the process, but at present, slow delivery is a fact that libraries and users must accept. The best the library can do is to provide well-qualified staff, allocate sufficient resources to minimize the time required for processing, and make online users aware in advance of some of the problems in obtaining documents.

Although interlibrary loan and general reference services are most likely to feel the direct impact, online searching can also affect other areas. For example, libraries have reported some impact on collection development, mainly in terms of new periodical subscriptions. Journals not on the library's subscription list can show up in online search results often enough to warrant purchase by the library. This does not occur with great frequency, but for a library with limits on new subscriptions, even a few such cases may mean some hard decisions.

The new online search service is also likely to have at least some impact on staff in other library areas. Reference librarians are most likely to be involved with user questions, but questions also come up at the circulation desk, in branch libraries, at general staff or faculty meetings in an academic library, and so on. All library staff need not be knowledgeable in the mechanics or philosophy of online searching, but they should at least be aware of its existence and able to refer patrons to the appropriate staff or department. This will mean some form of in-house introduction to the service, but it is worth the effort.

Response by Users

The library should anticipate responses by actual and potential users. One type of response, noted earlier, is the attraction of those who have never or rarely used the library before. These users are not likely to be familiar with general library policies or procedures or with the location and functioning of services. Interest for some will be restricted largely to the online service, but others may create additional demands in other areas of the library.

If a new online service is widely promoted, the response may be considerable. The library should be prepared for a wide range of reactions on the part of users, from minimal expectations by some to those who greatly overestimate the potential. Underestimaters are generally not a problem once they are adequately informed of how the service can help them, but it is sometimes difficult to deal with those who expect more than the system can give. Some first-time users think that full documents, not just citations, can be obtained in an online search. Many library users do not even know what printed indexes can do, so it is understandable that they would be in the dark about the purpose of online sources.

The best guard against misconception is well-designed promotion. Promotional materials and presentations must be brief enough that users will read and listen to them, and yet detailed enough to convey accurately the purpose of the service and what it can and cannot do. Even with a well-designed program, some users will retain unrealistic expectations. If a presearch interview between searcher and user is required, many of the remaining misconceptions will surface at that time and can be dealt with before the search is conducted and the results delivered.

An online search service requires users to interact with the library and its staff in unaccustomed ways. Most services ask patrons to complete a formal search request form, defining the topic, supplying relevant keywords and synonyms, citing pertinent articles if known, and so on. Although many users may carry out a roughly similar procedure when they conduct a search in manual sources, it is often a mental rather than a written process. Some users have difficulty articulating their needs so formally. In online, the user and library staff member are usually coparticipants in articulating and executing a search strategy. For the user, this is a new experience. For the library, it requires more formal arrangements for setting up presearch interviews and scheduling online appointments than is typical in traditional library service. The library must learn to deal with last-minute appointment cancellations, user "no shows," and those who arrive an hour early or an hour late. If users will be present during online sessions, the searching staff must be ready to deal with those who want to give advice on how the search should be conducted or on what is being done incorrectly. Some users will reevaluate their search topic as the session progresses and will want to change the focus of the search. If a service levies connect-time fees, a certain number of users will become extremely anxious when a staff searcher pauses online to reformulate strategy or when the results seem scant in relation to the amount of time spent online. Staff must become skilled in dealing with all these reactions.

Organizational Structure

How important is formal organization in operating an online search service? That depends on both the scope of the operation and the size of the library. In a small facility serving a limited number of users, there will be few options for defining such matters as the relationship between online searching and general reference, the organization of staffing, and the division of responsibility. But in larger settings, these become critical decisions for a library.

Several major concerns relate to the overall pattern of organization. An institution with many branch or remote departmental libraries must define the role of each geographically separate unit in the provision of online searching. Although this issue will not be applicable even to all larger libraries, a concern with greater universality will be the position of the online service within the organizational structure of the main library. Libraries generally follow one of two courses: Either the online service is set up as a separate unit, or it is integrated into the reference department. There are advantages and disadvantages to each. Some of the criteria for selecting one structure are administrative, such as budgeting, supervision, and so on. But equally important considerations have to do with online operation staffing patterns and their implications for the relationship between online searching and general reference service. Beyond these basic organizational decisions are other questions related to staffing, such as level, selection of personnel, and division of responsibility among online searchers.

The three major areas noted above—the role of geographically separate units, the place of the service within the overall library structure, and the organization of staff responsibilities—constitute a basic core of decisions central to the organization of a search service. The resolution of these matters establishes the basis on which the service will be administered and a framework within which policy and procedural decisions will be made.

Centralized versus Decentralized

For the library with branch locations, a major decision concerns providing service only through the central library or through some or all of the other sites as well. This decision has two parts: actual performance of online searching and administration of the service. If the library decides to provide online searching at more than one location, it can still be flexible about how decentralized administrative decisions and general policy will be.

The strongest argument for decentralized searching is that it places the service geographically closer to library users. In a large urban public library system, a search service offered only at the central library can be a considerable inconvenience for many users. Another strong argument, particularly in academic settings with departmental branches, is that the greatest subject expertise in the library is likely to be dispersed through the branches, and a decentralized service, therefore, can better draw on that expertise. However, in libraries other than academic the situation is often reversed. Particularly in large public library systems, the greatest special expertise is often found in the large central library, with the branches serving more generalized functions. The best approach thus depends on the roles of the branches and the main library.

One area in which decentralization almost always is at a disadvantage, however, is in operating expenses. Each location needs separate equipment, manuals, database guides, and so forth to perform effectively. For some libraries, these extra expenses put the possibility of decentralized service out of reach. For others, the additional expense may be viewed as a relatively minor trade-off for the service benefit.

The solution for some libraries lies between fully centralized and fully decentralized searching. The central location can perform most searches but can delegate responsibility for specialized requests to the branches. Or the branches can perform general searches, referring those that require special expertise to the main library. In either case, the library is drawing on the strength of the branches for conducting searches most appropriate to their emphasis, while relying on the central library to support areas in which the branches might be weaker. The main difficulties here are deciding which searches should be handled at what level and the logistics of referral. Referral of searches from one geographic location to another requires clear mechanisms for communicating between the locations. For most referrals, in addition, the searcher will not have the opportunity to speak directly with the person for whom the search is being conducted. This can mean greater possibility for misunderstanding or miscommunication. If the user is willing to or can travel to the site of the search, these problems are minimized, but not all users will be able or willing to make the journey.

A library's choice between centralized and decentralized service depends on such factors as extent of the geographic area, level of expertise and skill among staff, and ability to establish effective channels for conveying requests and results between locations. If some amount of searching will be conducted in all or some branches, a decision must be made about the extent to which administration is centralized or decentralized. It is generally most effective if overall administration is centrally coordinated since ordering supplies and such are often more cost-effective when channeled through a central unit. It is also best if policies and procedures are centrally coordinated. If each location is left to devise a charging scheme on its own, for example, users might begin to travel simply to take advantage of lower rates. Widely disparate policies regarding user status can also lead to much moving about. Because the branches might be serving different audiences, some flexibility in policy and procedure may be warranted, but it is generally more effective if decisions are at least sanctioned at a central level.

Separate versus Integrated

As already noted, libraries have generally either established a separate unit or have integrated the service within the general reference department, although there are other possibilities. Whether provided at one location or several, to what extent should the online service be separately identifiable from, as opposed to integrated within, another department or division of the library?

"Separate" does not necessarily imply total administrative independence from any other department or unit. An online service can be separately identifiable, say for budgeting, but still hierarchically within another department or division. A service that is completely integrated into another unit often does not have specific budget allocations for supplies, documentation, and so on. The staff that performs online searching provides other types of library service as well, usually general reference, and the responsibilities of the supervisor of the online service are also likely to extend into other areas. A separate service, on the other hand, normally has a clearly identifiable budget and the staff is likely to be involved only with online searching. The unit supervisor may answer to the head of reference or another department, but his or her responsibilities will be devoted entirely to administering the online service.

In a small library, the separate versus integrated question is of lesser importance; in some, integration is the only option with respect to staffing. In the one-person special library, the librarian is obviously responsible for providing all other services as well. But in larger settings, the question of a separate versus integrated service can take on considerable importance.

Concerning administration and the budget, there are practical advantages to the online search service as a separate unit. A separate unit is likely to have somewhat greater autonomy, and decisions that relate to its operation may be made more quickly and easily than if the service were part of another unit. A separate service can also make budgeting easier. True costs of operation can be identified far more accurately than if expenses are absorbed into broader departmental budget lines. More distinctive information about the cost of providing service makes it easier to monitor financial and staffing requirements.

The best argument for integration is that online searching is essentially an extension of the work performed in traditional reference service. As such, acquisition of an online search manual can be justified as the purchase of just another tool to aid the librarian in providing reference service. Similarly, salaries and other expenses can be viewed as among the normal costs of providing general reference to users. Some manuals and other materials are useful both in online searching and for traditional reference work, and an integrated unit can allow more cohesive development of the reference collection and can more easily avoid duplication of expensive sources suitable for both online and traditional service. Allocation of space and financial resources may be more effectively administered and competition more controlled if the online service is integrated within a broader unit.

Staffing

In all the arguments for integration or separation, the most important consideration in many ways is staffing. In libraries with an online service as a separate unit, staff responsibilities are often exclusively involved with searching. In many libraries with an integrated service, searching responsibility may be spread among all or most of the staff along with other duties. In practical terms, the former approach has certain advantages. Staff whose responsibilities are dedicated wholly to online searching are likely to develop a higher level of technical expertise and familiarity with all aspects of the service than those who perform only part time. To involve as many staff as possible, a reference department can easily spread searching responsibility too thin, and the overall result can be a lesser quality of service. Even when there is an ample amount of searching, there can still be a problem in dividing staff members' time between online and more traditional duties. Especially when the service is new and online is still a novelty for the staff, some will almost inevitably want to focus more of their time and attention on searching than on other duties. If left unchecked, this can lead to an imbalance in the overall provision of reference service.

Those who favor integration of staff responsibilities argue that if online searching is viewed as an extension of traditional reference service, separate staffing can be a barrier to overall performance. It is logical for reference staff to be as skilled in the use of online databases as in the use of other types of reference sources. And selecting just an elite few for searching work can lead to some resentment on the part of those not included.

However the service is run, friction between online searching and general reference must be avoided. The two staffs should at least be knowledgeable about what the other can and cannot do, so that queries can be referred to the appropriate people. Even with the search service as a separate unit, a close working relationship and mutual dependence between the units should be maintained. A separate service does not necessarily rule out online searching in the more traditional reference context as well. While a separate unit is available to handle complex or detailed searches, the general reference staff can regularly use online to answer specific queries, to provide brief lists of citations, and for a variety of other purposes.[1] Ready-reference use can serve as a pivotal link between traditional reference and a separate online searching unit.

The Successful Online Searcher

In selecting staff for an online search service, a library's general approach should be influenced by several factors:

Whether initiation or expansion of the service will require an increase in the size of the library staff as a whole.

The extent to which the library will make an effort to select searchers from among existing staff.

The degree to which search staff will be involved only with the online service as opposed to having other duties as well.

The importance attached to subject background in dividing searching responsibility among the staff.

There have been a number of attempts to identify the attributes of a successful online searcher.[2] Personality traits and work habits can vary widely among successful searchers, but the following qualities seem important:

Ability to use the technology and to learn systems and their retrieval capabilities.

Good memory for technical detail.

Superior communication skills and an ability to listen as well as to explain.

Ability to approach a problem logically and analytically.

Ability to make quick decisions and reformulate analyses of problems and approaches to them.

Perseverant but tempered by an attitude of economy and the ability to know when to quit.

Ability to deal with patrons in a "firm but gentle" manner when a situation warrants.

Constant willingness to learn on one's own and to share the benefits of those efforts with others.

An individual with all these attributes would not only be a good online searcher, but probably successful at anything else he or she tried as well. But it is important for an online searcher to have a balance of technical ability and communication skills. Assuming an adequate level of technical expertise, much of the success in online searching depends on the searcher's ability to understand users and their needs, to make users feel at ease in an interview and in an online environment, and to make his or her observations and comments clear. An ability to master the system is the foundation for technical expertise, but equally important is an ability to employ this knowledge as a bridge between user needs and the system capabilities: to analyze an information need, translate it into an online search strategy, and rethink the problem and change directions quickly when confronted with unexpected results.

A propensity for self-education cannot be overemphasized. Systems and databases change, and new ones are constantly added. Searchers may find out about these when they attend formal system and database update training sessions, but since such meetings can be few and far between, it is necessary to rely on newsletters, professional journals, revisions to manuals and other guides, participation in local user groups, and in-house sessions if searchers hope to perform online searching in the most effective manner possible. The library may assist in this effort by allowing time for such activities, but in the end, a large part of self-education will rest on individual commitment.

Among the searching staff, there should be clear policy and procedure regarding the division of responsibility. Responsibility should be divided into two levels: actual searching and attention to other activities required to support an online service. A fundamental issue related to searching is specialization versus generalization in terms of subject responsibility. Some libraries emphasize the former, in which searchers specialize in particular subject areas, usually corresponding to their own academic background. Some libraries prefer not to divide responsibility along subject lines. Others try to maintain some degree of flexibility, drawing on special subject expertise when it is available among the staff and for more difficult searches, but without making subject coverage the primary factor in division of searching responsibility.

If the library considers subject background an important attribute, this will influence not only the division of responsibility, but also the selection of individuals to staff the service. Some argue that system skills and personality traits are more important than subject background, but there are undeniable advantages of searchers having familiarity with the subject content of the databases they are searching. An example by Randolph Hock illustrates what can happen if a staff member is searching in unfamiliar territory:

> If the searcher does not know how to spell *methyl* or does not know that alkenes and olefins are the same, then good-quality chemical searching will be almost impossible. The chemist requesting the search is going to figure that the search might as well be done by a chemist rather than a librarian.[3]

The issue, then, can be one of credibility. The importance of subject background is most often discussed in terms of the hard sciences and technology, but it can apply to all areas. However, it is difficult to organize staffing around this principle in all but the largest settings.

Whatever degree of specialization is adopted, numerous tasks other than searching will need attention. Especially when first introducing a program, many libraries mistakenly equate operation of an online search service with the simple performance of online searching. The execution of searches is only one part of the operation. Table 16-1 shows the breadth of activities normally involved in operating a service.

If a search unit is fairly large, all staff need not be involved in all aspects of the service. Almost by definition all searchers are likely to be involved in each of the tasks listed in the "searching" category in Table 16-1. In administrative matters, input by as many searchers as possible is valuable, but responsibility for shaping this input and expressing it in final form will usually fall on a smaller number of staff, often a single individual serving in the capacity of coordinator.

Preparation of promotional materials and delivery of formal presentations about the service to classes and other groups may be a specialized responsibility, with some staff more actively engaged than others. All search staff should take part in at least some training and continuing education activities, both in-house and externally, but the responsi-

TABLE 16-1. STAFF ACTIVITIES IN AN ONLINE SEARCH SERVICE

Searching
    Presearch interviews
    Formulating initial search strategies
    Executing searches
    Logging searches
    Postsearch interviews and/or evaluation
Administrative Matters
    Developing policy and procedure guidelines
    Budgeting and preparation of reports
    Maintaining contacts with retrieval services, equipment vendors, and so on
    Collection development of manuals, search guides, and so on
Promotion and Training
    Preparing promotional materials
    Making presentations to various groups about the service
    Attending training and continuing education activities
    Conducting in-house training and continuing education activities
Record Keeping and Support
    Scheduling appointments
    Monitoring the stock of supplies, forms, and so on
    Maintaining general files
    Filing revisions into manuals
    Ordering supplies, manuals, and so on
    Reconciling retrieval-service and other vendor invoices
    Accepting user payment of fees for searching, and writing receipts
    Delivery of offline search results
    Compiling statistics

bility for conducting basic training and orientation of new staff will normally be assigned to one person, often the coordinator. Internal continuing education activities, on the other hand, can often draw on the search staff as a whole for sharing the benefits of each individual's special expertise or interests. Bookkeeping and support tasks are crucial to smooth operation of a service, but searchers should be free of as many of these responsibilities as possible.

In an online service with a small staff, the extent to which all responsibilities can be spread around will be limited. Most large online search services have found that having a staff coordinator, whose time is devoted entirely to the online service, is indispensable. The staff coordinator is usually responsible for carrying out many of the administrative tasks in Table 16-1, for organizing promotional efforts and in-house training and continuing education activities, and for overseeing operations of the unit in general. It is best if the coordinator also remains active in conducting online searches, but in a large-scale operation, the full-time demands of coordinating the activities of other staff may make this difficult.

The importance of efficient organization in any operation should never be underestimated. The success of online searching largely depends on the staff and its level of commitment to provide quality service. And the formal structure, above all else, must be one that fosters, not discourages, this dedication.

Costs and Cost Recovery

Numerous costs are involved in establishing and operating an online search service. For the smoothest all-around operation, the necessary funding should be assured ahead of time and specified for the service rather than being absorbed in an existing budget. The allocation for and expenses of online searching should be clearly identifiable even if the service is administered under another unit.

Four major aspects of financing an online search service are of concern to libraries. The "fee versus free" debate is examined in Chapter 15; here we look at the other three—initial costs in establishing a service, ongoing expenses once the service is up and running, and alternative charging structures that libraries have adopted to recover all or part of their expenses on an ongoing basis.

Initial Costs

The primary costs for setting up an online search service are outlined in Table 16-2. Although the importance of each factor will vary (equipment might be available in one library, but must be purchased in another, for instance), to accurately assess how much money will have to be spent before the service is initiated and the first search conducted, each library should examine all of the cost factors in Table 16-2.

Equipment

The two pieces of equipment essential for initiating an online search service are a terminal and a modem or acoustic coupler. Some terminals contain built-in modems; with others, a separate unit must be purchased. Access to a telephone line is also necessary. Some modems can be plugged directly into a telephone jack; acoustic couplers require a telephone set.

A terminal unit can take on any of several forms, including a simple CRT, a microcomputer or minicomputer, or a teleprinter. Although online searching can be conducted entirely on a microcomputer or CRT terminal without a hard-copy printing device, most libraries will want to have hard-copy capability available, which means buy-

TABLE 16-2. COSTS OF THE ONLINE SEARCH SERVICE

	Initial Costs	Ongoing Costs
Equipment	Terminal Modem Printer Telephone Microcomputer software	Depreciation replacement of existing equipment Acquisition of additional equipment Maintenance and repairs
Facilities	Furniture Installation of telephone and electrical outlets Other refurbishing	Expansion of existing facilities Refurbishing
System Charges and Telecommunications		Online connect time Database royalties Online and offline citation charges Packet switching network charges Long-distance telephone charges to nearest packet switching node
Supplies	Printer paper and ribbons Log books, accounting ledgers, receipt books, etc. Microcomputer diskettes	Printer paper and ribbons Log books, accounting ledgers, receipt books, etc. Microcomputer diskettes

Documentation	Manuals Thesauri and other search aids Subscriptions to professional journals and newsletters	Manuals Thesauri and other search aids Subscriptions to professional journals and newsletters
Training and Continuing Education	Workshop registration fees Travel expenses System charges for online practice	Training existing staff on additional retrieval services and databases Training new staff System charges for online practice on new or additional databases Professional developments: attendance at meetings, etc.
Promotion	Printed materials Slide, videotape production System charges for online demonstrations	Printed materials Slide, videotape production System charges for online demonstrations
Staff (service coordinator, searchers, support staff)	Salaries, wages Fringe benefits	Salaries, wages Fringe benefits
Other Expenses	Institutional memberships Advance payments to information retrieval services General overhead: space, lighting, administrative, etc.	Institutional memberships Annual advance payments to information retrieval services General overhead: space, lighting, administrative, etc.

ing a printer. A single-page display of a CRT is very limited, and in conducting a long search, it is convenient to have a hard-copy printout to consult. Without hard-copy capability, the user will either have to rely on offline prints ordered through the vendor or manually copy the results from the display screen—usually an impractical and time-consuming option.

Equipment costs vary greatly, and there is little point in trying to establish more than broad ranges here. At one time, probably the most heavily used terminal model in online searching was the Texas Instruments 745 portable teleprinter, still in use in many libraries. This communicating printer, with no visual display unit, transmits and receives messages at 300 baud through an acoustic coupler hookup affixed to the machine; it retailed for as much as $1,700 at one time. With the decline in the price of technology, a visual display terminal, modem, and attachable printer can now be bought for considerably less than that amount. This equipment will be basic, so if other options are added, such as 1200-baud communications, better quality hard-copy printing, or a more sophisticated terminal, the total cost can increase sharply.

In the selection of a printer, quality of print is highly important. A primary consideration is whether characters are formed by a series of closely spaced dots (dot matrix printers) or through one of several techniques that result in fully formed "letter-quality" characters. Libraries have often been reluctant to distribute documents printed on a dot matrix printer because of poor legibility. However, other considerations—such as cost—have favored the dot matrix printer for online searching. In general, dot matrix printers are much less expensive than letter-quality models. Some can be purchased for only a few hundred dollars. Although the price of letter-quality models has been coming down (some are available for under $1,000), they are still far less durable than most dot matrix printers in the same price range. A letter-quality printer durable enough to handle a high volume of online search activity is still an expensive item. In addition, letter-quality printers, regardless of price, generally print at a much slower rate than do most dot matrix printers. This can be a serious problem for an online search service, and for many libraries it makes the use of a letter-quality printer impractical.

On the brighter side, the print quality of dot matrix technology has improved dramatically. Some models that print quite legible copy may run about $600 to $700. For considerably more money, the Toshiba P1350 prints a dot matrix so closely spaced, and at a rate of 100 characters per second, that the print is barely distinguishable from fully formed, letter-quality characters. Another factor favoring these printers is their superior graphics capabilities, a feature of growing importance for numerical data retrieval, analysis, and display, as well as chemical substructure and other visual presentation requirements.

Costs also vary greatly for terminals. With separate terminal, modem, and printer components, an adequate visual display unit can be acquired for a few hundred dollars. At the other extreme, a library can purchase a microcomputer. When not used for online searching, the microcomputer can be in service for word processing, accounting, and so on. Its purchase can be justified in many ways, but it will, of course, increase the initial cost of equipment. The basic price for most models used in libraries, including a built-in or separate display unit, will probably be in the $1,500 to $3,000 range, plus the costs of search-related software. So, for a service that can be launched for about $1,000 to $1,500 worth of hardware, the library, depending on needs and commitments, can also rather easily spend $4,000 to $6,000 or more.

In purchasing any equipment, several things should be kept in mind. First, and self-evident, purchase only equipment that the library can afford. Second, rental or lease-purchase may be an option, although it will be more expensive in the long run. Third, costs do not stop with the purchase; the higher the purchase price, generally the more costly the maintenance and repairs. Four, shop around before buying. Even after a model has been chosen, the price can often be negotiated, especially if the product is handled by several different distributors.

Physical Facilities

Equipment costs will probably be the most substantial initial capital outlay, but other expenses can be considerable. It may be necessary to allocate money for physical facilities, such as the purchase of desks, chairs, and tables. Filing cabinets will be needed to store records of searches, receipts and invoices, brochures, and other documents about retrieval services, databases, equipment, and so on. Shelving will be needed to store larger documents such as system manuals and database thesauri. Additional telephone jacks or electrical sockets may have to be installed, lighting may need to be adjusted if video display terminals are used, and carpeting may have to be installed or, more often, removed to reduce the effects of static electricity. Try to balance economy with concerns for comfort in the work environment. Equipping the service with all the battered leftovers out of storage will not be conducive to a pleasant working environment.

Supplies and Documentation

At least a small expenditure for supplies will be necessary at the outset of a search service. Some money will be needed for printer ribbons and paper, and for various forms and bookkeeping materials—search request forms, log books or forms, accounting ledgers, receipt books if users are charged, and so on.

The library may also have to spend several hundred dollars on documentation when a service is initiated. System manuals from the retrieval services are necessary, and the library should purchase additional aids specific to the databases it will use frequently. Database aids can be extremely useful if they are selected with care. Avoid buying expensive thesauri and other materials for databases that will seldom or never be used. Subscriptions to a select number of professional journals and newsletters are well justified. Several journals focus directly on online databases and information retrieval, *Online, Online Review,* and *Database* among the more prominent.

Training and Promotion

Since the online skills of searchers will be a key ingredient in the success of a service, training should be a very high priority. Self-education may be an admirable trait in a searcher, but it should not take the place of initial formal training. The staff can obtain initial training on the major systems used in libraries through several sources. The most popular are the information retrieval services themselves, which periodically conduct sessions in various parts of the country. In addition, some state and regional networks conduct training on the major systems. The Bibliographical Center for Research (BCR) in Denver, for example, has two professional staff members who spend a good deal of their time conducting training throughout the Midwest and Rocky Mountain region on BRS and DIALOG. Some library schools offer intensive training on the use of selected systems. From whatever source, the initial training generally lasts one and one-half to two full days. Prices vary, but usually are in the $75–$150 range per person.

Depending on timing and the library's location, staff members may have to be sent to another city to be trained. That means expenses in the form of mileage reimbursement, overnight lodging, and meal and miscellaneous expenses for staff.

Once trained, the staff should have ample opportunity to practice searching before the service becomes operational. Fortunately, most retrieval services and some networks offer a fairly liberal number of hours of free searching to any individual who has attended one of their basic training sessions. But if the library plans immediately to search in several databases, this amount of free time will not allow searchers to gain even basic familiarity with very many databases before beginning to accept requests from users. Therefore, the library should be prepared to spend as much as several hundred dollars per searcher for online connect charges, telecommunications, and print charges to support adequate practice time.

There will also be some initial promotional expenses, depending on how widely the library wishes to make the service known. (Promotional activities are detailed later in this chapter.)

Salaries and Other Costs

The salaries of online searching staff can be viewed as an indirect cost of providing a search service. The important point is that enough time and attention must be allowed for staff to carry out the many tasks required in setting up a new service. Selection and installation of equipment, review and purchase of documentation, ordering of supplies, and training and promotion all require staff time.

As indicated in Table 16-2, expenses involved in initiating a search service include advanced payments to retrieval services and institutional membership fees in user groups. Advance payments, usually made to secure better discount rates, are not required in all cases, and in any event are not a "lost" expense if the library consumes the amount within a specified period. The money, however, must be on hand to send in if the library's contractual options require or favor prepayment.

Ongoing Expenses

As a comparison of costs in Table 16-2 indicates, many of the start-up and ongoing expenses of operating a search service are the same. Annual ongoing expenses can be less than, more than, or the same as those during the first year of the service. Because of the similarities, continuing expenses are not described here in detail except as they differ in scope or magnitude from initial costs.

No equipment will function perfectly or forever. The annual costs for maintenance contracts, from a manufacturer, supplier, or third party, may run 10 to 15 percent of the original purchase price. Although most equipment used by libraries in online searching is durable and will last for years, it will eventually need to be replaced, of necessity or by choice. Technological change and other factors can hasten replacement, such as the abandonment by many libraries of 300-baud modems in favor of 1200-baud devices. Given the present pace of change in technology, all equipment should be continuously scrutinized for usefulness and cost-effectiveness. If the scope of a service increases, the library may want to add more sophisticated peripheral equipment and establish additional work stations.

After a time, improvements in physical facilities may be needed. The amount of space might have to be increased, additional furniture acquired, and existing pieces replaced. As with equipment, these expenses are difficult to budget if the library operates on an annual appropriation basis. When reserves cannot be cumulated for capital expenditure or facility improvement, it is all the more important that a library constantly monitor its needs so that appropriate allocation can be budgeted for the forthcoming year.

The most substantial direct costs incurred on an ongoing basis are system use and telecommunications charges for searching. Connect charges, database royalties, and per-citation charges vary according to the retrieval service and databases used. Whatever the service, the library will probably make the online connection through a packet switching network. TYMNET, TELENET, and UNINET, the most commonly used, are priced between $6 and $11 per hour.

Packet switching nodes are not located in all cities, so the library may have to incur long-distance telephone charges to the nearest one. Some services have a direct dial option. At $20–$25 per hour, this can be the least expensive option for a library that does not have local access to a packet switching network. These telecommunications charges are separate from, and in addition to, the online connect charges assessed by the retrieval service, which will be substantially higher. Connect-hour charges, including time-dependent database royalties if assessed separately, vary enormously from one service to another and across databases. For most bibliographic databases, the fees range from $50 per hour up, although some will be less expensive. Per-citation charges usually range between 10¢ and 25¢ each, depending on the database. The composite of all these charges, on a per-search basis, can be as low as a few dollars for a quick search in an inexpensive database to more than $100 for a complex search in an expensive database.

The library will have to maintain adequate appropriations for supplies and documentation on a continuing basis. With experience, the library will become more adept at projecting the need for supplies. And while costs of documentation may be highest when first setting up a service, they are by no means a one-time expense. If the library incorporates additional retrieval services, it will have to purchase system manuals or search aids for any new databases. Subscriptions to key professional journals and newsletters should be maintained and new ones possibly added.

Training costs will continue even after the service is operational. If additional retrieval services are added, staff will have to be trained, and if new, inexperienced staff is hired, they too will need instruction. Some libraries train new staff members in-house, with the responsibility often falling to the coordinator of the service. Although in-house training can save on certain direct expenses, such as registration fees and travel, its overall cost-effectiveness is questionable. The in-house trainer will have to spend about two full days away from other duties, and the library will not receive the free online practice time provided by retrieval services and networks. Practice time for a new searcher, with online costs at regular rates, can easily exceed the amount of money it would cost to register the person in a retrieval service or network training session.

If searchers are to remain on top of things and if the service is to expand its database coverage, some of the staff should attend advanced workshops, update sessions, and special database training. As many as possible should become actively involved in local user groups and at least some should attend major annual national meetings. All this activity will result in better service, but, of course, it costs money.

Ongoing costs will involve updating promotional brochures or producing new ones if the library wants to target a new audience. Online demonstrations are generally most frequent during the first year or two of operation while the service is still establishing itself. However, in a setting with a fairly transient population—such as an academic community—the need to conduct demonstrations is constant.

Fee-based Alternatives

The extent to which a library plans to recover the costs of an online service will depend on its financial resources. In setting up a charging plan, the first step is to anticipate the total cost of the service by taking into account all of the factors listed in the Ongoing Costs column in Table 16-2. The next step is to decide the extent to which the service costs as a whole, and each of the individual expenses, can be absorbed within the library's operating budget. The remaining amount and the cost factors involved must then be examined and a charging formula set up for recovery of that amount.

Although virtually every ongoing expense in Table 16-2 could be examined individually with respect to its inclusion in a cost-recovery plan, it is possible to identify some major groupings of expenses. Direct costs are out-of-pocket expenses incurred through charges assessed by telecommunications facilities and online retrieval services. Many libraries view these as part of a single category of expenses, but some do make distinctions between them for purposes of cost recovery. Some search services, for example, recover retrieval service connect-hour charges and per-citation charges, but absorb telecommunications costs.

Indirect costs can be grouped into three categories: secondary ex-

:quipment, supplies, demonstrations, and so on); staff salaries, ιd benefits; and general overhead (space, utilities, general administration). As with direct expenses, many libraries view these as part of a single larger, nondistinct category and treat them identically in cost-recovery plans.

There is a continuum along which libraries are likely to include or exclude each group of expenses within a cost-recovery plan. At one extreme is full library subsidy of virtually all expenses associated with operation of the service. At the other is full cost recovery of all expenses. Most libraries fall somewhere in between. Probably the single most prevalent cost-recovery formula used in libraries is full recovery of all direct expenses combined with full subsidy of all indirect expenses.

Once the library has projected the expenses it expects to incur over a given period, has decided on the amount it needs to recover from users, and has selected the various cost factors to be included for full or partial recovery, the next step is to decide on an actual charging policy. In selecting a charging formula, two important parameters should be considered. One is whether charges will be based on time or will be a uniform flat fee for each search, or some combination of the two. The other is whether the charges will be specific to each database or generalized across databases. These options, noted in Table 16-3, have both advantages and disadvantages.

Time-dependent versus Flat-rate Fee

The direct online expenses that a library incurs will depend on the retrieval services and databases used, the amount of time spent online, and the number of citations printed or displayed. But for any search, some definite costs can be identified. Except for per-citation charges, most retrieval services use time-dependency as the basis for their charg-

TABLE 16-3. OPTIONAL BASES FOR CHARGING STRATEGIES

	Database Specific	Generalized, Non-Database-Specific
Time-dependent	Time-dependent, database specific charging	Time-dependent charging generalized across all databases
Flat rate	Flat-rate fee for each database	Flat-rate fee, generalized across all databases
Combined	Base rate flat fee, time-dependent charging beyond the base amount for each database	Base rate flat fee, time-dependent charging beyond the base amount, generalized across all databases

ing plans. Each search is charged according to the amount of time spent online, with an added component to recover per-citation costs.

Many libraries carry over this time-dependency as the principle basis for their own charging scheme. Each user is charged according to the amount of time spent online, usually supplemented with an additional per-citation charge.

This approach can also be used to recover indirect expenses. (Some libraries with a time-dependent charging plan for recovery of direct expenses use a flat-rate surcharge for recovery of indirect expenses. To arrive at this figure, the library calculates the amount of indirect expenses it needs to recover and divides that figure by the number of searches it plans to perform.) The simple, if somewhat imprecise, method for doing this is to figure out all the indirect expenses a library wishes to recover and express the total as a percentage of direct expenses. For example, suppose that:

1. A library expects that 1,000 searches will be conducted during the upcoming budget year.
2. The direct expenses (excluding per-citation charges) for 1,000 searches are projected to be $15,000.
3. Per-citation charges will be recovered from users at actual cost on a search-by-search basis.
4. The library will try to recover some portion of indirect expenses in this way:
   a. One-third of the salary and benefits of one full-time searcher whose total annual salary and benefits amount to $21,000; hence, recovery of $7,000.
   b. $500 to cover equipment maintenance.
   c. $500 as a reserve fund for eventual purchase of new equipment.
   d. $250 toward the purchase of documentation.
   e. $750 toward training fees and travel to conferences.

The amount of indirect expenses that this library wishes to recover is $9,000. If this amount is divided by the anticipated direct expenses of $15,000, the result is 60¢ of indirect expense to be recovered for each $1 of direct online costs incurred during a search. Using this as a basis for recovering the desired portion of indirect costs, the library would simply add 60¢ to each search for every $1 of direct online expense for that search. The total charge for a search with direct online costs of $10 would be $16 plus per-citation charges; for a search with direct online costs of $30, the user fee would be $48 plus per-citation charges, and so on.[4]

The main advantage of time-dependent pricing, especially in terms of direct costs, is that the user is charged an amount that fairly accurately represents, on a case-by-case basis, the costs to the library. The main disadvantages are the wide variations that occur in the cost of searches and the fact that a user will not know how much a search will cost until after it has been completed.

For these and other reasons, some libraries choose a flat-rate fee, charging the same amount for each search, regardless of how long it takes or how much it costs the library. Per-citation costs may be calculated into the standard rate, but are usually charged separately.

To arrive at the standard fee, the amount that must be recovered over a given period is divided by the number of searches anticipated during that time. The library in the above example recovering only direct online costs would divide the anticipated expenses of $15,000 by 1,000 searches to arrive at a flat rate of $15 per search. If the library wished to recover $9,000 of its indirect expenses, this amount would be added to the $15,000 before dividing by 1,000, resulting in a total per-search fee of $24.

The main advantages of the flat-rate fee are that it standardizes the per-search charges and, even when per-citation charges are extra, it allows the user a fairly clear idea of the total costs *before* the search is conducted. The disadvantages are possible wide discrepancies on a case-by-case basis—since the rate is based on an average—between the amount a user pays for a search and the actual search costs to the library. A user whose search takes only a few minutes will pay more than the actual costs, thereby subsidizing more complicated searches that take more time and cost far more than the standard rate. Another disadvantage is that a flat-rate fee structure can be more sensitive to inaccuracies in budget projections. If the actual average cost of searches exceeds the anticipated average, revenues from a flat-rate plan will fall short of expenses. Time-dependent pricing in a full cost-recovery plan, on the other hand, does not rely on the average cost of a search as a basis for calculating charges. And since higher per-search costs will be balanced by proportionally high per-search charges, there is greater protection against revenue shortfalls.

Some plans use certain elements of each charging method. The most common is to charge a flat rate for up to a certain number of minutes spent online, and then charge on a time-dependent basis when a search exceeds that amount of time. For example, a library might charge a base fee of $10 for the first ten minutes, and an additional $1 for each minute beyond ten. This kind of setup is not easy to budget, especially when a service is new and the library does not have a clear idea of the type and length of searches, but after a use pattern develops, this approach has two real advantages. The basic fee can be established so that the user has a fairly good idea of what he or she will have to pay.

At the same time, the time-dependent factor, because of the additional revenue generated for more time-consuming searches, allows the base fee to be set at a lower level than the overall average cost of a search. Under this plan, users with comparatively simple requests will not be subsidizing the cost of more complicated searches to the extent they do in a strictly flat-rate structure. In addition, for those searches that would otherwise tend to increase the average, time-dependent charging beyond a specified amount means that unexpectedly higher expenses will be balanced by higher revenues. This kind of "hybrid" approach does require some careful planning to realize its benefits, but the result can be a more equitable plan for most users and one that is less sensitive to inaccurate projections than a strictly flat-rate fee structure.

Generalized versus Database-specific Charging

Connect-hour rates, time-dependent database royalties, and per-citation charges vary appreciably among retrieval services and databases. In general, commercially produced scientific, technical, and business databases are more expensive than those in the social sciences, arts, and humanities, especially when the latter are produced by government or not-for-profit agencies.

Whether a library adopts a time-dependent or flat-rate charging plan or some combination, it will have to decide if charges will be calculated for each database or generalized across all of them. The generalized plan is easier to explain to users and leaves less room for misunderstanding about the rate at which a search will be charged. Some libraries also think that access in the library should not be priced according to such things as subject content or profit versus nonprofit status of the database producer.

The generalized, non-database-specific charging does have some problems, however. From the library's viewpoint, it is more difficult to budget for, since fees will be based on a projected average cost across databases for which the library itself is charged at widely varying rates. In addition, whether time-dependent pricing or flat-rate fee structures are used, generalized non-database-specific charging will penalize those whose searches are conducted in the less expensive databases while subsidizing those in the more expensive databases.

In time-dependent charging plans, database-specific pricing ensures a closer balance between user fees and direct library costs. For indirect expenses, however, an equity problem can occur if their recovery is calculated as a percentage of direct costs. For example, indirect costs for a 15-minute search in a $150 per hour or a $60 per hour database are not likely to be much different. But if the library charges indirect expenses as a percentage of direct costs, the user who searches in the $150 database will be charged two and one-half times as much for indirect expenses. Some libraries get around this by using a flat rate to recover indirect expenses and charging direct costs on a time basis.

No charging plan for online searching is perfect. The individual library must decide which factors it considers most important and plan accordingly.

Partial Subsidy of Direct Costs

Sometimes libraries cannot afford to provide free searching but can subsidize all direct, and some indirect, expenses in one of two ways: Some searches are provided free according to preestablished criteria, with full recovery of direct costs for others, or a uniform subsidy is applied to all searches.

In the first method, the library has to decide which searches will be free. A few use a quota system to determine this. Every library user is allowed a designated number of free searches over a given period and is charged beyond that. More frequently, libraries use user status or unavailability of print as criteria. An academic library, for example, might provide free searching to faculty but charge all other users. A library might allow free searches if no adequate print source is available.

Some libraries distinguish on the basis of complexity. For a very complex search, even if a print source is available, the search might be free since superior results presumably would be gained from the online database. If the request is straightforward and involves one basic concept that is an index entry in an equivalent print source, the user would be urged to conduct a manual search and would be charged if he or she still wanted the search performed online.

Some libraries waive or at least reduce fees if the searcher is newly trained or working with a new or little-used database. Such distinctions, however, are difficult to implement as standard policy.

All these criteria can be set before a search is actually performed. But some criteria can be applied during or after a search. Even in a totally fee-based service, a library should not charge back unexpected online costs that occur as a result of technical breakdowns, such as a system crash. Nor should users be charged for "bad" searches resulting from a staff member's misunderstanding of the search or simply poor performance. (Even the best searchers have an occasional off-session!) Some libraries even waive fees when a search yields results that a user judges to be of little or no value. A library using this policy, however, should keep in mind that "unhelpful results" are not the same thing as a "bad search." Some searches will yield no results regardless of the searcher's performance.

Waiving of fees in these instances may be a good public relations gesture on the part of the library, but such a policy may also be above and beyond the call of duty. One practical difficulty is in defining what does or does not constitute a "useful" set of results. In a search of a bibliographic database, for example, success cannot always be tied strictly to quantity or even quality of the citations retrieved. Also, in some searches the user hopes *not* to retrieve citations, as a search in a dissertation database. A doctoral student exploring a possible topic might well regard retrieval of no citations as a positive result.

The second way to absorb some direct costs is uniform subsidy, applying the same structure to all searches, regardless of complexity, user status, and so on. This method can be approached in three ways: straight percentage subsidy, front-end subsidy, and upper-limit subsidy (see Table 16-4 for descriptions and examples of these differences).

Some libraries use variations on these approaches. The library at California State University, Chico, has a "10/10/10" charging plan; the library pays the first $10 of direct costs of a search, the user pays the next $10, if necessary, and the library pays the third $10, with the user paying all additional online costs beyond that amount. Since simple searches can be conducted within the first $10 limit, some users obviously get free searches. Those between $10 and $30 are heavily subsi-

TABLE 16-4. UNIFORM SUBSIDY OPTIONS

	Description	Example
Straight % Subsidy	Library subsidizes a straight percentage of the costs of each search	Library subsidizes 40% of the cost of each search
Front-end Subsidy	Library pays up to a specified number of minutes spent online or up to a specified amount of costs for each search; user pays the remainder	Library pays for the first 10 minutes online or the first $10 of each search; user pays any costs above that amount
Upper-limit Subsidy	User pays up to a specified number of minutes spent online or up to a specified amount of costs for each search; library pays the remainder	User pays for the first 10 minutes online or the first $10 of each search; library pays any costs above that amount

dized by the library, and even for searches beyond $30, the library still makes a significant contribution.[5]

In addition to telecommunications and hourly connect costs, some libraries also partially subsidize online and offline citation charges. The possible approaches are about the same as those in subsidizing time-dependent charges. For example, a library can subsidize a straight percentage of the total citation charges for each search. It can also provide front-end subsidy, either paying a set amount, as the first 5 or 10 cents, or paying the full costs up to a certain number of citations, perhaps 25 or 50, with the user paying the entire costs of additional citations after that. In the upper-limit subsidy, the library might pay the cost of each citation above a standard rate, or the user might be required to pay full costs up to a specified number of citations. Of all citation subsidy plans, regardless of online approach, probably the most common is to fully subsidize up to a specified number of citations, after which the user pays the full costs of each additional citation.

Many libraries use both methods—free searches according to pre-established critera and uniform subsidy. Generally, libraries that absorb any part of direct online costs absorb a significant, not a nominal, amount.

Partial subsidy plans require skill in forecasting and budgeting. They also require careful estimation of total costs and accurate projections of the distribution use at various intervals of online time and costs. Any meaningful departures from such projections can result in a subsidy by the library that is considerably more (or less) than anticipated. However, the ability and willingness to absorb some portion of direct costs allow the library greater flexibility in its approach to charging, and also may help to alleviate some of the uneasiness caused by charging for a library service at all.

Promotion

Some libraries spend much effort promoting their online search service, and others devote little or no attention to this aspect. Ideally, the amount of time and money put into promotion should be closely correlated with the anticipated scope and level of the service provided. If a library's resources can support only a limited service or one available only to certain groups of users, an all-out publicity campaign would not be necessary.

Although promotion should be a continuing activity, care in planning is especially crucial when the service is first established. Studies of online searching consistently show that the most effective form of promotion in attracting new users is word-of-mouth. Part of this involves interaction between users and librarians, but an even more important part involves user-to-user communication. If initial efforts go awry and lead to an unmanageable demand level or serious misunderstandings on the part of many users about what the service can do, the library will have dug itself into a very deep hole. Bad news always seems to travel faster than good, and word of ineffectiveness, misleading advertising, and so on can spread rapidly throughout a community of potential users. With corrective countermeasures, a negative image can be overcome in time, but the library will have to expend much more effort in promotional campaigns than if the problems had been avoided in the first place through more careful planning.

Promotion of online services can be approached in two major ways: (1) form, examining the many products and services that a library can use to promote its online service, and (2) process and content. Promotion may take on many different forms: brochures and fliers, posters, demonstrations and presentations, radio announcements and newspaper articles, and so on. Different forms of promotion may serve different purposes and have different requirements, but basic principles must be taken into account in their design and use. Whether preparing a poster or a presentation, certain guidelines are essential to effective promotion. The emphasis in this section is mainly on these general guidelines, less importantly on various forms.

Part of Marketing

Promotion may be viewed as one part of the broader concept of marketing. In the field of librarianship, concepts of marketing and promotion are far too often viewed as synonymous, and are also equated with advertising. Marketing, promotion, and advertising are related, but not the same. Advertising is one part of promotion, and promotion is one aspect of marketing. In terms of online searching, the concept of marketing implies coordination of many activities: an understanding of the scope, capabilities, and needs of the service itself; an awareness of the impact of the service on the library as a whole; and knowledge about the needs, perceptions, and behavior of existing and potential users. Marketing takes into account all of these influences, the interplay between them, and implications for the provision of service. Effective promotion is not achieved simply through an all-out publicity blitz, but rather through a process that draws on broader principles for its organization, content, and timing.

Market Segmentation

One of the important principles in marketing is identifying which groups of individuals are most likely to use a product or service. Not all library users will be equally likely candidates. But even within the broad category of "users," basic distinctions must be made. An advanced scholar engaged in research and a student writing a term paper for a freshman English course might both be candidates for an online search, but their needs will obviously be quite different. Promotion will be most effective if the library recognizes such distinctions.

Potential users may be identified by such qualifiers as status (faculty member, graduate student, undergraduate, for instance), subject interest, and—perhaps an even more important consideration—the nature and complexity of the information need. The needs of some users for some searches will center around an almost inexhaustive list of sources; in other cases, "a few good citations" might do the job. These important distinctions must be kept in mind when designing promotional materials, media announcements, or presentations.

A library's marketing analysis should extend beyond the mere identification of user categories according to "need." Equally important are other characteristics of a defined user group: attitudes and level of knowledge about library and information research in general, perceptions of the role and capabilities of computers in assisting in research, and level of awareness about the online service. In preparing promotional materials and activities, these factors are just as important to take into account as are distinctions based on user status, subject interest, or anything else.

Promotional Content

The design of promotional content is a key element in effectively—and accurately—representing a product or service. Certain criteria should always be kept in mind. For one, promotion should be framed in terms of potential user needs and problems, not in terms of the technical aspects or jargon of information retrieval. Users are interested in results; basically, they want to know what the system can do for them, not how it works.

The best way to capture interest, then, is for promotional materials and presentations to speak directly to user needs. Some fliers and brochures designed by libraries use captions such as "Bibliographies for Term Papers" for immediate appeal to certain audiences. This example also stresses the importance of directing content toward specific segments of the user community. A flier describing applications of online searching for undergraduate term papers is not likely to merit even a second glance from doctoral students. Although some brochures should describe the service in general, these should be supplemented with more specialized material aimed at different segments of the user community.

Specialized promotional materials should use language and examples familiar to the target user group. A brochure for those in the business community will obviously be more effective if examples from business-related databases are cited than if chemistry databases are used.

The library should also balance brevity with thoroughness. Hard-copy materials, media announcements, and presentations should be short enough so that the user is not required to spend a great deal of time and effort reading or listening to them, yet the content should be informative and thorough enough to capture interest and should instruct the user about where to go and how to get an online search initiated.

With brevity and thoroughness in mind, the content of promotional materials should center around two aspects: emphasizing the advantages of an online search and presenting a realistic picture of what the service is and how it can be of use. Advantages commonly cited include saving the user a great deal of time and effort, the overall individuality and custom-tailored nature of the service, scope of sources available, ease with which multiple sources can be consulted, and the ease with which different concepts and key terms may be combined in a search.

Promotion should also state the limitations of a service, leaving little room for the user to formulate unrealistic expectations. Any limitations should be expressed in as positive a manner as possible, not as urgent warnings or red-letter restrictions. Dates of coverage, for example, should note terms of inclusion, not exclusion. Potential misunderstandings can be avoided by emphasizing what the search results *will* be, not what they will *not* be. If the final results of a search are produced only via offline prints supplied by the retrieval service through the mail, the promotion should carefully avoid any word of "instant results." If the library charges for online searching, this *must* be indicated in any promotion. The user should be given at least some idea of the general range he or she can expect to pay.

Effective promotional design is both an art and a business. If the library is aware of its potential user market, their needs, and perceptions, it can design promotional materials and activities that attract attention and elicit enthusiasm from a broad range of potential users.

Point-of-need Promotion

Timing and location are two important aspects of promotion, with the emphasis on delivery of promotional materials and activities at the point of greatest need. Location is the critical factor for such materials as posters, fliers, and brochures describing the service in general; they should be permanently displayed at strategic sites in the library. A prime spot for posters, for example, is where printed indexes and abstracts are shelved. The reference desk, if located apart from the online service, and the circulation desk are somewhat less critical, but as points of traffic, they are still valuable for placing general fliers or brochures. More specialized materials directed at specific user segments are effective when placed at or near the work environment or commonly used meeting places.

Timing relates to such things as special mailings, media announcements, and presentations. The most effective time to make a presentation to a class of undergraduates, for example, is when students are ready to start a term paper assignment. Even a well-designed presentation will be less effective if delivered too far in advance of an assignment or after most students have completed their papers. Articles in campus newspapers will be noticed more if they appear part of the way through a term than during the first week of classes or during finals. Special mailings to faculty members are likely to receive the greatest response when coordinated with the beginning of research sabbaticals, during preparation of grant proposals, immediately following receipt of research funding, or in other instances where particular faculty members are beginning a project. Timing may require some intelligence work on the part of the library, but the value of this promotional aspect should not be overlooked.

Part of a Broader Purpose

Libraries tend to promote online searching in its own context, apart from the other, more traditional services of the library. This approach can have some drawbacks, as Maloney observes:

> The active promotion of database searching, in the absence of a marketing program for the repertoire of informational services offered by libraries, has created an imbalance. The active promotion of one service at the expense or neglect of other services offered by the profession has resulted in a high degree of visibility for that one service . . . the service establishes a separate identity, both in the minds of the librarian and the user, apart from the "other" services which continue to be offered in a more traditional format.[6]

An intensive, narrowly focused promotion campaign can certainly make users aware of the search service, but it can also foster a lopsided view as to what the library as a whole has to offer. It fails to capitalize on an opportunity to use one very attractive service as a basis for heightening user interest in a much broader range of services.

In presentations and promotional literature, associations can be made between online searching and other library services—document delivery, for instance. The library should ask itself whether the purpose of its online search service is just to provide the user with a list of books and articles or whether, more accurately, the service is an intermediate means to facilitate the use of the documents themselves. If the latter is true, such efforts should not be overlooked in promotions of online searching.

Promotion presentations provide an excellent opportunity to use online searching as a focus around which to organize the promotion of other library services. Many potential users may not even be aware of the printed indexes and related reference sources in their field of interest, or may never have considered the value of assistance available from the general reference staff. A presentation on online searching should center first and foremost on that activity, but blended into the discussion should be the broader range of services the library offers.

User Feedback

User feedback is an important aspect of marketing and promoting an online search service. Carried out periodically, broadly based surveys and interviews are most useful. But procedures can also be built into the search service itself that require less effort but still result in valuable information. With a carefully designed search request form (see Figure 16-1 in the next section), the library can obtain data about who is using the service and why, and can use this information for refining or redirecting its promotion. Answers to a question on the form asking how a user learned about a service can provide insight about the effectiveness of different kinds of promotion. Postsearch evaluations also give important information, pinpointing the strengths and weaknesses of a service and measuring the satisfaction level of users. They can ascertain the effectiveness of other aspects of the library's promotional activities as well. A question for first-time users about their actual experience with the service as compared with their preconceptions can help to determine if promotion materials and activities accurately represent the service and its capabilities.

All of these factors play an important role in promoting an online search service, regardless of the particular vehicles used. No matter how carefully promotion is planned, some users will be oblivious to any and all efforts. But by taking into account the factors noted here, the library's promotional campaign stands a better chance of success than one organized around occasional publicity blitzes, or a limited range of promotional materials. The most effective promotional vehi-

.. the end, is the service itself. Well-organized promotion will enhance a service that provides high-quality assistance to users, but no promotional efforts will carry a service with a continuing reputation for poor performance.

Policy and Procedure

Some libraries provide online searching on a very informal basis with few "rules and regulations" regarding logistics. Users drop in at any time and request a search; if a staff member is available, the search is conducted immediately. Some users want to discuss their needs in detail; others just want to fill out a form or write up a description and leave it for the searcher. Some may want to be present when the search is being done; others prefer not to be.

In a small setting where the volume of activity is low and where librarians and users generally know one another and have frequent opportunity to interact, the informal policy works well. But in an environment with a much larger pool of potential users, it is usually necessary to operate under a more formal structure. A certain formality ensures a smoother work flow and greater consistency in the internal organization of the service itself. But formal policies and procedures in most libraries are also established to produce the best possible results for a user. This is achieved through such formal mechanisms as standard search request forms, presearch interviews, and the presence of the user during online sessions, providing more effective communication between user and searcher. These mechanisms should assist the user in articulating and refining an information need and should help to ensure that the searcher understands the user's request.

Many policy and procedure decisions will have a bearing on internal efficiency and on the effectiveness with which users and searchers communicate about an information need. Some of the more important are:

Policies and procedures manual

Drop-in versus scheduled appointments

Search request forms

Presearch interviews

Presence of the user at the online session

Delivery of results

User evaluations

Record keeping

Policies and Procedures Manual

Most libraries have standard policies and procedures governing online searching, but few go so far as to make up a manual. In a survey of 200 libraries offering online searching in the northeastern United States a few years ago, only six had developed a written policy manual, and most of those had only partially completed the manual or had addressed policy only in a general manner.[7] These manuals may be more common today, but it is a fairly safe bet that many libraries are still without them.

Listed below are the main points that should be covered in a policies and procedures manual for online searching. Any of these issues can present a problem if the library does not deal with it on a policy level. Without a written document, the library runs a greater risk of inconsistently applying policies even in such elementary matters as who can use the service and under what circumstances, to say nothing about the possible confusion over finer details.

POLICIES AND PROCEDURES MANUAL
A. Statement of purpose and goals
B. Access
    1. Available to whom?
    2. On what criteria are requests accepted or denied, and by whom? Does user have appeal rights?
    3. Limit on number of requests submitted by single user over given period?
    4. Priorities for handling requests by category of users.
C. Service Level
    1. What information retrieval services are used?
    2. Searching will be offered in what subject areas, on which databases?
    3. What criteria decide the searching of one database over another if both are pertinent and available?
    4. Are there limits for number of databases searched, time spent online, or citations printed for one search request?
D. Request Acceptance
    1. By what method(s)? Any exceptions?
    2. On-the-spot searches or appointments only?
    3. Who schedules appointments?
    4. Standard maximum turnaround time between acceptance of request and search performance?
    5. Rescheduling policy for user no-show at presearch interview or online session.
E. Presearch Interview/Strategy Preparation
    1. Are presearch interviews required?
    2. Guidelines for search strategy preparation: offline thesauri used or left to disgression of searcher?
F. User at Online Session
    1. Presence required, prohibited, or optional?
    2. In user absence, policy for payment or rescheduling if user feels results are inadequate.

G. Results Delivery
   1. Forms and mechanisms.
   2. How are citations provided in hard-copy form: offline from retrieval service, locally printed while online, downloaded and printed locally at later time?
   3. Results provided in machine-readable form?
   4. Does user pick up results or are they mailed?
   5. Postsearch interview required?
   6. Standard turnaround time between execution and result delivery?
   7. Procedure for undelivered results (whether not picked up or undelivered through mail).
H. Confidentiality
   1. Measures to ensure privacy of search requests and results.
I. Charges
   1. Fee schedule for charges.
   2. Payment procedure.
   3. Criteria for waiving, postponing, refunding payment. On whose authority?
   4. Procedures for conducting searches for users with outstanding fee balances.
J. Record Keeping
   1. Are search copies kept on file? For how long?
   2. What types of statistics will be compiled? When? By whom?
K. Personnel and Division of Staff Responsibility
   1. Do staff members search in all subject areas or is there specialization?
   2. Lines of authority for user complaints.
   3. Who authorizes work schedule changes and policy and procedure exceptions?
   4. Who decides on purchase of documentation?
   5. Who is responsible for support tasks (scheduling appointments, and so on)?
   6. Policy regarding meetings, workshops, training.
L. Demonstrations
   1. Policy regarding temporary removal of equipment for off-site demonstrations.
   2. Who approves demonstrations? Under what circumstances?
   3. Amount of lead time required to schedule in-house demonstrations? Who is informed?
M. Service Evaluation
   1. How is effectiveness judged?
   2. How will evaluation questionnaires relate to job performance evaluation of searchers?
   3. How are improvements in service to be made?
   4. How are changes in policies and procedures to be implemented?
N. Forms
   1. What forms filled out by searcher? User? Support staff?
   2. Disposition after use?

(Policies and procedures manual should contain a copy of each form used and examples of how they are to be completed.)

With clearly expressed statements, a written manual can reduce ambiguity and the chance of differing interpretation of policy and procedure among the staff. The manual becomes an authoritative source that can easily be referred to when a decision is needed regarding a particular request or incident. If necessary, the written document can also be shown to a user in case of a dispute. A frustrated user may still be dissatisfied, but there will at least be concrete evidence that the policy or procedure guiding a decision was general to the service rather than an arbitrary ruling directed personally against the user.

A written manual can be used as an educational tool for new staff, and it can codify some of the standards against which the performance of the service as a whole will be measured. In orienting new staff members, the written manual reduces the amount of time and effort that existing staff will have to spend explaining policy and procedure. In evaluating the performance of a service, the manual can serve as one of many instruments of measurement. Its chief contribution will be in terms of stated standards regarding such matters as turnaround time.

Drop-in versus Scheduled Appointments

A library can allow users simply to walk in at any time and have a search conducted immediately, in effect, a "while you wait" service, or users may be required to schedule an appointment in advance. This assumes that a presearch, person-to-person interview will be conducted and/or that the user will be present during the actual online session.

If a search service does require the user's presence, the drop-in-only approach is almost impossible. Even in a library with very few online search requests, it is unlikely that all of them can be performed "on the spot." Scheduling appointments allows for smoother work flow and better budgeting of time. If appointments are scheduled at adequate intervals, there will be less pressure on staff when a search is being conducted than if other users are lined up outside. Also, scheduling can discourage frivolous spur-of-the moment search requests.

In services with a low volume of activity, appointments are often handled informally. A user calls or stops by to see when a search can be conducted. The staff member assesses his or her schedule, and the two agree on a time, often later that same day.

Larger libraries seldom can exercise this degree of informality. When the volume of activity is high and there are several searchers on staff, appointments are best channeled through one person, usually a member of the support staff who is responsible for maintaining a master schedule.

The library must also decide whether drop-in search requests will be accepted on a time-available basis. If there is a lag in the schedule, a user fails to show for an appointment, or a search takes less time than expected, an unscheduled search may be allowed, but acceptance of on-the-spot requests should never be allowed to disrupt the schedule.

The unscheduled search that runs into the next time period inconveniences those who made appointments in advance. Also, unscheduled search requests should not be allowed to interfere with other staff duties.

Search Request Forms

Completion of a search request form by users is standard operating procedure in most online search services. This serves two major purposes. It forces the user to think about his or her information need and express it in a way that will best draw on the requirements and capabilities of online retrieval, and the information supplied by the user provides the basis for a searcher to formulate search strategy. If the user does not attend a presearch interview or the online session, the search request form is the sole source of user-supplied information. If the user does participate at either or both stages, the information may be refined during face-to-face discussion, but the description supplied on the form will be the starting point for that discussion.

There is no single standard search request form in use in libraries. Search services have, however, made their forms available over the years, so that libraries establishing a new online search service have guidelines to follow. Differences in forms are usually in level of information detail and specificity of individual questions. See the search request form example in Figure 16-1, which is fairly brief (many are longer).

The most useful search request form should include data in these six areas:

1. Introductory information, including: internal control data (request number, date, appointment date and time with searcher, searcher's name or initials); user identification data (name, address, phone, and social security or other identifying number); user characteristics (status, department, occupation, education level, experience with service, purpose of search).
2. Search description: title, narrative description, key terms and concepts, synonyms, excluded terms and concepts.
3. Relevant bibliographic data (if known): authors on topic, relevant organizations, journal titles likely to carry articles, citations, manual sources searched, likely online databases.
4. Search limits: restrictions on dates of coverage, language, geography, publication format; broad or narrow search; expected number of citations.
5. Results delivery: pickup or mail desired; urgency.

COMPUTER SEARCH SERVICE

Please read the attached *Guide for Readers* before filling out this form.

Name_____   Today's date_____

Department _____   Home address_____

Phone no. _____   _____

Appointment date and time_____

Searcher_____   Database(s)_____

Status (please check one) ____Undergraduate ____Graduate (MA) ____Graduate (PhD)

____Faculty ____Other

Describe in paragraph form the topic you want searched. Identify the basic area of concern and indicate any special aspects, models, end uses, or applications which are of interest. A list of specific terms is also helpful but is not enough in itself; we need to know how these terms relate to each other. Also indicate aspects or applications related to your topic which you want to exclude.

PLEASE RETURN THIS APPLICATION FORM TO THE REFERENCE DESK AT LEAST 24 HOURS BEFORE YOUR SEARCH APPOINTMENT.

The cost of a computer search is based on the amount of time required to search a particular file, the number of references printed offline by the high speed printer at the computer location, and the communication charges. Most searches cost between $10 and $40, but since each search is unique there is no way to determine exact costs in advance.

I hereby authorize the search described above to be performed and assume responsibility for the charges.

Signature_____

Date_____

Please do *not* sign until the search consultation is completed

Figure 16-1 Search Request Form used at the University of Kansas.

6. Payment: user limits; account number for charging; signature for agreement to pay.

The design of the form should take into account the characteristics of the primary user community and its needs. A form used by a public library is likely to differ from one used in an academic facility, and both are likely to differ from that used in a corporate, medical, or other type of library. The form's design should also take into account the uses to be made of the information supplied by the user. Obviously, the primary use will be as a basis for devising a search strategy, but there are other purposes as well. Data can convey a great deal of information about who is using the service, as well as how, when, and why. By exclusion, data can also help to identify groups who are not using the service and suitable applications for which the service is currently underutilized. On the basis of such analysis, the library may wish to redirect its promotion to reach those groups.

Presearch Interview

Many libraries consider face-to-face dialogue between a searcher and a user essential before the actual search. Through discussion of an information need and how an online search can help to meet it, the chances of misunderstanding are reduced and the likelihood of successful results increased.

While mutual understanding and successful results are the overall goals of the interview, they can best be realized when several specific objectives are kept in mind. Together, the following make up the purpose for the presearch interview:

To ensure that the searcher understands the user's information need.

If necessary, to assist the user in refining the information need.

To understand the preconceptions of the user about online searching, to develop realistic expectations, and to dispel any misconceptions the user might hold about the nature and results of the online search process.

To assess and explain the appropriateness, benefits, and limitations of online searching in terms of the specific information needs of the user.

To determine the user's level of familiarity with the topic and to determine the level of comprehensiveness suitable for the search.

To select appropriate systems and databases for the search and to formulate an online strategy.

To explain the mechanics and capabilities of online retrieval to the extent that the user's participation during the session will be a help rather than a hindrance.

To explain the policies and procedures of the service so that there will be no after-the-fact "surprises" for the user.

To promote an overall sense of cooperation between user and searcher.

In meeting these objectives, the presearch interview may require only a few minutes, or it may require a half-hour or more. For frequent users with whom searchers have established rapport over a period of time, the interview may be dropped altogether. But for the less frequent or first-time user, there are several areas that should be discussed before going online.

After briefly introducing the service, the searcher should discuss the purpose of the search and the description of the topic with the user. The searcher should already have had time to look at the topic description as stated on the request form, but it is important that the two examine the statement together and discuss it in greater detail. This will allow the searcher to make sure that the description accurately conveys the topic the user wants to investigate.

From the discussion, a searcher can formulate search strategy. It is important that the user be a part of the process, serving as clarifier of the information need. This may mean that the searcher may have to describe general principles concerning the mechanics of online searching, such as Boolean logic and truncation, qualifying parameters, and so on. The searcher will also have to select the most appropriate database(s), and the user should be told the general scope of such files as well as any important limitations in coverage. If a database is organized around a controlled vocabulary for retrieval, the user should understand why the exact terms stated in the search request might be replaced by other terms when the search is completed. The user can even help the searcher translate the original terminology into the required controlled vocabulary.

The user who learns something of the mechanics involved in searching should be able to think about his or her topic in terms of capabilities and limitations of online retrieval. A user who has at least an appreciation of techniques may be better able to understand the results of the search as well. Searcher and user may discuss the roles of each during the online session, the user giving advice and perhaps making certain decisions during the search, and the searcher serving as the expert in retrieval techniques.

Users should also have an understanding of the overall policies and edures of the service. If it is fee-based, the method for charging should be explained as well as paying procedures. Variations according to time spent online and number of citations retrieved should be discussed, plus policy restrictions, if any, on amount of time spent online or number of citations printed.

Options for delivery of results should be outlined and lag time estimated. The user should be informed from the start that in all likelihood the library will not have every document cited in the bibliographic search. This is a good time to discuss interlibrary loan possibilities.

The presearch interview should be a positive precursor to the online session, blending contributions of searcher and user to ensure the best possible results.

User at the Online Session

Most librarians favor a user's presence during an online search session. In fact, many think this is more crucial than the presearch interview. In general, users tend to be more confident of the results if they see what is going on at each stage. Studies indicate that satisfaction with results is measurably higher among users who are present during the search.[8]

Participation during the session is one more mechanism to ensure success. If an online strategy begins to give results that are unsatisfactory, the problem can be solved immediately instead of after the search is completed and the results delivered. When unexpected problems crop up, even in a relatively simple search, the user's presence can often make the difference between a good search and a poor one. In particularly difficult searches, in fact, the user may be the final arbiter in deciding when to continue and when to quit.

There are many advantages to be gained from the user's presence at an online search, but the searcher will do well to keep in mind the inevitability of running across "problem users." They are people who:

Consider themselves experts in use of the service and dictate every step.

Are indecisive, made more so by the ticking of the online meter.

Are unsure of their decisions and constantly modify their search requests, sometimes reaching a point where they become confused about the original need.

Are "chatty," so interested in the whole process that they do not want to miss anything and insist on a play-by-play explanation of each step.

If possible, such users are best spotted in the presearch interview, and, difficulties straightened out before the "meter starts ticking."

Delivery of Results

When search results consist of a few bibliographic citations or very brief information, it is easy to print them locally from the online connection while the user waits. But for more lengthy data, local printing can be costly in both time and money. The printing can take more time than the search itself, incurring telecommunications and system connect charges all the while.

Therefore, libraries still rely heavily on the information retrieval services for delivery of results in hard-copy form, printed at the service's facilities and sent to the library via mail. With this method, the library must decide how the printouts are to get to the user. A number of libraries prefer pickup by the user over mailing the results. This is because, even with an effective presearch interview, the results may contain a few surprises for the user in terms of format or presentation. The pickup method allows another chance to clarify the results if necessary, and assistance is easier if a staff member is on hand to look at the printout instead of discussing it over the telephone.

User Evaluations

Many libraries have developed a form on which users evaluate aspects of an online search performed for them. A user evaluation form can be an excellent tool to identify causes of dissatisfaction and to gain broader impressions of user regard for the service. It also tells the users that the library is concerned about the quality of service it provides. Some libraries distribute an evaluation form along with search results; others send it later under separate cover.

Unlike other stages in the online search process, the evaluation form requires after-the-fact participation by users. The library exercises fairly good control over the search process before the evaluation stage and can thus insist on formal search request forms, participation in a presearch interview, and presence at the actual session, and the user obviously has an incentive to comply in order to receive the desired information. But once the results are obtained, not surprisingly, the user has little incentive to participate further.

There is actually no effective way to "require" users to return evaluation forms, and a certain proportion simply will not. However, the likelihood of response can be improved by designing the form according to some basic principles:

It should be brief, one side of a sheet of paper, or two sides of a single sheet at most.

It should require little time and effort to complete.

As many of the questions as possible should be multiple choice, requiring the user simply to select the most appropriate answer.

General language should be used as much as possible, avoiding specialized vocabulary other than perhaps a few key terms (such as database, citations) that were fully explained and used repeatedly during the presearch interview and the online session.

The top of the form should carry a brief, positive statement about the purpose of the evaluation and the importance of responding.

Response will be improved if little effort is required of the user. This makes the self-addressed, stamped (if possible) envelope effective.

The questions on the form depend on what the library wants the form to accomplish. In a report on activities of the ALA Reference and Adult Services Division (RASD) MARS Committee on Measurement and Evaluation of Service, Richard Blood summarized the committee's consideration of the rationale for evaluation as:

> The Evaluation Committee feels that the primary goal of evaluating online services is to identify and analyze instances of poor search results and user dissatisfaction and to ascertain the modifications that can be made to improve the performance of online services.[9]

The committee also recognized that individual libraries might wish to expand on this purpose and include additional questions as appropriate. Some would argue, in fact, that analysis should uncover not only what is wrong about a service, but also what is right. Some libraries design their evaluation forms to measure satisfaction on the basis of databases searched, user status, search purpose, previous experience with the service, method of learning about the service, and so on. This kind of analysis can provide valuable management information, pinpoint specific areas in which improvements need to be made, and even suggest future directions in promotional strategies. Some libraries try to get all this information from the evaluation form; others rely on several different forms.

Listed here are several general categories and more specific criteria that often form the basis for questions asked on a user evaluation form. Whatever material and wording are used, the questions should relate to the actual uses that will be made of the responses. Keep in mind that brevity will increase the likelihood of return.

Background Information
    Name (optional)
    User status
    Department, division, company
    Purpose of search
    For first-time users, where they learned about the service
    Database or databases searched
Process
    Clarity/suitability of design of search request form
    Overall value of presearch interview
    Overall value of being present at the online session
Results
    Number of citations listed on hard-copy printout
    Percentage of citations relevant to user's information need
    Percentage of the relevant items cited that user was aware of prior to online search
    Relevant items of which the user was aware prior to the search that were not cited, though they should have been given the database used
    Clarity of the format in which results were presented
    Acceptability of the time lapse between the search and delivery of the result in hard copy
Costs
    Reasonableness of charge, given the results
General
    Value of the online search in general
    Clarity of progression of overall process from start to finish
    Estimated amount of time saved over an equivalent manual search
    Increased use of other library resources by respondee as a result of use of online search service
    Likelihood of repeat use by respondee
    Respondee willingness to recommend the service to others
    Open-ended question seeking comments about any aspect of the service or the online search

Most questions on an evaluation form require subjective judgments on the part of users, such as an often-asked query on how much time the user felt was saved by the online search, which the author of the MARS Committee report judged to be a "meaningless" question lacking in "diagnostic value relative to the criteria for evaluating online services" since it is so hypothetical.[10] But answers to questions such as these may provide a key to user perceptions of the service, and perceptions can be critical in determining whether a user is satisfied with an online search.

Record Keeping

Record keeping for the online service, as for most others in the library, might best be described as a series of tasks most people prefer not to do.

But without a record of events and solutions, there is little basis for dealing consistently and effectively with problems as they occur.

In addition to greater internal efficiency, records serve other purposes. Many libraries retain copies of search request forms for a couple of years in case a user returns and wants the same search or an update performed. Stipulations for many grants require retention of financial records for several years.

The extent of record keeping in a search service depends on the volume of activity and complexity of the overall operation. In a fairly active service, record keeping will usually consist of the following forms and activities:

> Forms
>> Appointment logs
>> Search request forms
>> Search strategy worksheets
>> Search logs
>> Receipts and records of payment
>> User evaluation forms
>> Vendor invoices
>> Statistical reporting forms
> Activities
>> Accepting requests and scheduling appointments
>> Recording data onto search logs
>> Receiving payment
>> Reconciling invoices, and accounting
>> Analyzing evaluations
>> Compiling statistics and preparing reports
>> Filing

Many of these activities and forms pertain to responsibilities of support staff. The focus in this section is on some activities more likely to be carried out by the searchers themselves, in particular, the use of search logs and the preparation of statistical reports.

The maintenance of search logs serves several purposes. They provide brief documentation of searches conducted, often serve as the basis for verifying vendor invoices, and provide certain statistical data that, when compiled, lend insight into the patterns of use of an online service. Information is generally recorded onto a search log immediately after an online session. A typical log provides space for some introductory identification data, such as search request number, date, requestor, and searcher. Space is provided for recording data about the search: the telecommunications network used, system and databases accessed, amount of time online and number of citations printed, and costs. Some search logs also include space for recording user charges and payment information. Insofar as possible, the searcher should only have to check appropriate columns or write in coded information, as this will reduce the amount of time required to record a search.

For purposes of verifying billing information from the search log, a search should be recorded as each entry into a single database, since that is how charges are usually reflected on vendor invoices. Thus, a single request might in fact be recorded as several "searches." Depending on the statistical uses of data recorded on the search log, however, an argument can also be made that a search should be defined as the handling of a single request, regardless of how many databases are accessed.

The debate over how to define a search has been going on ever since libraries began to provide the service. Some libraries have worked out a numbering plan that allows each entry into a database to be recorded separately, yet ties together all such entries related to a single request. This accommodates use of the search log for purposes of verifying vendor invoices, but also permits data to be combined for each request when required for other types of evaluation.

The search log can serve as a primary source of information in compiling statistics about the pattern of use of the service. By summing columns of recorded data at periodic intervals, the library can study broad trends in the use of the service in general, the distribution of use by systems and databases, the distribution of expenses by cost component, and so on. By themselves, these are interesting statistics, but they are more valuable when combined with other data from search request forms and user evaluations. By tying together all these pieces, the library can determine many things about the use of the service. The possibilities are almost limitless, and the following are but a few representative purposes that can be aided by analyses of the data recorded on various forms.

Peak periods when requests are submitted can be ascertained, and staffing scheduled accordingly.

Level of use can be evaluated in terms of securing a more favorable discount option.

Budgeting can become more accurate.

Fees for service can be adjusted in accordance with considerations of revenues, expenses, and level of subsidy.

Charging schemes can be restructured to more accurately reflect the distribution of vendor charges among various cost factors.

Groups who are not using the service but might benefit from doing so can be identified and targeted more specifically in future promotion.

It should be stressed that these are but a few of the many purposes for which information from various forms can be used. Some libraries have computerized much of their record keeping, and this can make for far easier manipulation and analysis of data. But whether manual or automated, record keeping and statistical analysis should be purposeful, not carried out simply as a matter of busywork. Library staffs have too much to do and too little time to expend effort on generating information that will have no application.

The principles and strategies in this chapter assume the need for formal organization in the operation of an online search service. As noted throughout, the extent to which formal structure is needed will depend on many circumstances, most importantly the scope of the service and the volume of activity. A small library that has a total staff of two and receives a search request every once in a while will obviously not have the same need for formal organization as a library with a high volume of activity and many searchers on staff.

Regardless of volume or staff, the provision of online searching is like that of other library services: The better organized it is, and the more familiar staff and users are with policies and procedures, the more likely it is that the result will be high-quality service.

Notes

1. For a description of some of the uses of online searching in ready reference activity, see Linda Friend and Bruce Bonta, "Reference Use of Online Databases: An Analysis," in *National Online Meeting Proceedings—1981*, New York, March 24–26, Martha E. Williams and Thomas H. Hogan, comps. (Medford, N.J.: Learned Information, 1981), pp. 213–220.
2. See, for example, Ann Van Camp, "Effective Search Analysts," *Online* 3 (April 1979): 18–20.
3. James J. Maloney, ed, *Online Searching Technique and Management* (Chicago: ALA, 1983), p. 87.
4. For further detail on costing for recovery of indirect expenses, see Helen Drinan, "Financial Management of Online Services—A How-to Guide, *Online* 3 (October 1979): 14–21.
5. Sara D. Knapp, "Beyond Fee or Free," in Online Services column, Danuta A. Nitechi, ed., *RQ* 20 (Winter 1980): 118–119.
6. James J. Maloney, "Would You Buy a Used Database Search from That Librarian? The Promotion of Database Searching in the Marketing of Information," in *National Online Meeting Proceedings—1982*, New York, March 31–April 1, Martha E. Williams and Thomas H. Hogan, comps. (Medford, N.J.: Learned Information, 1982), pp. 323–324.
7. Mary E. Pensyl, "The Online Policy Manual," *Online* 6 (May 1982): 46.
8. See, for example, Ruth Traister Morris, Edwin A. Holtum, and David S. Curry, "Being There: The Effect of the User's Presence on MEDLINE Search Results," *Bulletin of the Medical Library Association* 70 (1982): 298–304.
9. Richard W. Blood, "Evaluation of Online Searches," *RQ* 22 (Spring 1983): 267.
10. *Ibid.*, p. 274.

Index